Socialism and Populism in Chile, 1932-52

PAUL W. DRAKE

Socialism and Populism in Chile, 1932-52

UNIVERSITY OF ILLINOIS PRESS
Urbana   Chicago   London

Publication of this work has been supported by a grant from
the Oliver M. Dickerson Fund. The Fund was established by
Mr. Dickerson (Ph.D., Illinois, 1906) to enable the University
of Illinois Press to publish selected works in American history, designated by the executive committee of the Department of History.

Library of Congress Cataloging in Publication Data

Drake, Paul W.   1944-
    Socialism and populism in Chile, 1932-52.

    Bibliography: p.
    Includes index.
    1. Socialism in Chile—History. 2. Populism—
Chile—History. 3. Popular fronts. 4. Chile—
Politics and government—1920-   I. Title.
HX198.5.D7   335'.00983   77-17414
ISBN 0-252-00657-7

For my mother and father, Mary and Lyle

Contents

Tables

Abbreviations Used in Text

AD	Democratic Action (Venezuela)
APRA	American Popular Revolutionary Alliance (Peru)
ARS	Revolutionary Socialist Action
CGT	General Confederation of Workers
CIT	Confederation of Inter-American Workers
CNS	National Syndical Confederation
CORFO	Development Corporation
COSACH	Nitrate Company of Chile
COVENSA	Chilean Nitrate and Iodine Sales Corporation
CTAL	Confederation of Latin American Workers
CTCH	Confederation of Chilean Workers
CUTCH	Central Federation of Chilean Workers
FECH	Student Federation of Chile
FJS	Socialist Youth Federation
FOCH	Federation of Chilean Workers
FRAP	Popular Action Front
IWW	Industrial Workers of the World
MIR	Movement of the Revolutionary Left
MNS	National Socialist Movement
NAP	New Public Action
ORIT	Inter-American Regional Organization of Workers
PC	Communist Party
PDC	Christian Democrat Party
PN	National Party
PNR	National Revolutionary Party (Mexico)
POR	Revolutionary Worker's Party
POS	Worker's Socialist Party
PS	Socialist Party of Chile
PSA	Authentic Socialist Party
PSP	Popular Socialist Party
PST	Socialist Workers' Party
SNA	National Society for Agriculture
SNM	National Society of Mining
SOFOFA	Society for Factory Development
UP	Popular Unity
USP	Popular Socialist Union
USRACH	Republican Social Union of Wage Earners of Chile

Preface

This field research on the rise of socialism and populism was under-
taken in Chile during 1969, 1970, and 1973. Among the many scholars and public figures who aided the study, I especially want to acknowledge those who assisted in Chile. John P. Harrison smoothed my
introduction to that irresistibly charming but deeply troubled country.
Carlos Fortín and Jorge Tapia Videla provided indispensable guid-
ance in the project's early stages. Among other scholars, Raúl Urzúa
and Álvaro Jara were also particularly generous with their time and
suggestions. The interviews, documents, and advice supplied to me by
former and present leaders of the Socialist Party were invaluable.
Above all, it is a pleasure to thank Clodomiro Almeyda, Carlos Charlín
Ojeda, Alejandro Chelén Rojas, Mario Garay, Julio César Jobet and
his wife Elisa, Manuel Mandujano, and Astolfo Tapia Moore. Also
helpful were the descendants of Socialist Party founder Marmaduke
Grove Vallejo, his son Hiram and daughter Blanca Elena. Other
aspects of this history were illuminated for me by Jorge Barría, Aníbal
Jara, Carlos Keller, and Germán Urzúa Valenzuela. In the United
States, the manuscript was improved at various stages by the insightful
comments of John J. Johnson, Joseph L. Love, John D. Wirth, Theodore H. Moran, Frederic C. Jaher, and Stephen J. Stein. I would also
like to recognize the contributions of my research assistant, Terry
Dewitt.

Of the many institutions whose holdings and personnel facilitated
my work, the Biblioteca del Congreso, the Biblioteca Nacional, and the
Dirección del Registro Electoral in Chile deserve special mention. The
staff at the National Archives in Washington, D.C., were also gracious.

The study was made possible by a grant from the Foreign Area
Fellowship Program, to which I am indebted for its support of my
initial research and writing efforts. Further labors were generously
funded by awards and support from various divisions of the Univer-

sity of Illinois at Urbana-Champaign, including the Center for Latin American and Caribbean Studies, especially its research project on regional integration in Latin America, which operated under a grant from the Center for International Comparative Studies, in turn supported by the Ford Foundation; in addition, I am grateful for a summer faculty fellowship and four grants from the Graduate Research Board.

Finally, to all the other Chileans, North Americans, and institutions who aided my endeavors, I want to underscore my gratitude. It goes without saying that none of the above bear any responsibility for the statements, opinions, and defects which follow, but they all share the credit for any merits this study may have. And, last but most of all, I wish to thank my wife, Susan, for her tireless help, incisive criticisms, intellectual contributions, and constant encouragement.

1

Introduction

From the 1930s to the 1970s, Chile was politically unique in Latin America. It alone sustained an electoral democracy which included officially Marxist parties as the major leaders of the workers. When representative democracy existed at times in the rest of Latin America, explicitly nationalist, populist parties usually spoke for the urban masses. Despite differences in political systems and parties, Chile shared with its neighbors a heritage of common Ibero-American economic, social, and cultural features. That legacy encouraged Chilean practices and policies recognizable in other parts of the hemisphere since Chile's unusually open political system also operated under the stresses and strains of an underdeveloped country seeking a more productive and equitable national economy and society. Like other less-developed areas in the twentieth century, Chile became more urban, industrial, and pluralistic; it became more "modern," though not in any linear, smooth, or synchronized progression. As elsewhere, retarded and uneven development urged simultaneous solutions to economic backwardness, social inequalities, and political neglect of the lower classes. Allocation of scarce resources between industrialization and social welfare became a primary political issue after World War I. Because of the multiparty system encompassing the Socialists and Communists, Chile's reform experience echoed many issues of modern European history, such as the role of labor parties in coalition politics. Because of the economic and social context, it reflected many of the challenges encountered throughout the Third World, and especially Latin America, such as political trade-offs in late industrialization. Through an analysis of both that pluralistic electoral system and that Latin American socioeconomic setting, the Chilean case can enrich the comparative study of the rise and role of mass-based movements. By emphasizing the social aspects of political history, it will be argued that Chilean socialism and its popular-front coalitions during the formative interwar years bore many traits in common with Latin American populism.

To adjust to indigenous realities, the Chilean Socialists adapted, like all their counterparts in Europe and elsewhere, to particular national conditions and thus deviated from their own fundamental interpretation of Marxian goals. They made adjustments to Chilean political-cultural traditions, social structure, and economic underdevelopment. As a result, at least in the beginning in the 1930s and to lesser degrees thereafter, the Socialist Party (PS) not only displayed many similarities to its namesakes abroad; it also closely resembled Latin American populist movements. As will be elaborated further on, "populism" has principally been used in Latin America, with some flexibility, to refer to three broad, interrelated political phenomena. First, the term has been applied to an identifiable style of mobilization, leadership, campaigning, and propaganda; this approach places a premium on personalism, paternalism, nationalism, and immediate gratification of mass needs. Second, it has described a heterogeneous social coalition aimed in large part at the working classes but including and led by significant sectors from the middle or upper social strata. Third, it has become associated with an eclectic set of policies adopted during certain periods of "modernization"; these programs for national integration respond to the problems of underdevelopment by incorporating the workers in the process of accelerated industrialization through mild redistributive measures. Presumably, a movement strongly exhibiting all three characteristics would fit within a reasonably acceptable definition of Latin American populism. Such classification is potentially a question of degree, and other movements might be said to have some "populistic" mobilization, social, or policy traits mixed in with contradictory elements. The Chilean Socialists engaged in highly populist campaign techniques, social alliances, and program proposals on their own in the 1930s. They also joined multiparty, polyclass coalitions which pursued populist development programs through the 1940s. Consequently, this study will examine both populist proclivities within the PS and populist patterns within the larger Chilean reform experience.

Within Chile's multiparty system, the Marxists rose and fell twice from the 1930s to the 1970s. In the first phase (1932-52), Chilean socialism flowered and decayed under the leadership of the Socialist Party, usually in uneasy alliance with the Communists (PC). The thirties and forties formed a coherent historical period not only for the PS but also for the nation as a whole. Economically, the Depression turned attention toward greater internal industrial development.

Subsequent economic policies and trends flowed from these responses to the Depression and to later similar international disruptions, mainly World War II. Socially, the period from 1932 to 1952 witnessed rising numbers, organization, and assertiveness among the urban middle classes and workers. The contemporary onslaught of urbanization began outstripping the absorptive capacity of the cities' economies. At the same time, the increasingly urban economic elites devised new defenses to cope with ripening complexities. Politically, the modern leftward movement of the electorate and the multiparty spectrum took shape in the 1930s. Although Chilean socialism had roots in the nineteenth century, the rise of the contemporary Marxist electoral movement began during the Great Depression.

As an anti–status quo party, the Chilean Socialists broke into the national arena in the 1930s with intensely populist appeals behind a charismatic *caudillo* from the armed forces. The young party also evidenced weaker but significant populist social and policy tendencies. In Chile as elsewhere, socialism and populism were not necessarily mutually exclusive forces. While emphasizing the workers and revolutionary socialist objectives, the party also developed a mixed constituency encompassing the middle classes and programs seeking to reconcile industrial growth and welfare reforms. As a mixed breed of socialism and populism, the PS rapidly became one of the most dynamic mass movements yet to appear in the hemisphere.

In less than a decade of mobilization, the Socialists took a share of executive power through the Popular Front of 1938. The historic monopoly of the rightist parties, mainly the Conservatives and Liberals, was superseded by the centrist Radical Party, usually backed by the Marxists. Through the administrations of the Radical presidents (1938-52), the PS and the most articulated working groups were assimilated into a subordinate position in the existing multiparty and bureaucratic system. As before populism had shown a capacity for disruptive, paternalistic mobilization, it now revealed a capacity for integrative, clientelistic institutionalization. After mobilizing newly emergent social groups in fresh political ways through strongly populist appeals, the PS was institutionalized through multiparty populist coalitions and policies. This integration of the Marxists and the most organized sections of urban labor was accomplished through popular-front politics. Such coalitions with centrist reformers were partly a Chilean variety of European multiparty experiences in the era. At the same time, popular-front politics was a Chilean version of the common Latin American populist approach—which threaded through many divergent political systems—of multiclass coalitions simultaneously pursuing industrialism and welfarism. During the thirties and forties, the levels of social and political mobilization of the lower classes in Chile were sufficient to provoke the accommodation of a few previously excluded groups but not to force the displacement of established elites. Meanwhile, the Socialists' entrance into the upper echelons of the national political network through increasingly moderate alliances and programs pulled their party closer to the image of social democrats in the 1940s. Beyond hard-won but minor reforms, PS participation in government in the forties did not come close to producing their desired transformations in capitalist society. Rather, it led to the fragmentation and decline of the party. Chile's exceptionally open party democracy presented the Socialists with the classic dilemma of making their participation and ascent possible but blunting their radical programs and appeal. Nevertheless, throughout their career the Socialists preserved an initial, long-range commitment to Marxian revolutionary change. Therefore they incessantly complained that neither their party's approximation to Latin American populism in the 1930s nor its attempts at reformist democratic socialism in the 1940s lived up to its ideals. Partly for that reason, the PS tried in the following decades to move beyond populism and popular-front politics to stress more radical strategies and policies.

In the second phase (1952-73), Socialist discontent with previous frustrations spawned efforts to become more revolutionary Marxists. Leftist reform movements became more concerned with massive redistributive goals and structural reforms partly because import-substituting industrialization was running into bottlenecks; by the 1950s it had clearly failed to provide the employment, growth, or national independence expected. At the same time, additional contenders and issues jammed the political arena. The growth of population and the cities accelerated. Building on foundations laid during the earlier popular-front period, urbanization of the society and economy multiplied the politically active lower social sectors and their demands. Rural-to-urban migrants, peasants, and women emerged as social-political forces of greater consequence. Pressures from such groups and their political representatives soon rose beyond the threshold where traditional upper- and middle-class sectors were willing to accommodate them. Both responding to and feeding those pressures, the Marxists steered a more independent course from 1952 into the 1970s. This time, the PS climbed to power with far more emphasis on ideology and class conflict but without abandoning the democratic institutional framework or certain populistic carryovers from the past. Calling for a "workers' front" under their own leadership rather than broader coalitions behind centrist reformers, the Marxists ran Socialist Salvador Allende Gossens for the presidency four times. Those campaigns by the Socialist-Communist alliance moved well beyond earlier populist techniques, combinations, and programs. Meanwhile, the Christian Democrats displaced the Radicals as the leading center-left force and competed with the Marxist alternative. In those same years, the old limited electorate expanded enormously, primarily thanks to the enfranchisement of women. As elsewhere in Latin America, escalating and intensively politicized competition for limited resources reduced the likelihood of broad populist coalitions by the end of the 1960s.

One alternative was a sharp turn to the left, attempted through the Marxist election to the presidency in 1970. By that time, accelerated social and political mobilization was straining an inflation-ridden economy of scarcity and overloaded political institutions to the breaking point. This prompted elites fearful of their own emasculation or ejection to prefer repressive exclusion of their opponents rather than integrative inclusion. As a result, the Socialists failed again, crushed by a brutal military coup d'etat dedicated to political and social demobilization. This study explores the roots of that tragedy by investigating the origins, ascent, incorporation, and corrosion of the Chilean Socialists from the 1930s to the 1950s.

Socialism and Populism

The revolutionary socialism to which the Chileans aspired embraced demanding ideals that were seldom adhered to in any party or country. The Socialists adopted Marxism as their ideological orientation but not as a dogma. According to their ideals, Marxist socialist parties should be independent working-class vehicles, opposed to the dominance of the upper and middle social strata. They may, however, encompass segments of the middle classes as subordinate members. Therefore the Chileans sought to base their movement more on trade unions than on congressional or intellectual circles. They stressed class conflict as a basic premise and as the engine of change. Social revolution was the ultimate goal. Although they employed the means of formal political democracy, they wanted to transform that system into full economic and social democracy, so they retained the possibility of armed upheaval as a final necessity. Their theory of national development, then, was conflictual rather than integrative. It aimed at the overthrow of the domestic and foreign capitalist elites by the workers, rather than merely the integration of the poor into the more modern sector. The PS looked to massive state control of large-scale private property as a method of economic growth and redistribution. By their lights, the purpose of this collectivism was the creation of an economy free from the profit motive and a society free from class exploitation. Their vision of socialism rejected both reformist democratic models in Europe and revolutionary communism in the Soviet Union. To achieve their ends, the Chileans tried to build a tautly structured, programmatic party. In their view, socialist parties should emphasize rigorous ideological considerations and disciplined organization over personalist or purely pragmatic politics. Theoretically, they should have a global orientation and try to denigrate nationalism. During the unfolding of their movement and through later critiques of their own past, Chileans introduced these notions of how an idealized socialist party ought to behave. Therefore, contrasts between Socialist aspirations and actions in this study will be based on standards set by the Chileans themselves, not on any foreign ideal types or examples. The argument that Chileans exhibited populist traits in their adaptations of socialism to local conditions does not imply that they were, in any sense, inferior to or totally different from foreign counterparts, who also adjusted to their own distinct national situations. The varieties of socialism in theory and practice around the world caution against generalizations or universal expectations. Nevertheless, socialist movements theoretically and historically have been seen as a reaction to the harsher consequences of industrialization; socialism, particularly as an ideal type, usually seeks to reorder the relations of production to achieve greater distributive justice in relatively industrialized societies. Populism, on the other hand, is viewed frequently as a response to inequalities in areas still in the incipient stages of industrialization. Contemporary Chilean socialism surfaced in an underdeveloped country shocked by the worldwide Great Depression. Partly for this reason, the Chilean party originally bore the imprint of Latin American populism as well as the stamp of socialism.[1]

The comparative literature about populism—especially in Latin America but also elsewhere—contains a slim core of common thinking. Scholars have applied "populism," as a descriptive term, to

1. For major critiques of their own past by Chilean Socialists, see Julio César Jobet and Alejandro Chelén Rojas, *Pensamiento teórico y político del Partido Socialista de Chile* (Santiago, 1972); Julio César Jobet, *El Partido Socialista de Chile* (2 vols., Santiago, 1971); Alejandro Chelén Rojas, *Trayectoria del socialismo* (Buenos Aires, 1967); Oscar Waiss, *El drama socialista* (n.p., 1948). Some comparisons can be sampled in Luis E. Aguilar, ed., *Marxism in Latin America* (New York, 1968).

movements espousing ideologies as diverse as liberalism, socialism, and naziism in countries as varied as Russia and the United States. Although it never approaches the rigor of a "model" or ideology, populism captures a constellation of characteristics recognizable in particular Latin American political movements, especially during certain periods of social and economic "modernization." A more rigid, schematic concept would probably distort the untidiness of the historical reality, which the term populism, even with its ambiguities, helps illuminate. Particularly in the Latin American context, populism refers to a set of political actors, policies, attitudes, styles, and reactions commensurate with certain twentieth-century conditions. As an identifiable type, populism need not bear the burden here of any negative or positive connotations. Such a movement frequently emerges from crises in previously agrarian societies beginning to break out of the cocoon of rather tight, patrimonial upper-class rule. After the loosening of traditional controls, populism may erupt as a response to the problems of simultaneous economic modernization and social mobilization. It is one possible answer to the challenge of generating indigenous economic growth with the inclusion of the underprivileged majority. In this sense, populism can be a protest by both impoverished countries and deprived social groups. Not uncommonly, populism lashes out against the power of foreigners to direct or disrupt the native economy. Rather than relying totally on foreign models such as capitalism or communism, populists try to formulate autogenous recipes for development. Populism, then, may be both a reaction against the industrial systems of the more-developed world and a drive for industrialization at home. It seeks to close the gap between the rich and the poor internationally and domestically at the same time. As a result, populism has both a nationalist and a class orientation in the Third World. It aims at improving production by the nation as well as consumption by the lower classes. Populism seems most likely to take hold in less-institutionalized societies with acute tensions and disaffected but largely unorganized populations. At the same time, populist politics is facilitated by levels of national development beyond a critical minimum. Such mass movements become more possible after openings have appeared in the antique aristocratic system, through either erosion or explosion. Also, the partial advances of urbanization, education, and industrialization provide the necessary mobilizable mass, institutions, and issues. For example, when the growth of manufacturing lags behind urbanization and education, the generation of populist leaders from the middle or upper strata and of followers from the lower classes becomes increasingly likely. In other words, the failures and dislocations of modernization, rather than its absence, tend to produce populism.[2]

The populist "syndrome," as outlined in various studies, includes many elements frequently found in Latin American politics. First, charismatic, paternalistic leaders with lower-class followers or clienteles are more important to a populist party's dynamism than are programmatic appeals. These leaders often reach down to the masses because they are alienated from their own higher social sectors. Second, populism tends to be more a "mass" than a "class" movement. Particularly in countries lacking prior middle-class revolutions and massive urban concentrations of industrial workers, reform movements reach beyond a narrow proletariat base. A party may include peasants, artisans, segments of the middle groups, and even defectors from the upper class. The middle classes seem especially prone to pull away from such coalitions after their own objectives have been realized. Third, populist parties seldom give top priority to intricate, long-range plans for structural change. Rather, they emphasize spontaneous, piecemeal reforms and dashing slogans which seem to promise quick material and psychic payoffs. There is a dimension of utopianism in populism. Fourth, such movements are normally "anti" movements. They are defined primarily by what they oppose. Evil forces, which may be perceived as bankers or colonial oppressors, must be destroyed to liberate their victims. However correctly identified, such villains are typically pictured more clearly than are the benevolent forces and systems intended to replace them. Fifth, populists tend to be moralistic and redemption oriented. They extol the virtues of the common people and denounce the standards and guilt of the old ruling groups. Sixth, populism has a penchant for ideological eclecticism. This is understandable in movements with heterogeneous constituencies and goals. Populists in countries less developed than the industrialized West usually combine components of liberalism, anarchism, socialism, and even corporatism. Seventh, the strategy for development tends to be integrationist. Conceptually, this approach differs from conservative programs which favor the

2. All the sections on populism and Latin American examples rely, in particular, on the following sources: Ghita Ionescu and Ernest Gellner, *Populism: Its Meanings and National Characteristics* (London, 1969); Torcuato Di Tella, "Populism and Reform in Latin America," in Claudio Veliz, ed., *Obstacles to Change in Latin America* (London, 1965), pp. 47-74; Francisco C. Weffort, "El populismo en la política brasileña," in Celso Furtado et al., *Brazil:hoy* (2nd ed., Mexico, 1970), pp. 54-84; Octavio Ianni, *Crisis in Brazil* (New York and London, 1970); A. E. Van Nierkerk, *Populism and Political Development in Latin America* (Rotterdam, 1974).

capitalist elites at the expense of the working classes and from revolutionary programs which attempt to destroy the bourgeoisie and
replace them with the workers and peasants. Instead, populists try to
subsidize both the entrepreneurial sector and the masses and to help
the latter become increasingly incorporated into decision making and
benefits. There is an attempt to share the costs of development, with
a higher proportion to be paid by wealthier natives and foreigners.
Social welfare is at least as high a priority as material growth. Finally,
populist movements usually produce disappointing results. Seldom
revolutionary, populism prompts adjustments in the established political system rather than its overthrow. The response of dominant social
groups and institutions to the participation and rising expectations of
the workers helps determine the form and outcome of these innovations in mass politics. Populism may be accommodated, squelched, or
radicalized. It is likely to be more effective at mobilizing protests by
the underprivileged than at securing their organized participation in
national decision making or at delivering substantial benefits to them.
A populist party may lack the intellectual toughness and institutional
durability to bring about fundamental social reforms. It may have a
meteoric career or become an institutionalized part of the political
system, whether in the upper echelons or in the opposition. Populism
can possibly deter more militant labor politics in the short run but
generate greater worker radicalism over time. It can conceivably lead
to reform or revolution, or merely reinforce the status quo. In the
process, a rather impromptu populist movement can evolve into a
more structured form, such as a socialist party.[3]

By contrast, varieties of nonpopulist parties include those overwhelmingly appealing to one social class, for example the Communists, who focus on the proletariat. By the same token, technocratic
or aristocratic parties such as the nineteenth-century conservatives
and liberals, which do not emphasize the masses or redistributive
changes from the rich to the poor, fall outside the populist category.
In addition, pragmatic, mainly middle- to upper-class reform parties,
such as the Chilean Radicals, with little reliance on charismatic leaders,
public paternalism, manual laborers, or crusades for redemption of
the down-trodden, are not seen as populists in and of themselves.
Neither are simply clientelistic, aggregative machine parties lacking
strong social or ideological orientations. A purely bread-and-butter
labor party might be a mixed case. At the other extreme, fervently

3. Alistair Hennessy, "Latin America," in Ionescu and Gellner, pp. 28-61; Weffort,
pp. 54-84; Charles W. Anderson, *Politics and Economic Change in Latin America*
(Princeton, 1967), esp. pp. 174-83.

ideological movements, such as the Nazis or, again, the Communists, would also be excluded. Since such typologies are anything but air-tight, however, all the above movements could conceivably display some "populistic" traits. For example, particular personalistic, prop-agandistic, social, or policy currents within the otherwise highly struc-tured, ideological, and revolutionary movements led by Mao Tse-tung and Fidel Castro might be diagnosed as populistic tendencies; so might selected inclinations among European socialist parties, where personalistic leaders and compromising coalitions as well as programs are scarcely unknown, although operating in distinct national environments.

More specifically in Latin America, several mass movements ex-hibiting many populist symptoms—some peculiar to the term's usage in this region—have appeared since World War I. In the twentieth century, history demonstrates that populist parties in the hemisphere usually fused middle- to upper-class leaders with urban working-class followers. They mainly promoted reforms in the cities. This con-trasted with the rural base of populism in many world areas. Latin American laborers, especially the less-organized groups, tended to be the recipients rather than the originators or directors of these move-ments. In most cases, such parties were not finely structured, firmly ideological phenomena growing out of the prior and largely au-tonomous demands and organizations of the workers. Instead, a charismatic leader forged and held together the multiclass amalgam. Such a leader characteristically possessed a patchwork ideology that stressed immediate solutions for lower-class grievances. Personalism and nationalism were the essential forces; class loyalties and ideologi-cal purity were of secondary importance. Populists tried to unite the middle and lower classes against the "imperialists" and "oligarchs." These movements were normally associated with campaigns for import-substituting industrialization. This served as a mild form of economic nationalism and as a response to spiraling urbanization. Not surprisingly, Latin American populists displayed ideological and strategic ambiguities and contradictions. Usually through peaceful means, they pursued social change in conservative countries with powerful elites firmly opposed to pluralism, equality, or displacement. Populists espoused nationalism in countries still in search of nation-hood. They advocated redistribution of benefits and income from the wealthy few to the deprived many in societies lacking industrial abun-dance. They promoted mass mobilization in countries with a nonpar-ticipant political culture. In the twentieth century, the new urban groups remained under the influence of a rural, seignorial, Roman

Catholic, Ibero-American heritage. They came from a tradition of enforced social and political subordination, having served landlords, clergy, generals, *patrones*, and *caudillos*. This apparent propensity for deference, while not unique to Latin America or Chile, cropped up even in the hemisphere's burgeoning cities and even in seemingly participatory ideological movements. Although difficult to measure, these cultural continuities from the colonial, rural, peasant past to the urban present were widely recognized; they were associated with the heritage of a patrimonial state which replicated the hierarchical, authoritarian, paternalistic relations historically existing between the upper and lower social orders. To whatever extent such behavior and attitudes persisted among the workers, these orientations were assumed by many politicians, who offered the lower classes a fatherly, patronizing approach. Through such appeals, populist movements proved more effective out of government than in it. With their patron-client connections, personalism, and heterogeneity, they were particularly prone to vitiating compromises and cooptation. They were also susceptible to opportunism, factionalism, and fragmentation, obviously characteristics scarcely monopolized by populists. For all the above reasons, such movements encountered severe difficulties in institutionalizing themselves as enduring parties or lasting members of the national governing establishment. As a mechanism for massive social change or stable political development, populism usually fell far short of its promises. This was true even when populists were much more dedicated to meaningful reforms than were other viable political alternatives. In most cases, Latin American populism had socialist overtones, and, in Chile, socialism had populist overtones.[4]

If it can be shown that the Chilean Socialists, with their party label and Marxist aspirations, began as a highly populist movement, then the ubiquity of that political style from roughly the 1930s into the 1960s in Latin America can be further confirmed. With adequate caution, parallels may be drawn between many aspects of the mobilization of the masses in such diverse countries as Chile, Peru, Venezuela, Argentina, and Brazil. For example, in Peru, Víctor Raúl Haya de la Torre led the American Popular Revolutionary Alliance (APRA), a manifestly populist movement which inspired and allied with the Chilean Socialists. APRA emphasized personalism and nationalism.

4. Hennessy, pp. 28-61; Osvaldo Sunkel, "Change and Frustration in Chile," in Veliz, *Obstacles*, pp. 116-44; Francisco José Moreno, *Legitimacy and Stability in Latin America* (New York, 1969). Another study which appeared too late for full consideration here but which merits consultation is Octavio Ianni, *La formación del estado populista en América latina* (Mexico, 1975).

It concocted a pliable ideology including elements from Marxism, liberalism, corporatism, and the indigenous past. This program, which became increasingly moderate from the 1930s to the 1960s, sought the simultaneous expansion of industrialization and social welfare. Appealing to discontented regional as well as social groups, APRA claimed to speak for both "manual and intellectual workers." Although Peru trailed Chile in economic and social development, APRA emerged as one of the earliest and strongest populist movements in the hemisphere. It was able to organize and preserve its following within the party but not to take charge of the national government. Though it became the largest party in Peru and nearly took power as early as the 1930s, it never occupied the presidency. One key reason for APRA's failure was its inability to effectively mobilize large segments of the lower classes, especially peasants and rural-urban migrants. Even more important was resistance to APRA's participation by the upper class and the regular military.[5]

In Venezuela, the Democratic Action (AD) movement began in the interwar years with strong socialist leanings. It moderated and finally took and held office with the support of urban labor in the 1950s. The personalistic leader of AD, Rómulo Betancourt, like Haya de la Torre, was a former student rebel and intellectual. He was also a close friend of the Chilean Socialists.[6]

Argentina was a country with levels of urbanization, industrialization, literacy, labor growth, middle-class expansion, and political activism comparable or superior to those of Chile. As did the Liberal populist Arturo Alessandri Palma in Chile, the Argentine reformer Hipólito Irigoyen paved the way from World War I on for the coming of mass politics. In contrast to Chile, where the military removed itself from overt political activity at the start of the 1930s, Argentina experienced a restoration of conservative rule backed up by the armed forces during and following the Depression. Partly for that reason, populism did not crystallize in Argentina until the 1940s. Then a reformist military officer, Juan Domingo Peron, ignited a powerful multiclass movement based on the urban masses. He propounded a hodge-podge, nationalistic ideology, using his personal magnetism to freeze the loyalty of the workers to *peronismo*. Like Apristas in Peru and Marxists in Chile, Peronists came to account for roughly a hardcore third of the electorate. Although opposed by the Argentine

5. Harry Kantor, *The Ideology and Program of the Peruvian Aprista Movement* (Berkeley, Calif., 1953); Peter F. Klarén, *Modernization, Dislocation, and Aprismo* (Austin, Tex., 1973); Robert J. Alexander, *Aprismo* (Kent, Ohio, 1973).

6. Robert J. Alexander, *The Venezuelan Democratic Revolution* (New Brunswick, N.J., 1964).

Socialist Party, Perón attracted some admirers among their Chilean namesakes. Comparisons between Perón and Marmaduke Grove Vallejo, the Chilean Socialist leader from the military, would be valuable in studying about labor politics in Latin America.[7]

In Brazil between 1922 and 1930 there was political ferment among the younger military officers, which was not unlike that in Chile. Although President Getúlio Vargas (1930-45) cast himself as the father of the poor in the latter years of his reign, populism did not become the lifeblood of politics until the 1950-64 period. Even then, it flourished mainly in the larger cities of the south. One reason may have been that Brazil as a whole lacked many of the preconditions for political change. It was far less developed, particularly in terms of education and labor organization, than Chile or Argentina at the time of the Great Depression. Political parties with reformist, leftist ideologies were not as well established in Brazil. Even when populism took hold, it proved to be a flimsy specimen compared to the mass organizations constructed in Argentina and Chile. Brazil's inclusion of the lower classes in politics bore many of the same traits but was more vulnerable to easy dismantling by the military.[8]

Viewing the Chilean Socialists, at least in their early years, as populists clarifies the ways in which the party originally attracted a constituency and subsequently behaved within the national political system. However, the long-standing dedication of many PS members to Marxian class struggle against imperialism and capitalism should not be underestimated. This radicalism encountered greater emphasis and success in the years after 1952, the starting point for most accounts of contemporary Chilean politics. The following history will examine the preceding two decades as an intrinsically significant period of change and as the seedbed for more recent developments.

The Chilean Political Setting

From 1932 to 1952, Chile's accommodating political culture and system made a greater impact on the Marxists than vice-versa. Politics remained remarkably adaptable and stable despite the inclusion of avowedly revolutionary parties. This resiliency continued in large part

7. Similarities between Perón and Grove may have been more than coincidental. Colonel Perón was a military attaché in Chile during 1936-38, at the height of popularity for Grove and the Popular Front. Ernst Halperin, *Nationalism and Communism in Chile* (Cambridge, Mass., 1965), p. 123; Samuel L. Baily, *Labor, Nationalism, and Politics in Argentina* (New Brunswick, N.J., 1967); George Blanksten, *Perón's Argentina* (Chicago, 1953).

8. Thomas Skidmore, *Politics in Brazil* (New York, 1967).

because the upper class had cultivated a respected tradition of peace-ful electoral and bureaucratic procedures long before those institu-tions were seriously tested by social conflict. In the long view, insti-tutionalization or routinization preceded mobilization, a phenomenon awaiting more careful examination by historians of nineteenth-century Chile. In the twentieth century, the Marxist parties were assimilated into that system, not unlike their counterparts in Western Europe. In spite of the Chilean Left's excoriation of parliamentary politics and the inevitable dilemmas such methods presented to an ostensibly revolutionary movement, the Marxists failed to develop coherent alternative strategies. Since more radical options were ap-parently unattractive, unlikely to succeed, and not the only avenue open, the Socialists and Communists played by the existing rules of the game. After previous decades of aristocratic republicanism, those "rules" of multiparty politics placed a premium on heterogeneous coalitions to win presidential elections and to form congressional majorities. Success in both branches of government was extremely important because of the heritage of a strong legislature in frequent conflict with the chief executive. Furthermore, from the 1925 con-stitution through the 1950s a modified d'Hondt system of propor-tional representation for congressional and municipal elections en-couraged party proliferation and electoral pacts. Under this system, total votes were tabulated for all candidates as well as all parties on a particular list. Voters could cast ballots for the entire list, a party, or the individuals thereon. Then a complicated electoral quotient or "dividing number" was used in each electoral district to determine which lists had won how many seats and which candidates on the winning lists had been elected by virtue of their intralist ranking in the individual voting. In short, this system promoted individual and party coalitions to accumulate votes behind a particular combined list. Thanks to the quotient mechanism, parties in many districts had leftover votes; through coalitions, these excess ballots could be added to the contributions of their allies, often mini-parties who could not have survived alone. Personalities as well as parties were important in drawing votes to lists, but few could flourish in isolation. Although later revised in 1958-62, these electoral regulations, along with other political requirements, often conditioned Marxist behavior, regard-less of party ideologies or the expressed desire of more radical mem-bers to reject the inherited rules of the game.[9]

    9. Federico G. Gil, The Political System of Chile (Boston, 1966), esp. pp. 49, 215-16; Alberto Edwards Vives, La fronda aristocrática (6th ed., Santiago, 1966); Maurice Zeitlin, "The Social Determinants of Political Democracy in Chile," in James Petras and Maurice Zeitlin, eds., Latin America: Reform or Revolution? (New York, 1968), pp. 220-34.

Moreover, the Marxists, like all other Chilean parties, worked within an electorate restricted to literate males twenty-one years of age or older. Only in stages did women receive the franchise, first in the 1935 municipal elections, then in the 1949 congressional contests, and finally in the 1952 presidential race. The exclusion of women from most elections until 1952 reduced potential voters to some 49% of the population. In the 1930s and '40s, nearly 50% of the population was under twenty-one years old, so that shrank the voting pool further to about 25% of all Chileans. Those between eighteen and twenty-one years of age only won the ballot after the 1970 presidential contest, as did illiterates. According to national censuses, illiteracy over all ages fell from 37% in 1920 to 25% by 1930 and continued to hover around that figure in following decades. Illiteracy was slightly higher for women than men and much higher in rural than urban areas. Since most workers voting legally were in the cities, the Marxists concentrated their efforts there. For males of voting age, illiteracy dropped below 20% in the period. Nevertheless, this added factor cut the potential electorate again from roughly 25% down to a final eligible group of some 20% of the population. Of those eligible, usually fewer than half managed to overcome the difficulties of registration to actually inscribe themselves on the electoral rolls from the congressional election of 1918 through that of 1949. With slightly greater turnout for presidential than congressional contests, 9.9% of the total population registered for the 1920 presidential race, 9.5% for 1932, 10.3% for 1938, and 11.2% for 1946. Afterward, registration jumped to 17.6% of the population in 1952 and 36.2% in 1970. Of those registered, close to 80% usually cast ballots. In other words, between 7% and 9% of the total population voted for presidential candidates from 1932 until the beginning of rapid electoral expansion in 1952.

These restrictions on the franchise and the standard propensity for the underprivileged to register and vote less than the middle or upper classes slanted electoral power toward the wealthier groups. Nevertheless, all the contemporary observations, political appeals, and statistics from the interwar years establish that workers were voting to a significant extent. For example, at most 30% of the national population from World War I through World War II might be ranked above the category of manual laborers. Assuming sex and age patterns among the upper and middle classes roughly similar to the national averages, even though birth rates were apparently somewhat lower among the more affluent, subtracting women would shrink that electoral pool to some 15% of the nation and subtracting those under 21 years of age would reduce the eligible non–working-class voters further to perhaps

7% of the population. Even granting very few illiterates in the higher social strata and a greater propensity to register than the normal figure beneath 50%—and even if nearly all those registered actually cast ballots—it is hard to conceive of middle- to upper-class voters accounting for any more than 4 to 5% of the national population. Yet 9% of the total population voted, for example, in the 1938 presidential victory of the Popular Front.

Such imprecise national extrapolations certainly suggest that Chilean politicians knew their audience when they appealed for worker votes. It also indicates that studying parties and elections can illuminate the political and social attitudes of those workers who did vote, and it may well serve as one of the few measures available of broader worker orientations, since voters and leaders apparently reflected a wider constituency not enfranchised. Even more suggestive is local community data on voting. The 1940 census offered an imperfect but useful occupational breakdown of the active population into (1) *patrones,* including a mixed group of wealthy employers, small property owners, artisans, and the self-employed, many of whom were actually working class; (2) *empleados,* salaried, middle-class, white-collar employees primarily engaged in "intellectual" labor; and (3) *obreros,* wage-earning workers mainly involved in manual labor. The third category was the most reliable indicator of social class. In the urban community of Puente Alto in the province of Santiago, as one example, the census calculated 930 *patrones* (563) and *empleados* (367) combined, as opposed to 3,503 *obreros* among active males. In the 1938 presidential election, Puente Alto cast 1,715 votes, many obviously from workers. However narrowly based, elections provided the major political outlet for the working class in the era. Curiously, leftist demands to broaden this franchise to include illiterates or threats to resort to nonelectoral means were rare. The stability of this circumscribed, cooptive system required restraint on the part of reformers as well as conservatives.[10]

Economic conditions also helped shape the relationship between the state and the socialist movement. The Marxist parties arose in an economy with a small proletariat. From 1932 to 1952, agriculture continued to occupy a larger share of the economically active popula-

10. Atilio Borón, "Movilización política y crisis política en Chile," *Aportes,* no. 20 (Apr., 1971), pp. 41-69; Ricardo Cruz-Coke, *Geografía electoral de Chile* (Santiago, 1952), pp. 12-13; Robert McCaa, comp., *Chile. XI censo de la población (1940)* (Santiago, n.d.), esp. pp. 138 ff; Chile, *Geografía descriptiva de la vista panorámica en la exposición histórico-cultural del progreso de Chile* (Santiago, 1934), p. 76; Chile, Dirección General de Estadística, *Resultados del X censo de la población* (3 vols., Santiago, 1931), I, pp. 57-61; León Alterman P., *El movimiento demográfico en Chile* (Santiago, 1946), p. 92.

tion than did any other sector. However, that proportion claimed by agriculture and fishing declined from 39% (1930) to 35% (1940) to 31% (1952). During the same years, industry's share rose from 16% to 17% to 20%. As urbanization outpaced industrialization, the biggest occupational increase was in the service sector: from 1930 to 1940, the population economically active in the production of goods fell from 64.5% to 61.0%, while those in the services rose from 35.5% to 39.0%. Throughout the thirties and forties, only 5-6% of the population was engaged in mining. The rest were employed in miscellaneous activities such as administration, the military, and the liberal professions. Compared to the United States in 1940, Chile had inordinately high percentages of the active population in agriculture, mining, and services. For example, only 26% of the U.S. working population in 1930 was engaged in agriculture. Chile's decline of primary (agriculture, fishing, and mining) activities and growth of the secondary (industry and construction) and tertiary (services) sectors was even more evident in terms of national income. By the mid-1940s, agriculture accounted for some 33% of the active population but only contributed about 16% of national income; industry employed over 17% of the work force and produced roughly 20% of national income. From 1940 to 1954, industrial production as part of real national income rose 246%, government services 249%, and agriculture only 35%.[11] This trend continued so that by the 1960s urban industry, construction, and services totaled 78% of the gross national product, compared to 12% for agriculture, fishing, and forestry.[12]

So long as socialism and populism contributed to import-substituting industrialization, the political economy of Chile was able to tolerate ideologically incompatible forces. The political system was most able to satisfy competing demands and clienteles when prosperity, often dependent on foreign stimuli, was greatest. The Socialists and Communists capitalized on discontent over dependency, stagnation, inequality, and inflation when they were seeking office. Con-

11. Chile, Dirección General de Estadística, *Sinopsis geográfico-estadística de la República de Chile* (Santiago, 1933), pp. 102-3; Corporación de Fomento de la Producción, *Geografía económica de Chile* (4 vols., Santiago, 1950, 1962), II, pp. 160-63; Corporación de Fomento de la Producción, *Renta nacional, 1940-1945* (2 vols., Santiago, 1946), I, pp. 133-39; Corporación de Fomento de la Producción, *Cuentas nacionales de Chile: 1940-1954* (Santiago, 1957), pp. 29-58; Sergio Aranda and Alberto Martínez, "Estructura económica: algunas características fundamentales," in Aníbal Pinto Santa Cruz et al., *Chile, hoy* (Mexico, 1970), pp. 55-172. A general socioeconomic history is Julio César Jobet, *Ensayo crítico del desarrollo económico-social de Chile* (Santiago, 1955). Also consult the recent economic survey by Markos Mamalakis, *The Growth and Structure of the Chilean Economy* (New Haven and London, 1976).

12. Charles H. Daugherty, ed., *Chile: Election Factbook* (Washington, D.C., 1963), p. 4.

versely, they suffered from those same problems when serving in the executive branch. From 1952 to 1973, the Marxists placed more emphasis on state control and redirection of production and distribution, whether in foreign or domestic hands. Consequently, compromise through the mediating state in an era of slower industrial growth became more difficult.

The Chilean economy was highly dependent on the foreign sector, which was both an incentive and a constraint for nationalistic reform movements. Foreign ideologies and international strategies also made an impact. This could be seen in the Socialists' rapprochement with the United States in the 1940s and confrontation in the 1970s. The state relied on the foreign sector to help oil the wheels of government, patronage, and the economy. According to government calculations for the end of the 1920s, roughly 40-50% of annual national production was sold abroad, though this undoubtedly underestimated domestic subsistence production. Similarly derived figures for 1940-41 showed some 22% of the national product being exported, a sign of greater self-sufficiency.[13] At the start of the 1930s, for every $100 per capita of domestic commerce in Chile there was $90 per capita of foreign commerce; in the United States the figures were $750 and $75. So the ratio between domestic and external commerce in Chile was 10 to 9, that in the U.S. 10 to 1.[14] With the Depression, the importance of foreign trade declined somewhat. This indicated greater elaboration of the internal economy and less vulnerability to international fluctuations. Exports as a percentage of Chile's total disposable goods and services slid from 28.8% (1925-29) to 16.3% (1930-33) and then rebounded slightly to 23.1% (1934-39), 22.2% (1940-45), and 22.6% (1946-50).[15]

Copper and nitrates together consistently accounted for nearly 80% of Chile's foreign sales in the twentieth century. After World War I, nitrates began losing their preeminent position to copper. In the 1920s, nitrates comprised roughly 50% of exports and copper 30%.[16] The real shift came after the Depression; by 1937 nitrates claimed 18% and copper 55%.[17] The percentage of the active mining popula-

13. Chile, *Geografía*, p. 66; P. T. Ellsworth, *Chile, an Economy in Transition* (New York, 1945), p. 13. The long-range significance of Chilean dependency is argued in André Gunder Frank, *Capitalism and Underdevelopment in Latin America* (New York, 1966).

14. Charles A. Thomson, "Chile Struggles for National Recovery," *Foreign Policy Reports*, IX, no. 25 (Feb. 14, 1934), pp. 282-92.

15. Aníbal Pinto Santa Cruz, ed., *Antecedentes sobre el desarrollo de la economía chilena, 1925-1952* (Santiago, 1954), p. 86.

16. Fredrick B. Pike, *Chile and the United States, 1880-1962* (South Bend, Ind., 1963), p. 197.

17. Raúl Simón et al., *El concepto de industria nacional y de protección del estado* (Santiago, 1939), p. 26.

tion working nitrates and iodine fell from 48% in 1930 to 25% by 1940.[18] And by the 1960s, copper provided 60-70% of foreign exchange, nitrates less than 10%.[19]

Moreover, this leading economic sector was increasingly owned by foreigners. In 1920, U.S. capital controlled 82% of copper, Chilean 11%, French 3%, and British 1%. By the end of the 1920s, U.S. capital controlled over 90% of copper production for export. Bethlehem Steel Corporation monopolized iron ore. During the same period, the Guggenheims bought out most British interests and came to dominate over 85% of nitrate production. By the start of the 1960s, roughly 90% of copper production was still in the domain of North American companies, principally Anaconda and Kennecott. Then Christian Democrat President Eduardo Frei Montalva (1964-70) achieved 51% Chilean control and Salvador Allende (1970-73) full nationalization.[20]

From World War I on, the United States also became dominant in the broader range of Chilean foreign investment and trade. Average foreign investment as a percentage of the total capital existing in Chile accounted for 36% (1925-29), 52% (1930-33), and 40% (1934-39), and then declined to slightly over 20% (1940-51). Although an increasing amount went into manufacturing, the overwhelming bulk of foreign capital always remained in mining. For example, by the end of the 1940s, nearly 70% of direct foreign investment in Chile was still in mining and only some 5% in manufacturing.[21] Total U.S. investments in Chile surpassed those of Great Britain after World War I and came to provide over 60% of all foreign capital in Chile by the 1920s.[22] According to British competitors, in 1921 U.S. investments in Chile, mainly in copper and iron ore, exceeded all U.S. investments in any other South American country.[23] By the end of the 1920s, North American companies had major investments in mining, utilities, telephones, railroads, tobacco, sugar, food processing, textiles, banking, commerce, and the merchant fleet. By 1937, on the eve of the Popular Front victory, total U.S. investment in Chile had reached an estimated actual value of $500,000,000, including $410,000,000 in mining and $12,000,000 in commerce and manufacturing. Actual British invest-

18. Flavián Levine B. and Juan Crocco Ferrari, "La población chilena como fuerza de trabajo," *Economía*, año VI, no. 14 (1st trimester, 1945), pp. 15-85.

19. Daugherty, p. 4.

20. Pike, pp. 233-34; Chile-American Association, *Chile in 1930* (New York, 1930), pp. 20-24; Markos Mamalakis and Clark Winton Reynolds, *Essays on the Chilean Economy* (New York, 1965), pp. 219-23; Theodore H. Moran, *Multinational Corporations and the Politics of Dependence: Copper in Chile* (Princeton, 1974).

21. Pinto, *Antecedentes*, pp. 78-82.

22. Pike, pp. 233-34.

23. Great Britain, Department of Overseas Trade, *Report on the Industrial and Economic Situation in Chile* (London, 1922), p. 8.

ment had declined to roughly $300,000,000, with $140,000,000 in public debt, $100,000,000 in nitrates, and the remainder mainly in railroads.[24] Over the years, U.S. direct investments continued to climb, rising nearly 80% from 1940 to 1960.[25]

After World War I, the United States passed Great Britain first as the leading exporter to Chile and then as the leading importer from Chile. By the 1920s, the U.S. accounted for 54% of Chile's foreign trade. That position as the prime trading partner continued in the early 1960s, when the U.S. purchased over one-third of Chile's exports and supplied nearly one-half of her imports. Chile was traditionally very dependent on that foreign trade for manufactured consumer goods and increasingly after World War II for food and capital goods. The importation of capital goods, mainly from North America, as a percentage of total investment amounted to 48% (1925-29), 45% (1930-33), 40% (1934-39), 33% (1940-45), 58% (1946-50), and 61% (1951-53). This heavy reliance made political life very sensitive to external pressures and to international market oscillations. For example, negative trade balances in 1919 and 1930 precipitated political upheavals.[26]

Within this economic context, an attempt to merge political and social history must begin with an examination of population characteristics and class structure. The total national population tripled from the turn of the century to the 1970s: 3.2 million in 1907, 3.7 in 1920, 4.3 in 1930, 5.0 in 1940, 5.9 in 1950, 7.4 in 1960, and 9.7 in 1970.[27] From 1925-29 to 1945-49, the total population increased 36.4%. From 1925 to 1952, Chile's population, with an average growth rate of 1.5%, grew less than that of most of Latin America.[28] In Chile, the 1920s was a decade of relatively high population growth, averaging 1.4% per year, while in the 1930s growth slowed to 1.3%, and in the period 1940-54 it rose to 1.8% per year. By the 1960s, declining mortality pushed the yearly growth rate to about 2.5%, nearly the Latin American average.[29] Birth rates were higher in the rural than urban areas

24. Chile-American Association; "South America III: Chile," *Fortune,* XVII, no. 5 (May, 1938), pp. 74-83, 148-72.

25. José Cademártori, *La economía chilena* (Santiago, 1968), pp. 271-73.

26. Great Britain, Department of Overseas Trade, *Report on Economic and Commercial Conditions in Chile* (London, 1936), pp. 12-13; Pinto, *Antecedentes,* p. 76; Daugherty, p. 4; Pike, pp. 160-61.

27. Chile, Dirección General de Estadística, *Población total por provincias. Chile. 1885-1960* (Santiago, 1964); Jorge Ivan Tapia Videla, "Bureaucratic Power in a Developing Country: The Case of the Chilean Social Security Administration" (Ph.D. diss., University of Texas, Austin, 1969), p. 25.

28. Pinto, *Antecedentes,* pp. 14-15, 115.

29. Corporación de Fomento, *Geografía,* II, pp. 109-20; Chile, Dirección General de Estadística, *Sinopsis,* pp. 40-41; Daugherty, p. 4.

and higher among the lower classes. The lowest birth rates in the thirties and forties appeared in the wealthiest and most urban provinces per capita (Aconcagua, Santiago, and Magallanes), which, however, also had very elevated population growth rates because of massive inmigration from the other provinces and because of low death rates.[30]

Population shifts offered an increasing base to the urban left. According to national censuses, Chile's population rose from 43% urban in 1907 to 46% in 1920, 49% in 1930, 53% in 1940, 60% in 1952, and over 70% by the 1970s. During that 1940-52 period of rapid urbanization, the urban population increased 42%, the rural barely 3%, thanks to rural-to-urban migration. Santiago received 78.5% of all interprovincial migration in those years and grew by 48%, more than any other province. Yet the 1940s was a period of decline for the Marxists and the 1950s a period of rebuilding. The economic crisis of the 1930s contributed more directly to their expansion than did the demographic shift of the 1940s.[31]

Within that population, the grudging acquiescence of the upper classes as well as the support of the masses made populist socialism and political order reconcilable. Relations among social groups are basic to the concepts of both socialism and populism. For convenience, the following analysis will divide society into upper, middle, and lower strata. The three categories are based on essentially social and economic criteria, mainly occupations. Subjective judgments of observers in the era are also used. Following the political perceptions of Chileans in the period and the classical European pattern, it will be argued that the upper class associated most closely with the Right, the middle strata with the Center, and the urban workers with the Left. This clustering of social-political forces is not meant to define or use "social class" in a highly rigorous or mechanistic way, though there will be both numerical and qualitative attempts to measure the social texture of politics. Individual as well as group deviations from this handy tripartite correlation will also be stressed.[32]

It is difficult to define and calculate the size of social classes in Chile with great precision. Excluding an inactive population of over three million, the 1930 census counted the active population as 1,241,013. Using the three imperfect occupational categories described previously, the census found 369,364 employers or self-employed (29.8%

30. Flavián Levine B. and Juan Crocco Ferrari, "La población chilena," *Economía*, año V, nos. 10-11 (July, 1944), pp. 31-68; Alterman, pp. 59-65.

31. Chile, Universidad, Instituto de Economía, *La migración interna en Chile en el período 1940-1952* (Santiago, 1959), pp. 1-15; Tapia Videla, p. 25.

32. Joan E. Garcés, *1970. La pugna política por la presidencia en Chile* (Santiago, 1971).

of the active population), 172,600 employees (13.9%), and 699,049 workers (56.3%), of which roughly half were rural laborers.[33] By 1940, out of a total active population of 1,768,721, the census labeled 468,465 *patrones* (26%), 229,148 *empleados* (13%), and 1,071,108 rural and urban *obreros* (61%).[34] A better estimation by consistent social class criteria rather than the simple occupational data above found that the true property-owning, entrepreneurial, employer, wealthy upper class accounted for 9.3% of the active population in 1940 and 9.6% in 1952; meanwhile, the middle-class employees, professionals, and small proprietors rose from 11.6% to 13.8%, and the actual rural and urban laborers dropped from 79.1% to 76.6%[35] An observer during the Popular Front (1938-41) perceived the genuine upper class as even smaller, including only some 5,000 families, living mainly in central Chile, owning the largest estates, factories, and independent mines. That upper class also penetrated another some 5,000 families of almost equally successful lawyers, merchants, and businessmen, who were identified with the upper middle class. Below them were 19% of the population in the middle strata, mainly white-collar employees, and roughly 80% in the total worker category.[36] An estimate for the late 1950s placed the capitalist elites at 4.7% of the population, urban employees at 18.6%, and the workers at 76.7% (47.7% urban and 29.0% rural).[37] From all such attempted measurements, it seems reasonable to assume for the thirties and forties that the true upper class accounted for less than 10%, the middle class perhaps 15-20%, and all manual laborers at least 70%.

Beyond occupational, educational, racial, and familial distinctions, one of the sharpest class dividers was income. It was very unevenly distributed, even among the social groups beneath the upper crust. For example, one estimate for 1934 pegged the average yearly income of middle-class employees at 6,000 pesos, of nitrate and railroad workers at over 4,000, of factory workers in Santiago at 3,500, and of agricultural laborers at 2,400. Even with payments in kind, such as housing, rural workers were always far at the bottom of the scale.[38] By the 1940s, agricultural workers' annual wages were still the lowest,

33. Chile, Dirección General de Estadística, *Resultados del X censo*, III, pp. ix-xi.

34. McCaa, pp. 116-38.

35. Héctor Varela Carmona, "Distribución del ingreso nacional en Chile a través de las diversas clases sociales," *Panorama Económico*, año XII, no. 199 (Feb., 1959), pp. 61-70.

36. Hubert Herring, *Good Neighbors* (New Haven, 1941), p. 206.

37. James Petras, *Politics and Social Forces in Chilean Development* (Berkeley, Calif., 1969), p. 31.

38. Raúl Simón, *Determinación de la entrada nacional de Chile* (Santiago, 1935), pp. 75-76.

with industrial laborers receiving about three times as much as farm workers, and miners four times. Furthermore, the wages in industry, mining, and transportation rose far more than in other sectors during the 1940s. Meanwhile, white-collar salaries averaged roughly triple wages. White-collar employees in industry, government, and the private sector earned about seven times the income of peasants in the 1940s. "Middle-class" income in those years, according to some interpretations, rose more than that of any other social group, more than twice as much per capita as the income of workers. In other words, during the reformist governments of the 1940s an already inequitable income distribution became more regressive. An emphasis on subsidizing high-cost industry proved incompatible with large material benefits for the working class, whose standard of living was also depressed by endemic inflation. By 1954, one estimate was that the average per capita real income of the property-owning upper class rose more than did that of the urban and rural workers during the 1940s and was nearly three times that of the middle class. Worse, upper-class per capita income was about twelve times that of workers; and, even more glaring, an agricultural landowner's average income was roughly eighteen times that of an agricultural laborer. Of the active population, approximately 72% received incomes less than the minimum salary posted by the government. By the late 1950s, one calculation concluded, 9% of the active population claimed 43% of the national income. Whatever the precise figures, it is clear that gaps between classes were wide, that ample grounds for social-political hostilities existed, and that reform movements had done little to rectify those inequalities by the 1950s.[39]

Socialism and populism arose through the electoral shift to the left of all these social-political forces. From the 1930s into the 1970s, this leftward movement persisted, erratically but recurrently. This mutation in voting habits accompanied the gradual decline of the nineteenth-century conservative parties and the rise of new reform leaders. It included the transferral of traditional elite forces to more reformist candidates and positions as well as the regrouping of the disadvantaged sectors behind the socialist emblem. In addition, new centrist reformers arose as brokers between the Right and the Left. Votes for the leftist parties increased over time, and those receiving reformist votes also adopted increasingly radical programs.

During this growth of the Left, Chile's traditional ruling groups

39. Varela, "Distribución del ingreso nacional en Chile," pp. 65-70; Corporación de Fomento, *Geografía*, II, pp. 230-31; Corporación de Fomento, *Renta*, I, pp. 139-43; Ricardo Lagos Escobar, *La concentración del poder económico* (Santiago, 1961), pp. 166-68.

proved quite durable and, within limits, adaptable. The upper class or elite stratum was composed of the rural and urban privileged elements, mainly in agriculture and industry. The agricultural barons maintained a system of latifundia. According to the 1930 census, 6.8% of all the farms surveyed accounted for 81% of the value of all farms. One percent (less than 600 families) of all farms occupied 62% of all farm lands, while another 82% occupied only 4% of farm lands.[40] In the 1940s, 1,464 landowners possessed 68% of the national agricultural land, and that concentration was even greater in the three central, latifundia-dominated regions.[41] Popular-front–style movements made no change in that pattern. It was estimated in the 1950s that 9.7% of the agrarian landowners held 86.0% of the arable land, while 74.6% held only 5.2%. By the 1960s, when agrarian reform finally began, another survey showed 0.7% of the agricultural proprietors controlling 61.6% of the arable land. Nor was landownership unique in its tendency toward monopoly; the same pattern of concentration of ownership carried over into mining, industrial, and banking enterprises.[42]

Traditionally, the agricultural elites received favored treatment from the state. Benefits included easy credit, foreign trade rights, property laws, government posts, protection from unionization, and low taxes. For example, in the early 1940s taxes from agriculture accounted for barely over 1% of total government revenues. Meanwhile, mining contributed 14-21%, industry, 12-15%, and import-export rights, 19-37%. All the other sectors gave tiny amounts, but none so small as agriculture, especially compared to its allocation of benefits from government.[43]

However, agriculture's share of government favoritism, national production, and the active population declined from the Depression on, and especially in the 1940s. Per capita agricultural production fell. Chile went from a food surplus to a food deficit. In the forties—measuring net annual income per active person—fishing, construction, services, and agriculture supported the lowest per capita incomes; finance contributed 546% more per capita than did agriculture, mining 297% more, commerce 247%, government 230%, industry 142%, and transportation 100% more. From 1940 to

40. Chile, Dirección General de Estadística, *Sinopsis,* p. 127; Chile, *Geografía,* pp. 32-33.

41. Cruz-Coke, p. 35.

42. Pike, p. 281; Lagos Escobar, pp. 95-98.

43. Corporación de Fomento, *Renta,* II, p. 215; Adolfo Matthei, *La agricultura en Chile y la política agraria chilena* (Santiago, 1939), pp. 232-33.

1954, the active population in agriculture, while still far larger than that of any other economic sector, increased only 1.5%.[44]

While agricultural production rose only 8% from 1939 to 1948, national production climbed 38% and its industrial component 60%. Industrialization really gained momentum with the Depression. From 1925-29 to 1945-49, the index of total national production increased 59.1%, while that for industry soared 125.9%. Most of that import-substituting industrialization came in the form of consumer products, which still accounted for 95% of Chilean industry by the end of the 1940s. Protected industrialization as a mainly spontaneous reaction to international economic disturbances helped reduce the proportion of imports to total trade from 46% in 1932 to 38% in 1936. Manufactured imports were down to 31% of their 1929 level by 1940. Although nondurable imports, especially textiles, dwindled from 1929 to 1949, other imports for domestic industry expanded as a portion of foreign trade. For example, 36% of industry's primary materials were imported in 1939 and 26% were still imported in 1948; industry also remained heavily dependent on foreign capital and equipment.[45]

The responses of the agriculturalists and industrialists to new pressures from mass politics will be studied in organizations such as the National Society for Agriculture (SNA), the Society for Factory Development (SOFOFA), exclusive social clubs, and other traditional pillars of the upper class, such as the Roman Catholic Church. These elites congregated in the central provinces and in the Conservative and Liberal parties. The upper sectors shared enough values, political affiliations, and socioeconomic interconnections to unite on major issues. Although cohesive, they were neither intractable nor monolithic. While often repressive, their more distinctive characteristic was their ability to ameliorate and to absorb rising competitors. One reason for flexibility was that the mining base of the economy provided more of a foundation for foreigners than for the native upper class. Nevertheless, these domestic elites dominated the national economy and society, as well as politics, in the nineteenth century. Especially after World War I and then the Depression, they lost their direct monopoly over electoral and administrative politics to challengers representing the middle and lower strata and had to accommodate industrialization, minimal mass desires, and centrist reformers. These concessions safeguarded upper-class foundations and the

44. Corporación de Fomento, *Renta*, I, p. 139; Corporación de Fomento, *Geografía*, II, pp. 299-304; Corporación de Fomento, *Cuentas*, pp. 27, 70.
45. Pinto, *Antecedentes*, pp. 14-15, 91-93; Corporación de Fomento, *Geografía*, II, pp. 299-304; "South America III," p. 156; Ellsworth, p. 129.

overarching goal of social stability. That relative flexibility lasted, more or less, until the 1970s, when the Marxists took power directly within the constitutional system legitimized by the dominant groups for decades. Then the elites scuttled cooptation or conciliation in favor of overt coercion.[46]

Contacts and cooperation between the established elites and the urban middle-class leaders of leftist coalitions fostered political tolerance and trading even when it did not breed alliances. The middle sectors vacillated between the Right and the Left. Never a well-defined, unified social layer, they played an ambivalent role in politics. (In this study, terms such as "middle class," "middle classes," and "middle sectors" are used interchangeably with no intention of connoting any group behavior patterns; they are used merely to set off a social cluster distinct from the upper and lower strata.) The middle class was distinguished from the upper by income, ownership of the major means of production, family, and culture, although members of some occupations, such as lawyers and high-level bureaucrats, might belong to either stratum. In addition, illiteracy and manual labor kept the workers separate from the middle groups, although certain highly paid artisans might be perceived as middle class and some marginal merchants as lower class. The *capas medias* were primarily drawn from the professions, the intermediate levels of business and commerce, the lesser ranks of industry and mining, the military, the bureaucracy, education, and white-collar occupations. Essentially urban, the middle strata were also influential in provincial towns and in agricultural areas not monopolized by latifundia. There was a hazy division between the upper middle class—mainly liberal professionals, who accounted for only 2% of the active population in 1930—and the lower middle class—mainly white-collar employees, with the latter often more attracted to the Left. The role of these middle groups will be probed through examination of such institutions as professional organizations (which also enrolled upper-class members), student associations, employee unions, and the secretive Masonic Order, which included some anticlerical elites. More dependent than the upper class on achieving their ends through politics, the middle strata, in the opening decades of the twentieth century, were frequently identified with the followers of the moderate Radical Party. After the Depression, they were also prominent among the Socialists. Shifting alliances among social strata were as crucial to political changes as were inbred animosities. The workers depended on middle-class leaders of the

46. José Antonio Viera-Gallo and Hugo Villela, "Consideraciones preliminares para el estudio del estado en Chile," *Cuadernos de la Realidad Nacional,* no. 5 (Sept., 1970), pp. 3-24; Petras, pp. 97-101.

Left. In turn, those leaders depended on labor for their political credentials and electoral victories. From World War I into the 1940s, the middle sectors were prone to rally urban workers as a battering ram for opening up the old aristocratic system. From World War II on, the middle classes, especially the upper professional segment, were more likely to defend their gains against incursions from below. It was always difficult, however, to delineate a firm middle-class position; large chunks of the middle strata could always be found on both sides of political divisions.[47]

The middle classes also contributed to the growth of Chilean socialism in the 1930s and 1940s through their prominent role in the military. Within the Latin American context, the Chilean military's bitter withdrawal from open politics after the Great Depression and its abstinence until the 1970s provided a major explanation for flexibility and stability beneath an atmosphere of ideological and social conflict. Overt resistance to populism by the armed forces, which occurred at times in countries such as Peru, Argentina, and Brazil, did not erupt in Chile from 1933 until 1973. However, the military's toleration of civilian political rule and Marxist participation carried with it tacit limitations, such as anticommunism. Restraint did not exclude the officers from all influence. Containment of conflicts within the electoral arena deterred the Marxists from more violent routes to power. It also constrained the conservative groups from denying the Marxists offices won at the ballot box. At the same time, the threat of a nonelectoral Left, seen in intraservice and military-worker clashes in 1931, the socialist coup in 1932, Marxist militias in the 1930s, and admiration for communist Cuba in the 1960s, made the electoral Left a more palatable alternative for the traditional parties and the armed forces. By the same token, the threat of a nonelectoral Right, seen in postelection brinkmanship, conservative militias, and coup conspiracies, made the peaceful road more attractive for the Left. To both civilians and officers, however divided internally, making adjustments in Chile's malleable political system appeared preferable to risking naked con-

47. John J. Johnson, *Political Change in Latin America* (Stanford, Calif., 1958), pp. 1-14, 66-76; Jose Nun, "The Middle-Class Military Coup," in Claudio Veliz, ed., *The Politics of Conformity in Latin America* (London, 1967), pp. 66-118; Luis Ratinoff, "The New Urban Groups: The Middle Classes," in Seymour Martin Lipset and Aldo Solari, eds., *Elites in Latin America* (New York, 1967), pp. 61-93; Enzo Faletto and Eduardo Ruiz, "Conflicto político y estructura social," in Pinto et al., *Chile,* pp. 213-54; Chile, Dirección General de Estadística, *Sinopsis,* pp. 102-3; Jorge de la Cuadra Poisson, *Prolegomenos a la sociología y bosquejo de la evolución de Chile desde 1920* (Santiago, 1957), pp. 109-14; Luis Cruz Salas, *Historia social de Chile: 1931-1945. Los partidos populares: 1931-1941* (Santiago, 1969); Amanda Labarca H., "Apuntes para estudiar la clase media en Chile," *Atenea,* XCIX, nos. 305-6 (Nov.-Dec., 1950), pp. 239-57; Oscar Álvarez Andrews, *Chile monografía sociológica* (Mexico, 1965); Petras, pp. 28-32, 135-57.

flict. Although it had held the system together at critical junctures over the decades, the military proved willing to smash it in 1973. Then the alternative to Chile's gradualist reform tradition, with all its flaws and merits, turned out to be reaction, not revolution.

The initiatives, responses, and weaknesses of the lower classes also molded Chilean socialism and its role within national politics. The critical distinction was between rural and urban labor, although there were also important subgroups within each category. The largest segment of workers toiled in the countryside, but rural labor remained electorally dormant throughout most of the 1930s and 1940s. The term "peasants" will be used as shorthand to refer to a complex work force. In agriculture, the three main groups of laborers were (1) *inquilinos,* who were affixed to the great estates owned by the elites and accounted for about half of rural workers; (2) *afuerinos,* who were migratory laborers and suffered even greater poverty; and (3) small property owners or *minifundistas.* In 1938, the average *inquilino* earned between eight and twenty cents a day.[48] By the early 1940s, with the percentage of the active population in agriculture declining, each worker in mining, industry, transportation, or construction had a purchasing power at least twice that of a laborer in the fields.[49] Although peasants became more independent from conservative landowners as the century wore on, they were never as important an electoral force for the Left as were urban laborers.

Therefore, throughout this study analyses of the "workers" will normally refer to the politically participant laborers in the cities and mines. In most cases, peasants will be dealt with separately. The roles of the urban laborers or "masses" will be approached through their trade union, protest, and party activities. During this era, they normally supported the Democrats, Socialists, and Communists. The struggles of the lower classes gave impetus to populism and socialism. Because of their organizational and political debilities, they tended to look to higher social sectors for assistance. Restrictions on lower-class—especially peasant—organization and voting inhibited political effectiveness of the workers. These handicaps made it easier for the socialist movement to be incorporated by the traditional system. Constraints on lower-class politics also made it harder for their parties to extract major benefits for the masses. One calculation of average real wages for industrial workers measured in 1950 escudos showed the

48. "South America, III," p. 166. Two recent studies dealing with the agricultural sector deserve much fuller attention than it was possible to give them as this book was going to press: Arnold J. Bauer, *Chilean Rural Society from the Spanish Conquest to 1930* (New York, 1975) and Brian Loveman, *Struggle in the Countryside: Politics and Rural Labor in Chile, 1919-1973* (Bloomington, Ind., 1976).

49. Levine and Crocco, "La población chilena como fuerza de trabajo," pp. 65-66.

following bleak picture: (1) 30.4 escudos in 1914-16, (2) 29.2 in 1922-24, (3) 26.9 in 1938-40, (4) 28.8 in 1944-46, (5) 32.3 in 1951-53, (6) 26.2 in 1957, and (7) 34.0 in 1960-61.[50] Despite some improvements, grave problems with health, nutrition, housing, alcoholism, illegitimacy, and infant mortality persisted throughout the era. For example, infant mortality took 235 of every 1,000 live births in 1932. By 1942, Chile still had the highest recorded rate of infant mortality in the Western world, 195 per 1,000.[51] The participation of the lower classes and their representatives in the national bargaining system often decreased the militance of their programs and organizations. The mobilization of the masses severely menaced the established hierarchy only when their activism spilled over institutional boundaries.

By the turn of the century, the presence and organization, if not the leadership, of the urban working sectors in politics opened new possibilities. Their increasing visibility as a political issue and availability as a political resource presented both threats and opportunities to the upper and middle classes. In spite of debilities and repression, Chilean labor participated politically, pressed demands, and joined industry in fueling inflation. One reason was that nonagricultural workers suffered less population pressure than in much of Latin America. The absence of a great labor surplus was the result of a relatively low population growth rate and of the emergence of the strongest proletarian concentrations in the underpopulated mining zones of the north.[52] In addition, workers in the mines and cities forged tough, independent unions, albeit fenced in by a thicket of government regulations.

Probably more than any cultural habit of deference, the occupational structure and the legal industrial relations system kept labor weak and dependent upon political-party allies. The artisan sector, those in enterprises of four workers or less, accounted for approximately 71% of the industrial labor force in 1925 and then declined to 63% in 1930, 51% in the 1940s, and 46% by 1960. The 1924 labor code, hammered out without consulting the trade unions, granted legal recognition to a democratic labor movement independent of state domination. However, that charter made unions far weaker than employers in the bargaining system. First, the code permitted industrial unions organized by place of work mainly for blue-collar laborers

50. Oscar Muñoz Gomá, *Crecimiento industrial de Chile, 1914-1965* ([Santiago?], [1968?]), p. 194.

51. Chile, Dirección General de Estadística, *Sinopsis,* p. 72; Levine and Crocco, "La población chilena."

52. Aníbal Pinto Santa Cruz, *Chile, un caso de desarrollo frustrado* (Santiago, 1962), p. 130.

(*obreros*), but not in factories with fewer than twenty-five workers and not in federations among plants for purposes of collective bargaining. In the period from the 1920s through the 1940s, this excluded the vast majority of Chilean labor and manufacturing establishments from formal unionization. As a result, unions remained atomized, and most bargaining took place between an individual plant union and an individual, seldom responsive, employer. Second, the code allowed professional unions organized by craft mainly for skilled blue-collar workers and white-collar employees (*empleados*). Spanning more than one factory, these unions were smaller and weaker than the industrial organizations, which alone had the right to share in profits and engage in full-fledged strikes.

Third, public-sector unions were prohibited, although they often grew up anyway. Indeed, the restrictiveness of the labor code always left large numbers of unions without legal standing. Fourth, peasant unions were outlawed on paper until 1947 and in practice until 1967. Fifth, there was no provision for national labor federations, which took shape outside the legal framework until the Allende government of the 1970s. Sixth, the code's distinction between blue-collar *obreros* and white-collar *empleados* divided the union movement. It also prompted some skilled workers to seek advancement through congressional elevation from *obrero* to *empleado* status instead of through labor militance. One reason was that *empleados* won higher legal minimum wages and social security benefits. Seventh, the code regulated the internal organization of unions, for example requiring that those workers serving as union leaders also had to labor full time at their place of employment. Consequently, one of the few inducements to become an overworked, underpaid, harassed labor leader was political motivation. Eighth, union finances were regulated and inspected. For instance, funds squirreled away for strike purposes were not allowed. In all respects, fund raising was exceedingly difficult. Ninth, the state played a generally powerful role in union affairs and negotiations. It used discretion in applying the labor laws, mediated disputes with employers, set minimum wages, and established social security provisions. Under Chile's chronic inflation, this came to mean that government policies were probably as important as union activities in determining labor's real income.

Because of all these economic, social, and legal inhibitions, labor had to rely very heavily on politicians. By the same token, the politicians representing labor had to place great stock in their ability to win elections, receive appointments, and thus influence government policies. Successful parties supplied the labor movement with union leaders, lawyers to guide them through the maze of regulations, congressional and bureaucratic supporters, legislative reforms, finances, media sympathy, and often the impetus to either labor unity or disunity. Although the 1924 laws banned union political activities, unions actually took part in many ways. The dual necessity to serve the interests of the local union as well as those of the national party left labor leaders with divided loyalties. Union politics was highly competitive, and labor organizations not only leaned on friendly parties but also contributed to their success, thus avoiding simple subservience to them. Popular-front politics did not reform the restrictive labor code but it did encourage union expansion in the cities, which mainly took place because of the promotion of industrial growth. In the thirties and forties, urban unions grew significantly and became the mainstay of the political Left. After the Depression, the Marxists oriented unions toward party and electoral activities more than they devoted their parties to union affairs. While the employer elites were mobilizing to contend with these new challenges, labor unions were achieving unparalleled expansion in the 1930s. Legal unions grew from 433 organizations with 56,259 members in 1932 to 1,888 organizations with 162,297 members in 1940, according to one tabulation. These were impressive gains by labor, but those organized in unions remained a tiny percentage of the work force: roughly 8.0% in 1932, 9.0% in 1940, 12.5% in 1952, and 9.6% in 1959. This slow expansion in unions, as in the electorate, facilitated political stability.[53]

Although they were subordinate, the laborers participated actively in reform parties such as the Democrats, Communists, and Socialists. Appeals to the pragmatic benefits of clientelistic ties with party and government institutions, to deferential loyalty, to liberalism, to nationalism, and to class conflict and ideological radicalism all evoked favorable responses among varying segments of the lower strata. To the extent that populism and socialism from 1932 to 1952 depended on the idealism or opportunism of leaders from above worker ranks, it indicated the frailty of the handicapped lower classes as political actors, a situation obviously not unique to Chile. On the other hand, these forms of political expression also revealed the determination of the workers to demonstrate dissatisfactions with and, paradoxically, through the system. They rewarded those who tried to better their lot and who empathized with their problems. Both followers and leaders used each other to their own, and sometimes mutual, advantage.

53. Alan Angell, *Politics and the Labour Movement in Chile* (London, 1972), especially pp. 1-8, 42-77, 117-42; James O. Morris and Roberto Oyaneder C., *Afiliación y finanzas sindicales en Chile, 1932-1959* (Santiago, 1962), pp. 15-23; Chile, Dirección General de Estadística, *Sinopsis,* p. 240.

The workers were as heterogeneous in their political motives as any other social sector. Nevertheless, it seems safe to conclude that most of the laborers voting Socialist in the crises of the 1930s were initially attracted to charismatic leaders in their choice of a party. That political attraction, as in many movements and countries, became more a tradition and a routine than a revolutionary act or statement. Socialism in the 1930s was a popular set of symbols, as yet inadequately defined. Populism, under the banner of socialism, won a majority of the politicized workers when the economy lost its capacity to absorb labor and to fulfill rising industrial and consumer expectations.

These economic and social divisions must be contrasted with other sources of political friction. Traditionally, Chilean politics split more on clientelistic, religious, and regional issues than along socioeconomic fault lines. For example, in the nineteenth century the Right defended clerical prerogatives and the Left denounced them. Also, well into the twentieth century political cleavages sprang from regional diversities and inequalities. Chile can be cut into three layers, with the north and south ranged against the dominant center. The north was an arid region dependent primarily on mining exports. The south was a rainy, forested zone of recent development with farming, grazing, and pastoral exports. Both geographic extremes were more thinly populated and settled later than the central core of cities and latifundia. Influence and wealth were heavily concentrated in the central region, where Santiago was located. For example, of Chile's forty-eight presidents from 1817 through 1970, forty-two were born in the middle third of Chile, and twenty-four of those were born in Santiago.[54]

For a more elaborate examination of the regional dimensions of political patterns, the three sections of the country can be sliced into eight subdivisions, with two in the north, three in the center, and three in the south. The Great North contained the major nitrate and copper mines and the best-organized workers in Chile. It was one of the most urbanized zones, with a majority of the population living in ports and mining towns. Becoming more underpopulated, the Great North dropped from 8% of the national active population in 1930 to 5% in 1952. However, in 1930 it accounted for 57% of the national active population engaged in mining and, in 1940, for over 15% of all union members. It boasted some of the highest average wages for workers and was least dominated by latifundia. Given the zone's desert isolation and its nineteenth-century history as part of Peru and Bolivia, it

54. Richard B. Gray and Frederick R. Kirwin, "Presidential Succession in Chile: 1817-1966," *Journal of Inter-American Studies*, XI, no. 1 (Jan., 1969), pp. 144-59.

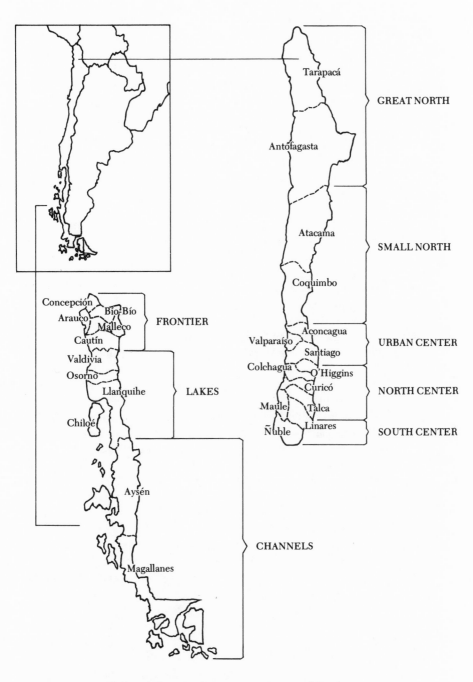

GREAT NORTH

SMALL NORTH

URBAN CENTER

NORTH CENTER

SOUTH CENTER

Tarapacá

Antofagasta

Atacama

Coquimbo

Aconcagua

Valparaíso

Santiago

Colchagua

O'Higgins

Curicó

Maule

Talca

Ñuble

Linares

Concepción

Bío-Bío

Arauco

Malleco

Cautín

FRONTIER

Valdivia

Osorno

Llanquihue

LAKES

Chiloé

Aysén

CHANNELS

Magallanes

Chilean Political Divisions: Provinces and Regions

shared with the extreme south the strongest regional sentiments in Chile. These resentments were compounded by its large contributions to the national treasury and small share of power and finances in the government. Highly dependent on international market fluctuations and foreign firms, the Great North provided fertile territory for the Left, especially the Communists.

In the Small North, the economy was better balanced between mining and agriculture. In the 1940s, 60% of its population was rural. Of all regions, it shared with the Great North the highest birth rate and the lowest wealth per capita, as measured by property evaluations in 1930. The Small North was a bastion for the Radicals.

The Urban Center harbored most of the middle classes, industry, commerce, government, and many of the largest *haciendas* or *fundos,* normally owned by the aristocratic families. In this region, nearly all the indexes of "modernization" available in the national censuses, such as urbanization, wages for workers, literacy, health, and communications, tended to be high, followed by those of the Great North and the southern provinces of Concepción and Magallanes. In the 1930 census, the Urban Center was counted as 77% urban, based on inhabitants in cities of 2,000 or more. While containing only 36% of the national active population, the region claimed over 50% of those engaged in industry, commerce, domestic services, public administration, and the liberal professions. By the 1940s, it claimed over 50% of the national unionized population. In Santiago province alone, population grew 32% in the 1920s to account for 16% of the national total by 1930. Santiago's share of the national population rose to 19% by 1940, 30% by 1952, and roughly one-third by the 1960s. From 1940 to 1952, its population grew 38% while the national total rose only 17%. The proportion of national industry in Santiago climbed from about 37% in 1930 to 50% in 1942 and 65% in 1952. However, labor remained less unified, organized, and combative than in the mining areas, partly because it was more diversified in Santiago and was counterbalanced by the white-collar middle class.

The North Center was the dominant agricultural zone and the stronghold of the conservative *latifundistas.* Also agricultural and dotted with large estates, the South Center was the most consistently conservative zone. At the start of the 1930s, these two agrarian regions held 21% of the total active population and over one-third of those employed in agriculture and fishing; they were only 30% urban, and they displayed some of the lowest rates of literacy, average wages, unionization, and wealth per capita. In the Frontier, south of the three central zones, regional resentments were deep-seated. Industrial Concepción had struggled to rival Santiago in the nineteenth century.

The coal mines and less extensive agriculture of the Frontier added to the region's distinctiveness and its propensity to back reformers. With 15% of the national active mining population and a higher proportion of its workers unionized, Concepción, in relative terms, was an even stronger center for labor and the Left than was Santiago.

The Lakes zone attracted numerous German immigrants and was heavily agricultural without a strong legacy of latifundium-based elites. Still over 70% rural by the end of the 1940s, it had one of the highest rates of birth and infant mortality. Finally, the fragmented Channels region was as removed from the national hub as was the Great North. After full incorporation as juridical provinces, the Channels also became a bailiwick for the Marxists in the 1930s. It had the lowest population density of all Chilean regions. From World War I on, the Channels developed as a new industrializing, urbanizing area of sheep and cattle raising, coal, and oil companies. There was significant foreign participation, mainly British, in these ranches and meat-freezing plants, similar to the U.S. role in the northern mines. Consequently, residents of both Chile's polar extremes were receptive to leftist economic nationalism. The southernmost province of Magallanes alone was 78% urban by 1930. Based on evaluations of property subject to taxation, it had the highest wealth per capita, over three times that of the second highest (Valparaíso-Santiago). Magallanes also had very low rates of birth, illegitimacy, and infant mortality. It boasted one of the most vigorous labor movements and the only full-blown regionalist party. Building on an earlier socialist movement shaped by European immigrants and Argentine socialists, the PS carved out an enduring domain in Magallanes. Both economic and historic factors turned these outlying areas against the three core regions.[55]

In the twentieth century, Chileans increasingly identified with na-

55. The province of Chiloé could be placed in the Channels region as well as the Lakes, since it was really distinct from either zone. A singular case, Chiloé was noted for an unusually strong Catholic Church, vast expanses of wilderness, few large landholdings, and little of the more modern industrialization and labor features common to the commercial agricultural businesses of Aysén and especially Magallanes. The latter two provinces formed more of a natural regional unit, especially for the purposes of political geography and analysis. Both Aysén and Magallanes were excluded from the 1920 electoral units, but later entered the electoral rolls together and are treated thenceforth in the text as a regional entity, as they were perceived by many politicians. From the beginning, individualistic Chiloé was included in the Lakes category, although its insertion in either the Lakes or the Channels would have made no fundamental difference in the basic regional political patterns treated in this study. See Cruz-Coke, esp. pp. 14-34; Gil, esp. pp. 4-13; Levine and Crocco, "La población chilena como fuerza de trabajo"; Alterman, pp. 59-68; Corporación de Fomento, *Geografía*, II, pp. 217-23; Cademártori, pp. 244-57; Chile, Dirección General de Estadística, *Resultados del X censo*, III, p. xi; Angell, p. 30; Armand Mattelart and Manuel A. Garretón, *Integración nacional y marginalidad* (2nd ed., Santiago, 1969).

tional over local or regional political references.[56] This was partly because of the Left's inculcation of social and ideological loyalties. Regional voting patterns for the Left or the Right could be explained as often by economic differences among regions as by simpler regional party traditions based on geographic location and provincial sympathies. For example, disagreements between northern miners and central agriculturalists stemmed from both socioeconomic and regional animosities. Urban groups, however, tended to vote at variance with rural groups, regardless of regional affiliations. At the same time, all parties had mixed followings and tried to rally support on the basis of provincial grievances against the core area. In many cases, outlying elites backed reform coalitions and the rural poor remained bound to traditional conservatism, with neither group necessarily voting like their social class counterparts in other sections of Chile. Certain regional patterns persisted. Moreover, all parties tended to stake out electoral fiefdoms in particular regions, such as the Socialists in Magallanes, a pattern not fully explicable by social class characteristics. Whereas the Radicals had relied heavily on regionalist support, the Socialists appealed more to social discontent; they built their movement in the 1930s on a combination of adherents from the urban core, the middle and lower classes, and the outlying provinces.

Regionalism retained a vibrant appeal for both the Right and the Left during a period of accelerating power for the unitary central government. Rightists used regional problems to cloud social class issues; they urged all provincials to unite behind them against the centripetal force of state intervention after the international Depression. Conversely, leftists tried to use regionalism as another way to focus on class conflicts; they rallied especially the provincial middle and lower classes against the central elites. Like populism in many countries, Chilean socialism was partly an outgrowth of uneven development between the central metropolis and the less-integrated provinces, whose resources were often drained to the dominant core or abroad. The discontented regions also provided the Socialists with electoral assets beyond the shallow base of the urban proletariat, which was especially important given the party's weakness with the peasants. In the rise of Chilean socialism and populism, more traditional political factors, such as regionalism and personalism, played a part along with more modern generators of political attitudes, such as social conflicts during urbanization and industrialization.

56. Arturo Valenzuela, "The Scope of the Chilean Party System," *Comparative Politics*, IV, no. 2 (Jan., 1972), pp. 179-99.

The Chilean Socialists

From their birth in the 1930s through their eclipse in the 1970s, the Chilean Socialists, in varying degrees, displayed some identifying characteristics. In the broadest sense, there was constant tension between socialism and populism, which was revealed in their incessant contradictions, conflicts, and divisions over ideology, membership, and methods. Ideologically, the party remained attracted to utilitarian and redistributive socialist theories reminiscent of those frequently encountered in the Third World. Although open to new ideological currents, the Socialists always embraced vehement nationalism while opposing Soviet Communism and distrusting social democrats. Throughout its career, the PS exhibited more solidarity with Latin American leftist movements than with international socialism. The party retained programmatic continuities, such as commitments to antiimperialism, industrialization, and social welfare. It always appealed to both social and regional grievances. In terms of composition, middle-class intellectuals led a mixture of mainly lower- but also some middle-class followers. Personalism and clientelism, expressed publicly and in intraparty affairs, were continuing features. While forming myriad coalitions over time, the PS maintained hostility toward the traditional Right and the upper class. Never resolved was the party's theoretical ambivalence toward the means to reaching power and creating socialism tempered by its pragmatic devotion to the democratic bargaining system.[57] Other enduring traits might be mentioned, such as flirtations with the military. Qualifications could be placed on all the above features, such as the Socialists' preference for coalitions with centrist reformers in the thirties and forties but with the Communists thereafter.

Although possessing many populist traits, the multifaceted Socialists also exhibited ever-present ideological and class components. And the PS lacked many tendencies often ascribed to populism, such as antiintellectualism, adoration of the indigenous past, and fear of modern technology. Moreover, many Socialists opposed populist proclivities within the party and tried to move beyond them.

The historical antecedents for the convergence of socialism and populism in Chile are described in Chapter 2. Openings appeared for new forms of lower-class politics through the erosion of the traditional elite system from World War I through the Depression. Chapter 3

57. Halperin, pp. 142-44; Jobet, *El Partido Socialista de Chile*, I, pp. 115-24; Salomón Corbalán González, *Partido Socialista* (Santiago, 1957); Norbert Lechner, *La democracia en Chile* (Buenos Aires, 1970), esp. pp. 82-85.

examines the birth of the modern socialist movement in 1932, during Chile's greatest twentieth-century crisis prior to the 1970s. The new political and social alignments emerging from those upheavals influenced national development for decades to come. Those political relationships among social groups, whether in conflict or cooperation, are analyzed in Chapters 4 and 5.

After its inception, the Socialist Party grew rapidly in the 1930s through populist appeals and coalitions with other reform vehicles. The social composition of the party remained fairly constant. The original leaders, and most later ones, were usually from neither the lower classes nor the most successful layers of the middle to upper strata. These middle-class leaders, often dissatisfied with their social status, reached out to the masses. The workers had become available politically as a result of the modernization and urbanization of Chile since the turn of the century. Socialist coalitions with more moderate parties were facilitated by middle-sector leadership, but middle-class dominance of the PS did not necessarily mean moderation; the intellectuals and professionals may have made the party as radical and no more primed for cooptation than it would have been under worker or union leadership. Social class did not correlate clearly with left-right divisions within the PS. There were, however, undeniable differences between the middle- and lower-class members. The party found it very difficult to go beyond the creation of a shaky alliance to actually forge an integrated, lasting movement of the middle and lower strata against the foreign and domestic economic elites. It had more success as a heterogeneous mass movement while rising to power in the 1930s (covered in Chapters 6 and 7) than while serving in various coalition administrations in the 1940s (treated in Chapters 8, 9, and 10).

The Socialist Party demonstrated its capabilities by mobilizing the masses in the 1930s. This earned its entrance into the established multiparty and bureaucratic network by the 1940s. The party's flexible ideological and social definition smoothed the formation of checkered social and party coalitions and its incorporation into the national bargaining system. In the process, the PS grappled with the dilemma of mobilization and institutionalization. The Marxists wanted to convert their ability to raise mass expectations and organizations into institutional strength and programmatic achievements through disciplined parties with ongoing access to national decision making. However, they did not want bureaucratization within the party and its involvement in the national government to smother its dynamism as an anti–status quo movement. In the thirties and forties, participation by the Socialists and Communists fortified, rather than undermined, the traditional state. However, that participation failed to produce massive benefits for their followers and did not insure enduring power for their leaders. Instead, by 1952 the Socialists had splintered and declined, and the Communists had been outlawed. The worker movement which had been mobilized in the 1930s and partially institutionalized by the 1940s was nearly defunct at the start of the 1950s. Mobilization and institutionalization were both double-edged swords for the Left. Mobilization raised demands, followers, and the claims of the Socialists to a share in political power. On the other hand, it threatened to outrun their capacity for control and their ability to deliver on promises. Mass mobilization could destabilize or capsize governments the Marxists served in, especially if it ever achieved the sudden pace experienced in some Latin American polities. And mobilization could trigger repression from traditional elites or the insecure middle classes. Institutionalization also presented opportunities and hazards. It offered continuity, sinecures, administrative avenues to serve and recruit more supporters, and involvement in the drafting and implementation of reform programs. On the other hand, participation in standard multiparty coalitions, practices, and governments turned the Marxists away from disruptive social activism. Therefore the leftists complained that they had been socialized into the norms of bourgeois democracy by the institutionalization of their movement into structured parties, unions, and state agencies. The programs for which they had sought support and offices were compromised. Consequently, institutionalization dimmed their luster as a protest movement. Given these trade-offs, it is not surprising that the Chilean Socialists never resolved the dilemma of participating in a gradualist, absorptive, and fundamentally conservative system with the avowed purpose of radically transforming it by mobilizing the masses.[58]

In their second phase (1952 to 1973), the Marxists rejected governing coalitions behind centrist reformers. Instead, they tried to revive the independent momentum of the 1930s to bring about more "revolutionary" reforms. The Socialists argued that populism, import-substituting industrialization, and bureaucratic clientelism were stages left behind as the party matured. The result of the Marxists' resurgence was the government of Socialist Salvador Allende in

58. Samuel P. Huntington, *Political Order in Changing Societies* (New Haven, 1968); Joseph L. Love, "Political Participation in Brazil," *Luso-Brazilian Review*, VII, no. 2 (Dec., 1970), pp. 3-24; Henry A. Landsberger and Tim McDaniel, "Mobilization as a Double-Edged Sword: The Allende Government's Uneasy Relationship with Labor, 1970-1973" (paper presented at the Latin American Studies Association Fifth National Meeting, San Francisco, 1974).

1970-73. It concluded with the banishing of the Marxist parties—of socialism and populism—by the military. The Epilogue briefly reviews this second era of the socialist movement and suggests continuities with the past.[59]

From the 1930s into the 1970s, the Socialists, despite major successes, failed twice to impose their vision of a new Chile. They fell short of their ultimate objectives both because of the forces opposed to them and because of their own dilemmas. They also failed to become an all-encompassing party of the masses or, even in conjunction with the Communists, to embrace a vast majority of the working class. No single, integrating, nationalist, populist party took hold in Chile. Neither did one unified, Marxist, majority party of the lower classes. Nevertheless, the Socialists and Communists, through the Chilean system, probably gave a greater voice to lower-class deprivations and aspirations than did any other movements there. They also outshone all other Marxist electoral parties in Latin America. They articulated, inspired, and enacted unprecedented reforms for the Chilean workers. In retrospect, the PS and PC had far more success than most Chileans would have predicted in 1932 or in 1970. That they ended their first era in frustration and their second in disaster is not as surprising as the fact that they pursued such nearly impossible goals for so long.

Exploring the early career of the Chilean Socialists illuminates the broader question of the forces at work in the nation's political life. It provides one prism through which to view over two decades of Chilean history. It also serves as a vantage point for observing the roles of the lower classes as pawns and participants, issues and actors. From a comparative perspective, studying Chilean socialism and populism should contribute to a general understanding of working-class politics, especially in Latin America and other areas on the periphery of the West. In the final analysis, Chile was not unique in the failure of its populist or even socialist movements to realize their versions of a just society.

59. Interviews with Julio César Jobet and Clodomiro Almeyda, Santiago, 1970; Regis Debray, *The Chilean Revolution* (New York, 1971), esp. pp. 68-69.

2

The Erosion of Traditional Politics: World War I to the Great Depression

The traditional political structure in Chile underwent several decades of disintegration before socialism and populism seized the initiative at the start of the 1930s. Socialist and populist precursors helped undermine aristocratic republicanism; the decline of that nineteenth-century system, in turn, opened the way for a new era of mass politics. The traditional stability of the Parliamentary Republic (1891-1925) resulted from limiting the political participation of lower social groups. Prosperity, which checked the dissatisfaction of the middle and working classes, rested on the precarious base of mining exports more than on internal development. However, the stable political arrangements of the Republic proved inadequate to deal with twentieth-century economic frustrations and the changes brought about by urbanization and industrialization. The crises of the 1930s were conditioned by the manner in which challenges to traditional politics first arose under the Parliamentary Republic.

The Parliamentary Republic: Defensive Politics

Through the first decade of the twentieth century, the Republic provided the upper class, especially the landed elites, with a patrician, European party style and safe political sinecures. The privileged sectors obtained narrowly channeled state action in economic development, mainly credit, and in social welfare, mainly declarations of charitable intentions. The Republic was designed to defend established interests rather than to respond quickly to new economic forces or demands from other social groups. To operate, the system required the subordination of underprivileged sectors, compromise between rural and urban elites, relative prosperity, a politically satisfied military, and a compliant president.[1]

1. Edwards Vives, esp. pp. 15-19, 210; Moreno, pp. 145-46.

The elites maintained a passive, ceremonial presidency through their control of parliament and by electing presidents from their own ranks. Presidential nominees disdained national charismatic or programmatic campaigns. Instead, they won office through the delivery of votes by local *caciques,* or bosses. All elections were handled through a network of patron-client linkages from the farm and village to the capital city.[2]

The lasting parties which most clearly represented upper-class interests and divisions were the Conservatives and the Liberals, which often sported myriad labels. While the Conservatives identified with the Church, the Liberals appealed more to anticlericalism. Although the leadership of the two parties came from nearly identical social backgrounds, there was a slight tendency for the Conservatives to pose as the champions of agriculture and the Liberals, of more urban groups. In the early twentieth century the frequently divided Liberals dominated Chilean politics by holding the center between the Conservatives, their social allies, on the right, and the Radicals, their political allies, on the left.[3]

The political supremacy of the upper class coincided with their domination of the rural and urban economies, largely independent of government regulation. Economic interests, extended families, and social ties crossed rural-urban boundaries and wove bonds of consensus between diverse elite groups vulnerable to division. The exclusive economic interest organizations, mainly the National Society for Agriculture (SNA) and the Society for Factory Development (SOFOFA), helped consolidate elite leadership. In addition, the privileged groups interacted through prestigious social organizations such as the Union Club in Santiago. The Church, the military, and select schools still provided support for the dominant groups, although those connections diminished after 1900. All these elitist organizations not only furthered unity among the privileged few but also introduced them to rising members of the middle strata.[4]

The Politics of Ascent

A respectable product of its era, the Parliamentary Republic fortified a tradition of party accountability and electoral regularity which

2. Wilfredo Mayorga, "Los caciques electorales," *Ercilla,* no. 1706 (Feb. 28, 1968), p. 15; Wilfredo Mayorga, "Los últimos caciques," *Ercilla,* no. 1709 (Mar. 20, 1968), p. 15; Pike, pp. 86-122.
    3. Julio Heise González, "La constitución de 1925 y las neuvas tendencias político-sociales," Chile, Universidad, *Anales* . . . , no. 80 (4th trimester, 1950), pp. 140-50; Carlos Vicuña Fuentes, *La tiranía en Chile* (2 vols., Santiago, 1938), I, pp. 15-26; Germán Urzúa Valenzuela, *Los partidos políticos chilenos* (Santiago, 1968), pp. 130-33.
    4. Heise González, pp. 134-43; Domingo Melfi, *Sin brújula* (Santiago, 1932), pp. 64-80.

allowed the gradual entrance of ascending groups. The urbanization of society and the economy which had been occurring since the last decades of the nineteenth century expanded the middle classes. More a social bracket than a conscious, coherent class, the middle sectors were torn between imitating and placating the elites or pressing them for greater concessions. The middle groups simultaneously sought acceptance from the upper class and support from the workers, and thus they played an ambiguous role in politics as well as in society.[5]

Lacking economic or social resources comparable to those of the elites, the middle groups attached themselves to upper-class political patrons or built their own electoral and bureaucratic strongholds. Although significant numbers of the middle classes supported all parties, they were most frequently identified, as a group, with the Radicals. This heterogeneous party was the most ardent opponent of the Conservatives, particularly on clerical and educational issues. Portraying themselves as the instrument of the middle sectors, the Radicals were best known for attracting teachers, bureaucrats, other white-collar employees, merchants, professionals, and small mine owners. In addition to some blue-collar workers, the Radical Party also encompassed segments of the elites, particularly in the outlying provinces resentful of Santiago's dominance. The political aims of the middle classes and their party spokesmen did not exceed the boundaries of the Parliamentary Republic until prosperity sagged and social pressures from below intensified.[6]

The Politics of Protest

The transition from a rural to an urban economy deteriorated the workers' relations with the middle and upper classes. This lack of social integration was most evident in the isolated mines. There, paternalism and electoral direction by traditional bosses began to break down in the early twentieth century. As a result, the flow of labor from the countryside to the cities and the mining towns created new political possibilities. No longer were workers so scattered in the rural areas or protected and controlled by personal ties to a landed *patrón*. The first clusters of such laborers formed in the nitrate and copper mines of the north, the coal zones of the south, and port cities such as Iquique and Valparaíso. Because Chilean industry was still at a low level of development, however, the urban workers did not form a cohesive proletariat. Rather, the workers were dispersed in the major

5. Johnson, pp. 66-76; Vicuña Fuentes, *La tiranía*, I, pp. 8-9.
6. Guillermo Feliú Cruz, "La evolución política, económica y social de Chile," Chile, Universidad, *Anales . . .* , no. 119 (3rd trimester, 1960), pp. 45-85; Alberto Cabero, *Chile y los chilenos* (Santiago, 1926), pp. 286-87.

cities; most were engaged in small-scale trades and manual occupations, often itinerant, and some acquired skills and artisan training.
Whatever their occupations, their economic plight was severe and
their living conditions squalid. The workers' precarious economic
situation was reflected in their lack of effective social organizations
and political participation.[7]

In the opening decades of the twentieth century, agricultural labor
remained nearly totally excluded from independent political action.
By contrast, the desperation of miners and urban workers erupted in
larger and more militant strikes, notably in the maritime, railroad, and
mining trades. In response to the emergence of unions and working-
class parties, the government either harshly repressed the laborers, as
in the massacre of hundreds of nitrate workers in Iquique in 1907, or
passed remedial legislation that was seldom implemented.[8]

The first efforts at national unionization culminated in 1909 with
the founding of the Federation of Chilean Workers (FOCH). It was
led by typographer Luis Emilio Recabarren Serrano. Concentrated in
the mines, the FOCH's strength was more local than national. Moderate at its beginning, the federation sought higher wages and better
working conditions through cooperation with the government. Immediate gains were negligible. The growth of union organizations and
the will to strike in the face of violent opposition, however, revealed
the increasing discipline and political determination among laborers.
Moreover, the emergence of a worker-led movement with socialist
aspirations established one possible pattern of mass politics for the
future.[9]

The parliamentary party closest to the workers was the moderate
Democrats, which also represented lower-middle-class sectors. Most
of the leaders and later political organizations of labor grew out of this
party. In 1912, former Democrat Recabarren founded the tiny
Worker's Socialist Party (POS), which took root in outlying geographic
zones of raw material specialization, production which was mainly for
export and usually tied to foreign firms. The nucleus of the POS was
in the mining north, and it had appendages in the coal zone and the
far southern meat-producing areas. It had little support in the major

    7. James O. Morris, *Elites, Intellectuals, and Consensus* (Ithaca, N.Y., 1966), pp.
112-15; Guillermo Viviani Contreras, *Sociología chilena* (Santiago, 1926), esp. pp. 82-84;
Pike, pp. 102-20; Heise González, pp. 168-89.
    8. Luis Vitale, *Historia del movimiento obrero* (Santiago, 1962), pp. 40-50; Julio César
Jobet, "Movimiento social obrero," in Chile, Universidad, *Desarrollo de Chile en la primera
mitad del siglo XX* (Santiago, 1953), pp. 51-71.
    9. Jobet, "Movimiento social obrero," pp. 51-71.

cities and almost none among peasants. The POS broke with the Democrats to reject coalitions with the parties of the elites and to advocate a more socialist program. Afterward, Recabarren linked the POS with the FOCH, but his attempt to build a more organized, independent, ideological labor movement failed to drain much worker support from the Democrats. Although still frail, the nascent protests and organizations of the workers helped undermine the Parliamentary Republic.[10]

Pressures on the Parliamentary Republic, 1915-19

By 1915, an incipient leftward movement of the Chilean electorate had taken shape, building toward a long-term trend. New social issues and demands first affected congressional elections in 1915, when the parties of the Left made significant gains over their showing in 1912. Although the Conservatives held fast with nearly 22% of the national votes, the more leftist parties began growing at the expense of the Liberals, who fell from 54% in 1912 to 42% in 1915. The Radicals climbed from 17% of the electorate in 1912 to 21% in 1915, the Democrats rose from 5% to 8%, and the POS attracted a handful of votes.[11]

The 1915 congressional elections were also significant because in them Arturo Alessandri Palma introduced Chileans to the disruptive possibilities of populist politics. Linking a man of the upper sectors to the masses, this new style offered solutions from a national *caudillo* rather than a local *cacique*. A former conservative Liberal deputy, Alessandri was a handsome lawyer who campaigned for senator from the northern mining province of Tarapacá in 1915. He was the candidate of the Liberal Alliance, a coalition of center-left parties. Breaking with custom, Alessandri fought for the seat on impassioned speaking tours designed to bypass local conservative bosses and personally reach the voters. He won primarily as the reformist candidate of the middle to upper-middle classes and as a protest against the north's domination by the center. Dubbed the "Lion of Tarapacá," in the province of greatest labor discontent, he also captured a lower-class following there. He did so with the support of the Radicals and Democrats and despite the opposition of the POS. Prototypes of socialism, the POS and the FOCH failed to counteract Alessandri's

10. Angell, p. 24; Julio César Jobet, *Recabarren* (Santiago, 1955), pp. 30-49, 87-100; Arturo Olavarría Bravo, *La cuestión social en Chile* (Santiago, 1923), pp. 92-104.

11. Chile, Dirección General de Estadística, *Política, administración, justicia y educación* (Santiago, 1938), p. 1; Vicuña Fuentes, *La tiranía*, I, pp. 42-50.

populist appeal to the workers, even with their warnings that he was a demagogic oligarch.[12]

World War I, by devastating the Chilean economy, gave impetus to Alessandri's formula for mass politics. By the end of the war, the plummeting international market for Chilean nitrates caused a severe depression, unemployment, and inflation. Dissatisfaction with reliance on the foreign sector and with the elites' management of the economy undercut the Parliamentary Republic.[13]

The war years also brought foreign reformist and revolutionary ideas which sharpened the thinking of Chilean intellectuals and politicians. The League of Nations advocated social reforms. Chileans were influenced by the restlessness of European laborers and by the Russian Revolution. They saw the power of industrialized nations, as well as the inequities of industrial society. Greater state involvement in economic and social problems was a world trend at odds with the premises underlying the Parliamentary Republic.[14]

Alessandri and the Liberal Alliance capitalized on wartime discontent by challenging the conservative forces in the parliamentary elections of 1918. A mixture of opportunism and reformism, the Alliance was based on the Radicals and enveloped the more progressive Liberals and most Democrats. Using the populist tactics pioneered by Alessandri, the Alliance forged an emotion-charged alignment of the middle and lower sectors with segments of the elites behind a program of incremental reforms. They won votes as a result of Alessandri's charisma as well as of specific promises or by bosses collecting obligations from clients. The national personalization of politics furthered the electoral shift to the left which had surfaced in 1915. The Alliance captured the lower house of Congress. Meanwhile the conservative forces retained control of the more powerful Senate, largely thanks to their grip on the rural vote, and were slow to grasp the severity of liberal populism's challenge to their rule.[15]

12. Elías Lafertte, *Vida de un comunista* (Santiago, 1961), pp. 114-17; Claudio de Alas, *Arturo Alessandri* (Santiago, 1915); Augusto Iglesias Mascaregno, *Alessandri, una etapa de la democracia en América* (Santiago, 1960); Edwards Vives, pp. 221-25; Vicuña Fuentes, *La tiranía*, I, p. 35; Cabero, *Chile*, pp. 255-56.

13. Frank Whitson Fetter, *Monetary Inflation in Chile* (Princeton, 1931), pp. 23, 39, 134-73; Alberto O. Hirschman, *Journeys toward Progress* (Garden City, N.J., 1965), pp. 218-35; Carlos Keller R., *Un país al garete* (Santiago, 1932), pp. 7-11; Cabero, *Chile*, pp. 306-9, 413; Chile-American Association, pp. 31-33.

14. Arturo Alessandri Palma, *Mensaje leído por S.E. el Presidente de la República* (Santiago, 1921), pp. 24-25; Heise González, pp. 100-25, 192-95; Olavarría Bravo, *La cuestión social*, pp. 6-9, 143-62.

15. In 1918, the Conservatives, Democrats, and POS essentially maintained their 1915 percentages, while the Liberals regained some votes. Most significant for the

The Election of 1920: Liberal Populism and Alessandri

Alessandri ran for president as the populist candidate of the Liberal Alliance in 1920. He believed that "rapid evolution" was required to "avert revolution."[16] He argued that an active president was needed to integrate the middle and lower classes into national politics; a strong, expanded state could include and regulate more social sectors and economic activities. Among many promises, Alessandri vowed to lessen discord by reducing parliamentary instability, Church connections with the state, currency depreciation, dependence on fluctuating export revenues, and neglect of the provinces, middle classes, and workers. Alessandri's personalistic style and identification with discontented social groups, more than his specific proposals, upset the political elites.[17]

To a large extent, Alessandri and his more conservative opponents represented two elite responses to social change and its accompanying disorders. They both wanted to restore harmony to the social order, but Alessandri placed more emphasis on ameliorative reforms and the Right still preferred coercion to concessions. Even when both agreed on the social legislation required to ease class antagonisms, Alessandri favored rallying the masses behind those reforms, whereas the traditional politicians wanted to resolve those issues in the gentlemanly fashion of the past, without the intrusion of the lower classes.[18]

The elites on the Right—the Conservatives and most of the Liberals—formed the National Union coalition to oppose the Liberal Alliance. The Right reacted with outrage to Alessandri's hauling divisive social issues from the halls of Congress into the streets. His denunciations of "oligarchs" and "gilded scoundrels" provoked the

---

future, the Radicals rose again, from 21.2% in 1915 to 24.7% in 1918. Chile, Dirección General de Estadística, *Política* (1938), p. 1. For example, the coal-mining zone of Lautaro had previously been a bastion of the conservative forces, with the miners voting as ordered by the owners. From 1918 on, however, this district shifted toward the Left. Edwards Vives, pp. 207-32; Heise González, pp. 156, 165-67, 191-97; Guillermo Feliú Cruz, *Alessandri, personaje de la historia* (Santiago, 1950), pp. 54-55.

16. Arturo Alessandri Palma, *Recuerdos de gobierno* (3 vols., Santiago, 1952), I, pp. 33-37.

17. Alessandri, *Recuerdos*, I, pp. 25-45, 395-404; Alessandri, *Mensaje* (1921), pp. 17-80; Arturo Alessandri Palma, *El alma de Alessandri* (Santiago, 1925), pp. 86-119; *El Mercurio*, June 23 and June 25, 1920; C. H. Haring, "Chilean Politics, 1920-1928," *Hispanic American Historical Review*, XI, no. 1 (Feb., 1931), pp. 1-26.

18. Vicuña Fuentes, *La tiranía*, I, pp. 20-35, 56-82; René León Echaíz, *Evolución histórica de los partidos políticos chilenos* (Santiago, 1939), pp. 153-54; Ricardo Boizard, *La democracia cristiana en Chile* (Santiago, 1963), pp. 42-52; Arturo Alessandri Palma, *El Presidente Alessandri* (Santiago, 1926), pp. 272-76; La Asamblea Radical de Iquique, *Don Arturo Alessandri* (Iquique, Chile, 1920); interview with Aníbal Jara, Santiago, 1970.

Right to brand Alessandri a traitor to his class and a communist, which furthered the polarization of political rhetoric.[19]

The Right tempered their social intransigence, however, with programmatic flexibility. The National Union wrote a platform nearly indistinguishable from that of the Liberal Alliance in promises of educational, economic, and labor reform. The elites resisted rapid middle-class ascension, but, at the same time, tried to draw the middle sectors away from a coalition with urban labor. Therefore they played on middle-class fears and their desires to identify with the upper classes instead of with the workers. Also, the privileged groups dreaded a shift of worker loyalties from employers to the new reformers and resented disrespectful lower-class behavior. Nevertheless, the Right had to acknowledge and court the workers because the Liberal Alliance, including renegade segments of the upper class, was stirring mass support. The National Union, through its platform and its opposition to Alessandri's populism, hoped "to avert class antagonisms artificially created as an electoral resource."[20]

The National Union's candidate, Luis Barros Borgoño, was a cautious, proper member of the traditional upper class. His elegant, antiseptic, aloof campaign contrasted starkly with the daring, passionate, face-to-face style of Alessandri. On one level, it was a contest over social images and political practices. On another, it was a time-honored conflict of the anticlerical and regional forces against the Conservatives and the "Santiago aristocracy." New appeals to the masses went hand-in-hand with traditional vote-buying by both sides. The 1920 election constituted a transition from past to future politics.[21]

The military, like all social groups, was both aroused and divided by the 1920 campaign. Plots simmered within the armed forces in 1919-20, but the military's social, political, and geographic cleavages made them an unlikely alternative to the electoral process. Alessandri

19. *El Mercurio*, June 1-25, 1920; *Catilina* (Santiago, 1920); *La política de la Alianza Liberal juzgada por sus propios hombres* (Santiago, 1920); Luis Durand, *Don Arturo* (Santiago, 1952), pp. 180-88.

20. Quoted from the National Union in Ricardo Donoso, *Alessandri, agitador y demoledor* (2 vols., Mexico and Buenos Aires, 1952, 1954), I, pp. 245, 246-50; *El Mercurio*, June 1, June 6, June 8, June 13, June 17, and June 23, 1920; Marcial Sanfuentes Carrión, *El Partido Conservador* (Santiago, 1957), pp. 61-70; Olavarría Bravo, *La cuestión social*, pp. 59-85; Morris, *Elites*, pp. 35-36, 126-54; Melfi, *Sin*, pp. 24-25.

21. *South Pacific Mail*, May 6, 1920; *El Mercurio*, Oct. 13, 1932; *Campaña presidencial de 1920. Candidatura del señor don Luis Barros Borgoño* (Santiago, 1920); John Reese Stevenson, *The Chilean Popular Front* (Philadelphia, 1942), pp. 32-33; Alberto Edwards Vives and Eduardo Frei Montalva, *Historia de los partidos políticos chilenos* (Santiago, 1949), pp. 183-87; Mig Zaleg, *Recuerdos provincianos, apolíticos, del año 1920* (Rancagua, Chile, 1931), pp. 11-38.

appealed most to members of the army, units stationed in the north, and younger officers who, in contrast to their conservative superiors, were often from the middle classes. Through membership in the Masons, the younger, progressive officers associated with upper-middle-class politicians, particularly those from the Radical Party.[22]

The heterogeneous Radicals and their middle-class supporters identified with Alessandri's style and promises. Partly by joining the Masons on the eve of the presidential contest, Alessandri bolstered his credentials with the middle sectors and anticlerical reformers. The class coalition of the Liberal Alliance widened when professional and white-collar associations collaborated with worker organizations. The middle sectors were angered by economic deterioration and dismayed by the minimal sympathy of the conservative elites. Therefore most of the middle classes in 1920 expressed their discontent by forming a temporary political alliance with the workers. However, the middle groups did not make a long-range commitment to reforms for the lower classes or to a protracted battle against entrenched privileges. For example, the short-lived Middle Class Federation, formed in 1919, complained far more about upper-class resistance to their mobility than about the plight of labor. In essence, the middle groups adopted a dual strategy. They politically denounced the "reactionary oligarchy" but continued to pursue a "bond of blood or friendship" with the upper class.[23]

Student politics in 1920 exhibited significant middle-class populistic traits. The Student Federation of Chile (FECH) joined mounting labor protests and thus helped stitch together the middle and lower classes. For example, FECH leaders conducted special classes for workers. Inspired by anarchism and socialism-communism, the students made common cause with the Industrial Workers of the World (IWW) and the FOCH. The conservative forces, acting through the Union Club and the government, attacked the FECH headquarters. They repressed students as well as workers, and thereby drove the two

22. Venturana Maturana Barahona, *Mi ruta* (Buenos Aires, 1936), pp. 2-16; Alejandro Walker Valdés, *La verdad sobre el motín militar* (Santiago, 1919), pp. 40-186; Arturo Olavarría Bravo, *Chile entre dos Alessandri* (4 vols., Santiago, 1962, 1965), I, pp. 92, 180; Carlos Sáez Morales, *Recuerdos de un soldado* (3 vols., Santiago, 1934), I, pp. 50-55; Terrence Stephen Tarr, "Military Intervention and Civilian Reaction in Chile, 1924-1936" (Ph.D. dissertation, University of Florida, Gainesville, 1960), pp. 4-9; Wilfredo Mayorga, "París contra Ibáñez," *Ercilla*, no. 1579 (Aug. 25, 1965), pp. 4-6; Vicuña Fuentes, *La tiranía*, I, pp. 54-58, 108, 139-43, 171-72.

23. Jaime Eyzaguirre, *Fisonomía histórica de Chile* (Mexico, 1948), pp. 157-58; Pike, pp. 284-87; Wilfredo Mayorga, "Rafael Luis Gumucio, el amigo," *Ercilla*, no. 1731 (Aug. 21-27, 1968), pp. 41-42; Alessandri, *Recuerdos*, I, pp. 41-47; Morris, *Elites*, pp. 35-41; Olavarría Bravo, *Chile*, I, pp. 64-81; Vicuña Fuentes, *La tiranía*, I, pp. 56-58, 65-108, 171.

groups closer together. Attracted to worker causes, romantic idealism, and charismatic leaders, the student generation helped create nationalistic, personalistic, vaguely ideological mass politics in Chile.[24]

The restless lower classes, although divided in their loyalties, transferred their anxieties from local to national expressions of discontent by 1920. Labor struck more than one hundred times, and strikes escalated through the depression's depths in 1919 and continued into 1920. Although Chile's balance of payments rebounded from a deficit of over 200 million pesos in 1919 to a surplus of over 1,000 million pesos in 1920, nitrate production and employment continued to fall through the presidential election period. That unemployment rippled throughout the rest of the economy. Also, from 1919 to 1920 price inflation, especially for necessities, took its greatest leap since 1913. From an index of 100 in 1913, the general cost of living in Santiago spurted from 143 in 1919 to 168 in 1920. The average prices for kilos of rice and flour nearly doubled. Influenced by the economic crisis and by the Russian Revolution, the FOCH adopted a Marxist position in 1919. It called for the abolition of the capitalist regime. According to the FOCH and the POS, Alessandri signified "the ascension to power of a new oligarchy deceiving the working masses with false promises of a false evolutionism that tries to obtain the support of the working classes in order to become their masters tomorrow."[25] To counter Alessandri's populism, they nominated Recabarren for the presidency, making him the first labor candidate in Chilean history. During the campaign, Recabarren suffered repeated persecution, including incarceration, by the government. He had no chance of victory. His FOCH was strongest with laborers in mines, factories, and transportation. The rival IWW (1919-25), building on Chile's anarchosyndicalist tradition and U.S. examples, was concentrated among port workers in Valparaíso and the north, primary school teachers, bakers, leather workers, and construction workers. The FOCH was larger and more radical. It claimed nearly 80,000 members to the IWW's 9,000. Both the FOCH and the IWW outdistanced many of their followers in revolutionary beliefs and commitments.[26]

24. Frank Bonilla and Myron Glazer, *Student Politics in Chile* (New York and London, 1970), pp. 31-75, 110-15; Wilfredo Mayorga, "La generación sacrificada," *Ercilla*, no. 1681 (Aug. 23, 1967), p. 13; Wilfredo Mayorga, "Todos fuimos anarquistas," *Ercilla*, no. 1676 (July 19, 1967), p. 15; Wilfredo Mayorga, "La difícil generación del 20," *Ercilla*, no. 1720 (June 5-11, 1968), pp. 43-44; Jobet, *Recabarren*, pp. 105, 141-42.

25. Vitale, *Historia*, pp. 12-19, 40-64; Chile, Dirección General de Estadística, *Sinopsis*, pp. 199, 265, 284-85; Cabero, *Chile*, p. 413; Fetter, pp. 39, 141-51.

26. Oscar Álvarez Andrews, *Historia del desarrollo industrial de Chile* (Santiago, 1936), pp. 223-26; "Los jefes del socialismo: Carlos Alberto Martínez," *Bases*, no. 2 (Nov., 1937), pp. 5-10; Jorge Barría, "Chile. La cuestión política y social. 1920-1926," Chile,

The ideologies and organizations of the FOCH, POS, and IWW paled before the personal appeal of Alessandri. The workers, even from the FOCH, responded more to Alessandri's oratory and to his emotional identification with the common man. In extreme cases, some workers believed that Alessandri personally would ease their toil and feed their families; others knelt to kiss his hand and brought sick children to be cured by his touch. For many workers, the messianic Alessandri represented a political awakening, for others, a distraction, but for nearly all he appeared as the most tangible, viable, and exciting alternative in 1920.[27]

The first phase of the indirect election was the voting for presidential electors. Suffrage restrictions excluded women, illiterates, police, military, clergy, prisoners, and those absent from their registration district, naturalized in a foreign country, or under twenty-one years of age. That left nearly 20% of the population eligible to vote. Of the 10% of the nation who were actually registered, those casting ballots in 1920 amounted to only 4.5% of the total population, compared to the 3.9% who had voted for president in 1915. The absolute number of voters (166,115) for president in 1920 was higher than that for president (139,176) or parliamentary deputies (149,813) in 1915 but lower than the totals for deputies in 1918 (183,017) or 1921 (197,267). Until a stronger presidential system was installed in 1925, voter turnout was normally higher for parliamentary elections. Also significant in 1920 was the abstention rate, which exceeded 50% of registered voters, higher than in the presidential election of 1915 (25% abstention) or the parliamentary elections for deputies in 1915 (19%), in 1918 (46%), or in 1921 (47%). Much of the low turnout in 1920 might be explained by antiquated registration lists and procedures, corruption, *cacique* control, the indirect character of the presidential balloting, higher voter identification with local than with national figures, the realization that the parliament was more powerful than the presidency, apathy among voters who believed that the differences between Alessandri and Barros Borgoño were largely stylistic and rhetorical, and the fact that many people who filled the streets for Alessandri—such

---

Universidad, *Anales . . .* , no. 116 (4th trimester, 1959), pp. 56-73; Morris, *Elites,* pp. 99-118, 144-51, 204-5; Cabero, *Chile,* pp. 135, 387-94; Stevenson, pp. 25-29; Wilfredo Mayorga, "Todos bailamos el año veinte," *Ercilla,* no. 1561 (Apr. 21, 1965), pp. 4-5; Angell, pp. 26-27.
    27. Wilfredo Mayorga, "Don Arturo y los cuarteles," *Ercilla,* no. 1745 (Nov. 27–Dec. 3, 1968), p. 41; Ricardo Boizard, *Voces de la política, del púlpito y la calle* (Santiago, 1939), pp. 13-18; René Olivares, *Alessandri, precursor y revolucionario* (Valparaíso, 1942), pp. 22-24; Durand, *Don Arturo,* pp. 180-86; Olavarría Bravo, *Chile,* I, pp. 81-82; Cabero, *Chile,* pp. 250-58; Vitale, *Historia,* pp. 50-64.

as students, workers, and women—could not vote. Beyond all these factors, the modest turnout in 1920 cautions against exaggerations about the level of voter interest, the depth of political divisions, and the extent of any "revolution" in electoral behavior. Alessandri reflected significant new attitudes, issues, and support, but he lost the popular vote to Barros Borgoño, 49.4% to 50.0%.[28]

Alessandri accelerated social divisions in Chilean politics, but the voting returns suggested he prospered more as a regional than as a class candidate. Alessandri's clearest advantage over Barros Borgoño, who dominated the traditional core, was in the extremities of Chile, as Table 1 shows.[29]

TABLE 1: VOTES FOR PRESIDENT BY REGION, 1920

Region	Alessandri	Barros Borgoño	Recabarren
Great North	71.8%	21.5%	6.6%
Small North	54.4	45.5	0.0
Urban Center	45.0	54.8	0.0
North Center	34.4	65.5	0.0
South Center	44.1	55.6	0.0
Frontier	62.6	37.4	0.0
Lakes	50.1	49.6	0.0
Total	49.4%	50.0%	0.4%

In addition to capturing the outlying provinces, Alessandri surpassed Barros Borgoño in the urban areas nationwide, but less so in the central regions. Alessandri carried the major urban communities in the northern and southern regions with resounding majorities, often in excess of 70%. In the three central zones, however, he lost many cities, notably Valparaíso and Viña del Mar, while taking Santiago with 57%. Apparently, political divisions still reflected historical regional jealousies as much as national social antagonisms. Alessandri ran worst in the central bastions of latifundia and best in the peripheral zones of mining, industry, and smaller agriculture.[30]

28. Chile, Dirección General de Estadística, *Resultados del X censo,* I, p. 40; Chile, Oficina Central de Estadística, *Política y administración* (Santiago, 1922), pp. 41-47; Chile, Oficina Central de Estadística, *Censo electoral 1921* (Santiago, 1922); Chile, Oficina Central de Estadística, *Política y administración* (Santiago, 1918), p. 33; Chile, *Recopilación de leyes,* VII (Santiago, 1914), pp. 283-84; *El Mercurio,* June 26 and June 27, 1920; Cruz-Coke, pp. 12-19; Lester W. Milbrath, *Political Participation* (Chicago, 1965), pp. 97-105.

29. Surprisingly, neither Recabarren nor Alessandri ran very well in the southern coal zones. The missing percentage in the national total belonged to blank or scattered ballots. Chile, Oficina Central de Estadística, *Censo Electoral 1921.*

30. Alessandri, *Recuerdos,* I, pp. 26-28. Alessandri was a more consistent victor over Barros Borgoño in the outlying provinces than in the urban districts regardless of regional location. The table below shows the split between the two candidates in the

In his campaign and near-victory by ballots, Alessandri relied on the resentful provinces, miners, the urban middle and lower classes, and sectors of the elites. His showing was an important step toward urban, populist, mass politics. But Alessandri did not fully eliminate *cacique* authority, the parliamentary system, or traditional voting habits and patterns.[31]

Fear of the masses, not the masses themselves, elected Alessandri to the presidency. During the tense weeks after the popular vote, a tribunal of honor deliberated on who should be president in light of the close electoral count. Mass demonstrations for Alessandri, joined by the POS and the FOCH, spawned rumors of general strikes and civil war. The campaign slogan "Either Alessandri as President or the Revolution" acquired an ominous ring. In the election, the Right had proved that they could still purchase and attract enough votes to lay claim to the presidency. Now the Left showed that popularity with the masses was also a powerful claim. National Union attempts to silence

---

fifteen electoral districts that contained a city of over 5,000 population (the percentage of urban growth for each city in 1907-20 is noted in parentheses beside the city). Listing the cities geographically from north to south reveals that regional position, more than the urban setting, tended to be associated with high votes for Alessandri:

	Alessandri	Barros Borgoño
Great North		
Iquique (−5.4%)	75.7%	21.0%
Tocopilla (−2.3%)	80.4	19.6
Urban Center		
Quillota (+6.1%)	37.0	63.0
Quilpué (+12.3%)	41.5	58.5
Valparaíso (+8.9%)	45.6	54.4
Santiago (+32.4%)	57.1	42.7
San Antonio (+98.8%)	45.5	54.5
South Center		
Chillán (−8.0%)	61.9	39.1
Frontier		
Talcahuano (+25.2%)	100.0	0.0
Concepción (+11.3%)	72.6	27.4
Lota (+34.3%)	33.4	66.6
Lautaro (+25.6%)	52.4	47.6
Temuco (+44.4%)	80.0	20.0
Lakes		
Valdivia (+43.6%)	68.4	32.6

Álvarez Andrews, *Historia*, p. 234; Chile, Dirección General de Estadística, *Resultados del X censo*, I, p. 47; Chile, Oficina Central de Estadística, *Censo electoral 1921*.

31. Vote-buying and cheating were widespread on both sides, but most observers saw far more fraud by the National Union. *South Pacific Mail*, July 1, 1920.

the *alessandristas* were unsuccessful. Military sympathies were uncertain. The elites became convinced that confirming Alessandri was preferable to continuing social disorders. Moreover, Alessandri's upper-class opponents knew he would be a restrained "revolutionary"; he promised the landowners, for example, that labor reforms and unions would be limited to the urban areas. The conservative elites decided to grant Alessandri a symbolic victory only to quiet the lower classes; the Right, given its control of the powerful parliament through domination of the Senate, had no intention of allowing the new president to become a dynamic reformer, even within the limits of what reform meant to Alessandri.[32]

Alessandri in Office, 1920-24

The parties and organizations associated with the workers gained under President Alessandri. In the 1921 parliamentary elections the Liberal Alliance's popularity rose. The voters doubled the percentage the Democrats had won in 1918 and raised the Radicals to the highest point in their history. The Worker's Socialist Party's share of the votes climbed to barely over 1%. Although labor unions still encountered persecution, it eased and they grew vigorously. The IWW and new unions for teachers and employees flourished. Most significant, the FOCH, followed by the Federation of Railroad Workers, expanded rapidly and joined the Communist International in 1921. The POS officially became the Communist Party of Chile (PC) in 1922. Many workers, particularly skilled laborers and artisans, did not follow this radical move by Recabarren and drifted toward independent socialism, but a majority of organized labor went along.[33]

Alessandri reached office with the aid of the workers but seldom governed with them or for them. His concept of mass politics was limited to electoral mobilization. Whereas past governments had ruled directly with the social groups they claimed to represent, there was a divorce between Alessandri's electoral supporters and most of his administration.[34]

32. Chile, Congreso Pleno, *Boletín y actas de las sesiones celebradas por el Congreso Nacional en 1920 con motivo de la elección de Presidente de la República* (Santiago, 1921), pp. 24-29; *South Pacific Mail*, Oct. 14, 1920; Lafertte, *Vida*, pp. 150-52; Stevenson, pp. 33-34; Pike, pp. 171-74; Olavarría Bravo, *La cuestión social*, pp. 255-64; Alessandri, *Recuerdos*, I, pp. 41-57; Sanfuentes Carrión, p. 72; Boizard, *La democracia*, pp. 25-37; Vicuña Fuentes, *La tiranía*, I, pp. 88-110.

33. In the 1921 election the Conservatives received 19% of the votes, Liberals 35%, Democrats 12%, and the Radicals 30%. Chile, Dirección General de Estadística, *Política* (1938), p. 1; Cruz Salas, pp. 15-16; Hernán Ramírez Necochea, *Origen y formación del Partido Comunista de Chile* (Santiago, 1965), pp. 127-28; Jorge Jiles Pizarro, *Partido Comunista de Chile* (Santiago, 1957); Morris, *Elites*, pp. 107-11, 204-6.

34. Oscar Bermúdez Miral, *El drama político de Chile* (Santiago, 1947), pp. 16-17; Edwards and Frei, pp. 187-91.

Alessandri blamed his disappointing presidential record primarily on congressional obstructionism. Vowing to oust the "old men of the Senate," Alessandri scuttled tradition once more in the 1924 parliamentary elections. With a brash exercise of presidential powers, he personally roused the people to defeat the National Union. Using Alessandri's tested *caudillo* style, the Liberal Alliance further chipped away at *cacique* sovereignty and won both houses of parliament. The contest was so heated that the military served as guardians at the polls. This exposed the armed forces to the seamier side of politics. Alessandri's election intervention shocked the elites, undermined constitutional stability, and emboldened military critics of the parliamentary system. The upper classes on the right had conceded the presidency in 1920 and now saw the citadel of their political dominance—the parliament—slipping from their grasp. With traditional politics under siege, both sides curried military favor.[35]

Military Intervention, 1924-31

Breaking their long record of aloofness from partisanship, the armed forces marched into open politics. They were divided in loyalties but united in dissatisfaction. Through inaction, corruption, and petty squabbling, the civilian politicians had tarnished the legitimacy of the Parliamentary Republic. As in 1919-20, political upheaval in 1924-25 coincided with a double-digit jump in the general cost-of-living index.[36] The younger, middle-class, intermediate-rank officers stunned the nation in mid-1924 by packing the galleries of parliament to ram through Alessandri's reform legislation, notably a new labor code and better pay for the military. The movement was headed by Majors Marmaduke Grove Vallejo and Carlos Ibáñez del Campo, both Masons. Their superiors, led by General Luis Altamirano Talavera, who was connected to the upper class and belonged to the Union Club, rapidly assumed leadership of the protest to guide it into more conservative channels. His authority damaged, Alessandri resigned and left Chile, while Altamirano and a junta took charge of the government. The upper-class conservatives quickly established their influ-

35. Enrique Monreal, *Historia completa y documentada del período revolucionario, 1924-1925* (n.p., 1927), pp. 25-53; Juan Pablo Bennet, *La revolución del 5 de septiembre de 1924* (Santiago, [1926?]), pp. 6-12; Carlos Vicuña Fuentes, *En las prisiones políticas de Chile* (Santiago, 1946), pp. 8-9; Alessandri, *El Presidente*, pp. 182-222; Carlos Sáez Morales, *Y así vamos . . .* (Santiago, 1938), pp. 17-20; Sáez, *Recuerdos,* I, pp. 60-77; Cabero, *Chile*, pp. 257-63. For this and all succeeding sections on the Chilean military during the 1920s, see Frederick M. Nunn, *Chilean Politics, 1920-1931* (Albuquerque, N.M., 1970).

36. Chile, Dirección General de Estadística, *Sinopsis*, pp. 284-85; Fetter, p. 39; Moreno, pp. 150-51; Carlos Pinto Durán, *La revolución chilena* (Santiago, 1925), pp. 43-47.

ence over the junta in hopes of restoring the social tranquility and
political tidiness of the pre-1920 period. By trying to reconstruct the
past, however, the elites mortgaged their future.[37]

In January, 1925, Ibáñez and Grove eschewed obedience to the
military hierarchy and replaced the conservative Altamirano government with a junta of their own. The new regime promised a wave of
reform. They returned Alessandri to the presidency. The traditional
elites discovered that the military, as well as the presidency and the
parliament, was unreliable.[38]

The second junta and Alessandri's return produced important
reforms, highlighted by the constitution of 1925. The constitution
codified Alessandri's promised labor and welfare legislation, gave
more economic leverage over private property to the state, and promised the provinces more administrative responsibilities. It separated
church and state and elevated the powers of the president over those
of parliament. Disgruntled conservatives were compensated by the
new quotient system for congressional and municipal elections. The
complicated quotient system safeguarded elite control of and exaggerated representation for rural voting wards. It also encouraged proliferation of parties and electoral pacts. But presidents were to be
elected directly and all voting was made obligatory; this boosted the
stakes in presidential elections and weakened *cacique* control. The rise
of modern *caudillos*, epitomized by Alessandri, helped create strong
executive government; that new state structure, in turn, reinforced
the trend toward personalistic national politics by requiring a dynamic
leader. By invigorating the presidency, the 1925 constitution encouraged populism and ended the Parliamentary Republic.[39]

After the constitution was ratified by more than sixteen to one in a

37. Frederick M. Nunn, "Military Rule in Chile: The Revolutions of September 5,
1924, and January 23, 1925," *Hispanic American Historical Review*, XLVII, no. 1 (Feb.,
1967), pp. 1-21; *Historia íntima de la revolución* (Santiago, n.d.), pp. 9-48; Bennet, pp.
28-29, 50-57, 101-222; Monreal, pp. 53-81; Vicuña Fuentes, *La tiranía*, I, p. 19, 139-210;
Sáez, *Recuerdos*, I, pp. 80-81, 104-75; Guillermo Edwards Matte, *El Club de la Unión en sus
ochenta años (1864-1944)* (Santiago, 1944), pp. 58-59. See idealistic, reformist articles by
Grove in *La Nación*, Oct. 4, Nov. 6, Nov. 11, Nov. 20, and Dec. 8, 1924. Raúl Aldunate
Phillips, *Ruido de sables* (Santiago, [1971?]).

38. Emilio Bello Codesido, *Recuerdos políticos* (Santiago, 1954), pp. 8-167; Emilio
Rodríguez Mendoza, *El golpe de estado de 1924* (Santiago, 1938), pp. 337-38; Ricardo
Boizard, *Cuatro retratos en profundidad* (Santiago, 1950), pp. 12-26; Boizard, *La democracia*, pp. 40-70; Ernest Würth Rojas, *Ibáñez. Caudillo enigmático* (Santiago, 1958),
pp. 64-87.

39. Chile, *Constitución política* (Santiago, 1925); Chile, *Recopilación de decretos-leyes*,
XIII (Santiago, 1925), p. 468; Alessandri, *El Presidente*, pp. 486-503; Gil, pp. 215-17;
Moreno, p. 153; Cruz-Coke, p. 61; Francisco Cumplido, "Constitución política de 1925;
hoy, crisis de las instituciones políticas chilenas," *Cuadernos de la Realidad Nacional*, no. 5
(Sept., 1970), pp. 25-40; Fernando Campos Harriet, *Historia constitucional de Chile*
(Santiago, 1956).

plebiscite, Alessandri left the government in charge of an interim chief executive and departed from Chile prior to the 1925 presidential election. Behind the scenes Ibáñez held the effective power but wanted to consolidate his position before assuming the presidency directly. The emerging *caudillo* ordered the parties to unite behind a civilian candidate. In hopes of salvaging the democratic process, most of the Radicals and Democrats reluctantly joined the Liberals and Conservatives in nominating Emiliano Figueroa Larraín, an apolitical aristocrat. Although Ibáñez outwardly accepted Figueroa's nomination, he wanted a second candidate to please the middle and lower classes and to keep politics divided and the ferment of reform alive; this allowed Ibáñez to play all factions against each other and thus seem even more the indispensable man. The Left wanted their own candidate, even if he could not win, to build a constituency for the future. A young army doctor, José Santos Salas Morales, became Figueroa's opponent. His reforms and free spending as Minister of Health in the second junta, particularly the reduction of lower-class rents, had endeared Salas to the younger military and the masses. His campaign was launched by a transitory, vaguely leftist, middle- and lower-class coalition, USRACH, the Republican Social Union of Wage Earners of Chile. The coalition was led by middle-sector employees, teachers, students, and intellectuals as well as some workers. USRACH included anarchist and corporatist thinkers; it proposed mildly socialist reforms. Because the labor unions favored Salas, the Communists also endorsed him. This marked the first time they combined with many Democrats and some disaffected Radicals in an electoral alliance. The Communists were able to join because Moscow permitted its international parties to engage in collaboration politics from 1921 through 1927.[40]

Salas's token candidacy, as expected, netted only a minority—28.4% of the votes against 71.3% for Figueroa. Salas, appealing to some of the same groups as Alessandri had in 1920, also won two of his three highest percentages in the Great North and the Frontier regions. But the Urban Center, which was one of the three lowest zones for Alessandri, was the second highest for Salas. As primarily a candidate of the capital city, Salas established a vote pattern which suggested that social divisions were gaining on regional resentments as the bases of leftist strength, as is shown in Table 2.[41]

After the presidential balloting, new congressional elections in 1925

40. Bello, pp. 168-217; Alessandri, *Recuerdos,* II, pp. 193-273, 329; Sáez, *Recuerdos,* II, pp. 16-34; Monreal, pp. 438-52; Vicuña Fuentes, *La tiranía,* II, pp. 80-90; Chelén, *Trayectoria,* pp. 61-66.

41. Chile, Dirección del Registro Electoral, "Elección extraordinaria de Presidente de la República" (Santiago, [1925?]).

TABLE 2: VOTES FOR PRESIDENT BY REGION, 1925

Region	Figueroa	Salas
Great North	55.9%	43.4%
Small North	84.5	14.8
Urban Center	64.1	35.3
North Center	82.6	16.8
South Center	89.9	9.9
Frontier	76.4	23.5
Lakes	80.0	19.8
Total	71.3%	28.4%

continued the leftward trend seen in 1921 and 1924. The combined total for Democrat, USRACH, and Communist candidates reached 22% of the electorate.[42]

Although Salas lost, his candidacy exposed the weakness of traditional party control of presidential politics. An unknown who became a popular figure in the few months of the second junta, he demonstrated that government handouts could create an instantaneous following. In the two-man race, Salas clearly attracted many anti-Figueroa voters who, though they may not have been committed to the Left, had nowhere else to direct their votes. Nevertheless, Salas's strong vote showed openings for a populist coalition combining regional and class-oriented politics.[43]

Figueroa ruled poorly and uncomfortably as Ibáñez's front man until 1927. Then Figueroa resigned, and a hasty, contrived election placed the stamp of popular, constitutional legitimacy on Ibáñez's authority. All the traditional parties, as well as USRACH, lent at least tacit support to his presidential bid. Only Elías Lafertte Gavino, a worker who had emerged as the Communists' leader after Recabarren's mysterious suicide in 1924, put up token opposition. Ninety-seven percent of the ballots cast in 1927 were recorded for Ibáñez.[44]

42. Although even official figures disagreed slightly for the 1925 elections, all concurred in a shift to higher votes for presidential than for congressional candidates. The major parties in the 1925 parliamentary deputies contest garnered approximately the following percentages: Conservatives 22%, Liberals 32%, Radicals 21%, and the Democrat coalition 22%. Chile, Dirección del Registro Electoral, "Elección" (1925); Chile, Oficina Central de Estadística, *Política y administración* (Santiago, 1927), p. 41; Sergio Guilisasti Tagle, *Partidos políticos chilenos* (2nd ed., Santiago, 1964), pp. 28, 81, 141; Urzúa Valenzuela, *Los Partidos,* p. 65; Pinto Durán, *La revolución,* pp. 128-219.

43. Sáez, *Recuerdos,* II, pp. 36-37.

44. The non-Ibáñez votes reached percentages well above the national average in the central urban areas of Valparaíso and Santiago, the urban zone of Concepción, and sections of the mining north, where the rates of abstention were the highest in Chile. Chile, Dirección General de Estadística, *Política y administración* (Santiago, 1929), p. 3; René Montero Moreno, *La verdad sobre Ibáñez* (Buenos Aires, 1953), pp. 35-133; Ramírez Necochea, *Origen,* pp. 143-60; Rodríguez Mendoza, *El golpe,* pp. 391-405.

Ibáñez was president at the end of the traditional political system and before the consolidation of a new one. Alessandri had articulated a reformist vision, and Ibáñez enacted many of his proposals. Both presidents contributed to the dismantling of traditional politics. Ibáñez's virtual dictatorship was based on both military and civilian supporters. By creating corporatist institutions to fill the void left by the bankruptcy of parliamentary politics, Ibáñez tried to discipline society for economic growth. He persecuted and exiled party leaders from all social levels. The temporary return of economic prosperity was financed largely through enormous foreign credits, mainly from U.S. investors. The upper class was pleased with foreign funding, low taxes, and stability. They accommodated themselves to Ibáñez's program of industrialization through tariff protection, which especially satisfied the urban elites and middle classes. On the other hand, the upper class was chagrined by its loss of many government posts and exiled leaders. Ibáñez, who claimed to represent the 1924 ideals of the younger officers, aided the middle sectors with jobs, housing, social security, and pensions. Like Alessandri, he displaced numerous aristocratic officeholders with newcomers from the middle strata and the outlying provinces. Major beneficiaries of the expanding budget were the middle classes in the bureaucracy and the military.[45]

Ibáñez was one of the first Latin American presidents to turn from opposing labor organizations to harnessing them through state-sponsored unionization. He silenced worker grievances with repression in the name of anticommunism and with government surrogates for autonomous unions. Undercutting the leftist trend in worker politics, he easily crushed the FOCH, the PC, and the USRACH. In so doing, he revealed the frailty of existing lower-class organizations. Centralized, paternalistic union organization fit the dictator's semi-corporatist model: he felt unions should serve the state as well as the workers. The heavy hand of government alienated some workers, but others were attracted by legal reforms, the increased real buying power of day wages, massive public works, and Ibáñez's magnetism.[46]

Ibáñez's ability to rule depended on popular acceptance as much as on dictatorial powers. Above all, he thrived on the mystique of efficient management of society and the economy, but then the fragile

45. Chile-American Association, pp. 7-40; Chile, *Geografía,* pp. 89-94; Townsend y Onel, *La inquisición chilena, 1925-31* (Valparaíso, 1932); Luis Correa Prieto, *El Presidente Ibáñez* (Santiago, 1962), pp. 149-51; Emilio Rodríguez Mendoza, *Como si fuera ahora . . .* (Santiago, 1929), pp. 438-39; Vicuña Fuentes, *La tiranía,* II, pp. 182-83.

46. Chile, Dirección General de Estadística, *Veinte años de legislación social* (Santiago, 1945), pp. 2, 139-41; Congreso Nacional del Partido Comunista, *En defensa de la revolución* (Santiago, 1933), pp. 35-38; Montero Moreno, *La verdad,* pp. 102-33.

foreign buttresses of economic growth began to break with the arrival of the Great Depression in 1929-30. An economic quake unleashed the festering social antagonisms contained since 1925. As a result, disorders pushed the president toward excessive reliance on force and cost him his claim to legitimate rule.[47]

The essentially oligarchic system which had reigned at the turn of the century was cracking near its foundations. Politically, the conservative elites lost the security of the presidency, the parliament, and the military. The constitution of 1925 curtailed the perquisites of the Church and other supports of the elites and, in effect, instituted a presidential republic. The social exclusiveness of the upper class was diluted, primarily by the ascension of individuals from the middle strata. With their historic defenses and political resources reduced drastically, the traditional ruling groups received an additional blow in 1930, when the Depression struck hard at their economic underpinnings. Out of the resulting chaos came a new style of national politics and a new breed of mass parties and leaders.

Impact of the Great Depression, 1930-31

The Great Depression caused political instability and change previously unmatched in the twentieth century in Chile. The crisis first and most emphatically hit the foreign sector of Chile's economy, where trade suffered more than anywhere else in the Western world. By 1932, exports tumbled to less than 12%, and imports to less than 20%, of their 1929 value. Dependent on foreign control of exports and subject to fluctuations of the New York market, Chile painfully paid the price of vulnerability. By 1931, sales of nitrates and copper, which accounted for nearly 90% of the nation's exports and which were controlled almost 100% by U.S. corporations, were falling precipitously. Ibáñez had purposely concentrated nitrate production and export in the Nitrate Company of Chile (COSACH). A joint venture between the Guggenheims of New York and the Chilean government, COSACH adopted the most mechanized production methods. These practices reduced the number of workers as well as the market for foodstuffs in the northern nitrate fields. When the Depression arrived in force in 1931, it multiplied unemployment and nearly halted production. COSACH became the villain much blamed by Chileans for the economic collapse. This criticism spilled over to

47. Boizard, *Cuatro*, pp. 62-87.

other foreign companies, since they dominated copper, iron ore, and many other markets also lost in 1930-31. Overall, the decline in mineral production from 1929 to 1931 exceeded 50%.[48]

As economic organization, production, and distribution became primary political issues, the public focused on additional ways in which foreign dependence was damaging. The foreign loans, mainly from the United States, which had underwritten Ibáñez's prosperity and government revenues, shriveled from 443 million pesos in 1929 and 682 million in 1930 to 54 million in 1931, 22 million in 1932, and finally zero in 1933. Consequently, government revenues plunged from 1,268 million pesos in 1929 to 515 million in 1932, and government expenditures from 1,190 million to 704 million, resulting in an involuntary 1932 deficit of 189 million pesos. A bankrupt Chile could not prime the economy or import necessities; neither could it finance the government or service the astronomical foreign debt.[49]

Out of the crash of the foreign sector and mining came unemployment and, for many, near-starvation. Unemployment in mining alone exceeded 60,000, out of a total of some 77,000 in 1930. By 1932 national unemployment surpassed 129,000, out of a national estimated work force of nearly 1,300,000. After rising under Ibáñez in the 1920s, the real purchasing power of wages slid in 1930 and plummeted in 1931. According to one estimate, real salaries fell some 40% from 1929 to 1932, while the prices of staples nearly doubled. Underemployment worsened, too, since many industries slashed working hours and wages. Labor's hardships exposed the inadequacies of the social laws passed in the 1920s. In desperation, laborers began deserting the mining camps. Most often they migrated to Santiago or to their rural families. The gypsy-like caravans of the unemployed, which paralleled the southward wave of the Depression, frightened the upper and middle classes and radicalized some fellow workers.

48. Chile, Dirección General de Estadística, *Sinopsis,* pp. 115, 184-236. By August, 1931, over 90% of the nitrate industry was merged into COSACH, under effective Guggenheim control. The Chilean government owned half the capital of COSACH in stocks and insisted that a majority of the workers and employees be Chileans. Where the old Shanks extraction process had required forty workers, the new Guggenheim production method needed only six. "Nitrogen," *Fortune,* VI, no. 2 (Aug., 1932), pp. 43-70, 90-91; Thomson, pp. 282-92; Chile-American Association, pp. 22-34; Pike, p. 209; Mamalakis and Reynolds, pp. 14-15, 230-32; Álvarez Andrews, *Historia,* pp. 246-306; Carlos Keller, *Un país,* pp. 35-45, 162-63; Ellsworth, pp. 3-8; *Hoy,* no. 11 (Jan. 29, 1932), pp. 17-18; Enrique Zañartu Prieto, *Hambre, miseria e ignorancia* (Santiago, 1938), pp. 32-55.

49. Ellsworth, pp. 4-35; Chile, Dirección General de Estadística, *Sinopsis,* pp. 114-17, 264-65, 270-75; André Siegfried, *Impressions of South America* (New York, 1933), pp. 81-87.

The wanderers fared little better in the cities or the countryside than they had in the mines. In response, the poverty-stricken government cut public works and offered little more than bread lines.[50]

Agriculture's northern and foreign markets soon evaporated along with handsome prices, profits, and credits. The landowners, like the miners, cried for special assistance from the Ibáñez government. Though naturally cushioned against adversity and therefore less ravaged than mining, *hacendados* and the SNA were increasingly discontented with Ibáñez.[51]

Industry and business felt the Depression less and nearly a year later than mining and agriculture, and recovered faster. Having grown rapidly in the late 1920s, urban industry was now heralded by the nation as well as by its own spokesmen as the salvation from economic catastrophe. Ibáñez had aided industry with protection, credit, subsidies, low (but rising) taxes, and control of labor. In 1930-31, the depletion of foreign capital and materials was somewhat offset by the opportunities created when competitive foreign imports declined. Foreign exchange became scarce not only to buy ingredients needed in manufacturing but also to purchase finished goods. Since national production was increased out of necessity, the Depression was a boon, especially in the long run, as well as a bane for industry. The industrialists' SOFOFA criticized Ibáñez for insufficient protection, credit, and foreign exchange so that industry could revive the economy by displacing manufactured imports.[52]

Ibáñez's rigid policies compounded Chile's economic woes. He

50. In 1930-31, wages in mining fell the most, those in industry less so and only briefly, and wages in agriculture least of all, starting from a much smaller base. Simón, *Determinación*, pp. 58-85; Ellsworth, pp. 14-15; Pike, p. 209; Chile, Dirección General de Estadística, *Sinopsis*, pp. 180-81, 215, 235-39; Zañartu, *Hambre*, p. 98; Santiago Wilson Hernández, *Nuestra crisis económica y la desocupación obrera* (Santiago, 1933); Leonardo Guzmán Cortés, *Un episodio olvidado de la historia nacional* (Santiago, 1966), pp. 15-16; El Comité Central del Partido Comunista, *¡Contra la dictadura fascista de Ibáñez!* (n.p., 1931), pp. 1-2; Julio Gaete Leighton, *Tarapacá y Antofagasta ante las consecuencias del pasado* (Iquique, Chile, 1931), pp. 57-74.

51. The SNA claimed that this was the worst crisis in the history of Chilean agriculture, and so pressed the government for protection, subsidies, credit, lower interest rates, reduced taxes, and higher commodity prices. La Sociedad Nacional de Agricultura, *Memoria* . . . (Santiago, 1932), pp. 5-25, 126-58; George M. McBride, *Chile: Land and Society* (New York, 1936), pp. 219-23; Jaime Larraín, *Orientación de nuestra política agraria* (Santiago, 1932), pp. 7-29; Chile, Dirección General de Estadística, *Sinopsis*, pp. 134, 154-57; Ellsworth, pp. 12, 75-76.

52. The number of declared business bankruptcies peaked in 1931. Mario Bravo Lavín, *Chile frente al socialismo y al comunismo* (Santiago, 1934), p. 110; La Sociedad de Fomento Fabril, *Plan de fomento de la producción* (Santiago, 1932), pp. 2-7; Chile, Dirección General de Estadística, *Sinopsis*, pp. 214-35, 268-71; Álvarez Andrews, *Historia*, pp. 322-30; Simón, *Determinación*, pp. 60-61, 73, 81-83; Ellsworth, pp. 1-37, 49-75, 161-62.

clung to COSACH and the gold standard. Heavily reliant on income from mining exports, the government budget had only a tiny surplus in 1930 before its resounding deficit of 1931. Seeking a balanced budget, Ibáñez tried to raise taxes and lower expenditures; both policies accelerated opposition to his regime, especially among bureaucrats, the military, and those employed in public works.[53]

Repudiation of Military Government

Despite the need for an economic solution and the decay of national parties during his tenure, Ibáñez turned to the traditional politicians to restore public confidence in July, 1931. He invited Liberals and Radicals from the right wings of their parties to form a cabinet of respected jurists and lawyers. Instead of propping up Ibáñez, however, the cabinet, led by Radical Juan Esteban Montero Rodríguez, exposed to the public the full extent of government bankruptcy. It also briefly revived many political freedoms. When the cabinet fell, civilian rule and Montero, not the exiled Alessandri, became the national rallying cry of protestors.[54]

All social groups joined the demonstrations against Ibáñez, but the middle classes participated most and the laborers least. In the vanguard, student protestors divided into two factions: (1) the Renovation group of moderates and conservatives associated with the Catholic University, and (2) the Advance group of leftists, mainly Marxists, associated with the national university. Legions of the middle classes, including teachers, doctors, lawyers, clerks, intellectuals, women, and even government bureaucrats, joined the students in strikes and marches. Political parties, even the Communists, played little role in the downfall of Ibáñez. The working classes, most of whom had been either cowed or captivated by the *caudillo* and his labor policies, rallied neither to him nor to most of the protests. Like the military, the mass of the workers took longer than the middle and upper classes to abandon Ibáñez.[55]

53. Carlos Ibáñez del Campo, *Mensaje con que el Presidente de la República da cuenta al Congreso Nacional* . . . (Santiago, 1931); Chile, Dirección General de Estadística, *Sinopsis*, pp. 114-18, 156, 218, 280-333; Álvarez Andrews, *Historia*, pp. 279-330; Keller, *Un país*, pp. 49-57, 98-99; Pinto, *Chile*, pp. 114-17; Antonio Cifuentes, *Evolución de la economía chilena desde la crisis hasta nuestros días* (Santiago, 1935), pp. 3-18; Zañartu, *Hambre*, pp. 90-97.

54. *El Mercurio*, June 15-23, 1931; Montero, *La verdad*, pp. 152-59; Sáez, *Recuerdos*, II, pp. 113-32.

55. Raúl Marín Balmaceda, *La caída de un régimen, julio de 1931* (Santiago, 1933), pp. 18-63; *El Mercurio*, July 24-27, 1931; El Comité de Estudiantes Universitarios, *Camaradas universitarios* (n.p., 1931); El Comité de los Estudiantes Universitarios, *Camaradas universitarios* (n.p., 1931); El Comité de Estudiantes Universitarios, *Al tirano y*

Faced with a barren choice between violent repression of demon-
strators or abdication, Ibáñez resigned and fled Chile at the end of
July, 1931. The celebrating crowds jeered and assaulted the
Carabineros (national police) and regular military personnel on the
streets. This derision departed from the deep tradition of public
admiration for the armed forces; it appalled, shamed, and angered
the officers. Consequently, they were ordered to their barracks by a
civilian provisional government until tempers cooled. Antimilitarism
was so fervid that civilian militias formed to maintain order and
prevent the military's return to domestic activity.[56]

The provisional government set presidential elections for October,
1931, but a September revolt of the naval squadron in the Small North
jolted the nation. The sailors protested the lowering of their salaries
through government budget cuts. From internal demands for better
pay and working conditions, the rebels escalated to broader calls for
higher taxes on the rich and redistribution of credit to the needy.
Hoping to gain support from leftist groups on the mainland, they
urged aid for the unemployed, protection for industrialization, and
subdivision of agricultural land. In reply to an unyielding government
ultimatum, the frustrated mutineers declared solidarity with the
workers, the FOCH, and the Communist Party. They called for "social
revolution."[57]

Beginning as a limited, reformist, middle-class uprising against low
wages and indifferent superiors from the upper class, the naval rebellion became increasingly radical in response to government overreaction. The panicky interim administration and nervous elites drew
parallels with the Russian Revolution; they tagged the rebellion a

sus secuaces (n.p., 1931); Enrique Molina, *La revolución, los estudiantes y la democracia* (Santiago, 1931), pp. 3-12; H. Ochoa Mena, *La revolución de junio* (Santiago, 1931), pp. 105-63; César Godoy Urrutia, *Manifiesto al magisterio de Chile* (Santiago, 1931), pp. 1-4; C. H. Haring, "The Chilean Revolution of 1931," *Hispanic American Historical Review*, XIII, no. 2 (May, 1933), pp. 197-203; Waiss, *El drama*, pp. 8-9; Congreso Nacional, *En defensa*, p. 35.

56. Guzmán Cortés, pp. 15-29; *El Mercurio*, July 27, 1931; Renato Valdés, *Tres cartas* (Santiago, 1932), pp. 3-8, 29-43; Tobías Barros Ortiz, *Recuerdos oportunos* (Santiago, 1938), pp. 2-13; Raúl Marín Balmaceda, *El 4 de junio de 1932* (Santiago, 1933), p. 9; Henry Grattan Doyle, "Chilean Dictatorship Overthrown," *Current History*, XXXIV (Sept., 1931), pp. 918-22.

57. José M. Cerda, *Relación histórica de la revolución de la armada de Chile* (Concepción, Chile, 1934); Patricio Manns, *La revolución de la escuadra* (Santiago, 1972); Almirante Von Schroeders, *El delegado del gobierno y el motín de la escuadra* (Santiago, 1933); Jacobo Nazaré, *Destrucción* (Valparaíso, n.d.), pp. 45-109; Bureau Sudamericano de la Internacional Comunista, *Las grandes luchas revolucionarias del proletariado chileno* (Santiago, 1932), pp. 10-24; Donoso, *Alessandri*, II, pp. 54-74; Ochoa Mena, pp. 194-95; Gustavo Mujica, *Rebelión en la armada* (Santiago, 1959.)

threat from communism and militarism. In fact, the Marxist Left and the organized workers neither fomented the mutiny nor succeeded in taking advantage of it, but their solidarity statements and rallies fed the fears of the middle and upper classes. In the minds of many, these events reinforced a relationship between military and leftist dangers. People associated the younger officers' calls for change in 1924-25, some of the reforms of Ibáñez, and the mutiny with the fear that any challenge to constitutional authority might usher in revolution.[58]

With widespread public support, the government defeated the rebels by ordering the air force to drop bombs near the squadron. Military leaders regretted that political problems had smudged their honor, disturbed the hierarchy, and produced a clash between two branches of the armed forces. The incident heightened both the military's distaste for politics and civilian desires for constitutional order.[59]

Revival of Traditional Politics: The Presidential Election of 1931

In the wake of Ibáñez's fall, discontent with the economy and disillusionment with the old parties created unprecedented political opportunities. In a rare and rapid breeding, parties divided and splinter groups and new contenders emerged. Never in Chilean history had there been a comparable period of political confusion and innovation.[60]

The Left was most active. The Communists, divided over a successor to Recabarren since 1927 and over the international Trotskyist schism since 1929, split decisively into Stalinist and Trotskyist camps; both claimed to be the official party. Several tiny socialist parties, cast along both fascist and Marxist lines, sprang up. The old unions revived and new ones arose. The masses, however, were disoriented by the economic disaster and political tumult. General strikes, for example, were unimpressive in numbers and effect. It was unclear who spoke for the workers. Neither on the left nor the right did political parties, despite their activity, play a major role in the selection of the next president.[61]

58. *El Mercurio*, Sept. 1-5, 1931; *Bandera Roja*, Oct. 1, 1931; *El Chileno*, Sept. 16, 1932; Boizard, *Cuatro*, pp. 132-35, 194-203; Guzmán Cortés, pp. 45-121; Sáez, *Recuerdos*, III, pp. 36-41, 86-87.

59. *El Mercurio*, Sept. 7, 1931; *Bandera Roja*, Oct. 17, 1931; Von Schroeders, pp. 6-167; Waiss, *El drama*, pp. 14-15.

60. Echaíz, *Evolución histórica*, pp. 166-74.

61. Partido Socialista, *Partido Socialista Marxista* (Concepción, Chile, 1931). The so-called Trotskyist wing of the Chilean PC, which was led by Manuel Hidalgo from 1927 to 1931 and became a separate party thereafter, actually placed more emphasis

The upper and middle classes, in an unusual electoral alliance, backed the bland and sober Montero for the presidency. The ancient enemies—the Conservatives and Radicals, Catholics and Masons —joined forces. Most important, the alliance was not backing an aristocrat, as had the uneasy coalition behind Liberal Figueroa in 1925, but an affluent Radical. Most elite politicians in the Conservative and Liberal parties favored Montero in 1931 because the cataclysmic events since 1920 had rendered some of the old party divisions irrelevant. The conservative elites feared Alessandri, populism, anarchy, communism, and the military more than they did the Radicals. Instead of running a divisive candidate of their own, the Right hoped to contain the crisis within the orderly channels of traditional politics by endorsing a popular Radical.[62] Moreover, the demure Montero was a nineteenth-century, laissez-faire liberal devoted to strict legality and was scarcely a threat to established interests. A lawyer, Montero was related to *hacendados*, connected to banking interests, and a member of both the Masons and the Union Club.[63]

Although Montero had the support of the historic parties, an extraordinary convention of the professional associations actually nominated him. The leading groups were the Medical Association of Chile, the College of Lawyers, and the Institute of Engineers. It was an attempt by the middle and upper classes to move beyond party and military politics. Both the Association of the Middle Class and the National Society for Agriculture endorsed a presidential candidate—Montero—for the first time. Student groups took no official stand but, as children of the middle and upper classes, most supported Montero.[64]

A Convention of the Left challenged the consensus around Montero. It charged that he could not be a candidate of national unity since

---

on electoral methods, reformist coalitions, parliamentary politics, and protection for national industrialization than did the Lafertte wing, which was more loyal to the Comintern. Stephen Clissold, ed., *Soviet Relations with Latin America, 1918-1968* (London, 1970), pp. 16-124; Congreso Nacional, *En defensa*, pp. 42-46; Melfi, *Sin*, pp. 31-32.

62. *El Mercurio*, July 29-30, Aug. 3, Aug. 19, Aug. 30, and Sept. 22, 1931; *El Diario Ilustrado*, Oct. 3-5, 1931; *El Chileno*, Oct. 3, 1931; Boizard, *La democracia*, p. 116.

63. Vicente Vico et al., *Hidalgo-Alessandri-Montero* (Chillán, Chile, 1931); Wilfredo Mayorga, "Cuando Montero 'se somete,' " *Ercilla*, no. 1598 (Jan. 19, 1966), pp. 18-19.

64. Pharmacists, dentists, accountants, employees, teachers, and architects were also prominent in the Montero campaign. They mainly operated through their professional associations, reflecting a strong 1930s' tendency to define politics along functional, occupational, and corporatist lines. *El Mercurio*, Aug. 7-16 and Oct. 6, 1931; La Sociedad Nacional de Agricultura, *Memoria* (1932), p. 29; Melfi, *Sin*, pp. 28-40. Fearful of rumors that Communist money was pouring in to fund the Left, the Right appealed to U.S. businessmen in Chile to aid Montero. United States, Department of State Archives, Record Group 59, "Chile, 1930-1944" (Washington, D.C.), Santiago, Aug. 28, 1931, pp. 1-2, 825.00/694.

he represented only the upper-middle and upper classes. The convention nominated Alessandri. Spearheading the campaign were the Democrats, several renegade Liberals and Radicals, and a handful of the new socialist-labeled parties, noncommunist unions, and artisan groups. Alessandri conducted a poorly organized, whirlwind tour reminiscent of 1920 in its intensity and content. Both the Right and the Left agreed that the Lion of Tarapacá was essentially unchanged. Conservatives complained that he was "the same *caudillo* who preaches disorder, who looks with pleasure on anarchy, who proclaims the subversion of all values."[65]

In truth, both Montero and Alessandri were centrist candidates whose platforms, for example the planks espousing monetary stability and protected industrialization, differed little. Above all, the two contenders established symbolic identification with opposing social sectors. Again, Alessandri projected an image as the idol of the poor and the nemesis of the rich. One of his campaign managers commented that his forays among the masses were not those "of a candidate but . . . of a god." In 1931, most of the urban working classes were still Alessandri's, but he could not count on the middle sectors or the Radicals.[66]

The Stalinist and Trotskyist Communist parties each presented a presidential candidate as well. The Stalinists, loyal to Moscow and followers of the post-1928 Comintern line against coalition politics, nominated Elías Lafertte as a defiant gesture. With no illusions of winning, the campaign effort was designed to mobilize workers, toughen party discipline, and "unmask the electoral farce." The regular PC hoped to keep laborers from voting for Alessandri, "who presents himself as the father of the workers," or the "traitor" Manuel Hidalgo Plaza, a dark *mestizo* from the working class who represented the Trotskyist faction. Orthodox Communist rallies of the unemployed, many of whom could not vote because they had migrated from their electoral districts, were sizable. The Lafertte platform, not unlike Alessandri's, emphasized aid for the unemployed, leniency for the naval rebels, and dissolution of COSACH. The Communists were far more radical, however, in the specifics of their demands and particularly in calls for an end to imperialism and for armed revolution. Also

65. *El Diario Ilustrado,* Oct. 5, 1931; *El Mercurio,* Aug. 28, Sept. 20, Sept. 22, and Oct. 3, 1931; Guzmán Cortés, pp. 113-46; U.S., Dept. of State Archives, Santiago, Oct. 2, 1931, pp. 3-4, 825.00/699; Guillermo M. Bañados, *Las ideas se combaten con ideas . . .* (Santiago, 1933), pp. 3-4.

66. *El Mercurio,* Aug. 28, Sept. 7-27, and Oct. 1-2, 1931; *El Diario Ilustrado,* Oct. 3-4, 1931; *South Pacific Mail,* Aug. 13, Sept. 3, Sept. 17, and Sept. 24, 1931; Alessandri, *Recuerdos,* II, pp. 434-39; Olavarría Bravo, *Chile,* I, pp. 300-301; Vico; Osvaldo Labarca Fuentes, *Los enanos de la libertad* (2nd ed., Santiago, 1932), pp. 65-83.

stressed were differences with the Hidalgo Communists and defense of the Soviet Union. Theoretical debates over Russian ideological disputes, rallies in honor of Sacco and Vanzetti, and a trip by Lafertte to Uruguay before election day made scant impact on most hungry, unemployed workers. Government harassment and Alessandri's magnetism also hurt the Communist campaign. Though the party denigrated electioneering, it was shaken when it failed to attract its expected share of ballots. The Communists failed again, as they had during the naval revolt, to take advantage of political openings on the left during the Depression or to attract a majority of the workers.[67]

The dissident Communist candidate Manuel Hidalgo had a program as radical as Lafertte's, but he forged a slightly broader coalition of support. A few Democrats and fledgling Socialists joined Hidalgo's campaign, although most Socialists abstained from the election or defected to Alessandri. Hidalgo, like Lafertte, interpreted the contest as an opportunity to galvanize workers and their class consciousness. He sought to establish a claim on the workers over his Stalinist rival.[68]

Montero won a landslide national victory, with 63.8% of the votes to 34.7% for Alessandri, 0.8% for Lafertte, and 0.4% for Hidalgo. Of all the provinces, Montero lost only Tarapacá, Alessandri's stronghold in the mining north. In contrast to 1920, Alessandri ran better in the urban areas of Valparaíso and Santiago than in the Frontier zone. His three strongest regions were the same as Salas's in 1925: the Great North, the Urban Center, and the Frontier. As Table 3 shows, urbanization was an increasingly important factor in leftist strength. At the community level, Alessandri ran slightly better in the mining than in the urban centers in 1931. The Communists scored exceptionally well, in comparison with their national totals, in the northern nitrate and

TABLE 3: VOTES FOR PRESIDENT BY REGION, 1920, 1925, 1931

	Montero	Alessandri		Salas	Lafertte	Hidalgo
Region	1931	1920	1931	1925	1931	1931
Great North	38.6%	71.8%	57.4%	43.3%	3.2%	0.5%
Small North	72.5	54.4	25.7	14.8	1.0	0.3
Urban Center	60.4	45.0	37.7	35.3	0.8	0.8
North Center	71.9	34.4	27.5	16.8	0.3	0.1
South Center	83.9	44.1	15.9	9.9	0.0	0.1
Frontier	67.2	62.6	31.7	23.5	0.9	0.0
Lakes	76.3	50.1	23.3	19.8	0.3	0.0
Total	63.8%	49.4%	34.7%	28.4%	0.8%	0.4%

67. Siegfried, pp. 74-77; *Bandera Roja*, Aug. 13–Oct. 17, 1931; *El Mercurio*, Oct. 3-4, 1931; Bureau, p. 43.

68. Congreso Nacional, *En defensa*, pp. 18-19, 46-47; *El Mercurio*, Aug. 17-20, Aug. 23-26, and Sept. 19–Oct. 4, 1931; *South Pacific Mail*, Oct. 1, 1931.

port areas and the southern coal-mining districts.[69] The Lafertte faction was disappointed that Alessandri's populism, albeit now laced with "socialistic" rhetoric, still drew most of the urban workers and miners away from the Communists. But the Stalinists were delighted that they had topped Hidalgo. Lafertte received fewer votes in 1931 than he had in 1927, if the non-Ibáñez votes in 1927 are presumed to have largely been for Lafertte. By any measure, the Communists' pre-Ibáñez support declined during his reign, and it did not notably revive with the global Depression.[70] Bemoaning both Communist parties' weakness with labor, Hidalgo's supporters commented: "This campaign demonstrated that the radicalization of the masses and the Communist Party are two totally different and absolutely independent phenomena. . . ."[71]

Traditional Response to the Crisis, 1931-32

The return of the traditional ruling groups to presidential power failed to ease the economic crisis, calm the ferment on the Left, or dispel the climate of fear. Immediately after Montero took office, a clash between the military and rioting workers reinforced and revealed the nightmares of the privileged sectors. During the Tragic Christmas of 1931, miners, urban workers, and some hired hands from *fundos* attacked an army barracks in the Small North. Elites in the riot zone had traditionally kept the workers unorganized. Rather than a planned, organized revolutionary deed, the assault was an anomic expression of desperation. Some local Communists participated, but party involvement was wildly exaggerated. Both the workers and the military panicked; more than thirty of the rebels and several Carabineros and soldiers died. This led to bloody reprisals in a neighboring community, where soldiers, with no violent provocation, summarily executed nearly twenty alleged Communists. Although the Great Depression had not yet sparked the revolution promised in Communist propaganda, elite overreactions to lower-class protests meant that Montero would probably not lead a government of national unity which encompassed the popular as well as the prosperous classes.[72]

69. Chile, Dirección del Registro Electoral, "Elección extraordinaria de la República" (Santiago, [1931?]); *El Mercurio*, Oct. 5, 1931; *El Diario Ilustrado*, Oct. 5, 1931.
70. Bureau, p. 43; *Bandera Roja*, Oct. 17, 1931; *El Mercurio*, Aug. 10, 1931; *El Diario Ilustrado*, Oct. 5, 1931; *El Chileno*, Oct. 7, 1931; U.S., Dept. of State Archives, Santiago, Oct. 7, 1931, pp. 2-6, 825.00/702; Osvaldo Quijada Cerda, *La pascua trágica de Copiapó y Vallenar* (Santiago, 1932), p. 14.
71. Congreso Nacional, *En defensa*, pp. 46-47.
72. The major worker complaints included unemployment, price inflation, and

From Ibáñez to Montero, Chile passed from tyranny to impotence. Nicknamed "Don One-Step," Montero, with his plodding devotion to constitutionality and government austerity, did little to resurrect the economy. It continued to worsen in 1932. Mineral production, employment, and exports fell more sharply than in 1931. The cost of living, particularly prices for daily necessities, soared to dizzying heights by mid-1932.[73]

The middle and lower classes were further alienated because Montero surrounded himself with archetypes of the moneyed, familial, proclerical elite. Employees, students, and even professionals from the middle strata joined laborers in escalating protests.[74] Discontent spawned feverish but ineffectual political activity. "Socialism," a vague connotation of positive state action as the salvation for all the disadvantaged, became the new political touchstone. The term was so in vogue that a group of Liberals included it in their program; even the government considered announcing its devotion to socialism. Alessandri helped popularize the notion by arguing for an undefined "state socialism." Because they were unable to spur Montero to action, support of his administration from Radicals and Liberals dwindled. Soon only the Conservatives were united behind the government. Out of disappointment with the resurgence of party politics and with standard political channels the impulse to conspire was born. "The crisis of authority," to which only Ibáñez had supplied a partial solution since World War I, was breaking another government. By 1932, the ineptness of Montero and the traditional elites helped clear the path for the modern, leftward movement of Chilean politics, which was marked by the rise of indigenous socialism.[75]

---

company stores. Quijada, pp. 1-17; *Zig-Zag* (Jan. 2, 1932), pp. 67-73; *El Mercurio*, Dec. 29-31, 1931; *Bandera Roja*, Feb. 14 and Feb. 21, 1932.

73. Ellsworth, pp. 6-29, 162-72; Simón, *Determinación*, pp. 58-86; Chile, Dirección General de Estadística, *Sinopsis*, pp. 155-57, 184, 199, 213, 232-38, 281-301; *El Mercurio*, Dec. 4 and Dec. 15, 1931; Sáez, *Recuerdos*, III, pp. 69-109; Melfi, *Sin*, pp. 40-113; Miguel Aránguiz Latorre, *El 4 de junio* (Santiago, 1933); La Sociedad Nacional de Agricultura, *Boletín*, LXIV (May, 1932), pp. 215-17; Leopoldo Arce G., *La crisis chilena* (Santiago, 1932), pp. 62-65; Jorge de la Cuadra Poisson, *La revolución que viene* (Santiago, 1931), pp. 27-44; Juan E. Montero, *Mensaje del Presidente de la República al Congreso Nacional* (Santiago, 1932); Carlos Pinto Durán, *Plan de gobierno de la república* (Santiago, 1932), pp. 7-52.

74. Liga de Asalariados Pro-Patria, *¿Revolución o paz? Año 1932* (n.p., 1932), pp. 3-40; Edwards and Frei, pp. 214-15; Labarca, *Los enanos*, pp. 151-85; Congreso Nacional, *En defensa*, pp. 48-49.

75. *La Opinión*, Mar. 21, Mar. 31, Apr. 1-11, May 10-13, June 3, and Sept. 21, 1932; *El Mercurio*, Nov. 6 and Dec. 11, 1931, Apr. 8-11 and May 22, 1932; *Hoy*, 1931-32; Sáez, *Recuerdos*, III, pp. 70-129; Melfi, *Sin*, pp. 17-19.

3

The Birth of Chilean Socialism, 1932

From June through October of 1932, politics, whether channeled through the barracks or the ballot box, moved rapidly leftward and recast the electoral spectrum for decades to come. Socialism in populist trappings captured widespread loyalty among the urban masses; it provoked profound readjustments in traditional politics. These transformations were accelerated by the Socialist Republic, born out of the conspiracies against Montero.

Conspiracy against Liberalism

The proliferating conspiracies against the laissez-faire government centered on three groups. Sharing an antipathy toward both communism and Montero, the conspirators hoped to avoid the former by deposing the latter. Their other common traits were middle-class backgrounds and ambitions, some Masonic support, and an amorphous belief in "state socialism." The first group of subversives was led by Carlos Dávila Espinoza, a journalist who had been Ibáñez's ambassador to the United States. Dávila attracted *ibañistas* and some army officers. In May, 1932, he published a plan which for the first time gave specific content to the flurry of proposals advocating "socialism." Dávila suggested a technocratic, warlike mobilization of the state to plan and organize the capitalist economy along corporatist, "functional" lines; this implied a hierarchical, compartmentalized, compulsory system of command and representation based on semi-official occupational and regional interest groups rather than autonomous individuals, classes, or parties. He believed that rationalizing the private economy through state intervention could avert "class warfare." His plan was a blueprint for economic change to forestall violent social change, and he hoped to replicate the industrial prosperity and social peace of the United States through some of the state mechanisms fashioned under European fascism. Accordingly, Dávila stressed emulating the North Americans' economic centralization, order, and efficiency rather than attacking their investments such as COSACH. The least radical of the conspirators, Dávila argued that "it is not for snobbism, nor only for reasons of morality and justice that we propose a step toward state socialism; it is to save yet the private economy. . . ."[1]

The other two conspiratorial groups were the *alessandristas*, who were essentially pursuing personal ambitions, and the socialists. This third group came out of the largest of the new leftist parties founded after the fall of Ibáñez in 1931, the New Public Action (NAP). Eugenio Matte Hurtado, the Grand Master of the Chilean Masons, led the NAP. Resigning his post in the lodge as the conspiracy approached fruition, Matte reflected Masonic concern about the national crisis and the return to government of the Conservatives and clericals. The NAP was composed of professionals, along with some students and workers, who were not orthodox Marxists. They shared many state capitalist and corporatist precepts with the *davilistas* and *alessandristas*. Nevertheless, the NAP's "Program of Immediate Action" stressed state control of the economy for the benefit of the workers, anti-imperialism, and anticapitalism. Their populist slogan was "Feed the People, Clothe the People, House the People." They were as undecided about the means to power as about the precise goals. Given the weakness of labor and leftist organizations, Matte and his followers decided to make a revolution for the proletariat rather than by the proletariat. This paternalistic approach focused their efforts on the military, which was seen as the only force capable of cracking the existing government and thereby opening the way to later socialist transformations.[2]

Socialism in Uniform: June 4, 1932

An opportunity for a coup soon presented itself because Montero alienated the armed forces. The military disliked the government's

1. *La Opinión*, May 3 and May 5, 1932; Carlos G. Dávila, *Chile no está arruinado* (n.p., 1932); Carlos G. Dávila, *Latin-American Trade Development with the United States* (New York, 1928), pp. 6-16; Carlos G. Dávila, *North American Imperialism* (New York, 1930); René Montero Moreno, *Confesiones políticas* (2nd ed., Santiago, 1959), pp. 75-82; Sáez, *Recuerdos*, III, pp. 96-269; Bravo Lavín, pp. 73-85; U.S. Dept. of State Archives, Santiago, May 9, 1932, 825.00/730.

2. Jack Ray Thomas, "The Socialist Republic of Chile," *Journal of Inter-American Studies*, VI, no. 2 (Apr., 1964), pp. 203-20; *El Mercurio*, Jan. 10-13, 1932; Nueva Acción Pública, *Declaración de principios y estatuto orgánico* (Santiago, 1932); "Los jefes del socialismo: Schnake," *Bases*, no. 1 (Oct., 1937), pp. 9-16; Partido Socialista, *4 de junio* (Santiago, 1933), pp. 1, 3; René Frías Ojeda, *Ubicación histórica del cuatro de junio* (Santiago, 1939), pp. 11-30; Alejandro Bravo G., *Cincuenta años de vida masónica en Chile* (Santiago, 1951), pp. 14-15; Cruz Salas, pp. 253-54.

denunciations of *ibañistas,* reductions in defense expenditures, and mismanagement of the economy and the social unrest. Then Montero transgressed the military's hierarchy and pride by summarily demoting Marmaduke Grove. After turning against Ibáñez and living in exile until 1931, Grove had been made commander of the air force by the Montero administration. On June 3, 1932, Montero accused Grove, probably unjustly, of collaborating with subversives. In response, Jorge Grove Vallejo, his brother and a socialist conspirator, joined Marmaduke's fellow officers to convince him that the military would stand by him against this political interference in internal affairs.[3]

Conspirators of all hues converged on Grove, but the socialist group and the NAP converted him to their cause. Grove began June 3 basically the same idealistic officer who had led the rebellion against the Parliamentary Republic and the Altamirano junta in 1924-25. At heart an *alessandrista,* he believed that more rapid evolution was required to avert revolution. Through the night of the 3rd, however, fellow Masons Matte, brother Jorge, and other *napistas* sold Grove their brand of socialism. It was only slightly more radical than Alessandri's promise of a welfare state. Linked to these persuasive conspirators through familial, social, and political ties, Grove became convinced that the suffering of Chile could be alleviated by installing a socialist state. The propaganda, rumors, and speeches of the recent trying months had paved the way to such a conclusion. The public, or so it seemed, was demanding socialism, however defined. As anarchists had long believed, one dramatic deed might smash the social shell and unleash the mass forces of national rejuvenation. Grove became, practically overnight, "the socialist *caudillo.*"[4]

Once the decision was made to escalate from defiance against his firing to a full-blown coup, Grove and the rebels consolidated their backing from the Air Force. They also secured the acquiescence of the army, the Carabineros, and the navy, who wanted at all costs to avoid civil war among the armed forces. To cement army support, the conspirators included Dávila and a retired general in the junta along

3. Jorge Grove Vallejo, *Descorriendo el velo* (Valparaíso, 1933), pp. 5-11. All these sections on the Socialist Republic benefited enormously from Carlos Charlín O., *Del avión rojo a la república socialista* (Santiago, 1972) and numerous conversations with the author, Santiago, 1970. *¿Por qué cayó Grove?* (Santiago, 1932), pp. 1-2; Ramón Vergara Montero, *Por rutas extraviadas* (Santiago, 1933), pp. 91-137; Arturo Alessandri Palma, *Rectificaciones al tomo IX* (Santiago, 1941), pp. 101-9; Ricardo Donoso, *Desarrollo político y social de Chile desde la constitución de 1833* (Santiago, 1942), pp. 194-202; Oscar Cifuentes Solar, "Declaración," *Núcleo,* no. 6 (Nov. 1, 1934), pp. 3-20; Sáez, *Recuerdos,* III, pp. 138-42.
4. Sáez, *Recuerdos,* III, pp. 142-81, 326-28; Partido Socialista, *Grove a la presidencia* (Santiago, 1937), pp. 15-16.

with Matte. Grove would be Minister of Defense. Word leaked to various workers' groups, and crowds in Santiago began calling for socialism.[5]

On June 4, airplanes swooped over the rooftops of Santiago. Leaflets proclaiming the inauguration of the Socialist Republic of Chile rained on the city. Rejecting both capitalism and communism, the rebels promised government action to end the Depression and calm discontent. Their program advocated national aid for the economy against foreign imperialist exploiters and special aid for the poor against domestic oligarchic exploiters. The declaration closed with a vow that the new regime would insure "national conservation" because the crisis faced Chile with a forced choice: "Either the final disaster or a change of regimes." Even though they ejected Montero by force, the socialists were demanding greater responsiveness from the existing evolutionary system, not a revolutionary revamping of society.[6]

The Socialist Republic

Socialism as a governing ideology was transmitted suddenly to the Chilean public, through a lightning coup more than through painstaking years of preparation. Not wholly alien, Chilean socialism was a populist amalgam of old and new political ingredients, of domestic and foreign elements. The junta mixed military and civilians, professionals and artisans, liberals, corporatists, anarchists, anarchosyndicalists, and Marxists. An improvised experiment, the Socialist Republic had neither the time nor the inclination to pursue long-range, ideological plans for national recovery and renovation. It offered piecemeal reforms and stirring oratory to Chileans who were more in need of comprehensive programs. It lacked clear leadership and mass organization, especially outside the capital city. For an ostensibly revolutionary regime, the Republic achieved scant participation of the workers or even backing from the peasants. Lasting only twelve days, the junta's impact was far more emotional than material. According to an appalled army general, many despairing Chileans, in that moment, had a vision of "a Socialist Republic, an affectionate mother who would take care of administrating the common good for the benefit

5. Marmaduke Grove Vallejo, "Discurso . . . ," *Núcleo*, no. 1 (June 1, 1934), pp. 1-20; Alessandri, *Recuerdos*, II, pp. 453-64; Partido Socialista, *4 de junio*, p. 3; Durand, *Don Arturo*, pp. 296-97; Thomas, "The Socialist," pp. 203-20.
6. *El Mercurio*, June 5, 1932; Marín Balmaceda, *El 4*, pp. 37-48; Sáez, *Recuerdos*, III, pp. 111-81.

of all her children, without odious distinctions, without privileges for anyone, with a spirit of justice previously unknown among us, and with truly miraculous results."[7] The Republic awakened such momentous hopes and fears that it made an indelible impression on Chilean politics.

The junta divided between Dávila, the moderate leader, and Matte and Grove, who headed the radical majority. Matte was a severe, distinguished, passionate but calculating rebel from the upper classes. Matte was cerebral; Grove instinctual. At the end of the 1920s, Grove had joined Alessandri and other exiles in efforts to overthrow Ibáñez. From Argentina, Grove flew over the Andes in 1930 in an airplane painted red to connote its revolutionary mission. The invaders, however, were betrayed and exiled to Easter Island. They escaped from there to Tahiti and then back to Europe, only to return home after the fall of Ibáñez. An impulsive, generous *caudillo,* Grove electrified the popular imagination in 1932. He soon personified the Socialist Republic. Ibáñez once said of Grove, "He was born a revolutionary, as others are born blond or brunette."[8] One of Grove's radio speeches broadcast the millenarian exuberance of some of the June revolutionaries: "2000 years ago Jesus Christ promised a better life, but we are more practical than the deluded Jesus Christ. We not only promise but will provide a better life at once. We shall realize our program even if half of the people of Chile perish in the attempt. Chile will establish a socialist republic which shall be followed by the other Latin American countries."[9]

Four key figures backed Matte and Grove. Oscar Schnake Vergara, a vibrant young organizer of students and workers with an anarchosyndicalist background, served as General Secretary for the junta. Eugenio González Rojas, a Mason, was Minister of Education. Carlos Alberto Martínez Martínez, a worker and experienced labor leader, headed the agricultural colonization program; and Alfredo Lagarrigue Rengifo, from a middle-class family of positivist thinkers, drafted the junta's plans for a functional state organized by occupational groups or syndicates and ran the Treasury. Their attempts to restructure Chile with decrees grew more radical after Dávila, who

7. Sáez, *Recuerdos,* III, pp. 7-8, 182-221; interviews with Charlín, Santiago, 1970.

8. Frías, pp. 3-5; Grove, "Discurso," pp. 4-6; Marmaduke Grove Vallejo, *Toda la verdad* (Paris, 1929); Partido Socialista, *Grove, el militar y el ciudadano* (Santiago, 1937), pp. 8-9; Donoso, *Alessandri,* II, pp. 14-27, 104-5; Eugenio Matte Hurtado, "Sobre el programa de la Nueva Acción Pública," Chile, Cámara de Senadores, *Boletín de sesiones extraordinarias, 1932-1933* (Santiago, 1933), pp. 395-403.

9. U.S., Dept. of State Archives, Santiago, June, 1932, p. 3, 825.00/311.

opposed the nationalization of nitrates and tried to reassure U.S. interests, left the junta. Unity was unlikely in such a medley of idealists and adventurers.[10]

The Socialist Republic was a moderate, rather middle-class breed of socialism, more radical in appearance than actuality. It stressed state planning more than class conflict. The government intended more to stimulate private enterprise than to expropriate the means of production. Rather than dividing up the great estates, it promoted agricultural colonization. The junta contemplated the redistribution of income rather than wealth. While closing the Congress fabricated under Ibáñez, the Socialist Republic retained most political liberties and kept censorship to a minimum. By emphasizing both immediate assistance for the masses and efficient, technical reordering of the economy along vaguely corporatist lines, the junta advocated both disruptive welfarism and orderly production. The dominant socialist-populist strain was evident in the slogan "Bread, Roof, and Overcoat" for the impoverished. The technocratic tendency was voiced in the junta's determination to provide a government of "energy, youth, efficiency, and discipline." In essence, the Socialist Republic proposed to aid the lower classes with an expanded state, one planned and managed by technical experts.[11]

The inherent contradictions of the Socialist Republic riddled its indecisive economic policies, particularly for banking and nitrates. The junta largely blamed the unrelenting depression on U.S. imperialists. Viewing the banks as the nerve center for Chilean and foreign capitalists, Grove and Treasury Minister Lagarrigue wanted to transform the Central Bank into a state bank to give them control of

10. According to a report from Dávila to the U.S. ambassador, Grove agreed that foreign interests, with the possible exception of COSACH, would not be harmed. U.S. Dept. of State Archives, Santiago, June 6, 1932, p. 435, 825.00 Revolutions/72; Thomas, "The Socialist," pp. 203-20; Sáez, *Recuerdos,* III, pp. 182-203.

11. The junta's basic announced program included the following: dissolving Ibáñez's Congress and COSACH; reducing the size of the armed forces and employing them in civic action; taxing the rich to end the government deficit and help the unemployed; expropriating with compensation certain underutilized agricultural lands for colonization by the unemployed; reopening closed mines and factories; imposing state regulation of internal and external commerce; stopping evictions of poor renters unable to pay; halting the state of siege and the punishment of naval rebels ordered under Montero; redistributing credit to the middle and lower classes; raising salaries and benefits for public employees; recognizing the Soviet Union; promoting inter-American solidarity; cutting luxury imports; controlling bank deposits; developing gold mining to ease unemployment and the gold shortage; and reorganizing the state and the economy along functional, corporate lines. *La Opinión,* June 5, 1932; *El Mercurio,* June 5, 1932; *La junta de gobierno al país* (Santiago, 1932); Partido Socialista, *4 de junio,* pp. 1, 3-4; Julio César Jobet, "Revolución socialista del 4 de junio de 1932," *Arauco,* no. 8 (June, 1960), pp. 49-50.

currency, gold, and credit. The Central Bank denied the junta loans to combat unemployment, a reversal of its policies under Montero. The Central Bank's major contributors and holders were private commercial banks and foreigners, mainly National City Bank, Guaranty Trust, and the U.S. Federal Reserve. Alarmed protests from Chilean and U.S. financial elites, as well as the U.S. Embassy, dissuaded the junta from encroaching on those credit resources. Instead, the socialists had to rely on inflationary spending policies. The junta was also frustrated in its plans to nationalize COSACH, plans which were being drawn up only hours before the socialists were ousted.[12]

The upper class opposed not only the Socialist Republic's specific proposals but also the way it degraded the "oligarchy" and coddled the ragged and hungry. At first, though, the elites tried to bend with the times and minimize conflict. The owner of the prestigious newspaper *El Mercurio,* for example, suggested that Chilean socialism was merely a new brand of evolutionary reformism which could be tamed and tolerated: "The Socialists of today are the Radicals of yesterday and the Liberals of the day before yesterday. The vanguard has changed in name, but its nature is the same. As much can be said of those stigmatized today as oligarchs: they are the same ones that yesterday were Conservatives and the day before yesterday Ultramontanes. Between them both is the center, which today is Radical and yesterday was Liberal. The names change: humanity does not."[13] One of the country's leading capitalists, the newspaper magnate answered the protests of his workers by announcing the "socialization" of the enterprise. Similarly, the junta sought to calm the elites; the socialists vacillated between attacking the rich on behalf of the masses, whose support was needed, and trying not to unduly alarm the upper and middle classes, whose acquiescence was needed. Assurances to the Church that the clergy would suffer in neither person nor property elicited statements of support for the junta from the archbishop. However, such attempts at conciliation on the part of the elites soon faded and were dwarfed by their resistance. Industrialists criticized the uncertainty of plans for state intervention in the economy and trimmed their production plans accordingly. SOFOFA complained about employees and workers who, inspired by the junta, were press-

12. Ernest Galarza, "Socialists Seize Government in Chile," *Foreign Policy Bulletin,* XI, no. 33 (June 17, 1932), pp. 1-2; Partido Socialista, *4 de junio,* pp. 3-4; Ellsworth, pp. 38-39; Mario Antonioletti, *La moneda, el crédito y los bancos* (Santiago, 1934), pp. 9-10; Donoso, *Alessandri,* II, pp. 106-7; Sáez, *Recuerdos,* III, pp. 185-229; U.S., Dept. of State Archives, Santiago, June 9, 1932, p. 437, 825.516/126, Santiago, June 9, 1932, p. 438, 825.516/129.

13. *El Mercurio,* June 9, 1932.

ing socialist demands. At the same time, landowners opposed schemes for colonization and for reduction of tariffs on imported foods. Like some other elite institutions, the Supreme Court closed down to protest the Socialist Republic. A proposed progressive tax on wealth and inheritances also drew upper-class fire.[14]

The upper classes' deeper anxieties about the Socialist Republic stemmed from age-old fears of and disdain for the working classes. The elites derided the boisterous, shabby crowds that roared beneath the balconies of the presidential palace. Violent attacks on the Union Club and rallies outside churches augmented upper-class dread. The U.S. ambassador observed the disarray and despondency of the conservative elites: "They nurse their respectability behind the barred doors of the Union Club. The hope of intervention by the United States is often expressed in their conversations."[15] Warning of impending anarchy or communism, the rightist elements blamed the armed services for the existence of the Socialist Republic, and they secretly began organizing their own paramilitary forces.[16]

The middle classes were divided between the elites and the Socialist Republic. The same professional groups—the College of Lawyers, the Medical Association, and the Institute of Engineers—that had mobilized middle-sector strikes against Ibáñez called without success for similar demonstrations to bring down the junta. Some other professionals, intellectuals, teachers, and white-collar employees considered themselves socialists after the frustrations of 1931-32. Others were at least amenable to the concept of state paternalism. The junta's declarations, moreover, threatened only the income of the extremely wealthy and the privileges of big capital, often foreign. Smaller manufacturers, merchants, and farmers were not dismayed, especially when the new government promised to give them preference in the distribution of credit and greater support against foreign competition. Rent relief eased burdens on the middle as well as the lower classes. Public employees envisioned higher salaries and fewer layoffs.[17] In addition, the junta attracted many middle-class professors

14. El Personal de la Empresa de "El Mercurio" en Asamblea, *Considerando* . . . (n.p., 1932); Agustín Edwards, *Recuerdos de mi persecución* (Santiago, 1932), pp. 99-101; La Sociedad de Fomento Fabril, *Boletín*, no. 6 (June, 1932), pp. 269-70; Fidel Araneda Bravo, *El Arzobispo Errázuriz y la evolución política y social de Chile* (Santiago, 1956), p. 299; Partido Socialista, *4 de junio*, pp. 1-3; Jobet, "Revolución socialista," pp. 49-50.

15. U.S., Dept. of State Archives, Santiago, June 13, 1932, pp. 440-41, 825.00 Revolutions/85.

16. Rafael Luis Gumucio V., *No más* (Santiago, 1932); Javier Vial Solar, *El diluvio* (Santiago, 1934), pp. 11, 85-87, 123-43; Edwards Matte, *El Club*, p. 65; Sáez, *Recuerdos*, III, pp. 207-8; *Dávila de cuerpo entero* (Santiago, 1932).

17. *El Mercurio*, June 6 and June 9, 1932; Congreso Nacional, *En defensa*, pp. 55-56; Partido Socialista, *4 de junio*, p. 2; Sáez, *Recuerdos*, III, pp. 186-205; Thomas, "The Socialist," pp. 203-20.

and students by enacting university reforms to give them greater say in administration. Like the rest of the middle class, however, university students, including FECH leaders, were split over the junta, and as many conspired against the Socialist Republic as rallied to it.[18]

It was impossible for most workers to know much about the junta's definition of "socialism." They did, however, recognize the government's identification of and sympathy with their problems. The junta's appeal was based on concrete deeds as well as scorching language and utopian promises of a classless society. The most dramatic single act of the regime for the lower classes typified its immediatist, populist character. Prompted by Grove, the junta returned to manual workers clothes and work implements, such as sewing machines, which the poor had been unable to redeem after pawning them to the Department of Popular Credit. Other actions also found favor with the masses. The junta restricted the right of landlords to evict impoverished tenants. It established a colony on a *fundo* in the south for hundreds of the unemployed. Food allotments for the bread lines increased. The regime released many of the laborers condemned after the naval mutiny and Tragic Christmas of 1931. In reciprocation, unions, such as the Federation of Railroad Workers, began tendering support. Petitions asking for nationalization and worker control poured in from the factories of Santiago and the mining north. Some of these demands were signs of rising enthusiasm for the junta; others constituted pressure on the regime from the Communists. The junta, with its rallies, gestures, symbols, and heroes, made a greater impact on the unorganized workers than on union members. The dispensing of goods and exhortations, rather than elaborate blueprints for the restructuring of Chilean society, became the hallmark of the Socialist Republic. Although not revolutionary, such magnanimous welfare measures and the charisma of Grove endeared the junta to many urban workers. In populist fashion, spontaneous payoffs from the top down seemed more important than structural changes in the traditional hierarchy of economic and political power.[19] Referring to the actions of the junta, one proponent of socialism complained that the wildly popular term was only dimly understood as a promise of short-range benefits: "Sixty percent of our citizens understand by socialism an improvement in the living condi-

18. Interview with Astolfo Tapia Moore, a member of that student generation and later Socialist Party leader, Santiago, 1970; Henry Grattan Doyle, "Chile in a New Revolution," *Current History*, XXXVI (July, 1932), pp. 477-80; Bonilla and Glazer, pp. 84-85.
19. *El Chileno*, June 19, 1932; "Los jefes . . . Martínez," p. 10; *La junta*; Partido Socialista, *4 de junio*, p. 1; Quijada, p. 31; Jorge Grove, pp. 24-44; Thomas, "The Socialist," pp. 203-20.

tions of the worker. A little more salary, a little less unemployment, a little more food for the unemployed, a small moratorium on rent payments, return of pawned goods. . . ."[20]

The official Moscow-oriented Communists opposed the Socialist Republic; the "Trotskyist" Communist Left lent the junta conditional support. After their years of organizational efforts, the official Communists were distraught at Grove's ability to draw the workers away from them. Their leader Lafertte expressed the PC's anguish over the June 4th movement: "For the constitutional government it was a coup; but it was something more for the Chilean Communists. . . the triumphant forces stole the presidential table-service that night, from the Communists they stole something more valuable and delicate than the table-service: the name Socialist Republic."[21] In hopes of regaining the initiative in leftist labor politics, the Communists dared the junta to prove its socialist coloring by enacting a list of more than seventy radical proposals. The official Communists charged that Grove was the new mask of the bourgeoisie and imperialism. Demanding a headquarters from the government, they seized part of the university. Grove replied with anticommunist speeches and at the same time tried, to no avail, to pacify the PC. Frightening the middle classes with propaganda and labor agitation, the Communists harassed the junta and denied it potential supporters among students and workers. The Stalinist Communists failed, however, to mobilize the masses or mount a clear alternative.[22]

Their rivals, the Communist Left, also made drastic demands on the junta—such as immediately arming the masses—but did not fight the regime. These so-called Trotskyists, who conflicted with the regular PC over personalities and tactics as much as ideology or strategies, saw the Socialist Republic as an opportunity to reach the workers through its popularity and thus promote revolution. The approaches of both the official and dissident Communists added to the clamor of rhetoric and rallies. This created the false impression that the Republic was losing control of the revolutionary masses.[23]

The military, which accepted Chilean *socialismo* and some plans to help the poor, feared that the junta was either contaminated with Communists or at least could not control them. Bombastic Com-

20. Oscar Álvarez Andrews, *Bases para una constitución funcional* (Santiago, 1932), pp. 5-9.

21. Boizard, *Cuatro*, pp. 139-42.

22. Robert J. Alexander, *Communism in Latin America* (New Brunswick, N.J., 1957), pp. 186-87; Sáez, *Recuerdos*, III, pp. 188-93; *El Mercurio*, June 8 and June 11, 1932; Waiss, *El drama*, pp. 15-16.

23. Congreso Nacional, *En defensa*, pp. 53-56; "Manuel Hidalgo, primer embajador socialista," *Rumbo*, no. 2 (July, 1939), pp. 13-16.

munist propaganda claimed that soviets of peasants, workers, miners, Indians, sailors, and soldiers were sprouting rapidly. Even a red carnation Grove donned at a worker rally was used by anticommunists to build the case for ousting the Socialist Republic. Anticommunism justified counterrevolution and set limits on the armed forces' willingness to move toward the left or to allow such movement. At the same time, officers were apprehensive that, like the naval rebellion, the Republic would foment leftist notions and weaken discipline among the servicemen. Other officers, particularly in the army, hoped to replace Grove with Ibáñez. All opposed disorder in the streets. Without positive and widespread military support, the Socialist Republic was isolated and doomed.[24]

Perhaps above all the Socialist Republic fell because it lacked public confidence and organized mass support. The government's permissiveness toward the rhetorical Left as much as its own radicalness undermined its position. Internal divisions and uncertainties also hurt the junta, as did the opposition of powerful interests. Added to domestic opponents were U.S., British, and French antagonists. All three foreign governments cooperated with international bankers and corporations to block any junta plans for nationalization. They warned the socialists that any interference with foreign holdings such as nitrates and copper would cause Chilean deposits to be frozen and credit for international transactions to be withheld. The United States denied recognition until the junta's stance toward foreign interests could be clarified. When Chile's oil supply fell critically low, a Standard Oil tanker held up deliveries; the junta pleaded in vain for help from socialist countries like Russia. Near the end of the Socialist Republic, the British dispatched a cruiser toward Chile as a signal to the junta and its adversaries in the navy. Although foreign overreactions compounded the junta's woes, the Socialist Republic was made and unmade by the Chilean military and a handful of civilians, not by the masses or foreigners. When the Santiago garrison and the navy moved against the Republic, it had little recourse. The regime's influence beyond Santiago was minimal. There were no organized, solid party or social forces to defend the administration. After losing his position in the junta, Dávila convinced the uneasy military, particularly the infantry, that Grove and Matte had carried the movement to extremes. On June 16, 1932, the Army ousted the first socialist government of Chile.[25]

24. Von Schroeders, pp. 138-63; Montero Moreno, *Confesiones*, pp. 85-86; Sáez, *Recuerdos*, III, pp. 189-204; U.S., Dept. of State Archives, Santiago, June 13, 1932, pp. 440-41, 825.00 Revolutions/85.
25. U.S., Dept. of State Archives, Santiago, June 5, 1932, 825.00 Revolutions/64,

Grove and Matte considered calling on the air force or the masses to resist, but finally decided to surrender peacefully. Exiling both men to Easter Island, the armed forces announced that the Socialist Republic would continue under new management now that it had been cleansed of "communist" elements. Dávila was put in charge of a civilian junta resting on the shoulders of the military. Dictatorial order was imposed immediately, but a spate of worker protests broke out over Grove's removal. Some of the Communist Left and socialists backed the strikes and demonstrations, which were particularly force-ful among transportation and construction workers, especially in Valparaíso and Santiago. However, Dávila quickly snuffed out dissent.[26]

The Military Withdraws from Political Intervention

For 100 days, Dávila tried to revive Ibáñez's model of development: authoritarian state intervention and efficiency powered by foreign—U.S.—assistance. With foreign loans unavailable, he relied on infla-tionary credit expansion. Dávila established a National Economic Council to organize and plan the private economy along functional, sectoral (agriculture, commerce, etc.) lines and to foster industry. The Depression continued, however, and discontent permeated all social sectors. Relying on the tolerance of the military, Dávila's version of "socialism" as state capitalism ended in September, 1932.[27] The military replaced him with General Bartolomé Blanche Espejo

Santiago, June 5, 1932, 825.00 Revolutions/69, Santiago, June 9, 1932, p. 438, 825.516/129, Santiago, June 10, 1932, 825.516/131, Santiago, June 13, 1932, 825.516/127, Santiago, June 13, 1932, 825.516/138, Washington, June 15, 1932, 825.00 Revolutions/100, Santiago, June 16, 1932, 825.00 Revolutions/102, Santiago, June 16, 1932, 825.516/151; United States, Department of State, *Foreign Relations of the United States. Diplomatic Papers. 1932* (5 vols., Washington, D.C., 1948); Ronald E. Raven, "El 4 de junio: Birth of a Legend" (M.A. thesis, Wayne State University, Detroit, 1973), pp. 25-61; Cifuentes Solar, pp. 18-19. *¿Por qué cayó Grove?*, pp. 1-13; Partido Socialista, *4 de junio*, pp. 3-4.

26. *El Mercurio*, June 17, 1932; interview with Charlín, Santiago, 1970; Alexander, *Communism*, p. 187; Sáez, *Recuerdos*, III, pp. 207-11; Thomas, "The Socialist"; Pedro Elías Sarmiento, *Descorriendo el velo de los hermanos Grove en la Isla de Pascua* (Valparaíso, 1938).

27. U.S., Dept. of State Archives, Santiago, June 16, 1932, 825.00 Revolutions/103, June 24, 1932, 825.00 Revolutions/125, July 7, 1932, 825.00 Revolutions/143, July 14, 1932, 825.00 Revolutions/157, Aug. 17, 1932, pp. 2-3, 825.00/1234; Carlos G. Dávila, *We of the Americas* (Chicago, 1949), pp. 1-8, 66-68, 127-36; Carlos G. Dávila, "The Montevideo Conference. Antecedents and Accomplishments," *International Concilia-tion*, no. 300 (May, 1934), pp. 121-58; Dávila, *Chile*, pp. 1-28; Alfredo Guillermo Bravo, *El 4 de junio: el festín de los audaces* (2nd ed., Santiago, 1932), pp. 94-101; Carlos Orrego Barros, *La organización gremial y el poder político* (Santiago, 1932), pp. 6-36; Wilfredo Mayorga, "Crisis con sangre," *Ercilla*, no. 1682 (Aug. 30, 1967), p. 15; Ellsworth, pp.

as a caretaker chief executive to preside over new presidential and congressional elections set for October. The armed forces announced that Dávila had been cashiered because he had been more dictatorial than socialist.[28]

Blanche promised to carry on the "socialist aspirations" of the nation until the elections. Everyone, it seemed, had become a "socialist." But there was a public outcry against further military officeholding. The army then decided to end Blanche's brief tenure and military participation in open politics.[29]

The army and civilians in the mining north precipitated Blanche's downfall. This regionalist, almost separatist, revolt fused all political forces, including *napistas* and Communists, behind the demand for civilian, stable government. The rebels ordered the Santiago garrison to stop meddling in politics and soiling the military's and Chile's reputation. The PC in Santiago chastised workers and party members for backing regionalist, civilianist movements instead of revolutionary goals; this revealed the Communists' own regional splits. The garrison in Concepción, another leftist-voting, anti-Santiago area, and even military and civilian groups (such as *alessandristas*) in the capital city joined the uproar against Blanche. Echoing the disillusionment and bitterness of most of the armed forces, Blanche resigned. He urged his fellow officers to never again enter the political arena. The military withdrew to its barracks, as the Minister of War proclaimed, "forever." Meanwhile, the civilian president of the Supreme Court formed an interim government until order based on legitimate rule could be reestablished by the ballot box.[30]

The Election of 1932

The 1932 election brought a return to political normality after more than a decade of disintegration. At the same time, a new style of politics—populist socialism—christened the modern leftward move-

17-19, 43-51, 80-82, 161-65; Zañartu, *Hambre*, pp. 30-31, 98-152; Keller, *Un país*, pp. 22-27, 110-11; Álvarez Andrews, *Historia*, pp. 352-53; Congreso Nacional, *En defensa*, pp. 59-63; *El Mercurio*, June 20-26, July 1-10, July 23-25, Aug. 16, and Aug. 31, 1932; *La Opinión*, June 18 and Sept. 13-15, 1932.

28. Germán Luco, *Desde Alessandri hasta Alessandri* (Concepción, 1932), pp. 8-10; Sáez, *Recuerdos*, III, pp. 213-99; Decreto Ley No. 476, in Chile, Tribunal Calificador, "Elecciones extraordinarias generales" (Santiago, 1933), p. 9.

29. *El Mercurio*, Sept. 14-17, 1932; Montero Moreno, *La verdad*, pp. 175-77.

30. Wilfredo Mayorga, "Chile bloqueado por los chilenos," *Ercilla*, no. 1702 (Jan. 31, 1968), p. 15; *El Mercurio*, Sept. 28–Oct. 3, 1932; *Bandera Roja*, Oct. 22, 1932; *El Chileno*, Oct. 15, 1932; Congreso Nacional, *En defensa*, p. 70; Bravo, *El 4*, pp. 20-45, 83-93; Sáez, *Recuerdos*, III, pp. 271-318.

ment of the Chilean electorate. 1932 also saw a proliferation of parties and candidates, a more common trend in later Chilean political life. In the congressional contests many infant parties boasting new creeds and leaders challenged the historic organizations. Five candidates aspired to the presidency: Conservative Party President Héctor Rodríguez de la Sotta; Liberal Enrique Zañartu Prieto, former Treasury Minister under Dávila; Liberal Arturo Alessandri; exiled Socialist Marmaduke Grove; and Communist Elías Lafertte. This array made the election an invaluable microcosm for analyzing the origins of populist movements and the reactions of traditional groups to accommodate them. For the first time in Chilean history, two major candidates, Alessandri, the spokesman for liberal populism, and Grove, the paladin of socialist populism, based their campaigns on appeals to the mass vote.

The election was held under far more trying economic conditions than during Alessandri's first victory in 1920. National production, wages, and employment were still declining by October, 1932, despite some partial recovery in industry. The volume of exports hit bottom in November, 1932. The greatest jumps since 1900 in the fluctuating cost-of-living index paralleled the periods of political upheaval in 1919-20 (a 25-point rise in the index), 1924-25 (up 16 points), and 1931-32 (up 18 points). From September to October, 1932, alone, the cost-of-living index in Santiago jumped 7 points. Meanwhile, wholesale prices fell from an index of 100 in 1928 to a low of 74 in October, 1931, and then soared to 178 by the end of 1932. Inflation nearly doubled the currency in circulation during 1932.[31]

In response to the economic crisis, most Chileans looked to state intervention, industrialization, and economic nationalism as the keys to recovery. Disillusionment with free enterprise swept the political spectrum. The need for state expansion in the economy was agreed upon far more than were how much expansion, under whose control, and for whose benefit. Heterogeneous foreign influences mingled in every proposal to overhaul the capitalist economy. Most of the Right, however, stressed corporatist-fascist notions of state regulation and the Left emphasized socialist models. As the Left pressed for greater state action to help the masses, the Right demanded that an expanded state control restless social groups.[32]

31. Ellsworth, pp. vii-51, 161-65; Chile, Dirección General de Estadística, *Sinopsis,* pp. 116-17, 155, 213-18, 233-38, 284-85; Hirschman, pp. 216-43; Chile, *Geografía,* pp. 46-58.
32. Álvarez Andrews, *Bases,* pp. 14-97; Daniel Martner, *Economía política* (2nd ed., Santiago, 1934), pp. 171-78; Guillermo González Echenique, *Reflexiones de la hora presente* (Santiago, 1934), pp. 45-59.

The desire to extend state participation in the economic sector focused on import-substituting industrialization. It was promoted by the Right and the Left under the banner of economic nationalism. Industrialization, however, was essentially a pragmatic defense against the disappearance of foreign goods, capital, revenues, and exchange. The limited objectives of this brand of economic nationalism posed no threat to foreign capital or ownership; nor did it provide the impetus for even relative economic self-sufficiency, although it did direct more attention to internal development. Nevertheless, even tepid economic nationalism blended state activism and industrialization and appealed to major elements in all social and political factions. It thus facilitated agreements on how to overcome the crisis.[33]

The other main issue of the 1932 campaign—removal of the military from politics—was expressed by all factions in terms of restoring pride in Chile's superiority to less-stable Latin American nations. Antimilitarism also dwelt on the recent failures of officers in the government. One goal of constitutionalists on the Right was to halt the swing to the Left by containing the military. Conservative barrages against the military and Ibáñez were also attacks on Grove, socialism, communism, and disorders which provided openings for the masses.[34] A despondent Liberal said in retrospect that "it is in the nature of things that [military] interventions only clear the route for socialism to advance. . . ."[35]

Upper- and middle-class leaders ready to use force to defend de-

33. In addition to foreign possession of Chilean raw materials, even national industries relied heavily on imported primary materials, often already semiprocessed abroad. Wilson, pp. 33-40. ". . . the main sources of Chilean income from exports are in non-Chilean hands. Consequently a considerable proportion of statistically shown exports may be described as 'false' exports since the proceeds from them do not return to Chile either in goods, money, or services. . . . nitrate, copper, iron, and even the wool and frozen meat of Magallanes, are all in foreign hands, while the greater part of everyday commerce is carried on through the medium of foreign agents and merchant houses." Great Britain, Department of Overseas Trade, *Economic Conditions in Chile* (London, 1932), p. 13. Francisco Rivas Vicuña, *Nacionalismo social* (Santiago, 1932), pp. 5-13; Ellsworth, pp. 16-25, 128; Mamalakis and Reynolds, pp. 14-16, 70, 190, 227-36, 279-81.

34. Ricardo Cox Balmaceda, *Discurso* (Santiago, 1932), p. 4; *Unión Republicana* (Valparaíso, 1932), pp. 2-31; Bravo, *El 4*, pp. 5-88; Gumucio, *No más; El Chileno*, Oct. 20, 1932. The feeling that Chilean politics had degenerated into a disgraceful comedy was captured by U.S. humorist Will Rogers on a visit to Santiago: "I have been accused of coming to Chile with an ulterior motive, and therefore I will leave early tomorrow, because I do not want to be president. I understand in this matter that the President fears to send his clothes to the laundry because he does not know if he will be in the Moneda [the presidential office] when they send his clothes back to him." *La Nación*, Oct. 15, 1932.

35. Ladislao Errázuriz, *Los deberes del Partido Liberal en la hora actual* (Santiago, 1934), pp. 5-6.

mocracy and to maintain public order without recourse to the regular military formed Republican Militias. These paramilitary groups attracted scores of sincere, conservative constitutionalists devoted to restraining the armed forces. However, the militias' attacks on the Left, in which they denounced "communists" as much as "*caudillos,*" showed that antimilitarism was suffused with the desire to deter social conflict and to cage socialism and populism.[36]

Severely divided but uniformly resentful of the criticism heaped upon them, the armed forces refrained from further overt political activity. Although most military officers regretted their plunge into politics, several still entertained political ambitions. Even those still tempted to seize the state feared conflicts among the services and did not want to assume an unsavory police role. They realized that the heavy military participation in government since 1924 had burdened them with the blame for subsequent failures. The Chilean military could not offer itself as a fresh alternative in the 1930s, unlike military groups on much of the continent, since it had been in power when the Great Depression arrived. More-conservative leaders of the armed services and those from the outlying provinces were particularly determined to uproot interventionist tendencies and escape the stigma of 1931-32. Most of the officers felt betrayed by the civilians who had encouraged their political activism.[37]

Upper-Class Adaptations

In 1932 the upper class accepted attitudes, strategies, reforms, and alliances they had rejected in the past. Although pessimism drove some to embrace outmoded traditions, most, with varying degrees of reluctance, tolerated the need for new solutions. Although the threat of socialism, communism, and revolution was exaggerated, the elites' perception and use of that threat was an important motivation for

36. Rather typical leaders of the Republican Militia were Eulogia Sánchez (an engineer and businessman from Santiago educated at the Catholic University who belonged to the Union Club and Auto Club) and Diego Sutil (a businessman, financier, and landowner from Santiago who belonged to the SNA, Union Club, and Club Hípico). La Milicia Republicana, *Albúm conmemorativo de su presentación pública* (Santiago, 1933); Jorge de la Cuadra Poisson, *La verdad de la incidencias milicianas* (Santiago, 1935); Wilfredo Mayorga, "Cuando el PS gritaba viva el ejército," *Ercilla,* no. 1613 (May 4, 1966), pp. 14-15; Alain Joxe, *Las fuerzas armadas en el sistema político de Chile* (Santiago, 1970), pp. 28-130; Wilfredo Mayorga, "La Milicia Republicana," *Ercilla,* no. 1609 (Apr. 6, 1966), pp. 18-19; Wilfredo Mayorga, "El fantasma de Vignola en Santiago," *Ercilla,* no. 1606 (Mar. 16, 1966), pp. 18-19.

37. Unión Social del Personal en Retiro de las Fuerzas Armadas de Chile, *Declaración de principios* (Santiago, 1932); Bravo Lavín, pp. 7, 146-72; Sáez, *Recuerdos,* I, p. 8.

political flexibility. The Right had ceded some ground to reform advocates in the immediate post–World War I years and now went significantly further. When the conservative groups had touted Montero in 1931, they had sought to resurrect a previous status quo. In 1932, they were trying to preserve the existing one. The elites argued for "reform and not restoration" because the only apparent choice left was between evolution and the dreaded "creole socialism."[38] In opting for increased changes, the upper class was in effect acknowledging that measured concessions were the minimum price for social stability.[39]

The upper class and the Right, more than in 1920, now focused their political arguments on the best way for the state to participate in economic growth and social welfare. The religious issue had been muted by the 1925 constitution. During the Parliamentary Republic, the privileged few had feared an expanded state as a potential threat to their private enclaves; now they feared more the threat of new groups against their interests and state stability. The radical reform proposals of emerging social-political elements made the issue of private versus state capitalism of the 1920s appear mild by comparison. Consequently, the upper class accepted greater state penetration of the economy. At the same time, they tried to fortify their own corporate structures. The elites sought to dampen class antagonisms and voter unrest by stabilizing the economy under state auspices. They hoped to promote harmony by lowering their traditional opposition to the incorporation of disadvantaged social and regional groups. In retrospect these accommodations appear minimal, but they were costly to the upper class: these adjustments were tantamount to relinquishing future electoral preeminence to the middle classes and their populist followers.[40]

The elites' economic leaders hoped that state-sponsored, nationalistic industrialization would breathe new life into their rural as well as their urban interests. They envisioned natural benefits in promoting Chilean capitalists against foreign competition in the name of nationalism. By 1932, most upper-class leaders were not defending

38. Pedro Lira Urquieta, *El futuro del país y el Partido Conservador* (Santiago, 1934), pp. 9, 20; González Echenique, esp. pp. 62-74.
39. José María Cifuentes, *La propiedad* (Santiago, 1932), esp. pp. 69-70; Gabriel Amunátegui Jordán, *El liberalismo y su misión social* (Santiago, 1933), pp. 12-14; Guillermo Subercaseaux, *La política social nacionalista moderna* (Santiago, 1932), p. 1; Errázuriz, pp. 3-11.
40. Partido Liberal, *La crisis* (Santiago, 1932), pp. 1-8; Lira Urquieta, pp. 9-29; Agustín Edwards, *Las corporaciones y la doctrina liberal* (Santiago, 1934), pp. 6-7.

the traditional balance of the state and the private economy as much as fighting to bend the emerging system to their needs.[41]

Many agriculturalists campaigned for state aid to industry as complementary to aid for themselves. They argued that boosting agricultural exports would garner more foreign exchange and that priming industrial production would reduce spending for foreign goods. As industry expanded, so would its demands for primary materials, many of which came from agriculture. The agrarian elites also hoped that industrialization would ease rural population pressures and incipient demands for land reform. The mines had been the usual escape from overcrowding in central Chile, but as a result of the depression the demand for labor in the mining areas had been reduced. Consequently, workers returning to their home districts gorged the labor market and swelled discontent with latifundia. Many *hacendados*, therefore, welcomed reform efforts to build up industry and mining, for example by eliminating COSACH.[42]

The Society for Factory Development joined the National Society for Agriculture in advocating state aid to both sectors of the economy. The industrialists claimed top priority by arguing that, as they perceived was true in the United States, waste, poverty, and, above all, social conflict could be avoided through centralized, planned industrialization with compensatory benefits and guarantees for the workers.[43] The SOFOFA pleaded its case in nationalistic terms: "The industrial consolidation of the country is the best expression of its economic sovereignty. Without one's own industry there is no true independence."[44] On the issues of economic nationalism and civilian government, the elites' arguments superficially mirrored those of many middle- and lower-class leaders in 1932.

Middle- and Lower-Class Anxieties

The middle classes, in contrast to 1920, seemed more concerned with protecting their positions than with challenging the elites. Although divided, the middle groups generally clung to the parties, programs, and candidates of the past. Both the upper- and lower-middle sectors welcomed elite acceptance of reformist ideas embodying statism, industrialization, and economic nationalism, still consid-

41. Partido Conservador, *Programa y estatutos* (Santiago, 1933), pp. 1-15; Amunátegui Jordán, pp. 12-14.

42. Larraín, *Orientación*, pp. 1-29; Thomson, p. 286; Keller, *Un país*, pp. 122-25.

43. La Sociedad de Fomento Fabril, *Plan*, pp. 1-2; La Sociedad de Fomento Fabril, *Rol de industriales de Chile* (Santiago, 1932), p. 72.

44. La Sociedad de Fomento Fabril, *Boletín*, XLIX (Sept., 1932), p. 415.

ered somewhat "socialist" notions. Students, for example, were too split to take any official stand in the election. As nearly as can be determined, the middle classes tended to stay with the Radicals and Alessandri. On the other hand, many professionals and employees, lacking elite connections or defenses, suffered from unemployment and price inflation and therefore empathized with labor's distress. Government handouts and housing assistance were needed for white-collar employees as well as manual workers. Proportionate to their number in the work force, *empleados* were losing almost as many jobs as *obreros*. According to Alessandri, "The unemployment of the middle class . . . because of its social ambience, and its higher standard of living, is perhaps the most painful. . . ."[45] Since doctors and lawyers were often employed, at least partly, by the state, they were also harmed by the Depression's depletion of public revenues. Many members of the middle groups favored "socialist" expansion of the state as a primary employer. While most of the middle sectors, especially the upper-middle class, accepted a political alliance with the elites to ride out the crisis, others moved toward the new political challengers leading the lower classes.[46]

In 1932 the working classes were the most disadvantaged and agitated sectors of society. Among other things, they were carrying the burden of the Depression. The issue of civilian rule as a dividing line among the candidates meant little to the workers, but how the state would be used to promote recovery was extremely relevant. As expected, the lower class was the least-organized sector of society and the least able to make its views prevail. Unions, largely confined to the urban areas, were weak and ineffectual; they had never been as strong as they appeared, and the Depression had disrupted their efforts to rebuild after Ibáñez had dismantled them. In numbers, labor unemployment exceeded that of any other group by at least five times. Mine workers now jobless had been politicized for years by the Communists and Alessandri. In their southward trek, these migrants spread radical ideas which increased pressures on the central government and on the archaic system of land tenure. Even some agricultural workers were provoked to ask for higher pay and better treatment, but proposals for land division from some urban reformers were aimed less at peasant

45. Arturo Alessandri Palma, *Mensaje leído por S.E. el Presidente de la República* (Santiago, 1933), p. 74; Chile, Dirección General de Estadística, *Resultados del X censo,* III, pp. ix-xi; *Crónica,* Mar. 23, 1932; *El Mercurio,* Oct. 30, 1932; La Fracción Comunista del Grupo Avance, *¿Quién dividió el grupo avance?* (Santiago, 1932), pp. 9-14; Johnson, *Political Change,* pp. 79-81; Ellsworth, pp. 7-15; Bravo Lavín, p. 145.

46. Wilson, pp. 39-54; U.S., Dept. of State Archives, Santiago, Feb. 16, 1932, 825.00/33.

grievances and more at reducing unemployment by establishing colonies for the middle and working classes from the cities. Most political competition centered on the urban workers. The older parties appealing to those workers had lost their dynamism, and newer ones offered verbal claims rather than structured realities. The Communists expressed disgust at the common belief of workers that the forthcoming voting would finally solve lower-class problems. By all accounts, the urbanized masses had been looking for a savior throughout the recent kaleidoscope of coups and were searching for one when they went to the polls.[47]

The working classes, counting the peasants, clustered at all points on the political spectrum. They responded to four distinct appeals: (1) promises of protection of order, family, and religion, and provision of charity from traditional patrons and bosses on the Right; (2) promises of secular, liberal populism from the equally paternalistic Alessandri; (3) promises of more radical, socialist populism from Grove, who also evoked a somewhat deferential following; and (4) promises of Marxist revolution from the Communists. The urban workers and miners, who were the stalwarts of the new politics and therefore the major lower-class focus of this study, were most attracted to the latter three options.

Political Options: The Right

With the 1932 political roster divided into three segments by the addition of the Marxists, two candidates represented the Right, one the Center, and two the Left. The Conservatives ran Rodríguez de la Sotta, the party's president, who represented its most recalcitrant members. Nevertheless, his half-hearted candidacy also showed that, because of the rise of the new Left, the rightists "in self-defense are adopting more liberal policies toward labor, property, and the distribution of wealth. . . ."[48] Rodríguez de la Sotta was a token candidate to hold the intransigent and more progressive factions of the party together. Most Conservatives urged forgoing past antagonisms to assure Alessandri's victory. Others still found such an endorsement unthinkable, although they may have favored another Liberal or a Radical. Fundamentally, they agreed with Liberals and Radicals on

47. González Vera, "Meditación electoral," *Célula*, no. 5 (Oct. 26, 1932), pp. 1-2; *Manifiesto de la asamblea demócrata departamental de San Fernando* . . . (San Fernando, Chile, 1932), pp. 3-4; *Bandera Roja*, Oct. 29, 1932; Congreso Nacional, *En defensa*, pp. 80-81, 116-17; Vial Solar, pp. 115-16; Ellsworth, pp. 14-15, 74; Zañartu, *Hambre*, pp. 138-41; Keller, *Un país*, pp. 123-44.
48. U.S., Dept. of State Archives, Santiago, Aug. 17, 1932, p. 4, 825.00/1234.

the need for cooperation to surmount the crisis. Even the Conservative nominee stressed that the battle lines now should be drawn against socialism, not liberalism. Rodríguez de la Sotta's campaign literature portrayed him as a friend of the working class. He conceded that social justice, as well as government discipline for agitators, was needed to quell labor unrest.[49] Since Rodríguez de la Sotta was an instrument for party unity rather than for presidential victory, one leading Conservative, a vitriolic past opponent of Alessandri, implied that the elites should desert their own candidates to guarantee their old nemesis a majority: ". . . it will be necessary for many citizens to sacrifice not only their preferences, not only legitimate desires, but also very just and well-founded feelings of repugnance and aversion."[50] To many, Alessandri seemed necessary to provide the legitimacy and authority to withstand the types of disorders and attempted coups which had issued in the Socialist Republic.

Enrique Zañartu Prieto, who was from the landed aristocracy, ran as a more reformist candidate of the elites. He was backed by many Liberals, indebted landowners who favored his paper-money policies, and regionalist groups, especially in the south. As part of the trend toward leftist political labels, one Liberal faction campaigned for Zañartu as a "socialist." By this they meant that he wanted to amplify state activity in the economy to better the lot of the middle and lower classes and to expand credit for agriculturalists and other social groups outside the elites of central Chile.[51]

Political Options: The Center

Chile had changed far more than Alessandri, who served as a common denominator in the elections of 1920 and 1932. Alessandri boasted that he was "the same as in 1920." He tried to hold the middle and lower classes on that basis while attracting elites with the argument that he was the only man, because of his charisma, who could both win and govern. Never belonging to the revolutionary Left or the reac-

49. Héctor Rodríguez de la Sotta, *Crisis política, económica y moral* (Santiago, 1932); Bartolomé M. Palacios, *El Partido Conservador y la democracia cristiana* (Santiago, 1933), pp. 29-30; Partido Conservador, *Programa,* pp. 1-15; Vera, "Meditación," pp. 1-2; *El Diario Ilustrado,* Oct. 7-29, 1932; *El Mercurio,* Oct. 12-29, 1932; *El Debate,* Oct. 30, 1932; *La Opinión,* Oct. 31,1932; *Bandera Roja,* Oct. 22, 1932.
50. *El Diario Ilustrado,* Oct. 23,1932.
51. *Célula* (Oct. 26, 1932), p. 1, (Jan.-Feb., 1933), p. 8; Enrique O. Barbosa, *Los liberales democráticos y la candidatura de don Enrique Zañartu Prieto* (Santiago, 1932), pp. 1-3; Enrique Zañartu Prieto, *El proyecto Ross* (Santiago, 1933); Zañartu, *Hambre,* pp. 3, 24-30, 54-75, 138-69; *Chile Pan-American* (Dec., 1932), p. 115; Vera, "Meditación," pp. 1-2; *Bandera Roja,* Oct. 22, 1932; *La Opinión,* Oct. 6 and Oct. 9, 1932; *El País,* Oct. 29, 1932; *El Mercurio,* June 23, 1920, Sept. 26 and Oct. 6-26, 1932.

tionary Right, Alessandri remained a moderate reformer. By 1932, the leftward shift of the political spectrum had left him straddling the center. Alessandri's program, style, and political affiliations had changed little over the years. As one admirer said, "Even his name has acquired the power of a talisman, and operates magically."[52] However, the social sectors attracted to him were balanced differently, for in 1932 more elites and fewer workers rallied to Alessandri.[53] Alessandri's tone had mellowed somewhat, but his backers insisted that he was still in the vanguard because "that which was called 'justice' yesterday, today is named 'socialism.'"[54] Not surprisingly in the aftermath of the 1932 upheavals, the restoration of order was at least as frequent a theme in his campaign as the advancement of reform. Alongside promises from 1920 and 1931 of aid for the workers, his newspaper ads stressed that "The Triumph of Alessandri is the Triumph of Civilian Rule." While some rightists still reviled the ex-president as the destroyer of the tranquil past, one former Conservative opponent complimented Alessandri's less inflammatory tone in 1932: "Serenity is now dominating the restless spirit of this impulsive man, who yesterday presented himself as a threat and today desires to be useful to his country."[55]

Alessandri's political base—the Radicals and Democrats—was officially the same as in previous elections. These parties announced that they were endorsing Alessandri and a statist, nationalist program with "socialist tendencies," which included many planks from past campaigns.[56] Unofficially, many Liberals, and even some of the nascent socialists flocked to the Lion of Tarapacá. Reformers calculated that he had a better chance to win than Grove, and some observers contrasted Alessandri, a "moderate socialist," with Grove, the "socialist-nationalist."[57]

Alessandri's appeal as a reformist strongman who could guarantee stability after the exhaustion of other alternatives spanned all social strata in 1932. Speaking for many enlightened elites, *El Mercurio*

52. Inés Echeverría de Larraín, *Alessandri* (Santiago, 1932), p. 100.
53. Samuel Gajardo Contreras, *Alessandri y su destino* (Santiago, 1951), pp. 229-32; Sáez, *Y así*, pp. 33-34; Alessandri, *Rectificaciones*, pp. 113-29; Vera, "Meditación, " pp. 1-2; *El Mercurio*, Oct. 23, 1932.
54. Echeverría, pp. 7, 100-103.
55. *El Diario Ilustrado*, Oct. 6, 1932; *El Mercurio*, Oct. 5-8, Oct. 19, and Oct. 23-29, 1932; *La Nación*, Oct. 2, 1932; Alessandri, *Recuerdos*, III, pp. 3-5; Luco, pp. 10-16; Gajardo, pp. 229-32; Stevenson, pp. 89-93.
56. *El Mercurio*, Sept. 2, 1932.
57. Henry Grattan Doyle, "The Chilean Elections," *Current History*, XXXVII (Dec., 1932), pp. 344-45; *El Mercurio*, Sept. 30–Oct. 8, Oct. 21, and Oct. 26-27, 1932; Pinto Durán, *Plan*, pp. 15-28; Olavarría Bravo, *Chile*, I, pp. 234, 243, 303-5.

praised the candidate as a consistent evolutionary whose reforms did not stimulate "class hatred" but were "a balm to relieve it." The newspaper added that the upper class had misjudged him and could see now how "innocuous" his proposals were compared to newer demands.[58] Nearly all Chileans applauded his attacks on COSACH and monetary instability. The ephemeral Union of the Middle Class endorsed him, and the middle strata probably provided his strongest supporters. Many workers also welcomed Alessandri's assurances of government assistance and some continued to revere him as the hero of 1920. Alessandri still encouraged his reputation as the champion of the middle and lower classes, but by 1932 the workers were discovering new spokesmen.[59]

Political Options: The Left

The Socialist campaign for Grove was thoroughly personalistic even though the candidate himself was in exile. The Socialists hoped to replace Alessandri with Grove as the new idol of the masses: "Grove signifies with deeds in 1932 what was a liberal and demagogic formula with Alessandri in 1920. Alessandri was the political orator who electrified the masses and precipitated the evolution from an agrarian feudalism toward a rhetorical and pseudo-socialized democracy. He was a stage in social laws . . . Grove signifies in 1932 much more. In ten more years perhaps those who combat him will see in him the moderator of new advances and of vital economic courses. . . ."[60] The Socialists explicitly portrayed Grove as a *caudillo*. They offered him as a "messianic formula" to end foreign exploitation of Chile and, thus, the Depression.[61] Public opinion was running against military men, but Grove's candidacy was riding another tide, that of Chilean socialism. Indeed, it often seemed that the entire campaign was a struggle among all contenders, except the Conservatives, for the claim to the socialist label. An extreme example of the cult arising around the name of Grove likened him to Christ, who was called "the first socialist revolutionary."[62] Another enthusiast claimed: "The race loves Grove, as yesterday . . . [it loved] Alessandri . . . by instinct, intuitively, subconsciously, the nation divines the heroic quality, religiously heroic, the mythical quality of . . . Grove, *caudillo* of the Chilean

58. *El Mercurio*, Oct. 6, 1932.
59. *El Mercurio*, Oct. 5-7 and Oct. 19-29, 1932; *El Imparcial*, Oct. 31, 1932; *El Debate*, Oct. 16, 1932; *La Nación*, Oct. 2, 1932; La Fracción Comunista, pp. 8-9; Vera, "Meditación," pp. 1-2.
60. *La Opinión*, Oct. 1, 1932.
61. *La Opinión*, Oct. 11, 1932.
62. *La Opinión*, Oct. 15, 1932.

Left."[63] Combining populism and socialism to carve out a constituency between the *alessandristas* and the Communists, the newborn Socialists decked the walls of Chile with the slogan "Grove to Power."[64]

The neophyte socialist parties which had manned the June 4 revolution formed a unified committee, led by the NAP, to direct the campaign. The other parties, which had also appeared after the fall of Ibáñez or the emergence of the Socialist Republic, were Revolutionary Socialist Action (ARS), Socialist Order, the Unified Socialist Party, and the Marxist Socialist Party. The prominent leaders of the campaign hailed from the Socialist Republic (Carlos Alberto Martínez, Oscar Schnake, and Eugenio González) and from a school teachers' union (César Godoy Urrutia). Through their electoral barnstorming, they hoped to build a mass-based party. A few renegades from other parties, usually Radicals, Democrats, and former *alessandristas,* also participated. The *grovistas* had, however, a negligible party organization behind their crusade.[65]

Grove received, as he had during the Socialist Republic, the conditional backing of Hidalgo's Communist Left, the Trotskyists. These dissident Communists believed that since Grove had captivated the workers, their party's only hope was to work through his socialist movement. The Communist Left planned to transform the workers' "disorientation" toward Grove from an evolutionary, electoral force into a revolutionary movement to expand their own base of support. In the process, Hidalgo brought some labor organizations into the campaign.[66]

The Socialist program made *grovismo* and *socialismo* synonymous, partly by highlighting the dramatic deeds of the Socialist Republic. They denied charges that Grove's brand of socialism meant militarism, but their campaign did not match those of Rodríguez de la Sotta, Zañartu, and Alessandri in pounding at the issue of civilian rule. Instead, the Socialists stressed the need for state action on behalf of economic nationalism, antiimperialism, industrialization, and urban as well as rural labor.[67]

Socialist propaganda stressed manual laborers, especially those in

63. *La Opinión,* Sept. 30, 1932.
64. *La Opinión,* Oct. 3, Oct. 9, and Oct. 22, 1932; *El Mercurio,* Oct. 30, 1932; Congreso Nacional, *En defensa,* pp. 65-66.
65. "Los jefes . . . Schnake," p. 15; *La Nación,* Oct. 4, 1932; *El Mercurio,* Sept. 25, Oct. 7-8, and Oct. 13, 1932; Jack Ray Thomas, "Marmaduke Grove and the Chilean National Election of 1932," *The Historian,* XXIX, no. 1 (Nov., 1966), pp. 22-33.
66. Congreso Nacional, *En defensa,* pp. 63-66, 149-61; La Fracción Comunista, pp. 5, 14.
67. *La Opinión,* Oct. 6-12 and Oct. 22-26, 1932; *El Mercurio,* Oct. 26, 1932; *La Nación,* Oct. 2, 1932.

the cities, more than the middle classes, but the leaders' definition of "workers" included nearly all social sectors except the upper class. The *grovistas'* concept of "socialism" was similarly elastic; it fundamentally relied on Marxist and utopian ideas of social equality. For most Chileans, socialism during the Great Depression vaguely signified state mobilization to heal the economy and to lessen the suffering of the disadvantaged groups. Both within and without the Grove camp, the socialist umbrella sheltered notions of social justice, conceived variously as charity, the welfare state, or revolutionary changes. Socialism referred to collective rather than individual organization and action. Some self-proclaimed socialists defined this collectivism in terms of functional (sectoral or occupational) groups, while others prescribed it in the form of social classes or, simply, national unity. A few professed socialists could even have been labeled antisocialist socialists, since they were undercutting more dogmatic ideologists by appropriating the trademark for milder programs. Socialism, in some cases, connoted an organic, corporatist state that would provide material growth without class conflict. For many claimants to socialism, the doctrine was merely a reformist political catchword. It suggested limited measures such as national credit institutions and social security. Some cast it in the idiom of Christian morality. For others, socialism was a combative ideology, very similar to communism but without international affiliations. In this view, socialism signified class conflict, sweeping nationalizations and expropriations by the state of natural resources, utilities, and basic industries, and radical changes in property and power relationships. It implied violent revolution. More important than the myriad intellectual offshoots of socialism was that it became, to many deprived Chileans, a symbol of hope. For some a badge of class consciousness, it suggested dividing politics along class lines and appealing for votes on that basis. Although politicians from reactionaries to revolutionaries tried to take advantage of the workers' identification with the symbol of socialism, Grove became its embodiment.[68]

The mixed appeals of ideology, class politics, *grovismo*, and nationalism—socialism leavened with populism—naturally attracted a heterogeneous following. Labor organizations, notably younger workers in Santiago and Valparaíso, collected money and distributed

68. F. B. Clever, *¡Atras!* (Valparaíso, 1932), pp. 5-16; Clodomiro Cabezas Cabezas, *Nuestro socialismo* (Santiago, 1932); Frente Funcional Socialista, *Manifiesto del Frente Funcional Socialista* (Santiago, 1934); Armando Quezada Acharán, *El socialismo* (Valparaíso, 1932), pp. 5-7; Michael Harrington, *Socialism* (New York, 1970), esp. pp. 6-7; Pike, pp. 257-65; Álvarez Andrews, *Bases*, pp. 5-10; *La Opinión*, Oct. 7-8 and Oct. 24-28, 1932.

propaganda for Grove. Noncommunist unions and remnants of the IWW movement were especially active. The unemployed joined hunger marches in the urban centers. Some port workers vainly tried to get a boat to Easter Island to retrieve Grove prior to the balloting. Many women who had had their sewing machines returned under the Socialist Republic worked for Grove and urged their husbands to vote for him. Some intellectuals, professionals, merchants, and employees also lent support. Meanwhile, the official Communists bemoaned the loss of labor to Socialist campaigners, who the PC charged were "inebriating the workers with electoral demagogy."[69]

The regular Communists, or Stalinists, with Lafertte as their candidate, still derided the electoral route but hoped to triple their 1931 showing. Lafertte's main goal was to hold these orthodox Communists together, safe from the allure of coalitions, whether with Hidalgo, Alessandri, or, most commonly, Grove. When the Communists complained that many workers had faith that a decree, a coup, or an election could conjure up socialism as by the wave of a wand, they in effect conceded that many of their organizational efforts and revolutionary promises had been fruitless. According to these Communist complaints, class consciousness was still far weaker than they had imagined. The PC drive was also hobbled by persecution; their newspapers were shut down and their presidential and congressional candidates were briefly jailed. Still, after years of building the party and the FOCH, Lafertte at least hoped to outpoll Grove, who had been a major public figure for only five months.[70]

The Communists tried to outbid the Socialists with a program more radical on every point. For example, the PC's land reform proposals were more sweeping and its wage demands more generous. With calls to "arm the proletariat," the Communists went beyond the "reformism" of the *grovistas*. Accordingly, the traditional upper- and middle-class leaders thought the Communists more dangerous than the Socialists. This assessment was partly because of ingrained anticommunism and partly because the Socialists were more willing to work within the electoral system and less eager to promote class struggle. But Grove's charisma and actions spoke louder to many in the working classes than did the Communists' more radical words. There was some truth in Hidalgo's charge that the official PC was

69. *Bandera Roja,* Oct. 29, 1932; *La Nación,* Oct. 2, 1932; *La Opinión,* Oct. 12, Oct. 22, and Oct. 28, 1932; *El Mercurio,* Oct. 5, Oct. 9, and Oct. 11, 1932; *Célula* (Oct. 26, 1932), p. 2; Mayorga, "El fantasma," pp. 18-19; Durand, *Don Arturo,* pp. 301-2.

70. *Bandera Roja,* Oct. 22 and Oct. 29, 1932; La Comisión de Agit. Prop. del C. C. del Partido Comunista, Sección Chilena de I.C., *Plan de estudios de un curso de capacitación* (Santiago, 1933), p. 6; Lafertte, *Vida,* pp. 249-55; Boizard, *Cuatro,* pp. 143-44.

mistaking its own propaganda for reality and confusing the real exploitation of the masses with the unreal radicalism of the masses.[71]

Outcome of the 1932 Elections

The votes for president produced three major surprises. All provided evidence, which will be elaborated in the next chapter, that the electorate had moved to the left. First, and most unexpected, Grove finished second out of the five candidates with 17.7% of the ballots cast. Second, Alessandri won a resounding majority with 54.7%. Third, Rodríguez de la Sotta (13.7%) and Zañartu (12.4%), the right-wing candidates, failed to attract the votes anticipated. Not surprisingly, Lafertte drew only 1.2% of the voters.[72]

Reactions to the election results varied. Alessandri attributed his victory, as in 1920, mainly to the middle classes, the workers (especially the miners), and the outlying provinces. Many elites, including those in the agricultural regions and the Conservatives, expressed pleasure at Alessandri's victory; even many who had opposed the ex-president now rallied behind him. In addition, many foreign investors, who had feared Alessandri in 1920, now praised his reelection.[73]

The regular Communists found some solace in their higher number of votes than in 1931, but they were despondent over the workers' belief in elections and in Grove. Lafertte's appeals on class and ideological grounds had failed. A great deal of work would be required to change the attitudes, indeed the political culture, of the workers, or the Communists themselves would have to change. The Hidalgo group felt their alliance with the *grovistas* had reaped fewer electoral and revolutionary results than hoped. The Communist Left lamented that rather than convincing the workers that in the circumstances Grove was merely a useful tool, they had witnessed and aided the wholehearted conversion of the masses to *grovismo*.[74]

The Socialists were disappointed by Alessandri's triumph but still expressed the hope that he would revive the reformist spirit of 1920. Mainly, the Socialists were thrilled by Grove's strong showing. Fur-

71. Congreso Nacional, *En defensa*, pp. 65, 71; *Bandera Roja*, Oct. 22 and Oct. 29, 1932; *El Mercurio*, Oct. 24, 1932.
72. Chile, Dirección del Registro Electoral, "Elección extraordinaria de Presidente de la República" (Santiago, 1932); *La Nación*, Oct. 31, 1932.
73. *El Mercurio*, Nov. 2, 1932; *El Diario Ilustrado*, Oct. 31 and Nov. 3-4, 1932; *La Nación*, Oct. 31, 1932; *El Debate*, Nov. 13, 1932; La Sociedad de Fomento Fabril, *Boletín*, no. 11 (Nov., 1932), pp. 503-5; *South Pacific Mail*, Nov. 3, 1932; *New York Times*, Nov. 1, 1932, pp. 1, 5.
74. According to Lafertte's Communists, Grove received his votes from workers, the unemployed, and white-collar employees. *Bandera Roja*, Oct. 29 and Nov. 5, 1932; Congreso Nacional, *En defensa*, pp. 67-69.

thermore, as the U.S. Embassy observed, "Undoubtedly Grove's supporters are more numerous than shown by the actual vote."[75] His high electoral percentage was crucial to demonstrating and developing a base for building a mass party which could launch other, sustained campaigns. The Socialists argued that the 1932 successes were merely a prelude to the formation of a new workers' party which would one day restore the Socialist Republic to power.[76]

Grove and Matte returned to the mainland on election day. Surprised to learn that he had been a presidential candidate and had come in second, Grove claimed a "moral victory."[77] He stressed that the Socialists would continue the struggle through legal, electoral means: "I do not speak of taking power by assault, but of preparing ourselves to conquer it in the way that the bourgeois parties have done. . . . We will work in the light of day, and we will overcome."[78] Shortly thereafter, on April 19, 1933, the miniscule socialist parties which had managed the Grove campaign united to found the Socialist Party of Chile (PS).[79]

Alessandri took office and reestablished legitimate presidential authority. The combination of his personalism and elected constitutionality allowed Alessandri to prevail where others had not.[80] On the surface, the 1932 election returned Chile to the security of traditional modes and formal democracy. Changes at a deeper level, however, had remolded electoral politics and would continue to do so. The socialist-populist forces claimed a permanent place in the political spectrum. In the process, they spearheaded a lasting shift of the electorate to the left. How that basic alteration in mass politics occurred, and the responses of the traditional political sectors to the new challengers, held the key to the political future. The following two chapters explain these political transformations through an analysis of social groups and the parties and policies with which they identified during the Great Depression.

75. U.S., Dept. of State Archives, Santiago, Oct. 31, 1932, 825.00/771.

76. *El Mercurio*, Oct. 30 and Nov. 1, 1932; *La Opinión*, Oct. 30 and Nov. 1, 1932; Marmaduke Grove Vallejo, "La elección presidencial de 1932," *Claridad*, Apr. 24, 1938, p. 2.

77. *El Mercurio*, Nov. 1, 1932.

78. *La Opinión*, Nov. 12, 1932.

79. The personalistic nature of the multiform Socialist movement after the election was seen in the appearance of a Santiago publication called *Grove*, which lauded him and a program for a collectivized society. U.S., Dept. of State Archives, Santiago, Nov. 9, 1932, 825.00/776; Julio César Jobet, *El socialismo chileno a través de sus congresos* (Santiago, 1965), pp. 125-34; *La Opinión*, Nov. 3, 1932.

80. *Hoy*, no. 50 (Nov. 4, 1932), p. 1; Alessandri, *Recuerdos*, III, pp. 8-21; Alessandri, *Rectificaciones*, pp. 115-23; Moreno, pp. 159-61.

4

The Social Dimensions of the Move to the Left, 1931-33: The Traditional Parties

To approach the socioeconomic bases of Chilean political alignments and of the shift toward the left during the Great Depression, the composition of the competing parties must be analyzed at two levels. First, the sources of votes for the various candidates and their parties will be probed. Second, the sources of leadership for those parties will be examined. Then these data will be used to explore both the traditional parties and the parties of the workers.

Voting Patterns: 1932

The role of the 1932 elections in marking a new political era can be seen in the high level of voter participation. In 1932, about 10% of the population—slightly over half those eligible—were registered. This 16% increase in the absolute number of people registered since 1920 was approximately equal to national population growth, with some additional gains due to an improving rate of literacy. Between the presidential elections of 1931 and 1932, registration increased most in the highly urban provinces of central Chile (Aconcagua, Santiago, Coquimbo), where nearly half the nation's voters were located. Registration and voting fell in the north, where workers fled the ravages of the Depression, and thus many probable leftist voters were absent. Of all Chileans registered and able to vote, the number who actually exercised the franchise more than doubled from 1920 (166,115) to 1932 (343,892). The rise in numbers voting from 1931 (285,810) alone represented nearly a 20% increase. Of those officially registered in 1932, 80% cast ballots for president (compared to 73% in 1931 and 76% for deputies and 74% for senators in the simultaneous 1932 congressional elections). This confirmed and accentuated a trend, first seen in 1925 and continuing into the 1970s, of greater voter interest in presidential than congressional elections. The 1932 vote for president constituted a higher percentage of those registered and a higher percentage (8%) of the total population than in 1920, when 4.5% of the total population voted, or 1931.[1]

The 1932 congressional returns revealed a striking extenuation of the leftward trend—crucial to understanding the emergence of socialism and populism—that had first surfaced in 1912-15. The Right reached bottom in 1932, and the new Left started growing at the expense of the Radicals and Democrats. In 1912, the Right— Conservatives and Liberals—accounted for nearly 76% of the electorate. In 1925 they slipped to 52%. Even adding the total for minor rightist parties to that of the Conservatives and Liberals, the Right had fallen to 37% of the electorate in 1932. The Electoral Registry noted this, and counted what is designated as the "Center"—Radicals and similar groups—as 20% and the "Left"—Democrats, Socialists, and various ill-defined other parties—as 33%. Besides fresh voting shifts, one reason for the 1932 results was the decline of the Liberals. However, after dividing and dwindling for many years, their fragmentation into three main factions in 1932 explained only part of their poor showing. More fundamental political changes were taking place. Even following reunification from 1933 on, the Liberals failed to recoup their old voting strength, rising in deputy elections to only 20.7% in 1937 and then sliding back to 13.9% in 1941 and 17.9% in 1945 and 1949. In fact, the Right as a whole never exceeded its 1932 percentage by much in future congressional elections. Thus the really significant new pattern in 1932 was the launching of the Marxist electoral Left, which endured as a force from that time on despite varying electoral and party tactics of opponents. In addition to the major parties, independents, tiny factional groups, and scattered candidates polled a record high vote in 1932, demonstrating the erosion of traditional politics. In many ways, these 1932 outcomes signified the end of one electoral era and the inauguration of another, as Table 4 shows.[2]

1. Chile, Dirección del Registro Electoral, "Elección" (1932); Chile, Dirección del Registro Electoral, "Elección" (1931); Chile, Tribunal Calificador, esp. pp. 15-25; Chile, Dirección del Registro Electoral, "Poder electoral de la República" (Santiago, 1932); Chile, Oficina Central de Estadística, Censo electoral 1921, pp. 107-8; Chile, Dirección General de Estadística, Sinopsis, pp. 32-33, 41, 89; Chile, Dirección General de Estadística, Resultados del X censo, I, p. 40; Chile, Geografía, pp. 75-76; Chile, Recopilación de decretos-leyes, XIII, p. 468; Luis Valdés Larraín, El sufragio (Santiago, 1940), pp. 370-81, 471-72; Cruz-Coke, p. 13; U.S., Dept. of State Archives, Santiago, Oct. 25, 1932, p. 4, 825.00/775.

2. The table excludes the 1924 and 1925 results, which continued the 1921 patterns with only minor changes although the Democrats and Radicals fell sharply in 1932 from their 1924-25 gains. Also omitted are the miniscule percentages for the POS or Communists: 0.4% (1915), 0.3% (1918), and 1.4% (1921). Votes for Communists were

TABLE 4: VOTES FOR DEPUTIES, 1912-32

	1912	1915	1918	1921	1932
Conservatives	21.6%	21.5%	19.3%	19.2%	17.2%
Liberals	54.0	42.4	46.4	35.4	17.3
Radicals	16.6	21.2	24.7	30.4	18.4
Democrats	4.8	7.9	6.5	12.4	13.7
Socialists	0.0	0.0	0.0	0.0	6.4
Independents and others	3.0	7.0	3.1	2.6	26.0

The leftward trends in 1932 can best be grasped in comparison with previous elections. With Alessandri a relatively constant factor from 1920 to 1932, voters on the Right shifted to support him in 1932 and many of his former admirers moved on to the more radical Grove, an ex-*alessandrista*. The combined tallies of Rodríguez de la Sotta and Zañartu in 1932 compared to the vote for Barros Borgoño in 1920 show that the "conservative" constituency dropped 23.9%. In other words, as Table 5 shows, almost half the votes on the Right in 1920 disappeared in the presidential election of 1932. The "Marxist" category shows Recabarren's percentage in his symbolic campaign of 1920 and the combined percentages of Grove and Lafertte in 1932. Lafertte alone tripled Recabarren's 1920 percentage, and he received six times as many actual votes.

The shift to Alessandri in 1932 in areas which had traditionally voted conservatively is evident not only in the national totals but also at the regional, provincial, and community levels. Alessandri gained in previously antagonistic zones more than he built on past strengths.

TABLE 5: VOTES FOR PRESIDENT, 1920 AND 1932

Year	"conservatives"	Alessandri	"Marxists"
1920	50.0%	49.4%	0.4%
1932	26.1 (−23.9)	54.7 (+5.3)	18.9 (+18.5)

hard to calculate because they were repeatedly forbidden from running under their party name, for example in 1932 when, nonetheless, they won a handful of elections in worker districts of the mining north and Santiago. The Socialist group in the table includes the NAP and three of the other micro-parties on the Grove campaign committee; they won seats in the Great North (where one was elected as a "federalist"), the Urban Center, and Concepción. All the major party categories include most of the dispersed factions of the parent bodies. The designations Right, Center, and Left are those used by the Electoral Registry. Chile, Tribunal Calificador; Chile, Dirección General de Estadística, *Política* (1938), p. 1; Chile, Dirección General de Estadística, *Sinopsis*, pp. 34-35; Zarko Luksic Savoia, *La conducta del votante y sus razones sociales* (Santiago, 1961), p. 48; Urzúa Valenzuela, *Los partidos*, p. 73; Guilisasti, p. 81; Cruz-Coke, p. 53; Cruz Salas, pp. 310-12.

Out of sixty-one comparable *comunas,* or local voting districts, that Alessandri lost in 1920, he improved his showing in all but eight in 1932. Results in some of these *comunas,* particularly those in rural areas, were clearly manipulated by local elites. In the rural communities of Purén and Los Sauces, for example, Alessandri's share of the votes jumped from 0% in 1920 to nearly 90% in 1932. On the other hand, in the forty-eight comparable *comunas* which Alessandri won in the 1920 election, in 1932 his percentages fell in over half. Clearly, a flexible elite was, under new circumstances, willing to transfer the votes of its clients in order to return its former foe to the presidency.[3]

Comparisons with the 1931 election also provide clues to the transformation in 1932. Alessandri tended to improve most in 1932 where he ran poorly in 1931. Conversely, in the zones where Alessandri lost support from 1931 to 1932, Grove, almost without exception, scored well above his national percentage; this was particularly true in Santiago. Grove also made a strong showing in *comunas* where Hidalgo had won votes in 1931.

Comparing the 1932 congressional and presidential results provides further evidence that conservative voters chose presidential alternatives to the left of those they had selected in previous post–World War I elections. The national vote for president was higher than that for Congress, but the Right's presidential candidates receiver fewer numerical votes than their congressional entries. As a result, the Right's candidates for deputy attracted 36.5% of the ballots while their presidential candidates together mustered only 26.1%. This gap represented a defection of both Liberals and Conservatives to Alessandri. The comparison between congressional and presidential results also underscores the personalistic nature of the Socialist campaign; Grove roughly doubled the congressional votes received by the parties backing him.

The 1932 regional results, summarized in Table 6, show that the *grovistas* did not simply represent another protest of the geographic extremes against the center of Chile. In contrast to Alessandri in 1920

3. The label "conservatives" is used in Table 5 without a capital letter to distinguish the relative political position from the Conservative Party. *Comuna* figures have been culled and cross-verified from both official and newspaper sources. In cases when only newspaper returns were available, they were only used when checked with more than one paper, when listed therein as final results, and when not contradicted by the cumulative official results for that particular *comuna's* department and province. Since electoral districting and the way results were reported changed more than once in the interwar years, comparisons at the provincial and departmental levels over time are a bit unreliable, and only a limited number of *comunas* can be compared from one election to the next. In addition to the government sources cited previously, see *La Nación,* Oct. 31, 1932; *El Mercurio,* Oct. 31–Nov. 1, 1932; *El Diario Ilustrado,* Oct. 31, 1932; U.S., Dept. of State Archives, Santiago, Nov. 2, 1932, p. 2, 825.00/774.

TABLE 6: VOTES FOR PRESIDENT BY REGION, 1932

Region	Rodríguez	Zañartu	Alessandri	Grove	Lafertte
Great North	2.0%	3.9%	78.7%	11.9%	3.2%
Small North	6.6	20.0	56.9	15.6	0.6
Urban Center	13.5	7.5	44.3	33.4	1.2
North Center	25.9	12.5	54.4	6.0	1.2
South Center	18.0	23.7	55.9	1.9	0.5
Frontier	10.0	15.7	65.6	7.2	1.1
Lakes	16.5	18.9	58.6	5.4	0.5
Total	13.7%	12.4%	54.7%	17.7%	1.2%

and 1931 and to Salas in 1925, Grove ran best in the Urban Center. His electoral showing correlated better with social and economic factors other than historic regionalist resentments. Alessandri, in 1932, increased his 1920 percentages in every region except the Urban Center. The ex-president gained most in the latifundia-dominated regions, where he had been weaker in the past. He held his traditional bailiwick in the far north, which also remained Lafertte's strongest area. As in 1925 for Salas and 1931 for Alessandri, the South Center remained the most impenetrable zone for the Left. Alessandri's continuing regionalist appeal, Zañartu's regionalist, agriculturalist base, and Rodríguez de la Sotta's reliance on the central provinces of the rural elites are also evident.

Regional and social cleavages both coincided and conflicted in the voting patterns. By 1932 social divisions were overshadowing regional considerations, to a significant extent, at least on the Left (even in the votes for Grove). Urbanization and the Great Depression had intensified class voting. For many reasons, casting ballots along class lines was to be expected in a society as stratified as Chile. This was particularly true when the Depression aggravated social divisions, which began to be perceived more politically. Elections became increasingly important to social groups as the state, especially the presidency, amplified its role in the economy. At the same time, politicians such as Alessandri, the Communists, and the Socialists urged voters to think in class terms and to vote with their reference groups and against the representatives of their social enemies. Class positions increasingly influenced, but did not determine, voting decisions. Traditional, personal, and regional loyalties were still deeply ingrained. Also, class distinctions among parties, platforms, and candidates were not sharply defined. With all contestants basically agreeing on the electoral process and its norms, parties emphasized the accumulation of votes from multiple groups more than the class solidarity of their voters. Even though the elites displayed a proclivity to align with the

Right, the middle strata with the Center, and the urban workers with the Left, all political groups were socially heterogeneous. Moreover, with Chile's multiparty system, each social layer had more than one alternative clearly aimed at its sympathies. For example, workers searching for a candidate appealing to the laboring classes might have chosen Alessandri, Grove, or Lafertte.[4]

Some evidence that socioeconomic factors played an important role in 1932 is supplied by the high incidence of votes for the Right in rural provinces and for the Left in urban areas. This rural-urban split was only partly influenced by regional location. More important, the urban factor and relatively high votes for the Left tended to coincide with a composite of indexes of modernization tabulated in the 1930 census, for example, low numbers of latifundia, fewer declared Catholics, and high rates of literacy, industrialization, unionization, and population growth. By the same token, the Right scored better in provinces with a high percentage of their employed population in agriculture, the Left in those with a high percentage in mining or industry. Also noteworthy was the difference between Grove and Lafertte in those mining and industrial provinces. Grove's average percentage of votes was lower in the mining (12.5%) than in the industrial (20.6%) provinces. Conversely, Lafertte garnered a higher average in the mining (2.5%) than in the industrial (1.3%) provinces.[5]

Votes for the Left were also normally higher than average in the provinces hardest hit by the Depression. For example, the extreme misery and unemployment in the mining north reinforced the traditional propensity to vote for the Left because of resentment against the Santiago elites, even after many of those out of work had migrated south. Nearly all the provinces in which day wages were still declining in 1932 were mining and industrial areas which gave many votes to Grove and few to Rodríguez de la Sotta and Zañartu. Interestingly, Grove ran best in both the northern provinces and Santiago; his appeal crossed regional boundaries on the basis of socioeconomic grievances.[6]

The greater effect of the Depression on mining and industrial than on agricultural workers reinforced the urban-rural dichotomy. Chile,

    4. Bravo, *El 4,* pp. 7-45; Wilson, p. 46; Seymour Martin Lipset and Stein Rokkan, eds., *Party Systems and Voter Alignments* (New York, 1967); Robert R. Alford, *Party and Society* (Chicago, 1963), p. 302; Angus Campbell et al., *The American Voter* (New York and London, 1960), pp. 369-73.
    5. Chile, Dirección General de Estadística, *Resultados del X censo,* I, pp. 40-47, 51-61, II, pp. 257-62, 309-99, III, pp. xi, xiii; Chile, Dirección General de Estadística, *Sinopsis,* pp. 88, 129, 181, 183, 216, 240; Álvarez Andrews, *Historia,* pp. 246-48, 291, 314.
    6. Chile, Dirección General de Estadística, *Sinopsis,* pp. 236-38; Vial Solar, pp. 116-19; Gaete, pp. 59-69.

roughly 3% more urbanized in 1932 than in 1920, was approximately evenly divided between rural and urban populations by 1932. This shift adversely affected the Right, which relied heavily on the captive rural vote. While not based on a scientific sample, Table 7, which shows the average of each candidate's percentage of the total vote in selected highly urban (75-100% "urban" according to the national census) or rural (90-100% "rural") *comunas,* tends to corroborate the trends evidenced by regional and provincial data and thus further spotlights the influence of urban or rural settings on political patterns.[7] Considering data from multiple sources, the overall pattern of leftist reliance on the urban areas was undeniable, although incidental and traditional factors also played a part. Many of Grove's most favorable urban communities were in Santiago, where the Socialist Republic and the embryonic Socialist parties had the greatest impact. Nevertheless, even outside Santiago the Socialist strongman's support tended to be compacted in urban zones. Among just those *comunas* included in Table 7, his average in the urban districts was 68% above his national total and six times his average in those extremely rural communities.

In 1920 Alessandri ran better in the urban than in the rural *comunas* used in Tables 7 and 8, although heavily rural districts also contributed significantly to his vote total. But in 1932 Alessandri scored slightly better in these rural than in these urban communities, which points to the same propensity already displayed by regional and provincial data. As seen in Table 8, rightist losses from 1920 to 1932 were greater in the urban areas, where the new Left was making such strong gains. These urban conservative losses were not fully reflected in

TABLE 7: VOTES FOR PRESIDENT IN SELECTED URBAN AND RURAL *COMUNAS,* 1932

	Rodríguez	Zañartu	Alessandri	Grove	Lafertte
Urban *comunas*	11.4%	6.0%	53.8%	26.2%	2.6%
Rural *comunas*	17.9	20.9	56.1	4.7	0.8

TABLE 8: VOTES FOR PRESIDENT IN SELECTED URBAN AND RURAL *COMUNAS,* 1920 AND 1932

	"conservatives"	Alessandri
Urban *comunas,* 1920	44.0%	56.0%
Urban *comunas,* 1932	17.4 (−26.6)	53.8 (−2.2)
Rural *comunas,* 1920	56.2	43.8
Rural *comunas,* 1932	38.8 (−17.4)	56.1 (+12.3)

7. See Appendix A: Methodological Note on the Construction of the *Comuna* Tables.

increments for Alessandri, in part because Grove was recording such high percentages in the cities. The decline in rural conservative percentages, on the other hand, almost directly translated into higher shares for Alessandri. Regional, provincial, and community data indicate that the movement to the left occurred in both areas, but primarily in the urban electorate.

Votes for Grove were a general urban as well as a social-class phenomenon. For example, Grove relied more heavily on the central province of Santiago than did any other candidate; he drew 47% of his national vote from that province alone, while the other presidential hopefuls all took less than 30% of their national ballots from there.[8] Santiago accounted for over 25% of the total national presidential vote in 1932, compared to 17% in 1920. Considered 80% urban by the 1930 census, Santiago province was the most urbanized in Chile. It contained 23% of the national population. Within Santiago province, Grove ran best in the heavily urbanized *comunas*. In those highly urban districts, he exceeded his national average most in the three communities most noted for relatively large concentrations of industrial and other workers: San Miguel (where Grove polled 46.6% of the votes), Quinta Normal (46.1%), and Renca (49.3%). Though at a lower level than in the worker zones, Grove also topped his national percentage in highly urban Santiago *comunas* with large middle- to upper-class components, namely Providencia (30.2% of the votes for Grove) and Nuñoa (24.0%). Outside Santiago, he also ran well in the prosperous urban coastal community of Viña del Mar, where he captured 41.3% of the ballots. A high vote for Grove was possible in such middle-class areas because the socialist *caudillo* appealed to middle- as well as lower-class voters. Also, even in these relatively well-to-do *comunas* there was a social mix that included the servant and working classes. Grove added new groups, apparently many from the middle sectors, to a Marxist-labeled constituency that had previously relied mainly on miners.

Although not a national sample, those three Santiago working-class *comunas* can be contrasted with the average of each candidate's percentage of the total 1932 vote in selected *comunas* with unusually high components of miners or peasants, regardless of regional location; Table 9 does this.[9] The Right and Alessandri now clearly dominated in these selected peasant zones, further indicating that Marxism and populism appealed mainly to workers outside agriculture.

---

8. From Santiago province in 1932, Alessandri received 20% of his national vote, Rodríguez de la Sotta 29%, Zañartu 17%, and Lafertte 22%. From Santiago province in 1920, Alessandri won 17.0% of his national votes and Barros Borgoño 16.6%

9. See Appendix A.

TABLE 9: VOTES FOR PRESIDENT BY TYPE OF *COMUNA*, 1932

	Rodríguez	Zañartu	Alessandri	Grove	Lafèrtte
Industrial *comunas*	9.7%	6.5%	35.2%	47.3%	1.3%
Miner *comunas*	2.8	6.3	74.7	12.2	3.4
Peasant *comunas*	22.6	17.7	55.0	4.4	0.1
National total	13.7%	12.4%	54.7%	17.7%	1.2%

Alessandri, it seems, retained popularity in the mining *comunas* largely because of his personal following there. As already evidenced at the regional and provincial levels, the strong showing of the Center and the Left in the mining sectors is underscored by the miniscule percentage there for the Right (see Table 9). The most significant *comuna* difference between Grove and Lafertte was the former's greater strength in industrial areas and the latter's relative strength in mining zones. The Communists, as they themselves noted, had more success in the mining than in the urban industrial sectors because there was greater organization and a longer tradition of struggle in the mines. The PC had higher percentages in the older nitrate and coal districts than in the newer copper areas, whereas the Socialists were far stronger in copper and coal districts than in nitrate communities. These figures suggest that Grove scored better with the less-organized workers, the middle- and lower-middle classes, and the unemployed in the industrial zones than in the mining communities. Contemporary observers of the election confirmed these trends.[10]

The Socialists also outdistanced the Communists in the congressional elections. Eugenio Matte, for example, outpolled any other senate candidate in Santiago, running especially well in the predominantly working-class *comunas* identifiable there. Although new parties entered Congress in 1932, the traditional organizations retained control. The Conservatives, Radicals, and Liberals elected the highest numbers of candidates. The Democrats, although deeply and irrevocably split over issues of ideology and coalitions, remained the largest "leftist" group in Congress. Congressional candidates linked as friends or foes in the public mind with Ibáñez and military rule won almost as often as they lost; the election was not a referendum on the ex-dictator and militarism. These issues did not influence voters as much as did party loyalties, personalities, and deeper social and economic factors.[11]

The leftward movement of the Chilean electorate in 1932 constituted a social and political realignment. There was a strong tendency

10. Bureau, pp. 24-32; *Bandera Roja*, Oct. 29, 1932.
11. Chile, Tribunal Calificador; Donoso, *Alessandri*, II, pp. 120-22.

among both the upper and lower classes to vote for a candidate who had programs and identifications to the left of their past inclinations. Apparently, Alessandri, who had toned down his previous populism, appealed more to the middle classes than any other candidate, and Grove, more to the urban workers. Rodríguez de la Sotta gathered a strong elite vote, one often based on elite control of the rural masses. Zañartu was principally a rural, regionalist candidate. Lafertte's vote seemed nearly completely from workers and was concentrated in the mining areas. Compared to the Communists, Grove's surprising showing came mainly from populist rather than directly class-based politics; leaders from the middle strata won the political loyalty of many of the urban masses. In the midst of an economic and institutional crisis, the Socialists captured mass loyalties partly with promises of immediate gratification, utopian slogans, a revolutionary ideology, and the theme of economic nationalism. More important, they succeeded because of Grove's personal magic. Given his physical absence and lack of party backing, Grove's vote tally was all the more impressive. Nonpopulist alternatives like the more ideological Communists failed to hold the worker vote in 1932. So did moderate populist alternatives like Alessandri. What succeeded was the combination of two forces previously opposed—socialism and populism—now personified by Grove.[12]

The 1932 election revived a system of peaceful transfers of political offices, signaled the end of open military intervention until the 1970s, and permitted the birth of a socialist constituency. Released by the flexible realignment of the traditional groups and pulled by the Socialists' initiative on the Left, the electorate moved away from its old moorings. To analyze further the social sources of these political changes, it is necessary to investigate the social composition of party leadership.

Leadership Patterns: 1931-33

Tables 10a-10g, which show aggregated social background characteristics for political leaders during the Great Depression, do not precisely define the social classes dominating the various parties. Rather, the tables indicate relative differences in the social positions of the groups presented. For instance, the leaders of the traditional parties—Conservatives, Liberals, and Radicals—tended to belong to higher-class organizations and occupational sectors than did the leaders of the parties on the Left—Democrats and Socialists. Negative

12. Sáez, *Recuerdos*, III, p. 313.

TABLE 10: BACKGROUND INFORMATION ON CHILEAN POLITICAL LEADERS, 1931-33[13]
(Conservatives, Liberals, Radicals, Democrats, Socialists, and candidates who won from
all parties in the 1932 congressional elections)

Table 10a: Percentage of Leaders of Each Group from Each Province
(Each province's percentage of the national population in 1930 is noted in parentheses.)

Province	Cons.	Libs.	Rads.	Dems.	Socs.	1932 Cong. Winners
Tarapacá (3%)	0%	0%	1%	0%	5%	1%
Antofagasta (4%)	0	1	1	4	0	1
Atacama (1%)	0	1	4	4	5	4
Coquimbo (5%)	2	2	10	2	2	5
Aconcagua (11%)	18	10	8	12	6	16
Santiago (23%)	55	59	23	32	42	28
Colchagua (7%)	0	6	7	0	7	4
Talca (5%)	7	8	3	9	8	9
Maule (5%)	2	2	5	4	3	3
Ñuble (5%)	0	4	8	4	4	4
Concepción (8%)	6	1	10	18	5	11
Bío Bío (4%)	4	2	6	4	2	3
Cautín (10%)	0	0	6	5	10	3
Valdivia (6%)	6	1	6	4	2	5
Chiloé (4%)	0	0	4	4	2	2

Table 10b: Percentage of Leaders of Each Group in Various Primary Occupations

Occupation	Cons.	Libs.	Rads.	Dems.	Socs.	1932 Cong. Winners
Agriculture	30%	35%	23%	0%	6%	30%
Business & Commerce	28	19	14	25	11	23
Industry	7	7	7	7	2	11
Professionals	75	73	77	39	57	62
Bureaucrats	0	1	7	11	7	2
Employees	2	1	7	21	20	6
Workers & Artisans	0	0	0	21	7	4

Table 10c: Percentage of Leaders of Each Group Who Occupied Major Political
Positions before or during 1932

Position	Cons.	Libs.	Rads.	Dems.	Socs.	1932 Cong. Winners
Minister	20%	78%	47%	61%	13%	17%
Senator	31	25	25	25	7	4
Deputy	80	68	68	68	6	14

13. See Appendix B: Methodological Note on the Construction of the Tables of
Background Information on Political Leaders.

Table 10d: Percentage of Leaders of Each Group with Given Educational Background

Institution	Cons.	Libs.	Rads.	Dems.	Socs.	1932 Cong. Winners
University of Chile	49%	64%	65%	21%	44%	47%
Catholic University	42	2	0	0	9	12
Foreign institution	15	11	8	11	7	10
Military institute	0	2	5	0	4	3
Below university level	11	11	13	39	24	23

Table 10e: Percentage of Leaders of Each Group Who Were Members of Given Organizations

Organization	Cons.	Libs.	Rads.	Dems.	Socs.	1932 Cong. Winners
Union Club	61%	78%	43%	0%	0%	37%
SNA	41	34	13	0	2	24
SOFOFA	9	13	7	7	4	5
Viña del Mar Club	6	6	2	0	0	4
Auto Club	7	7	4	0	0	4
September Club	0	14	4	0	0	4
Regional organizations	9	13	12	0	0	18
Professional organizations	40	35	45	11	34	29
Employee or worker organizations	0	0	2	79	11	17

Table 10f: Average Age of Leaders of Each Group, in 1932

Cons.	Libs.	Rads.	Dems.	Socs.	1932 Cong. Winners
44	49	45	47	34	42

Table 10g: Number of Leaders of Each Group in the Above Tables

Cons.	Libs.	Rads.	Dems.	Socs.	1932 Cong. Winners
54	85	93	28	54	141

associations are clearer than positive ones. For example, it is obvious that the owner of a *fundo,* a factory, or a Union Club membership did not belong to the lowest stratum. A miner rather clearly ranked in the working class. On the other hand, some small merchants or artisans might fall in the lower or middle layers. A professional or someone with a university education might belong to the middle or upper sectors. Family connections and income are key variables absent from the tables. Moreover, the findings given are minimal in the sense that lack of information that a particular leader was a *latifundista* does not necessarily mean that he wasn't one. The tables should also be interpreted with caution because they tell who participated but not who wielded power.[14]

From Table 10a, it is evident that these political leaders were generally concentrated in Santiago, which is one reason for resentment in the outlying areas. The 1932 congressional winners reflected a geographic pattern more similar to the distribution of the national population than did the party leaders as a whole. Although political command was hoarded in Santiago and its environs, affiliations with peripheral regions, while not a legal requirement, naturally facilitated success in outlying congressional elections.[15]

Rather stark differences between the three traditional parties and the two farther left appear in Table 10b on occupations. Large landowners ("Agriculture") were much more common in the leadership of the traditional organizations. Workers, artisans, and employees cropped up· far more frequently among the top Democrats and Socialists. At the same time, however, certain similarities crossed the political spectrum. Professionals played a prominent role in all groups. Leaders came primarily from the professions and the urban provinces regardless of party affiliation; these common traits facilitated political cooperation. According to the data available, there was scant participation by less-integrated groups from the more-underdeveloped provinces and lower-status occupations.[16]

14. Another study of party leadership in Chile, which measured social backgrounds every ten years from 1917 to 1967, found 1937 the greatest period of turnover, with a dramatic influx of new blood. Throughout those fifty years, among all presidents of the Conservative Party, 70% had aristocratic family names, 55% belonged to the Union Club (vs. 61% of the entire 1932 sample presented here), and 90% had university degrees (vs. roughly 89% of the 1932 sample here). Conversely, members of the Communist central committee had no aristocratic family names, no memberships in the Union Club, and 60% without secondary education in the 1920s but 53% with university degrees by the 1957-67 period. Over the years, Communist leadership became less working class and more intellectual, professional (especially lawyers), and petty bourgeois. Jean Reimer, *Circulación de las elites en Chile* (Santiago, [1971?]); Labarca H., pp. 243-46. Numerically minor parties, notably the Communists, were left out of the tables here because of insufficient data to derive meaningful percentages, but the information available on them will be offered in the text.

15. Chile, Dirección General de Estadística, *Resultados del X censo*, I, pp. 41-45.

16. "Agriculture" refers only to large landholders, some owning more than one *fundo;* small proprietors or agricultural laborers are not included. "Business and Com-

Table 10c shows that, with the exception of the Socialists, these political leaders were largely men elected or appointed to high government posts in the past or in 1932. The number of positions held prior to the 1932 election by the winners in that year was far lower than the number held by most other party leaders. This difference indicates the emergence of a new congressional group, thanks partly to voter rejection of past leaders. A fresh political moment had arrived, not only through infant parties but also through the election of an inexperienced battery of leaders from the traditional parties.[17]

In Table 10d, the political significance of attending the Catholic University is highlighted by contrasting the Conservatives with the other parties. Although the leaders of all the traditional parties attained higher educational levels than those on the Left, even some of the historic party chieftains lacked university training. Also interesting was the relative insignificance of education at a foreign institute of higher learning as a political divider.[18]

Table 10e on economic and social organizations is the most revealing about background differences among party leaders. The first six organizations listed were commonly identified with the upper class. They correlated strongly, as the table shows, with political affiliations to the right of the Democrats and Socialists. Professional organizations, the eighth category, were associated with both the upper and middle classes. The last category, mutual aid associations and unions devoted to employees or workers, also demarcated social groups and distinguished the two leftist parties from the three more traditional ones. Finally, Table 10f draws attention to the comparative youth of the Socialist leaders in 1932 and the slightly younger average of the congressional winners.[19]

merce" does not distinguish between large or small enterprises. "Industry" signifies factory owners, along with a few important executives of industrial firms. "Professionals" encompasses numerous skilled occupations, including many lawyers as well as doctors, dentists, military officers, architects, and engineers. Government "Bureaucrats" is largely repetitious of one segment of the employees' category, although professionals and others are also contained here. "Employees" covers both public and private white-collar occupations. Finally, "Workers and Artisans," as manual laborers, is the only category usually considered lower class. Milbrath, pp. 16-17, 126-30.

17. Ministerial and congressional positions are included for all years up to 1933, including those won in the 1932 election; therefore the percentages reveal something about both the source of leaders in the sample (often those victorious in the 1932 elections) and the previous governmental posts held by these leaders. Of course, the previous positions counted for the winners in 1932, in contrast to those for the parties, exclude seats won in the 1932 election.

18. "Foreign" usually refers to education at a foreign university but sometimes also indicates attendance at a non-university institution abroad. "Below university level" means that the leader never reached any university institution; his formal education may have stopped at any level below that or may never have begun.

19. All the memberships discovered in the listed organizations in 1932 or previously

Overall, these tables portray parties which include a vertical slice of the social strata but have a horizontal or class bias to their social composition. The findings suggest that social class, although having a pronounced influence, did not always determine the political affiliations of leaders. On the other hand, the social images which suffused Chilean politics are partly reflected in the leadership profiles. There is a strong social gradation from the Right to the Left. There are important implications for both conflicts and coalitions. The voting data as well as the leadership tables display a social and political gap between the three more traditional parties and the two on the Left. Therefore, the roles of the Conservatives, Liberals, and Radicals—and the groups and policies associated with them—in the move to the left and in the confluence of socialism and populism will be treated first. The Socialists, Democrats, and similar groups, such as the Communists, will be analyzed in the next chapter.

Upper-Class Flexibility, 1931-33

When new mass movements arose out of the crisis at the start of the 1930s, the traditional groups' responses to the new contenders helped determine the manner and outcome of their entrance into the political system. Relative flexibility on the Right was as critical a variable in political change as militancy on the Left. Most of the upper sectors in the early 1930s had built on a tradition of selective flexibility since the nineteenth century. In the thirties and earlier, the Chilean elites could often be intransigent and repressive. Repeatedly, however, they went through learning experiences, as in the years following World War I, which taught them that conciliation of new forces and ideas was preferable to confrontation. This occurred when new groups, such as organized labor, established their ability to persist and disrupt in the face of stubborn opposition. In response, the more sophisticated upper-class leaders made gradual concessions to soothe social antagonisms and to safeguard their fundamental privileges. Most of the upper sectors began making new strategic adjustments in the early 1930s which led to the future acculturation of populism and socialism.[20]

---

are included. The most complete information was found on the first three organizations. Regional clubs and organizations are such entities as "agriculturalists of Cautín" or "sons of Tarapacá." Professional clubs and organizations include the Institute of Engineers, the Medical Association, etc. Employee or worker organizations are mainly trade unions. There was scant difference found between the average and mean ages of the leaders, so the averages alone are used.

20. Paul W. Drake, "The Political Responses of the Chilean Upper Class to the Great Depression and the Threat of Socialism, 1931-1933," in Frederic Cople Jaher, ed., *The Rich, the Well Born, and the Powerful: Elites and Upper Classes in History* (Urbana, Ill., 1973), pp. 304-37; Pinto, *Chile*, pp. 130-31; Pike, pp. 388-91.

The upper classes and the Right, out of necessity and choice, became more adaptable from World War I to 1932. A former Conservative later observed, "The Right, in our country, has one great virtue, and that is that it promptly absorbs experiences and succeeds in grasping the form of events to introduce itself into them."[21] By the 1930s, the established elites were shifting from ostentatious, direct rule to more indirect methods. The state, electoral politics, and, to a smaller degree, the economy and society were becoming less oligarchic in form. The elites' willingness to bend with change was greatest in the political realm, less evident in economic matters, and minimal in the social order. The economic Right was usually more willing than the political Right to tolerate the rise of new leftist parties and leaders, who were far less an immediate threat to the owners of property than to the holders of government seats. However, this often pragmatic attitude of the privileged few toward political innovations also reflected a growing openness in their economic and social relations with the groups below them. But in all spheres the upper classes' tractability had definite boundaries. Their parties and organizations opened contacts and negotiations with struggling groups and ideas. Often, these were changes in degree, not in kind, differences in strategies, not goals or beliefs. The elites still worked to preserve essentials, such as the structure of land tenure and credit institutions. The upper strata and the Right simultaneously admitted new participants and concepts into old institutions while fortifying those institutions to defend their basic interests.[22]

Upper-Class Economic Adjustments

Spurred by the Great Depression, the economic elites turned more toward state solutions, industrialization, and economic nationalism. With Chile's critical source of wealth, mining, largely in foreign hands, it was not surprising that rural and urban domestic capitalists adopted such compromising solutions. Many elites hoped that these proposals would promote social and political tranquility: "Consequently, either one encounters formulas that permit modifying the existing capitalist regime with greater equity and spirit of justice, or the revolutionary

21. Boizard, *La democracia,* p. 101.
22. Wilhelm Mann, *Chile luchando por nuevas formas de vida* (2 vols., Santiago, 1935), I, pp. 146-47; Domingo Amunátegui Solar, *El progreso intelectual y político de Chile* (Santiago, 1936), pp. 6-12; Edwards Vives, pp. 15-19, 207-8; Siegfried, pp. 69-86; Lagos Escobar, pp. 114-65; Vicuña Fuentes, *La tiranía,* I, pp. 20-26, 63-64, II, pp. 182-83; Melfi, *Sin,* pp. 76-77, 112-13; Robert T. McKenzie and Allan Silver, "The Delicate Experiment," in Lipset and Rokkan, eds., pp. 115-25; Joseph LaPolombara and Myron Weiner, eds., *Political Parties and Political Development* (Princeton, 1966), pp. 3-42.

tide will be uncontainable."[23] Stated simply, the bargain struck in the 1930s involved ceding officeholding to middle-class representatives and encouraging industrialization, but preserving immunity for the countryside.

In the main, rural elites reacted to populism by trying to quarantine it in the cities. Despite their displeasure and some resistance, the SNA and most large landholders endured selected urban reforms, restricted food prices, and increased aid to industry as the costs of restraining social discontent. Benefits for urban groups were tolerable in part because the landowners had ties with industrial, financial, and commercial elites. Increasingly, many of the landholders themselves lived in the cities. Although they hoped to revive the importance of agricultural exports, most of the *latifundistas* realized that future growth would depend heavily on the expansion of the urban market. The interlacing interests of many rural and urban sectors were also seen in the purchase of land for prestige and as a hedge against inflation by urban economic magnates and rising members of the middle classes. This tendency helped diminish the enthusiasm, for example of Radicals, for agrarian reform, although land redistribution was tempting as a way to swell the market for urban-produced goods and to slow migration to the cities.

Rural elites and the urban upper and middle classes also shared similar concerns because they all depended on the state. They relied on foreign inflows to state coffers to provide government revenues, credit, and salaries. This dependence on foreign capitalists through the intermediary of the state helped confine economic nationalism to demands for higher taxes on foreign enterprises and for import-substituting industrialization. In return for their acquiescence in greater state aid to the urban economy, the rural elites retained their control over government agencies concerned with agriculture. As in the nineteenth century, they continued to receive government subsidies in the form of generous credits from the state Mortgage Bank (Caja de Crédito Hipotecaria). By keeping down taxes on the land, the agriculturalists continued to receive more benefits at a lower cost than any other sector in the 1930s. Moreover, the *hacendados* maintained an effective veto over national land policies and the organization of rural labor. Their ability to postpone mobilization of the peasants by the populists and Marxists allowed the landowners to meet declining prices for agricultural products by pruning costs such as salaries and

23. Cuadra, *La revolución*, p. 22; Carlos Keller R., *La eterna crisis chilena* (Santiago, 1931), pp. 15-19, 233-49; Gil, pp. 196-97; Aníbal Pinto, "Desarrollo económico y relaciones sociales," in Pinto et al., *Chile*, pp. 5-52; Cifuentes, *La propiedad*, pp. 26-80; Subercaseaux, *La política*, pp. 6-15.

benefits for the workers. The landowners also responded to lower prices by raising productivity, mainly through mechanization, which was sometimes subsidized by the government. Both responses accelerated the urban migration of the bulging rural population. This migration produced new potential recruits for populists in the cities. On the other hand, ceilings on food prices kept a lid on urban labor discontent and wage demands, which pleased industrialists. The president of the SNA, Jaime Larraín García Moreno, and a few landowners tried to lessen discontent in the countryside by promoting a policy of the *"buen patrón"* to care more charitably for peasants, for example with better housing. There were even a few proposals for colonization projects to dodge more drastic agrarian reforms. The vast majority of *latifundistas,* however, hoped to cope with changes in the 1930s by cooperating with urban elites and reformers, rather than by improving the lot of the rural masses. Transactions with past political opponents became increasingly necessary as voting strength tilted toward the cities. Control of the rural vote became less and less an assurance of political domination. Nevertheless, landholding, while declining in economic importance by the early 1930s, still conferred significant political power and great social status.[24]

The SNA, closely linked to the Right and to the government bureaucracy, illustrated the tendency of the privileged groups to expand and fortify their traditional organizations. At the same time, they sought new supports from the state. The SNA was Chile's most powerful and oldest economic interest organization. It was also the one most directly involved in politics. Earlier, it had founded both the Society for Factory Development and the National Society of Mining. These organizations were social clubs as well as pressure groups. Membership overlapped, although not extensively. In any case, the rural and urban economic leaders were frequently connected by social, banking, and party ties as well as by the interest organizations. Although at odds on numerous specific issues, the rural and urban sectors could agree on larger goals, such as defense against socialist

24. La Sociedad Nacional de Agricultura, *Memoria* (1932), pp. 5-31, 123-28, 158-60; La Sociedad Nacional de Agricultura, *Boletín,* LXIV (July, 1932), pp. 327-31; Chile-American Association, pp. 36-38; McBride, pp. 129-81, 219-71, 373-82; Gene Ellis Martin, *La división de la tierra en Chile central* (Santiago, 1960), pp. 91-94, 134-36; Almino Affonso, "Trayectoria del movimiento campesino chileno," *Cuadernos de la Realidad Nacional,* no. 1 (Sept., 1969), pp. 15-31; Robert R. Kaufman, *The Politics of Land Reform in Chile, 1950-1970* (Cambridge, Mass., 1972); Larraín, *Orientación,* pp. 1-29; Alessandri, *Recuerdos,* III, pp. 58-59; Chile, Dirección General de Estadística, *Sinopsis,* pp. 126-27; Chile, *Geografía,* pp. 93-94; Enzo Faletto, Eduardo Ruiz, and Hugo Zemelman, *Génesis histórica del proceso político chileno* (Santiago, 1971), pp. 37-38; Armand Mattelart, Carmen Castillo, and Leonardo Castillo, *La ideología de la dominación en una sociedad dependiente* (Buenos Aires, 1970), pp. 137, 122-23; Aranda and Martínez, pp. 138-46.

reforms. All these interest organizations established closer relationships with state agencies and each other in the early 1930s because there was, more and more, a divorce between economic and electoral power. The old political parties were weakening and the new ones, from the point of view of the elites, were unreliable. These interest organizations tried to attract new members while tightening their internal control by existing cliques. Control inside the SNA and similar institutions was even more oligarchic than the social profile of the members would indicate. At times, notably during the Depression, the SNA and its companion organizations influenced continual national decision making on economic matters more than did the political parties. Therefore, the parties offered not only a potential challenge to the interest organizations; they also, to a degree, absorbed people into an electoral, rhetorical aspect of the political process which was not always the center of national decision making. On the other hand, parties provided access for those not included in organizations such as the SNA.[25]

The improved stature of the industrial groups corresponded to changing elite attitudes as well as to pressures for economic innovations from populists on the new Left. Even the Archbishop of Santiago endorsed a national industrialization campaign. For several reasons, this campaign coincided with the rise of populist politics. Both industrialization and new forms of working-class politics were responses to the Great Depression. Both populists and urban economic elites saw the expansion of industry as a panacea. In the long run, industrialization was viewed as a way to promote social and political quiescence. Economic nationalism served the intrinsic interests of the industrial leaders in the SOFOFA at the same time that it appealed to the anxieties of the middle and lower classes. Both populists and industrialists favored greater state attention to urban needs, to the middle class, and to modernization. These groups debated, however, whether the campaign to rationalize production and industrial relations meant greater benefits for the workers or more scientific use of the workers. Industrialization aggravated social relations which made new political alternatives more attractive to labor groups. Out of labor-management conflicts, however, came greater elite willingness to accept limited participation by organized labor. The more farsighted

25. Genaro Arriagada, *La oligarquía patronal chilena* (Santiago, 1970), pp. 27-32, 49-82; Pedro Luis González, *50 años de labor de la Sociedad de Fomento Fabril* (Santiago, 1933), pp. 3-4; La Sociedad Nacional de Agricultura, *Boletín,* LXIV (Dec., 1932), pp. 605-7; Lagos Escobar, pp. 95-165; Matthei, pp. 209-33; Robert E. Scott, "Political Parties and Policy-Making in Latin America," in LaPalombara and Weiner, pp. 331-67; Erico Hott Kindermann, *Las sociedades agrícolas nacionales y su influencia en la agricultura de Chile* (Santiago, 1944), pp. 16-97.

industrialists tolerated bread-and-butter labor advances so long as
they contributed to more efficient production and did not give the
workers or their leaders excessive political weight or benefits at the
expense of the upper class. Industrialization raised incentives for
bringing the working class into politics and for enacting labor reforms; greater worker benefits and orderly participation might
remove conflicts from the industrial arena. More progressive industrialists hoped that lower food prices and other reforms for the workers would preempt more extreme demands from the Left, produce a
healthier work force, and make the masses consumers of items beyond
bare necessities.[26] One advocate of industrialization advised manufacturers not to fear the state or certain labor advances: "We must
not forget that without unions there would never be a corporative
regime, nor control, and the danger of a social revolution would
be permanent. . . . Without abundant population there will be no
domestic market; even with sufficient population, but without good
salaries and wages, there will be no domestic market. . . . Such is
the tight connection of the social and the industrial questions, and
the contribution that labor laws ought to make to industrial
development."[27] Thus industrialists had shared goals as well as conflicts with both landowners and urban laborers. Although opposing
the populists and their worker followers, the industrial elites, with
different motives, adopted some parallel proposals for their own
ends.

Social Preservation and Accommodation

Although remaining socially aloof, the upper sectors were neither
monolithic nor closed to all outsiders. Their social and familial institutions tried to preserve upper-class homogeneity but also admitted
some newcomers. One observer remarked in the 1930s: "The change
of social stratification signified for the aristocracy only the renovation

26. Industrialization as an economically nationalist solution to the problems highlighted by the Great Depression was somewhat deceptive because "even many of these
so-called national industries are financed and directed by foreign interests." Great
Britain, Department of Overseas Trade, *Economic* (1932), pp. 42-43; La Sociedad de
Fomento Fabril, *Boletín*, XLIX (Jan., 1932), pp. 3-26, (Feb., 1932), p. 65, (May, 1932),
pp. 213-19, (June, 1932), pp. 269-70, (Nov., 1932), pp. 503-5; La Sociedad de Fomento
Fabril, *Rol*, pp. 4-75; La Sociedad de Fomento Fabril, *La Sociedad de Fomento Fabril de
Chile* (Santiago, 1935), pp. 1-3; La Sociedad de Fomento Fabril, *Plan*, pp. 1-7; González,
50 años, pp. 3-31; Álvarez Andrews, *Historia*, pp. 1-7, 246-81, 310-11, 348-57; Morris,
Elites, pp. 151-53, 263-69; Santiago Macchiavello Varas, *Política económica nacional* (2
vols., Santiago, 1931), II, pp. 100-102; Keller, *La eterna*, pp. 169-85; *El Mercurio*, Dec. 24,
1931–Jan. 30, 1932; Mann, II, pp. 38-63.

27. Álvarez Andrews, *Historia*, pp. 350-51.

of its components, but it could not take away its class character."[28] Organizations, schools, and parties not only defined one social group as opposed to another but also provided for social exchange. Interaction among upper- and middle-class politicians generally reduced the likelihood of political polarization or isolation of the upper sector. While such interaction promoted compromises on new ideas and reforms, it also helped the middle and upper classes close ranks in the crisis.[29]

The Union Club and its social-political role exemplified this mixture of continuity and change in elite organizations. It was the traditional epitome of upper-class exclusiveness in the public eye, but it was also open to the upwardly mobile. Among politicians who were club members, Conservatives and Liberals dominated. On a lesser scale the Radicals were also well represented. This indicated both that the upper classes were welcoming the rising upper-middle class into the club and that many Radical leaders were themselves upper class. Absent from the club were the Democrats, Socialists, and Communists. Foreigners, particularly economic leaders from the United States and Europe, and high military officers were prominent members. Like other elite institutions, the Union Club was both a means and a reflection of social-political advancement.[30]

Aristocratic families and schools also simultaneously defended the upper strata and brought them into closer contact with the middle classes. Blue-blood names—Zañartu, Errázuriz, Larraín, Irarrázaval—still studded Conservative and Liberal party rosters. However, politics was slipping out of the grasp of great families, so marriages and *compadrazgo* (co-godparenthood) were sometimes used to bring potential challengers from the middle and even lower classes into the fold.[31] The leaders of the traditional parties had more education than those on the Left, but they did not find a university degree crucial to their status. Private secondary schools traditionally defined and unified the upper class more than university affiliations. For example, the elitist Colegio de San Ignacio had been a breeding ground for presidents, among them Figueroa and Montero. But the growing importance of professional skills and credentials in a more

28. Mann, I, pp. 79-80.
29. Vial Solar, pp. 149-50; Vicuña Fuentes, *La tiranía*, I, pp. 15-19, 63-64, II, pp. 183-88.
30. Edwards Matte, *El Club,* pp. 7-69; Club de la Unión, *Septuagésima sexta memoria* (Santiago, 1932), pp. 8-20; Rodríguez Mendoza, *El golpe*, pp. 300-301; Montero Moreno, *La verdad,* pp. 109-11.
31. Sáez, *Recuerdos,* I, p. 46; Keller, *Un país,* pp. 17-19; Domingo Melfi, *Dictadura y mansedumbre* (Santiago, 1931), pp. 8-20.

complicated, industrialized society brought more upper- and middle-class individuals together in the universities.[32]

As a political issue, the Church no longer kept most Conservatives and Liberals apart. It had even lost much of its potency as an issue for the Radicals. The Church's influence with the masses and usefulness as a control device for the elites was slight and was primarily reduced to the rural areas. The clergy tried to enroll more followers among the middle and lower classes by cooperating with the separation of church and state in 1925 and by endorsing material reforms as well as spiritual rewards. Old political-religious battles shifted to new issues and new parties. In particular, the Church and its defenders now fought the Masonic elements among the Socialists more than among the Liberals and Radicals. Even many conservative Catholics, influenced by the social encyclicals and the challenge of Christian Democracy, assumed more reformist postures around the Great Depression. Another motivation was to keep the Catholic vote united. In the process the Church and the Conservatives hoped to assuage worker discontent and thus undercut socialism and populism.[33]

The dwindling social and ideological strength of the upper class in the military rendered the armed forces an unreliable source of support. After the Socialist Republic, many segments of the upper and middle classes, notably liberal professionals, opposed future military incursions into overt politics, especially as a potential opening for the Left. The elites joined the middle sectors in forming Republican Militias to deter military intervention. Although some upper-class leaders on the Right later considered resorting to the military, there were, from 1932 on, severe constraints on the elites' willingness and ability to call on the armed forces.[34]

Political Realignment on the Right

The traditional elite political parties liberalized their positions after 1920, especially during 1931 and 1932. As demands rose for social

32. Olivares, *Alessandri,* p. 66; Melfi, *Sin,* pp. 81-83; interviews with Raúl Urzúa, Santiago, 1970, 1973.

33. *La defensa del obrero* (Santiago, 1932), pp. 2-16; Alessandri, *Mensaje* (1921), pp. 19, 38-41; Rafael Luis Gumucio V., *El deber político* (Santiago, 1933), pp. 1-19; Francisco Javier Ovalle Castillo, *Hacia la política chilena* (Santiago, 1922), p. 7; Viviani Contreras; Araneda, pp. 25-31, 152-54, 181-229; Gaete, pp. 3-13; Vicuña Fuentes, *La tiranía,* I, pp. 170-71.

34. La Milicia Republicana, pp. 1-44; Cuadra, *La verdad;* Acción Nacionalista de Chile, *Ideología* (Santiago, 1932), pp. 3-12; René Montero Moreno, "Los principios comunistas . . . ," *Memorial del Ejército de Chile* (Jan., 1932), pp. 45-53; Gumucio, *No más;* Montero Moreno, *La verdad,* pp. 148-49; Boizard, *Cuatro,* pp. 23-25, 54-57; Joxe, pp. 57-59, 72-73, 112-30; Bravo Lavín, pp. 8-79, 130-89; Sáez, *Recuerdos,* II, pp. 138-41, III, pp. 318-19.

and economic as well as political justice, the "economic" Left of 1932, the Socialists and Communists, made the "political" Left of 1920 appear far preferable. The conservative parties, while continuing to defend essential social and economic privileges, came to accept the 1925 constitution and participation for all manner of parties and candidates. The endorsement of various statist solutions by the Conservatives and Liberals, formerly steeped in nineteenth-century orthodoxy, spelled the demise of traditional right-wing politics. The resolution of the church-state controversy in 1925 erased the major barrier to a close partnership between the two parties. As the tables on social background showed, the leadership profile of these two rather homogeneous parties closely paralleled the composition of their constituency, except for dependent peasant voters. A shared creed and social attributes united the leaders of the rightist parties more than the Radicals or the parties on the Left. Their conversion to coalitions with reformers, such as Alessandri and the Radicals, was facilitated by increased elite contact with the middle classes and by the upper-class origins of many reform leaders. Of course, neither the Radicals nor the middle sectors were always obtainable as allies, for their availability depended on their current political strategy.[35]

The Conservative Party in 1932-33 was undecided on how much liberalization to assimilate and how to reconcile its recalcitrant and progressive factions. A party leader gave this strategic advice:

> The sad truth is that we do not have . . . recourse to a movement of popular opinion. This is the painful reality; we are absolutely impotent to impede any legislative attack that might be mounted against us. In order to obstruct or postpone, we must live [by] negotiating, making combinations, ceding constantly in order to save the basics, tolerating inconveniences, resisting impulses, subduing . . . impetuous urges of those who do not recognize the bitter reality. We need to perform such distressing labor because to give battle today, without the forces to conquer, would be reprehensible madness.[36]

Consequently, most Conservatives began to argue that they, too, offered the common people a centrist party advocating solutions in between individualism and state socialism. To preserve social peace and counter populist socialism, they proposed, in effect, greater employer and state paternalism, often cast in a corporatist mold.[37]

35. Alessandri, *Recuerdos*, III, p. 48; Edwards and Frei, pp. 221-25. González Echenique, pp. 60-74; Melfi, *Sin*, pp. 15-16.

36. Gumucio, *El deber*, p. 17.

37. *El Chileno*, Aug. 15-29, 1931, Nov. 12, 1932; *El Debate*, Oct. 16, 1932; *El Mercurio*, Oct. 22, 1932; Partido Conservador, *Programa*, pp. 3-15; Gumucio, *El deber*, pp. 1-24; Sanfuentes Carrión, pp. 57-102; Morris, *Elites*, pp. 126-207; Ricardo Boizard, *Hacia el ideal político de una juventud* (Santiago, 1931), pp. 3-15; Boizard, *La democracia*, pp. 42-43.

Although less socially exclusive in their appeal and leadership than in 1920, the Conservatives, as is evident in the leadership tables, still epitomized the Catholic elites in politics. They were concentrated in the geographic center of Chile, where latifundia and traditional aristocracy dominated. Given their strongly upper-class occupational, educational, and organizational profile, the Conservatives were clearly taking new directions in 1931-33 because of fresh political strategies, not because of basic social changes on the Right.[38]

The clearest evidence of a turn to the left within the Conservative Party was the emergence in 1931-33 of a nucleus of young reformers, who created the Falange later in the 1930s and then, in the 1950s, the Christian Democrats. Their elders had tried to counter liberal reformism with Christian charity. Now the new Conservative generation hoped to outbid Socialism and Communism with Christian reform. They wanted to offer the middle and lower classes an alternative in between "the oligarchic cancer . . . [and] the masonic pestilence." Some even called for "Christian Socialism." In the nineteenth century, the clerical and anticlerical forces fought over who would lead the aristocratic system; now forces similarly opposed fought over who would lead the reform system. Like their counterparts in the secular socialist camp, the future *falangistas* were motivated by the Depression and by foreign ideas, such as reformist Catholic thought and, to a lesser extent, the idealistic aspects of fascism. These Conservative reformers advocated statist, nationalist, corporatist transformations to achieve progress without class conflict.[39]

The leaders of this rebellion within the Conservative Party resembled many of the Socialists in their inspiration, youth, and middle-class roots among students and professionals. Among Conservatives, their more modest origins—often from the outlying provinces—left them slightly alienated from the aristocratic party chieftains. Principally from the Catholic University, many of the Falange founders were baptized politically through the Renovation student group which had

38. Januario Espinosa, *Figuras de la política chilena* (Santiago, 1945), pp. 120-22; Lira Urquieta, pp. iii-xii, 9-29, 35-72.

39. George W. Grayson, Jr., *El Partido Demócrata Cristiano Chileno* (Buenos Aires, 1968); Ricardo Boizard, *Historia de una derrota* (Santiago, 1941), pp. 67-68, 143-51; Ricardo Boizard, *Doctrinas sociales* (Santiago, 1933), pp. 4-14; Boizard, *Cuatro*, pp. 169-214; Guilisasti, pp. 199-201; Luis Vitale, *Esencia y apariencia de la democracia cristiana* (Santiago, 1933); Partido Liberal, *La crisis;* Edgardo Garrido Merino, *Espíritu y acción del liberalismo* (Santiago, 1934), pp. 3-24; Edmundo Montecinos Rozas, *Apuntaciones para el estudio de la evolución de los partidos políticos chilenos y de su proyección jurídica* (Santiago, 1942), pp. 9-10; Amunátegui Jordán, pp. 6-14; Edwards, *Las corporaciones*, pp. 3-14; Morris, *Elites*, pp. 146-71; Barbosa, pp. 1-3; Errázuriz, pp. 3-11; José Maza, *Discurso* (Santiago, 1932).

been active in the FECH campaign against Ibáñez. Others had participated in largely unsuccessful efforts in the 1920s and early 1930s to attract labor to a Christian movement. The appearance of these future Christian Democrats, arising as an alternative to the Radicals and the socialist Left, forecast the lines of combat in reform politics for a later time.[40]

Historically, the Liberals had advertised a somewhat more urban, industrial, anticlerical program than the Conservatives, but their leaders were at least as likely as the Conservatives to be landowning elites concentrated in the central rural zones. Such social similarities facilitated the alliance formed between the two parties in the early 1930s, although the unification did not become official until the 1960s. The Liberals shared the Conservatives' desire to reconstruct the elite parties into bulwarks of the center against the socialist Left. Therefore many Liberal factions adopted more reformist, statist positions, although others clung to the old Manchester individualism. To maintain their relevance in a post-liberal era, most party leaders grafted mild welfare-state provisions onto their perennial program for otherwise laissez-faire government. These concessions to save the private economy and social structure from their own shortcomings marked a critical turning point for the Liberals:[41] "The Liberal Party calls together its men in . . . an hour that is an open parenthesis toward a future which one perceives indistinctly and which surely we will not be able to stop . . . in this instant . . . [there is] a necessity for change and reform, for social readjustment. . . . In this hour of uncertainty . . . the Liberal Party initiates a new stage."[42]

Fledgling minor parties advocating a mixture of corporatism and reform also attested to the ferment on the Right in these years. These parties also hunted for a political path between a discredited liberal system and the new threat of a socialist order. The most significant group was the National Socialist Movement (MNS, or Nazis). Like

40. These leaders of the future Falange included Eduardo Frei Montalva, Bernardo Leighton Guzmán, Radomiro Tomic Romero, and Ricardo Boizard Bastidas. Boizard, *La democracia*, pp. 36-37, 109-79, 200-202; Bonilla and Glazer, pp. 82-100; Grupo Universitario Renovación, *Renovación. Declaración de principios.* (Santiago, 1932); Marcos Chamudes, *Chile, una advertencia americana* ([Santiago?], [1972?]), pp. 27-31.
41. Partido Liberal, *Quinta convención* (Santiago, 1932); Partido Liberal, *Proyecto de estatuto orgánico del Partido Liberal* (Santiago, 1931); Partido Liberal, *Programa y estatuto* (Santiago, 1933); Partido Liberal, *La crisis;* Edgardo Garrido Merino, *Espíritu y acción del liberalismo* (Santiago, 1934), pp. 3-24; Edmundo Montecinos Rozas, *Apuntaciones para el estudio de la evolución de los partidos políticos chilenos y de su proyección jurídica* (Santiago, 1942), pp. 9-10; Amunátegui Jordán, pp. 6-14; Edwards, *Las corporaciones*, pp. 3-14; Morris, *Elites*, pp. 146-71; Barbosa, pp. 1-3; Errázuriz, pp. 3-11; José Maza, *Discurso* (Santiago, 1932).
42. Amunátegui Jordán, pp. 6-7.

many Chileans during the Depression, the Nazis were propounding foreign solutions in nationalistic dress and seeking a messiah. However, their head, Jorge González von Marées, lacked the talent and charisma of a mass leader. Borrowing ideas mainly from German and Italian fascists but also from the Peruvian Haya de la Torre, González von Marées promised to install antiimperialist socialism without Communist participation. The Nazis added such proposals as redress of regional grievances and landholding reforms to their eclectic program. Their leaders were young, urban, and frequently professionals. Although they usually came from a higher social background and from more right-wing parties than did the Socialists, the Nazis bore some resemblances to the leftists. Both tried to unite the lower and middle classes behind them; the Nazis appealed to "workers with muscles and with brains." They listed their congressional candidates in 1932 as two lawyers, a merchant, an employee, and a worker. In competition with the Socialists, however, the MNS underlined the groups' even greater differences: the Nazi emphasis on "class cooperation," modification rather than destruction of capitalism, and opposition to Marxism and Masonry.[43]

Conclusions on the Upper Class and the Right, 1931-33

The distinguishing feature of the privileged groups' responses to new mass movements in the early 1930s was their acceptance of evolutionary changes and reforms. Their rather flexible reaction to intensified demands to accelerate economic growth and to include the lower classes in national life showed that traditional and modern modes were being blended in the upper class. It was not really a modernizing upper class, but neither was it opposed to partial modernization. Their accommodation of pressures for change may have preserved more of their privileges than overt, intractable resistance would have.

Most of Chile's traditional leaders hoped that economic change

43. *La Nación*, Oct. 15, 1932; *El Imparcial*, Oct. 22, 1932; *El Mercurio*, June 26, 1932; *El Movimiento Nacional-Socialista de Chile* (Santiago, 1932); *El Movimiento Nacional-Socialista de Chile* (Santiago, 1933); Jorge González von Marées, *El Movimiento Nacional-Socialista de Chile* (Santiago, 1932); Jorge González von Marées, *La concepción nacista del estado* (Santiago, 1934); Wilfredo Mayorga, "Cuando el PS," pp. 14-15; Wilfredo Mayorga, "Jorge González von Marées," *Ercilla*, no. 1740 (Oct. 23-29, 1968), pp. 41-42; Wilfredo Mayorga, "La fugaz violencia del nacismo," *Ercilla*, no. 1611 (Apr. 20, 1966), pp. 18-19; interview with Carlos Keller, Santiago, 1970; Keller, *La eterna*, pp. 22-44; Keller, *Un país*, pp. 12-33, 56-73, 122-50; Carlos Keller R., *Como salir de la crisis* (Santiago, 1932), pp. 1-32; Carlos Keller R., *Nuestro problema monetario* (Santiago, 1932), pp. 21-32; *Hoy*, no. 13 (Feb. 12, 1932), pp. 4-5; Partido Agrario, *Declaración de principios y programa* (Temuco, Chile, 1934); *¿Qué es el Partido Agrario?* (Talca, Chile 1935).

would avert social change. They also believed that moderate state capitalism could preempt state socialism. In the process of economic modernization, the integration of the rural and urban economic leaders was sufficient to avoid sharp conflict. Consequently there was a reasonably smooth transition in emphasis from declining rural to rising urban enterprises. This compromise between agrarian and industrial sectors helped forestall potential threats from below. Furthermore, this accord was constructed within democratic boundaries, buttressing continuities that contributed to political stability.[44]

The alliance between the two upper-class parties in 1931-33 and the compatibility of proposals from the agriculturalists' SNA and the industrialists' SOFOFA provide indirect or fragmentary evidence of interlocking elites. Since this analysis focuses on the political elites, overlapping between the rural and urban economic leaders is mainly inferred from background information on party leaders. It is also known that there were insufficiently studied, imperfect, but intricate connections through families and through boards of directors of corporations, banks, and government agencies. The leadership tables showed that the Right was very active in the interest associations representing the economic elites. The data behind the leadership tables reveals that six of the nine Conservatives who were either prominent in industry or the SOFOFA were also large landholders or members of the SNA. Of the sixteen Liberals in the sample who were important industrialists or SOFOFA members, twelve were also major landholders or SNA members. However, only four of the twelve Radical leaders who were industrialists or belonged to the SOFOFA also possessed great estates or SNA memberships. Available evidence for the early 1930s does not definitively prove that the upper classes were tightly interwoven, but it does point to significant linkages and mutual interests. The shared values and political affiliations of the rural and urban upper classes clearly had some basis in shared social and economic foundations. In all probability, both the interpenetration of the upper classes and their penetrability—both their solidarity and their diversity—contributed to their perseverance. Because the upper sectors were rather closely knit but not sealed to all newcomers, they were able to accept change without being overwhelmed by it. Significantly, the elites sacrificed relatively little in order to appease middle-class aspirations.[45]

44. Petras, esp. pp. 53-55.
45. Mattelart, Castillo, and Castillo, p. 123; Pinto, "Desarrollo," p. 26; Lagos Escobar.

Contradictions of the Middle Classes: Precursors, Leaders, and Modulators of Political Change

As the Right urged the ambivalent middle classes to unite with the upper sectors against insurgency from below, the Left called on them to enlist in labor's struggle against the elites. Prior to 1932, the middle groups paved the way for the leftward movement of the electorate and the inclusion of populism and socialism by diluting the rigid, direct rule of the old elites. In addition, the middle sectors contributed new intellectual concepts of reform and progress. At all points on the political spectrum, the middle classes provided leaders. They lent support, respectability, and flexibility to movements on both the Right and the Left. Although the prevailing pattern in the middle strata during 1931-33 was to back the restoration of order prescribed by the Right, the major innovation was the defection of others, particularly in the lower-middle and white-collar employee ranks, to the side of the new Left.[46]

The widespread dependence of the middle classes on government largesse and employment made them natural proponents of state expansion. Proliferation of government and industry had been promoted by Alessandri and Ibáñez. It was now tolerated by the Right and obviously encouraged still more by the Left. Such political change and patronage expansion promised to alleviate the economic problems of the middle sectors without transforming the bases of production relations or the social hierarchy. The upper class planned to maintain access to the burgeoning state by reserving certain government agencies to itself and by conciliating middle-class reformers. Already taking education, government, and party posts formerly appropriated by the upper strata, some middle groups also saw an opportunity to displace foreigners in industrial management. They only favored labor demands for state solutions to social problems so long as such programs did not endanger their own standard or style of living. In an economy of scarcity, the intermediate groups, rather than upsetting the precarious system, usually hungered for greater relative security. Their disdain for manual labor and their social ambitions motivated them to cooperate with the upper class, but their low incomes and high unemployment, exacerbated by the Depression, created bonds with the workers. The economic dependence and weakness of the middle classes, especially those lacking reliable connections with the elites, did

46. Raúl Alarcón Pino, *La clase media en Chile* (Santiago, 1947), pp. 46-109; La Agrupación Económica-Social de la Clase Media, *Programa* (Valparaíso, [1931?]), pp. 3-12; Mann, I, pp. 70-80, II, pp. 111-13; Melfi, *Sin,* pp. 74-80; Siegfried, pp. 69-70, 174-75; Pike, 112-15; Durand, *Don Arturo,* pp. 178-80.

not determine where they would turn politically, but rather created countervailing pressures.[47]

All middle-class occupational groups were split between the Right and the Left. Regardless of their occupations, fervent Catholics tended toward the Conservatives. Many professionals, particularly doctors and lawyers, belonged to or received their livelihood from the privileged sectors; they often sympathized with the Liberals. Other professionals depended on the state and felt closer to the masses. Some doctors, for example, were exposed to welfare reform ideas in their schooling and to the suffering of the poor in their hospital and state health work. Therefore, as in many other countries, professionals and intellectuals often led leftist movements. Smaller manufacturers and businessmen wanted more equitable distribution of state credit, which had been promised by both Alessandri and the Socialist Republic. The lower-middle class, principally teachers, employees, and a few highly successful artisans, had long felt relative deprivation, joined union struggles, and contributed support to reform parties.[48]

Of the few middle-class landowners, some, particularly in the southern provinces, resented the elites, while others bought land to emulate the aristocracy. Novice landlords from the urban upper-middle class seldom lived on their estates or paid much attention to agricultural production. As a result, stable *patrón*-worker relations atrophied in central Chile. As the plight of agriculture and rural labor deteriorated, peasant migration to the cities increased. Even though leftist, populist politics rarely penetrated the countryside, worsening rural conditions helped supply new arrivals for charismatic urban politicians. At the same time, rural-urban migrants held down wages and unionization, which kept the urban lower classes discontented, disorganized, and susceptible to populist appeals. Rural social relations, in other words, mainly indirectly boosted the new Left.[49]

Middle-Class Social and Organizational Bases

The middle groups lacked class coherence, programmatic unity, and firm organizational defenses. For example, the 1930s' attempts to rebuild the Middle-Class Federation from 1920 floundered. The middle classes relied heavily on webs of interpersonal and clientelistic relationships. They spun vertical coalitions across class lines out of not

47. Heise González, pp. 151-65; Pinto, *Chile,* p. 133; Vicuña Fuentes, *La tiranía,* I, pp. 10-14; Johnson, *Political Change,* pp. 66-83; Congreso Nacional, *En defensa,* pp. 48-49; Eduardo Frei Montalva, *Chile desconocido* (Santiago, 1937), pp. 87-91.
48. Mann, I, pp. 71-75, II, pp. 87-113; Alarcón, pp. 107-8.
49. Martin, pp. 92-136.

only parties but also groups such as the Masons, student organizations, and the military. All contributed to the advance of the middle classes and of socialism and populism.[50]

The secretive Masons actively protected their members' interests, generated political leaders, and provided a nexus for coalition building. The lodge was a clientelistic organization for procuring high public offices and favors as much as a center for anticlerical and reform ideas. Masonic ties were important among families. They had great influence in the judiciary and the bureaucracy, the military and the Carabineros, education and student organizations, industrial, professional, and intellectual groups, and political parties. Although members ranged from the landed anticlerical elites to the artisan sectors, the Masonic lodges were most deeply rooted among professionals and the middle class.[51]

Many Masons moved to the left between 1920 and 1933. They shifted from a legalistic, juridical concept of reform to a socioeconomic definition. Previously associated in the public mind with the Liberals and, above all, the Radicals, the Masons now also became identified with the Socialists and Communists. The lodge members' study in the 1920s of new political ideas inspired many to sympathize with the Russian Revolution as well as the French. During the Depression, the Masons were trying to meet new aspirations, channel political anxieties, and keep the lodge united and relevant. They founded Masonic Action as an attempt to orient their members from different parties around a common reformist creed. Masonic Action stressed industrialization as well as health and education for the underprivileged. With the nineteenth-century church-state issues subdued, the Masons became more predominantly middle class and established new political credentials by reaching out to anticlericals in the socialist camp and labor politics.[52]

By the 1930s, political leaders who were Masons mainly belonged to

50. Vicuña Fuentes, *La tiranía*, I, pp. 12-13; Mann, I, pp. 80-82; Tapia Videla, p. 244; Montecinos, pp. 85-86.

51. Fernando Pinto Lagarrigue, *La masonería: su influencia en Chile* (3rd ed., Santiago, 1966), pp. 8-31, 284-317; José María Caro, *El misterio de la masonería* (Santiago, 1926); interviews with Charlín and Almeyda, Santiago, 1970; "¡La masonería traiciona a Chile!" *Trabajo*, Jan. 6, 1954, p. 4; Vicuña Fuentes, *La tiranía*, I, pp. 54-55, 100, 139-46, 170-75, 216-18; Bonilla and Glazer, pp. 54-55, 92, 136; Boizard, *Historia*, pp. 143-48; Edwards and Frei, p. 198; Walker, pp. 78-107; Alessandri, *Recuerdos*, I, p. 373. Some lodges specialized in particular groups, such as artisans or military officers, but most were mixed. Foreigners were also active members. Apparently, the lodges became more strictly middle class in the 1930s, partly because of the withdrawal of many upper-class Liberals and lower-class Democrats. Mayorga, "París," pp. 4-6; Wilfredo Mayorga, "Por qué falló el avión rojo," *Ercilla*, no. 1580 (Sept. 1, 1965), pp. 4-5.

52. Pinto Lagarrigue, pp. 8-31; Bravo G., pp. 4-13; *La Opinión*, Apr. 17, 1932.

the Radical, Socialist, Democrat, and Communist parties. All the elected presidents of Chile from 1920 to 1958 were Masons. However, the lodge was not monolithic, as seen by the memberships of Alessandri and Ibáñez, Montero and Grove. The Masonic affiliation of these political enemies also recommends caution in interpreting the real political distance among them. Although the organization did not officially participate in politics, its shrouded role has been controversial in Chile. Both the *alessandrista* movement of 1920 and the Popular Front of 1938 were aided by Masonic connections. The Masons have often been blamed by the Right for fomenting extremism and by the Left for toning down reform movements.[53]

The university students, who were increasingly middle class, helped create mass politics in Chile, particularly through the FECH. They served as precursors, activists, and formers of middle class–lower class alliances and movements. They shifted from spontaneous populist politics in 1920 to more ideological, partisan efforts tied to national parties—especially the Socialists, but also the Radicals, Nazis, Communists, and Falangists—in the 1930s. The students' devotion to worker causes became more sophisticated and structured, though they built on past friendships and coalitions. For example, one FECH leader from the 1920 period was Eugenio González. He helped found the Socialist Republic and the Socialist Party and attracted workers and students to both. Thus the generation of 1920 partly produced the leftist parties of 1931-33, which in turn shaped the new student movement of the subsequent Popular Front period.[54]

The military contributed to the leftward movement which generated populist socialism by ending the Parliamentary Republic in 1925 and passing labor legislation. After weakening the hegemony of the traditional elites and parties, the armed forces removed themselves as a live option in open politics. This left civilians, including Marxists, to

53. Like the Socialists and Communists in the 1930s and '40s, the Democrats in the 1920s had tried to reduce Masonic influences within their party. One earlier estimate was that out of 2,931 Masons in 1918, 577 were foreigners, and the remainder won 39 out of 118 deputy seats in the 1921 congressional elections. Masons also dominated the cabinets and many other government posts under Alessandri and Ibáñez. They shifted among certain parties and leaders to maintain their influence. Some Chilean electoral contests continued to be, beneath platform rhetoric, clashes between Masons and anti-Masons. Luis Donoso, *La masonería* (Santiago, [1934?]), pp. 30-44; Stephen Clissold, *Chilean Scrap-Book* (London, 1952), p. 63; René Olivares, *Ibáñez* (Valparaíso, 1937), p. 61; Heise González, p. 156; Vicuña Fuentes, *La tiranía*, I, pp. 42-44, 146-48, 178-215; Wilfredo Mayorga, "Las asambleas del hambre," *Ercilla*, no. 1567 (June 2, 1965), pp. 4-5, 10.

54. Many of the more radical student leaders came from the outlying provinces. Bonilla and Glazer, pp. 32-135; Mayorga, "La difícil," pp. 43-44; Mayorga, "La generación," p. 13; Julio César Jobet, "La juventud de 1930 y el socialismo," *Arauco*, no. 9 (July, 1960), pp. 29-32.

make the system work within the electoral arena. Primarily middle-class military leaders, especially in the army and air force as opposed to the more aristocratic navy, also contributed to political change by attracting the workers, first to Ibáñez and then to Grove. The military weakened the hold of the local *caciques* in politics, especially through the consolidation of the Carabineros as a national police force. Furthermore, as advocates of state responsibility, especially in the economic and social fields, most military politicians promoted industrialization and nationalism. The linking of military intervention with "socialism" was confirmed for some by the enmity between the regular army and the conservative Republican Militias. However, diverse military commanders retained ties with the Masons and the Union Club, with the middle and the upper classes. Divided on both ideological and social lines, the armed forces were not radical. Neither, however, were they prone to move against the creation of populist, leftist politics by middle-sector leaders.[55]

Coalition Politics

The middle classes' oscillation between the Right and the Left tempered political and social conflict. They helped direct working-class politics into structured channels and make it tolerable to potential opponents, whether other middle-class politicians, military, or elites. The civilianist movement, the Montero campaign, military activism, and the blossoming of new parties all showed the middle-class eruption into political leadership. Many who had been represented, as under Alessandri, now became representatives. Whether moderates or radicals, many middle-class leaders clearly were dissatisfied with their place in the existing structure. Those still most antagonistic toward the upper class transferred their protest from clerical to social and economic issues.[56]

As the traditional party claiming to speak for the middle classes, the Radicals were torn in the early 1930s between becoming the vanguard of the Right or the moderating force of the Left. Both the Right and the Left in Chilean politics tended to reach toward the center, whether it was Conservatives backing Liberal candidates for president or

55. Mayorga, "Cuando el PS," pp. 14-15; Unión Social del Personal; Montero Moreno, *La verdad*, pp. 146-49; Montero Moreno, "Los principios," pp. 45-53; Bravo Lavín, pp. 7, 145-66; Joxe, pp. 28-31, 40-43, 68-130; Boizard, *Cuatro*, pp. 12-25, 62-87; La Milicia Republicana; Cuadra, *La verdad;* Henry Grattan Doyle, "Fascism in South America," *Current History,* XXXVIII (Aug. 1933), p. 599.

56. For a sampling of the unprecedented number of new parties of all political hues led by the middle classes in 1932, see Chile, Tribunal Calificador; Frei, pp. 87-93; Johnson, *Political Change*, pp. 78-83.

Democrats supporting Alessandri. By the 1930s it could be said, "The country has advanced so much toward the left, that the Radical Party, which before was the most extreme, without changing ideas or tendencies, has become the party of the center."[57] Now the Radicals were able to dispute both the Right's representation of business and industry and the Left's representation of students and workers.[58]

Like a barometer reflecting new trends in Chilean politics, the Radicals progressed from a party primarily for the outlying regions and anticlericals in the late nineteenth century to one increasingly for the middle classes in the early twentieth. The party's most significant, lasting union strength developed among white-collar employees. In 1906, and then more vehemently in the 1930s, the Radicals officially but regretfully recognized the class struggle and affirmed their solidarity with the workers until enough social reforms could be achieved to restore harmony. This declaration, most clearly set forth in 1931, against the injustices of the capitalist system was usually downplayed in subsequent party statements, seldom guided policy, and proved far milder than the Socialists' ideas and propaganda. Indeed, the Radicals supported the conservative Alessandri administration in the 1930s until the consolidation of the Popular Front. Nevertheless, their evolution by the thirties from liberalism to state interventionism upset many of their more traditional members, especially landowners. It also kept the party in the thick of political change and bestowed respectability on the new Left. Increasingly, the Radicals led the drive for industrialization, which they came to see as the key to efficient development and to social as well as economic stability.[59]

The Radical leaders combined upper- and middle-class traits. In contrast to the other parties, the percentage of Radical leaders from the various regions of Chile closely approximated the national distribution of population in the provinces. Radicals were active in many of the same occupations and organizations as the heads of the elite parties. Their social rise, for example in the Union Club, coincided with their political ascent since World War I. The average year of

57. Gumucio, *El deber*, p. 16.

58. Boizard, *Historia*, pp. 35-36, 144-45; Urzúa Valenzuela, *Los partidos*, pp. 158-65; Petras, pp. 120-21; Oscar Waiss, *Presencia del socialismo en Chile* (Santiago, 1952), p. 13.

59. Gabriel González Videla, *El Partido Radical y la evolución social de Chile* (Santiago, 1938); Partido Radical, *Programa, estatutos, reglamento* (Santiago, 1933), pp. 3-27; Partido Radical, *¡Radicales en la acción!* (Vallenar, Chile, 1932); Alberto Cabero, *Recuerdos de don Pedro Aguirre Cerda* (Santiago, 1948), pp. 141-43; Enrique Vera Riquelme, *Evolución del radicalismo chileno* (Santiago, 1943), pp. 183-249; Francisco Conrado Barría Soto, *El Partido Radical* (Santiago, 1957); Pedro Aguirre Cerda, *El problema industrial* (Santiago, 1933); Angell, pp. 8, 160-61; Labarca Fuentes, pp. 152-43; Mann, I, pp. 147-48; *El Mercurio*, Dec. 10, 1931, June 18, 1932.

entry into the Union Club for Conservatives and Liberals in the sample of 1931-33 party leaders was 1912; the average year of entry for the Radical members of the club was 1920. The Radical leaders represented the middle classes indirectly more than directly; according to the available evidence, the social status of the party representatives was generally higher than that of the party's followers. The Radical leadership was quite similar to that of the Conservatives and Liberals but also revealed an important gradation of differences. In addition, they shared many traits with the founders of the Socialists, particularly the professionals, though the Radicals were far better connected to the elites. With a party membership of northern mine owners, southern landholders, urban professionals, bureaucrats, teachers, and other types, the Radicals were ideally suited to serve as political brokers.[60]

The Radicals were not the only party incorporating the middle classes as followers or, to a lesser extent, leaders. The middle sectors were also active in the parties which most clearly represented the workers. Of greatest interest was their contribution to the Socialists. These aspects of the middle-class role in accelerating but also domesticating the growth of socialism and populism will be explored in the following chapter on the Left and labor during the Great Depression.

60. Luis Palma Zúñiga, *Historia del Partido Radical* (Santiago, 1967), pp. 173-78; Urzúa Valenzuela, *Los partidos,* pp. 152-53, 164-65; Vicuña Fuentes, *La tiranía,* I, pp. 172-75; Cabero, *Chile,* pp. 286-87; Boizard, *La democracia,* pp. 143-45; Rodríguez Mendoza, *El golpe,* pp. 300-301.

5

The Social Dimensions of the Move to the Left, 1931-33: The Parties of the Workers

In 1931-33, the parties, organizations, and defenses of the workers were in a shambles. When the welfare of the lower classes was at low ebb, their resources were also exhausted. This weakened condition was even more true of rural labor, which will largely be excluded from the following discussion as outside political competition. Among workers in the cities and the mines there was a vacuum to be filled by new options, and political coalitions across social barriers were attractive.

Disorganization and internecine conflict raged among unions. The vast majority of workers were not organized; the existing unions were frail. Although the number of unions multiplied in 1932, some were little more than paper organizations. The mosaic included the FOCH, which never recovered from its trampling by Ibáñez. Its remaining strength among miners and transportation workers was complemented by a small following in manufacturing. Anarchosyndicalist unions tried to regain their followers in construction, leather, baking, printing, and maritime trades. "Legal" unions with shallow roots in the Ibáñez years and Catholic unions struggled to make an impact. As in the past, the unions vacillated between independent labor militancy, led mainly by workers themselves, and participation through elections and parties, led mainly by *caudillos* from the middle and upper classes.[1]

For unions, the 1930s became a decade of booming organization and consolidation. They developed stronger ties with political parties and the government. More than growing out of a powerful national

1. Luis M. Heredia, *Como se construirá el socialismo* (Valparaíso, 1936), pp. 62-63; *Acción*, (Oct., 1933), p. 2; Álvarez Andrews, *Historia*, pp. 223-25, 335-50; Jobet, "Movimiento social obrero," pp. 81-88; El Congreso, *En defensa*, pp. 43-46, 116-17; Morris, *Elites*, pp. xv-xviii, 36-41, 111-12, 204-63; La Fracción Comunista, pp. 6-10.

union movement, the Socialists helped create one. In the 1930s the Socialists' eclectic, nationalist approach to unionization prevailed over the Communists' international program. Most of the legal unions fostered under Ibáñez, frequently among industrial laborers, entered the Socialist fold. In addition, the Socialists enrolled numerous anarchosyndicalist groups and even a few former Communist union branches. Alessandri had attracted the workers when their organization was incipient, and Grove, when their organization regressed and needed rebuilding.[2]

Political Attitudes and Alternatives

In most cases, the urban workers who participated in politics adapted to the prevailing norms of the Chilean system. They took part in electoral contests, joined coalitions transcending party and social differences, followed paternalistic or charismatic leaders, and bargained pragmatically with state institutions. Hampered by inadequate education, elite hostility, and other restraints on their efficacy, workers were less directly engaged in politics than were members of the higher social strata. Above all, labor's presence was felt when it came time for demonstrations or voting. Appeals to workers for votes based on class criteria often came from middle-sector leaders competing for lower-class followers. These leaders created class alignments in politics more than they reflected them. Quite often, party and personal loyalties overshadowed class allegiances in determining political choices.[3]

In its political adolescence, labor had followed two distinguishable currents: populism as practiced by Alessandri and the clientelistic Democrats, and socialism as interpreted by Recabarren and the POS. By the 1930s, important elements of both strains fused in the Chilean Socialists, who thus became the dominant force in labor politics. The Socialist growth began in 1932, but, for the moment, the Democrats remained the largest party of the workers in Congress.

Compared to the Socialists, a high percentage of the Democrat leaders came from the artisan and worker sectors. Their leadership also included a notable number of employees, men without a univer-

2. Vitale, *Historia*, p. 73; Morris and Oyaneder, pp. 15-37; Cabero, *Chile*, pp. 165-66; Bureau, pp. 33-38; Bonilla and Glazer, pp. 32-58, 117-21; Heise González, pp. 159-65; Robert J. Alexander, *Labor Relations in Argentina, Brazil, and Chile* (New York, 1962), pp. 256, 285-98; Moisés Poblete Troncoso and Ben G. Burnett, *The Rise of the Latin American Labor Movement* (New York, 1960), pp. 38, 63.

3. *Bandera Roja*, Oct. 29 and Nov. 5, 1932; *El Debate*, Oct. 16, 1932; *La Nación*, Oct. 2, 1932; Ugarte, pp. 9-17; Melfi, *Sin*, pp. 25-27; Gumucio, *El deber*, p. 16; Tulio Lagos Valenzuela, *Bosquejo histórico del movimiento obrero en Chile* (Santiago, 1941), pp. 51-56.

sity education, and members of associational groups devoted to workers and employees. Conversely, no large landowners or members of the clubs identified with the upper class appeared in the Democrat sample. The Democrats had a greater worker-artisan component and tradition than any of the other parties in the leadership tables, but they lacked innovative intellectuals, a radically collectivist program, and charismatic leaders from their own ranks. Repeatedly, the Democrats had coalesced with the traditional parties. These temporary alliances cost the party dissident leaders and incubated other leftist movements. In the past, Recabarren and others had deserted the party because it collaborated with the elites and the Right; in 1931-33, new dissenters were leaving for similar reasons, while the Democrats joined the Liberals and Conservatives as the bulwarks of Alessandri's administration.[4]

As the Socialists' electoral strength waxed in the 1930s, the Democrats' share of votes for deputies plummeted: from 14% in 1932 to 9% in 1937 to 6% in 1941. Many of their younger, more leftist members formed a short-lived Democrat-Socialist Party or deserted to other organizations not affiliated with the Alessandri government. Most, however, departed to create the Democratic Party. Soon it joined the Popular Front and later, like most of the shreds of the Democrats, vanished. The antiquated practice of wooing workers through *fiestas,* mutual-aid organizations, and nonideological unions no longer sufficed. Clientelism alone preserved remnants of Democrat adherence, but it failed to withstand the added programmatic and personal appeals of the officially Marxist parties.[5]

Communist Failures

The orthodox Communists also failed to sway substantial numbers of workers during the Great Depression. Earlier, the PC had been accepted as a partially legitimate party, for example serving in the Congress and helping draft the 1925 constitution, but from 1928 to 1935 the sectarian revolutionary Comintern policy dictated noncollaboration with nationalist reformers. Consequently, the Chilean Communists took many stances unsuited to immediate national realities and thus damaged the credentials which they had built up through years of hardship. They dwelt in a dream world of peasant-

4. Héctor de Petris Giesen, *Historia del Partido Democrático* (Santiago, 1942), pp. 59-63, 83-106; Julio César Jobet, "Alejandro Escobar Carvallo y el movimiento obrero chileno," *Arauco*, no. 84 (Jan., 1967), pp. 53-60; Jobet, *Recabarren*, pp. 8-33, 87-100.
5. Aquiles Concha, *A mis electores* (n.p., [1932?]); *Manifiesto de la asamblea demócrata;* Urzúa Valenzuela, *Los partidos,* p. 54; Mann, I, p. 107.

worker soviets. Propaganda about impending revolution was emitted from a skeletal national organization with a tenuous grip on scattered cells. Moreover, the anticommunism which ran deep in Chilean society made the party a hounded organization and a negative reference group. Their strength was overestimated by both their opponents and themselves.[6]

Communist attacks on the Socialists and all reformers cost the party support. The historical record indicates that most workers did not share the PC's sectarian ideological and class outlook. Compared to the Socialists, the Communists defined far more narrowly the social groups which could build a revolution. Accordingly the PC claimed that the decisive issue was who would lead the struggle: the middle class—meaning Socialists—or the workers—meaning Communists. The PC charged that the middle class was untrustworthy because it vacillated politically between the upper and lower strata. In particular, the Communists denounced middle-class elements, especially leaders, in the Socialist Party. They regarded the Socialists as infected with fascist-corporatist ideas, for example, nationalism and "functionalism" (organization of society and the polity into occupational and sectoral compartments), and they branded the PS a new disguise for imperialism. Like their brethren in other countries, the Communists also marketed their program as far more radical than that of the Socialists, notably about immediate confiscation of *fundos* and arming of the workers. Indeed, the most scathing indictments of the PS came not from the Right but from the regular Communists, who were losing the contest for the masses to these new contenders.[7]

Although biographical information is too scarce to include Communist percentages in the leadership tables, there is little doubt that their party officials came largely from the working class. As expected, the party played up this aspect of its composition. In fact, a majority of the PC's traceable 1932 congressional candidates were workers and artisans, with only a handful of employees, students, and professionals. Later, in 1937 and 1941, its victorious candidates showed a similar pattern, though with rising percentages from the middle sectors. The Communists described their 1932 congressional candidates in San-

6. *Bandera Roja*, Aug. 13, 1931; La Comisión de Agit. Prop., pp. 3-41; Bureau, p. 43; El Congreso, *En defensa*, pp. 13-28; U.S., Dept. of State Archives, Santiago, May 30, 1932, 825.00/1130; Galo González Díaz, *La lucha por la formación del Partido Comunista de Chile* (Santiago, 1958), pp. 8-10; Raúl Ampuero Díaz, *La izquierda en punto muerto* (Santiago, 1969), pp. 33-34.
7. Juan Siquieros, *El grovismo* (n.p., [1933?]); *Bandera Roja*, Aug. 13, Aug. 20, Aug. 27, and Oct. 17, 1931, Oct. 22 and Oct. 29, 1932.

tiago as three construction workers, two unemployed white-collar employees, one railroad worker, one transportation worker, one roving merchant, one student, one primary school teacher, one Carabinero, one unemployed northern worker, one chauffeur, one shoemaker, and one theater owner, a wealthy contributor to the PC. Municipal alderman candidates in Santiago in 1935 included six manual laborers, one teacher, one employee, and one writer. In 1937, identifiable elected congressional candidates were four workers, one former university student, and one professional. By 1941, elected congressional candidates included six workers, three teachers, two professionals, one theater owner, one intellectual, one merchant, and one employee; there was now a majority from the middle class. A small sample of PC leaders in 1931-33 indicated that most came not only from the lower classes but also from the provinces outside Santiago. They often had scant education. Many belonged to numerous unions but never to the organizations associated with the upper class. Beneath the leadership, Communist members and voters were also overwhelmingly from the laboring sectors, particularly in the mines and the north, where the party had begun. The PC also counted on port workers, bakers, metal workers, the unemployed, the unskilled, and construction workers, although the last group was slipping away. Since the Communists depended heavily on workers in the nitrate and coal zones, the Depression's decimation of those areas hurt severely. The PC doubtless had more influence with the workers than electoral figures showed.[8]

Even in the Communist Party, where leaders normally came from labor, the middle classes were asserting their role in a few posts at the start of the 1930s. Present to a lesser extent than among the Socialists, they nevertheless influenced decision making far out of proportion to their numbers within the PC. These middle-sector Communist leaders came from the USRACH and other past student-worker coalitions. Although Lafertte, from the lower class, was the PC's perennial candidate, Carlos Contreras Labarca, a lawyer and Mason, led the party. He came from the 1920 FECH generation and was secretary-general of the PC from 1931 to 1946. As the first nonworker to ever head the POS or the PC, Contreras Labarca represented new middle-class,

8. When the POS became the PC, many artisans and more-skilled workers left the party. It acquired some peasant support in the early 1920s under Alessandri but lost it under Ibáñez, except among some rural laborers close to the cities. Cruz Salas, pp. 11-16; *Bandera Roja,* Aug. 13 and Oct. 17, 1931, Oct. 22, 1932; Bureau, pp. 30-38; La Comisión de Agit. Prop. pp. 3-5; El Congreso, *En defensa,* pp. 43-46; Gaete, pp. 31-60; Boizard, *Cuatro,* pp. 89-144; Reimer.

student, teacher, employee, intellectual, and professional dimensions in the Communist movement, which nonetheless remained dominantly working class in overall leadership and orientation.[9]

At the start of the 1930s one measure of the Communists' weakness was the abandonment of the regular party by the Trotskyists. This Trotskyist label was imposed on the Communist Left by the regular party more than it was embraced by the rebels. Actually, they were more willing to cooperate with the Chilean political establishment than were the Lafertte Communists. This schism in international Communism aggravated a long-standing feud within the Chilean party that focused on a struggle between Lafertte and Hidalgo for Recabarren's mantle. In addition, the international rupture coincided in Chile with the leftist dilemma caused by the Socialist challenge. Although the two Communist parties maintained equally radical programs, only the Hidalgo group aligned with the Socialists occasionally because of the PS's undeniable worker base. If there was any measurable difference in social composition between the competing Communists, the dissidents may have been slightly more working class. For example, out of twelve identifiable Communist Left candidates in the 1935 municipal elections, ten were workers (six from construction or related fields) and the two others were chauffeurs. The Communist Left's core was found among municipal and construction workers, especially carpenters, iron workers, painters, electricians, and plasterers, but neither the dissident Communists nor the fading anarchosyndicalists, who also retained many followers among these laborers, could prevent large numbers of them from joining the Socialists. The Communist Left also made one of the earliest, most important efforts to recruit rural labor; however, the attempts of party leader Emilio Zapata Díaz, a construction worker, to organize peasant leagues around Santiago met with very limited success. The dissident Communists also attracted a few middle-class members, such as employees and professionals, primarily around the party's base in Santiago. It initially enrolled more students than the regular PC, mainly through the *Avance* group which had battled Ibáñez from the University of Chile. Nevertheless, most of the rebel Communists' leaders, like Manuel Hidalgo, came from the lower classes. By working their way up through the Democrats, then the FOCH and the POS, they scaled high posts within the Communist movement. Losing their

9. Since monthly quotas from worker members were the mainstay of PC funding, their decline during the Depression prompted the party to try to expand its base. To a lesser extent than in the PS but also noteworthy were the offspring of immigrants attracted to the Communists. Cruz Salas, pp. 13-35; Bureau, pp. 38-42; González Díaz, *La lucha*, pp. 28-34.

match with the regular PC, Hidalgo and a majority of the Communist Left had joined the Socialist Party of Grove by 1937, thus augmenting the working-class component of the PS.[10]

"Creole Socialism"

The Socialist Party, formally founded in 1933, boasted a long list of diverse ancestors. Some members traced its origins back to nineteenth-century reformers and the Democrats. Like the Communists, the Socialists claimed Recabarren and the POS as antecedents. The POS had preceded the Russian Revolution, thus imparting an indigenous flavor to Chilean Marxism. It had spread the language and concepts of socialism among the workers. At the same time, the Socialists were descendants of the *alessandristas* and military reformers. However, perhaps the party's richest legacy came from the anarchist and anarchosyndicalist tradition among students and workers. That tradition had its roots in "resistance societies" at the end of the nineteenth and start of the twentieth century: concentrated in Santiago and Valparaíso, these organizations attracted mainly artisans working in fields such as printing, baking, shoemaking, carpentry, and transportation; port workers and immigrants were also common adherents. The journey by many labor leaders from anarchism to anarchosyndicalism to socialism evidenced a progressive acceptance of more structured, political, and statist means to achieve rather constant revolutionary ends. The IWW was an offshoot of this anarchosyndicalist inheritance, and so was the USRACH, which, in the 1925 and 1927 elections, had tried to unite the salaried middle and lower groups behind populistic heroes from the military. The last serious anarchist attempt at organization was the General Confederation of Workers in 1931; it made inflated claims of over 15,000 members, mainly among better-paid workers and skilled artisans. As the role of artisans in industrial occupations declined and as the Socialists and Communists gathered strength, all such anarchist-anarchosyndicalist movements faded to insignificance. Nevertheless,

10. Like the Communists, the Communist Left, which began its separate existence in 1931, included in its leadership some sons of immigrants; at least five of the party's eighteen directors were from immigrant families. Cruz Salas, pp. 13-145; *Izquierda,* June, 1934–Aug., 1936; "Manuel Hidalgo," pp. 13-16; Vitale, *Historia,* pp. 76-79; El Congreso, *En defensa;* Waiss, *El drama,* pp. 7-19; Oscar Waiss, *Socialismo sin gerentes* (3rd ed., Santiago, 1961), pp. 3-6; Humberto Mendoza, *¿Y ahora?* (Santiago, 1942), pp. 7-9; U.S., Dept. of State Archives, Santiago, Oct. 14, 1940, 825.00/1265. The striking similarity in names between the Mexican peasant leader Emiliano Zapata and the Chilean Emilio Zapata is apparently coincidental. Manuel Hidalgo and Emilio Zapata, *2 discursos en el parlamento* (Santiago, 1933).

that strain in labor politics left its imprint on the future, for example contributing leaders like Contreras Labarca to the PC and Schnake to the PS. The direct, immediate precursors of the PS, however, were the Socialist Republic of June 4, 1932, and the fledgling parties which created that regime and managed Grove's subsequent presidential campaign.[11]

Of the parties which formed the Socialists, Matte's New Public Action (NAP) was the prototype. The NAP combined humanitarian, liberal, socialist, and even facist thought. It proposed evolutionary study of social issues and education of the workers through night schools ("Popular Universities") and unions. These ideas flowed from the Masonic creed and the student movement. The NAP emphasized spiritual renewal and individualism more than materialism and collectivism and preferred social "cooperation and solidarity" to class conflict. They advocated greater state control of the major means of production, but not the abolition of private property. They envisioned a "functional," "corporative regime" organized on the basis of economically integrated regions. Eclectic idealists, they borrowed heavily from Haya de la Torre's Peruvian APRA party, which distilled Indo-American socialism and antiimperialism. Even in countries like Chile that were unsuited to put such emphasis on the Indian, APRA's populist blend of socialism and nationalism made an enormous impact. Intellectuals and professionals, especially lawyers, led the NAP. In addition to high-ranking Masons like Matte and Alfredo Lagarrigue, a few leaders were workers and former FOCH organizers, like Carlos Alberto Martínez; two rather typical leaders were doctors Natalio Berman Berman, born of Jewish parents in Russia, and Oscar Cifuentes Solar, a Mason and Minister of Health in the Socialist Republic. An essentially middle-class movement, the NAP tried to act for the workers in politics.[12] As one observer noted:

> One of the characteristics which distinguishes genuinely Latin American socialism, represented in Chile by the NAP and similar parties, is the peculiar tactic which they employ in the class struggle. It consists as much in a restriction as in an extension of the front . . . on the one hand, it tries

11. Angell, pp. 16-29; Julio César Jobet, *Los precursores del pensamiento social de Chile* (2 vols., Santiago, 1955); Jobet, *Recabarren,* pp. 34-37, 101-49; Alejandro Chelén Rojas, *Tres hombres. Carlos Marx, Recabarren y Grove* (Chañaral, Chile, 1940), pp. 29-33; Chelén, *Trayectoria,* pp. 77-78; Alejandro Escobar Carvallo, *Un precursor socialista* (Santiago, 1932), pp. 5-15; Wilfredo Mayorga, "El jesuita rebelde," *Ercilla,* no. 1713 (Apr. 17, 1968), p. 15; Mayorga, "Todos bailamos," pp. 4-5; Mann, I, pp. 109-11, 141-42; Heredia, pp. 62-63.

12. *Acción,* June-Aug., 1932; Nueva Acción Pública; Jobet, *El socialismo chileno,* pp. 9-10; *El Mercurio,* Aug. 15 and Sept. 2, 1931; Mayorga, "Las asambleas," pp. 4-5; Cifuentes Solar, "Declaración," pp. 3-4; Espinosa, *Figuras,* pp. 53-54.

to form a unitary Latin American group within the world of socialism, leaving the union of the "proletariat of all countries" only as an ulterior perspective. And, on the other hand, it calls to the struggle not only the proletariat, but also . . . the intellectuals of the middle class . . . this is because the Latin American workers, given their cultural backwardness, would not have, according to the words of don Eugenio Orrego Vicuña—one of the principal sustainers of the union between manual and intellectual workers—sufficient preparation to make the factories function and to resolve the urgent and intricate problems of the economy. . . . Therefore Latin America has "the essential task" of obtaining for the struggle of the proletariat the cooperation of highly educated elements which belong to other "exploited" social groups.[13]

The four other micro-parties which eventually became the Socialists were the Marxist Socialist Party, Revolutionary Socialist Action, Socialist Order, and the Unified Socialist Party. The Marxist Socialist Party, an offshoot from USRACH, was typical of these groups. It included representatives from APRA at its first congress. A mixture of doctors, lawyers, teachers, small merchants, employees, and some laborers, the party had as its leader Eliodoro Domínguez, an intellectual and former anarchosyndicalist. Another leader was Jorge Neut Latour, an ex-member of the Communist Left and a lawyer who had defended workers, notably in the 1931 Tragic Christmas conflicts and the trials which grew out of them. The Marxist Socialists cultivated ties with both the Communist Left and the emerging Socialist Party. The other socialist precursors also blended Masons, teachers, students, and labor leaders. Despite multiple ideological differences, one common denominator was the advocacy of evolutionary state socialization of the means of production. These parties believed that such state intervention would allow it ultimately to redistribute wealth to the underprivileged and to achieve social justice and stability. In 1933 unification of these diverse parties was hastened as a means of mutual defense against sporadic repressive measures by the Alessandri administration, which at various times jailed or exiled Grove, Schnake, and other leftist leaders.[14]

The Socialist Party was born of a coup, weaned through an election, and initiated as a formal organization in April, 1933. Even given certain precursors, its emergence was, by any criteria, sudden. As attested by Grove's conversion, the PS was partly a historical acci-

13. Mann, I, pp. 149-50.
14. Cruz Salas, pp. 64-69, 106-7, 251-83; *La Opinión,* Apr. 20 and Apr. 21, 1933; *El Mercurio,* Aug. 4 and Aug. 15, 1931; *Bandera Roja,* Aug. 20, 1931; Orden Socialista, *Principios fundamentales* (Santiago, 1931); Jobet, *El socialismo chileno,* pp. 9-10; Hidalgo and Zapata, p. 10; Quijada, pp. 20-21.

dent. Rising rapidly, it made exaggerated claims of nearly 50,000 followers in its first year. During the 1930s one reason the party flourished and became the largest single representative of the working class in politics was that it exuded youthful dynamism. Alternatives to it were debilitated and tarnished. In addition, the Socialists benefited from dismay over Alessandri's marriage with the Right. Fear of the Nazis also propelled some Chileans into the Socialist camp. Because of the Socialists' nationalism, many reform-minded citizens preferred them over the Communists or Radicals. Never joining an International burnished the PS's favorable image. The party did, however, establish links with a gamut of leftist, nationalist, frequently populist Latin American parties, including APRA of Peru, Democratic Action of Venezuela, the Socialists of Argentina, Liberal factions in Colombia, and the Revolutionary Party of Mexico. In their own country, the Socialists at various times formed coalitions with everyone to the left of the Conservatives and Liberals.[15]

Initially, doctrine played only a minor role in the Socialists' success. Even though official party documents usually stressed revolutionary Marxist class struggle against capitalism and imperialism to create a statist, collectivist society, these principles were softened by other statements from the heterogeneous PS and its spokesmen, by party actions, by immersion in the electoral democracy, and by adjustments to local socioeconomic and historical conditions. The passage of time also toned down publicly radical positions; for example, early demands for state expropriation of most latifundia and major foreign as well as domestic enterprises were scaled down and never acted upon during the Popular Front. Despite appearances and the firm Marxian commitments of some Socialists, their movement was honeycombed with competing and contradictory ideological currents. In the early 1930s Socialist thought grew out of improvisation as much as intellection. To most Chileans in 1931-33, "socialism" meant little more than state expansion and sympathy for the workers. One conservative newspaper complained: "Among us socialism is in vogue. They [the socialists] attribute to it curative properties for all our ills. . . ."[16] Although more ideological and union-based than many populist movements in Latin America, the PS exhibited some of the hybrid thinking usually associated with populism. During the formative years, ele-

15. Partido Socialista, *33 años por el socialismo* (Santiago, 1966), ۲۰. 6-7; Julio César Jobet, *El socialismo en Chile* (Santiago, 1956), pp. 5-6; Alejandro Chelén Rojas, *Flujo y reflujo del socialismo chileno* (Santiago, 1961), pp. 10-12; Partido Socialista, *4 de junio*, pp. 1-4; Partido Socialista, *IV congreso extraordinario del Partido Socialista* (Santiago, 1943), pp. 9-11.
16. *El Debate*, Sept. 4, 1932.

ments from other foreign models were folded in with European socialism. New ingredients were added to take into account the realities of economic development which was inferior to that achieved earlier in the more industrialized West, and there were extracts from past Chilean reform movements. Furthermore, party ideology was overshadowed by concrete promises to gratify the immediate needs of the middle and lower classes: "The simple watchwords and objectives captured the masses, a bit disillusioned with the intellectualized juggling of the Communists. . . . The Socialist Party has demonstrated . . . a simple, frank . . . party line, which even the man in the street understands. . . ."[17]

The Socialists announced that they were not strictly Marxist-Leninist but were merely interpreting national problems from a Marxist point of view. Paradoxically, their strident nationalistic program was woven out of foreign strands. Officially, the party's early public position approximated nationalist communism. Declarations included maxims such as ultimate armed revolution and a transitory dictatorship of the proletariat. Such radical language, however, was a guide neither to the behavior nor to the beliefs of most party leaders. Rather, the PS's early radical Marxist line partly served to give it revolutionary credentials comparable to those held by the rival Communists. At the same time, it distinguished the PS from more moderate competitors, mainly the Radicals. For the founders' generation, Marxist theory represented more of a protest symbol than a precise ideological commitment. Although not unique to the Chilean party, this tension between long-range aspiratons and short-range operations, between appearance and substance, was central to the prolonged Socialist effort to maintain its revolutionary image without losing its foothold in gradualist electoral politics. This dilemma of pursuing avowed revolutionary ends through evolutionary means was less troublesome while constructing the party as an opposition force than while serving later in coalition governments. In part, it reflected the dilemma of trying to appeal to the lower classes with revolutionary imagery and to the middle groups with evolutionary behavior.[18]

Different members of the Socialist Party adhered to different varieties of Marxism. On a world scale, they tried to be more revolution-

17. Waiss, *El drama*, pp. 19-20.
18. Miriam Ruth Hochwald, "Imagery in Politics: A Study of the Ideology of the Chilean Socialist Party" (Ph.D. dissertation, University of California at Los Angeles, 1971), pp. 88-89, 122, 228-31; Marmaduke Grove Vallejo, *La relegación de Grove* (Valparaíso, 1933), pp. 27-28; Marmaduke Grove, *Manifiesto socialista* (Santiago, 1934), pp. 5-6; Partido Socialista, *4 de junio*, pp. 1-4; Julio César Jobet, "Tres semblanzas de socialistas chilenas," *Arauco*, no. 69 (Oct., 1965), pp. 22-42; *El Mercurio*, Oct. 2 and May 28, 1931, May 28, 1932; Edwards and Frei, pp. 234-38.

ary Marxists than European social democrats, but without imitating the Communists. Though basically reformist, Chilean socialism resembled today's heterodox Third World varieties; it enveloped both a utilitarian emphasis on state-induced industrial growth and a humanitarian emphasis on state programs for redistribution.[19]

Many moderate party members, such as Grove, tended to admire humanistic French socialism or the British Labour Party at least as much as Marxism. The PS was similar to the Labour Party in seeking a mixed state and private economic system. The Chileans, like the British, courted groups beyond the working class and fought the Communists for control of the unions. In many ways, Chilean socialism remained linked to liberalism in its emphasis on both welfare and individualism. For example, some Socialists opposed class inequalities because they hindered individual liberties and mobility. Their agrarian reform proposals favored the creation of family farms as much as collective units, technical modernization, and higher standards of living for the peasants. Some Socialists battled for equality of opportunity, a meritocracy, rather than a Marxian socialist society. Compared to the British Labour Party, however, the Chilean Socialists wanted greater state control of property. Theoretically, the Chileans were more amenable to nondemocratic tactics. The PS believed that Chile had to industrialize further and build a more honest, representative democratic system before British Labour–style politics could be practiced fully.[20]

Anarchism, anarchosyndicalism, and corporatism were other European ideas that influenced Chilean socialism. To an unprecedented extent, the backgrounds of the party's members merged the two previously antagonistic currents in the labor movement, anarchosyndicalism and Marxism. Many Socialists hoped to unite syndicalism and Marxism by emphasizing unionization over congressional politics, but that never came to pass. There were also some anarchist roots to early arguments by a few Socialists for decentralized, "functional," syndicalist organizations arranged and administered by geographic production units and types of work. But, overall, there were only minor anarchist undercurrents coursing through Socialist thought. The PS was too statist, nationalist, and Marxist to satisfy any real anarchists or anarchosyndicalists, who were nearly moribund politically by the 1930s.[21]

19. Julio César Jobet, "Origenes y primeros congresos del Partido Socialista," *Arauco*, no. 12 (Oct., 1960), pp. 5-19; Partido Socialista, *Grove a la presidencia*, pp. 2-31; Halperin, pp. 142-44, 229.
20. Hochwald, pp. 94-95; Julio César Jobet, "Trayectoria del Partido Socialista de Chile," *Arauco*, no. 63 (Apr., 1965), p. 9; Jobet, "Tres semblanzas," pp. 23-28.
21. Partido Socialista, *4 de junio*, p. 2; Grove, *Manifiesto;* Bonilla and Glazer, pp.

Like socialism, corporatism permeated the political spectrum in the early 1930s. It even made an impact on a few Socialists. As was typical in Chilean politics, these corporatist impulses were hitched to the desire for a semiauthoritarian, personalistic figure to impose a government of order above the storm of multiparty politics. The Right usually saw recasting government and society along functional, economic sectoral lines as a way to circumvent populist, working-class pressures and safeguard the power of regional and employer elites. Conversely, the Left saw it as a way to sidestep the conservative congress and augment the influence of labor organizations. Instead of universal suffrage, some PS leaders preferred "functional socialism" as a way to organize the state. Even the name "Socialist Party" barely won out over "Integral Socialist Party" at the founding in 1933. Most Socialists, however, resisted the faddish corporatism as a new cloak for the status quo.[22]

In addition to European examples, many American reform movements influenced the Chilean Socialists, at least to a minor extent. Some party leaders felt an affinity with the New Deal of U.S. President Franklin Roosevelt,[23] and many identified with the Mexican revolution. Throughout the 1930s, both Chilean Socialist and Communist leaders developed close ties with the architects of Lázaro Cárdenas's Mexico. The Socialists admired Luis Carlos Prestes, the Brazilian army rebel and Communist leader, and compared Grove to him. They borrowed from the socialist writings of the Argentine Juan B. Justo and the Peruvian populist and Marxist José Carlos Mariátegui. Without a doubt, the greatest American influence on the Chilean Socialists in these early years was Haya de la Torre and his American Popular Revolutionary Alliance (APRA). *Aprista* leaders and student activists made numerous contacts with Chilean Socialists. A leading APRA intellectual, Luis Alberto Sánchez, sat in on meetings of both the Chilean Socialists and the Nazis. *Aprista* influences could be discerned in many PS doctrines and symbols, such as continental antiimperialism and the party insignia of an Indian hatchet emblazoned on a map of South America. Like the Socialists, APRA promised simultaneous economic modernization and social equalization. It also appealed to both the middle and lower classes. Even though the Indianist orientation of the APRA theorists was played

37-38; Mayorga, "Cuando el PS," pp. 14-15; Mayorga, "Todos fuimos anarquistas," p. 15; Mayorga, "Todos bailamos," pp. 4-5; Chelén, *Trayectoria*, pp. 77-78; Leonard I. Krimerman and Lewis Perry, eds., *Patterns of Anarchy* (Garden City, N.Y., 1966).

22. *Consigna*, Apr. 20, 1935; *Claridad*, Apr. 19, 1938; *La Opinión*, June 5, 1932; *Acción* (Oct.-Dec., 1933); Grove, *Manifiesto*, p. 18; Partido Socialista, *4 de junio*, p. 2; Álvarez Andrews, *Bases*, esp. pp. 5-14; Edwards and Frei, p. 239; Edwards, *Las corporaciones;* Mann, I, pp. 120-23; Echaíz, pp. 166-74; Cruz Salas, pp. 113-14; Fredrick B. Pike and Thomas Stritch, eds., *The New Corporatism* (Notre Dame, Ind., 1974).

23. Partido Socialista, *4 de junio*, p. 3.

down in Europeanized, mestizo Chile, it was still incorporated in Socialist appeals for "the cultural and political coordination of the Indo-American proletariat and . . . the creation of an antiimperialist Indo-American economy. . . ."[24]

Less significant than its bonds with APRA was the PS's relationship to the largest, most successful Latin American socialist party prior to its birth, that of Argentina. Although the Chileans established an enduring friendship with their Argentine namesakes, their roots in different national contexts and historical epochs always kept the two parties distinct. Compared to their counterparts across the Andes, the Chileans were both more populist and more Marxist. They always criticized the Argentines for remaining European-style moderate social democrats, even during years when the Chileans themselves drew close to that pattern. Throughout, personalism and nationalism were more important in Chilean socialism. In contrast to the Argentines, the Chileans placed greater emphasis on control or expulsion of foreign capital and on import-substituting industrialization, even at the cost of rising consumer prices. They were more willing to contemplate the hypothetical possibility of armed struggle. Both socialist organizations were dominated by middle-class leaders, but, over time, the Chileans became more of a working-class party and the Argentines less of one. For multiple reasons, the Chilean Socialists became more of a leftist, national, successful party in the long run.[25]

Mingling these various models and ideologies, the Chilean Socialists, like many populist movements, stressed an attack on the status quo even more than elaborate, integrated proposals for an alternative system. For the early 1930s, an appropriate way to summarize their program is to outline its criticisms of the prevailing order. The party protested inequalities among both domestic social groups and nations. It united these grievances by simultaneously excoriating oligarchs and imperialists, who, according to the Socialists, were conspiring against the common people.[26]

24. Grove, *Manifiesto*, pp. 5-6; Partido Socialista, *Grove a la presidencia*, pp. 20-31; Partido Socialista, *4 de junio*, pp. 1-4; Hennessy, pp. 28-61; Pike, p. 204; Bonilla and Glazer, pp. 82, 98-99, 121, 135; Hochwald, pp. 88-89; Vial Solar, pp. 197-99; *Consigna*, 134-37; Luis Alberto Sánchez, "Marmaduke Grove," *Zig-Zag*, año XLVII, no. 2424 (Sept. 8, 1951), p. 39; *El imperialismo extranjero en Chile* (Santiago, 1937), pp. 16-19; Eliodoro Domínguez, *¿Qué quiere el socialismo?* (Santiago, 1937), p. 20; Alejandro Chelén Rojas, *Aspectos históricos de la revolución mexicana* (Chañaral, Chile, 1938), pp. 12-14; U.S., Dept. of State Archives, Santiago, Oct. 29, 1938, 825.00/1085; *Célula* (Mar., 1933), p. 3.

25. *Consigna*, Mar. 27, 1937; Robert J. Alexander, *Latin American Political Parties* (New York, 1973), pp. 109-22.

26. Jobet, *El Partido Socialista de Chile*, I, pp. 116-20; Ionescu and Gellner, pp. 1-4.

From their antioligarchy stance, the Socialists hoped to unite the majority of Chileans, the middle and lower classes, against the wealthy few. They argued that there were only two meaningful classes within this capitalist society: those who owned the means of production and those who sold their labor. By this definition, at least 90% of all Chileans, from ditch diggers to doctors, should have joined the Socialist Party. In contrast to the narrowly proletarian Communists, Grove and the PS leaders envisioned a national movement of the "masses." Only a few Socialists argued against the leadership that the party should be composed almost totally of manual laborers.[27]

The PS endorsed traditional antioligarchy tenets in Chilean politics as well as innovative demands for redistribution of income, land, and power. For example, Matte and others perpetuated the Masonic tradition of anticlericalism, especially in regard to education.[28] Despite their belief in state authority, a few Socialists echoed the old provincial outcry for administrative decentralization. Socialists in the peripheral provinces were likely to represent local interests and clienteles more than ideological and class concerns commensurate with party declarations in the capital city. The Socialists drew parallels between foreign (British and North American) exploitation of the northern mines and foreign (British and Argentine) investments in the landed companies of the extreme south. They charged that these were internal colonies, whose surplus capital was siphoned off to Santiago and foreigners. The party especially claimed Magallanes as a southern province of concern. There the PS opposed the latifundia and oligopolistic livestock and processing companies, whose owners usually resided in distant Santiago. Land reform in Magallanes was urged as a way to aid small capitalists, colonists, and the workers—a reasonable but not notably Marxist proposal. Thus this became a regional, class, and nationalist issue, melding traditional and modern concerns.[29]

Socialist nationalism thrived on the issue of antiimperialism. As the party realized, "socialism" and "nationalism" were the two most popular political commodities in the 1930s, with nearly all candidates trying

27. *Acción* (Dec., 1933), p. 3; *El Socialista*, no. 8 (Concepción, Nov., 1934), p. 3; *Jornada*, Nov.-Dec., 1934; Partido Socialista, *La línea política del Partido Socialista* (Santiago, 1941); Partido Socialista, *4 de junio;* Ampuero, *La izquierda*, pp. 34-35; Jobet, "Orígenes," pp. 7-9; Congreso Nacional, *En defensa*, pp. 39-42.

28. Julio César Jobet, *Socialismo y comunismo* (Santiago, 1952), pp. 3-4; Partido Socialista, *4 de junio;* Grove, *Manifiesto*, pp. 9-14; *La junta; La Opinión*, June 5, Oct. 7, and Oct. 22, 1932; *Consigna*, July 27 and Dec. 7, 1935.

29. *Jornada*, Dec. 22, 1934; *La Opinion*, Mar. 21 and Apr. 4, 1932; Jobet, *El Partido Socialista de Chile*, I, pp. 87-88; Partido Socialista, *4 de junio*, p. 2; Chelén, *Trayectoria*, pp. 191-92; Oscar Schnake Vergara, *El Partido Socialista y el problema de las tierras de Magallanes* (Santiago, 1937).

to capitalize on these sentiments.[30] One PS leader, in an exceptionally condescending and frank public analysis, described their attempt to fuse and lay claim to the dual symbols of Chilean populism:

> . . . the great masses, although they do not find themselves capable of defining what is socialism, have acquired, nonetheless, a marvelous sensitivity for feeling it. For them, socialism is simply the contrary of present reality. . . . they have a socialist faith. . . . they believe in socialism in the same way that simple minds believe in God. . . . At this moment . . . there exists in Chile . . . political confluence in which many organizations appear identical in their immediate proposals. Many organizations have realized that only on the basis of socialism and nationalism can one continue to appeal to the masses, and the speeches, symbols, and publications make it difficult for the mass-man to distinguish among what is said by a Socialist, a Communist, a young Conservative, and even a Nazi.[31]

Socialist nationalism produced denunciations of the Soviet Union in addition to the United States.[32] Like APRA, the PS embraced Latin American as well as Chilean nationalism, tracing its vision of continental solidarity back to Simón Bolívar.[33] As the most significant nationalistic grouping yet to arise in Chilean politics, the party attracted adherents beyond the narrow boundaries of industrial labor. In a Marxist vein, the Socialists appealed to class conflict. At the same time, in a populist vein, they appealed to national unity of the middle and lower classes against the perceived oligarch-imperialist clique.[34]

The PS helped make economic nationalism and foreign penetration fundamental political issues for the Chilean future. Party leaders swore to achieve the "second national independence": liberation from excessive reliance on foreign markets, credits, and industries. Simultaneously, they hoped to promote import-substituting industrialization, nationalization of foreign enterprises, and labor benefits. However, they gave industrial growth top priority. In Marxist terms, the Socialists felt that they had to encourage more socialized production before more socialized appropriation and distribution were really feasible, but reconciling state stimulation of high-cost industries and social welfare was difficult. The PS faced the dilemma of simultaneously trying to improve Chile's position compared to wealthier foreigners and the masses' position compared to wealthier nationals.[35]

30. *Acción* (Oct., 1933), pp. 4-5; Partido Socialista, *4 de junio.*
31. Though far exceeded in Socialist literature by rather rote declarations of Marxist party doctrines, such openly paternalistic statements seem to be as revealing about the attitudes and appeals of many party leaders in the era. *Consigna,* May 6, 1937.
32. *El Mercurio,* June 5 and June 11, 1932.
33. Partido Socialista, *4 de junio.*
34. Interviews with Jorge Barría, Santiago, 1973, and Astolfo Tapia, Santiago, 1970; Jobet, *El Partido Socialista de Chile,* II, pp. 177-78; Halperin, pp. 39-40; Hennessy, pp. 28-61.
35. Jobet, "Orígenes," pp. 5-19; Grove, *Manifiesto,* pp. 5-22; Partido Socialista, *4 de*

Their emphasis on state planning to achieve economic modernity and social justice was as much a response to the failings of the private economy as an outgrowth of Marxist tenets. Their economic ideas welded together concepts from both the Socialist Republic and Dávila's administration. Some proposals—such as a national economic council to oversee planning and foment industry—foreshadowed the Popular Front's program.[36] Supporting protected industrialization was a way to build the Socialists' factory labor constitutency as well as the national economy. They were aware of the danger of confusing their advocacy of "industrial rationalization" to benefit the workers with conservative advocacy of state capitalism to rescue the economic elites. Given the pitfalls in the party's hopes to synchronize industrial growth and redistributive changes for the underprivileged, the PS's economic programs, along with their many vehemently socialist elements, also shared policy approaches and problems with what might best be labeled developmental populism.[37]

Opposition to the status quo included displeasure with traditional party politics. The PS was founded to provide a leftist electoral alternative untainted by the Communists or the chicanery of the old reform parties. Its leaders wanted to avoid becoming just "one more

---

junio, pp. 2-4; Mario Antonioletti, *Cooperativismo* (Santiago, 1954), pp. 121-50; Gregorio Guerra, "Revolución y crisis de la racionalización," *Cuadernos de la Economía Mundial,* no. 6 (1932), pp. 1-32; Andrés Garafulic Y., *Carnalavaca* (Santiago, 1932).

36. One fundamental document with a strongly socialist approach was the party's official "Program of Immediate Action" of 1933-34. It must be assessed in conjunction with other statements from the era, but its main points are worth noting: (1) In social services, expand the state's role in feeding, clothing, and housing the people and in holding down the prices of primary necessities; (2) In agriculture, have the state take over most latifundia and redistribute those lands to be worked collectively, limit the legal size of landholdings, protect small producers, plan agricultural production, and improve the standard of living of peasants; (3) In mining, make all mines and natural resources with no current owner the exclusive property of the state; (4) In general economic policy, achieve an "equilibrium" between agriculture and industry, determine the major enterprises ready for rapid "socialization" by the state, and establish heavy state regulation of all economic activities, including production quotas, credit, banking, transportation, communication, wages and salaries, social security, mechanization, electrification, internal and external commerce, and foreign capital; (5) In international politics, defend the special nature of the Latin American "revolution" and build toward a "Socialist Republic of America," adhere to no other international affiliations, denounce all "imperialisms" and especially "panamericanism," and open national relations with Russia; (6) In nitrate policy, support a state-administered monopoly as a first step; and (7) In cultural policy, promote socialist doctrines, state control of all the means of communication and education, enlarged cultural and educational institutions, technical education, and Latin American cultural studies. Jobet, *El socialismo chileno,* pp. 127-34; Partido Socialista, *4 de junio;* Jobet, "Trayectoria," p. 9; Pinto, "Desarrollo," pp. 28-29.

37. Domínguez, *Qué,* p. 23; *Ruta,* no. 1 (Feb. 16, 1935), p. 3; Jobet, *El socialismo en Chile,* pp. 5-7; Oscar Schnake Vergara, *Política socialista* (Santiago, 1938), pp. 52-58.

party" in the Chilean panorama.[38] It was a point of pride that most PS leaders were young and new to politics.[39] One Socialist senator later attributed the party's early success to its leadership by "a new group of men, free of complicity with the past, uncontaminated by the stupid and black intrigues of the so-called traditional parties. . . ."[40]

Part of the attempt to differentiate themselves from regular political parties was reflected in efforts to lead a redemptive movement as well as a political cause. The PS promised a rekindling of the national spirit and a new era of honor and decency in government. There was a tinge of the moralistic, revitalizing character common to mass, populist movements seeking total solutions to social stress. Hence, an evangelistic tone embellished some party propaganda. Indeed, a handful of Socialists were former followers of evangelical religions, and a few supporters of Grove compared him to Jesus Christ. In 1935, Grove defined his party's socialism in this way: "More than a program, it is all faith; all a concept, all a political, economic, and social religion to be realized." Nearly revivalist undercurrents were seen in the exclusion from party membership of "lazy ones, drunks, or thieves." Socialists claimed, "Party life improved those who possessed some vice, and, in general, elevated everyone above his weaknesses." Exemplary behavior within the organization was seen as preparation for the altruistic society to be created. Most of these appeals to morality centered on Grove. Propaganda portrayed him leading an honorable, sober, disciplined, kindly life. Grove stood for "dignity," in contrast to the corrupt image of the more-experienced parties and the violent stereotype of the Communists. Extolling the Socialist Republic as "Twelve Days of Integrity in Government," the PS celebrated June 4 as its birthday. The program during that republic included a "Tribunal of National Sanction," which had been devised initially by Grove and other young military officers in the mid-1920s to compile lists of allegedly immoral public officials. In a moralistic, rather middle-class cadence, the Socialists stressed the "responsible," high-minded nature of their movement: "The Socialist Party is a group of honorable and sincere men with blind faith in a better future." These themes implied that a movement of the lower classes could be "respectable." Those who joined could take pride in being Socialists and siding with the virtuous common people against the snobbish upper class. Some

38. Oscar Schnake, "No somos un partido más," in Comité Regional del Partido Socialista de Santiago, eds., Homenaje al 6th aniversario del Partido Socialista (Santiago, 1939), pp. 5-6; Partido Socialista, Grove a la presidencia, p. 7.

39. Partido Socialista, 4 de junio, pp. 1-2; Jobet, El socialismo chileno, pp. 125-27.

40. Alejandro Chelén Rojas, El partido de la victoria (Chañaral, Chile, 1939), p. 5.

Socialists attributed the party's popularity more to its moral rectitude and rejuvenating enthusiasm than to ideology.[41]

Another aspect of their deprecation of traditional politics was ambivalence about electoral as opposed to violent routes to power. They retained a nostalgic fondness for their dramatic seizure of the executive branch in June, 1932. Officially, the party always maintained that its commitment to bourgeois democracy was only tentative and merely a means to the end of socialism. Torn between being Marxist or populist, revolutionary or reformist, many members were undecided whether to work within or against the prevailing system. In actuality, the PS never prepared for armed revolution but devoted itself to elections. After being ousted by the military at the end of the Socialist Republic, Grove and other leaders foreswore future involvement with takeovers by armed force. Thereafter, the party's cultivation of good relations with segments of the armed services was designed more to neutralize any military opposition to Socialist participation in regular politics than to conspire. The PS hoped to avoid the sort of hostility which the APRA in Peru had experienced from the army. The Socialists' lasting tension between evolutionary means and revolutionary goals was not surprising in a highly stratified society with democratic traditions challenged by severe economic difficulties. In the 1930s, more impatient rightists as well as leftists thought Chile's problems required swifter, nondemocratic answers. Accordingly, the authoritarian tendencies found in some populist movements in Latin America and elsewhere were not absent from Chilean socialism. Such inclinations, however, were far overshadowed by the party's pragmatic immersion in the inherited democratic system.[42]

Composition of the Socialist Party

In large part, the heterogeneity of the Socialists accounted for the party's ideological and tactical diversity. The dominant leaders were mainly from Santiago. Only a small number engaged in worker or

41. Partido Socialista, *4 de junio*, pp. 1-4; Grove, *La relegación*, pp. 27-28; Partido Socialista, *Grove a la presidencia*, pp. 2-15; Jobet, "Tres semblanzas," pp. 22-42; Jobet, *El socialismo en Chile*, pp. 5-6; Jobet, *El socialismo chileno*, pp. 125-34; *Ruta*, no. 2 (Mar. 2, 1935), p. 1; H. E. Bicheno, "Anti-Parliamentary Themes in Chilean History: 1920-70," *Government and Opposition*, VII, no. 3 (Summer, 1972), pp. 351-88.

42. *El Socialista*, no. 8 (Concepción, Nov., 1934), p. 3; *La Opinión*, Oct. 7 and Nov. 12, 1932, Apr. 25, 1933; *Consigna*, June 30, 1934, p. 3; Bicheno, pp. 351-88; Domínguez, *Qué*, pp. 23-24; Mayorga, "Cuando el PS," pp. 14-15; Schnake, *Política*, pp. 29-49; Jobet, "Origenes," pp. 5-19; Juan F. Fernández C., *Pedro Aguirre Cerda y el Frente Popular chileno* (Santiago, 1938), pp. 47-73.

artisan occupations. Taken in its entirety, the Socialist leadership profile fell between those of the Radicals and the Democrats, though all three contained significant middle-class components. For example, as the tables showed, the PS leaders were primarily in the liberal professions—less so than the Radicals and more so than the Democrats. Compared to the Democrats and Communists, the prominent Socialists were notably not from the working classes. Compared to the Radicals, however, they were excluded from the organizations associated with the elites. To oversimplify, the Radicals were a middle-class party that included the upper class, and the Socialists were a middle-class party that included the lower class. The top Socialists had seldom participated in government or congressional posts prior to 1933, except during the Socialist Republic. The PS founders sprang from a new political generation. Of all the parties sampled, the Socialists seem to have had the most solidly middle-class leadership. Yet the Socialists, not the Democrats or the Communists, attracted the largest working-class following in the presidential election of 1932 and thereafter throughout the 1930s.[43]

The Socialist middle-class leaders were markedly younger and less connected to the upper class, for example through ownership of *fundos* and membership in clubs, than their counterparts in the other parties in the tables. These middle-sector Socialists mainly came from what the Communists labeled, with great derision, the "petty bourgeoisie." A significant number belonged to the higher, wealthier strata of the middle classes. Many belonged to the Masonic lodge, an organization which often linked professionals and intellectuals with students. In the upper ranks of the PS, doctors and journalists as well as white-collar employees were common. At the University of Chile, for example in the medical school, anarchist thought had a long history of influence, and it led some students and professionals first into alliances with workers and then into the Socialist Party. Though it was not noticeable in the leadership profile, some younger military officers continued lending important support to the PS. Dissatisfied with the status quo, these middle-class leaders of the Socialists chose to challenge it, but whether they mainly wanted to transform the system or to press for their greater acceptance into it remained in doubt in the 1930s.[44]

43. Jobet, *El socialismo chileno*, pp. 125-27; Urzúa Valenzuela, *Los partidos*, p. 194; Robert Michels, *Political Parties* (New York, 1962), pp. 15-18, 107, 140, 230-58.

44. Partido Socialista, *4 de junio*, pp. 2-4; Jobet, "La juventud," pp. 29-31; Mayorga, "Cuando el PS," pp. 14-15; El Congreso, *En defensa*, pp. 39-42; Bonilla and Glazer, pp. 43-65, 110-34.

The Socialist leadership reflected the general move of the middle classes into more direct, commanding political participation at the outset of the 1930s. Although determined to champion the cause of the workers, the PS leaders exhibited mixed motives. Major reasons why these middle-sector types chose that party over other options were their youth, limited access to the national government, and deteriorating socioeconomic positions which seldom included ties to the elites. At the same time, they preferred the Socialists to other parties because of their historical experience, ideology, and idealism. Socialism was fashionable, particularly among intellectuals, teachers, students, and professionals. For many middle-class party leaders, the material life that had seemed bountiful in 1929 had taken a sudden downturn. Through 1931-32, their discontent refocused from the military to the traditional socioeconomic structure, from demands for civilian rule to protests against social and economic injustices. Disillusioned with the historic parties, these middle-class rebels created a new one. Some, especially as the 1930s wore on, hoped the PS would satisfy their electoral and bureaucratic ambitions. Many of the middle-class leaders who headed the Left were marginally less successful than those who steered other parties. They empathized with the workers because of their own, personal intellectual propensities and relative deprivation of status and economic position. For example, a relatively high number of Socialist leaders were from first- or second-generation immigrant families; for immigrants and their descendants, politics was one means of expressing their status anxieties and of obtaining some of the perquisites available to more successful, integrated members of the middle and upper classes. Thus their status and position could become more commensurate with their economic, educational, and occupational backgrounds. Other frustrated middle-class leaders sided with the Left partly out of resentment against discrimination and snubs at the hands of the upper class. Contact between the wellborn or wealthy and the middle class, for example in schools, could breed either cooperation or contempt. Whatever their motivations, some of the middle-class Socialist leaders contended that they were locking arms with the lower classes in equal opposition to the "oligarchy." Other party directors, recognizing the subordination of the labor groups within the PS, argued that the workers were poorly educated and ill prepared to manage the movement or the nation and its economy. Matte, for example, had lost some of his idealism when he tried to topple Montero solely by actions of the workers and ended having to rely upon the military. Such critical appraisals of the workers implied a paternalistic approach to labor politics.[45] In the 1930s, it was clear that many Socialist leaders were influenced by Eugenio Orrego Vicuña, a writer who preferred middle-class leaders for the proletariat: "In truth, I do not conceive of socialism (in the epoch of construction, you understand) except as a hierarchy in which the workers and the peasants are in the base and the intellectuals act in the superior structure, filling the functions of organization, education, discipline, and articulation."[46] In retrospect, a leading Socialist intellectual passed a harsh but perceptive judgment on the roles of the middle classes in the party:

> . . . the Socialist Party, in spite of its apparent revolutionary vigor, exhibited vacillating attitudes and . . . inclinations toward compromises and transactions; within its leadership, one noted a marked electoralism and a strong appetite for the positions of popular representation. It had not yet succeeded in assimilating its Marxist conception and outlining for itself a consistently socialist policy. Finally, the socioeconomic conditions of the country did not show themselves favorable to costly revolutionary activity. There existed a small working class, immature and with scant consciousness; an immense peasantry, removed from any restlessness; and a vast middle class, or petite bourgeoisie, with clear predominance in the political action of the working masses. The petite-bourgeois tendencies prevailed over the proletarian and through the Popular Front encountered their natural channel.[47]

The few Socialist leaders from the working class usually had backgrounds in mutual aid and anarchist or anarchosyndicalist labor movements. Other labor leaders switched from the Communists, especially the Trotskyist wing. Although some leaders with a labor heritage may have resented the party's dominance by middle- to upper-class elements, these differences seldom produced open eruptions in the early years.[48]

From printed sources, voting materials, and social background data, it seems evident that a far smaller percentage of Socialist leaders

45. One estimate, mainly based on surnames, was that at least one-third of the officers of the tiny parties which united to form the PS were descendants of immigrants; out of 70 participants at the founding of the PS, 10 were apparently from immigrant stock. Cruz Salas, pp. 12-14; Faletto, Ruiz, and Zemelman, pp. 63-82; Bonilla and Glazer, pp. 64-67; Chamudes, pp. 28-30; Guerra, p. 5; Mann, I, pp. 149-51; La Agrupación, pp. 3-4; Labarca Fuentes, pp. 185-86; Jobet, "Origenes," pp. 7-9; Jobet, "La juventud," pp. 29-31; Michels, pp. 18-34, 238-42.

46. Eugenio Orrego Vicuña, El escritor y la sociedad (Santiago, 1937), p. 10. Also see Eugenio Orrego Vicuña, Perspectiva del desenvolvimiento socialista en América y en el mundo (Santiago, 1932); Mann, I, pp. 149-50.

47. Jobet, "Trayectoria," p. 9.

48. Jobet, "Origenes," p. 9; interviews with Jobet, Santiago, 1970; Bonilla and Glazer, pp. 56-57.

than voters were workers. Contrasting these findings to those on the Democrats and Communists, it is obvious that neither the parties with the most radical program nor the most leaders from the lower classes were doing best among the workers. Factors besides class allegiances and ideology were strongly influencing political alignments. Fragile common political beliefs, rallying symbols—more than common social, family, or economic bonds—banded the Socialist leaders and followers together. Concurrently, relations among unequal social groups, rather than class conflict, may best explain the emergence of the Socialist amalgam. Therefore, the social composition of the PS at the intermediate membership level between the leaders and the voters needs to be explored to ascertain more precisely who the Socialists were and what factors accounted for their origins and associations within the party.

Data on the 447 original, official members of the Socialist Party in Santiago in 1933 shows that at this level, as well as among the top leaders, the Socialists primarily came from other than working-class occupational strata. Of the 440 occupations which were clearly listed by the members themselves, only about one-third were apparently from the worker or even artisan sectors. Middle-class occupations, as nearly as can be determined, engaged a majority of the founding members, as can be seen in Table 11.[49] Truly an intermediate group, the original party membership contained a far higher proportion of

49. This membership list only contained a handful of the same names used in the leadership tables presented earlier; they were two separate groups. Of the 447 members inscribed in the founders' registry, 433 noted clearly their occupations. Seven of these 433 original members listed two occupations of apparently equal importance; therefore, a total of 440 occupations are used in the membership table. Some of the occupational categories combine slightly mixed types—for example both private and public white-collar employees are included in the "employees" category. In other instances, the Spanish job description written by the members could be variously interpreted: "practicante," for example, could have applied to an intern, nurse, or assistant chemist. In the vast majority of cases, the occupations are recorded here as direct translations of the job descriptions listed by the party members. Not only were a majority of the clearly classifiable occupations (admittedly a limited indicator of social class) ranked above the working class, but also a majority of the unclassified occupations in the table were, in all likelihood, associated with non-worker strata. In other words, even an extremely cautious interpretation of the founders' registry indicates that a majority of the original members of the Socialist Party in Santiago in 1933 were engaged in occupations strongly identified with the middle classes. Only a few of the founding members recorded information beyond occupation, such as age and residence. For the 35 members who listed their ages as well as occupations, the average and mean age in 1933 came to 36 years. Over time, an obviously incomplete tabulation was kept in the registry of those original members who, after 1933, left the party or were expelled; of the 35 members so designated, 28 were clearly not from the working class. Partido Socialista, "Rejistro de fundadores" (Santiago, 1933); interviews with Carlos Charlín and Manuel Mandujano Navarro, both signers of the registry in 1933, Santiago, 1970; Jobet, *El socialismo en Chile,* pp. 5-7.

TABLE 11: SOCIAL GROUPINGS OF SANTIAGO SOCIALIST PARTY MEMBER
        OCCUPATIONS, 1933

Apparently from the middle classes or above:

121 employees	4 journalists
22 teachers	3 architects
21 accountants	3 engineers
17 merchants	2 agriculturalists
13 students	1 intern, nurse, or
9 doctors	assistant chemist
7 lawyers	1 subengineer
7 industrialists	1 chemist

Total   232

Apparently from the laboring classes:

30 carpenters	3 tailors
22 mechanics	3 hatters
21 electricians	3 typographers
11 chauffeurs	2 braziers, coppersmiths,
9 shoemakers, sellers, or repairmen	boilermakers, or tinkers
7 painters (in construction)	2 day-laborers
6 plasterers	2 gardeners
6 plumbers	1 closer of shoes
4 varnishers	1 asphalt layer
4 seamstresses	1 railroad worker
4 furniture makers	1 tinsmith
4 bakers	1 construction worker
3 bricklayers	1 factory worker
3 cabinet makers	1 paver

Total   156

Probable class position or job definition less obvious:

9 women working at home	1 commission merchant or
8 telegraphers	commission agent
7 draftsmen	1 actor
6 builders	1 photographer
2 brokers or agents	1 timber merchant, lumber
2 contractors	dealer, or carpenter
2 iron workers	1 innkeeper or landlord
2 writers	1 musician
2 seamen	1 steam, steamer, or steamboat
2 traveling merchants	worker
1 painter (undefined)	1 glass dealer or blower
1 painter (artist)	

Total   52

workers than did the leadership but almost certainly a lower proportion than did the Socialists' overall public following and voters. The
membership wedded the middle and lower classes politically.

The middle-class members, somewhat like the leaders, enrolled in the PS because of idealism, political traditions and ambitions, and their relatively weak, dependent position in society. These middle-class Socialists came mainly from occupations that did not require a university education. Precariously clinging to a white-collar ledge barely above labor, some members of the middle classes were beaten down by the Depression. Unemployment was high for salaried employees in 1931-33; the Depression squeezed credit, rents, and commerce. Many of the school teachers who joined the party had been driven from their jobs by the Depression or the Alessandri government. Poorly paid, they lacked status commensurate with their educational training. Moreover, some teachers, such as Eliodoro Domínguez, had a history of labor struggles through anarchosyndicalist unions. Thus a new alignment with workers in the PS offered no serious forebodings or obstacles to experienced segments of the middle groups. Stronger than the lower classes, the middle strata were more capable of erecting political movements to serve their needs through the state.[50] As future Christian Democrat President Eduardo Frei observed in the 1930s:.". . . this middle class formed itself in its first stage in the past century in the ranks of the most advanced doctrinaire liberalism, and afterward in the Radical Party. . . . Today . . . following a universal process, it is integrating the ranks of socialism."[51]

Of the identifiable working-class Socialist members, most came from small trades (shoes, bread) or independent fields (furniture, electricity) rather than highly organized or factory and mining sectors. The new party had the most success with labor where the Communists were weak. For example, the PS made little impact in the mines until later in the 1930s. Then it established a strong following in the rising copper industry, while the Communists preserved their enclaves in the declining nitrate fields and in the coal mines. In the beginning, the Socialists elicited the greatest response from urban skilled laborers and artisans, such as typographers and chauffeurs, who were above the rank of the common workers. In 1933, a majority of these Santiago PS worker members came from the construction industry. Initially, construction suffered more from the Depression than any other major industry, but then it expanded during the rest of the thirties. Unemployment was especially high in the building trades and available evidence indicates that wages there continued to fall into 1933.

50. Eliodoro Domínguez, *Un movimiento ideológico en Chile* (Santiago, 1935), pp. 21-28; Godoy, *Manifiesto*, p. 2; El Congreso, *En defensa*, pp. 48, 59, 81; Sáez, *Recuerdos*, III, pp. 105-8; *Bandera Roja*, Oct. 22, 1932; Hochwald, pp. 94-100.
51. Frei, p. 93.

The anarchists and the IWW had strong antecedents in construction, as well as in other worker groups represented in the Socialist membership, for instance bakers. Having established good relations with these laboring sectors, Eugenio González and Oscar Schnake helped bring them into the party. Mutual-aid and pre-political "resistance" societies had long influenced artisan, industrial, and port workers in Santiago and Valparaíso; these working groups lacked a firm socialist ideology and were attracted to the Democrats, Alessandri in 1920, and then Grove in 1932. In addition, some of the party's worker members defected from the Communist Left and even the regular PC.[52]

The structure of underdevelopment, the Depression, and political traditions largely explain the relatively low worker component in the avowedly Marxian Socialist Party. Chile was in the incipient stages of industrialization, still passing from the artisan to the factory phase. Outside the mines, the country lacked a large, experienced, highly organized, classic proletariat. Unions were feeble. Among workers, small-scale trades prevailed and laborers were dispersed within the urban areas. Almost half the nation's workers were still in the countryside, where leftist politics rarely penetrated. Among early members of the PS, many of the workers were artisans or itinerant laborers rather than factory or intensively organized workers. The unionized groups which adhered to the Socialists were seldom former Communists, which indicated that the gulf between anarchist-anarcho-syndicalist and communist laborers persisted under new labels. Above all, the workers who flocked to Grove and the Socialists had traditionally followed middle-class, even military, figures, in some cases the same names now affiliated with the PS.

The populist character of the party, evident in its birth and doctrines, was also seen in the vertical social composition of its membership. Like most Socialist parties competing in elections, the Chileans strove to attract social sectors beyond the laboring class. Given the timidity of peasant mobilization, the weakness of urban labor, and the sudden appearance of the Socialists, recruitment beyond the working sectors had to be particularly successful in Chile. Under these conditions, the level of labor activism in the party was impressive. Poorly integrated social groups such as minimally organized workers, some rebels from the naval uprising, and youth were among the party's members. There was a social gap between the leaders—with their

52. *Bandera Roja*, Oct. 29, 1932; El Congreso, *En defensa*, pp. 116-19; Ellsworth, pp. 12-13; Partido Liberal, *La crisis*, pp. 9-10; Mayorga, "Todos fuimos anarquistas," p. 15; Cruz Salas, pp. 17-18; Hochwald, pp. 56-57; Angell, p. 16.

declared class identification and ideology of eventual proletarian revolution—and the followers of the PS.[53]

Lacking a long period of gestation (for example on a union base), a naturally large and easily mobilizable worker constituency, and a firm ideology, the Socialists built their movement in other ways. The eclectic character of the party facilitated coalition politics, both among social groups and with other parties. The heterogeneous PS was held together by Grove, who encapsulated the ambiguities and dynamism of the movement. *Caudillismo* became a persistent feature of the Socialist Party, never more so than when Matte was hailed as a secular saint and Grove emerged as a folk hero. More than purposefully shifting ideological positions—though this was the result—the masses from 1931 to 1933 swung to a new charismatic leader. According to a later PS senator, "If well it is true that the Socialist Party . . . counted upon intellectual values of the highest order, nonetheless its growth was due in the first place to Grove, to that emotional attraction he exercised over the people. . . ."[54]

Grove's magnetism, more than ideology or class interest, propelled the young party past its Democrat and Communist rivals. Although straightforward and persuasive, with a soldierly air of command, Grove's speaking style could not touch Alessandri's oratory; Grove's charisma stemmed from his daring deeds. Grove's father was a lawyer, a Radical, and a Mason in the Small North; he instilled anticlerical, regionalist, and reformist ideals in his son. As a rising young military student and then officer, Marmaduke led protests against injustices. Essentially a Jacobin and humanist, Grove progressed from *alessandrismo* and *ibañismo* to the protean *socialismo* bubbling out of the ferment of 1932.[55]

Throughout the political skirmishes which convulsed the 1930s, Grove provided the new party's cohesive force. In the process, he reinforced the masses' belief in vindication through the electoral route. Grove was the mystical tool consciously used to galvanize a

53. Ampuero, *La izquierda*, pp. 34-35; Vial Solar, p. 199; Mann, I, pp. 117, 149-51; Bonilla and Glazer, pp. 68-69; Michels, pp. 90-107, 277-98.

54. Chelén, *Trayectoria*, p. 85.

55. Sáez, *Recuerdos*, III, p. 60; Partido Socialista, *Grove, el militar*, pp. 1-7; Vicuña Fuentes, *La tiranía*, I, p. 162; Vergara Montero, *Por rutas*, pp. 141-45; Correa Prieto, pp. 103-10; Grove, *Toda;* Jack Ray Thomas, "The Evolution of a Chilean Socialist: Marmaduke Grove," *Hispanic American Historical Review,* XLVII, no. 1 (Feb., 1967), pp. 22-37; Jack Ray Thomas, "Marmaduke Grove: A Political Biography" (Ph.D. dissertation, Ohio State University, Columbus, 1962); Tito Mundt, *Yo lo conocí* (Santiago, 1965), pp. 190-92; interviews with Grove's children, Hiram and Blanca Elena, Santiago, 1970; Manuel Bedoya, *Grove, su vida, su ejemplo, su obra* (n.p., [1944?]).

mass movement and pave the way for doctrinal penetration. Even the more revolutionary Socialists, who chafed at Grove's populism, usually acknowledged his utility as a unifying symbol and spokesman. Billing Grove as the savior of the downtrodden, the Socialists claimed that his "voice has a humble intonation, a familiar vibration, that evokes in us the voice of the father."[56]

Grove himself was an idealist, but no ideologist. The best evidence is that he never read Marx and never accepted orthodox Marxism. He was more enthusiastic about nationalism and the middle classes than about the international proletariat. Grove thought that class conflict should be avoided, and he believed that classes acted through representatives, not as units. In his opinion, the middle sectors were better prepared than the workers to lead the all-important industrial development of Chile and the accompanying quest for social justice. Some of Grove's ideas—such as forging a mixed economic system —owed a great debt, over the years, to the British Labour Party and to Roosevelt's New Deal. A few of the influences that molded fascists in Italy also found expression in Grove. He agreed with Mazzini's arguments about intellectual constructs only having value as they were expressed in action. In addition, Grove shared the view of Carlyle and others that great leaders, not impersonal economic or class forces, were the prime movers of history. In the PS, a personality cult flourished which portrayed the "leader" as the vehicle of mass aspirations, a concept at odds with more orthodox Marxism. Grove's style, more than his socialism, enthralled a mass audience. Largely through the attraction to Grove, voting socialist became a tradition for many in the lower and even middle classes: "for thousands of citizens, socialism was confused with the person of Marmaduke Grove."[57]

In the 1930s, the party's dependence on *grovismo* provides the major explanation for its extraordinary growth. However, that dependence on personalism stunted the PS's organizational and ideological maturation. Perhaps the Socialist Party was overly reliant on Grove, but without his populist appeal the party might never have existed at all.[58]

Though Grove's charisma was the critical element in the Socialist formula, other key leaders also contributed to the party's success.

56. *Acción*, no. 1 (Oct., 1933), p. 1; *Consigna*, Apr. 6, 1935; Mendoza, *¿Y ahora?*, pp. 179-82; interviews with Charlín, Mandujano, Alejandro Chelén Rojas, and Mario Garay, Santiago, 1970.
57. Jobet, "Origenes," p. 6; Jobet, "Tres semblanzas," pp. 23-28; Thomas, "Marmaduke Grove: A Political Biography," pp. 228-52; Grove, *La relegación*, pp. 10-36; Marmaduke Grove Vallejo, *Reforma agraria* (Santiago, 1939); *Lo que dijo Grove* (Santiago, 1934); Waiss, *El drama*, pp. 24-25; Bicheno, p. 371; Georgina Durand, *Mis entrevistas* (2 vols., Santiago, 1943), II, pp. 238-41.
58. Interview with Astolfo Tapia, Santiago, 1970.

Eugenio Matte, "the true Chilean Robespierre," was the architect and intellect of the PS until his premature death in 1934. Born into the upper strata, Matte had always tried to help the poor, whether as a student, journalist, lawyer, or professor. The PS later compared him to others who, "like Moses and Christ," had sacrificed their high social standing to serve the masses. In his student days, he supported union causes and night classes ("Popular Universities") for workers. Like most of the Socialist founders, he had been thrilled by Alessandri in 1920 and appalled by the conservative coup d'etat in 1924. Matte progressed from Masonic moralizing to greater concern with radical material as well as spiritual reforms, but he eschewed consistent Marxism. Instead, he retained an almost mystical belief in the ability of "renovating forces" to transform Chile overnight. He also argued that an arduous period of industrialization, education, and transition was needed before the workers and Chile would be ready for unadulterated socialism, but he urged the masses to place their faith in that socialism rather than in Christianity. Symbolizing the new spirit of youth, Matte drew many students and idealists to the Socialists. His sudden death at the age of 37 deprived the party of an eloquent, meteoric leader.[59]

The secretary-general of the Socialist Party was Oscar Schnake, a dynamic young orator with an anarchist background. While Grove generated most of the energy publicly, Schnake usually guided the party machinery. During the two years following the birth of the PS, he was frequently in hiding, prison, or exile, where he met Haya de la Torre. One party pamphlet attributed to Schnake the "purity of a lay saint of the revolution" and exhorted the faithful to appreciate "his paternal affection toward the party and toward all its members." A rebellious medical student and coal strike leader in 1919-20, Schnake had helped bring the FECH and the workers together through the IWW. His connections with other Socialist leaders were fortified in 1925 when he joined Eugenio González and Carlos Alberto Martínez in USRACH to help Manuel Hidalgo organize worker demonstrations demanding the ouster of the Altamirano junta and the return of Alessandri. Schnake, a synthesizer and compromiser, passed from the Radicals and then from Santos Salas to ultimately become a Socialist.

59. Matte, "El Programa," pp. 184-94, 395-96; Sáez, *Recuerdos,* III, pp. 128-29; Mundt, p. 213; Mayorga, "París," pp. 4-6; Wilfredo Mayorga, "Caímos por no armar el pueblo," *Ercilla,* no. 1603 (Feb. 23, 1966), pp. 14-15; Partido Socialista, *4 de junio,* p. 3; Natalio Berman B., "Eugenio Matte Hurtado," in Comité Regional del Partido Socialista, pp. 11-14; Julio César Jobet, "Semblanza de Eugenio Matte Hurtado," *Arauco,* no. 15 (Jan.-Feb., 1961), pp. 41-43; Frías Ojeda, pp. 16-17; interview with Charlín, Santiago, 1970; *La Opinión,* Apr. 16, 1933.

Rather than trying to solve doctrinal differences among the Socialists, he pragmatically promoted harmony behind specific goals. Schnake believed that his party's unique contribution and best means of mass mobilization was unifying the middle and lower classes: "unity of purposes (struggle against imperialism and the national oligarchy); unity of social sectors separated until yesterday; unity of action incarnated in a *caudillo*. . . ."[60]

Other middle-class leaders of the party included intellectuals and professionals. Eugenio González was a professor, a Mason, and a past president of the FECH from the 1920 period. Like many Socialist leaders, González had anarchosyndicalist ties and had been exiled by Ibáñez. Ricardo Latcham issued from the same Catholic youth movement which had cradled the Falange, but he chose the Socialists. Latcham was noted for his skills as an author and for his denunciations of North American mining control. Natalio Berman was a doctor with mixed religious and Marxist notions of humanitarianism. A former *alessandrista*, Berman helped launch the PS in Concepción. Another doctor was Salvador Allende Gossens, a minor figure at the time who later rose to great prominence. Allende, himself a Mason, came from a family of lodge leaders, Radicals, anticlericals, and liberal professionals; his brother-in-law was Grove's brother, and the families were close. At the national university in the late 1920s, Allende began identifying with the poor and studying Marxism while living with other medical students from the provinces in working-class slums of Santiago. As vice-president of the FECH and an active participant in the Advance student group protests against Ibáñez in 1931, he was arrested. In 1932 he was inspired by the Socialist Republic and much affected by the death of his father, at whose funeral Allende publicly vowed to dedicate his life to "social struggle." To pursue that goal, he chose the Socialists over the Communists because of the former's freedom from international ties. In 1933, at the age of twenty-four, Allende became one of the youngest founders of the PS in his home of Valparaíso, where he was working for the public health department.[61]

60. Schnake, *Política*, pp. 10-23, 74-79; Schnake, "No somos," pp. 5-6; Mayorga, "Todos fuimos anarquistas," p. 15; Mayorga, "Cuando el PS," pp. 14-15; Frías Ojeda, p. 18; Monreal, p. 229; Vera Riquelme, pp. 208-10; Julio César Jobet, "La personalidad de Oscar Schnake y los primeros años del Partido Socialista," *Arauco*, no. 73 (Feb., 1966), pp. 2-20; U.S., Dept. of State Archives, Santiago, Oct. 29, 1938, 825.00/1085; John Gunther, *Inside Latin America* (New York and London, 1941), p. 253.

61. Natalio Berman B., *Digo lo que pienso; hago lo que digo* (n.p., n.d.); Natalio Berman B., *Berman al servicio del pueblo* (Santiago, 1945); Ricardo A. Latcham, *Chuquicamata, estado yankee* (Santiago, 1926); Julio César Jobet, "La personalidad socialista de Eugenio González Rojas," *Arauco*, no. 42 (July, 1963), pp. 8-11; Eugenio González Rojas, *Hombres*

PS leaders with working-class backgrounds included Carlos Alberto Martínez, a former printer who came from a lower-class family. Martínez was active in mutual-aid and syndicalist societies for workers, often in alliance with students. He helped Recabarren develop the FOCH but left the POS when it turned Communist. Persecuted as a union leader and labor politician, Martínez remained an independent socialist until the Depression. Another laborer, a shoe repairman, was Augusto Pinto. Self-educated, Pinto had been an IWW leader in 1920.[62]

Largely because of their heterogeneity, the Socialists surpassed the other political options presented to the workers in the 1930s. Without resolving the contradictions inherent in the uneasy marriage between Marxism and populism, the Socialists led the leftward movement of the Chilean electorate. They were more personalistic and middle class than the Communists, more Marxist and lower class than the *alessandristas*. The beginnings of national development, seen in urbanization and industrialization, both laid the groundwork for the emergence of the Socialists and placed limits on the party's programs and composition. The electoral shift toward the left and the appearance of the PS helped the workers, over time, play a greater role in Chilean politics, but seldom in leadership positions. More than draining worker support from the ideologically snarled Communists, the Socialists drew laborers away from the Democrats and Alessandri. At the same time, they added new social elements to the Marxist-labeled Left.[63]

In the 1930s, the mixed socialist and populist beginnings of the modern electoral Left bequeathed an equivocal and difficult legacy to the future of mass politics in Chile. Although it was possible the Socialists' populist approach might reduce the chances of class conflict and more radical alternatives in the short run, it might also heighten those chances in the long run. Conceivably, Grove and the PS could have, over the years, used populist tactics to simply break into the multiparty establishment and the bureaucracy or to spread ideological education and construct a more class-based movement. That latter possibility would grow as industrialization proceeded and the labor base available to the Left expanded. In the beginning, the Socialists

(Santiago, 1935); Debray, pp. 63-70; Baltazar Castro, ¿*Me permite una interrupción?* (Santiago, 1962), pp. 137-40, 162; Mayorga, "Todos fuimos anarquistas," p. 15; Mayorga, "La generación," p. 13; Boizard, *La democracia,* p. 145.

62. "Los jefes del socialismo: Carlos Alberto Martínez," pp. 5-9; Mayorga, "Todos fuimos anarquistas," p. 15; Cruz Salas, pp. 15-16.

63. Jobet, *El socialismo chileno,* pp. 9-48; Waiss, *El drama,* pp. 7-24; Weffort, pp. 54-84; Ianni, *Crisis,* pp. 5-7, 50, 82-99, 102-9, 197-205.

had the potential to aid social peace—by funneling the masses into their movement and giving them reforms—or to foment social disruption. The party vacillated between independent, ideological, class politics—emphasized rhetorically—and mass-based, reform coalitions—emphasized in practice. Whether the Socialists would undermine or integrate the existing system, social and economic as well as political, by working within it posed the question of the efficacy of evolutionary means to declared revolutionary ends.[64]

64. Di Tella, pp. 47-74; Waiss, *El drama,* pp. 19-24.

6

The Growth of Chilean Socialism through Coalition Politics, 1933-38

The socialist movement gained popularity as a protest against the conservative Alessandri administration, in office from 1932 to 1938. Relying on the elites, the Right, and extraordinary executive powers, Alessandri enforced political and social order. At the same time, he constrained the military by shuffling commands, retiring conspirators, and rewarding loyalists. At his inauguration, the new president pointedly refused to review the troops; of more significance was his support of the Republican Militia as a check on militarism and leftist agitation. Alessandri made it clear, however, that in his opinion a majority of the officers were honorable and deserved praise. The president's ability to tame the military in this fashion demonstrated the vigor of public antimilitarism. It also showed the firmness of the armed forces' decision to abide by popular opinion and abstain from open politics. Under Alessandri, political stability and economic recovery commenced rapidly, this time with an emphasis on protected industrialization.[1]

Alessandri's National Reconstruction

Although one of the countries hardest hit by the world Depression, Chile rebounded quickly. By 1939, Chilean factories were producing nearly 60% more goods than in 1930. The number of officially registered unemployed fell from 123,200 in December, 1932, to 58,500 in July, 1933, and continued downward thereafter to less than 5,000 in 1936. Above all, national recovery was a result of the revival of the

1. *Hoy*, no. 50 (Nov. 4, 1932), p. 1; Alessandri, *Mensaje* (1933); Alessandri, *Rectificaciones*, pp. 113-58; Alessandri, *Recuerdos*, III, pp. 8-21; Moreno, pp. 159-61; Olivares, *Alessandri*, pp. 128-44; Domingo Amunátegui Solar, *La segunda presidencia de Arturo Alessandri* (Santiago, 1961); Leonidas Bravo Ríos, *Lo que supo un auditor de guerra* (Santiago, 1955), p. 54.

international economy. Despite the government's generally orthodox and austere economic policies, recuperation was facilitated by a few domestic measures of Alessandri and his Finance Minister, Gustavo Ross Santa María, who encouraged manufacturing, construction, and exports. That recovery, however, did not entail solutions to nagging issues such as economic nationalism and distribution. As a result, economic reconstruction calmed politics and kept the conservative parties in the saddle momentarily without stalling the growth of the Left. Through populist nationalist appeals, broad social-political coalitions, and programs promising greater inclusion of the workers in the process of industrialization, the administration's opponents made gains in the 1930s.[2]

The Alessandri government's dealings with foreign interests most disappointed the Left in the areas of mining and utilities. As one of the administration's first acts, it replaced the controversial COSACH with COVENSA, the Chilean Nitrate and Iodine Sales Corporation. This new corporate arrangement brought the Chilean government into marketing operations. But the leftist parties complained because it maintained production and sales primarily (about 60%) in the hands of the owners, the Guggenheims of New York. Moreover, the state was regulating the declining nitrate industry rather than the rising copper producers. Finance Minister Ross's nitrate reorganization guaranteed the government 25% of the gross profits. In turn, those earnings were automatically committed to service on the foreign debt rather than to industrialization or to social welfare for the middle and lower classes.[3]

In addition, the government's opponents criticized Ross's deal with the U.S.-owned Chilean Electric Company for falling short of nationalization. Under pressure from Ross, the company expanded its Chilean operations to provide better service and included nationals on the board of directors. It also granted a small share of profits to the government.[4]

Government critics lambasted Alessandri's treatment not only of foreigners but also of the middle and lower classes. Economic recovery

2. Ellsworth, esp. pp. vii, 1-52, 96-100, 128-65; Thomson, pp. 287-91; Herring, p. 201.

3. "South America III," pp. 158-62; *Chile Pan-American* (Jan., 1933), pp. 1-2; Great Britain, Dept. of Overseas Trade, *Report on Economic* (1936); Zañartu, *El proyecto;* Mann, II, p. 151; Bermúdez, pp. 31-34; Jorge de la Cuadra Poisson, *Magia financiera* (Santiago, 1938), pp. 21-87; Aníbal Mena L., *Fuerte antinacionalismo del gobierno. Delictuoso constitución de la COSACH* (Santiago, 1933); Mariano Riveros Cruz, *La industria salitrera frente al proyecto de ley sobre Corporación de Ventas de Salitre y Yodo* (Santiago, 1933).

4. Herring, pp. 198-204; Partido Radical, *El Partido Radical ante el "acuerdo de caballeros" Ross-Calder* (Santiago, 1936); Julio Dell'Orto Prieto, *Un chileno al servicio de Chile* (Santiago, 1937).

benefited the upper strata most and the workers least. Consequently, the discontent stemming from the Great Depression persisted. Alessandri's restricted state action, constrained by the low level of exports and his financial orthodoxy, failed to satisfy the middle sectors. While monetary devaluation helped Chile respond to the resurgence of the world market, it intensified price inflation at the expense of the salary- and wage-earning groups. The income and employment situation of the middle classes, however, was better than that of labor.[5]

The Alessandri administration also favored the middle classes over labor by enacting protective welfare legislation for white-collar employees in 1937. This provided minimum salaries, unemployment compensation, and retirement benefits far in excess of any granted to blue-collar workers. Reflecting real social distance between "employees" and "workers," this continuing juridical distinction laid the foundation for that gap to widen in the future. The Socialists opposed such discriminatory social legislation as a wedge between the middle and working classes, whom they were trying to unite for political action.[6]

Early Growth of the Socialist Party, 1933-35

The infant Socialist Party grew too fast to integrate new members into a coherent structure. It developed with an entrenched leadership trying to impose discipline on a fluid, inchoate mass base. To attract and unite followers, the party relied on the spontaneous leadership talents of national and local *caudillos*. Despite inherent instability and disorganization at the base of the party, the PS was hierarchical in the sense that all major decisions emanated from a highly centralized, rather authoritarian leadership. Although less socially, ideologically, and organizationally rigid than the Communists, the Socialists also allowed little real democratic participation from the grass roots, a perennial source of grumbling. Theoretically run by "democratic centralism," the PS was dominated at the top by the elected central committee and its secretary-general. Beneath were intermediate regional and sectional committees to pass instructions on down to the tiny "nuclei," or cells, organized by community or place of work, at the bottom of the pyramid. However, seldom did this machinery function as smoothly as intended. A disjunction existed between the elaborately organized high command and its weak lines to volatile local

5. Hirschman, pp. 241-45; Pinto, "Desarrollo," pp. 19-20; Johnson, *Political Change,* pp. 81-82.
6. Cruz Salas, p. 188.

units. Therefore, unstable support from below, poaching by other parties, and Socialist divisions were likely.[7]

The leaders dominated the PS largely through patron-client relationships and their effectiveness in the national electoral system. Within the upper spheres of the party, the ability of Socialist commanders to deliver or deny personal supporters to PS causes promoted divisive *caudillismo* and factionalism. Such patronage relationships were vital to followers seeking favors from the party or the government. In all parties, patron-client linkages were important and increasingly formalized in the 1930s as the state expanded its impact on the lives of all Chileans.[8]

Within the leadership circle, top Socialists jockeyed for power by forming cliques based at least as much on personal as on ideological bonds. Though often sincere, ideological disputes were also—as in any political organization—weapons manufactured to use against opposing intraparty factions. One such internal secret grouping in the 1930s was the anti-Masonic Grand Circle, dominated by dissident student leaders. Another short-lived fraternity was the Bolívar Lodge of the Liberators of America, which forged unity among the party's highest leaders.[9]

The personalistic nature of party leadership favored the wealthier Socialists. Better able to recruit clienteles and to campaign for public offices, men of means naturally came to dominate a party devoted to elections and in need of congressional immunity to shelter its leaders from persecution. While this system facilitated the election of representatives from a party dedicated to the workers, it did not promote the election of many workers themselves. The middle class prevailed among the party's electoral nominees and central committees throughout the 1930s, although worker participation was also significant. In addition, there was some evidence that the PS's congressional representatives tended to be even more dominated by nonworkers than did its central committee. From 1932 to 1937, the party had two workers and six professionals in Congress, compared to seven workers, three employees, and five professionals in the central

7. Cruz Salas, pp. 75-77; *Consigna,* Mar. 30, 1935; Partido Socialista, *Estatutos* (Santiago, 1936); Gil, pp. 290-92; interviews with Garay, Santiago, 1970, 1973.

8. Julio Enrique Guiñez Carrasco, *Interpretación de la evolución social y política de Chile desde 1932 a 1952* (Concepción, Chile, 1963), pp. 101-3; interviews with Chelén and Charlín, Santiago, 1970.

9. Some leaders of the Grand Circle left the PS in the early 1940s to form the short-lived Socialist Workers' Party and then joined the Communists. The Bolívar Lodge tried to forge bonds among the PS, the Communist Left, other Latin American reform parties such as APRA, and sympathetic army officers. Waiss, *El drama,* pp. 26-28.

committee. School teachers (mainly from primary and secondary schools rather than universities), professionals, and white-collar employees always outnumbered wage laborers or artisans on the central committee. In the 1935 municipal elections, teachers, lawyers, journalists, small businessmen, and employees were joined on the PS lists by smaller numbers of tailors, railroad workers, manual laborers, and union leaders.[10]

Recruitment of more followers from the middle classes perpetuated the social makeup of the PS. Doctors, lawyers, and teachers continued to join the party. Its Socialist Youth Federation (FJS), founded in 1934, attracted some urban and rural laborers and even named a worker as its first secretary-general. Nevertheless, the FJS's greatest impact was among urban middle-class students, who won the presidency of the FECH for the PS in 1936.[11] Some small farmers in southern Chile also rallied to the party, mainly because of its defense of the family farm against latifundia concentrated in the central regions.[12] Economic recovery and industrialization, as well as the gradual return of foreign investments, swelled both the middle- and lower-class pools to be tapped by the Socialists, especially in the growing cities.[13]

While retaining their predominantly middle-class leadership, the Socialists became more heavily working class in composition throughout the 1930s. In contrast, the Communists were increasing their percentage of middle-class leaders and followers. The Socialists' union policy favored the amalgamation of the organized middle- and lower-class groups. Partly because the PS was less tightly organized and more dominated by its congressional leadership than was the PC, there always existed a wider "division between union and party" in the Socialist camp. Just as the PS grew electorally more by taking voters away from older parties than by mobilizing new participants, so it grew in the labor movement mainly by outbidding old leaders, such as the Democrats and anarchosyndicalists, rather than by creating new unions. One of the Socialists' first conquests was the short-lived National Syndical Confederation (CNS), formed in 1934 mainly out of existing legal unions from the Ibáñez years; by 1935 it claimed

10. Chelén, *Trayectoria*, pp. 184-92; *Consigna*, Apr., 1935; Jobet, *El socialismo chileno*, p. 24; interviews with Mandujano and Charlín, Santiago, 1970; Cruz Salas, pp. 11-12; Hochwald, pp. 57-58.
11. *Consigna*, 1934; Raúl Ampuero Díaz, *La juventud en la frente del pueblo* (Santiago, 1939).
12. *Consigna*, Dec. 21, 1935.
13. U.S., Dept. of State Archives, Santiago, Nov. 4, 1938, pp. 6-8, 825.00/1090; Faletto, Ruiz, and Zemelman, pp. 54-60.

some 60,000 adherents, probably an exaggeration. In the 1930s the weakness of clear ideological or class politics among laborers helped open the way to dominance of the worker movement by largely middle-class Socialists.[14]

The process of economic and social modernization which expanded the Socialists' potential constituency in the cities failed to make much of an impact in the countryside. Despite some rural unionization and strike campaigns by the Left in 1933-34, the peasants remained the least politically mobilized portion of the lower class. Although they pioneered with promises of agrarian reform, neither the Socialists nor the Communists broke sharply with the past leftist tradition of restricting most changes to the cities. They did not mount a frontal assault on the landed elites. Socialist organizers complained that peasants were far harder to recruit than urban workers and found rural laborers much more likely to still be dispersed, illiterate, and submissive to conservative bosses. Apparently the few peasant supporters attracted by the Socialists were poorly organized and believed that Grove would give them land. Hidalgo's Communist Left also later brought into the PS a small contingent of rural workers. Even when they incorporated some peasant groups, the Socialists, like the other parties, failed to develop leaders who were peasants.[15]

The continuing Socialist recruitment from both the middle and lower classes produced some social tensions within the party. A few working-class members even complained that the dominant intellectuals and professionals were exploiting the PS for personal gain. In response, the party urged its "bourgeois" members to be less aloof toward party regulations, doctrines, functions, and worker members. By the same token, the PS cautioned the workers that busy middle- and upper-class Socialists could not be expected to spend as much time with internal affairs. Such Socialists, it was argued, were indispensable because of their training. Therefore, they should be trusted despite their roots in higher social spheres.[16]

The Socialists also expanded by fanning out from the capital city to the underprivileged regions. In the process, they became a truly national party, although still mainly urban. Fragmentary evidence indicates that the PS developed much the same social composition in the outlying provinces as in Santiago, though with fewer workers in

14. *Acción* (Oct., 1933), p. 2; Jobet, *Recabarren*, pp. 159-61; Morris, *Elites*, pp. 258-59; Cruz Salas; Angell, pp. 103, 121.
15. *Acción*, Apr. 9, 1933; U.S., Dept. of State Archives, Santiago, Apr. 10, 1934, pp. 2-3, 825.00/839; Partido Socialista, *A los camaradas de Bío-Bío* (Los Angeles, Chile, 1934), pp. 1-3.
16. *Consigna*, Dec. 21, 1935.

the early years. While playing on regionalist sentiments, the PS argued that socialism, rather than the decentralization within the capitalist system championed by conservative groups, was the solution to provincial problems.[17]

In the far north, the Socialists began luring middle- and lower-class followers away from the entrenched Radicals and Communists. The party's greatest successes there came among industrial and, gradually, mining workers.[18] In the far south, the Socialists scored faster gains because those newly occupied zones were not yet firmly controlled by the older parties. In provinces such as Magallanes and Aysén, the PS made inroads against regionalist candidates by stressing the special problems of local laborers. The party also ran workers as candidates in municipal and congressional elections and thereby established a special following among meat-packers, farm laborers, and colonists as well as a broader following as defenders of provincial interests. As in other provinces, a regional strongman and his local clientele helped make Magallanes a permanent bailiwick for the PS.[19]

From these social and regional bases, the PS early entered multiparty coalitions. Constant internal party debates raged over the ideological, social, and tactical justifications for such alliances. Most Socialists, however, considered pacts, at least transitory ones, necessary to win elections, defend themselves against political harassment, and amplify their voice in Congress. Their first congressional coalition was the Bloc of the Left. It existed in 1934-35, prefiguring the Popular Front. Dominated by the Socialists, the Bloc included the Democratics (the more reformist half of the divided Democrat Party), the Communist Left, and a splinter group from the left wing of the Radicals and had hopes of winning the whole Democrat and Radical parties away from the Alessandri government.[20]

Intraparty opposition to such political-social coalitions was a leading cause of the first, miniscule split in the Socialist Party. In 1934 a small group of Marxist revolutionary intellectuals in the Santiago branch of the PS began arguing for violent, proletariat revolution instead of class coalitions and electoral gradualism. They denounced "populist parties," meaning Nazis and *apristas,* as too nationalist, corporatist, and merely reformist. Decrying tendencies toward populism within

17. *Acción,* July 8, 1933; Partido Socialista, *Boletín Socialista* (1936); *El Socialista* (1932-34); *Consigna,* June 22, 1935.
18. Lucy Casali Castillo, "Los partidos populares como expresión del norte de Chile," *Occidente,* año XIV, no. 121 (Nov.-Dec., 1959), pp. 23-29.
19. *El Socialista* (1935); *El Socialista* (1938); *El Mercurio,* Apr. 9, 1935; interview with Charlín, Santiago, 1970; interview with Barría, Santiago, 1973.
20. Cruz Salas, pp. 288-89.

the PS, these radical writers complained that middle-class opportunists and demagogues were stifling their attempts at ideological
purification of the party through democratic dialogue. These dissenters, known internally as the Revolutionary Socialist Opposition,
maintained close connections with the Communist Left. Expelled
from the PS in 1935, the intellectual rebels formed a tiny vanguard
group dubbed the Socialist Left. In 1938, they joined with a handful of
dissidents from the Communist Left, after Hidalgo's group joined the
PS (1936-37), to found the Trotskyist Revolutionary Worker's Party
(POR), which affiliated with the Fourth International. Led by municipal workers and intellectuals, the microscopic POR circulated on the
fringes of left-wing politics for decades thereafter. In 1934-35, the
regular PS charged those middle-class intellectuals with using the
abrasive slogan of "workerism" to gain support from lower-class
Socialists for their personal ambitions.[21]

Although the Socialists established their viability as a national party
from 1933 to 1935, they were not yet a major electoral power. They
won some by-elections, notably Grove's victory in the race for Matte's
vacated senate seat in 1934. In the 1935 nationwide municipal elections, however, the Socialists garnered less than 2% of the votes. Their
best showing of all came in Magallanes. Municipal contests, the only
ones where voters included women and foreigners, who both dispro-
portionately favored more conservative candidates, underestimated
potential PS strength in congressional or presidential elections.
Moreover, government persecution and faulty party organization
hindered PS effectiveness. The Socialists themselves estimated that
only about 20% of their followers were registered to vote. Worse,
many of their supporters were illiterate and therefore denied the
franchise. After the disappointing results in 1935, the party devoted
itself more to electoral work, which would pay off in future balloting.[22]

Throughout the 1930s, the Socialists pinned most of their hopes for
attracting the masses on the intentionally mythical, symbolic, colorful

21. *Acción Socialista*, Apr.-July, 1934; *Consigna*, Apr. 20, 1935; Cruz Salas, pp. 52-53,
61-62, 78.
22. Only 8% of the population voted in 1935, roughly 5% for the Right and 3% for
the Left. While the Conservatives and Liberals scored slight gains, the Radicals and
minor parties ran poorly. The PS vote pattern was mixed, showing some victories or
high percentages in Santiago, the distant provinces, mining communities, urban districts, and even a few scattered rural zones. From incomplete local returns, it appears
that the party ran worst in the central and southern regions dominated by latifundia.
The Left expressed dismay at the female voting pattern. Chile, Dirección General de
Estadística, *Política* (1938), p. 1; *Consigna*, Apr. 13 and Apr. 20, 1935; *El Mercurio*, Apr.
8-9, 1935; Chile-American Association, pp. 1-3, in U.S., Dept. of State Archives, Santiago, Apr., 1935, 825.00/882.

figure of Grove. Justifying this populist emphasis on a militaristic, daring "leader," one PS writer in 1935 argued that it was necessary to provide singular command for the "revolution" and to win the loyalty of the lower classes: "The mentality of the common people is simple. It is always stirred by that which it understands, by that which excites its emotions, and by that which tends to satisfy quickly its most burdensome needs." Along with more mundane as well as more ideological appeals, this paternalistic approach expanded the party's following.[23]

Communist Popular-Front Initiatives, 1935-36

Dismayed at their inability to compete successfully with the Socialists, the Chilean Communists began suggesting more flexible doctrinal and social strategies in 1933. The Latin American Conference of Communist Parties in 1934 proposed heterogeneous alliances with reform parties. In this transition toward the popular-front strategy, the Chilean PC in 1934-35 called for a "united front" of peasants and the proletariat against fascism. Nevertheless, in April, 1935, the party still officially preferred "economic and political strikes, mass battles and actions, guerrilla struggles, insurrection" to electoral-congressional methods of gaining influence. Only when the Comintern officially endorsed the popular-front policy did the Communists, in late 1935, begin knitting that coalition together in Chile. It demanded cooperation with reformers from "the petty bourgeoisie and the progressive national bourgeoisie" instead of doctrinaire, independent preparation for revolution.[24]

Conditions within Chile were ripe for the popular-front approach. Repression by the Alessandri government, more than the threat of full-blown fascism, made alliances of convenience attractive to the Communists. Above all, a popular front offered the PC a way to overcome its weakness among the workers and the electorate at large.[25]

The adoption of the popular-front formula produced changes in Communist Party ideology, social composition, tactics, and political fortunes for decades to come. Their new devotion to building an electoral machine to deliver votes to themselves or their allies caused

23. *Consigna*, Apr. 6, 1935.
24. Partido Comunista, *Hacia la formación de un verdadero partido de clase* (Santiago, 1933); *Frente Único*, 1934-35; *Principios* (1933-34); La Comisión de Agit. Prop., pp. 3-41; Bureau, pp. 18-38; Cruz Salas, pp. 32, 80, 109, 265-97; Ramírez, pp. 12-14; George Dimitroff, *¡Frente popular en todo el mundo!* (Santiago, 1936).
25. Eudocio Ravines, *La gran estafa* (2nd ed., Santiago, 1954), pp. 133-99; Unión Social de Chile, *Procedimientos comunistas para obtener adaptos a su causa* (Santiago, 1933), pp. 3-7; Fernández C., pp. 46-74; González Díaz, *La lucha*, pp. 9-34.

the PC constituency to soar from barely 2,000 in 1931 to over 53,000 by 1941. In relative terms, the party became more populistic. Communists joined many Socialists in embracing the previously scorned doctrine that a proletariat, socialist revolution had to await a "bourgeois," democratic, industrial revolution in "semi-feudal" Chile. Beginning in 1935-36, the PC identified its program with Chilean multiclass interests by emphasizing national economic modernization over social conflict.[26]

The appeal of the Communists' more moderate, nationalistic program attracted new allies and party members from social strata above the worker level. While retaining its worker-dominated composition, the PC now added intellectuals, students, professionals, white-collar employees, merchants, lesser industrialists, and even middle-class women as sympathizers and members. Even a handful of upper-class Chileans joined or secretly funded the party, some for idealistic reasons and some to provide insurance against labor conflicts. These middle- to upper-class converts and contacts brought the Communists greater political legitimacy.[27]

Although the PC now restrained labor militance and strikes in order to court higher social groups and less-radical parties, it also made gains with the workers. Apparently many blue-collar Communists accepted the argument that they should sacrifice immediate material benefits for themselves in favor of later rewards through victories for the Popular Front. In the mid-1930s the Communists began winning the loyalty or at least cooperation of labor leaders formerly independent or tied to the Radicals, Democrats, or Socialists. The party's ability to provide financial and legal advice, deals with the Ministry of Labor and the bureaucracy, and electoral leverage expanded its influence in the worker movement far beyond official membership.[28]

Within the party, some working-class Communist leaders resented newer arrivals from the higher social spheres. In contrast to the Socialists, however, the worker group or its representatives always kept the upper hand in the PC. At times, middle-class Communists were reprimanded for excessive independence from the proletariat. Even Secretary-General Contreras Labarca depended upon the party segment more closely associated with the workers.[29]

26. Elías Lafertte and Carlos Contreras Labarca, *Los comunistas, el Frente Popular y la independencia nacional* (Santiago, 1937); Ravines, pp. 167-99; Cruz Salas, pp. 32, 80, 109-10, 265-97; Boizard, *Historia*, pp. 134-35.

27. Marta Vergara, *Memorias de una mujer irreverente* (Santiago, 1961), pp. 93-130; Ravines, pp. 167-99.

28. Ravines, pp. 178-85.

29. Vergara, pp. 109-55.

The Communists' approach to their prospective allies was to win over a leadership clique within each party. Then they bolstered that faction's arguments for the Popular Front by supplying votes to its candidates.[30] The Communists' ability to deliver worker votes, even to conservative Radicals, was demonstrated in the 1936 by-election for senator from two southern provinces, the first victory for the Front. This success convinced many wavering Radicals of the advantages of aligning with the Marxists. The Communists and Socialists produced enough leftist votes to elect a Radical millionaire wheat grower, Dr. Cristóbal Sáenz Cerda, senator. Ironically, the defeated government candidate was a self-made Democrat who lacked the aristocratic name and inherited wealth of his Marxist-backed opponent.[31]

Forging the Popular Front Party Coalition

The Communists commenced construction of the Popular Front by appealing to both the humanitarianism and the opportunism of the Radical Party's left wing, which was centered in Santiago. Even more conservative, older, landowning Radicals—who usually opposed the Front—increasingly heeded Communist overtures as Alessandri awarded the best patronage positions to the Conservatives and reunited Liberals. By promoting a Radical over a Socialist as the Front's presidential nominee, the Communists increased the Radicals' ardor and the coalition's prospects for electoral success; the PC could thereby gain access to power without fearing that the new president might favor the PS over them or might be so reformist as to undercut them with the workers.[32]

As the largest reform party in Chile, the Radicals were the key element in the Popular Front. They provided respectability, experience, organization, voters, and money. Although rooted in the middle sectors, the party gave the Front a link with the upper class, mainly through its landed right wing. The Front, a multiparty coalition rather

30. Carlos Contreras Labarca, *Unidad para defender la victoria* (Santiago, 1938), p. 17; Chamudes, pp. 77-79; Ravines, pp. 167-77.
31. Luis Mandujano Tobar, *Luis Mandujano Tobar, candidato a senador por Cautín y Bío-Bío* (Santiago, n.d.); U.S., Dept. of State Archives, Santiago, Apr. 28, 1936, pp. 1-4, 825.00/922.
32. Some of the more adamant Radical opponents, frequently from the provinces, were never persuaded to coalesce with the Communists and instead formed the short-lived Doctrinaire Radical Party to back the government against the Front in 1938. Partido Radical, *Convención extraordinaria del Partido Radical* (Santiago, 1937); Partido Radical Doctrinario, *Manifiesto del Partido Radical Doctrinario a los radicales del país* (Santiago, 1938); Enrique Burgos Varas, *A los radicales de mi patria* (Santiago, 1938); Carlos Contreras Labarca, *El programa del Frente Popular debe ser realizado* (Santiago, [1940?]), pp. 35-37; Stevenson, pp. 64-75; Halperin, pp. 47-49; *La Hora*, 1936-37.

than one mammoth populist party stretching from the urban workers to the rural aristocrats, wove the disparate elements of Chilean politics together.[33]

Like many Radicals, some Socialists were wary of the Popular Front. Initially the Socialists preferred to build leftist unity on their own Bloc of the Left rather than the Communists' Popular Front. They were leery of the Front because of Communist raids on their followers and because of the likely preponderance of the Radicals.[34] The PS wanted to pull middle-class reformers over to socialism, not consign it to their tutelage. Reluctant Socialists warned that the workers and peasants might not be "mature" enough politically to withstand the seductions of middle-class electoral alliances. They cautioned that joining the Front might kill the hope of uniting the masses within the PS.[35]

Led by Schnake and the moderates, the most ardent Socialist proponents of the Front were concentrated in Santiago. They argued that coalescing the workers with the middle class was not unduly risky. They claimed that Latin American parties like themselves, for example the APRA in Peru and the PNR (National Revolutionary Party) in Mexico, were internal "popular fronts" before the multiparty formula was proposed. At the same time, these Socialists conceded that the Popular Front would not produce real socialism. Nevertheless, they praised the coalition as a necessary vehicle for avoiding worse alternatives. In their view, it promised to achieve incremental reforms for the workers until revolutionary change became more possible. Some Socialists, as well as Radicals, were inspired to emulate European fronts in the decade. Furthermore, the PS leadership hoped that the party could grow through affiliation with the Front and thus eventually carry the coalition beyond reformism to genuine socialism. In the final analysis, the Socialist decision to enter the Front rested on the pragmatic electoral realization that their party was incapable of defeating the Right single-handedly.[36]

The Socialists' grudging acceptance of the Popular Front led to modifications in their program. From 1935 on, the party's public pronouncements and behavior became less overtly Marxist and revolutionary. Ironically, its leadership at the same time encompassed

33. Palma, *Historia,* pp. 173-78; Ernesto Loyola Acuña, *La verdad en marcha* (Talca, Chile, 1938), pp. 62-63.
34. Partido Socialista, *La línea,* pp. 21-22; *Consigna,* May 1 and Sept. 7, 1935; Cruz Salas, pp. 78-110, 265-94.
35. *Consigna,* May 9, 1936; de Petris, p. 115; Waiss, *El drama,* pp. 20-24.
36. Schnake, *Política,* pp. 59-96; *Frente Único,* 1934-35; *Consigna,* Feb. 1, Mar. 14, and Nov. 14, 1936; Jobet, *El socialismo chileno,* pp. 33-37; Chelén, *Trayectoria,* pp. 92-95; Fernández C., pp. 47-73; Thomas, "Marmaduke Grove: A Political Biography," pp. 237-80; Luis Zúñiga, *El Partido Socialista en la política chilena* (Santiago, 1938), pp. 15-27.

more and more orthodox Marxist thinkers, particularly with the influx of younger recruits and of former members of Hidalgo's Communist Left in 1936-37. Like the regular Communists, the PS's increased emphasis on democracy over socialism, nationalism over class struggle, and social reforms over redistribution of property and power was designed to pull the middle classes away from the grasp of the Right or fascism. For example, previously strong Socialist demands for state expropriation of latifundia and foreign mineral holdings were muffled as the 1930s progressed.[37]

Although increasingly committed to electoral mobilization and multiparty bargaining, the Socialists retained the theoretical possibility of armed struggle. The party's declaration of adherence to the Front cautioned that bourgeois democracy was only a temporarily useful instrument which could not lead to ultimate power for the proletariat. Since the Socialists did not seriously prepare to seize power with violent means, the threat served chiefly to keep their ideological aspirations alive, burnish their revolutionary luster, and compensate the more leftist party members. It also established the potential of retaliation in case the opposition tried to deny their electoral victories.[38] As Grove said, "To the ballot boxes or to arms!"[39] Socialist Deputy Carlos Alberto Martínez affirmed in 1937 that "we fight by every means ... by legal means if sufficient; by revolution if necessary."[40]

As a result of participation in the Popular Front and greater attention to standard party and electoral recruitment practices, the Socialist Party grew rapidly. From a few hundred party branches throughout Chile up to 1935, the PS ballooned to 1,500 units in 1936 and to 5,000 in 1937, aided by the Popular Front congressional campaigns. Meanwhile the Socialist Youth Federation soared from 1,000 chapters in 1935 to 3,500 in 1937, nearly 9,000 in 1938 with the presidential victory of the Front, and 12,000 by 1939.[41]

Along with some minor parties, the new Confederation of Chilean Workers (CTCH) also joined the Front. Prior to the founding of the CTCH in 1936 as a by-product of Popular Front unity, Chilean unions were split into three main camps. From over 100,000 purported members in the 1920s, the Communists' FOCH had been decimated, leaving a residue mainly among miners in nitrates and coal. The even

37. Partido Socialista, *Programa* (Santiago, 1936); Schnake, *Política*, pp. 29-49; Cruz Salas, p. 114.
38. Jobet, *El socialismo chileno*, pp. 33-37.
39. *Consigna*, Mar. 14, 1936.
40. Quoted in Cruz Salas, p. 266.
41. Ampuero, *La juventud*, p. 37.

coal. The even weaker anarchosyndicalist General Confederation of
Workers (CGT) maintained fewer than 6,000 members, primarily in
construction and printing trades in Santiago. The third major group
was composed of the legal and new unions in the mushrooming
National Syndical Confederation, which was strongest among industrial laborers and white-collar employees; the CNS was heavily dominated by the Socialists. In addition, there were significant unaligned
unions, such as the bakers and railroad workers, also debilitated first
by Ibáñez and then by the Depression.[42] In the 1930s this dispersed
union movement gained strength despite government opposition,
rather than under extensive state tutelage as Ibáñez had envisioned.
According to the best estimates, the number of unions grew from 421
in 1930 to 433 in 1932, 549 in 1933, 635 in 1935, and 1,888 in 1940.
During the same years, membership, at least on paper, increased from
55,000 to 56,000 to 69,000 to 78,000 to 162,000. In other words, the
number of unions and their members more than tripled from 1930 to
1940. Most of that growth took place in the cities and only to a much
lesser extent in the mines and the countryside. In the process, these
unions developed closer ties with leftist political parties than with
government offices. Their gradual growth and institutionalization in
the thirties were facilitated by the umbrella of the CTCH. It united
lower- and middle-class unions. The new confederation incorporated
the FOCH, the CNS, the Association of Chilean Employees, most
independents, and even a few peasant unions, although the tiny CGT
rejected affiliation.[43]

The CTCH augmented labor unity but diminished labor militance.
Initially the confederation's major purpose was to promote Popular
Front electoral victories, for which it restrained worker demands and
strikes. Instead of echoing older FOCH demands for revolution
against capitalism, the CTCH's 1936 declaration called for industrialization, a more socially progressive welfare regime, and antifascist
coalitions with the middle strata. Since fascism was not a paramount
threat in Chile, these coalitions were actually more important for the
growth of the leftist parties against the traditional Right, a logical
objective in light of the rules of the national political system and the
labor code. Indeed, most of the CTCH leaders were politicians whose
first loyalty was to their party, and in the 1930s the CTCH produced
more gains for the Socialists and Communists than for its worker

42. *Consigna*, June 1, 1935; *Acción* (Oct., 1933), p. 2; Thomson, p. 286; Heredia,
pp. 11-63.

43. Jobet, *Recabarren*, pp. 159-64; Angell, pp. 7-8, 40-42, 108-9; Morris and
Oyaneder, pp. 15-25; Jorge Barría, *El movimiento obrero en Chile* (Santiago, 1971),
pp. 85-89.

members. Within the confederation, the Socialists held a slender majority and the secretary-generalship.[44] Through the CTCH and other avenues, many workers derived benefits and joined party leaders in helping launch the Popular Front. In particular, government repression of a major strike by railroad workers in 1936, which included reprisals against the leftist press and parties, sparked the final solidification of the Popular Front.[45]

The Masons also helped weld the Front together. Leading Masons from the Communists, the Socialists, and the Radicals were principal draftsmen of the coalition; and the Front nominated a prominent Mason, Pedro Aguirre Cerda, for the presidency, even though he had scant public following outside the lodges.[46]

In the mid-1930s the Grand Master of the Chilean Masons promoted prudent reform coalitions as an antidote to revolutionary ferment. His view coincided with that of many Radicals, who believed that their participation in the Front could pacify social discontent and the Marxists more efficiently than could coercion by Alessandri or Ross. They argued that their party "within the Left, is called upon to discharge the role of a regulating force, one which makes possible the desired transformation by means that preserve democratic rights and avoid social explosion. . . ."[47] The Grand Master's reform proposals also reflected Radical thought and presaged the Popular Front platform. For example, he advocated secular education, limited controls on foreign enterprises, agricultural colonization, respect for civil liberties, and state protection for efficient national industries. In urging these reforms, the Masonic leader claimed to speak for both the middle and lower classes and the provinces against the Santiago-based regime of Alessandri. The Grand Master blamed the government's conservatism, mistakes, and harshness for the growth of extremism and communism. Therefore he implored Radicals, Socialists, and even progressive, younger Liberals to set aside their doctrinal differences in the cause of unity.[48]

Predictably, the Popular Front was organized through a network

44. *Claridad,* Apr. 10 and Apr. 15, 1938; Contreras, *Unidad,* pp. 16-18; Vitale, *Historia,* pp. 18-20, 73; Morris, *Elites,* pp. 236-63; Stevenson, pp. 71-75; Angell, pp. 108-22.

45. Bermúdez, pp. 41-50; *Frente Popular,* 1936-40.

46. Boizard, *Historia,* pp. 143-48; Bonilla and Glazer, pp. 92, 136; Vicuña Fuentes, *La tiranía,* I, pp. 42-44, 146-48, 178-215; Mayorga, "París," pp. 4-6; Olivares, *Ibáñez,* p. 61.

47. *Hoy,* no. 278 (Mar. 18, 1937), p. 10.

48. Gran Logia de Chile, *Tercera conferencia dada por el serenísimo gran maestro . . .* (Santiago, [1935?]); Gran Logia de Chile, *Cuarta conferencia dada por el serenísimo gran maestro . . .* (Santiago, [1935?]).

of party leaders far more than as any outgrowth of demands or initiative from the masses. Neither did it really integrate the middle and lower classes within the movement. The Communists and Socialists expressed regret that the Front was the product of classic political bargaining and *caudillismo* rather than "conscious" mass action to which the parties responded. On the other hand, it was a step beyond earlier populism. Now the leaders were taking the workers more into account and offering them concrete programs as well as flashy slogans and symbols.[49]

The leadership of the Front's national executive committee was placed in the hands of the Radicals, the largest member party.[50] They also had the most influence on the coalition's compromise program. To reach a minimal consensus, the Marxist members moved more toward the right than the non-Marxists did toward the left. By doing this, the Marxists defined themselves more as conciliatory democratic parties pursuing populist policies.[51]

The official program of the Popular Front was watered down from an earlier draft by the CTCH. The confederation's blueprint had also been temperate, listing higher wages and production as its top priorities, but it had leaned more toward state socialism and economic nationalism. For example, CTCH calls for suspension of payment on the foreign debt became Popular Front suggestions for reduction of payments.[52]

Despite the populist slogan of "Bread, Roof, and Overcoat," the program of the Popular Front, and even the Socialist Party, was dedicated more to state planning for modernizing production than to redistribution. Front declarations stressed recovering natural resources, promoting industrialization, and updating agriculture with a modicum of land reallocation. These goals might have been better represented by the slogan "Copper, Factories, and Land."[53]

The Front's economic program for state-induced industrialization united the middle- and lower-class groups and parties, despite the danger of tariff protection inflating consumer prices. The economic elites could believe that welfare for the workers would increase production and consumption. The workers could believe that welfare for the industrialists would raise employment, wages, and independence

---

49. Partido Comunista, *Ricardo Fonseca* (Santiago, [1952?]), pp. 83-84; *Consigna*, May 22, 1937.

50. *Reglamentos del Frente Popular* (Santiago, 1937).

51. U.S., Dept. of State Archives, Santiago, Oct. 29, 1938, 825.00/1085; Cruz Salas, pp. 268-69.

52. *Claridad*, Apr. 10 and Apr. 15, 1938.

53. Boizard, *Historia*, pp. 148-49.

from foreign capital.[54] In turn, catching up with the more industrialized West was broadcast as part of a larger campaign of economic
nationalism. More leftist Radicals echoed the Marxists in urging the
nationalization of some foreign holdings, public utilities, latifundia,
and basic industries. Although the program's details were hazy, the
slogan "Chile for the Chileans" capsulized the Front's emphasis on
nationalism rather than class conflict.[55] The more moderate supporters of the Front viewed such economic nationalism, designed to
recover more of the national wealth for Chile, in mild terms: "The
Popular Front is acting within the limits of the capitalist economy and
the formulas that it proposes are, also, of the capitalist order. . . . we
are not proposing a socialized economy; we are seeking a solution to
the problem of imperialism within the very rules . . . of the capitalist
system."[56]

The Front's social reforms were expected to flow from these
economic changes. Although expressed in generalities, the program
promised better incomes, housing, health, and education. In the
main, the Front repeated promises heard since World War I. It called
for greater attention to regional as well as social grievances, especially
when campaigning in the distant provinces, and vowed to give underprivileged groups not only enhanced material benefits but also expanded participation in national decision making. For example, it
proposed "direct participation of the working class" in managing
government agencies concerned with labor.[57] In most respects, however, observers agreed that "the platform of the Popular Front is
sufficiently vague so that the Conservative Party itself could operate
under it and later point with pride to its well-kept promises."[58]

Test of the Popular Front: 1937 Congressional Elections

The 1937 congressional contests were the first major test of strength
between the two increasingly polarized political camps. In their more
flamboyant propaganda, the government forces portrayed their conflict with the Popular Front as "two civilizations that confront each
other: the ferocious and bloody mongol directed from Moscow and
the Christian. . . ."[59] By 1937, the electorate was numerically nearly a

54. Cruz Salas, pp. 125, 154-55.
55. Partido Radical, *El Partido Radical ante,* pp. 3-10; González Videla; Héctor
Arancibia Laso, *La doctrina radical* (Santiago, 1937).
56. *El imperialismo,* p. 56.
57. Schnake, *Política,* p. 26; Aquiles Concha, *A mis amigos y correligionarios de la
provincia de Atacama* ([Santiago?], [1937?]); Enrique Turri, *Frente Popular* (n.p., n.d.).
58. U.S., Dept. of State Archives, Santiago, Oct. 29, 1938, p. 4, 825.00/1085.
59. *El Diario Ilustrado,* Mar. 2 and Mar. 5-8, 1937; U.S., Dept. of State Archives,
Santiago, Feb. 17, 1937, pp. 2-6, 825.00/975, Mar. 10, 1937, pp. 1-3, 825.00/980.

third larger than in 1932. Eighty percent of the registered voters cast ballots for congressional deputies, compared with 76% in 1932. Despite inflation, shortages, and the emergence of the Front, the Right retained majorities in both houses of Congress and made slight electoral advances.[60]

The political extremes, the Conservatives and Liberals at one end and the Socialists and Communists at the other, gained in the 1937 elections. The Conservatives and Liberals combined won 42% of the votes for deputies. Adding probable supporters from minor parties gave the Right a slender electoral and congressional majority. The Right's greatest strength remained in the central zones with high concentrations of latifundia. Marxist gains, highlighted by a major triumph in Santiago, were the only consolation for the Popular Front. Socialists (11%) and Communists (4%) both approximately doubled their 1932 percentages. Meanwhile, minor centrist groups and, most significant, the Radicals did not run as well as expected. From being the largest single party in Chile in 1932, the Radicals slid to third place, with 18.6% of the ballots, in 1937. In accord with past electoral patterns, the Radicals scored best in the outlying provinces, especially in the south. In spite of post-election doubts, the Radicals stayed within the Front as the best hope of reviving their ebbing electoral fortunes.[61]

Pleased with their 1937 gains, the Socialists redoubled their commitment to electoral pursuits. A good part of their success was attributed to Grove's having stumped for candidates for months.[62] Over 70% of the Socialist house and senate candidates were apparently from the middle sectors or above. They included doctors, dentists, lawyers, teachers, merchants, and white-collar employees, and also officers and lawyers for white- and blue-collar unions. A few candidates were recently nationalized Spaniards. Several nominees had been jailed during the earlier fight to topple Ibáñez. One Socialist contestant was president of the Evangelical Federation of Social Action; he urged his religious followers to join the PS. From the working class, the party fielded such nominees as mechanics, typographers, a miner who had been arrested during the 1931 Tragic Christmas, and a laborer in a refrigerated meat-packing plant in Magallanes.[63]

The Socialists' highest voting percentage came in Magallanes (57%),

60. Chile, Dirección General de Estadística, *Política* (1938), pp. 1, 5; U.S., Dept. of State Archives, Santiago, Mar. 20, 1937, pp. 1-2, 825.00/984.

61. Chile, Dirección General de Estadística, *Política* (1938), pp. 1, 5; U.S., Dept. of State Archives, Santiago, Mar. 17, 1937, 825.00/983, Mar. 18, 1937, 825.00/987.

62. *Consigna*, Mar. 13 and Mar. 20, 1937.

63. *Consigna*, Mar. 1, 1937; *El Diario Ilustrado*, Mar. 9, 1937.

where they defeated a regionalist candidate with their appeals to the provincial working class. Their second highest percentage (26%) came in the three urban departments of Santiago province, where they led all entries within the Popular Front slate. The PS also outpolled its national percentage in the northern mining zones and in other urban clusters such as Valparaíso and Concepción. By contrast, the party's worst showings generally came in the central agrarian provinces between Santiago and the far south.[64]

Following their success in the 1937 balloting, the Socialists began to receive a stream of new members, which would become a flood after the 1938 presidential victory. The PS tried to weed out the opportunists from the idealists to keep its aura as a fresh alternative to the older clientelistic parties. This influx aggravated growing pains and internal tensions. Party leaders even charged that some of the new arrivals were Communist infiltrators trying to foment divisions.[65]

The Communists' official 1937 figure of 4% of the votes was still confined to a very few areas. In the rural districts and even in Santiago, the party remained extremely weak. In roughly two-thirds of Chile's electoral departments, the PC tallied no official votes. It was estimated that over 40% of the Communists' national ballots were cast by longshoremen and factory workers in Valparaíso and Santiago. Within the capital city, the Communists' only votes (7%) came from the electoral district in which most of the factory workers lived; in the same district, the Socialists won 23%, far more than any other party. Another 40% of the PC's national vote total, as nearly as can be determined, came from nitrate and copper workers, principally in the far north; there, the Communists overpowered the Socialists. The remainder of the PC's national ballots came mainly from factory and mining areas in and around Concepción. In sum, the party's electoral support was concentrated in the zones with the highest levels of unionized labor. After 1937 the party grew in those same areas, particularly and intentionally among miners. The PC remained a far narrower party than the PS, geographically as well as socially. Contrasted to the Socialists, victorious Communist candidates in 1937 were more often from the working class. The backgrounds of those Communist winners were about evenly divided between workers and those of higher status occupations.[66]

64. *El Mercurio*, Mar. 6 and Mar. 8, 1937.
65. *Consigna*, May 1, 1937.
66. The Communists' actual vote total may have been slightly higher, perhaps over 5%, because some of their ballots were hidden under other party labels. U.S., Dept. of State Archives, Santiago, Mar. 14, 1939, p. 9, 825.00/568; Cruz-Coke, p. 107; Cruz Salas, p. 314.

The Ibáñez Alternative

A third movement, headed by Carlos Ibáñez, also obstructed the Popular Front's path toward the 1938 presidential election. Ibáñez's highly personalistic, populistic movement, although small, held enough potential supporters hostage to make victory for the Front unlikely. But major forces both within the Ibáñez camp, especially the Nazis, and within the Front, especially the Socialists, opposed unification. Despite their antifascist position, the Communists were the most eager for an accommodation between the Front and the *ibañistas*. The platforms of the two movements—which emphasized state planning, economic nationalism, and social welfare— were almost identical, but most of the politicians appeared irreconcilable.[67]

With its nonideological reformist appeal, the amorphous Ibáñez movement drew backing from all social and political sectors. According to the best available evidence, its core was middle class, notably provincials, bureaucrats, and retired military men. Ibáñez had almost no chance of being elected president. Nevertheless, a few economic elites provided covert financing. They did so to support the ex-dictator as a drain on the Front's votes and to cover themselves in case he became president through a fluke or a coup.[68] The most significant organized party behind Ibáñez was González von Marées's National Socialist Movement. The MNS criticized the traditional Right for trying, unsuccessfully, to stem the tide of Marxism with counter-productive repression and advocated reforms for the middle and lower classes to steal the Marxists' thunder.[69]

Even given the populist and fascist proclivities within the Ibáñez movement, the Socialists were enough of a mixture to harbor a handful of renegades who abandoned the mother party in 1937 to join his campaign. The defectors called themselves the Socialist Union. These rebels were led by middle-class professionals and intellectuals, among them Ricardo Latcham. Their followers were mainly teachers, public

67. Like the other two candidates, Ibáñez's antiimperialism was lukewarm; his supporters, like some in the other two camps, also solicited funding, apparently in vain, from the United States Embassy. U.S., Dept. of State Archives, Santiago, June 28, 1938, 825.00/1042, July 16, 1938, 825.00/1040; *Claridad,* 1938; Carlos Ibáñez del Campo, *Programa presidencial* (Santiago, 1938).

68. U.S., Dept. of State Archives, Santiago, May 11, 1937, pp. 4-5, 825.00/993, Oct. 29, 1937, p. 6. 825.00/1010, Apr. 20, 1938, p. 3, 825.00/1026, May 18, 1938, pp. 3-7, 825.00/1032, July 30, 1938, pp. 2-4, 825.00/1044.

69. Jorge González von Marées, *La mentira democrática* (Santiago, 1936); Jorge González von Marées, *La hora de la decisión* (Santiago, 1937); Mayorga, "La fugaz," pp. 18-19; Mayorga, "Jorge," pp. 41-42; Faletto, Ruiz, and Zemelman, pp. 82-86; *El imperialismo,* p. 17; Joaquín Edwards Bello, *Nacionalismo continental* (Santiago, 1968), pp. 154-62.

employees, and a few skilled workers. Increasingly from 1935 on, these dissidents had rankled at Grove's domination of the PS. With the formation of the Popular Front, this leadership conflict focused on the issue of closer relations with the *ibañistas* to unite the masses under one roof. That was a Communist proposal supported by the Socialist insurgents. The Socialist Union represented perhaps 20% of the PS in 1937. In the 1938 municipal elections, the tiny party received roughly 12,000 votes, compared to over 45,000 for the regular Socialists. Since it was largely confined to Santiago, formation of the Socialist Union represented only a minor loss for the regular party. Moreover, this loss was compensated for immediately by the formal absorption of the Communist Left into the PS in 1937. Maintaining much of their doctrinal orientation within the PS, these Trotskyists contributed to later left-wing divisions in the party. For the moment, however, they brought in additional workers to replace the heavily middle-class faction that had departed with the Socialist Union.[70]

Nomination of the Popular Front's Presidential Candidate, 1938

The defection of the Socialist Union was triggered by the regular party's decision to run Grove as their "pre-candidate" for the Popular Front presidential nomination. The Socialists argued that they had the right to name the nominee because their party was most truly representative of the mixed middle- and lower-class constituency of the Front. They claimed to "struggle for the liberation of a people and not of a class." They also nominated the popular Grove to galvanize mass support for the party and the coalition; his candidacy also provided a bargaining point with the Radicals to pull the Front more toward Socialist positions. Although a moderate Socialist, Grove as a candidate gave hope to more leftist party elements who feared Radical domination of the Front as a deception of the workers.[71]

The campaign for Grove—as "the heroic and generous *caudillo* of the popular masses," "the moral president of Chile," and "the purest expression of our nationality"—was far more personalistic and leftist than that for the Radical candidate, Pedro Aguirre Cerda; it was

70. Socialist Union support for Communist positions and the fact that some of the splinter group's leaders later joined the PC after their own party dissolved added to recurrent Socialist suspicions that such splits in the PS were engineered by Communist infiltrators. *Consigna*, Oct.-Nov., 1937; Cruz Salas, pp. 12-25, 79-98, 298; Carlos Contreras Labarca, *El trotzkismo* (Santiago, 1937); U.S., Dept. of State Archives, Santiago, Apr. 26, 1938, p. 7, 825.00/1030.

71. *Claridad*, Jan. 16, Apr. 9, and Apr. 13, 1938; *Consigna*, Aug. 14 and Nov. 13, 1937; Wilfredo Mayorga, "Las intrigas electorales de 1938," *Ercilla*, no. 1619 (June 15, 1966), pp. 18-19.

clearly a more populist alternative ultimately passed up. For example, Grove made far greater threats to nationalize foreign capital, as Cárdenas had done in Mexico. Blending Marxism and messianism, the Socialists vowed to uplift the masses "under the paternal and fraternal gaze of our leader."[72] An exceptionally effusive propaganda article in 1937 asserted that, for peasants and Indians, "Grove is their fatherland, their God and their law."[73]

The Radicals countered the Socialists' bid by insisting that a larger constituency gave their party priority in naming the presidential candidate. The Radicals chose Aguirre Cerda, from the right wing of the party, as their "pre-candidate." He had initially opposed his party's joining the Popular Front. Aguirre Cerda's candidacy signified the entrusting of the Front's leadership to its most moderate members, but his nomination also cemented the loyalty of most vacillating Radicals to the cause.[74]

A mild reformer with a middle-class background, Aguirre Cerda had become a wealthy landowner and proponent of industrialization. As a teacher, lawyer, wine grower, and Mason, he had married into the landed upper class. He frequently served in governments after World War I and acted as a leader within the Radical Party. During the 1930s Aguirre Cerda worked as a consultant to the party and its press, to numerous corporations, and to the interest associations for agriculture, industry, and mining. One of the few policy goals he shared with the more leftist leaders of the Front was devotion to economic modernization with an emphasis on industry.[75]

At the Front's Convention of the Left in April, 1938, Grove and Aguirre Cerda deadlocked for the presidential nomination. Behind the scenes, Grove, with some bitterness, learned that the Communists would not support him for standard-bearer. He also discovered that many Radicals would never back him even if he became the Front's candidate. After more than ten rounds of balloting, it appeared that the coalition might founder on the issue of a nominee. To salvage Popular Front unity, Grove electrified the stalemated convention by suddenly withdrawing in favor of his rival. In the euphoria of that moment, Grove was compensated by being named president of the Front to lead the campaign and to offset Aguirre Cerda's blandness with his own charisma.[76]

72. Partido Socialista, *Grove a la presidencia*, pp. 6-27; *Claridad*, Apr. 9, 1938.
73. *Consigna*, May 22, 1937.
74. Ravines, pp. 171-75; Boizard, *Historia*, pp. 35-36, 143-49; U.S., Dept. of State Archives, Santiago, May 19, 1937, p. 4, 825.00/994.
75. Cabero, *Recuerdos*, pp. 17-83, 116-49; Aguirre Cerda; Luis Palma Zúñiga, *Pedro Aguirre Cerda* (Santiago, 1963), pp. 9-76.
76. Thomas, "Marmaduke Grove: A Political Biography," pp. 276-82; Boizard,

The nomination of Aguirre Cerda illustrated the inescapable quandary and costs of such electoral coalitions, especially for the weaker members of the Front, the Marxists. The broadness of Aguirre Cerda's appeal mellowed the reformist content of the Popular Front at the same time as it enhanced its electoral chances.[77] Even the Right reacted favorably to such a conciliatory nominee. Conservative praise for Aguirre Cerda as a responsible moderate, however, was coupled with warnings that he was serving as a Trojan horse for the dangerous Marxists. This rightist distinction between the acceptable nominee and his evil supporters was calculated to woo as many Radicals as possible back to the government's side:[78]

> The ... Right does not fundamentally object to the candidate of the Popular Front as a person. ... He is, in reality, a man of the *Right*. A rich man, a great producer, a grand industrialist, a landowner of the type so detested by communism, his interests and his ideology locate him ... in the ranks of the citizens of order. As a Radical ... his party was always bourgeois democratic, with the same economic and social gradations as the other parties of that category, like the Conservative and the Liberal. ... its men belong to the same social and cultural categories as the men of Catholic conservatism and act, frequently, together in the same businesses. Both groups are composed, at the level of their intellectuals and producers, of professionals, doctors, lawyers, professors, etc., or industrialists, agriculturalists, merchants, who, in our small environment, often come together, maintain intimate personal relations, including families, and work, frequently, as associates or colleagues. Their political approximation, in the absence of vexatious questions like those of religious character, which so divided them in the past, is explainable.[79]

Although the Left was mainly pleased at multiparty unity behind Aguirre Cerda, a few dissenters, privately and at times publicly, reacted to his nomination as a betrayal of the workers by the Popular Front. For example, one *ibañista* expressed the suspicions of some disgruntled reformers when he alleged that Aguirre Cerda was deceiving the masses with hackneyed slogans: "'Bread, Roof, and Overcoat' means anything anyone could want, and, in consequence, means nothing ... it is a program like the transitory flattery of amorous seduction for the popular classes but one that leaves the road open for matrimony with the oligarchy."[80] Younger and more leftist Socialists

Historia, pp. 148-51; Fernández C., pp. 69-72; Galo González Díaz, *El congreso de la victoria* (Santiago, 1938), pp. 47-48.

77. Stevenson, pp. 71-85; Rafael Luis Gumucio V., *Me defiendo* (Santiago, 1939), pp. 19-23.

78. U.S., Dept. of State Archives, Santiago, Apr. 20, 1938, pp. 2-4, 825.00/1026.

79. *La Nación*, Apr. 25, 1938.

80. Tancredo Pinochet, *Aguirre Cerda* (Santiago, 1938), pp. 7-15, 64-65.

regretted Grove's withdrawal as a candidate. They wanted to use his popularity to build a more coherently Marxist, independent constituency opposed to the prevailing system. Instead, under leadership of Schnake and the moderates, the PS plunged into the traditional swirl of coalition bargaining and compromises. At least for the moment, the radical, mobilizing potential of populist socialism was giving way to its clientelistic potential for accommodation with existing political institutions. Nevertheless, after only six years of dedication to electoral politics, the Socialists and Communists were on the threshold of a significant share of presidential power.[81]

81. *Claridad*, Apr. 18, 1938; Mendoza, *¿Y ahora?*, pp. 179-82; Chelén, *Trayectoria*, p. 88; Faletto, Ruiz, and Zemelman, pp. 101-4.

7

Victory for the Popular Front, 1938

Alessandri's successful administration and the relative political peace in 1933-37 coincided, as had past tranquil periods, with a cycle of economic recuperation and expansion. As measured by export fluctuations, which reflected world market trends and reverberated throughout the Chilean economy, those previous years of economic growth were 1912-13, 1916-18, 1922-24, and 1927-29. Conversely, past periods of political unrest and change, such as presidential turnovers through elections and coups, had usually come during economic cycles of recession and contraction (1914-15, 1919-21, 1925-26, and 1930-32). In the same fashion, economic decline and discontent in 1937-38 were ushering in a new era of political transformation.[1]

Upper-Class Assertiveness, 1938

The upper classes in 1938 were overly confident of electoral supremacy and overly fearful of middle- and lower-class challengers on the new Left. Consequently, most of the privileged groups and the Right drew a hard line against the Popular Front. Despite tactical, religious, and policy disagreements, the upper sectors possessed enough shared beliefs and socioeconomic interconnections to act in unison. According to the U.S. Embassy in 1938: ". . . the wealth of Chile has hitherto been concentrated to a large extent in the hands of the aristocratic landholding class; and this class has gradually interested itself in industrial enterprises, so that it today still dominates not only the agricultural but also industrial and mineral activities of Chile (leaving aside the large American enterprises)."[2]

1. The correlation between economic and political cycles is, of course, imperfect (for example with a coup in late 1924), but is nonetheless striking. Corporación de Fomento, *Geografía*, II, pp. 354-56; Pinto, *Antecedentes*, p. 2.
2. U.S., Dept. of State Archives, Santiago, Nov. 4, 1938, p. 6, 825.00/1090.

From the beginning of the Great Depression, the economic elites emphasized their functional, *"gremial"* organizations over political parties when they perceived a threat to their interests. The 1930s was a decade of institutionalization for the capitalists as well as for the workers. Economic priorities and policies were becoming more salient political issues. In response, upper-class interest groups strengthened their institutionalized participation in government decision making related to their private sector.[3]

Under Alessandri's administration, the elite economic sectoral organizations increased their activities, mutual coordination, and role in government. For example, the SNA and the SOFOFA had joint representatives before the Central Bank and the state credit and export-import agencies. These national societies were solidifying a "parceling-out" of government authority relevant to their functional, occupational interests. So long as they retained their functional preserves, the elites could hope that a leftist capture of the presidency would not ruin them; perhaps at worst their political adversaries would consign other government fiefdoms to contending groups such as labor.[4]

A leading example of growing mobilization and institutionalization by the economic elites was the 1933 founding of the Confederation of Production and Commerce. It was constructed as a supraorganization to coordinate all the upper-class sectoral institutions. It pursued common goals, such as lower taxes, "harmony" instead of class conflict between capital and labor, and opposition to populist leaders of the masses. The confederation embraced all the major national interest associations: SNA, SOFOFA, National Society of Mining (SNM), and Chamber of Commerce. In addition, it enrolled regional groups, economic promotional agencies, and major enterprises. The president of the confederation, who was also head of the SNA, announced at the opening convention, "Today we are strong because we are organized, tomorrow we will be invincible because we will have improved our organization."[5]

At the same time, these economic elites made a direct, public bid to monopolize presidential power. They promoted the candidacy of

3. *Las fuerzas productoras ante la elección presidencial* (Santiago, 1938), pp. 1-2; Arriagada, pp. 28-32; Lira, p. 25.

4. For example, see La Sociedad de Fomento Fabril, *Industria*, año LVI, no. 1 (Jan., 1939), pp. 6-16; Mamalakis and Reynolds; Eldon Kenworthy, "Coalitions in the Political Development of Latin America," in Sven Groennings, E. W. Kelley, and Michael Leiserson, eds., *The Study of Coalition Behavior* (New York, 1970), pp. 103-40; Constantine Menges, "Public Policy and Organized Business in Chile," *Journal of International Affairs*, XX (1966), pp. 343-65.

5. *Sesión inaugural de la convención de la producción y del comercio* (Santiago, 1934).

Gustavo Ross, Alessandri's tough, talented Finance Minister. The economic leaders proclaimed that politics had become too important to relegate to their traditional party intermediaries. Presidents of the SNA, SOFOFA, SNM, Chamber of Commerce, Central Bank, and top corporations issued joint manifestos with the presidents of the Conservative and Liberal parties. They called for a technocratic "regime of order" to stifle class conflict and thus encourage economic productivity.[6]

The sentiments of elite economic organizations were echoed by upper-class social institutions. For example, the Union Club and the September Club made their enthusiasm for Ross known.[7] In spite of the rightist candidate's lack of religious devotion, some clergy openly worked and prayed for his election.[8]

Within the economic upper strata, the agricultural barons were usually more enthusiastic about Alessandri and Ross and more antagonistic to reforms than were the industrial magnates. Under Alessandri, the landowners and the SNA welcomed the "tight collaboration" with government departments. This was especially true in the Ministry of Agriculture, often filled with SNA officials, and in agencies concerned with credits and exports. The SNA also had privileged access to departments dealing with worker affairs. There, the landed elites prevented the extension of urban social security and unionization rights to rural labor. In addition, new taxes in the 1930s were imposed on consumers and industrialists, not landowners.[9]

Ross appealed especially to the more reactionary landholders. They believed that discipline and productivity were the best solution to demands for social reform in the countryside. These rural elites complained of "growing insubordination" and excessive migration to the cities, two signs of peasant discontent. Other landlords accepted the need for minor reforms. They endorsed colonization, better salaries, and improved housing. To preempt leftist programs for government intervention, the SNA encouraged benevolent landowner paternalism toward the peasants; it also tried to keep more peasants away from labor unions by enlisting them in the Society.[10]

The captains of industry naturally disagreed with the agricul-

6. *Las fuerzas productoras*, pp. 1-4.

7. *Hoy*, año VII, no. 360 (Oct. 13, 1938), p. 9; Boizard, *Historia*, p. 12.

8. U.S., Dept. of State Archives, Santiago, Aug. 26, 1938, p. 4, 825.00/1050.

9. La Sociedad Nacional de Agricultura, *El Campesino*, LXX (Apr.-July, 1938); *Las fuerzas productoras*, p. 7; "South America III," pp. 164-68; Alessandri, *Recuerdos*, III, pp. 58-59; Grove, *Reforma*, pp. 34-77.

10. La Sociedad Nacional de Agricultura, *El Campesino*, LXX, no. 4 (Apr., 1938), pp. 204-8, no. 5 (May, 1938), p. 243; Gumucio, *Me defiendo*, pp. 52-58; Matthei, pp. 45-47, 120-33.

turalists on specific economic priorities, such as tariff levels. Nevertheless, they shared a determination to defeat the Popular Front. SOFOFA's crusade for Ross was joined by the president of the national Chamber of Commerce; he pointed out that 1938 was the first time the merchants as a group had ever endorsed a presidential aspirant.[11]

United States businessmen in Chile, whose numbers were rising, also preferred Ross. They were less convinced than domestic elites, however, of the real distance separating the presidential combatants. All three candidates assured U.S. economic interests of favorable treatment by their prospective administrations; they intimated even better treatment if U.S. enterprises would contribute to their campaigns.[12]

Middle-Class Ambitions and Division, 1938

In the 1930s the middle class grew and hungered for a bigger slice of the political pie. Chile became more urban and the service sector expanded. While the percentage of the active work force in agriculture declined, that in industry and commerce increased. Moreover, the percentage in public administration nearly doubled from 1930 to 1940. This caused some Chileans to complain that "this country is suffering from a veritable fever of *empleomanía*."[13] Vitriolic conservatives charged that the middle groups and the Masons were seducing the masses with Marxism merely to create a bloated state to feed their own bureaucratic appetites. Though the middle class was still fundamentally bureaucratic, it acquired a firmer economic base. The proliferation of industries and small enterprises helped, as did the turnover in landholdings thanks to colonization and hard times, although the exhaustion of frontier lands intensified middle-class pressures on the latifundium system. The gradual return of foreign investment, especially from the United States, also multiplied middle-class occupations.[14]

Most segments of the middle strata joined and led the workers in the Popular Front because of economic and status grievances. But, as always, they remained politically divided. On election eve, Aguirre Cerda still complained that some members of the "middle class who

11. *Las fuerzas productoras,* pp. 19-30.
12. U.S., Dept. of State Archives, Santiago, Aug. 30, 1937, pp. 1-2, 825.00/1007, June 23, 1938, 825.00/1035-1/2, Aug. 27, 1938, pp. 1-6, 825.00/1051.
13. Alterman, pp. 95-96; Faletto, Ruiz, and Zemelman, pp. 46-54; Antonio Zegers Baeza, *Sobre nuestra crisis política y moral* (Santiago, 1934), pp. 3, 58-69.
14. Mann, II, pp. 112-33; McBride, pp. 275-77.

should be consistent and solidified with their class" were working for
Ross.[15] One reason so many from the middle sectors sided with the
Front was the distance between their income and that of the upper
class, which was even greater than the gap between middle- and
lower-class incomes. As evidence of the low pay scales of the middle
classes, it was estimated in 1937-38 that government white-collar employees earned from $16 to $80 per month, private white-collar employees in offices and shops an average of $23 per month ($276 per
year), and public school teachers about $36 per month ($432 per
year). Beneath the middle class, copper workers averaged around 95
cents a day ($314.45 a year, working an average of 331 days), nitrate
workers 72 cents a day ($205.20 a year, working 285 days), coal
workers 61 cents a day ($179.95 a year, working 295 days), and tex-
tile workers 51 cents a day ($146.37 a year, working 287 days). Accord-
ing to the 1937 industrial census, all workers in factories (often just
tiny shops) averaged $3.36 a week ($174.72 a year). In the building
trades, carpenters averaged 12 cents an hour, cabinetmakers 10 cents,
and masons and plumbers 8 cents. In the cities, skilled workers earned
roughly 64-80 cents a day, and unskilled workers 32-44 cents a day.
Worse, farm workers attached to great estates reportedly received
about 12 cents per day.[16] In addition to the mutual income concerns of
the culturally divided lower and middle classes, the rationalization and
concentration of the urban economy into larger and more monopolistic enterprises also created leftist recruits from groups such as shop-
keepers. Public and private white-collar employees worried that Ross
might trim the government payroll and favor the economic elites at
their expense. Although public school teachers usually identified with
the Radicals, primary-level instructors increasingly preferred the
Socialists and Communists. Students and intellectuals, primarily from
the secular University of Chile, rallied to the Front. The FECH endorsed Aguirre Cerda.[17]

The military was expected to abstain from the elections because of

15. *Claridad*, Oct. 23, 1938.
16. These calculations are based on an exchange rate of one peso = four U.S. cents.
Herring, pp. 206-8; "South America III," pp. 78-83.
17. These grievances were reflected in the ephemeral Political, Economic and Social
Organization of the Middle Class of 1934, which grew out of the middle-sector federation of 1919 and its attempted revival in 1931. The organization's heterogeneous
composition and statist program foreshadowed the Popular Front, and some of
its leaders favored making the PS into the official party of the middle class. La
Organización Política, Económica y Social de la Clase Media, *Programa mínimo provisional*
(Valparaíso, 1934); *Acción Socialista*, June 16, 1934; Stevenson, esp. p. 128; Diego Espoz,
Ante el abismo . . . (Valparaíso, 1936); Marta Infante Barros, *Testigos del treinta y ocho*
(Santiago, 1972); U.S., Dept. of State Archives, Santiago, Aug. 13, 1938, p. 2,
825.00/1047, Aug. 26, 1938, pp. 4-5, 825.00/1050.

its traditions and divisions. In the opening years of his administration, Alessandri had disciplined and downgraded the armed forces while boosting the elitist Republican Militia; that tactic left a residue of bitterness and military sympathy for the government's opponents. By 1938, however, the militia had disbanded and Alessandri had rebuilt the military in the face of the international tensions which were rising toward World War II. In so doing, he won most of the armed services back to the government's side. Many officers favored Ross because he promised order and seemed most likely to secure funds for new armaments. Others preferred Ibáñez, but not enough to mount a takeover. Despite their anticommunism, a few officers even sided with the Popular Front. It was assumed that most military leaders were not hostile enough toward the Front to obstruct its taking office. It also appeared likely, however, that the armed forces might intervene if the Front ever made sudden moves toward socialism.[18]

Urban vs. Rural Workers, 1938

Under Alessandri, there were relative, gradual increases in urbanization, literacy, and prosperity among the workers. These gains and rising political consciousness made the workers less susceptible to political or monetary inducements from bosses on the Right.[19] At the same time, continuing problems and deprivation amidst some gains made the urban workers favor the Left. Although real wages had been rising since 1933, they were still below pre-Depression levels and were not keeping pace with the cost of living. For example, average daily wages in ten major industries increased 16% from 1936 to 1937, while retail prices jumped 25%. Industrial and mining production and employment had largely recovered from the Depression but dipped in 1937-38. Even though the most impoverished workers were still in the countryside, they remained least attracted to the Popular Front.[20]

The failure of the Marxists and the Front to mobilize many peasants electorally or in joint action with urban labor persisted, despite stirrings in the countryside. The symbol of rural unrest was the 1934 uprising at Ránquil, near Concepción. This fight over lands by displaced peasants was harshly repressed and remained an isolated movement. The conflict left hundreds dead and official landowners

18. *Hoy*, año VII, no. 354 (Sept. 1, 1938), p. 19; U.S., Dept. of State Archives, Santiago, Apr. 26, 1938, pp. 9-10, 825.00/1030, May 25, 1938, p. 8, 825.00/1033, Oct. 15, 1938, p. 6, 825.00/1077.

19. Olavarría Bravo, *Chile*, I, p. 357; U.S., Dept. of State Archives, Santiago, Nov. 4, 1938, p. 6, 825.00/1090.

20. Ellsworth, pp. 1, 46-47, 162-72; Chile, Dirección General de Estadística, *Veinte*, p. 139; Sáez, *Y así*, pp. 223-47.

victorious, having enjoyed the aid of government forces.[21] Another sign of ferment was the emergence of a few rural labor unions. For example, vineyard workers won the right to legal organization in 1933. A Marxist National League for the Defense of Poor Peasants arose in 1935. Apparently some agricultural laborers, especially in the far north and south, often near previously politicized groups such as miners, backed the Socialists and the Front. Far more, however, supported Ross.[22]

In addition to obstruction from the Right, there were severe cultural and organizational hurdles to peasant mobilization. Nevertheless, it was surprising that the Chilean Left made such small and ineffective efforts in the countryside. Among major national politicians, Grove emphasized agrarian reform most. He attracted few rural workers, however. This weakness contrasted with the ideology of the Marxists. It also inhibited the express desire of many leftists to rely less on alliances with the middle and upper classes. Furthermore, Marxist deficiencies in the countryside were crippling since the peasants still constituted a plurality of the active labor force and of the conservative electorate.[23]

Regional Grievances, 1938

Although overshadowed by national economic and social problems, regional issues and attitudes also underlay the political cleavages in 1938: "The central provinces are consumers, they live at the expense of the others, which are producers, and they benefit from a privileged situation in every sense, while the provinces of the north and south are considered economically colonies of the capital."[24] The exports of the north and south paid for the imports of the central provinces. For example, in the 1930s the northern port of Antofagasta handled about eight times as many exports as imports and the central port of Valparaíso processed about six times as many imports as exports.[25] The north and south produced over 80% of all exports, and Santiago and Valparaíso consumed over 50% of all imports.[26]

21. Matthei, pp. 45-47, 120, 130-33, 261; Armando Hormachea Reyes, *El Frente Popular de 1938* (Santiago, 1968), pp. 33-34.

22. Almino Affonso et al., *Movimiento campesino chileno* (2 vols., Santiago, 1970), I, esp. pp. 23-28; Mario Mallol Pemjean, *La verdad sobre los dirigentes regionales de Iquique del año 1941 del Partido Socialista chileno* (Iquique, Chile, 1942), pp. 42-44; Contreras, *Unidad*.

23. Grove, *Reforma;* Lechner, esp. p. 60.

24. Matthei, p. 38.

25. Chile, *Geografía*, p. 67.

26. Roberto Vergara Herrera, *Descentralización administrativa* (Santiago, 1932), p. 8.

Such economic concentration in Santiago was extraordinary since the province accounted for less than 19% of the national population and only about 16% of national production. However, it consumed over 40% of the meat eaten in Chile and possessed nearly 50% of the nation's automobiles and twice as many commercial establishments per inhabitant as the other provinces. Moreover, since Santiago's major contribution to national output was through industry, it relied on primary materials from the other provinces or from abroad. For example, foreign exchange generated by the northern provinces was used to purchase products to be finished in central Chilean factories and then sold to the north at swollen prices. Provincial discontent based on these inequities was exacerbated by the economic difficulties of the 1930s, because central Chile recovered faster and more fully than did the more remote areas.[27]

Especially galling was the core provinces' disproportionate control of credit and finances, which were often channeled through government agencies. Santiago's prosperity and dominance resulted from its political power as much as from any objective economic conditions. In the early 1930s, while Santiago province received an estimated 52% of the loans granted in Chile, it possessed only 22% of the nation's total appraised property value. At the same time, Santiago had 58% of all mortgage loans and 32% of rural mortgage loans, but its farm lands comprised only 15% of the value of the nation's agricultural properties.[28] In the core provinces as a whole, the central landowners produced 50% of Chile's agricultural output in the 1930s. Without any compelling economic justification, they also received nearly 90% of the credit dispersed by the government's major mortgage institute. Therefore, when the Popular Front demanded a more equitable distribution of state credit, it addressed the grievances of all Chileans beneath the landed upper class and outside the core zone.[29] However, the Front's desire to allocate more credit to industry could be seen as a new bonanza for the Santiago elites. From 1930 to 1942, the capital city's share of the national active industrial population rose from 37%

27. Santiago also had the highest provincial rate of literacy, the major educational institutions, the most social services per capita, nearly 30% of the armed forces personnel, and almost 40% of the government bureaucrats. Adolfo Ibáñez B., *Santiago y las provincias* (Valparaíso, 1936), pp. 6-28; Raúl Rodríguez Lazo, *Aspectos sobre centralismo y descentralización en Chile* (Santiago, 1935), pp. 20-44; Vergara Herrera, p. 20; Keller, *La eterna*, pp. 146-49.

28. Loans of all types were more accessible in Santiago, where more money was loaned in proportion to deposits than in other provinces. In 1934, 51% of all Chilean property transfers took place in Santiago. Ibáñez B., pp. 13-23.

29. Matthei, pp. 232-34.

to 50%.[30] The outlying provinces also complained about excessive allocations from the expanding government budget to Santiago. For example—at least according to available figures for 1934—Santiago reaped far more than its fair (proportionate to population) share of public works expenditures.[31]

Another criticism from provincials was that the increasingly powerful politicians and bureaucrats were mainly from the capital city. Countless local and minor problems could be solved only by recourse to officials with connections at the seat of the national government. Everyone—businessmen, landowners, the poor—had to journey to Santiago to tap government largesse and to cope with complex state regulations. Even in the distant zones, public functionaries, frequently appointees from the capital city, were usually oriented toward their source of patronage rather than the local area.[32]

Alessandri failed to implement the 1925 constitutional provision for provincial assemblies. As a result, the panacea of "administrative decentralization" to increase provincial control over local decisions and decision makers remained a live issue. Although a ritual promise from all politicians, it rang loudest from the Popular Front in 1938.[33]

Small regionalist parties and erstwhile separatist movements cropped up in the far north and far south. In 1935, fifteen deputies briefly organized a loose "federal party" in Congress. Most provincials believed, however, that alignment with powerful national parties brought more central government attention to their area's problems.[34]

In the 1930s both the Right and the Left progressed beyond old jurisdictional reforms to call for "functional" reorganization of the provinces by economic production sectors. This was the concept of creating new regional administrative units based on contiguous provinces with similar economies. For the Right, this occupational-regional formula for national organization and economic development promised local government based on elite-dominated corporate interest groups rather than individual voters or social classes. In large

30. Alterman, pp. 103-4; Levine and Crocco, "La población chilena como fuerza," p. 50.
31. Ibáñez B., pp. 16-17.
32. Ibáñez B., pp. 18-28; Vergara Herrera, pp. 3-6; Guiñez, p. 101.
33. Rodríguez Lazo, pp. 20-45; U.S., Dept. of State Archives, Santiago, Jan. 19, 1938, p. 3, 825.00/1016.
34. *Programa de trabajo de los candidatos a regidores del Partido Regionalista de Magallanes* (Magallanes, Chile, [1938?]); *El Socialista*, año 3, no. 9 (Jan. 16, 1938), p. 1; *El imperialismo*, pp. 3-15; Matthei, p. 38; Vergara Herrera, p. 20; Casali, pp. 23-29; Humberto Beltrame Curubetto, *Aspiraciones populares* (Iquique, Chile, [1938?]).

part, such proposals sprang from fears of a takeover by populism and socialism at the national level. One right-wing Liberal promoted this corporatist regionalism as "a means to end the class struggle as a political weapon, and to give intervention in the administration of the provinces to the productive forces, instead of leaving it to the mercy of the agitators."[35]

Some conservatives also linked their regional protests with opposition to accelerated government intervention in the economy and society. They condemned a modernizing, centralizing, mass state because it threatened the autonomy of economic elites as well as outlying provinces. While the Left appealed to regional groups against the concentration of economic power in the clutches of the central upper class, the more traditional Right appealed against concentration in the tentacles of the central government.[36]

The Nazis and other tiny corporatist parties were in the forefront of rightist regionalism. Parties relying heavily on the regional issue made little headway, however. More successful were leftist parties out of power who combined regional protests with a larger movement for social reform, as seen in the Popular Front.[37]

Both 1938 presidential candidates appealed to provincial anxieties by promising expanded attention, credit, and public works. The Front carried the issue with greater vigor, in part because the Radicals had a reputation as defenders of regional interests. The Socialists placed far heavier emphasis on class than on geographic cleavages. They warned working-class voters against being sucked into alliances with local elites against the central provinces. Instead, the PS courted regionalist votes with promises of equitable socialist economic development and of middle- and lower-class solidarity against the central oligarchy. The Socialists' strongest bastion remained Magallanes, the province of the most virulent regionalism.[38]

The Right's 1938 Presidential Campaign

Immediately after Aguirre Cerda's nomination, the National Convention of the Right chose Ross. Only about 10% of the Conservatives (the Falange wing) and some 30% of the Liberals preferred a less abrasive and haughty personality. The dissenters feared that "his

35. Edwards, *Las corporaciones,* pp. 7-14; Vergara Herrera, pp. 24-26; Matthei, pp. 37-39.
36. Ibáñez B., pp. 18-28.
37. Vergara Herrera; Ibáñez B., pp. 1-3, 27-28; *¿Qué es el Partido Agrario?;* Partido Agrario, *Acción corporativo* (Chillán, Chile, 1941); *Unión Republicana* (Santiago, 1932); Unión Republicana, *Declaraciones de sus juntas generales de directorios* (Santiago, [1936?]).
38. *Consigna,* June 22, 1935; *Claridad,* Sept. 6, 1938; Nicanor Poblete, *Descentralización económica de las provincias* (Santiago, 1937); Infante, pp. 47-48.

reputation as an unscrupulous conservative" would aggravate social conflicts and solidify leftist unity. Whereas a wily conservative might easily have outbid the cautious Popular Front with a program of "Tory reform," Ross's stern, cold-hearted image made victory less certain.[39]

As the son of a rich industrialist and a fabled financier in his own right, Ross was vulnerable to the leftist caricatures of him as a merciless reactionary. The unprecedented numbers of business magnates publicly active in his campaign also lent credence to charges that he was the servant of domestic and foreign capitalists. Indeed, Ross personally represented the newer urban economic elites more than the older landed aristocracy.[40] Having lived most of his adult life outside Chile and having even accepted the presidential nomination from Europe, Ross fell prey to leftist propaganda that he was an antinational candidate. Satirists dubbed him "Monsieur Gustav." The Front tagged him a tool of U.S. imperialism, the "Minister of Hunger," the "last Pirate of the Pacific," and "the total antithesis of our nationality."[41]

Such polarized images obscured the similarity of the two main candidates' programs. In contrast to the Front, the Right did not issue a formal platform. Instead, they offered Ross as a paternalistic strongman to provide "order and work." His sparse, laconic speeches echoed most of Aguirre Cerda's promises, for instance expanded education and higher wages. Ross was at least as eager as his opponent for economic planning and intervention by the state but appeared more hesitant about economic nationalism. Like most spokesmen of the Right, Ross subordinated labor benefits and import-substituting industrialization to concerns about productivity and efficiency. More important, even when he advocated the same reforms as did Aguirre Cerda, Ross specialized in understatement, while the Front excelled at raising expectations.[42]

Although friendlier than the Popular Front toward foreign inves-

39. U.S., Dept. of State Archives, Santiago, Apr. 26, 1938, pp. 1-6, 825.00/1030, July 2, 1938, p. 3, 825.00/1038; *Hoy*, año VII, no. 322 (Jan. 20, 1938), pp. 12-13, no. 361 (Oct. 20, 1938), p. 13; "South America III," p. 170; Gumucio, *Me defiendo*, pp. 4-71; Partido Conservador, *Falange Nacional* (Santiago, 1938), pp. 6-14; René León Echaíz, *Liberalismo y conservantismo* (Curico, Chile, 1936).

40. Dell'Orto, pp. 29-43.

41. Ramón Morales C., *Democracia chilena triunfante* (Santiago, 1939); Sáez, *Y así*, p. 120; Cabero, *Recuerdos*, pp. 170-75; U.S., Dept. of State Archives, Santiago, July 30, 1937, pp. 1-3, 825.00/1004; Infante.

42. *Una revolución en la paz, 1932-1937* (Santiago and Valparaíso, 1937); *Doctrina rossiana* (Santiago, 1938); Gustavo Ross Santa María, *Palabras de un estadista* (Santiago, 1938); Víctor M. Villagra, *Discurso del presidente del Partido Liberal de Bulnes* (Chillán, Chile, 1938); Edecio Torreblanca, *Ante la próxima elección presidencial* (Santiago, 1938); Cuadra, *Magia;* U.S., Dept. of State Archives, Santiago, Apr. 26, 1938, pp. 3-4, 825.00/1030, June, 1938, pp. 2-6, 825.00/1045.

tors, Ross was also expected to extract more than Alessandri had from U.S. companies. He saw a pragmatic national need for more foreign exchange and capital as well as a likelihood of North American concessions to counter German penetration. According to business reports from the U.S. Embassy, Ross apparently planned "to milk the copper companies" because they were "taking out all their profits and leaving in Chile only wages and taxes." A visit to the United States just prior to his presidential campaign, however, had made Ross less inclined toward such economic nationalism. A pleased U.S. businessman commented, "I think that his trip to the U.S. has also made him more conservative than he used to be. . . ."[43] Some North Americans reportedly contributed to Ross's campaign.[44]

En route to Chile from Europe to accept his nomination, Ross told the Brazilian Minister for Foreign Affairs that his main electoral strategy was to purchase voters.[45] A Ross campaign chairman also assured the U.S. ambassador in Chile that the Right would buy enough lower-class votes to vanquish the Front. He conceded that Aguirre Cerda would win by a wide margin in an honest election. Easiest in the rural districts, such traditional bribery was more difficult in the cities, where leftist organizations were stronger and worker political consciousness was rising. In some urban districts, Popular Front inspectors and workers' militias watched the polling. Many urban laborers refused the bribes or voted for the Front even after accepting, despite threats of losing their jobs.[46]

The other major approach of the Ross campaigners was to win over supporters from the middle classes and the centrist political groups, including disaffected Radicals. Like the Popular Front, the Right promised to elevate the living standard of the middle strata and to lift more workers into the middle class as a means of softening social tensions. The conservative forces awakened the fears of the middle sectors by painting the Marxists as anarchic "hordes" endangering religion, family, property, and national sovereignty. While the Left used the Spanish civil war and the Mexican revolution as inspirations, the Right dwelt on their violence, suffering, and potential importation to Chile. Ross and Aguirre Cerda each vowed to save Chilean democracy from the other.[47]

43. Mr. Bogdan of the J. Henry Schroeder Banking Corporation, "Chile," pp. 9-13 in U.S., Dept. of State Archives, Santiago, June 23, 1938, 825.00/1035-1/2.

44. Stevenson, pp. 89-93.

45. U.S., Dept. of State Archives, Rio de Janeiro, June 3, 1938, pp. 1-2, 825.00/1034.

46. U.S., Dept. of State Archives, Santiago, June 28, 1938, 825.00/1042, Oct. 18, 1938, 825.00/1078, Nov. 9, 1938, 825.00/1092.

47. The Right included the more conservative Democrats as well as newer micro-parties, in addition to the Conservatives and Liberals. La Nación, Apr.-Oct., 1938; El

The Popular Front's 1938 Presidential Campaign

Whereas Ross's candidacy provoked polarization, Aguirre Cerda appealed to both the middle and lower classes without unduly frightening the upper strata. He realized, as Ross did not, that purchased votes were declining in importance. Instead, popularity with the masses was becoming the prevailing political currency. Although arousing few passions on either side, Aguirre Cerda exuded the calm, humble, paternalistic style of a kindly school teacher. As the campaign moved along, teachers, intellectuals, industrialists, and the middle class in general identified with his background, beliefs, and comportment. Aguirre Cerda's small stature and swarthy mestizo visage earned him the derision of the rich but the affection of the poor. Scorned as *"El Negro"* by the Right, he was embraced as *"Don Tinto"* (after the red wine he cultivated) by the Left. Consequently, Aguirre Cerda came to symbolize among his supporters the quintessence of *"chilenidad,"* in contrast to Ross's European gentility.[48]

Aguirre Cerda's soothing, compromising manner helped hold the unruly Popular Front together and attract independents as well as a few disgruntled rightists. On the other hand, the candidate lacked the dynamism to conduct a rousing populist campaign.[49] One U.S. observer remarked that "Aguirre Cerda has no popular appeal and being a rich man himself is, of course, unable to preach the gospel of Socialism in a very convincing way."[50] Aguirre Cerda said that he was "neither a *caudillo* nor a Messiah."[51] Party organization, not the magnetism of the nominee, propelled the Popular Front campaign. It was the Marxist ability to mobilize the workers against the old ruling parties that was changing the political composition of Chile.[52]

The charismatic element was provided by Grove, the Front's most significant campaigner except for its nominee, who was at times overshadowed by the Socialist *caudillo*. He accompanied Aguirre Cerda the length of Chile to deliver his fervent mass following to the coalition's

---

Diario Ilustrado, Oct., 1938; *Las fuerzas productoras,* esp. pp. 27-28; Torreblanca; Raúl Marín Balmaceda and Manuel Vega, *La futura presidencia de la república* (Santiago, 1938).

48. Cabero, *Recuerdos,* pp. 170-77; Morales; Boizard, *Historia,* pp. 35-37; *El Mercurio,* Oct. 8, 1938; Loyola, *La verdad,* p. 7; Castro, *¿Me permite?,* pp. 64-67; Fernando Alegría, *Mañana los guerreros . . .* (Santiago, 1964), pp. 205-9.

49. U.S., Dept. of State Archives, Santiago, May 18, 1938, pp. 6-7, 825.00/1032, May 25, 1938, pp. 2-8, 825.00/1033.

50. Mr. Bogdan of the J. Henry Schroeder Banking Corporation, "Chile," p. 2 in U.S., Dept. of State Archives, Santiago, June 23, 1938, 825.00/1035-1/2; Pinochet, *Aguirre,* pp. 19-65.

51. Cabero, *Recuerdos,* pp. 170-75.

52. U.S., Dept. of State Archives, Santiago, Oct. 29, 1938, 825.00/1085; Fernández C., pp. 71-73, 91.

standard-bearer. The evidence indicates that the working classes, rallied by the Marxists, were mainly voting for Grove and his brand of socialism in 1938, persuaded that Aguirre Cerda and the Popular Front were valid surrogates.[53]

The main divider between the Right and the Front in the campaign was the perceived character and abilities of the nominees and the composition of their social-political support. Platform distinctions were fuzzy. Instead of specifics, ideological and social symbols, identifications, and reference groups became the battleground. Voters were apparently making the choice based on an assessment of which candidate, given his social loyalties, was most likely to govern in their behalf.[54]

To a significant extent, the Front's campaign was devoted to proclaiming political and economic moderation. In response to the Right's warnings of impending "anarchy," Aguirre Cerda argued that the Front was actually the best guarantee of "order." He contended that reforms, not repression, were most likely to produce social tranquility.[55] Aguirre Cerda had no intention of expropriating domestic or foreign industries and was far more interested in agricultural efficiency than parcelization.[56] For example, the Front ran a newspaper notice to reassure landowners that their property, however large, would be safe so long as it was legally owned and intensively worked. Further compromising its reformist credentials, the coalition promised to lower taxes on industry and commerce as well as consumers. In his public enthusiasm for private property and civil order, Aguirre Cerda was barely distinguishable from Ross.[57]

Such moderation was connected to the Front's efforts to build a campaign chest from wealthy Radicals. Although unconfirmed, there were reports of quests for funds from North Americans, sweetened with assurances for U.S. companies.[58] There were also rumors of solicitation of contributions from Cárdenas in return for promises to buy Mexico's expropriated oil once Aguirre Cerda was elected.[59]

    53. El Diario Ilustrado, Oct. 1, 1938; Claridad, Oct. 25, 1938; Pinochet, Aguirre, pp. 84-86, 139; Boizard, Historia, pp. 148-51; U.S., Dept. of State Archives, Santiago, July 30, 1938, p. 2, 825.00/1044; Thomas, "Marmaduke Grove: A Political Biography," pp. 276-82.
    54. Boizard, Historia, p. 150.
    55. Claridad, Oct. 23, 1938; Manifiesto de las mujeres aguirristas de Coquimbo . . . (Coquimbo, Chile, 1938).
    56. U.S., Dept. of State Archives, Santiago, Oct. 29, 1938, 825.00/1085.
    57. El Mercurio, Oct. 4, 1938.
    58. U.S., Dept. of State Archives, Santiago, June 28, 1938, 825.00/1042.
    59. U.S., Dept. of State Archives, Santiago, Sept. 11, 1938, 825.00/1053, Sept. 14, 1938, 825.00/1062, Sept. 16, 1938, 825.00/1059, Sept. 21, 1938, 825.00/1067, Oct. 10, 1938, 825.00/1076.

Above all, the Front was bankrolled by the CTCH, not Washington, Mexico, or Moscow: union levies on members meant that it was primarily underwritten by large sacrifices out of small incomes.[60]

A few weeks before the balloting, the Popular Front brought victory within its grasp by securing the backing of the small but pivotal forces behind Ibáñez. The delivery of this support was largely explained by the Alessandri government's slaughter of youthful Nazis who tried to topple the administration in a foolhardy putsch. The abortive coup made less impact on public opinion than did the government's brutal suppression of it. While denouncing the insurrection, the Front made the election into a "plebiscite on the massacre."[61]

At the urging of the Popular Front, *ibañistas* switched from their discredited movement to Aguirre Cerda. Attempts by the Right to resuscitate the disabled Ibáñez campaign were fruitless. Even the Socialists grudgingly concurred in welcoming support from the Ibáñez-Nazi forces. By any standard, the inclusion of the Chilean Nazis in the antifascist Popular Front was incongruous, even though the MNS was more reformist than its European counterparts. The expanded alliance was another example of the Left's need and willingness to subordinate ideological to electoral considerations.[62]

Despite the collapse of the Ibáñez alternative, Ross remained a heavy favorite on election eve. Emotional polarization spread exaggerated fears of a leftist revolt against Ross or a rightist coup against Aguirre Cerda. Equally exaggerated were apocalyptic warnings that Ross would usher in fascism, or Aguirre Cerda communism.[63]

Results of the 1938 Election

The Popular Front won the 1938 election with 50.3% of the votes. According to the 1930 census, 12% of the population was registered; of those, 88% (a higher turnout than in 1932) cast ballots. In other words, about 5% of all Chileans elected Aguirre Cerda president.[64]

The traditional regional pattern of voting prevailed, as Table 12 shows. Aguirre Cerda ran best in the distant north and south and worst in the central latifundia-dominated zones. A blend of geo-

60. U.S., Dept. of State Archives, Santiago, Oct. 8, 1938, p. 5, 825.00/1074, Nov. 2, 1938, p. 5, 825.00/1086.

61. *Hoy,* año VII, no. 361 (Oct. 20, 1938), pp. 9-10, no. 358 (Sept. 29, 1938), p. 14; *Claridad,* Oct. 13, 1938; César Godoy Urrutia, *Los sucesos del 5 de septiembre* (Santiago, 1939); Boizard, *Historia,* pp. 97-125.

62. *El Mercurio,* Oct. 10, 1938; Fernández C., pp. 81-87.

63. *El Mercurio,* Oct. 23, 1938; U.S., Dept. of State Archives, Santiago, Sept. 21, 1938, pp. 7-8, 825.00/1067, Oct. 15, 1938, 825.00/1077.

64. Chile, Dirección General de Estadística, *Política* (1938), pp. 4-7; *Hoy,* año VII, no. 362 (Oct. 28, 1938), p. 9; *El liberalismo* (Santiago, 1939), p. 28.

graphic and social factors spelled victory. The Front's highest provincial vote came from the Socialist stronghold of Magallanes (88.6%),
and it also won the heavily populated urban provinces of Santiago,
Valparaíso, and Concepción. High provincial votes for Aguirre Cerda
coincided with indices of modernity, such as urbanization, unionization, higher average wages paid to workers, and low religiosity.[65]

At the community level, a victory of the urban over rural areas was
also evident, as can be seen in Table 13. Using occupational distribu-
tions from the 1940 census, it can also be seen that Aguirre Cerda ran
best in urban *comunas* with the highest determinable percentage of
industrial laborers among those districts selected for Table 14; he
scored second best in miner *comunas* and worst in the peasant areas
considered.[66]

TABLE 12: VOTES FOR PRESIDENT BY REGION, 1938

Region	Aguirre Cerda	Ross
Great North	64.4%	35.3%
Small North	61.0	38.5
Urban Center	48.0	51.3
North Center	32.0	67.7
South Center	31.2	68.6
Frontier	51.5	48.4
Lakes	43.6	56.2
Channels	68.5	31.4
Total	50.3%	49.4%

TABLE 13: VOTES FOR PRESIDENT IN SELECTED URBAN AND RURAL *COMUNAS*, 1938

	Aguirre Cerda	Ross
Urban *comunas*	61.5%	37.5%
Rural *comunas*	38.2	61.5

TABLE 14: VOTES FOR PRESIDENT BY TYPE OF *COMUNA*, 1938

	Aguirre Cerda	Ross
Industrial *comunas*	66.2%	33.6%
Miner *comunas*	55.6	44.2
Peasant *comunas*	26.9	72.6

Within the capital city, the Front surprised its opponents and displayed its mixed support by running well in both former rightist
enclaves and leftist districts. Aguirre Cerda netted a bare majority in

65. Levine and Crocco, "La población chilena como fuerza," pp. 59-85; McCaa,
pp. 16-202; Cruz-Coke, pp. 38-39, 101.
66. See Appendix A.

the middle- to upper-class urban communities of Providencia (50.1%) and Nuñoa (50.9%), while taking 47.3% of the vote in well-to-do Viña del Mar, for an average of 49.4% in these three unusually non–working class areas. Within Santiago province, Aguirre Cerda also carried the more clearly working-class areas of San Miguel (74.0%), Quinta Normal (69.9%), Renca (58.4%), and Puente Alto (67.9%), but by higher percentages.

Legitimizing and Defending the Electoral Victory, 1938

After the ballots were counted, the Front had to translate that demonstration of electoral supremacy into a constitutional assumption of the presidency. As in 1920, critical days passed between the election and the ratification of its verdict by the Congress. Bitter leaders of the Right immediately filed charges of electoral corruption against the Front. Refusing to recognize the victory, they announced that the electoral process was not fully over until the results had been legally verified.[67]

Initially, the Right's response to the electoral outcome was dominated by its most reactionary elements. Terrified of the Marxists, some predicted that Aguirre Cerda would be "the Kerensky of Chile."[68] They feared that future elections would never be held fairly with Communists and Socialists in the government. They knew their political prospects were glum even with honest elections; electoral dominance was slipping into the hands of the Left and the underprivileged social sectors. Other conservatives realized that the Front only threatened their control of the bureaucracy and the budget, not their private enterprises or way of life. Nevertheless, they used inflammatory charges and tactics to try to keep the Front out of office or to squeeze concessions from it.[69]

The major ploy of the more intractable rightists was to challenge the legality of the electoral returns. They hoped that their majority in Congress would approve a recount in favor of Ross. As a result, post-electoral uncertainty prompted organizing and arming by militant factions on both sides. Some conservative groups momentarily disrupted the economy; by design and panic, the stock market and the value of the peso fell, and in that pressure-cooker atmosphere, rumors of a coup spread.[70]

67. Boizard, *Historia*, pp. 152-61.
68. Infante, p. 102.
69. U.S., Dept. of State Archives, Santiago, Nov. 2, 1938, pp. 5-6, 825.00/1087, Nov. 9, 1938, 825.00/1093; *Hoy*, año VII, no. 362 (Oct. 28, 1938), pp. 31-32.
70. Infante, pp. 83-90; U.S., Dept. of State Archives, Santiago, Nov. 9, 1938, p. 8, 825.00/1092, Nov. 12, 1938, pp. 1-2, 825.00/1094.

Even during those days of confrontation, however, many more temperate leaders of the Right, those who would ultimately prevail, began to argue for cooptation. They maintained a stern exterior but did not want unyielding opposition to harden Aguirre Cerda's alignment with the Left. Instead they hoped to ease him away from the Marxists "through considerate handling and encouragement." Their chances for legal or extralegal denial of the Front's victory appeared slim. As a result, mounting numbers of conservatives chose a strategy of "seduction and flattery," and they tried to divide or domesticate the Front through accommodation, "the hoary, time-honoured stratagem of conservative forces." Many, haunted by memories of 1932, even preferred a tamed Popular Front administration to a military alternative. With the leftist electoral trend expected to continue, "wise rightists . . . realize that they must move over somewhat to the left in their policies, hoping in that way to induce the Popular Front to move more toward the right. . . ."[71] ". . . there has been a steady seepage of rightist elements into the Popular Front fold since the results of the elections were known (one of the most frequent comments by Rossistas is that the most strategic course of action for the conservatives is to 'take Aguirre Cerda over' the way they did Alessandri)."[72]

Several leaders of the rightist political parties began acknowledging the Front's triumph, in contrast to the intransigent public posture of the Ross commanders. The more supple conservative elites offered cooperation on certain mild reform measures. These peace feelers came first from more moderate members of the minor rightist parties, the progressive wing of the Liberals, and the Falange.[73]

Within days after the balloting, even a few of the more adaptable Conservative Party leaders publicly recognized the Front's triumph. They calculated that the social and political costs of reversing the Front's victory might be greater than the price of accepting it: "For the conservatives, since we can not count on either the masses or the armed forces, it suits us, even more than our adversaries, to maintain constitutional democracy."[74] A majority of Conservative chieftains, however, reacted with outrage to the electoral loss and they blamed the Falange. Attempts to punish the *falangistas* caused them to break away to form a small, independent, centrist party.[75]

71. U.S., Dept. of State Archives, Santiago, Oct. 29, 1938, 825.00/1085, Nov. 2, 1938, pp. 3-7, 825.00/1086.

72. U.S., Dept. of State Archives, Santiago, Oct. 29, 1938, 825.00/1085, Nov. 23, 1938, pp. 7-9, 825.00/1097.

73. Partido Liberal, *7.a convención* (Santiago, 1939), pp. 346-47; U.S., Dept. of State Archives, Santiago, Nov. 2, 1938, pp. 5-6, 825.00/1087.

74. Gumucio, *Me defiendo*, pp. 65, 15-21, 41-71.

75. U.S., Dept. of State Archives, Santiago, Dec. 6, 1938, pp. 3-4, 825.00/1102; Partido Conservador, *Falange*.

Alessandri and his government resolved to transfer office peacefully. Though the president officially withheld recognition of Aguirre Cerda's victory until the Right's electoral protests were adjudicated, his administration helped legitimize the triumph already acknowledged by public opinion. Shortly past midnight of election day, the Minister of the Interior, Aguirre Cerda's godfather, announced that the Front had won. That official declaration was not repeated in the tense days that followed. It was, however, communicated to Chilean legations abroad by the Minister of Foreign Relations. Thus the narrow electoral victory acquired international as well as national sanction.[76]

Conservative, upper-class groups who were not party leaders were even more flexible toward the president-elect. With less to lose than those holding government posts, the economic elites, especially in the cities, realized that their control over the major means of production and communication was not in jeopardy. The stock market and business panic after the election was brief.[77]

Foreign, mainly North American, economic interests also responded with restraint. The U.S. ambassador, in accord with the Good Neighbor policy, recommended conciliation. Of course foreign capital was jittery and sought clarifications from the Front. Some U.S. as well as Chilean companies feared retribution because of past "social slights" and economic discrimination against leaders of the Front. Aguirre Cerda knew that "these American enterprises have one and all lent aid and comfort to his defeated opponent. . . . "; however, he, along with some Socialist congressmen and other Front spokesmen, despite broad public approval of gradual nationalization of mineral holdings, public utilities, and marine transportation, assured U.S. diplomatic and business representatives that they intended "to govern along moderate lines." With such guarantees from the victors, foreigners generally decided to cooperate with the incoming administration.[78]

Some Church leaders also gracefully accepted Aguirre Cerda's victory. Bishop José María Caro sent a congratulatory telegram which helped legitimize the electoral results, and later, during the Front government, he became archbishop to smooth Church-state relations. In turn, the Front did not attack the Church.[79]

76. Wilfredo Mayorga, "Cuatro cartas de triunfo para don Pedro," *Ercilla*, no. 1622 (July 6, 1966), pp. 23-25; Florencio Durán Bernales, *El Partido Radical* (Santiago, 1958), pp. 70-71.
77. U.S., Dept. of State Archives, Santiago, Oct. 29, 1938, 825.00/1085.
78. U.S., Dept. of State Archives, Santiago, Oct. 29, 1938, 825.00/1085, Nov. 2, 1938, 825.00/1086, Nov. 9, 1938, 825.00/1093, Nov. 26, 1938, p. 3, 825.00/1100, Dec. 3, 1938, pp. 2-3, 825.00/1103, Dec. 6, 1938, 825.00/1102.
79. Mayorga, "Cuatro," pp. 23-25; Infante, pp. 106-7.

From election to inauguration day, the Front pursued a dual strategy of a firm defense and a conciliatory offense. Brinkmanship on both sides dominated the first weeks after the balloting. As Alessandri had in 1920, the Left used the specter of civil war to press for confirmation of its victory. Mass rallies stoked the fighting spirit of the Front and also convinced many conservatives and military officers that accepting Aguirre Cerda was preferable to civil strife.[80]

The civil war scenario was based not only on suppositions concerning the spontaneous combustibility of the working class; it also rested on the existence of paramilitary forces. Even the Radicals and the Falange, which also swore to defend the Front's claim on office, boasted token militias. Most disturbing to the Right were the militias of the Socialists, Communists, and Nazis, whose ideologies justified the taking of power by force of arms.[81] At the same time, the Front kept mass mobilization and confrontation under control so as not to support rightist fears of impending anarchy or revolutionary upheaval as a justification for military intrusion.[82]

Aguirre Cerda led the Front's simultaneous efforts to appease the established forces and to convince them that acquiescence was the best hope for the social order. His declared theme of "to govern is to educate" forecast only gradual social change. The victorious candidate reassured domestic and foreign elites that his primary economic objective was increased production, not redistribution or nationalization. Scoffing at fears of social convulsion, he argued that Chileans were too "patient" to engage in revolution. Aguirre Cerda encouraged the view that he would serve as a safety valve. "His position is and will be difficult: that of a renovator as conservative as he can possibly be. . . ."[83] Aguirre Cerda warned his adversaries: "I am the second Chilean President from the Radical Party . . . I will be the second and the last if those of the other side do not know enough to listen to reason and to make concessions, as the great leaders of their own group have advised. . . . Either I open a regulating channel for the desires of the people or after me comes the flood."[84]

During the post-election transition, the Communists joined the Radicals in emphasizing moderation. They welcomed the influx of more middle-class adherents after the balloting. The PC advised the

80. *El liberalismo,* pp. 27-28; U.S., Dept. of State Archives, Santiago, Nov. 9, 1938, pp. 6-8, 825.00/1092.

81. Wilfredo Mayorga, "Cuando el ejército 'dio pase' a don Pedro," *Ercilla,* no. 1687 (Oct. 4, 1967), p. 15.

82. Contreras, *Unidad,* pp. 18-24; Fernández C., pp. 92-93.

83. U.S., Dept. of State Archives, Santiago, Nov. 9, 1938, 825.00/1093, Nov. 23, 1938, 825.00/1097; Infante, pp. 83-114.

84. U.S., Dept. of State Archives, Santiago, Nov. 9, 1938, 825.00/1093.

Radicals to be less anticlerical and the Socialists, less extremist, so that more Chileans would feel comfortable with the Front.[85] Many Socialists also gave the impression that the Popular Front would merely be a Chilean "New Deal." Still, the PS was more combative than its allies and emphasized the threat of civil war more.[86]

The most important audience for the maneuverings of the Right and Left was the regular military. The armed forces rejected right-wing conspiracies because, first, the officers were divided in their loyalties whether to the conservatives, the Front, or simply the constitution. The military did not favor actions which would cause fighting among the branches of the armed services or against large numbers of civilians. Even the more aristocratic navy could not rally enough officers in its own ranks to support suggestions of a coup from some Ross supporters. Though a few high military officers favored the Front, part of this backing was really support for Ibáñez. Second, the civilian Right was also torn, with many leaders, including President Alessandri, unenthusiastic about military intervention. Third, there were traces of animosity toward Alessandri and the conservative groups for slights in the early 1930s. Fourth, the military still remembered with distaste its previous experience in government and the onus of the Great Depression and political chaos. Finally, the behavior of the Popular Front swayed the armed forces against marching back into power.[87]

The post-election tension eased when the military, in effect, expressed its preference for a peaceful transfer of the presidential sash to Aguirre Cerda. A few army officers were even ready to rebel if the Right snatched victory from the Front. In response to private inquiries from Ross, the commanders-in-chief of the army and the Carabineros indicated that a reversal of the electoral count would ignite more violence than they wanted to confront. In their reply to Ross, which soon became public, these generals argued that a majority of the armed forces, as well as the civilian population, had already accepted the Front's victory, and they urged Ross to withdraw his electoral protests to avoid social disturbances. The Carabineros, which had the lowest social-class composition of any of the armed services, were the most emphatic in rejecting potential support of the Right. In response, Ross, amply bitter, surrendered his fight for the presidency and

85. Lafertte and Contreras, *Los comunistas,* pp. 7-21; Contreras, *Unidad,* pp. 20-40.
86. U.S., Dept. of State Archives, Santiago, Dec. 6, 1938, 825.00/1102; Cruz Salas, p. 270.
87. Mayorga, "Las intrigas," pp. 18-19; Mayorga, "Cuando el ejército," p. 15; Cabero, *Recuerdos,* pp. 186-87; U.S., Dept. of State Archives, Santiago, Nov. 2, 1938, pp. 3-5, 825.00/1086, Nov. 16, 1938, pp. 2-6, 825.00/1096.

departed for Europe. The Right and the Left both immediately backed away from the brink of open conflict. Although not the result of full deliberations among all branches of the armed services, this military decision, almost as much as the election and more than the congressional considerations, resolved the issue of presidential succession.[88]

Inauguration of the Popular Front, 1938

The organization and inauguration of the Aguirre Cerda administration helped calm political fears and tempers. The incoming president's initial appointments reserved the key positions for moderates, mainly Radicals. Some critical slots even went to holdovers from the Alessandri years, "especially in those important posts that don't get much public attention." Most of the Marxists' appointments were "conspicuous rather than important." Nevertheless, Aguirre Cerda went farther in rewarding the Left than some Chileans had expected. For example, he named Schnake's wife mayor of Santiago and a Communist from the 1931 naval mutiny mayor of Valparaíso. The Socialists received the least important cabinet slots (Health, Development, and Lands and Colonization) and the Communists none. Meanwhile, the Radicals took the most significant and sensitive seats, Interior, Defense, Foreign Affairs, Treasury, Education, and Agriculture. Minor parties received token positions, such as the Democratics in the Ministry of Labor.[89]

By dominating the new administration, the Radicals realized their age-old dream of taking government positions from the rightist parties. The Radicals contrasted their takeover with earlier ascendance by individuals from the middle strata. They claimed that now the full middle class, with the proletariat behind it, was shoving the oligarchy out of the government. Allegedly, the true, non-"*arribista*" middle class, without desires to become aristocrats, was now in charge. The jubilant Radicals even vowed to oust existing middle-class government

88. Apparently, military support for the president-elect was also based on Front promises not to prosecute any Carabineros involved in the massacre of Nazis; one of President Aguirre Cerda's first acts was to declare amnesty for everyone involved in the putsch and the slaughter. Bravo Ríos, pp. 93-95; Thomas, "Marmaduke Grove: A Political Biography," pp. 308-9; Mayorga, "Cuatro," pp. 23-25; *El Mercurio*, Nov. 14-16, 1938; *El Diario Ilustrado*, Nov. 13-15, 1938; Infante, pp. 99-101; U.S., Dept. of State Archives, Santiago, Nov. 13, 1938, pp. 1-2, 825.00/1091, Nov. 14, 1938, 825.00/1095, Nov. 23, 1938, pp. 6-9, 825.00/1097.

89. The *ibañistas* rejected cabinet-level appointments, as did the Communists, but took minor domestic and foreign-service posts. The Nazis, Falange, and progressive Liberals stayed out of the spoils distribution. U.S., Dept. of State Archives, Santiago, Jan. 17, 1939, pp. 2-8, 825.00/1118; *La Nación*, Dec. 25, 1938.

servants of the elites unless those bureaucrats came over to the winning side where they belonged.[90]

For the Communists and Socialists, it became a cliché that the Left had won political but not economic power through the presidential succession. In reality, the Marxists had won very little of either kind of power in 1938. Following a slim electoral victory, the Front entered office with shaky unity and only partial control of the government. Moreover, Aguirre Cerda was a right-wing Radical. The Marxists were underrepresented in the cabinet. A hostile majority in the Congress, the bureaucracy, and other state institutions was braced against radical change. Without even considering domestic and foreign elite economic interest groups or the military, the constraints on Marxist participation and plans were formidable.[91]

Although the Marxists seized little immediate executive power, they did benefit from a rapid increase in their following. In the first months after the 1938 balloting, the leftist organizations and parties received a rash of new members. Labor leaders did not capture prominent positions in the Aguirre Cerda government, even though the unions had probably supplied the Front with its largest single bloc of votes. Within two months after the presidential election, however, the CTCH grew by tens of thousands, more than doubling its membership. Formerly unaligned unions and independent workers, not just those from the large mining and industrial firms, rushed to be affiliated with a winner; bandwagon politics suited a clientelistic system. Moreover, the burgeoning CTCH remained dominated by the Socialists and Communists, who divided the leadership nearly evenly. This union growth was part of the quick institutionalization of working-class groups under the Front.[92]

Such membership expansion ranked as the highest priority of the Communists in the Front. Although they accepted lesser posts, they rejected cabinet ministries. The PC outflanked the Socialists by supporting the new government but staying out of the higher administration: thus the Communists were less directly responsible for government actions and later suffered fewer complaints from their more impatient revolutionaries about timid government policies. Abstaining from the cabinet gave the PC more freedom to build its union support. It also restrained the Right and the military from anticommunist conspiracies against the administration.[93]

90. González Videla, pp. 24-30.
91. Lechner.
92. U.S., Dept. of State Archives, Santiago, Nov. 23, 1938, p. 3, 825.00/1097, Dec. 6, 1938, 825.00/1102.
93. For example, Communists took sub-cabinet positions in quasi-autonomous gov-

Some Socialists also balked at cabinet participation, but the majority leadership drew the party into the government. The "pro-abstention" minority came mainly from the North, Concepción, the Youth Federation, and the former Communist Left. At the PS congress in December, 1938, these dissidents accounted for about 30 of the 450 delegates. The "pro-abstentionists" endorsed the Popular Front coalition and the fulfillment of its program, but they prophesied that the Socialist Party would be unable to exert real power or achieve its objectives from its three minor cabinet stations. These pessimists feared that their party would be compromised, corrupted, and discredited.[94]

The Socialists would have preferred more powerful posts, especially the Ministry of Labor. Nevertheless, party leaders thought they could bring relief to all the underprivileged and establish reformist credentials through the Ministry of Health. They also saw an opportunity to benefit and proselytize small miners and industrialists, particularly in the northern provinces, through the Ministry of Development; and they hoped to reach agricultural laborers and small farmers through the previously ineffectual Ministry of Lands and Colonization.[95]

Conclusions on the Ascension of the Popular Front

Neither unmitigated populism nor socialism took full power through the Popular Front, though strong strains of both tendencies were seen in the coalition's rise, support, and programs. In essence, the new leftist forces were channeled into the ongoing system behind traditional reformers more devoted to economic than social change, an emphasis very similar to that of more avowedly conservative Latin American governments in the era. A period of highly populist mobilization of the middle and lower classes issued in an administration far less radical than its promises had implied. There was an inherent tension in the ability of such heterogeneous coalitions to attain high national offices because there was a tendency for those same coalitions to inhibit the enactment of the very programs for which the Socialists had sought office.

The process of moderation of the new Left began during the formation of the Front and sped up after electoral triumph. Through this moderation, the Socialists and Communists vaulted from electoral participation in 1932 to government executive participation in 1938.

ernment institutions such as insurance agencies. Stevenson, pp. 94-97; Carlos Contreras Labarca, *Por la paz, por nuevas victorias del Frente Popular* (Santiago, 1939), p. 27.

94. Chelén, *Trayectoria,* p. 92; Cruz Salas, pp. 79-80, 271.

95. Chelén, *El partido de la victoria,* pp. 23-27.

The PS and PC scaled those heights without upsetting the established political system or forcing a break with the traditional parties. Above all, this was possible because of the resilience of Chilean political culture and institutions, the adaptability of the established elites, and the compromises of the Marxists. Through the brokerage of the centrist groups and parties, institutionalization of a movement with pronounced populist characteristics but ostensibly committed to the destruction of the status quo commenced very rapidly. The 1930s was a decade of intense leftist mobilization, but it did not upset the political or social order.[96]

The Front's victory sanctified the tradition that the Left, including the Socialists and Communists, could enter the presidential chambers through electoral coalitions, and it left open troubling questions for both the Marxists and their opponents. The new administration had the potential to duplicate the achievements of contemporary and later populist regimes elsewhere in the hemisphere or to write a more unusual record of reform with strongly socialist leanings. For the Marxists, the Popular Front's ascension presented opportunities to exercise partial power and to build their parties. It also presented dangers of cooptation, frustration, and loss of prestige as a protest movement. At the same time, the Marxists' antagonism toward the establishment but willingness to participate in it threatened the privileged groups with displacement. However, it also gave the conservative elites the opportunity to harness the new Left and populism within the constraints of the traditional bargaining system.

At least in the short run, the election of Aguirre Cerda inherently delayed the radicalization of Chilean politics. It brought the dissident groups spawned during the Depression into the give-and-take of administration. It persuaded most of the Marxists and the workers to place greater trust in constitutional remedies. Concomitantly, it convinced almost all but the most obdurate conservatives of the necessity of gradual changes within legal bounds.[97]

As in the past, initial overreaction to the 1938 electoral victory of reform forces was followed by surprising moderation and accommodation. This occurred because of both the tenacity and sophistication of the Right and the caution and composition of the Left. The ascension of the Popular Front did not signal the dawn of social transformations. It did, however, mark the beginning of a new political era of accelerated state capitalism and institutionalization of the socialist forces.

96. Lechner, esp. p. 80.
97. Stevenson, pp. 136-37.

8

Institutionalization of Chilean Socialism through the Popular Front Administration, 1938-41

By the end of the 1930s, institutionalization of lower-class politics superseded mobilization. After taking office, the Popular Front downplayed the mobilization aspects of populism but maintained its broad, integrating social coalition and its compromising policies of simultaneous industrialization and social welfare measures for the urban middle and lower classes. While reflecting certain European multiparty patterns, popular-front politics also resembled Latin American populist phenomena. After the rather direct upper-class rule expressed in the Parliamentary Republic, Chile had struggled through a series of crises of authority since World War I. As in other Latin American countries, political uncertainty and social rigidity had accompanied changing socioeconomic realities. In the 1920s and early 1930s, this had led to military solutions to the legitimacy vacuum. Then the Popular Front alternative surpassed direct elite rule or military-backed dictatorships as an authentic means of political organization. Multiclass movements including urban labor became the organized, accepted, legitimate social base of government. Such social-political coalitions kept state institutions afloat so long as mobilization of still subordinated groups did not overload the flexible arrangements forged through the popular-front formula.[1]

The major political impact of the Popular Front was to institutionalize class-based politics. It integrated the Marxist parties, the unions, and their followers into the system through class cooperation more than through conflict. New contenders were incorporated without ejecting traditional participants. The elasticity of Chilean democracy opened electoral and bureaucratic avenues of participation to the

1. Faletto, Ruiz, and Zemelman, esp. p. 5; Lechner, esp. pp. 17-66.

organized working classes and especially their representatives. At the same time, it blunted their demands for social change. The inclusion of Marxist mass politics in the multiparty bargaining network deflected attacks against the system toward particular officeholders or laws. The workers and their leaders only obtained a secondary role in the distribution of power and benefits. However, the inclusion of the Marxists not only held out the promise of stability and perhaps cooptation; it also carried the possibility of Marxist growth and eventual takeover. An additional possibility was that by the time the Marxists grew powerful enough within the system to reach for the presidency on their own, they might be so socialized into traditional values as to no longer present a revolutionary threat. In any case, the peaceful coexistence fashioned by the early 1940s did not eliminate tensions within the system for either the Right or the Left.[2]

The populist elements were largely institutionalized in the Socialist Party and into the governing apparatus. Through involvement in the Aguirre Cerda administration, the Socialists shifted emphasis from the mobilization stage of populism to a more institutionalized, clientelistic phase. Mobilization indicated the disruptive, insurgent potentialities of populism. Now institutionalization showed its accommodative, integrative capacities.

Economic Changes under the Popular Front

The years 1930-53 formed a coherent economic period which began with the Depression and continued through reactions to it and to World War II regardless of the parties in office. Like Alessandri before him, Aguirre Cerda essentially pursued a model of state capitalism. In other words, the state actively encouraged private enterprise and often took the place of individual entrepreneurs in developing capitalism, which resulted in a mixed public-private economy. Such assistance primarily for the capitalist elites was far different from the redistributive goals of state intervention under a socialist model. In the thirties and forties, Chile's presidents grappled with common economic problems, especially in the foreign sector, so they all emphasized internal industrial modernization. Since Chile lagged behind more industrialized nations, the Popular Front identified the labor movement more with national economic development than with working-class social conquests. The new administration did not plan to meet the needs of the poor at the expense of the rich. Rather, Aguirre Cerda's government expected to improve the well-being of all Chileans through increased productivity, a time-honored

2. Petras, pp. 123-35; Lechner, pp. 80-81; Stevenson, pp. 136-46.

conservative vision. The Left failed to articulate or install an alternative economic recipe to that favored by the developmentalist Right.
The Front's only innovations were to amplify state intervention even
further, to increase the emphasis on industry, and to pay more attention to the labor component and full employment. However intended,
populism and import-súbstituting industrialization logically coincided. The influence of the Front over the workers facilitated "social
peace" during the government's acceleration of industrial capacity,
which allowed the administration to postpone immediate rewards for
the working class in the name of future benefits. Therefore, populist
electoral campaigns, based on appeals to the social discontent of the
underprivileged, issued in technocratic, developmentalist governments committed to production over redistribution.[3]

Diverse other Latin American regimes experienced economic
changes similar to Chile's during the thirties and forties, so international factors probably explained more about policy making than did
internal politics. The immediate constraint on the Popular Front was
the onset of World War II. This disruption of international transactions pared imports and resources available for new government
programs. The scarcity of manufactured imports inspired the drive
for indigenous industrialization, which was only partially hindered by
the dearth of foreign capital goods. From 1938 through 1941, Chile's
index of industrial production rose over 25%, while agricultural output virtually stagnated. The war years also accelerated a dramatic shift
from Europe to the United States as trading partners. As World War
II took shape (1938-40), British and German trade with Chile plummeted, while the United States nearly doubled its Chilean sales and
tripled its purchases. This dependence on the United States dam-
pened economic nationalism, even for the Marxist members of the
Front. For example, the governing coalition, afraid of alienating
the North American market, did not bleed the nitrate or copper
companies. On the beneficial side, the war created a huge demand
for Chile's mineral products and a large accumulation of foreign
exchange.[4]

World War II also fueled inflation, as did government priming of
the economy. After relative stability in 1938, chronic price inflation
soared again throughout 1939-42, when the cost of living rose 83%,
more than from 1931 to 1939. Instead of attacks on vested foreign and
national interests, the Popular Front opted for economic growth fed by

    3. Corporación de Fomento, *Geografía*, II, pp. 519-20; Corporación de Fomento,
Renta, I, p. 173; Durán, pp. 80-81, 124-26, 174-84; Pinto, *Chile*, pp. 108-25.
    4. Flavián Levine B., "Indices de producción física," *Economía*, año V, nos. 10-11
(July, 1944), pp. 69-98; Jorge González von Marées, *El mal de Chile* (Santiago, 1940), pp.
62-64, 154-72; Corporación de Fomento, *Geografía*, II, pp. 295-97; Herring, p. 239.

foreign loans and domestic credit expansion. These capital injections won political support from the economic elites and the middle classes, but consumers, especially the poor, suffered from rising prices. The main beneficiaries of depreciating currency were debtors, often landowners. Expansion of industry and construction was funded by domestic savings, monetary expansion, and loans from the U.S. Export-Import Bank. These policies furthered economic growth rather than national autonomy or social reform.[5]

Although mainly devoted to aiding oligopolistic industry, the Front, pursuing contradictory objectives, also tried to lighten the price burden on consumers. To intervene in the economy to control prices and output, Aguirre Cerda exhumed some neglected decree laws from Dávila's Socialist Republic. Resurrecting Dávila's state capitalist innovations allowed the Front to avoid having to run the gauntlet of the obstructionist Congress. These laws, for example the ones governing "overproduction," provided protection for inefficient national industries in saturated markets by restricting competition and stabilizing prices. They also allowed the government to clamp down on the prices of some primary necessities, mainly agricultural goods. One of Aguirre Cerda's first acts was a populist decree reducing the prices of milk and bread. These state interventions favored the urban over the rural economic elites even more than the mass of consumers.[6]

The thrust of state action by the Popular Front was to rationalize aid to private entrepreneurs in all sectors of the economy, especially industry and construction. Government expansion and planning linked the middle-class bureaucrats in particular agencies with the corresponding economic elites for the sector they served. All the interest group elites, even the labor organizations, carved out or retained bureaucratic fiefdoms related to their special fields. For example, landowners worked hand-in-hand with the new state activists in departments regulating the modernization of agriculture. Rather than establishing drastic new directions or highly coordinated plans, the Front merely introduced a multiplication of government activities to cope with an increasingly complex society. This semicorporatist state served as an umbrella over the compartmentalized, particular interests of sectors and groups. It did not become the envisioned conductor and integrator of the private economy.[7]

The central agent of these government policies was the new De-

5. Ellsworth, pp. 80-81, 106-22, 165; Corporación de Fomento, *Geografía*, II, pp. 321-22.

6. *Pan, techo, abrigo. Dos años de gobierno popular* (Valparaíso, 1941); Gregorio Talesnik Rabinovich, *Intervenciones del estado y control del precios por el mismo* (Santiago, 1941).

7. González von Marées, *El mal*, pp. 129-31; Barría, *El movimiento*, pp. 68-72.

velopment Corporation (CORFO). It was praised by the Front parties as their most significant achievement, but CORFO was dedicated to raising production, not the lower classes. This quasi-autonomous agency, whose purpose was to disperse credit in all branches and regions of the economy, sought to stimulate private enterprises so that they could stand on their own. CORFO worked to create at most a mixed, rather than a socialist, state-run economy. Through such a mechanism, the twin populistic aspirations of nationalistic industrialization and major benefits for the working classes were unlikely to be realized simultaneously. For example, CORFO investments were geared to promoting domestic manufacturing utilizing native resources and were seldom aimed at encouraging low-cost operations to improve the current standard of living of a majority of Chileans. As the most favored sector, industrialists saw their profits rise far more than wages for workers.[8]

The Front organized CORFO along functional lines as a combined state-private institution to represent all facets of Chilean society. In effect, the economic elites and their homologous departments of the government dominated. The ruling body of CORFO included government ministers, congressional representatives, presidential appointees, and members from all the state sectoral economic planning and credit agencies. In addition, there were official representatives from the SNA, SOFOFA, SNM, Chamber of Commerce, Institute of Engineers, and, last and least, the CTCH.[9]

Though hailed as an instrument of economic nationalism, CORFO was funded from foreign as well as domestic sources. Conservative congressional opposition convinced the Front to abandon its original plan of paying for CORFO by taxing wealthy Chileans, so the government relied more on small credits from the U.S. Export-Import Bank in CORFO's beginning years. These loans were available partly to pull Chile over to the allied side in World War II and normally had to be spent on U.S. goods and services. Export-Import Bank funding encouraged the government and CORFO to help North American as well as Chilean enterprises, particularly mixed foreign-national ventures. Dependence on these credits also dissuaded the Front from injuring U.S. industries. For example, the bank successfully discouraged a project to construct hydroelectric plants which would have competed with U.S. utility interests in Chile. At the same time, Aguirre

8. Luis Amadeo Aracena, *Ensayos económicos, políticos y sociales* (Santiago, 1941), p. 104; Corporación de Fomento de la Producción, *Cinco años de labor, 1939-1943* (Santiago, 1944), pp. 18-56; Ellsworth, pp. 91-93.
    9. Corporación de Fomento, *Cinco*, p. 9.

Cerda's continued servicing of Chile's already high foreign debt resulted in more being paid out to the United States than came in; a large part of these payments abroad, however, were financed through moderately increased taxes on the U.S. copper companies.[10]

Many conservative groups initially opposed the creation of CORFO, even though they later became some of its major beneficiaries. The political Right in Congress was most hostile, but the economic interest organizations, in particular the SOFOFA and the SNM, welcomed CORFO, especially when it began to operate in their favor.[11] Partly in order to coax the CORFO legislation through the obstinate Congress, the Communists and Socialists helped the government pacify the Right. The Marxists maintained social tranquility by subduing worker struggles and demands, especially in agriculture. In a trade-off between economic and social change, the Left sided more with industrialization during the Popular Front.[12]

The Socialists were among the major architects and boosters of CORFO, although some later complained that it served inefficient economic magnates more than the consuming masses. At least in the early years, however, the PS was deeply involved in giving the agency its developmentalist orientation. Schnake, as Minister of Development, negotiated loans with the United States to fund CORFO and stabilize Chilean exports. Especially during wartime shortages and other difficulties, many Socialists became more concerned with selling than nationalizing copper. Increasingly, they accepted the workers' and their country's role in the market system. Socialist leaders stressed the best way for Chile to profit from that role instead of trying to change it. In the name of industrialization, they compromised their devotion to economic nationalism and working-class advancement. The Socialists and their allies did not make CORFO a vehicle for their earlier economic programs, among them agrarian reform or expropriation of basic foreign and domestic industries; they were soon engrossed in pragmatic, day-to-day government administration. Consequently, the PS leadership became more enamored of technocratic projects and problem solving than of ideological conquests. In some-

10. Corporación de Fomento, *Geografía,* II, p. 522; Corporación de Fomento, *Renta,* II, p. 219; Corporación de Fomento, *Cinco,* pp. 22-38; Gunther, p. 235; Ellsworth, pp. 85-88; Cademártori, pp. 162-63; Stevenson, pp. 122-25; Fernando Casanueva Valencia and Manuel Fernández Canque, *El Partido Socialista y la lucha de clases en Chile* (Santiago, 1973), p. 304.

11. Wilfredo Mayorga, "El golpe de estado de 1939," *Ercilla,* no. 1701 (Jan. 24, 1968), p. 15. For example, see La Sociedad Nacional de Minería, *Boletín Minero . . . ,* LI, no. 468 (Apr., 1939), pp. 287-311.

12. Cruz Salas, p. 272; Corporación de Fomento, *Cinco,* pp. 36-38.

what populist fashion, they concentrated on immediate solutions rather than long-run strides toward socialism.[13]

Upper-Class Adjustments to the Popular Front

The Right and the upper class hemmed in the Front by fighting it doggedly in the political arena and demarcating permissible boundaries of economic and social reform. Within those limits, however, the unreconstructed political elites were far more uncompromising than the adaptable leaders of other institutions associated with the upper class. Except in party conflicts and extreme cases, the traditional elites mainly tried to lull or neutralize the Front and subsequent "populistic" coalition governments led by the Radicals in the 1940s. The upper sectors employed limited warfare but also, more significantly, conciliation and cooptation. For example, the elites throttled any strongly reformist initiatives by the Front in Congress and, at the same time, guided state expansion to their benefit through flexible approaches by private interest organizations.[14]

A good example of the disarming approach adopted by many conservative institutions outside the hostile political parties was the response of the Roman Catholic Church. At the insistence of even many conservatives in Chile, the Vatican removed the reactionary Archbishop of Santiago. Rome replaced him with the bishop from the north, José María Caro, who had congratulated Aguirre Cerda on his electoral victory. The new president had discreetly requested the Vatican to make that change in Church leadership.[15] Under Archbishop Caro, the Chilean Church won a reputation as the most progressive in Latin America. Caro took a position close to that of the Falange. While praising Aguirre Cerda and prudent, Christian reforms, he still drew a hard line against Marxism. This was not only an appeal to the poor, it was also an attempt to steer the far Right and the non-Marxist members of the Front away from extreme positions. In 1939, Caro even startled the landed elites by urging unionization, better living conditions, higher wages, and a share in profits for the peasants. Without denouncing the structure of land tenure, the archbishop said that exploitation of workers was a sin and warned that selfish landowners would be denied the sacraments. Such enlightened responses by traditional institutions countered Marxist reform proposals. The Church's mediating role also reduced the likelihood of total polarization or drastic challenges to the social order.[16]

13. Cruz Salas, pp. 156-59.
14. Mattelart, Castillo, and Castillo, pp. 117-19.
15. Durán, pp. 140-41.
16. José María Caro, *La iglesia está con el pueblo* (Valparaíso, 1940); Editorial "El

Agricultural and Industrial Elites

The landowners came to epitomize the increasingly preemptive, tolerant attitude of the economic elites toward the Popular Front. This flexibility was especially evident after the first shock of defeat subsided and coup attempts fizzled. Jaime Larraín, president of the SNA and the Confederation of Production and Commerce, was in the forefront of aristocrats who had feverently backed Ross but then arranged a *modus vivendi* with the Aguirre Cerda government. Through guarded cooperation, Larraín tried to reconcile the landholders and the administration. He prodded the SNA and its members to adapt to the Front's mild programs for peasant betterment: "It is impossible to stop social evolution. We must put ourselves on the side of social evolution in order to channel it."[17] In addition, Larraín urged the *latifundistas* to enroll more farm workers in the SNA and to take advantage of state support for agricultural mechanization and modernization.[18]

Like the Church and other elite institutions, the SNA edged away from reliance on political parties and their brawls with the Front. The landowners' organization wanted to be able to press its constituents' case with government regardless of who won elections. Such cooperation between the SNA and the state was facilitated by Radical leaders who were prominent landowners. Thus the heterogeneity of the Popular Front toned down its reform program. During the Aguirre Cerda administration, many landed Radicals joined the SNA for the first time and helped make it more receptive to rural reforms and the government more responsive to the agrarian elites. Differences between the Society and the government were mediated by Radical Cristóbal Sáenz, the wealthy estate owner who had won the first by-election for the Front in 1936. He became vice-president of the SNA and a member of Aguirre Cerda's cabinet. Supporting Larraín's policy of conciliation, Sáenz helped bury Popular Front plans for agrarian reform.[19]

Aguirre Cerda's own cordial relations with the landed elites were equally important. Some landowners attacked the President as a traitor and agitator against them and blamed the government when agricultural output fell while production in all other sectors, especially

---

Amigo del Pueblo," *El socialismo y el comunismo ante el sentido común* (4 vols., Santiago, 1939); Herring, pp. 218-20.

17. Hott, pp. 21-22; La Sociedad Nacional de Agricultura, *El Campesino*, LXXI, no. 1 (Jan., 1939), pp. 18-20; U.S., Dept. of State Archives, Santiago, Oct. 11, 1939, p. 3, 825.00/1177.

18. La Sociedad Nacional de Agricultura, *El Campesino*, LXXI, no. 5 (May, 1939), pp. 239-40.

19. La Sociedad Nacional de Agricultura, *El Campesino*, LXXI, no. 1 (Jan., 1939), p. 2; Durán, p. 100.

industry and mining, rose moderately. The Front, however, boasted of increasing rural credit and aid. The administration's restrictions on selected agricultural prices did little damage to production and sometimes pegged food and fiber prices above world-market levels. Despite some economic complaints, most landowners realized that Aguirre Cerda's highest priority in the countryside was social peace to facilitate production. He preferred landowner generosity as the best solution to peasant grievances. For example, Aguirre Cerda and other prominent Radicals reprimanded their Marxist allies for fomenting class hatred against the members of the SNA.[20]

From the 1930s until the 1960s, this accommodation between the Front and the landed elites set limits on Chilean social and political development, while institutionalizing the settlement that had taken shape between the rural and urban economic leaders after the Great Depression. Restricting government social reforms to the cities, it was a working arrangement typical of Latin American populism and import-substituting industrialization. In essence, prices for agricultural products were held down to placate the urban supporters of the centrist reformers and Marxists. This muted labor discontent against industrialists, and in turn the rural elites were shielded from peasant unionization. As a result, the archaic system of land tenure could endure while economic losses were sweated from rural labor. The government dispensed modest subsidies and credit to agriculture, which partly compensated for enforcing low prices, and the Right retained its rural voting base. In sum, urban unions and leftist parties gained from the relative decline of the agrarian sector, but the losers were the rural workers much more than the landed elites.[21]

During the first year of the Front, Marxist unionization of peasants jeopardized the tacit agreement between landowners, on the one hand, and urban industrialists, workers, and reformers, on the other. At the end of the 1930s rural unionization, especially by the Communists, boomed. The PC claimed nearly 400 rural unions with almost 60,000 members, concentrated among the poorest peasants, by late 1939. In the same year, the CTCH listed peasant organization as a high priority and enrolled thousands. The confederation demanded full legalization of rural unions. Socialist Deputy Emilio Zapata led the Marxists' National Peasant Federation, which superseded the smaller 1935 National League for the Defense of Poor Peasants, and then escalated rural mobilization to peak intensity. Strikes called during

20. U.S., Dept. of State Archives, Santiago, Oct. 28, 1939, pp. 2-3, 825.00/1179, May 8, 1940, 825.00/1210; Durán, pp. 54-59, 98-100; Levine, "Indices," p. 87; Ulises Correa, *Discurso pronunciado . . .* (Santiago, 1941), pp. 3-7.
21. Aranda and Martínez, pp. 125-34.

harvests were most effective for the workers because they were potentially catastrophic for the landlords. All the Front parties also tried to court the small, middle-class landowners. In former conservative strongholds, the governing coalition began winning rural by-elections, both by rallying the peasants and by private Radical acquisitions of estates. Increasingly in 1939, the left wing of the Front called for state intervention to improve peasant wages, living conditions, and independence from landlords. In response, the conservative elites implored the state to prevent the extension of legislation and unionization for urban workers to the countryside.[22]

In this confrontation, Aguirre Cerda ultimately sided with the SNA against the Marxists. The government declared a moratorium on peasant unionization and strikes, and Aguirre Cerda assured the SNA, "I understand perfectly that my policy should promote harmony and not social struggle."[23] In return, the landowners promised to improve labor conditions and to halt dismissals of farmworkers. In effect, the landholders became more tightly organized and influential while the peasants became less so.[24]

In terms of political economy, the Front, regardless of ideological coloration, chose to favor least the group least able to pressure it. Keeping the peasants down and on the margin of the cash economy reduced demands on scarce resources. In addition, maintaining peasant wages as the lowest in Chile restricted the internal market for both domestic and foreign goods. Although this constrained industrialization in the long run, it conserved savings and foreign exchange during the difficult opening years of World War II. Choking off peasant activism also avoided disruptions of food supplies to the cities; holding down the prices of basic foods and peasant demands to slow inflation and to mollify urban constituents could not work if rural unions dislocated production and extracted benefits.[25]

Despite protests, all the Front parties and the CTCH grudgingly

22. La Confederación de Trabajadores de Chile, *¿Por qué salimos a la calle el 21 de mayo de este año?* (Santiago, 1940); La Confederación de Trabajadores de Chile, *Manifiesto de la Confederación de Trabajadores a las clases laboriosas del país* (Santiago, 1940); La Confederación de Trabajadores de Chile, *Treinta meses de acción en favor del proletariado de Chile* (Santiago, 1939); Caro, *La iglesia*, pp. 1-9; Comité Regional del Partido Socialista, p. 40; Partido Comunista, *XI congreso . . .* (Santiago, 1940), pp. 32-37; Ernesto Loyola Acuña, *El hombre que frustró una revolución* (Talca, Chile, 1942), pp. 26-54; Affonso et al., I, pp. 37-41, 125-26; Angell, pp. 248-55.

23. La Sociedad Nacional de Agricultura, *El Campesino*, LXXI, no. 4 (Apr., 1939), p. 182.

24. U.S., Dept. of State Archives, Santiago, Mar. 24, 1939, p. 6, 825.00/1135.

25. La Sociedad Nacional de Agricultura, *El Campesino*, LXXI, no. 3 (Mar., 1939), p. 122; Corporación de Fomento, *Renta*, I, pp. 122-23; Hott, pp. 21-23; Levine and Crocco, "La población chilena como fuerza," p. 67.

accepted the government's suspension of agricultural unionization. The Marxists deplored the surrender to the SNA but went along so as not to cause trouble with the Right for the government.[26] Like disgruntled Socialists, some Communist leaders later attacked these years as a period of self-serving collaboration that benefited the middle and upper strata at the expense of the workers: "At the time we did not struggle with sufficient energy for the hegemony of the proletariat, and we committed an aberration of the Right; we accepted . . . the truce in the countryside . . . the compromise of not forming unions of agricultural workers, with the false idea of 'not creating difficulties for the government.'"[27]

By cooperating with centrist forces, namely the Radicals, at the cost of leaving the lower classes largely unorganized, the Marxists remained dependent on segments of the middle groups. At the time, urban industrial workers represented less than 20% of the active population, while peasants still accounted for over 35%. By narrowing the social base of leftist movements to mainly the cities, the Socialists and Communists could not defy traditional multiparty politics. The dilemmas and compromises encountered by socialism and populism in coalitions contributed to the perpetuation of the same problems. By scuttling challenges to the structure of underdevelopment, particularly in the countryside, the Marxists failed to transcend partial political dependence on the middle sectors and centrist parties.[28]

The industrial elites and the SOFOFA were even more receptive than the landowners and the SNA to the policies of Aguirre Cerda's administration. Like the SNA, the president of the SOFOFA disassociated his organization from the virulent attacks on the government by the political Right and welcomed CORFO. The industrialists played the chords of economic nationalism to encourage state intervention on their behalf, so long as government activism produced neither competition nor control. Less far-sighted urban elites still loathed state planning as a betrayal of laissez-faire. In response, the Radicals pointed out that their brand of state participation in the economy only helped private enterprise. The Radical Party asserted that it was "an undeniable fact that never have industry and commerce had larger profits than during the Government of the Left. . . ."[29]

26. U.S., Dept. of State Archives, Santiago, Mar. 24, 1939, p. 6, 825.00/1135, Aug. 28, 1940, p. 1, 825.00/1248; La Confederación de Trabajadores de Chile, ¿Por qué; La Crítica, Nov. 7, 1939; Contreras, El programa, pp. 40-80; González Díaz, La lucha, pp. 28-42; interview with Chelén, Santiago, 1970.

27. Volodia Teitelboim, "Algunas experiencias chilenas sobre el problema de la burguesía nacional," Principios, no. 59 (July, 1959), pp. 20-30.

28. Faletto, Ruiz, and Zemelman, p. 107.

29. Isauro Torres and Pedro Opitz, Defensa de los gobiernos de izquierda (Santiago,

Industrial leaders also favored the Front's urban social welfare measures so long as they discouraged labor agitation. Better wages, health, education, and housing for workers increased their productivity and consumption more than their costs to employers. At the same time, inflationary credit policies aided manufacturers while helping keep wages from rising commensurately with worker productivity. Therefore, it was not fully incompatible for populist politics to pursue import-substituting industrialization and welfare for urban labor simultaneously. One of the only production advantages possessed by a late-industrializing nation like Chile was "relatively cheap but not proportionately inefficient labor."[30] Through tariff protection, forced savings, and higher prices to consumers, industry prospered, mainly financed by sacrifices from the social sectors purportedly represented by the Popular Front.[31]

Middle Classes

The widening gap between the middle classes, notably white-collar employees, and the workers was a hallmark of the Front administration and subsequent Radical governments in the 1940s. The middle sectors received more state jobs, health care, housing, education, and other rewards than did the lower strata. The Front gave the middle groups greater assistance with their socioeconomic aspirations and better insulation from inflation than the workers. For example, the expansion of the social security system delivered benefits to white-collar employees at the expense of blue-collar workers.[32] Partly because of their special juridical status, their increased unionization, and government favoritism, employees saw their real income rise far more than that of laborers.[33]

The middle classes also improved their position by winning numerous new political offices. They did so by overcoming much of the bribery which had always guaranteed the upper class their seats in Congress. Initially, the decline of electoral fraud in 1938 was certainly more of a victory for the middle-class politicians who received votes

---

1942), p. 3; La Sociedad de Fomento Fabril, *Industria*, años LVI-LVII (Oct., 1938-39); Simón et al., pp. 3-28; Dale L. Johnson, "Industrialization, Social Mobility, and Class Formation in Chile," *Studies in Comparative International Development*, III (1967-68); Levine, "Indices," pp. 70-77; U.S., Dept. of State Archives, Santiago, Feb. 22, 1939, pp. 7-8, 825.00/1126.
   30. Ellsworth, pp. 145-46.
   31. Ellsworth, pp. 122-24.
   32. Pinto, "Desarrollo," pp. 21-27; Tapia Videla.
   33. Chile, Universidad, Instituto de Economía, *Desarrollo económico de Chile, 1940-1956* (Santiago, 1956), p. 4; Angell, pp. 66-68.

without paying for them than for the workers who stopped selling their franchise.

The most significant segment of the middle strata for the Front parties was the bureaucracy. Mainly as a result of state expansion in response to the Depression, the percentage of the active population in public administration doubled from 1930 to 1940, with the most rapid increase under the Front. Public employees now offered an organized social base to the Left, as they had to the Right in the past. The bureaucracy had an elaborate network from the far north to the far south. It provided effective government supporters and clienteles. Given the regressive tax structure of Chile, this apparatus thrived at the expense of the working classes and consumers. Bureaucrats often identified with middle-class "socialism," with the Radicals or Socialists, because of a belief in incremental reforms through state expansion. Consequently, they served as a moderating, mediating, stabilizing influence on the Left. Their political loyalties, however, tended to be transient and pragmatic. Bureaucrats usually gravitated toward parties in power or about to arrive there. Their bandwagon tendencies provided one explanation for the honeymoon period experienced by most new governments. Toward the end of a presidential term, those same governments deflated, when public employees began shifting toward the next likely winner, since Chilean chief executives could not immediately succeed themselves.[34]

Bureaucratization of the Popular Front was an integral part of institutionalization. Bureaucrats poured into the Front parties after the 1938 victory. In turn, members of those parties inundated the bureaucracy. The Radicals, through their identification with the middle class and their dominance of the administration, had the most success with the ballooning bureaucracy. That party soon represented a majority of public employees.[35]

Critics of the Front charged that the unseemly, partisan scramble for bureaucratic spoils had become worse than ever. Liberals berated "socialism" as merely an excuse to inflate the central government through which "the politicians found an easy means to satisfy the appetites of their electoral clientele."[36] Allegedly, government posts were doled out solely on the basis of party and personal affiliations, not merit: "political color, godfather relationships, friendships are the

34. Barría, *El movimiento*, pp. 90-92; Viviani, pp. 173-74; Petras, pp. 292-335; Salvador Valdés M., *Cinco años de gobierno de izquierda, 1939 a 1943* (Puente Alto, Chile, 1944), I, p. 85.

35. Angell, pp. 66-68.

36. *El liberalismo*, pp. 5-6.

decisive factors. . . ."[37] Obviously, such *"arribismo burocrático"* and clientelistic politics were not, in fact, new. The Front's only real innovation in the time-tested spoils system was to give the Left and labor their turn. Unionized workers, through however corrupt, paternalistic, and unequal a system, obtained a small share of influence beneath the economic elites. Without assailing domestic or foreign elites, the Front's expansion of the bureaucracy not only accommodated the middle class and party patronage holders but also, to a lesser extent, their worker clients.[38]

Outside the civilian bureaucracy, the other highly organized group permeated by the middle classes was the military. Throughout 1938-41, there were constant rumors that the Right or the Left was plotting a coup d'etat. Beyond traditions of civilian rule, middle-class, Masonic, and party ties helped the administration hold the armed forces in line. The moderation of government measures and the ineptitude of the Right also undercut conspiracies, and the Front also retired a few of the more adverse and politicized generals. Although many high-level officers were wary of the governing coalition, the rank and file regarded it fairly positively.[39]

Three other important factors discouraged military intervention. First, the Socialists and Communists realized that their scrupulous adherence to constitutional norms was necessary to deter armed conspiracies. Such strict propriety also hobbled their ability to fulfill promises of social reform and mobilization. Even slight missteps or impetuous acts were caricatured by the Right as illegal moves toward a dictatorship of the proletariat. Second, the Marxists again warned of mass retaliation if the Right resorted to violence. The PS kept the Socialist Militia visible as a potential counterpoise to coup attempts. Third, the government tried to court or neutralize the regular military by raising pay and benefits and rewarding loyal officers.[40]

Workers

In one of his last cabinet meetings in 1941, Aguirre Cerda paternalistically expressed regret for the Front's failure to live up to its covenant with the working classes: "We promised the people to pull them out of misery, to raise their social, economic, and moral level.

37. González von Marées, *El mal,* pp. 113-14.
38. González von Marées, *El mal,* pp. 97-113.
39. U.S., Dept. of State Archives, Santiago, Aug. 24, 1939, 825.00B/61, Sept. 26, 1940, pp. 1-2, 825.00/1253.
40. U.S., Dept. of State Archives, Santiago, July 11, 1939, 825.00/1159.

Apart from the intelligent and constructive action of some of my ministers, we have wasted time here with long debates and discussions, without ever arriving at practical and effective solutions for the great problems. It burdens my soul with profound sorrow, because I imagine that the people, whom I love so much, could think that I have deceived them."[41] The workers derived little from the economic trends during the Popular Front and even less from the Radical coalition governments which succeeded Aguirre Cerda. Through inflation and indirect taxes, the laboring groups paid for the government's development of industry and the bureaucracy. Employment in manufacturing failed to keep pace with urbanization. From 1940 to 1952, Chile moved from roughly 53% urban dwellers to over 60%, which was more than twice the rate of urbanization in the decade of the 1930s. Industrialization also failed to slash dependence on foreign capital or to boost wages along with production.[42]

Continuing worker support for the Front was not easily explained by material gains or class consciousness. Although it initially improved under the Front, the overall wage situation of workers was no better by the end of Aguirre Cerda's tenure than before the Great Depression. The standard of living of most of the lower classes stagnated or deteriorated. For example, the housing shortage was worse by the mid-1940s than in 1939. In comparison with unemployment under the Alessandri administration in the 1930s, the number of job-seekers registered with the government Labor Office more than doubled from 1937-38 to 1939-40 and then dropped beneath pre-Front levels in 1941-42. Even the few laborers who received real wage increments under Aguirre Cerda were concentrated in the extreme north and south, the urban center, and Concepción, where the ruling coalition did well electorally. Working-class beneficiaries were also concentrated in selected occupations—the highest average wages were paid in transportation, mining (about 60% unionized), and industry (about 50% unionized), the lowest in agriculture—again reflecting the Front's electoral base. Furthermore there was great variation within the urban sector: for example, workers in monopolistic, protected industries often received some of the highest wages (along with those in foreign-owned enterprises) and therefore shared the owners' enthusiasm for import substitution. Although the standard of living improved somewhat for highly organized miners, bakers, and construction workers, it stayed about the same or worsened for textile and

41. Olavarría Bravo, *Chile*, I, p. 555.
42. Johnson, *Political Change*, pp. 81-84; Ellsworth, pp. 86-158; Cademártori, pp. 118-273; Jobet, *El Partido Socialista de Chile*, II, pp. 53-68.

chemistry workers. Within the least-disadvantaged lower-class sectors, the best-organized benefited most.[43]

In the 1940s the relative gains of social groups under the series of Radical administrations, which the Socialists and Communists helped elect and worked with most of the time, can be gauged by income distribution. Although figures vary, the best estimates for the period agree on the increasingly regressive nature of income distribution. According to one calculation, real national income rose some 40% from 1940 to 1953; however, the workers (considered as about 57% of the active population) watched their real income rise only 7%. Meanwhile the real income of middle-class white-collar employees climbed 46%, and that of the upper-class property owners, financiers, and entrepreneurs, as closely as that group can be defined, soared 60%.[44] Another estimate showed middle-class per capita income rising from roughly four times that of the urban and rural workers in 1940 to five times that of the workers by 1957. In the same span of years, upper-class per capita income rose from nearly twelve times to over fourteen times that of the workers. For 1942, it was calculated that 77% of the work force did not earn sufficient income to support a decent life for one individual, as defined by government standards; only 0.3% earned enough to provide the minimum requisites for a family of four.[45]

Under Aguirre Cerda, the institutional advances for labor unions exceeded the material progress for laborers. The number of legal unions nearly tripled. During the first three months of the Front administration, more industrial and professional unions were created than during all the governments from 1925 to 1938. Many anarchosyndicalists, such as engravers, house painters, and plasterers, joined the CTCH, which they had spurned prior to the Front's victory. From 1941 to 1949, the number of total union members increased over 40%.[46] Industrialization as well as government toleration facilitated these mainly urban union gains. Nevertheless, most union members were still miners, artisans, or middle-class employees. The growth of manufacturing did not generate as large an industrial proletariat as the Marxist parties had hoped. From 1940 to 1954, the percentage of the economically active population in personal services

43. Pinto, "Desarrollo," pp. 21-27, 106-22; Herring, p. 221; Levine and Crocco, "La población chilena como fuerza," pp. 52-63; Contreras, *El programa,* pp. 58-60; Arturo Aldunate Phillips, *Un pueblo en busca de su destino* (Santiago, 1947), pp. 107-9.
44. Pinto, *Chile,* pp. 136-39, 185-98.
45. Varela, "Distribución del ingreso nacional," p. 405; Pike, pp. 273-74.
46. Cruz-Coke, pp. 38-39; Durán, p. 163; U.S., Dept. of State Archives, Santiago, Mar. 14, 1939, p. 8, 825.00/568; Comité Regional del Partido Socialista, p. 25.

rose twice as much as that in manufacturing. Absorbing rural-to-urban migrants, the population in personal services, where the picayune average wages were only superior to those in agriculture, saw its share of national salaries and wages decline during the Radical era, while the share of industrial workers increased.[47]

The Socialists, and to a lesser extent the Communists, far overshadowed the Radicals in the leadership of the CTCH. The Radicals had more success with public employee organizations, often independent from the confederation. In the 1940s, the Socialists retained the secretary-generalship of the CTCH, but the Communists made rapid gains on their rivals. The populist approach of the PS outdistanced the PC far more at the ballot box than in the union halls. Repeatedly, the Socialists complained that Communist labor leaders, though less numerous, were more experienced and skillful at union organization. The more painstaking efforts of the PC laid a firmer foundation for future dominance in the labor movement.[48]

Both the Socialists and Communists criticized domination of the CTCH by middle-class party leaders. Apparently, workers seldom participated in the decision making at the top of either their unions or parties. According to left-wing Socialists, such labor and party coalitions were emasculating the workers rather than radicalizing the middle sectors. Union leaders frequently treated the CTCH as an appendage of the PS, the PC, and, thus, the government. In most respects, the CTCH remained a political union created by the Popular Front parties largely as an electoral vehicle. The middle class not only occupied key command posts in the labor movement but also won preferential treatment for white-collar over blue-collar unions. Employee, professional, and intellectual associations multiplied, with many joining the CTCH. In contrast to the FOCH, the CTCH became far more of a mixed middle- and lower-class organization.[49]

The CTCH subordinated worker demands, strikes, and class conflict to support for the Aguirre Cerda administration and its program of industrial growth. Although left-wing dissidents criticized the Marxist parties for increasingly restraining labor activism the longer the Front was in office, the first year of Aguirre Cerda's tenure witnessed a growing number of strikes with a rising percentage settled

47. Petras, pp. 15-16; Levine and Crocco, "La población chilena como fuerza," pp. 60-64; Angell, pp. 68-70.

48. Angell, pp. 66-68, 110-11, 239-41; Partido Socialista, *Política sindical del Partido Socialista* (Santiago, 1939), pp. 34-35.

49. Partido Socialista, *Tesis política* (Santiago, 1939), p. 14; Partido Socialista de Trabajadores, *El camino del pueblo* (Santiago, 1942), pp. 43-46; Elías Lafertte and Carlos Contreras Labarca, *El Frente Popular vive y vencerá* (Santiago, 1941), pp. 31-32; Angell, pp. 107-10.

in favor of the workers. According to the CTCH, it was involved in 204 strikes and other labor-management disputes (193 resolved to the benefit of the workers) in 1937, its first year. In 1938, it was involved in 198 conflicts (184 successful for the workers) and, in 1939, in 267 conflicts (266 successful), still mainly in the urban areas. The CTCH became increasingly timid, and its complaints about lethargic reforms were overridden by its promise of "unconditional collaboration to the government of the Popular Front." For example, the union advocated higher pay for bureaucrats and the military almost as much as for manual laborers. Within the CTCH, the Communists were even more conservative and cooperative with Aguirre Cerda than were the Socialists. In this period both the PC and the PS believed that building the workers' unions and parties was worth some sacrifices by labor. The Marxists argued that support for the government was, in the long run, more in the best interests of the workers than disruptive demands for immediate benefits.[50]

Institutionalization through the Popular Front made the Marxist labor movement more participant but less radical. Unions were pleased with their greater representation in government agencies, such as the workers' social security administration which was headed by a Socialist. The Marxist parties and unions came to accept the 1924 legal industrial relations system although they had initially rejected it because it was devised by the traditional parties. The 1924 code handicapped unions in the bargaining process, subjected them to heavy state regulation, and encouraged labor to depend on political allies. Organized labor remained the primary base of the Marxist parties. Since the slim benefits diverted to the working classes by the Front went to those organized few, the PC and PS restrained their party protests about the neglect of the underprivileged majority.[51]

Regional Groups

Given its strength in the outlying regions, the impression existed that "the Popular Front government is essentially a government of the *provinces* against the *capital*."[52] However, Aguirre Cerda's reluctance

50. La Confederación de Trabajadores de Chile, *Manifiesto;* La Confederación de Trabajadores de Chile, *¿Por qué*; La Confederación de Trabajadores de Chile, *Treinta,* pp. 5-7, 37-38, 95-97; Partido Socialista, *Tesis,* p. 14; Comité Regional del Partido Socialista, p. 25; Contreras, *El programa,* pp. 44-82; Ravines, pp. 185-89, 375-77; Stevenson, pp. 94-97, 129-30; U.S., Dept. of State Archives, Santiago, Oct. 11, 1939, pp. 4-5, 825.00/1177; La Confederación de Trabajadores de Chile, *La Confederación de Trabajadores de Chile y el proletariado de América latina* (Santiago, 1939).

51. Morris, *Elites,* p. xviii; Angell, pp. 45-59; Petras, pp. 246-47.

52. U.S., Dept. of State Archives, Santiago, July 11, 1939, p. 8, 825.00/1159.

to pay more than lip service to provincial grievances kept alive regional resentments on both the Left and the Right. The Socialists
continued to cast themselves as the defenders of the far north and
south, especially the middle- to lower-class groups within those
peripheral areas. Liberals charged that increasing centralization
brought Santiago over 50% of the national income in 1939 while it
only produced 18% of the national product.[53]

Political Changes and Strategies by the Right

In contrast to the approach of the upper-class economic organizations, that of the conservative parties toward the Popular Front was
mainly implacable opposition, especially against the Marxists. Many
politicians on the Right tried to make the governing coalition appear
illegitimate in order to incapacitate it or to set the stage for a military
coup. The secondary strategy of the rightist parties involved intermit-
tent concessions to the Radicals in hopes of luring them away from the
Marxists. Through this dual approach, the Conservatives and Liberals
tried to prevent substantive reforms issuing from political gains. They
also worked to retain as many bureaucratic and electoral fortresses
as possible.[54]

The Front showed itself to be less combative during the first year in
office than it had been as the opposition. In response, the Right closed
ranks and put its adversaries on the defensive. The conservative
parties' main weapon, as it had been against Alessandri in the 1920s,
was their control of Congress. Aguirre Cerda responded to the congressional barricade by vigorously implementing existing and forgotten laws. He also postponed other reform projects until victory could
be won in the mid-term (1941) elections. His congressional opponents
activated the seldom-used device of impeachment accusations against
cabinet ministers to keep the administration off balance.[55]

Congressional barrages led a larger opposition campaign to undermine the government's legitimacy. Legislators and the conservative press put forth charges of illegality, tyranny, anarchy, incompe-
tence, and corruption and relentlessly warned of alleged incursions on

53. Carlos Müller Rivera, *El jefe de la brigada parlamentaria contesta, en defensa del
Partido Socialista, los ataques derechistas* (Santiago, 1940); Partido Liberal, 7. *a convención*,
pp. 179-80; González von Marées, *El mal*, pp. 106-9; Durán, pp. 112-13.
54. U.S., Dept. of State Archives, Santiago, July 11, 1939, p. 6, 825.00/1159;
Bermúdez, pp. 61-65.
55. Oscar Schnake Vergara, *América y la guerra* (Santiago, 1941), pp. 7-8; Durán,
pp. 198-207; Cruz Salas, pp. 221-22.

freedom of the press and assembly. Alarmist rumors of economic and political collapse abounded.[56]

The most damaging salvos from both sides were charges of antinationalism. Conservative groups condemned the Front as serving the dictates of international Marxism instead of the interests of Chile. They accused the leftists of importing violent revolutionary models from Mexico or even Spain and Russia. In vain, they tried to pass a bill outlawing the Communists. The Marxists replied with equal derision toward the conservative elites and also questioned their legitimacy as national political contenders. They called for tougher government measures against the Right. Some even suggested closing or replacing the obstructionist Congress, perhaps through a plebiscite. Above all, the Socialists and Communists portrayed their foes as lackeys of foreign capitalism, imperialism, and fascism.[57]

Amidst such polarization, both the Right and the Left tried to isolate each other by winning over the Center. While branding the Marxists extremists, the Right simultaneously scolded and courted the Radicals "like an erring son, who has made an unfortunate choice of friends, but will doubtless 'see the light' and return to the fold of conservatism in due time."[58] However, Aguirre Cerda and a majority of the Radicals and their middle-class followers refused to switch from the Marxists to the Right. These centrist forces remained fastened to the Left because they benefited enormously from their dominant role as leaders and brokers in the Front. Also, the Socialists and Communists made concessions, such as controlling union demands, to keep the coalition together.[59]

Within the Conservative and Liberal parties, there was constant debate between reaction and evolutionary reform as the best antidote for electoral losses to the Left. For example, more recalcitrant Liberals preferred to reverse party decline by totally discrediting the Marxists and their programs. They favored rebuilding by appealing to the discontented outlying provinces rather than the newly assertive lower social groups. These Liberals aimed at the provinces because the party did not have a single alderman left in Santiago by 1939. Less aristocratic, younger, more progressive Liberals, however, took command of the party by the end of the Popular Front. Like Conser-

56. Bermúdez, pp. 61-76; Partido Socialista, *Significado de la república socialista del 4 de junio* (Santiago, 1939), pp. 22-26.

57. Infante; Cruz Salas, pp. 222-23.

58. U.S., Dept. of State Archives, Santiago, July 11, 1939, p. 6, 825.00/1159.

59. Contreras, *Por la paz,* p. 23; U.S., Dept. of State Archives, Santiago, July 17, 1940, 825.00/1229, July 24, 1940, 825.00/1232.

vatives who espoused "Christian" paternalism, these Liberals hoped to stall the Marxist advance by claiming the leadership of moderate social change.[60]

A few rightist groups responded to the Front not only with party strategies but also with military conspiracies. Subversives from the *ibañistas* and the conservative parties found their man and their issue in General Ariosto Herrera Ramírez and his fervent anticommunism. A participant in the 1931 Tragic Christmas and an admirer of Mussolini's Italy after serving there as a military attaché, Herrera "pronounced" against the government in August, 1939. In response, leftist unions, parties, and paramilitary units rushed to the streets to confront the coup attempt. Forestalling the Herrera rebellion encouraged the belief of many Front members that the potential wrath of the masses prevented military takeovers of leftist governments. Most top coalition leaders, however, realized that the loyalty of key officers and the lack of broad armed-services support for Herrera were more significant reasons for the government's survival.[61]

The abortive coup convinced many on the Right and the Left to adopt more conciliatory postures. While still relying on congressional obstructionism, many conservatives increasingly tried to flatter and appease Aguirre Cerda. They saw him as a buffer against the more militant programs of the Marxists. The inept conspiracy also further convinced the Communists and Socialists that defending their government took precedence over pressuring it to keep the promises of 1938.[62]

The Popular Front's Political Changes and Strategies

The dominant themes of the Front experience were internal squabbling, progressive moderation, and institutionalization. Aguirre Cerda labored constantly to hold the coalition together. In the tussle for advantage, the Radicals, although passing some laudable, limited reforms, opportunistically entrenched themselves in the state apparatus. As a result, they grew electorally, mainly at the expense of the

60. Sergio Fernández Larraín, *El Partido Conservador en la vida nacional* (Santiago, 1940); Sergio Fernández Larraín, *33 meses de gobierno de Frente Popular* (Santiago, 1941); Sergio Vergara V., *Decadencia o recuperación* (Santiago, 1945), pp. 210-16; Partido Liberal, *7.a convención;* José Maza, *Liberalismo constructivo* (Santiago, 1942), pp. 3-15; González von Marées, *El mal,* p. 97; U.S., Dept. of State Archives, Santiago, Mar. 29, 1939, pp. 1-4, 825.00/1136.

61. Wilfredo Mayorga, "El golpe," p. 15; Wilfredo Mayorga, "Cuatro," pp. 23-25; U.S., Dept. of State Archives, Santiago, Aug. 26, 1939, pp. 1-4, 825.00/1170; Bravo Ríos, pp. 123-141.

62. U.S., Dept. of State Archives, Santiago, Aug. 30, 1939, pp. 2-4, 825.00/1172, Oct. 11, 1939, pp. 1-3, 825.00/1177; Cruz Salas, pp. 221-22.

Liberals and the two Democrat parties. The Radicals' electoral percentage rose from roughly 18% in the 1930s to over 20% in the 1940s. Under Aguirre Cerda, the party laid the groundwork for control of the executive branch for the next decade.[63]

The Radicals' social composition changed little, except for additional recruits from the bureaucracy and education. The basic party division was still between southern landowners, closer to the Liberals, and urban professional and middle-class groups, closer to the Socialists. In addition, a few workers were found in the rank and file. The Radicals fared poorly with university students, who were more attracted to the Marxists or the Falange.[64] Party factions fought with each other and Aguirre Cerda over policies and appointments. Leftist Radicals were often stronger in the party councils and rightist leaders in the government, which fueled endless quarrels. For example, in 1940 the left wing criticized the "millionaires' cabinet," which featured prominent Radical landowners publicly opposed to peasant unionization. In addition, provincial Radicals complained that *"arribistas"* in the capital city were snatching up the most prized posts. Perhaps for most Radicals, left and right, the "bureaucratic state" became an end in itself.[65]

The Communists, without equivalent government posts and perquisites, grew even more spectacularly than the Radicals or Socialists. To a lesser extent than their coalition allies, the Communists also underwent a process of bureaucratization and institutionalization, both within the party and into the government apparatus. They obtained access to the state, decision making, and credit and filled some sub-cabinet posts, such as municipal offices, consulates, and commissions. They established good relations with national executive officers and agencies, notably in the labor field. The PC participated in the functions and ceremonies of the presidential office. Since the Communists never deserted Aguirre Cerda, he reciprocated with important favors, for example, vetoing rightist attempts to banish the party. To preserve those institutional ties, the Communists maintained a low profile. Aguirre Cerda pacified the Right not only with conservative policies but also with a tight leash on the PC. In one case, he removed the appointed Communist mayor of Valparaíso when the

63. U.S., Dept. of State Archives, Santiago, Aug. 24, 1939, 825.00B/61, Sept. 5, 1940, 825.00/1250; Vergara V., pp. 204-20; Cabero, *Recuerdos,* pp. 245-58; Pinto, "Desarrollo," pp. 19-27; Pike, pp. 244-45.
64. U.S., Dept. of State Archives, Santiago, July 11, 1939, 825.00/1159.
65. *Convención provincial radical de Chiloé* (Ancud, Chile, 1940), p. 14; Partido Radical, *El Partido Radical en el gobierno;* Bermúdez, pp. 82-91; Stevenson, pp. 100-101; Partido Radical, *Posición política y estatuto del Partido Radical* (Santiago, 1941).

navy protested. Although the Communists shared executive power, they could only do so within very circumscribed limits and through self-abnegation.[66]

The Communists were able to become more fully a part of the existing multiparty system by moderating their program, relaxing their membership criteria, and emphasizing electoral campaigns behind tested personalistic leaders. Although maintaining the most radical posture of any coalition member, the PC stressed specific problem solving over grand ideological designs. Especially at the beginning and end of the Popular Front, the party, in response to shifting international policies, praised constitutional democracy and the family more than social revolution. It muzzled worker discontent. While remaining basically a party of miners and urban workers, the PC appealed to "progressive sectors" of the peasants, middle classes, and even elites to join the Front and the party.[67]

These nationalistic, elastic policies increased internal party tensions as well as Communist growth. The moderate programs and eclectic composition of the Popular Front aggravated friction between middle-class and working-class PC leaders. The party commanders were a discordant mixture of seasoned warriors from the proletariat, new middle-class orators and organizers, dissatisfied professionals, sympathetic intellectuals and artists, and sons of immigrants, frequently Jews. Mounting discontent in the dominant "worker" wing of the PC coincided with an abrupt shift in the Soviet position.[68]

In September, 1939, the Soviet Union signed a nonaggression pact with Germany and so deemphasized popular-front concessions to antifascist reformers until Hitler's invasion of the U.S.S.R. in June, 1941. While that Stalin-Hitler accord was in effect, the Chilean PC briefly revived the rhetorical radicalism and working-class exclusivity reminiscent of the Great Depression. For the moment, the Communists denounced middle-class reformers as seducers of the workers' movement. The apex of this symbolic campaign against the bourgeoisie was the party's declaration of Masonry's incompatibility with Communism. The PC forced middle-class leaders such as Contreras Labarca to renounce their lodge membership. Like the

66. Contreras, *El programa*, pp. 35-80; Correa, *Discurso*, pp. 8-10; Ravines, pp. 375-77; Durán, pp. 186-90.

67. Contreras, *Por la paz*, pp. 8-29, 47-65; Contreras, *Unidad*, pp. 42-44; Partido Comunista, *Problemas de organización* (Santiago, 1939); Elías Lafertte, *Como triunfaremos en las elecciones de 1941* (Santiago, 1940), pp. 9-12; Montecinos, p. 104; Cruz Salas, pp. 35-36, 164-68, 247-48; U.S., Dept. of State Archives, Santiago, Mar. 14, 1939, 825.00/568.

68. Cruz Salas, pp. 164-65; Vergara V., p. 266.

Socialists, the Communists agonized over the issue of intraparty class collaboration, but the spokesmen for the workers retained the upper hand.[69]

During the Stalin-Hitler pact, the Communists also hardened their ideological program, although their behavior remained gentle. They temporarily resurrected harsh criticisms of domestic and foreign capitalists. Although remaining in the Front, they lashed government timidity. The German attack on Russia in 1941, however, flipped the PC back into full public cooperation with its coalition partners and with any group potentially opposed to the Axis powers. Despite a few deviations, Communist participation in coalition administration mainly fortified, rather than threatened, the traditional state.[70]

Institutionalization of the Socialist Party

After accepting high offices, the Socialists wrestled with ways to move toward their ideological objectives through government participation. Like the Communists, their justification for winning and holding office was to redistribute wealth, benefits, and power to the underprivileged. However, the means to electoral success and survival, once the Socialists were ensconced in the executive branch, proved an impediment to the Marxists' long-range programmatic aspirations. There was scant likelihood now that the Socialists would adopt more violent means. Regardless of ideological claims, they were far more a reformist electoral movement—operating within the Chilean system—than a revolutionary vanguard. Consequently, the PS and PC groped for novel ways to squeeze socialistic reforms through the democratic maze. They tried to turn gradualist institutions to the tasks of sweeping social and economic change without breaking, or being broken by, those institutions.

This dilemma over means and ends, over the pace of change, constituted a trade-off or tension between institutionalization and mobilization. On the one hand, the Marxist parties' ability to hold office depended on their capacity to compromise, consolidate, and institutionalize their participation and reforms. On the other hand, their ability to lead the working groups toward structural transformations depended on their capacity to mobilize mass pressures for change, change which could either strengthen the Marxists' base of support or outrun and destabilize the Popular Front government in the face of tenacious resistance from the Right. Therefore, the Marx-

69. Contreras, *El programa*, pp. 72-80; González Días, *La lucha*, pp. 20-42.
70. Contreras, *Por la paz*, pp. 8-48; Chamudes, pp. 102-3; Partido Comunista, *XI congreso*, pp. 33-37; Cruz Salas, pp. 165-68, 247-48.

ists, especially the Socialists, tried to synchronize mobilization and institutionalization of the workers' movement while serving in the coalition administration.

The attempt to coordinate institutionalization and mobilization failed. Marxist integration into the political hierarchy was mainly achieved at the cost of postponing worker activism and reforms. During Aguirre Cerda's first year, the Socialists successfully operated in government ministries while simultaneously generating pressure on the administration from the streets, the factories, and the mines. Soon, however, they opted for institutionalization and gradual, piecemeal reforms, pushing economic growth over redistribution. They reduced mobilization, for example, by disbanding the Socialist Militia and curtailing peasant unionization. The PS emphasized building the party from the top down through government as much as through the creation of autonomous mass organizations. As a result, Chilean politics remained stable through gradual expansion.[71]

The Socialists were unable to resolve the dilemma of how to lead the masses toward socialism through the bourgeois state without falling to the reactionaries or getting stuck in the halfway house of democratic reformism. The PS was in a trickier position than its allies. The Radicals could concentrate on administration with fewer ideological qualms and less erosion of their social base. They blunted the Socialists' initiatives in the executive branch and outbid them for middle-class support. Conversely, the Communists could concentrate on mobilization of the working classes with less responsibility for administration.[72]

Institutionalization, like independent mobilization, was a double-edged sword. Participation in the higher echelons of government was also a means to build mass support, albeit along traditional clientelistic and electoral lines rather than through social conflict against the prevailing system. Like other parties, the Socialists used state agencies and spoils to proselytize and win elections. With functionaries blanketing Chile, the PS became a more truly national party geographically. Its enclaves within the state network also helped the Socialists dominate organized labor, despite Communist encroachments. Furthermore, serving in government not only moderated the PS but also gave it influence over administration. Even though Socialist participation generated few concrete benefits for the party's social constituency, it

71. Comité Regional del Partido Socialista, pp. 33-54; Partido Socialista, *Contestamos a los enemigos del pueblo chileno* (Santiago, 1939); Cruz Salas, p. 72; Petras, esp. pp. 292-335.

72. Partido Socialista, *Tesis*, pp. 5-13; Partido Socialista, *El Partido Socialista y su 6.° congreso ordinario* (Santiago, 1940), pp. 7-10; Bermúdez, pp. 88-99.

helped keep Aguirre Cerda loyal to his leftist allies. The corrosive effects on the PS of cumulative compromises were far more apparent after than during the Popular Front.[73]

At the highest level, the Socialists were integrated into the state structure through appointment to three cabinet slots for the duration of the Front. To exert as much influence as possible from those minor ministries, the PS replaced three rather weak Socialists with top party leaders at the end of 1939. Grove became secretary-general of the party, Schnake took over Development, Allende, Public Health, and Rolando Merino, Lands and Colonization. Despite their best efforts, however, their role in the cabinet did more to debilitate internal party leadership and to build up electoral and bureaucratic clienteles than to drive through reform programs.[74]

Institutionalization of the Socialists was at least as important below the cabinet level. The party was rewarded with about one-third of the intendants of provinces, several mayors (notably Schnake's wife in Santiago and Grove's brother in Viña del Mar), and many governors over districts within provinces, positions which facilitated the accumulation of local followers. Socialists received directorships or high posts in numerous government agencies, mainly the workers' social security office, the Department of Colonization, the Gold Placers Administration, the Commissariat of Subsistence and Prices, the Department of Public Housing, the nitrate and iodine corporation, and CORFO, not to mention countless jobs for local party organizers. Socialization of the Marxists into existing institutional norms also occurred through their gains and experience in Congress. Throughout the tenure of the Front, the Socialists complained about the insignificance of their allocations in the cabinet and insufficient numbers of governorships at the subprovincial district level. They were disappointed with their share of high-paying foreign service jobs, although Manuel Hidalgo, for example, became ambassador to Mexico. The PS also bemoaned the carryover of conservatives in perhaps half the intermediate-level government positions. Dissatisfied Socialists always argued for more high government and party posts for themselves as a means to hasten reforms. It was suspected, however, that some ambitious Socialists used reform demands to justify their hunger for office. Although not the bureaucratic feast that the Right charged, the Socialists' plums in

73. *La Crítica,* Oct. 25, 1939; Mallol; Cabero, *Recuerdos,* pp. 283-84; González von Marées, *El mal,* pp. 58-61; U.S., Dept. of State Archives, Santiago, Mar. 24, 1939, pp. 5-6, 825.00/1135, Aug. 2, 1939, 825.00/1164, Oct. 11, 1939, pp. 4-5, 825.00/1177.

74. Salvador Allende, *La realidad médico-social chilena* (n.p., 1939); U.S., Dept. of State Archives, Santiago, Sept. 30, 1939, pp. 2-3, 825.00/1176, Nov. 22, 1939, p. 5, 825.00/1185.

the Aguirre Cerda administration did represent significant integration of an officially revolutionary, Marxist party into the Chilean
state.[75]

"Bureaucratization" of the PS occurred in three ways: (1) the entrance of Socialists into the state bureaucracy, (2) the influx of bureaucrats into the Socialist Party, and (3) the entrenchment of moderate, authoritarian, hierarchical, bureaucratized leadership within the
upper levels of the party. Both the party and its role in national politics
became more institutionalized. The issue for the future was whether
the Socialists were taking over the state or it was taking over them.[76]

The Socialist Party received numerous new members in 1939-40,
many of whom were state bureaucrats, or aspired to be. This inflow of
public employees bolstered the impression that institutionalization
of the party and its role in the state spoils system was the ticket to PS
growth. However, many of these recruits from the bureaucracy were
prepared to shift to other vehicles when the PS no longer held executive offices. Basing itself somewhat more on the public sector, the
party became less ideological and more pragmatic. It promoted the
bureaucrats' interests, such as higher salaries. Some Socialist founders
and workers protested their displacement by middle-class "parvenus"
and "mediocrity."[77]

The newcomers provided increased support to the established,
more conservative PS leaders such as Schnake and Grove. The party
became less reliant on membership dues and more dependent on
funds from government posts or wealthy leaders. As a result, the PS
became less a vehicle of mass mobilization and more a clientelistic
employment agency devoted to electoral success almost as an end in
itself. Socialists in government or with close access to its patronage
powers and employees enhanced their control over the party. Some
also made personal gains and adopted a more comfortable life style.
Discipline imposed on the party by these personalistic, rather privileged figures caused dissident, often younger Socialists to protest the
decline of internal democracy as well as ideological devotion.[78]

75. Partido Socialista, *Manifiesto* (Santiago, 1940), pp. 11-12; Comité Regional del
Partido Socialista, p. 4; Marmaduke Grove Vallejo, *Grove explica el peligro de una falsa
unificación socialista* (Santiago, 1946), p. 4; *¿Qué es*, p. 8; González von Marées, *El mal*, p.
61; Stevenson, p. 99; U.S., Dept. of State Archives, Santiago, Jan. 4, 1939, 825.00/1114;
Weston H. Agor, *The Chilean Senate* (Austin, Tex., and London, 1971), pp. 147-53.
76. César Godoy Urrutia, *¿Qué es el inconformismo?* (2nd ed., Santiago, 1940),
pp. 20-27; Bermúdez, pp. 102-4.
77. Partido Socialista, *Sobre la moral revolucionaria* (Santiago, 1939); Partido
Socialista, *La línea*, pp. 23-24; César Godoy Urrutia, *¿A dónde va el socialismo?* (2nd ed.,
Santiago, 1939), pp. 5-14; Partido Socialista de Trabajadores, *El camino*, pp. 9-10;
Mallol.
78. U.S., Dept. of State Archives, Santiago, Sept. 30, 1939, pp. 2-4, 825.00/1176,

By the end of the first year of the Front administration, a battle was brewing within the Socialist Party over the consequences of internal and governmental institutionalization. Like older protest parties such as the Democrats, the Socialists had briefly broken new ground and then compromised themselves in the traditional, highly clientelistic system. Also like the Democrats, their absorption into the multiparty bargaining process provoked disgruntled internal factions to demand a return to leftist independence and a revival of the idealism and autonomous mobilization of past years. The party was torn. Government collaboration boosted the PS by expanding its mass base at all social levels but hurt it by dividing the leadership. By opening the bureaucracy to representatives of the working groups and by giving those groups benefits and subordinate participation, the PS role in the Front administration watered down class conflict. Conversely, it sharpened leadership conflict by heightening discord over goals, strategies, posts, and perquisites, within both the coalition and the party. Ultimately, these leadership disagreements led to PS ruptures and decline and dissipated the membership gains attained partly through state involvement. The electoral and institutional achievements of the Popular Front years neither produced great substantive gains for the workers nor guaranteed Socialist unity or popularity. As a result, some Socialist critics of institutionalization argued for a return to independent populist mobilization, while others favored greater emphasis on radical Marxist positions.[79]

Nov. 22, 1939, p. 5, 825.00/1182; Waiss, *El drama,* pp. 16-17, 32-33; Amadeo, pp. 91-96; Bermúdez, pp. 102-4; Cruz Salas, pp. 84-85; Alexander, *Latin American,* p. 131; Michels.
   79. Casanueva and Fernández, p. 10; Lechner, p. 85.

9

The Results of Institutionalization through the Popular Front, 1940-41

Institutionalization led to both the growth and the division of the Socialist Party and the Popular Front. By the end of 1939, discontent with the fruits of external and internal bureaucratization crystallized into the "Nonconformist" movement within the PS. The Nonconformists wanted fewer Socialists in the bureaucracy and fewer bureaucrats in the party. They blamed both evils on participation in the Aguirre Cerda administration. They protested against timidity in government policies and authoritarianism in intraparty direction. As a cure, these rebels against populism and institutionalization demanded that the PS withdraw from the Front unless their reform proposals were accepted in short order.[1]

César Godoy Urrutia, a primary school teacher and head of a teachers' union, became the leader of these more intellectual, idealistic, younger Socialists. As a former anarchist, Godoy still had more confidence in the undisciplined force of the masses than in the organized power of the state. According to Godoy, the Socialists' tactical compromises in the Popular Front were becoming strategic surrenders. His Nonconformists claimed that the workers, allegedly because they were immature politically and deficient in class consciousness, were being led into the arms of the capitalist state. In the rebels' view, populism had led PS leaders to degenerate into merely social democrats instead of moving on to more radical Marxism. Therefore, Godoy advised the party to escape cooptation and corruption by reviving and accentuating independent class struggle and ideological combat.[2]

1. Chelén, *Trayectoria*, pp. 76-87; Waiss, *El drama*, pp. 16-33; Partido Socialista, *Tesis*, pp. 7-30; U.S., Dept. of State Archives, Santiago, Feb. 22, 1939, pp. 2-5, 825.00/1126.
2. Godoy Urrutia, *¿Qué es*, esp. pp. 3-20; Godoy Urrutia, *¿A dónde*, esp. pp. 7-14; Partido Socialista de Trabajadores, *El camino*.

Ideological arguments for greater Socialist devotion to the working class and Marxism were inextricably mingled with the Nonconformists' personal animosity toward the party's moderate leaders, headed by Schnake and Grove. To a significant extent, both intraparty factions, concerned with private ambitions as well as public policies, used ritual ideological charges to struggle for PS and government posts. The role of such personalistic disputes, as opposed to deeper programmatic and strategic conflicts, apparently loomed even larger in later 1940s' Socialist divisions. In 1939 Godoy failed to defeat long-time personal rival Grove for secretary-general. Subsequently, the Nonconformists' resentment mounted against what they saw as the heavy-handed ruling clique.[3]

Secession of the Nonconformists, 1940

Unable to wrench the party leadership away from complicity with the Popular Front, some Nonconformists were expelled, and others seceded. In mid-1940 they founded the rival Socialist Workers' Party (PST), which took five of the regular party's fifteen deputies in Congress and none of its five senators. At most, the rival party siphoned away some 10% of the PS's membership and roughly 2% of its national electorate.[4]

Besides Godoy, the leaders of the PST tended to be former anarchists, Trotskyists, and members of the Communist Left. For example, Emilio Zapata, a worker, and Oscar Waiss, a lawyer, journalist, and former student leader, came out of Hidalgo's Communist faction; Orlando Millas had previously been head of the Socialist Youth; Dr. Natalio Berman brought in many of his worker followers, especially coal miners, from around Concepción. The northern mining districts and Magallanes also contributed to the formation of the PST. Other leaders included public and private white-collar employees, lawyers, teachers, accountants, and construction workers.[5]

The PST claimed to speak more for the working-class elements among the Socialists. The splinter party asserted that its members were "principally of worker origins."[6] Compared to the regular party,

3. Mallol, esp. p. 5; U.S., Dept. of State Archives, Santiago, Sept. 5, 1940, p. 1, 825.00/1250.

4. Partido Socialista, *Para deshacer la ola de calumniosas informaciones . . .* (Santiago, 1940); U.S., Dept. of State Archives, Santiago, Apr. 23, 1940, pp. 1-2, 825.00/1208, May 29, 1940, p. 4, 825.00/1214; Stevenson, pp. 101-2.

5. Cruz Salas, pp. 12, 73-98, 107, 304; Godoy Urrutia, *¿Qué es*, p. 13; Natalio Berman B., *El Diputado Berman defiende a los obreros del carbón* (Santiago, 1941); Berman, *Berman;* U.S., Dept. of State Archives, Santiago, Sept. 26, 1940, 825.00/1256.

6. Partido Socialista de Trabajadores, *El camino*, pp. 1-7.

a higher percentage of PST adherents may have been working class and a smaller percentage public employees or Masons. Above all, however, the PST resembled a miniature of the mother party and its internal contradictions.[7]

The PST cast itself as a social and ideological alternative to the regular party and the Popular Front by proposing a "Workers' Front." Similar to the Communist line prior to 1935, this strategy envisioned alliances only with truly working-class organizations and rejected coalitions with bourgeois parties like the Radicals or the Falange. However, the PST's reform program was substantively no more radical than that of the mother party, at least on paper.[8]

Neither the workers nor their parties responded enthusiastically to the PST's appeal to class loyalties and ideology. The renegade party lost by-elections and members rapidly; in a senatorial contest in Valparaíso, Godoy received only 2% of the vote. The PST was driven out of the CTCH, and the rebels were cut off from patronage jobs as well as electoral allies. Many national Workers' Socialist leaders began returning to the PS or fleeing to other parties. By 1941 the PST shed its principles, cooperated with the Popular Front government, and entered elections in league with the Radicals and Communists. The PST ran with the Front in the 1941 congressional elections and backed the Radical candidate for president in 1942. With little ideological or other reason left for existence, the frustrated PST was formally absorbed into the Communist Party in 1944.[9]

Secession of the Socialist Party from the Popular Front Coalition, 1940-41

Ironically, the regular Socialists quit the Popular Front party coalition shortly after the departure of the Nonconformists. The PS withdrew because of the continued inclusion of the Communists, not the conservatism of the Radicals. This Socialist turn against the PC grew out of domestic and international developments, but in part it was an escalation of long-standing ideological competition for the same constituency. Although remaining with the government, the Socialists said that alliance with the PC was unacceptable because that party was antinational and authoritarian. The Socialists hoped to isolate the Communists and cut short their surging influence with labor. The PS

7. Partido Socialista de Trabajadores, *El camino*, pp. 37-38.
8. Cruz Salas, p. 273; Chelén, *Trayectoria*, p. 99.
9. Partido Socialista de Trabajadores, *Construyendo el partido único* (Santiago, 1944); Partido Socialista de Trabajadores, *El camino;* Partido Socialista, *La línea*, p. 15; Waiss, *El drama*, pp. 41-43.

complained loudly about Communist raids on its leaders and followers. For example, it was alleged that the Communists had instigated
the split with the PST. Traditionally hostile relations between the two
Marxist parties were especially bad during the Soviet *détente* with Nazi
Germany.[10]

The rift with the Communists also arose out of the Socialists' dilemma as a populist-Marxist party in an industrializing country highly
dependent on international trade. The stringencies of World War II
exacerbated this dilemma. Paradoxically, the Socialists' commitment
to nationalist industrialization and growth compromised their opposition to foreign penetration. As a result of their antifascism and the
economic exigencies of World War II, the Socialists, like the APRA in
Peru, developed a more positive attitude toward the United States.
Their responsibilities in the Aguirre Cerda administration drew the
Socialists away from the Communists and closer to the "Colossus of
the North."[11]

Schnake led the PS into the vanguard of Chileans eager for better
political and economic relations with the United States. Hating the
Communists, he hoped to replace them in the labor movement with a
middle-class-based, democratic, socialist party. As Minister of Development, Schnake attended the Pan American Conference at
Havana in late 1940 and then visited the United States. His transformation during that trip personified the Socialist Party's shift to emphasizing economic growth in partnership with the Western Allies.
Schnake returned to Chile brimming with praise for the high standard
of living and political democracy in North America.[12]

The United States assumed a larger role as a diplomatic, military, and economic friend of Chile and the Popular Front when the
Export-Import Bank extended a $12,000,000 credit to CORFO in
June, 1940. That loan was used to buy U.S. industrial and agricultural
equipment. Then Schnake returned from his trip with the promise of
a second loan for $5,000,000, in large part granted to counter Axis
infiltration of Chile. The money was designed to release frozen credits
of U.S. firms and to service the foreign debt and reduce Chile's
foreign exchange deficit. This arrangement bore some similarity to
the Ross deal in the 1930s which the Marxists had denounced.

10. Partido Socialista, *El libro negro del Partido Comunista* (Santiago, 1941); Partido
Socialista, *La línea;* Jobet, *Socialismo y comunismo;* U.S., Dept. of State Archives, Santiago,
Aug. 12, 1939, pp. 5-6, 825.00/1166, June 7, 1941, pp. 1-10, 825.00/1366; Stevenson,
pp. 110-17.
11. Partido Socialista, *Manifiesto;* Herring, pp. 239-41.
12. Gunther, pp. 253-54; Cruz Salas, pp. 159, 248.

Schnake also brought back assurances of U.S. purchases of surplus production, especially nitrates, and a U.S. offer to guarantee the stability of the vital copper industry.[13]

Immediately upon his return to Chile, Schnake and the Socialists boasted of these international achievements and rocked Chilean politics with a vituperative campaign against the Communists. They excoriated the PC as an obstacle to greater cooperation with the United States and attacked their rivals' tolerance of fascism externally and promotion of labor unrest internally. Schnake denied Communist charges that his bargain with the United States was a surrender to imperialism or the bourgeoisie. According to the Socialists, his deal was necessary to maintain a bearable standard of living during the forced austerity of wartime; they said it would do more to help the workers, especially the miners, than would the "revolutionary gymnastics" of the Communists. The Socialists' anticommunism coincided with a temporary preference for maintaining production and employment through foreign support, not social conquests by the workers.[14]

The Communists responded to the sudden Socialist onslaught with equal invective, intensifying past efforts to stigmatize PS leaders as deceivers of the workers. They lambasted Schnake and Grove as lackeys for the United States, the Right, the SNA, the Union Club, the fascists, and the APRA. The PC also tightened its own bonds with the Radicals to try to dislodge Socialist functionaries from the government and the labor movement.[15]

By the start of 1941 the Socialists officially withdrew from the Popular Front coalition, while staying in the administration. Although the other coalition parties refused to expel the Communists, many of the unions in the CTCH sided with the PS and left the Front. Even several unions with heavy Communist influence applauded Schnake's negotiations with the United States as a source of concrete benefits. Nevertheless, the CTCH, which officially stayed in the Front, was permanently wounded by the Marxist feud.[16]

13. Denunciations, especially by the PC, of Schnake's loan's terms later led the Front to cancel it. Herring, p. 242; Schnake, *América;* Amadeo, pp. 120-21; Carleton Beals, *Rio Grande to Cape Horn* (Boston, 1943), pp. 300-301.

14. Partido Socialista, *Chile y América en la órbita espiritual del socialismo* (Santiago, 1941), esp. pp. 28-29; Partido Socialista, *La línea;* Schnake, *América.*

15. *Hoy,* año X, no. 485 (Mar. 6, 1941), pp. 2-4, 26; Carlos Contreras Labarca, *La traición de los jefes socialistas al descubierto* (n.p., 1941); Carlos Contreras Labarca, *¡Este es Schnake!* (Santiago, 1941), p. 6; Lafertte and Contreras, *El Frente,* pp. 33-36; U.S., Dept. of State Archives, Santiago, Aug. 24, 1939, pp. 5-6, 825.00/1171.

16. Angell, p. 110; Cruz Salas, p. 169; U.S., Dept. of State Archives, Santiago, Jan. 7, 1941, 825.00/1291, Jan. 16, 1941, 825.00/1299.

Leaders of the Socialist Party after Institutionalization

During the Popular Front, changes in Socialist behavior did not reflect any sweeping alterations in the party's social composition. Though some modifications in the mix took place, the PS remained a distinctively multiclass party fusing the middle and lower strata. This conclusion is based on observations by the Socialists and others, on party programs and actions, on electoral returns, on membership data, and on studies of PS leadership.[17] The following leadership table for 1940-42, Table 15, is constructed along the same basic lines and from the same general sources as the earlier one (Table 10, p. 109) on top political personnel in 1931-33. It catches the Socialist Party's internal and public leaders at the height of institutionalization, after the PST schism but before later divisions, and compares them with the leaders of the Conservatives, Liberals, and Radicals.[18]

TABLE 15: BACKGROUND INFORMATION ON CHILEAN POLITICAL LEADERS, 1940-42

Table 15a. Percentage of Leaders of Each Party from Each Provincial Unit
(Each provincial unit's percentage of the national population in 1940 is noted in parentheses.)

Provincial Unit	Cons.		Libs.		Rads.		Socs.	
Tarapacá (2%)	0%	(0%)	5%	(+5%)	2%	(+1%)	4%	(−1%)
Antofagasta (3%)	0	(0)	2	(+1)	2	(+1)	2	(+2)
Atacama (2%)	2	(+2)	2	(+1)	2	(−2)	2	(−3)
Coquimbo (5%)	0	(−2)	4	(+2)	10	(0)	2	(0)
Aconcagua & Valparaíso (10%)	15	(−3)	4	(−6)	12	(+4)	10	(+4)
Santiago (25%)	54	(−1)	53	(−6)	17	(−6)	19	(−23)
O'Higgins & Colchagua (7%)	2	(+2)	5	(−1)	4	(−3)	2	(−5)
Curicó & Talca (5%)	7	(0)	5	(−3)	8	(+5)	10	(+2)
Maule & Linares (4%)	0	(−2)	2	(0)	7	(+2)	4	(+1)
Ñuble (5%)	2	(+2)	9	(+5)	10	(+2)	6	(+2)
Concepción & Arauco (7%)	2	(−4)	0	(−1)	2	(−8)	8	(+3)
Bío Bío (3%)	2	(−2)	2	(0)	2	(−4)	4	(+2)
Malleco & Cautín (10%)	5	(+5)	5	(+5)	11	(+5)	13	(+3)
Valdivia & Osorno (6%)	2	(−4)	2	(+1)	4	(−2)	2	(0)
Llanquihue & Chiloé (4%)	2	(+2)	0	(0)	2	(−2)	8	(+6)
Aysén & Magallanes (1%)	0		2		2		0	

17. U.S., Dept. of State Archives, Santiago, June 7, 1941, p. 10, 825.00/1366.
18. See Appendix B.

Table 15b: Percentage of Leaders of Each Party in Various Primary Occupations

Occupation	Cons.		Libs.		Rads.		Socs.	
Agriculture	34% (+4%)		35% (0%)		36% (+13%)		6% (0%)	
Business &								
Commerce	17	(−11)	16	(−3)	10	(−4)	6	(−5)
Industry	7	(0)	11	(+4)	4	(−3)	0	(−2)
Professionals	71	(−4)	81	(+8)	72	(−5)	73	(+16)
Bureaucrats	2	(+2)	2	(+1)	11	(+4)	10	(+3)
Employees	5	(+3)	0	(−1)	12	(+5)	21	(+1)
Workers & Artisans	0	(0)	0	(0)	0	(0)	13	(+6)

Table 15c: Percentage of Leaders of Each Party with Given Educational Background

Institution	Cons.		Libs.		Rads.		Socs.	
University of								
Chile	37% (−12%)		63% (−1%)		59% (−6%)		38% (−6%)	
Catholic University	51	(+9)	11	(+9)	0	(0)	4	(−5)
Foreign institution	10	(−5)	14	(+3)	5	(−3)	15	(+8)
Military institute	0	(0)	2	(0)	4	(−1)	4	(0)
Below university								
level	17	(+6)	16	(+5)	27	(+11)	40	(+16)

Table 15d: Percentage of Leaders of Each Party Who Were Members of Given Organizations

Organization	Cons.		Libs.		Rads.		Socs.	
Union Club	34% (−27%)		65% (−13%)		22% (−21%)		0% (0%)	
SNA	27	(−14)	28	(−6)	13	(0)	0	(−2)
SOFOFA	0	(−9)	4	(−9)	4	(−3)	0	(−4)
Viña del Mar Club	2	(−4)	5	(−1)	0	(−2)	0	(0)
Auto Club	7	(0)	7	(0)	6	(+2)	0	(0)
September Club	0	(0)	16	(+2)	6	(+2)	0	(0)
Regional								
organizations	17	(+8)	26	(+13)	30	(+18)	13	(+13)
Professional								
organizations	27	(−13)	26	(−9)	36	(−9)	38	(+4)
Employee or worker								
organizations	0	(0)	0	(0)	1	(−1)	27	(+16)

Table 15e: Average Age of the Leaders of Each Party, in 1941

Cons.		Libs.		Rads.		Socs.	
43	(−1)	50	(+1)	46	(+1)	39	(+5)

Table 15f: Number of Leaders of Each Party in the Above Tables

Cons.		Libs.		Rads.		Socs.	
41	(−13)	57	(−28)	83	(−10)	48	(−6)

NOTE: The number in parentheses beside each party's percentage in a particular category is the change from 1931-33 to 1940-42.

The general social profile of the political elites by the end of the Popular Front was strikingly similar to that existing a decade earlier. There was, however, a relatively noticeable ascent of leaders from previously excluded social sectors and provinces. Throughout, both conclusions drawn from the 1931-33 or the 1940-42 tables and comparisons between them must be extremely cautious. Therefore only broad differences in composition among the parties and across time will be stressed. As seen in Table 15a, the dominance of the core urban provinces persisted, overwhelmingly among the leaders of the Right. Over 50% of both the Conservative and Liberal national leaders came from Santiago province in 1940-42. By contrast, fewer than one-fifth of the Radical and Socialist leaders were born there. As indicated in the tables and electorally, the Socialists dramatically shifted from a Santiago-centered, almost purely urban movement to a national party which recruited leaders and followers from nearly all provinces. In the 1940s they had only half the percentage of leaders from the capital city's province as in the 1930s. There was a slight decline in the dominance of the central zone for all parties.

Table 15b shows that the prevailing occupational patterns and distinctions among top political figures remained roughly constant from the thirties to the forties. The most noteworthy increases were in the landowner and professional groups, which were already significant. Bureaucrats, employees, and workers made only small gains from their previously low base. Apparently, state growth swelled the percentage of bureaucrats in parties more at the membership than at the leadership level. The representation of urban business and industrial elites at the pinnacle of the parties weakened, despite the urbanization of the population and the economy following the Depression. Whether from the upper or the middle classes, professionals still dominated all the parties sampled.

The Conservatives and Liberals exhibited a very similar occupational makeup to that of the Radicals, except for the latter's advantage among public and private white-collar employees. None of the three major traditional parties contained any identifiable leaders from the working class. All continued to have a high percentage—at least one-third—from the landed elites. Since the Depression, the Conservative leadership had become both more landed and more middle class. The Conservatives were inscribing more Chileans of modest means, though more at the party's base than at the summit.[19] If any slight distinction could be established between the Conservatives and the Liberals in the thirties and forties, it was that the latter's social compo-

19. Gumucio, *Me defiendo*, pp. 4-17.

sition looked even a bit more exclusively upper class. The Liberal roster
was dotted with aristocratic family names boasting landed and commercial wealth. Compared to the Conservative leaders, they were not
significantly more derived from the urban elites.[20] The Socialists were
set off from the traditional parties primarily by their low percentages
in the three most clearly higher-class occupations at the top of Table
15b. This difference was particularly graphic among large landowners. The Socialists' relatively high percentage of national spokesmen
from employee, worker, and artisan ranks also set them apart, and it
should be noted that the Radicals shaded off toward the Socialists at
the level of white-collar leaders.

Table 15c reveals an overall drop in the educational level attained by
party leaders, compared to 1931-33. This perhaps bespoke the rise of
middle-class and provincial groups within all camps. There was, however, still a gradation from the right to the left. Conservative and
Liberal leaders showed stronger educational credentials than the Radicals and Socialists, even though all tended to be far better educated
than the population at large. Attendance at the Catholic University
still marked the Conservatives; the Radicals drew no leaders from that
institution. Not surprisingly, the Socialists presented the most leaders,
even more than in 1931-33, with less than university schooling.[21]

Table 15d suggests that leader memberships in prestigious
economic and social organizations dwindled for all parties. The
reason is unclear. It may be related to the growing divorce between
elite parties and socioeconomic organizations, since interest groups
relied more on their own institutional bonds with the state. In any case,
the pattern distinguishing the Socialists from the three older parties
carried on. Even middle- to upper-class directors of the PS were
denied or actively rejected the status-conferring memberships of
their counterparts from more conservative parties. Conversely, the
Socialists' always relatively high participation in employee and worker
organizations was still growing. In terms of affiliations, the Radicals
again appeared as an intermediate group between the Right and the
PS. Regardless of party, increasing enlistment in regional organizations apparently reflected the generally enhanced importance of the
outlying provinces. Finally, Table 15e indicates that the average age of
party leaders changed little from the 1930s, except for the aging of the
enduring PS ruling group. Nevertheless, the Socialists remained marginally younger than their competitors.

20. *Consigna*, Mar. 30, 1935; Gran Logia de Chile, *Cuarta*.
21. Some lower-status professional occupations, such as accountants, did not require university degrees, so the apparent discrepancy between professional and university percentages is not significant.

The Socialist leadership can also be thrown into relief by comparing it with that of the Communists, who were not included in the table because of the spotty information available on a tiny sample. The prominent traceable Communists were more restricted in their regional origins than the Socialists. They came mainly from the north or the urban core. Almost none had occupations in business, commerce, industry, or agriculture. A few leading Communists were professionals, intellectuals, journalists, white-collar employees, and erstwhile student leaders. As before, the most striking contrast with the Socialists was the large proportion of workers. Many PC directors were full-time party officials. A vast majority had never reached the university level in their education, a very high percentage had union affiliations, a lesser number could be found in professional and regional organizations, and none in the elite social and economic institutions. In general, the Communist leaders remained more lower class than the Socialists and were less representative of a diverse national, mass constituency.

Compared to the encrusted Communist leadership, the Socialist ruling group was more fluid. Youth and newcomers gained access to the upper echelons of the PS with relative ease, which made the PS more volatile than the PC. Nevertheless, a hard core from the founders' generation, men who had arisen in the 1920s like Schnake and Grove, clung to power. Above all regular offices, the party created an honorific position of permanent "leader" for Grove. Beneath these authorities was a swarm of newcomers, a generation of young adults percolating up from the 1930s. They were idealistic, ambitious, and elbowing their way toward the top.[22]

Despite significant turnover in personnel, the Socialist leadership remained heavily middle class. Bureaucrats and lawyers augmented their influence from the 1940s on. Even trade-union leaders prominent in the party's inner councils were mainly of middle-class occupations, for instance, Bernardo Ibáñez Águila, secretary-general of the CTCH. The middle sectors always dominated the PS central committee:[23] for example, in 1941 that committee contained one merchant, one teacher, four professionals, three white-collar employees, and five workers or union leaders. During the Front's administration, the middle– to lower-middle–class Socialists were slightly stronger on the central committee than in the congressional delegation.[24]

22. Cruz Salas, pp. 89-91; Partido Socialista, *Estatutos* (Santiago, 1940).
23. Hochwald, pp. 57-58.
24. Cruz Salas, p. 12.

The Socialists' largely middle-class congressmen dominated their party more than did PC legislators. To the displeasure of some PS members, these elected Socialists overshadowed the union leaders and workers.[25] Congressmen, who were chosen by the national party and did not have to come from the districts where they were elected, still tended to be independent, personalistic, relatively wealthy, and loyal to their geographic area. Poorer candidates had little chance of being nominated or elected, which produced some class friction within the PS. Socialist senators and deputies, whose strength was based on their private clienteles, were often removed from the lower classes and impeded worker mobility within the party.[26]

Followers of the Socialist Party

During the Popular Front, Socialist Party membership grew by thousands, more than doubling from 1938 to 1941, despite factionalism and programmatic disappointments. The PS established hundreds of new local chapters after the 1938 victory, and new members soon outnumbered all those enrolled in the first five years of the party. One estimate placed total registered PS membership at over 50,000 by 1941. According to Grove, this windfall showed the efficacy of participation in coalitions like the Front. Moreover, he insisted, this influx came more from the laboring class than from the middle sectors or bureaucracy, and he denied charges that the PS was being inundated with opportunists. Grove offered membership data to indicate that the newcomers perpetuated the mixed middle- and lower-class character of the party, with an emphasis on workers. The Socialists accepted 2,246 new members from Santiago during the first five months of 1939: 69 women without any occupational designation, 87 public employees (including teachers), 567 private white-collar employees, 360 students, professionals, industrialists and merchants, and 1,161 manual laborers. Assuming the accuracy of Grove's figures, and grouping occupations as smoothly as possible with the earlier categories, the rough comparison of Table 16 can be made between the original Santiago members in 1933 and these new arrivals in 1939. Grove also tabulated 318 new members from the southern province of Valdivia for early 1939: 6 public employees, 22 private employees, 7 professionals, industrialists and merchants, and 283 (89%) manual workers, including 110 peasants. Although the data are open to suspicion because of the political motivation to appear highly working class,

25. Angell, pp. 122-41.
26. Chelén, *Trayectoria,* p. 190; Cruz Salas, pp. 12, 91-92.

TABLE 16: SOCIAL GROUPINGS OF SANTIAGO SOCIALIST PARTY MEMBER OCCUPATIONS, 1933 AND 1939

Occupational Group	1933	1939
Apparently from the middle classes or above	47.9%	45.1%
Apparently from the working classes	35.5	51.7
Class position unclear	16.6	3.1

this fragmentary membership evidence is the best available. It agrees with impressions from voting data. Significantly, Grove's figures indicated an increasing lower-class component in the PS membership, one far out of proportion to the worker and peasant share of leadership posts or benefits from the Popular Front.[27]

This Socialist membership growth partly stemmed from penetration of new regions. The PS tried to consolidate its following in far-flung provinces and thus to capture traditional conservative strongholds. Socialist government officials made special efforts to funnel benefits, such as new industries, ports, and cooperatives, into the distant provinces. For example, propaganda portrayed Schnake and other leaders as loyal men of the north—"the cradle of socialism in Chile"—dedicated to saving it from being "suctioned by voracious centralism." The party held congresses throughout Chile to study and promote the regional needs of workers, thus linking geographic and social discontent.[28] In the initial months of the Front, the PS finally established affiliates in every province. In the first year it organized 150 new nuclei, notably in outlying peasant and miner zones. Local leaders were often, however, attuned to regional rather than national, ideological concerns, and they frequently joined the PS as a ladder to jobs and mobility. Nevertheless, party composition was, in many cases, more lower class in the provinces than in Santiago. The Socialists' desire in the 1930s to be a vehicle for the working classes was becoming more of a reality, through institutionalization, by the 1940s.[29]

Within the working sectors, the Socialists, predictably, still did far better with urban than with rural laborers. They were strongest with copper and railroad workers, with skilled laborers in general, in contrast to the Communists. Both the PS and the PC were able to make

27. Grove's itemization of the occupations of the new Santiago members added up to two fewer than the total he gave of 2,246, with no explanation offered. Partido Socialista, *El Partido Socialista y su*, pp. 20-22; Gunther, p. 255.

28. Casanueva and Fernández, pp. 140-43; Partido Socialista, *Primer congreso regional del Partido Socialista en la provincia de Tarapacá* (Santiago, 1939); Müller.

29. Mallol, pp. 2-43; Partido Socialista, *El Partido Socialista y su*, pp. 20-22; Juan E. Castro D., *Conciencia socialista* (Antofagasta, Chile, 1939), p. 3.

gains because there were many thousands of unorganized and even unionized workers without fixed party affiliations.[30] Although still concentrated in the cities and mines, the Socialists increased their peasant recruitment. As the Socialist Youth Federation doubled in size, it enrolled many rural workers. The PS had the most rural success before Aguirre Cerda acceded to demands for the preservation of the Right's sanctuaries in the countryside. Even before that concession, the Socialists found the peasants to be rather conservative and hard to enlist into either unions or parties. Rural laborers were often more receptive to joining a union clearly geared to their immediate self-interests than a party preaching abstract ideology. Therefore, the moratorium on peasant unionization was a severe blow to Marxist efforts in the countryside. Beyond unions, the Socialists' appeals to the peasantry stressed the most paternalistic approach of those aimed at any social group. Party leaders thought that Grove's charisma, rather than elaborate programs, was the fastest way to mobilize the politically inexperienced peasants.[31] For example, one 1941 populist pamphlet, directed by the PS at the peasants, offered Grove as an object for worship:

> . . . this soldier . . . who has not felt a muscle in his face tremble before death . . . who listens to threats of shooting with a smile on his lips, this man . . . made of steel . . . often has the tenderness of a child, when listening to a worker describe his poverty. More than once Grove has dried a tear from his eyes, taking upon his shoulders the misfortune of the humble. . . . one ought to read his biography to gather its lessons. . . . we can see him in this instant, with . . . his clear eyes, hard in order to whip the enemies of proletarian demands and affectionate when shaking the weathered hand of a son of the common people.[32]

Moderation of the Socialist Party Program

The Socialists' program during the Front was heterogeneous and even contradictory because the moderation of the 1940s was grafted over the radical doctrines of the 1930s. In practice, the PS concentrated on incremental, *ad hoc* problem-solving within the domestic and international capitalist order, but the insistent refrain in party declarations was still rather rote revolutionary Marxism. For example, the Socialists had fully embraced a gradual, democratic transition toward

30. Partido Socialista, *Política sindical,* pp. 19-34; Partido Socialista, *Estatutos* (1940); Angell, p. 134.

31. Partido Socialista, *El Partido Socialista y su,* pp. 20-26; Comité Regional del Partido Socialista, pp. 39-40; Partido Socialista, *Política sindical,* pp. 19-33.

32. Partido Socialista, *Cartilla sindical campesina* (Santiago, 1941), pp. 5-7.

"socialism," however defined. Nevertheless, their proclamations reiterated the ultimate impossibility of an evolutionary path and the transitory necessity of a dictatorship of the proletariat.[33]

An even stronger party theme than Marxism, particularly in the face of World War II, was nationalism, both Chilean and "Indoamerican."[34] In 1940, this continental solidarity with other populist, nationalist movements resulted in the Socialists hosting the First Latin American Congress of Leftist Parties in Santiago. They excluded the Chilean and other Communists; the Radicals declined their invitation. Delegations arrived from other socialist parties, such as those of Argentina and Ecuador. Most important were representatives from less ideologically defined worker movements, such as the APRA of Peru, the Democratic Action of Venezuela (including Rómulo Betancourt), and the official Revolutionary Party of Mexico. Like the Chilean Socialists, they all professed the desire for economic independence for their countries as well as a unified American front with the United States against fascism—not likely compatible goals.[35]

Above all, the Socialists' revolutionary rhetoric gave ground to dry, detailed recommendations for economic growth. This metamorphosis responded to the economic difficulties of the times, the Socialists' changing perspective from the heights of executive offices, and their hopes of building a national majority. The PS asserted that its economic program would benefit all social sectors, not just the workers.[36] The party reconciled its economic developmentalism with social issues through such slogans as "only the industrialization of Chile will save the working class."[37]

In the·Front government, the Socialists' initiatives to boost the economy and the middle classes encountered more support from the Radicals and the Right than did their proposals for the workers. Socialist efforts on behalf of CORFO, economic planning, state banking, national shipyards, heavy industry, tourism, fishing, and roads

33. Partido Socialista, *Chile*, pp. 4-9; Partido Socialista, *Estatutos* (1940); Julio César Jobet, *El Partido Socialista frente a la penetración imperialista en Chile* (n.p., 1939); Julio César Jobet, *Significado del Partido Socialista en la realidad nacional* (Santiago, 1940); U.S., Dept. of State Archives, Santiago, Aug. 12, 1939, pp. 2-6, 825.00/1166.

34. Oscar Schnake Vergara, *Chile y la guerra* (Santiago, 1941); Chelén, *El partido de*, p. 12.

35. Partido Socialista, *Primer congreso de los partidos democráticos de latinoamérica* (Santiago, 1940); U.S., Dept. of State Archives, Santiago, Oct. 10, 1940, p. 2, 825.00/1261.

36. Partido Socialista, *Concepción económica del Partido Socialista* (Santiago, 1941), esp. pp. 3-25.

37. Brigada Parlamentaria Socialista, *Boletín informativo* (n.p., 1942), p. 121; Schnake, *América*, pp. 3-4; Partido Socialista, *Chile*, pp. 79-88.

overshadowed their actions on behalf of agrarian reform, low-cost
housing, and mass education.[38] In the name of economic productivity
and unity against fascism, most Socialist leaders, like many politicians
elsewhere in the world at that time, modulated their antioligarchy and
antiimperialist positions. For example, Grove assured the U.S. Embassy that his party, more than any other, backed the United States in
the Allies' cause and also complimented North American firms on
their fairness toward Chilean workers. At the same time, the Socialists
directed their programs and achievements more at the middle than
lower classes. The party's congressmen advocated at least as many
reforms—such as minimum salaries and readjustments for inflation—for accountants, public and private white-collar employees, and
the armed forces as for factory workers, miners, or peasants. As
the Front progressed, the PS tried to curry favor with the military
rather than reduce or confront it, partly by dissolving the Socialist
Militia. Instead of trying to divide latifundia among the peasants,
Socialist legislators proposed agrarian colonization programs mainly
for the middle classes. These colonies were targeted for public or
underutilized lands and included full compensation to previous owners. A further concession was Socialist acceptance of the Radicals'
expansion of secondary education for the middle strata more than of
primary schooling for the poor.[39]

The Socialists' own compromises, combined with the resistance of
their partners and opponents to reforms, resulted in a disappointing
balance sheet of achievements. The Popular Front compiled a
superior record of reform compared to past administrations but a
modest one compared to its campaign promises.[40] These failures and
frustrations evoked an acid assessment from Grove by 1941: "The
evils of yesterday . . . still have not been remedied. . . . its [Chile's] evils
have become worse with the accession to power of the so-called Left.
The common people remain sunk in hunger and misery; the odious
economic and social privileges are intact; it appears that nothing has
been done except to substitute some men for others in the Government and the Public Administration. . . . we continue in the period of
promises. . . ."[41] Blaming mainly the rightist opposition for these fail-

38. Stevenson, p. 127; Casanueva and Fernández, pp. 141-47; Partido Socialista,
Chile; Partido Socialista, *La línea;* Partido Socialista, *Manifiesto.*
39. U.S., Dept. of State Archives, Santiago, June 7, 1941, pp. 1-10, 825.00/1366,
June 17, 1940, 825.00/1220; Brigada; Partido Socialista, *La palabra de Oscar Schnake V. en
la convención radical de La Serena* (Santiago, 1939), pp. 9-12; Partido Socialista, *Significado,* pp. 4-29; Francisco Pinto Salvatierra, *Clase media y socialismo* (Valparaíso, 1941).
40. Stevenson, p. 136; *La Crítica,* Dec. 16, 1939.
41. Partido Socialista, *Chile.*

ures, the Socialists focused their tattered hopes to realize the Front program on increasing the strength of their party and the administration through the March, 1941, congressional contests. Rather than breaking with the government or adopting more radical means, the PS envisioned an electoral solution to the programmatic omissions of the Front.[42]

1941 Congressional Elections

Brinkmanship on both the right and the left escalated because the final outcome of the Popular Front experiment seemed to hang in the balance of the mid-term elections. The Right dreaded substantial losses, forecast by 1939-40 by-elections.[43] Consequently the Conservatives and Liberals threatened to abstain from the congressional contests. This boycott imperiled the legitimacy of the balloting and the security of the constitutional government. The Right claimed that abstention was necessary because the Front could not be trusted to conduct fair elections. The conservatives' underlying motivation was to pressure the government to curb new Marxist campaign efforts at rural and urban organization and strikes. Once again, the Right showed itself most bellicose when leftists probed its countryside preserves. By vowing to refrain from electoral participation, the opposition also sought to encourage the Radicals to follow the Socialists' lead by breaking with the Communists. Finally, a few conservative groups wanted the military dragged into open politics as an overseer in an atmosphere of electoral uncertainty, although the armed forces' presence could inhibit right-wing votebuying as well as left-wing activism.[44]

The Aguirre Cerda administration caved in to rightist demands. The government wanted to defuse an explosive situation caused by leftist mobilization and rightist resistance. The price of assuring that the conservative forces would continue to acquiesce and take part in formal electoral democracy was high. The Front quashed strikes, restrained the leftist press, restricted union political activities, and banned remaining paramilitary organizations. To further fortify its position and calm the opposition, the government used the armed forces to monitor the voting. Thus the Right's risky but shrewd

42. Cruz Salas, p. 274.
43. U.S., Dept. of State Archives, Santiago, Apr. 10, 1941, pp. 1-2, 825.00/1332, Mar. 23, 1942, pp. 1-2, 825.00/1629.
44. Los Partidos Liberal y Conservador, *¿Por qué nos abstenemos?* (Santiago, 1940); Loyola, *El hombre,* pp. 63-65; Lafertte and Contreras, *El Frente,* pp. 7-8; Partido Comunista, *Cartilla electoral* (Santiago, 1941).

threat obtained some of the concessions unlikely to be won on election day.[45]

With the military guarding the polls and discouraging corruption
and violence, the 1941 elections were probably the most honest in
Chile to that date.[46] Although restrained and divided, the members of
the original Popular Front won a resounding victory. The 1941 results
demonstrated the electorate's shift to the left which had continued
since the Great Depression. Despite the paucity of material rewards
from the Front, the masses were increasingly attracted to its member
parties. Apparently, many voters blamed the Right more than the Left
for the failures of the last three years. The Socialist Party, which
entered the lists alone, reached a career electoral peak. Losing the PST
apostates and leaving the Popular Front party coalition while continuing to serve in the administration did little direct, measurable electoral
damage to the Socialists. Some party dissidents contended that its
showing was not what might have been indicated in by-elections before the desertion of the PST and the breakup of the Front. Many
Socialists complained that numerous Communist voters and trade
union adherents would have supported them if they had chosen the
same combination of participation with relative independence as the
PC had in the Front. As critics charged, deep collaboration with a
lukewarm reformist government may have sown the seeds of internal
PS disintegration, always a potential problem at the leadership level,
but the 1941 balloting indicated that collaboration had not discredited
the party in the eyes of many voters.[47]

Counting the Socialists together with the Front, the Left won 59% of
the votes in 1941, roughly an 8% increase over their presidential tally
in 1938. Of the slightly more than 11% of the population which were
registered in 1941, 78% cast ballots. From the thirties to the forties, the
voting population grew only slightly more than the national population. Far greater than the increase in the size of the electorate from
1937 to 1941 were the gains by the three major original Front parties.
More than attracting new entrants into the electorate, the leftists were
taking voters away from minor parties and the traditional Right. The
allied rightist parties, including smaller organizations such as the
Democrats, Falange, and former Nazis and *ibañistas,* garnered 41% of
the ballots. The submergence of independents illustrated polarization. Among the major parties, the traditional Right captured nearly
31%—17.2% for the Conservatives and 13.5% for the Liberals, who

45. Loyola, *El hombre,* pp. 63-65.
46. *Hoy,* año X, no. 485 (Mar. 6, 1941), pp. 1, 9.
47. U.S., Dept. of State Archives, Santiago, Mar. 5, 1941, 825.00/1316, Mar. 23, 1942, pp. 1-2, 825.00/1629.

suffered the worst loss. The Front-swept into control of both houses of Congress and the Radicals won 20.7% nationally, the largest single party share in Chile. The Communists' percentage rise was most spectacular, from 4% of the electorate in 1937 to almost 12% in 1941. The Socialists jumped from 11.2% to 17.9%, second only to the Radicals in national totals. With votes for the PST (3%) and other socialist-leaning miniature parties added, the socialist total topped 20%. This stimulated the PS's vision of becoming the largest party in Chile.[48]

Table 17's comparison between the 1937 and 1941 congressional elections at the provincial level casts light on the dramatic movement to the left through institutionalization of the Popular Front.[49]

At the regional level, the traditional left-right pattern held in broad outline in 1941. As usual, the Left made some of its highest tallies in the north and south and the Right tended to score above average in the agrarian nucleus of the nation. Except in the most conservative region, the South Center, however, the original Popular Front beat the Right everywhere; it was a national victory for the administration.[50]

At the *comuna* level, the national character of the Front's triumph and its gains in the rural areas were also evident, as Table 18 shows. In contrast to the elections of the 1930s, the traditional Right and the major original Front parties did not display striking differences in 1941 along this rural-urban scale. In the 1938 presidential showdown, Ross had scored nearly twice as well in the rural *comunas* used in the table above as in the urban ones: 61.5% to 37.5%. Aguirre Cerda had recorded the opposite pattern: 38.2% in the rural communities and 61.5% in the urban. After three years in office, the governing coalition won solidly in both types of *comunas*, running only slightly better in the urban districts. The big gains for the coalition came in the rural areas, as attested by regional, provincial, and selected community data. By 1941 the combined Right still relied on a higher average percentage of rural votes than any one of the governing parties, but the Radicals and Socialists were close behind.

Grouping the *comunas* used in previous tables by the same occupational criteria, as in Table 19, further suggests voting differences

48. The PST lost all its deputies, except for Natalio Berman, with his personal following in Concepción. In eight provinces the PST received no percentage of the ballots and in four others less than 1%. Chile, Dirección del Registro Electoral, "Resultado general de las elecciones de Congreso Nacional . . . y de municipalidades . . ." (Valparaíso, 1942); U.S., Dept. of State Archives, Santiago, Dec. 22, 1941, 825.00/1509; Lechner, p. 80.
49. Chile, *Política* (1938), p. 5.
50. *Hoy,* año X, no. 485 (Mar. 6, 1941), p. 25.

between the Right and the Left.[51] In these tables both the Right and the Left showed a mixed voter composition across ecological occupational strata, but the different community categories used here also

TABLE 17: CONGRESSIONAL VOTES FOR PARTIES BY PROVINCE, 1937 AND 1941

	Conservatives & Liberals		Radicals		Socialists & PST		Communists	
	1937	1941	1937	1941	1937	1941	1937	1941
GREAT NORTH								
Tarapacá	12.8%	12.8%	16.9%	18.9%	14.4%	19.2%	20.0%	31.8%
Antofagasta	21.0	9.5	21.3	17.4	16.4	18.0	23.0	41.4
SMALL NORTH								
Atacama	47.2	19.7	29.2	55.1	0.0	25.2	3.8	0.0
Coquimbo	45.0	28.4	33.1	28.9	18.3	16.3	0.0	20.9
URBAN CENTER								
Aconcagua	75.2	43.7	23.6	22.7	0.0	17.7	0.0	15.0
Valparaíso	34.6	34.5	15.8	16.5	12.7	20.4	10.6	12.6
Santiago	41.7	30.1	12.6	14.8	20.7	22.2	6.5	10.9
NORTH CENTER								
O'Higgins	62.6	41.5	9.9	15.0	8.1	22.8	6.0	14.2
Colchagua	63.9	47.6	7.4	15.9	3.3	30.2	0.0	3.5
Curicó	79.5	45.8	20.0	18.9	0.0	12.9	0.0	16.8
Talca	63.2	40.5	25.4	14.5	0.0	13.4	0.0	13.2
SOUTH CENTER								
Maule	81.1	54.4	15.3	34.3	0.0	3.7	0.0	0.0
Linares	62.5	39.5	14.4	18.2	3.5	20.8	0.0	0.0
Ñuble	56.0	43.3	27.4	26.2	0.0	12.9	0.0	3.7
FRONTIER								
Concepción	20.1	12.4	20.4	20.5	13.5	29.4	7.6	11.8
Arauco	26.3	11.0	36.6	29.7	0.0	18.3	0.0	34.9
Bío Bío	52.4	38.7	27.0	29.7	0.0	14.7	0.0	2.4
Cautín	29.3	24.1	20.4	24.7	5.3	14.4	0.7	4.2
LAKES								
Valdivia	38.5	19.3	24.9	19.5	5.7	35.6	0.0	6.0
Llanquihue	66.3	41.3	18.1	18.3	0.0	37.1	0.0	1.9
Chiloé	57.3	43.3	28.7	37.4	0.0	14.2	0.0	0.0
CHANNELS								
Magallanes	8.2	0.0	0.0	37.7	56.9	42.9	0.0	0.0
Total	42.0	30.7	18.6	20.7	11.2	20.7	4.1	11.8

TABLE 18: VOTES FOR PARTIES IN SELECTED URBAN AND RURAL *COMUNAS*, 1941

	Cons. & Libs.	Rads.	Socs.	PST	Socs. & PST	Comms.
Urban *comunas*	24.5%	22.3%	17.5%	5.7%	23.2%	14.1%
Rural *comunas*	29.8	23.8	22.7	0.9	23.6	10.4

51. See Appendix A.

TABLE 19: VOTES FOR PARTIES BY TYPE OF *COMUNA*. 1941

	Cons. & Libs.	Rads.	Socs.	PST	Socs. & PST	Comms.
Middle- to upper-class *comunas*	39.4%	17.2%	14.4%	1.5%	15.9%	9.5%
Industrial-worker *comunas*	16.7	14.4	26.1	7.0	33.1	15.4
Miner *comunas*	15.5	23.6	13.9	3.0	16.9	39.0
Peasant *comunas*	44.1	14.4	24.4	0.8	25.2	6.6
National total	30.7%	20.7%	17.9%	2.8%	20.7%	11.8%

manifested distinguishing political tendencies. In the three urban *comunas* with significantly middle- or upper-class traits and low percentages of workers (compared to the national figures of the 1940 census), the combined Right won more than double the nearest competitor's average percentage in 1941. In those same three unusually non–working-class *comunas,* the Communists ran worst among the major parties. In the second community category, *comunas* with unusually high proportions of urban workers in manufacturing and construction, the regular Socialists and the PST averaged nearly double the percentage of the nearest challenger. In the third and most defined set of *comunas,* with a concentration of workers occupied as miners, the Communists received their highest average voting percentages. The PC surpassed any other political grouping there. Within the mining zones, they scored best in the major coal and nitrate communities, while the Socialists tallied their highest percentages around the key copper mines. In the final group, rural areas with high percentages of agricultural laborers or peasants, the two rightist parties together were still stronger than any single opponent. The Communists remained the weakest major contender. In just three years, the Socialists had risen to second place as a vote getter in these selected peasant *comunas.* The Right's fears of Marxist mobilization during the Popular Front were well founded.

From the 1930s to 1941, as indicated by data from both the provinces and these selected *comunas,* the Right's greatest losses accrued to the original Front parties in the rural, peasant, and mining zones. There was less seepage to the Front in the major urban areas. Yet in 1941 the Conservatives and Liberals remained healthiest in the central and agrarian regions. Conversely, the original Front parties held their advantage in the geographic extremities, with slight gains, while making giant strides in the central conservative regions. The government parties were still weakest in the core agrarian provinces, but their biggest increases occurred there. From 1937-38 to 1941 being in power raised the Left's voting strength in previously conservative zones more than in the provinces of their declared constituency, the urban middle and lower classes.

At the *comuna* level, the governing coalition's general pattern of 1938 persisted. The Front, counting the Socialists, ran well above its national percentage in 1941 in these selected urban, rural, miner, and industrial-worker communities. It scored significantly below its national percentage in peasant and middle- to upper-class areas in the tables. From 1938 to 1941, the greatest coalition increments came in rural, peasant, and miner zones. The Front even ceded a little ground in the urban worker and middle- to upper-class *comunas* in the tables.

Within the governing coalition, the Radicals continued to prosper to a large extent as a party of the less-privileged regions against the core of Chile. Their highest regional percentages came in the Small North, the Frontier, and the Channels. Among the *comunas* studied, the Radicals fared best in mining zones. The Communists, although remaining compacted regionally, became more of a national party. Compared to fourteen provinces in 1937, in 1941 only five gave the PC no percentage of votes. Heavy reliance on high percentages in mining provinces, especially Tarapacá and Antofagasta in the Great North, continued. By 1941, the party, which tripled its congressional representation, made respectable showings in a few highly agricultural provinces, but these were still the most likely to deny it support.[52] In the *comuna* tables, the PC gathered its highest average percentages in miner and industrial-worker categories. Nevertheless, the Communists, like the Socialists, exhibited some of their biggest percentage gains from the 1930s in rural peasant areas. One limited indicator of changes for the Marxists is given in Table 20, a comparison of the average voting percentages for Grove and Lafertte in 1932 with those for the two Socialist parties and the Communists in 1941. At the regional level, from 1932 to 1941 the Socialists' highest percentages shifted from the urban core, which remained vital in absolute numbers, to the far south, as Table 21 shows. By 1941 the PS had become a fully national party, winning respectable percentages in all provinces and regions. Although ten provinces had not registered any percentage of their votes for the Socialists in 1937, all gave the party measurable backing in 1941. The Socialists made their greatest advances in agrarian areas from the North Center through the Lakes, and the South Center remained their consistently worst region. Their percentage in the Channels skidded but stayed the highest of any zone.

52. *Hoy*, año X, no. 485 (Mar. 6, 1941), pp. 25-26, no. 486 (Mar. 13, 1941), pp. 11-25.

TABLE 20: VOTES FOR SOCIALISTS AND COMMUNISTS BY TYPE OF *COMUNA*, 1932 AND 1941

	Socs. & PST		Comms.	
	1932	1941	1932	1941
Urban *comunas*	26.2%	23.2%	2.6%	14.1%
Rural *comunas*	4.7	23.6	0.8	10.4
Middle- to upper-class *comunas*	31.8	15.9	0.8	9.5
Industrial-worker *comunas*	47.3	33.1	1.3	15.4
Miner *comunas*	12.2	16.9	3.4	39.0
Peasant *comunas*	4.4	25.2	0.1	6.6
National total	17.7%	20.7%	1.2%	11.8%

TABLE 21: VOTES FOR SOCIALISTS BY REGION, 1932-41

Region	Grove, 1932	Socs., 1937	Socs., 1941	Socs. & PST, 1941
Great North	11.9%	15.4%	15.7%	18.6%
Small North	15.6	9.1	18.0	20.7
Urban Center	33.4	11.1	18.1	20.1
North Center	6.0	2.8	18.1	19.8
South Center	1.9	1.1	12.5	12.4
Frontier	7.2	4.7	14.2	20.1
Lakes	5.4	1.9	29.9	30.6
Channels	—	56.9	42.8	42.9
National total	17.7%	11.2%	17.9%	20.7%

As in the 1930s, in 1941 the Socialists ran very well in the three most urban and (per capita) richest provinces (Aconcagua, Santiago, and Magallanes). Nationwide, however, they were less dependent on high percentages in urban provinces and increasingly characterized by regional strongholds without such strong socioeconomic identities.[53]

At the *comuna* level, the Socialists, like the Right, reaped high percentages in peasant districts and relatively low ones in mining zones. Unlike the Right, they tabulated very high rates in urban-worker communities and their lowest of all in the middle- to upper-strata areas considered in the tables. As the Socialists became devoted less to populist mobilization and more to institutionalization, the industrial-worker communities continued to provide the party's highest percentages and its largest single base, in terms of absolute voting numbers, from the 1930s' Depression through the 1940s. According to this very limited ecological evidence, the Socialists, in contrast with the Communists, remained far more a vehicle for urban laborers than for miners. This tendency was also reflected at the provincial level,

53. Levine and Crocco, "La población chilena," pp. 49-50.

in party commentaries, and through union alignments. In 1941 the really stunning Socialist gains issued from peasant and rural areas. As the PS claimed and as was indicated previously for the early 1940s at the leadership, membership, and provincial levels, *comuna* data suggested an increasingly lower-class party, particularly at the base.

Institutionalization internally and into the bureaucratic state, despite complaints from dissidents, did not convert the PS into more of a party of the central provinces and the middle to upper classes, at least as nearly as can be determined from the 1941 election data. Its participation in government had not damaged the party electorally in most key worker and peasant areas. Given the PS's rising voter support, the collaboration issue apparently alienated far more Socialist leaders, for ideological or personal reasons, than it did working-class followers. The 1941 results suggested a party of the masses on its way to greater definition as a projection of the working class and to preeminence within Chile's multiparty kaleidoscope. The Socialists and Communists needed far more strength among urban and, especially, rural laborers to speak authoritatively for the lower classes without forming coalitions reliant on centrist reformers. Nevertheless, both Marxist parties had made great progress since the Depression.

The Socialists were delighted with their impressive 1941 voter totals. Grove led the ticket by winning the highest number of ballots of any candidate in all of Chile in his reelection to the senate. However, the gap between the Socialists' share of the electorate and their representation in Congress taught them the perils of independence. In Chile's proportional quotient system, the top individual vote recipient on the multicandidate list which received the most votes was elected over a higher individual vote getter on a list with fewer total votes. This not only encouraged major parties to form electoral coalitions to aggregate votes behind one list but also allowed minor ideological, regional, or personalist parties to survive within alliances because all partners could add to a slate's total. In 1941 the Socialists ran on slates separate from the original Front, so the PS's vote totals in districts did not accumulate and translate into as many elected congressmen as they otherwise might have. With nearly 18% of the national ballots for deputies, the party only elected 10% of the deputies. By contrast, the Communists, thanks to multiparty lists, elected 11% of the deputies with less than 12% of the votes. The Radicals polled only a few thousand more ballots than the Socialists but elected nearly three times as many deputies. In large part because of these electoral rules and pressures, the Socialists did not chart a fresh, solitary course based on their disappointments with the Front and their popularity with the voters. Instead, the issue for the future was what kinds of coalitions the PS would accept.[54]

The high Marxist vote did not spur the government to more leftist action. Wartime economic constraints still postponed the fulfillment of the administration's program. The congressional results did, however, dissuade the Right from trying to undermine the government. The worsening international situation and the Marxist desire for a broad consensus against fascism also favored a domestic climate of compromise, so the conservative opposition increasingly sought a "generous truce" with Aguirre Cerda.[55] Lingering doubts about the reformist zeal of the invigorated Front ended when Aguirre Cerda died from tuberculosis in November, 1941, nine months after the congressional elections. At its crest of political power, the experiment of the Popular Front was over. The huge crowds of mourners at Aguirre Cerda's funeral indicated, as had the electoral results, that he had retained wide popularity with the common people.[56]

Conclusions

The coalition politics of the Popular Front, as a Chilean form of populism, channeled the desires and campaigns of the masses for social welfare into support for induced industrialization. At the same time, the government tempered state capitalism with piecemeal social reforms and some inflation compensation for the middle and lower classes. Economic modernization itself contributed to some overall social benefits, such as declining infant mortality, and despite scanty material gains for the working groups, they achieved greater organization and participation for themselves and their representatives. The workers were not merely used by ambitious politicians; the followers also used their leaders to create openings for advancement. Collaboration with the Front was far preferable to the chronic repression handed down by past administrations. Participation also gave the workers a sturdier organizational base for the future, albeit one dependent on government and party tolerance.[57]

Institutionalization proceeded rather smoothly because of the character of the Marxist parties and the Chilean system. Through electoral and administrative assimilation, the Socialists and Communists exchanged their earlier struggle for power for a struggle for

54. Cruz Salas, p. 316; Partido Socialista, *Una etapa de clarificación socialista* (Santiago, 1944), pp. 12-13; Partido Socialista, *Chile*, pp. 11-22; *El Diario Ilustrado*, Mar. 5, 1941.
55. *El Diario Ilustrado*, Mar. 2-6, 1941.
56. Cabero, *Recuerdos*, p. 337.
57. Cruz Salas, pp. 169, 319-20; Torres and Opitz, pp. 3-14; Valdés M., I, pp. 85-1.10; Alterman, pp. 38-39.

participation. In part, the international conservatism of the Communists and the populism of the Socialists made their moderation and integration possible. Both their ideologies and social composition were flexible enough to facilitate integration. Moreover, the PS and PC presented their demands for inclusion to a political system that was willing to admit them on its terms.

Chilean politics adapted to absorb the Marxists by modifying both them and itself. Flexible elites, institutions, and middle groups were ready, after a period of resistance, to share some of the spoils. By admitting the masses' own leaders, but not their more ambitious programs, the ruling groups hoped to mitigate rather than accentuate social-political conflict. It was a second-best choice to direct domination. Adding new layers and compartments to the state to accommodate the Front caused little damage to vested socieconomic elites. Thereafter, the opposing forces could do battle within the legal limits of bureaucratic and party politics while sharing a common, though highly unequal, stake in the system. Chile developed politically by allowing the democratic expression of social antagonisms. This deflected or regulated those antagonisms without removing their root causes. These arrangements made expanding political participation compatible with economic continuities and persistent social inequalities. By restricting unionization and the franchise, political institutionalization remained well ahead of mobilization.[58]

The informal allocations worked out through popular-front politics headed Chile toward a zero-sum game. Stability depended on an absence of frontal assaults on the existing distribution of power and perquisites. For example, rapid Marxist mobilization of the peasants threatened to overload the state's capacity to satisfy both the upper and lower classes. The Right as well as the Left always feared that the other side might try to finally resolve postponed conflicts by crippling or eliminating its opponents. Without unbridled repression from the Right or more revolutionary initiatives from the Left, the future promised a stalemate.

For populism and socialism, the Front brought both success and frustration. The Chilean Left channeled the populist mobilization of the lower classes into a Marxist framework but also into the established system. By so doing, the Communists and especially the Socialists may have endowed "mass politics" with the potential to be a more hardy agent of change, however gradual and limited, than in many Latin American countries. However, that process of political change had yet to prove that it could produce substantial social or economic reforms.

58. Lechner, pp. 17-22, 61-65; Kenworthy, pp. 121-39.

10

Decline of the Socialist Party, 1942-52

Mobilized in the 1930s and partially institutionalized by the start of the 1940s, the Marxist movement was nearly moribund by the 1950s. In the decade following the death of Aguirre Cerda, the Radical Party, through myriad coalitions which frequently included the Marxists, continued to govern Chile. Although the formal Popular Front was never revived, the political patterns developed in that experience persisted. Those patterns failed to gain sizable benefits for the working class and ultimately led to the disintegration of the Socialists and the proscription of the Communists. Despite the carryover of significant political refrains from the 1930s during the restraints of World War II and the economic difficulties of its aftermath, Chilean populism waned. Disruptive, activist, personalist appeals to the masses decreased in frequency as politics operated mainly through established party organizations and the Marxists weakened. Broad social coalitions emphasizing the workers became less sustainable as centrist groups turned away from an enervated national labor movement and drew closer to conservative elites and cooperation with the United States. Compromising policies integrating production and redistribution gave way to more single-minded dedication to economic growth as industrialism and welfarism appeared less compatible in an era when import substitution became ever more difficult and inflation ever more relentless. By the end of the forties, popular-front politics, despite real gains over previous alternatives, had left a disappointing legacy to its participants, especially the Marxists and workers.

President Juan Antonio Ríos Morales, 1942-46: "To Govern Is To Produce"

Socialist decline coincided with a World War II government consecrated to national unity, social stability, and economic productivity. Aguirre Cerda's successor perpetuated the late president's emphasis on industrialization but downplayed his accompanying concern with reforms for urban labor. Although not based upon a formal pact among the leftist parties, the presidency of Juan Antonio Ríos Morales represented an extension of popular-front politics along more conservative lines.

Businessman Ríos was even more closely identified than Aguirre Cerda with the anticommunist right wing of the Radical Party. Ríos's candidacy in 1942 was strictly a Radical Party decision, not a result of coalition deliberation. However, to avert the return of the Right, the Communists, Socialists, PST, centrist parties such as the Democrats and the Falange, and even some renegade Liberals, including Alessandri, threw their support to Ríos.[1]

In the 1942 election the Marxists backed Ríos's Democratic Alliance grudgingly. In their view, Ríos was at least preferable to the Right's nominee, Carlos Ibáñez. The ailing Conservatives and Liberals chose Ibáñez because they realized that a bona fide member of their own ranks stood little chance in a two-man contest. In addition, some rightists desired an authoritarian ruler.[2] The Communists distrusted both candidates but saw Ríos as more likely to lead a broad consensus over to the side of the Allies in World War II. With Russia and Germany at war, the PC further subordinated worker and peasant causes to the need for national unity against fascism, including cooperation with segments of the economic elites and the Right.[3] The CTCH, increasingly under Communist control even with a Socialist secretary-general, also worked for Ríos.[4]

The Socialists initially hoped to recapture independence or to at least bargain for greater influence by running Schnake as their own candidate. Of all the 1942 nominees, Schnake was most favorable to the interests of the Allies and the United States. After his skillful service in government, he was even viewed positively by some on the right and in the army. To the dismay of some Socialists, Schnake quickly withdrew in favor of Ríos because he believed that electoral coalition offered the only guarantee of defeating Ibáñez. Once again,

1. Lafertte and Contreras, *El Frente*, p. 6; Partido Socialista de Trabajadores, *El camino*, p. 39; U.S., Dept. of State Archives, Santiago, Dec. 4, 1941–Jan. 26, 1942, 825.00/1471–825.00/1568.

2. U.S., Dept. of State Archives, Santiago, Nov. 27, 1941–Jan. 26, 1942, 825.00/1488–825.00/1568; Raúl Aldunate Phillips, *Sentido moderno de liberalismo* (Santiago, 1943); Wilfredo Mayorga, "La derecha deseaba la dictadura," *Ercilla*, no. 1693 (Nov. 29, 1967), p. 15.

3. Sergio Sotomayor A., *Carta abierta de un ex militante al Partido Comunista* (Santiago, 1953), p. 56; Partido Socialista, *Una etapa*, pp. 74-83.

4. Partido Socialista, *Informe sobre posición política del Partido Socialista* (Santiago, 1943), pp. 15-16; U.S., Dept. of State Archives, Santiago, Jan. 20, 1942, 825.00/1551.

the rather stubborn realities of Chilean multiparty politics and loyalties seemed to leave the Marxists with little choice.[5]

Winning 56% of the vote, Ríos dedicated his administration to raising productivity as a response to wartime hardships.[6] Especially during Ríos's first year, overall production, prosperity, and employment fell. Throughout his tenure there were shortages, mainly in capital goods. From 1942 to 1944 the war and government restrictions kept imports down to 13% of national income. The cost of living far outstripped wage increases for workers. The general price index rose roughly three times as much from 1942 through 1945 as it had from 1938 through 1941. According to a later CORFO estimate for 1940-45, monetary national income soared 120% while real national income climbed only 8%. The 1942-43 recession was eased, however, by better economic relations with the United States. This improvement was a result of Chile's breaking with the Axis powers as the Socialists and others had advised. The war gradually boosted Chile's mineral exports, foreign exchange accumulation, employment for miners, and desire for greater industrial self-sufficiency. State support of private enterprise was furthered by U.S. trade, credits, and economic advice. For example, U.S. loans and missions went into CORFO projects to raise production in steel, oil, and fishing. Through cooperation with the Allies, Ríos was able to sustain the economy without trespassing on the incomes of industrialists, landowners, or upper-echelon bureaucrats.[7]

Favoritism for high-cost industry enriched a few at the expense of the mass of consumers. While the general index of production rose from a base of 100 in 1938 to 108 in 1942 and 112 in 1945, industry went from an index of 112 in 1942 to 130 in 1945, mining from 116 to 111, and agriculture from 95 to 105. Thirty-three percent of the active population earned a living in agriculture, but its per capita share of national income accounted for only 16%. Such policies benefited the upper and middle classes more than the workers or, obviously, the

5. U.S., Dept. of State Archives, Santiago, Dec. 16, 1941, 825.00/1486, Jan. 11, 1942, 825.00/1525; Jobet, *El socialismo chileno,* pp. 48-49.

6. Only 80% of the registered voters cast ballots in 1942, compared to 88% in the more ideologically defined and heated contest of 1938. The popular-front electoral pattern continued, with Ríos scoring better in the outlying than the central provinces and better in the selected miner and urban-worker than middle- to upper-class *comunas.* Chile, Dirección del Registro Electoral, "Elección extraordinaria de Presidente de la República" (Santiago, 1942); U.S., Dept. of State Archives, Santiago, Jan. 13, 1942, pp. 1-2, 825.00/1570, Feb. 7, 1942, 825.00/1597, Mar. 11, 1942, 825.00/1617.

7. Chile also contributed to the Allied cause by accepting a comparatively low price for copper exports while paying increasingly high prices for imports. Durán, pp. 314-82; Johnson, *Political Change,* pp. 84-86; Corporación de Fomento, *Geografía,* II, p. 321; Loyola, *El hombre,* pp. iii-iv; Partido Socialista, *Informe,* pp. 6-17.

peasants. According to one CORFO estimate, national income in 1943 was distributed 48.3% to bosses, property owners, landlords, investors, and the self-employed (who were not necessarily upper-class), 24.2% to salary earners (mainly white-collar employees), and only 21.2% to wage-earning workers (the remaining 6.3% went to social services and foreign mining). The middle strata also gained from the expansion of fiscal revenues, the bureaucracy, and education, but middle-class incomes rose little more than did those of urban workers during the war years. Nevertheless, middle- and lower-class interests were diverging and the Marxists failed to mount a credible alternative to the coalition government's increasingly conservative policies.[8]

Disintegration of the Socialist Party, 1942-46

During the Ríos years and throughout the 1940s, the right and left wings of the PS hamstrung each other and the party. The fragmentation and demoralization of the Socialists was an acute case of a broader political illness. All parties suffered from shopworn proposals, vacillation, opportunistic squabbles over power and spoils, and factionalism. The Socialists, however, were more susceptible than the Radicals or Communists to serious divisions. The Radicals were less ideologically oriented than the Socialists and more satisfied with their profits from government participation. Less tension existed between their programmatic aspirations and their clientelistic behavior. The Communists were more moderate and efficient than their Marxist rivals. For an ideological party, the PC's social composition, at all levels, was more orthodox. The Communists were also more pleased with their gains among labor unions and less mired in skirmishes over government plums. Both the Radicals and the Communists relied less on personalism to unify their ranks than did the Socialists.[9]

The Socialists seemed to have drifted farther than ever from their ideological moorings when Grove once again led them in backing a conservative Radical and helping staff his first cabinet. They placed three moderate Socialists, led by Schnake as continuing Minister of Development, in the same minor posts allotted to them under Aguirre Cerda, while the Communists once again gave the administration support without joining the cabinet. In 1942-43, the PS shared responsibility in a conservative cabinet composed not only of right-wing

8. Francisco Méndez, ed., *Chile: tierra y destino* (Santiago, [1947?]), p. 534; Durán, pp. 284-88; Vergara V., pp. 51-55, 108-12; Corporación de Fomento, *Renta*, I, pp. 16-17, 99.

9. Bermúdez, pp. 11-12.

Radicals and Democrats but also of aristocratic Liberals, including the president of the SNA.[10]

Under Ríos, however, the younger, more leftist Socialists, especially in Santiago, intensified their opposition to collusion with an increasingly conservative government and with the Communists. In 1938 some 80% of the party's members had approved entering the Aguirre Cerda administration, but in 1942 Grove, Schnake, Bernardo Ibáñez, and the PS leadership only defeated the anticollaborationists by sixteen votes (74-58) at the party congress. Grove was reelected secretary-general mainly thanks to the loyalty of the provincial Socialists. The dissidents, led by the Socialist Youth and Raúl Ampuero Díaz, demanded more devotion to socialism in national politics and to democracy and the workers within the PS. Once again, contending middle-class leaders promised the workers greater participation in return for intraparty support. Seeking both reforms and power, the rebels wanted the PS out of the government and the *grovistas* out of the party leadership. This internal division was better explained by *caudillismo* than by clear ideological or class conflicts.[11]

Alienation and rebellion among the masses following the Socialist Party were neither widespread nor the major causes of ruptures within. To the contrary, splits among party leaders mainly caused its mass base to crumble. These intraparty divisions did not cut clearly along class lines. In the 1940s, the Socialists vied with the Radicals for the middle-class and provincial votes while contesting the Communists for the worker votes. The PS lost ground on both fronts.[12] The party's instability estranged many middle-class supporters. Socialist insurgents desirous of leaving the administration, while perhaps appealing to disaffected workers, offended public-employee members concerned with job security. More to the point, the middle classes generally lost interest in crusades for social change. Instead, they wished to cement their positions in and links with the bureaucratic state, which offered a far more dependable source of problem solving than the mercurial Socialists. Among the various parties, the Radicals proved a more attractive and reliable guarantee of employment and patronage favors, for example for those in public works and

10. Partido Socialista, *Una etapa*, pp. 74-80; U.S., Dept. of State Archives, Santiago, Apr. 1, 1942, 825.00/1635.
11. Jobet, *El socialismo chileno*, pp. 48-55; Angell, pp. 140-41; Partido Socialista, *Informe*, pp. 14-15; *Congreso extraordinario del Partido Socialista* (Santiago, 1944), esp. pp. 7-14; *Hoy*, año XI, nos. 537-44 (Mar. 5–Apr. 23, 1944); interviews with Jobet, Almeyda, and Charlín, Santiago, 1970, and Barría and Jobet, Santiago, 1973.
12. Partido Socialista, *Una etapa*, pp. 11-13, 135-36; Cruz-Coke, pp. 83-85.

municipal unions. The Socialists' participation in government served as a conduit for some middle-class groups, like public school teachers, simply to align more consistently with the Radicals. Compared to the PS in the 1940s, the Radicals were more effective at recruitment through government institutions, and the Communists through independent mobilization.[13]

The Communists came to wield far more strength in the CTCH than did the Socialists, especially after the PS left its government posts and shattered into factions. The PC gained support among the working classes despite its cooperation with conservative elites in the name of antifascism.[14] The Socialists and Communists alike renounced strikes during wartime, accepted obligatory arbitration of labor disputes, supported extraordinary government police powers, favored industrialists, and condemned but tolerated the poverty of the masses. Even with a majority in Congress from 1941 to 1945, the original Front parties passed very little of the legislation long promised to urban and rural laborers, for instance broader social security coverage. Nevertheless, while some workers shifted away from the Socialists, most remained loyal to the Marxist parties and to the popular-front approach.[15]

Angered by conservatism at the top of the PS and erosion at the base, the Socialist insurgents consummated their rebellion at the 1943 party congress. There, beginning a fundamental shift, the young Turks elected Allende secretary-general over Grove by nearly a two-to-one margin. Allende was a compromise choice for the takeover, which was largely led by Ampuero. Born in the far south to a middle-class family of teachers, Ampuero was educated to be a lawyer in Santiago. As a youth leader, he was not a sparkling orator but rather a masterful intraparty debater and operator.[16]

Grove chastized the victors for youthful impatience and for cloaking personal ambitions under ideological principles. More favorable than the rebels to cooperation with both the government and the Communists, he maintained that industrial production had to be raised still further and World War II concluded before class conflict and expensive reforms for the workers could be promoted. He also

13. Partido Socialista, *Informe,* pp. 9-19; Casali, p. 28.
14. Vergara V., pp. 221-27; Carlos Contreras Labarca, *Unión nacional y partido único* (Santiago, 1943).
15. Partido Obrero Revolucionario, *¿A dónde va la C.T.CH.?* (Santiago, 1944); La Confederación de Trabajadores de Chile, *Memoria . . .* (Santiago, 1946), p. 15; Partido Socialista Auténtico, *Primer congreso extraordinario* (Santiago, 1946), p. 9; Angell, pp. 110-11.
16. Castro, *¿Me,* pp. 137-40; Jobet, *El socialismo chileno,* pp. 50-51; Partido Socialista, *IX congreso* ([Santiago?], 1943), pp. 3-13.

defended reliance on U.S. aid. Grove's adversaries, without proposing clear alternatives, condemned these economic and international arguments as rationalizations for the continued deprivation of the proletariat. Grove's efforts to impose discipline within the PS, more than his adherence to Ríos's conservative policies, caused his downfall, however. Initially, the new officers tried to keep him as a powerless but charismatic totem in the permanent position of "Maximum Leader."[17]

The new leadership withdrew the PS from the Ríos government. Roughly 80% of the party's members supported independence, hoping to recapture lost momentum and purify their doctrines. They argued that competing with the Radicals by dispensing favors from their posts in a conservative administration debased not only the party but also the middle and working classes, who were thus diverted into a quest for individual mobility instead of class struggle. Shifting from institutionalized clientelism back to rallying the masses through independent campaigns was risky. Leaving Ríos just after he had acceded to the demand by Socialists and others to support the Allies would deny the party its share of economic benefits about to arrive from the United States. The PS reassured modest functionaries, workers, and peasants that absence from the administration—where the party claimed to have held less than 5% of all public jobs in any case—would not exclude Socialists from all influence, aid, and employment. After their exit, party leaders envisioned selective criticism and support of the government from the outside.[18]

The split between the new ruling group around Allende and the *grovistas* was grounded more in tactical and personal than strategic and ideological differences. Neither party programs nor party methods veered to the left. Allende's new demands called for accelerated economic planning and amplified welfare measures, not immediate redistribution of power and wealth. While describing himself and his party as Marxist, Allende said that he favored a nationalistic, democratic government of the middle- and lower-class masses rather than a dictatorship of the proletariat. Leaving the cabinet did not involve a rejection of coalitions with centrist reformers; rather, it was an attempt to redefine the purposes and forms of collaboration and to exert greater independent weight within coalitions. The Socialists still

17. Grove, *Grove*, pp. 2-5; *Congreso extraordinario*, pp. 3-7; Salvador Allende, "Trayectoria del Partido Socialista," Partido Socialista, *Boletín Interno . . .* (Oct., 1943), pp. 3-7; Durand, *Mis*, II, pp. 244-49; Julio César Jobet, "El Partido Socialista y el Frente Popular en Chile," *Arauco*, no. 85 (Feb., 1967), pp. 13-47; Thomas, "Marmaduke Grove: A Political Biography," pp. 257-62, 330-34.

18. *Congreso extraordinario*, pp. 7-12; Partido Socialista, *Informe*, pp. 5-24; Partido Socialista, *IX*, pp. 3-15; Salvador Allende, *La contradicción de Chile* (Santiago, 1943), pp. 4-5.

preferred the left wing of the Radicals to the Communists. Whereas the PS had left the party alliance but stayed in the administration under Aguirre Cerda, it now exited from the government but remained affiliated with the coalition which had elected Ríos. In addition, the Socialists tried to weave closer ties with the centrist Falange.[19]

Grove and the Authentic Socialist Party

Retiring from the Ríos government failed to rekindle Socialist internal democracy, unity, or growth. The *grovistas* immediately abandoned the regular party to form the Authentic Socialist Party (PSA) in 1944. Socialist unity suffered a double blow because Godoy's PST formally joined the Communists just prior to the birth of the PSA. The regular PS and Grove's PSA were about equally heterogeneous in composition, although the offspring appeared somewhat more middle class.[20]

Now the fractured Socialists tumbled into their worst period of electoral decline. The regular party lost its two most famous leaders: although remaining a nominal member of the PS, Schnake went abroad as ambassador to Mexico and never returned to the domestic political limelight, and Grove's separate party confused the Socialists' followers. Between the two organizations, the PS held the bulk of the faithful and the union leadership. Meanwhile, the old Socialist *caudillo* and his PSA withered away. The Socialists had mushroomed rapidly in the 1930s largely because of the magnetism of Grove. The fortuitous combination of *grovismo* and *socialismo* had achieved a momentum that was never recaptured by the man or the party alone.[21]

The PSA was an expression of the Grove cult, mildly reformist and scarcely Marxist. It always stressed the need for the unity of all Socialists, of all reform parties, and of middle-class leaders with working-class followers. The Authentic Socialists forged closer alliances with the Radicals, the Communists, and the government than did the parent party. Throughout the Ríos administration, the PSA retained cabinet and minor posts such as Minister of Justice, one provincial intendant, and six departmental governors in 1946, viewing those positions as evidence of party success.[22]

19. Partido Socialista, *IV*, pp. 53-57; Partido Socialista, *Informe*, pp. 9-13; Partido Socialista, *Una etapa*, pp. 8-13, 69-76; Allende, *La contradicción*, pp. 3-40; Wilfredo Mayorga, "Primeros pasos falangistas en la Moneda," *Ercilla*, no. 1624 (July 20, 1966), pp. 17-19.

20. Jobet, *El socialismo chileno*, pp. 51-53.

21. Jobet, "El Partido," pp. 37-39; Thomas, "Marmaduke Grove: A Political Biography," pp. 330-36.

22. Grove, *Grove*, pp. 2-7; Partido Socialista Auténtico, *Primer;* Partido Socialista

After World War II and electoral disappointments, most Authentic Socialists either drifted out of political life or returned to the mother party. No longer the firebrand of yore, Grove lost his third bid for the senate in 1949. Thereafter, he went into retirement, and the PSA evaporated. Marmaduke Grove, the kindly, swashbuckling *caudillo* of the red airplane, the Socialist Republic, the Socialist Party, the Popular Front, and the Authentic Socialists, had been a catalyst in Chilean politics for thirty tumultuous years. In 1954, at the age of seventy-five, suffering from a lung infection, Grove died, modestly and alone, politically forgotten.[23]

Socialist Decline in the 1945 Congressional Elections

The 1945 congressional elections registered losses from 1941 for the original Popular Front parties, especially the Socialists, and roughly 6% gains each for the Conservatives and Liberals. Compared to the 1937 congressional contests, the combined rightist parties rose from 42% of the votes for deputies to nearly 44%. Although they did not equal their 1941 percentage, the Radicals exceeded their 1937 tally (18.6%) with 20.0% in 1945; so did the Communists, with 4.1% in 1937 and 10.2% in 1945. The combined Socialist parties, with 12.8% in 1945, fell almost back to the 1937 level of 11.2%. Together, the Radicals, Communists, and Socialists accounted for 43% in 1945, recreating the standoff with the Right prior to the Left's gains under Aguirre Cerda's administration. Table 22 summarizes these votes.[24]

Neither Socialist party alone was as electorally strong as the Communists by 1945. The regular PS (7.2%) barely outpolled the PSA (5.6%). For the Socialists, there was little evidence that participation or nonparticipation in the Ríos government was the key to electoral prominence.

TABLE 22: NATIONAL CONGRESSIONAL VOTES FOR PARTIES, 1941 AND 1945

Cons. & Libs.		Rads.		PS & PST		PS & PSA		Comms.	
1941	1945	1941	1945	1941	1945	1941	1945	1941	1945
30.7%	43.7%	20.7%	20.0%	20.7%	12.8%			11.8%	10.2%

Auténtico, *Sobre la unidad socialista* (Santiago, 1946); Manuel Eduardo Hubner et al., *Forjando la unión nacional* (Santiago, 1944).

23. Interviews with Blanca Elena and Hiram Grove, Santiago, 1970; Thomas, "Marmaduke Grove: A Political Biography," pp. 334-36; Jobet, "El Partido," pp. 38-39.

24. See Appendix A. Chile, Dirección del Registro Electoral, "Elección ordinaria general de senadores y diputados al Congreso Nacional" (Santiago, 1945).

At the regional level, the two Socialist parties fell least in their traditional strongholds of the Urban Center and the Great North from 1941 to 1945. They reverted to their previous weakness in the agrarian North Center and South Center. In 1945, the Socialists still ran best in the Channels and the Urban Center. The highest single voting percentages for the regular PS came from the provinces of Magallanes and Santiago. By 1945, the Socialists, who failed to attract any measurable percentage of the votes in some provinces, were sliding back toward a previous highly selective regional pattern, as Table 23 shows. At the community *(comuna)* as well as the regional level, the Socialists' descent left them strongest in their areas of traditional popularity, especially urban-worker zones, as seen in Tables 23 and 24. From 1941 to 1945, the combined Socialists fell more in those *comunas* designated highly rural by the national census than in those designated highly urban. Both parties showed a slight propensity to run better in the selected urban than rural communities in 1945. Among the communities included in Table 24, the two Socialist contenders slipped most in peasant districts. The table's middle- to

TABLE 23: VOTES FOR SOCIALISTS BY REGION, 1937, 1941, 1945

Regions	1937 PS	1941 PS	PS & PST	1945 PS	PS & PSA
Great North	15.4%	15.7%	18.6%	6.5%	14.9%
Small North	9.1	18.0	20.7	4.2	7.5
Urban Center	11.1	18.1	20.1	7.8	15.3
North Center	2.8	18.1	19.8	0.7	5.8
South Center	1.1	12.5	12.4	4.5	5.3
Frontier	4.7	14.2	20.1	4.8	8.2
Lakes	1.9	29.9	30.6	3.5	13.7
Channels	56.9	42.8	42.9	23.5	28.4
National total	11.2%	17.9%	20.7%	7.2%	12.8%

TABLE 24: VOTES FOR SOCIALISTS BY TYPE OF *COMUNA*, 1941 AND 1945

	1941 PS	PST	PS-PST	1945 PS	PSA	PS-PSA
Urban *comunas*	17.5%	5.7%	23.2%	9.0%	6.4%	15.4%
Rural *comunas*	22.7	0.9	23.6	6.9	5.9	12.8
Middle- to upper-class *comunas*	14.4	1.5	15.9	3.9	6.3	10.2
Industrial-worker *comunas*	26.1	7.0	33.1	17.1	7.1	24.2
Miner *comunas*	13.9	3.0	16.9	6.3	5.5	11.8
Peasant *comunas*	24.4	0.8	25.2	4.7	3.4	8.1
National total	17.9%	2.8%	20.7%	7.2%	5.6%	12.8%

upper-class *comunas,* normally more attracted to the Radicals than to the Socialists, and mining areas, traditionally the home of the Communists, also reduced their support of the PS and the PSA. Even in the copper communities, the Socialists, especially the regular party, sank well below previous percentages. Perhaps significantly, the Socialists lost least among the urban-worker *comunas* studied. Socialist support dwindled everywhere from 1941 to 1945, but regional, provincial, and communal data indicated that their most vigorous backing, particularly for the regular party, still came from urban labor areas. This relatively steadfast support ran counter to the notion that institutionalization and fragmentation had hurt the Socialists drastically with the proletariat. Given the political and industrial bargaining systems, some laborers no doubt regretted the PS's reduced access to the state. Others had previously resented the inability of state collaboration to deliver promised benefits, and still others evidently remained loyal throughout government participation and nonparticipation. If it had not been for the high regular party scores in city sectors with significant worker components, it is likely that Grove's renegade group would have beaten the parent organization.

The Socialists' Third Front, 1945-46

After Allende's transitional stewardship in 1943, the regular Socialist Party chose Bernardo Ibáñez as its secretary-general. From a rural working-class family in the south, Ibáñez had risen to middle-class status through education and leadership of teachers' unions. Following his persecution and unemployment under Alessandri in the 1930s, his ascent as a labor leader and his alignment with the Left and blue-collar causes were not based primarily on ideology or confrontation. On the contrary, Ibáñez, an ex-Communist, stressed a bread-and-butter approach to labor needs. His international labor connections and experience also aided his career. Ibáñez became a CTCH leader in 1936, a founder of the Confederation of Latin American Workers (CTAL) in Mexico in 1938 and thereafter second vice-president of the international organization, and, most important, secretary-general of the CTCH in 1939. Meanwhile he was a frequent visitor to the United States, where he toured universities as well as labor organizations and conferences at the invitation of the American Federation of Labor and the Congress of Industrial Organizations. As head of the Socialist Party, Ibáñez's roots among union leaders were unusual, but his middle-class orientation and very pragmatic, moderate outlook were typical.[25]

25. Bernardo was apparently no relation to Carlos Ibáñez. Bernardo Ibáñez, *El socialismo y el porvenir de los pueblos* (Santiago, 1946), pp. 47-51.

Prodded by Ampuero and the younger Socialists, in 1944-45 Ibáñez and other leaders tried to unite the party against indiscriminate coalitions with the Radicals or the Communists. By late 1945, many Socialists began advocating a vague "Third Front." Once again, rhetoric aside, this tactic was not a switch to the left. Rather, it was an attempt to carve out an independent reformist position, for example in conjunction with the Falange, in between the Right and the Ríos government alliance. Internationally, this "third position" brought the PS into closer contact with the Brazilian labor party of Getúlio Vargas and the Argentine Peronists, populist movements which the Chileans labeled "parties of socialist tendencies." The PS also nourished intimate personal and ideological ties with their "brother party," Democratic Action of Venezuela, and with the APRA of Peru. Domestically, the Socialists seized the chance to gain an edge over their Communist and Radical rivals by opportunistically entering the cabinet of an administration noted for its violent reactions against labor.[26]

Because of the failing health of President Ríos, another right-wing Radical, Alfredo Duhalde Vásquez, took over as interim chief executive at the end of 1945. His shaky government overreacted to Communist-led nitrate strikes in the north and solidarity rallies in Santiago; the repression caused bloodshed and alienated Authentic Socialist, Falange, and even some Radical members and supporters of his administration. Following wholesale cabinet resignations, the acting president tried to restore order and pacify the Left by pasting together a cabinet which included the armed forces and the regular Socialists. Having backed the previous labor protests against Duhalde, the PS now accepted four ministries and promises to respect union rights. The PC and the bulk of the CTCH attacked the cabinet, which included Bernardo Ibáñez. When the Communists retaliated with further demonstrations and strikes, mainly in the southern coal zone, Duhalde broke their resistance with troops.[27]

In large part, the Duhalde-labor episode sprang from conflicts within the Chilean Left. While Ríos was dying, the leftists were scuffling for advantageous positions for the 1946 elections, and for union supremacy. In spite of party declarations against joining any governments not committed to socialism, the PS participated in the Duhalde

26. Agustín Álvarez Villablanca, *El tercer frente* (Santiago, 1945), pp. 2-15; Partido Socialista Auténtico, *Sobre*, p. 12; Jobet, *El Partido Socialista de Chile*, I, p. 194; Ampuero, *La izquierda*, p. 21; Waiss, *El drama*, pp. 46-52.

27. Durán, pp. 400-405; Ibáñez, *El socialismo*, pp. 8-61; Partido Radical, *En defensa de los principios* (n.p., 1946); Alfredo Duhalde Vásquez, *Gobiernos de izquierda* (Santiago, 1951).

administration as a means of diluting the president's hostility toward labor and hounding their rival in the CTCH. The Communists reciprocated by successfully branding many Socialists as traitors to labor. At the same time, the PC prepared to enter the next administration and turn the tables by persecuting their rivals from ministerial posts. The Socialists also claimed to be joining the cabinet to lessen civil strife and forestall a coup by the military. Some PS leaders, like the Argentine Peronists, hoped to form an ill-defined "third force" with the armed services, since fresh party coalition possibilities were few. However, this adventure with Duhalde failed to bring the Socialists or their program to power. Instead, it left the PS further debilitated and vulnerable to a showdown in the CTCH.[28]

Division of the Labor Movement, 1946

Labor unity, forged by the same Marxist parties that now shattered it in 1946, had lasted nearly a decade. The end of World War II and the onset of the Cold War terminated cooperation within the Left. The Communist majority in the CTCH was no longer willing to accept a Socialist, Bernardo Ibáñez, as secretary-general. Consequently, one branch of the confederation broke away under Ibáñez and the Socialists. The other wing followed the Communists and won recognition from the old Ríos coalition—the Radicals, Falange, and PSA—as the official CTCH.[29]

Both Moscow and Washington contributed to this labor division, which left the Chilean workers less able to defend their interests. The Socialists blamed the rupture on the Communists' Cold War policy of increasing their control over Latin American unions even at the cost of splitting federations. In accord with a harder line from the Soviet Union, the PC tried to crush the Socialists. By the same token, the CTCH split resulted from Socialist determination to reduce the Communists' role in the Chilean and Latin American labor movement. Bernardo Ibáñez, a non-Marxist admirer of the welfare state and the British Labour government led the Socialists' anticommunist campaign. He was influenced by his international ties, particularly with APRA, AD, and the North American trade unions. Like Schnake before him, Ibáñez broke with the Communists in 1946 immediately

28. Chelén, *Trayectoria*, pp. 106-7; Partido Socialista Auténtico, *Primer,* esp. pp. 9-11; Partido Socialista Auténtico, *Sobre,* pp. 1-4; Partido Socialista Auténtico y Partido Comunista de Chile, *Pacto de acción política* (Santiago, 1946), pp. 3-14; Grove, *Grove,* pp. 8-12; Marmaduke Grove Vallejo, *Declaraciones del Senador Marmaduke Grove al "conflicto del carbón"* (Santiago, 1947); Bernardo Ibáñez, *Discurso pronunciado por el Secretario General de la Confederación de Trabajadores de Chile* (Santiago, 1946), pp. 8-9.
29. Angell, p. 227.

after a trip through Latin America, Europe, and the United States. He praised U.S. prosperity, electoral democracy, and labor unions. At the same time, Ibáñez also turned against the international CTAL of Vicente Lombardo Toledano in Mexico because of Communist influence on the organization. In response, the Communists charged that the Socialists were colluding with a North American- and AFL-led Cold War crusade to divide the CTCH and the CTAL.[30]

Indeed, the U.S. government, the AFL, the United Mine Workers, and their international representatives donated organizers and money from 1946 on to help divide Chilean and Latin American labor into communist and anticommunist camps. AFL-CIO support was critical to the survival of the Socialists' fraction of the CTCH. Ibáñez welcomed U.S. aid and closer ties with the AFL and the State Department, which grew out of the Socialists' pro-U.S. position during World War II. He portrayed the internecine labor struggle as a war between "totalitarian" and "democratic" forces. Although he aligned the Socialists with Western liberalism rather than Marxism, the party officially sided with neither super power in the Cold War. Ibáñez also became a hemispheric leader in the AFL's efforts to create a noncommunist inter-American labor organization opposed to the CTAL. In 1946-48, this campaign culminated in the establishment of the Confederation of Inter-American Workers (CIT), with the active participation of the Socialist CTCH and the Peruvian *apristas*. Ibáñez became chairman of the CIT and George Meany, of the AFL, vice-chairman. These international linkages soon led Ibáñez away from Chilean politics and into permanent involvement and employment with U.S.- and AFL-CIO–sponsored inter-American labor organizations in the 1950s.[31]

The 1946 breach in the CTCH left many laborers weakened organizationally and partially disappointed with having followed the Marxists and their presidential preferences. Criticizing leftist party politics, a few union leaders chose autonomy from either branch of the CTCH. Most member unions, however, adhered to one of the two federations.

30. With the switch from the war against fascism to the Cold War, in 1946 the Communists replaced Contreras Labarca as secretary-general with Ricardo Fonseca, a more combative leader more closely associated with the worker majority of the party. Sotomayor, pp. 57-59; Partido Socialista Auténtico y Partido Comunista, pp. 3-14; Ibáñez, *Discurso*, pp. 1-10; Ibáñez, *El socialismo*, pp. 3-63; Serafino Romualdi, *Presidents and Peons* (New York, 1967), p. 37.

31. The CIT was the precursor to the ORIT (Inter-American Regional Organization of Workers), in which Ibáñez also became a leader. Romualdi, pp. 37-42, 73-139, 323-32; George Morris, *CIA and American Labor* (New York, 1967), pp. 48-91; Bernardo Ibáñez, *El movimiento sindical internacional y la fundación de la C.I.T.* (Santiago, 1949), pp. 5-12; Partido Comunista, *El tercer frente ha sido alquilado por el imperialismo norteamericano* . . . (Santiago, 1946).

The Communist majority CTCH encompassed coal and nitrate miners, construction workers, port workers, bakers, and some industrial laborers. The smaller Socialist CTCH included workers in copper, public transportation, railroads, textiles, chemicals, and a few other industrial activities.[32]

Socialist Debacle in the 1946 Presidential Election

The special 1946 election to replace Ríos demonstrated the transition of Chilean politics from ideological and social struggles in the 1930s to more opportunistic jostling for party advantage in the 1940s. The Conservatives offered the freshest option with a social Christian centrist candidate, Eduardo Cruz-Coke. He probably attracted as much support from the Falange and Grove's PSA as from his own party. More traditional Conservatives joined the Liberals behind Fernando Alessandri Rodríguez, after flirting with again nominating his father Arturo. Even a few rightist Radicals and Socialists rallied to the younger Alessandri. Equally bankrupt, the Left once more sold the electorate the promises and alignments of the Popular Front. A left-wing Radical, Gabriel González Videla, staked his campaign mainly on the enthusiasm of the Communists. He promised to revive the reformist spirit of 1938. The PC claimed that popular-front politics was still necessary because the workers lacked radical class consciousness and retained enormous faith in electoral *caudillos*. For that reason, and to secure middle-class support, the Communists backed González Videla, a long-standing ally.[33]

Although most of the regular Socialists ultimately voted for González Videla, the party did not endorse him. The PS was too factionalized and dispirited to make a coherent, positive decision about the election. All presidential contenders solicited Socialist backing, including Conservative Cruz-Coke. A majority of PS leaders, however, found it unthinkable to team up with the Right or the Communists and therefore ran their own nominee, Bernardo Ibáñez, in a vain attempt to hold the disintegrating party together.[34]

The declining turnout for presidential elections was one sign of political disillusionment: it dropped from 88% of the registered voters in 1938 to 80% in 1942, and then to 76% in 1946. González Videla won

32. La Confederación de Trabajadores de Chile, *Memoria*, pp. 10-16; Ibáñez, *Discurso*, pp. 1-13; Angell, pp. 111-13.
33. Partido Comunista, *El tercer;* Partido Comunista, *Ricardo*, pp. 124-41; Bermúdez, pp. 153-57.
34. Ibáñez, *Discurso*, pp. 12-14; Partido Socialista Auténtico, *Primer*, p. 10; Agustín Álvarez Villablanca, *Objetivos del socialismo en Chile* (Santiago, 1946), pp. 41-46; Chelén, *Trayectoria*, pp. 103-11; Jobet, *El Partido Socialista de Chile*, I, pp. 190-98.

a plurality (40.1%). He ran weakest in the central agrarian zones south of Santiago, where the rightist candidates obtained their highest percentages. González Videla's provincial pluralities came in areas of traditional leftist strength such as the geographic extremities and the urban and mining zones. If Cruz-Coke (29.7%) and Alessandri (27.3%) could have combined their forces, the Right might have defeated the Left with a majority vote (57%).[35]

Vast defections left the Socialists' official candidate with only 2.5% of the national electorate. Ibáñez fell short of a plurality in every *comuna* in Chile. The older PS leaders were discredited. The Radicals and Communists were pulling away both the party's voters and its union followers and were once more in charge of the government. In every way, 1946 marked the nadir for the Socialist Party.[36]

In the aftermath of the electoral catastrophe, Ampuero took direct control of the PS as secretary-general. Allende and the long-discontented younger generation backed him. From 1946 to 1952, the regular party devoted itself to doctrinal redefinition and organizational reconstruction, but recovery did not come quickly or smoothly, for the Socialists suffered further divisions and distress after 1946. Nevertheless, the renovation begun by Ampuero paid major political dividends by the 1950s.[37]

Ampuero's recuperative regimen insisted on party independence and internal discipline. He steered the PS away from personalism and from political somersaults which only grasped at fleeting power or influence. Although Ampuero's takeover initiated a march away from populism and clientelism toward more explicitly Marxist socialism, it was a protracted and never completed evolution. Democratic socialism naturally required at least minimal conformity to the code and conduct prescribed by the national political system. Despite some claims to the contrary, the PS made no full turn against non-Marxist ideologies, against the middle classes, or against centrist reformers; the party could not cast aside its heritage. The new Socialist leaders pledged to cooperate with other reformist parties only if coalitions were not broad, compromising, or permanent. Henceforth, they planned to join only governments fully dedicated to socialism and the workers. Therefore, the PS spurned González Videla's invitation to serve in his administration. Even at this moment of renewal, however, there was no firm Marxian rejection of transactions with reform

35. Chile, Dirección del Registro Electoral, "Elección extraordinaria de Presidente de la República" (Santiago, 1946); Cruz-Coke, pp. 83-85, 96-109.

36. Partido Socialista Auténtico, *Primer*, pp. 10-11.

37. Chelén, *Flujo;* interview with Garay, Santiago, 1970.

groups linked to the bourgeoisie. The Socialists were still more willing to lock arms with middle-class, centrist parties than with the Communists. In 1946, they specifically ruled out alliances of any nature only with the Conservatives, the Liberals, and the Communists. The Socialists were more concerned with rebuilding by taking the working sectors back from the PC than with opposing the increasingly rightist Radical government. Their abstention from the González Videla administration sprang more from the inclusion of the Communists in his cabinet than from the appointment of Liberal ministers. Praising the President's campaign promises, the Socialists agreed to back selected reforms from outside.[38]

González Videla's Turn toward the Right, 1946-52

In 1946, as in 1920 and 1938, tension mounted between the counting of the ballots and the formal ratification of the new president. In the absence of a majority winner, Congress could select either of the top two vote-getters. González Videla guaranteed his certification by promising the Liberals cabinet posts and new restrictions on peasant unionization. Apparently, the Communists accepted his bargain with the Right as necessary if he was to take office at all.[39]

The immediate political result was the strangest cabinet in Chilean memory, combining "Manchester and Moscow." For the first time, the PC took cabinet posts, and in company with Liberals and Radicals. At the zenith of their influence, the Communists filled three relatively secondary slots: Public Works, Agriculture, and Lands and Colonization.

Under González Videla at least the illusion of greater prosperity existed from the recession of 1947 until the 1950s. Compared to the two previous Radical administrations, per capita real personal con-

38. Partido Socialista, *La palabra del Partido Socialista en la lucha sindical* (Santiago, 1947); Eugenio González Rojas and Raúl Ampuero Díaz, *La controversia permanente: socialismo y liberalismo. El socialismo único fundamento de la democracia. Carácter de la revolución chilena* (Santiago, 1957), pp. 39-40; Oscar Waiss, *Nacionalismo y socialismo en América latina* (Santiago, 1954), p. 121; Waiss, *El drama*, pp. 46-98; Humberto Mendoza, *Socialismo, camino de la libertad* (Santiago, 1945), pp. 79-93; Ibáñez, *Discurso*, pp. 13-14; Chelén, *Trayectoria*, pp. 111-13; Halperin, pp. 61-66.

39. Years later, the PC claimed to have opposed González Videla's bargain with the Right and charged that he made secret promises at the time to the rightist parties and to the United States to oust the Communists from his administration within a matter of months. Although he rescinded Aguirre Cerda's prohibition on rural unionization, González Videla kept faith with the Liberals and the landed elites by joining the conservative-dominated Congress in 1947 in passing special restrictive legislation which effectively stifled peasant organization until the 1960s. Partido Comunista, *Ricardo*, esp. pp. 142-49; Affonso et al., I, pp. 42-63, 125-26; Partido Socialista, *La palabra del Partido*.

sumption rose during the post-war years. Nevertheless, in that uneven economic period from 1946 through the early 1950s the growth rates of real production and real per capita income declined in comparison with the war years. Indeed, the overall growth rates of national production and income from 1930 to 1954 were so disappointing that pre-Depression levels were barely being reached by the end of the 1940s. The masses' standard of living improved little in the late forties. Increasingly, the distribution of national income favored white-collar employees and those who owned the means of production over urban and rural wage-earners. Newcomers to the labor market strained Chile's economic capacity, and population and price inflation grew more per year from 1938 to 1950 than from 1928 to 1938. After World War II, the rising inflation and expenditure of accumulated foreign exchange reserves contributed to high profits and an initial impression of well-being, but soaring prices hurt the working classes and, to a lesser degree, large segments of the middle strata. From a base of 100 in 1938, the general price index climbed to 238 in 1946 and then jumped to 417 by 1949.[40]

Certain sectors and indicators made striking gains under González Videla. As copper prices rose, Chile's terms of trade with other countries improved slightly. Real productivity of mining outshone the achievements of the war years. The United States was the major market for Chilean copper, and, as part of a larger pattern of cooperation with the González Videla administration, stockpiled that copper to help support prices. Foreign investment—nearly 70% from the United States by 1948—also increased, exceeding the 1940-45 period by over 7%. Although North Americans provided less credit than Chileans hoped for as former wartime allies, loans to CORFO did facilitate industrialization. Those credits and the appetite for more helped swing González Videla against the Communists and labor.[41]

González Videla also turned away from his electoral allies by his accelerated favoritism for industry and the urban elites. At the same time, the more prosperous middle groups defended their gains. They supported copper and industrial growth based on friendly relations with the United States more than socioeconomic reforms based on coalitions with the workers. While the importance of industry and the

40. Partido Radical, *14 años de progreso, 1938-1952* (Santiago, 1952), pp. 40-47; Corporación de Fomento, *Cuentas*, pp. 27-59; Corporación de Fomento, *Geografía*, II, pp. 297, 321-24; Chile, Universidad, Instituto de Economía, *Desarrollo*, p. 2; Pinto, ed., *Antecedentes*, pp. 34-35; Durán, pp. 383-86.

41. Corporación de Fomento, *Cuentas*, pp. 48-53; Corporación de Fomento, *Geografía*, II, pp. 299-304; Pinto, ed., *Antecedentes*, pp. 78-82; Johnson, *Political Change*, pp. 86-90.

service sector in national income rose, that of mining and agriculture shrank. Under González Videla, the government's share of national income and expenditures expanded even more than under Aguirre Cerda and Ríos. Growth of the bureaucracy and education pleased the middle classes. The swelling government was increasingly funded through indirect taxes, which ascended from a general level of about 55% of all taxes from 1940 to 1945 to over 60% from 1946 to 1952. Governments created by the "Left" continued to pay the bills primarily through regressive taxation and levies on foreign enterprises. They did not exact the costs of development from the domestic upper class.[42]

The Radicals and many in the middle classes came to prefer stability over mobilization now that they could effectively use the state to further their self-interests. Closer alliances with the traditional elites and rightist parties resulted. By 1950, however, spiraling prices spawned strikes and protests by the lower, salaried layer of the middle strata against the Radical government which had favored them over manual laborers. The differential impact of inflation caused variations within the larger pattern of middle-class support for González Videla and his conservative policies. White-collar unions, which blossomed after World War II, often opposed both blue-collar demands and the government's inflationary favoritism for the economic elites. Thus the middle sectors were divided by the end of González Videla's administration.[43]

In spite of dismal living conditions, government repression and the weakness of the Marxist parties and unions kept worker activism down from 1946 to 1952. Union collaboration with the bureaucracy, especially the Ministry of Labor, served to restrain more than fulfill worker demands. One Socialist complained that the institutionalization of labor into cooperation with government in the 1940s had produced a union movement almost as tamed by the state as those paternalized by Vargas in Brazil and Perón in Argentina. By the end of the 1940s, fewer than 300,000 workers out of nearly 6,000,000 Chileans were organized.[44] Sporadic economic reversals prompted by international market fluctuations were paid for by the working class through inflation, rising indirect taxes, and government austerity measures. The

42. Pinto, ed., *Antecedentes,* p. 96; Pinto, *Chile, un caso,* pp. 136-39, 195-97; Corporación de Fomento, *Cuentas,* pp. 28-45; Durán, pp. 383-86, 546.

43. Angell, pp. 150-63; interview with Germán Urzúa Valenzuela, Santiago, 1970. For further information on the Radicals in these years and thereafter, see Germán Urzúa Valenzuela, *El Partido Radical* (Santiago, 1961); Petras, pp. 131-38; Pinto, "Desarrollo," p. 27; Labarca H., pp. 250-56.

44. Waiss, *El drama,* p. 52; Ibáñez, *El movimiento,* pp. 5-12; Petras, pp. 128-37.

gap between workers and employees widened. According to figures advanced by the Radical Party, without adjusting for inflation, a blue-collar worker's average daily wage rose from 8 pesos in 1928 to 18 in 1938 and to 100 by 1950, while a white-collar employee's average monthly salary rose from 200 pesos in 1928 to 600 in 1938 and 5,700 in 1950. In terms of real purchasing power, the Radicals calculated that a worker's average daily wage could buy 8.8 kilos of bread in 1928, 8.7 in 1938, and 11.1 in 1950; an employee's average monthly salary, rising far more, could buy 222 kilos of bread in 1928, 292 in 1938, and 633 in 1950. Using 1938 as a base of 100, the Radicals concluded that the average price index for basic commodities had risen 532 points by 1950; meanwhile, the income index for an average daily worker's wages rose 525 points in copper, 612 in coal, 622 in nitrates, and 739 in textiles; the index for an average private white-collar employee's salary in Santiago, initially already well above the income of blue-collar workers, rose 1,159 points, that for a tenth-grade state bureaucrat, 591, and that for a top-grade public functionary, 1,685 points. Furthermore, it was estimated that white-collar salaries averaged triple blue-collar wages, and the peasants remained far poorer than any other sector. As the Radical era drew to a close, at least 60% of the total income-earning population still received less than the minimum income defined as necessary for subsistence by the government; at most, 8% of the working class received this income level or more. Roughly 63% of the active population eked out a living from 23% of the national income. The more affluent one-third of the population was mainly made up of the middle and upper classes.[45]

González Videla neglected the less-privileged provinces as well as social groups, both of which had been seen as the springboards for his election. From 1946 on, the provincial economic elites mounted a new protest movement against administrative and economic centralization. Although dominated by the Right, the movement crossed all social-political lines and included representatives of all the national interest groups, for example the SNA, SOFOFA, SNM, and CTCH. It provided further evidence of public alienation from the existing parties as solutions to Chile's problems. Clearly, ample grounds for a reform movement could be found in the discontent of the provinces as well as the middle and, especially, lower classes. However, the Marxists and their allies failed to generate an offensive from either base in the late 1940s.[46]

45. Partido Radical, *14*, pp. 37-47; Corporación de Fomento, *Geografía*, II, pp. 224-31.

46. Primera Convención de las Provincias de Chile, *Un paso hacia la descentralización administrativa del país* ([Valparaíso?], [1946?]); Cuadra, *Prolegomenos*, pp. 119-30.

Suppression of the Communist Party, 1947-48

Serving in the González Videla administration, the Communists held most labor demands in check and delivered few immediate benefits to their working-class followers. Nevertheless, party growth through government participation was rapid. Both union gains and electoral triumphs demonstrated PC expansion. In particular, the Communist leap from 10.2% of the vote in the 1945 congressional balloting to 16.5% in the 1947 municipal elections, which tripled the party's number of votes from the 1944 municipal contests, confirmed conservative fears. In 1947, the PC received double the vote of the PS. (Table 25 summarizes the 1947 voting.) The Communists reached an electoral summit through cabinet participation, as the Socialists had earlier, and then went into forced decline.[47] The Communists' electoral gains were mainly coming at the expense of Socialist strength in urban industrial zones. Compared to its showing in selected mining *comunas,* the PC still scored much lower (usually close to 20% of the vote) in selected urban *comunas* of industrial workers, but nonetheless normally above its national percentage. Mining areas still furnished the Communists' highest percentages. According to a Chilean study, they averaged 71% of the ballots in major coal-mining, 63% in major nitrate, and 55% in major copper communities. These main mining and industrial districts combined accounted for less than 10% of all Chile's *comunas* but a majority of the Communists' national votes.[48]

Like the Socialists before them, the Communists twisted on the horns of the dilemma between mobilization and institutionalization.

TABLE 25: NATIONAL MUNICIPAL VOTES FOR PARTIES, 1947

	Male Voters	Female & Foreign Voters	Total Voters
Conservatives	17.8%	30.0%	20.2%
Liberals	13.1	14.0	13.3
Radicals	20.8	17.0	20.0
Socialists	8.8	8.3	8.7
Authentic Socialists	0.2	0.2	0.2
Communists	17.7	11.8	16.5

47. A relatively high turnout of 84% of the registered voters cast ballots in 1947. The results from women and resident foreigners were reported separately because, up to that time, municipal elections were the only ones in which they could vote. Chile, Dirección del Registro Electoral, "Elección ordinaria de municipalidades" (Santiago, 1948).

48. The Chilean study used the copper communities of Chuquicamata, Potrerillos, and Sewell, the nitrate zones of Iquique, Pozo Almonte, Lagunas, Toco, and Pedro de Valdivia, and the coal *comunas* of Coronel, Loïa, and Curanilahue. Cruz-Coke, pp. 18-19, 78-82, 106-9; Partido Comunista, *Ricardo,* p. 152.

Success at obtaining mass support soon cost them their role in the administration. The Marxists were tolerated as government participants when they served as safety valves for working-class discontent, but they were unacceptable when they used their government positions to rally the masses and pressure the administration from below. As in Eastern Europe, the Communists thrashed their socialist and reformist trade-union rivals. The PC expanded its influence in education, agricultural ministries, and other state economic agencies, such as departments concerned with exports, price controls, and public works. It was feared that the Communists were tightening their grip on the national economy both from the top through government and from the bottom through unions. While they took over and reinvigorated many urban unions, the Communists had also renewed efforts at peasant organization by González Videla's second year in office. Once again, the ominous possibility of a worker-peasant alliance under Marxist auspices proved more than the traditional elites would accept.[49]

The conservative elites, as they had repeatedly been trying to do since 1936, convinced the Radical leaders to dump the Communists. The Radicals responded to rightist alarms partly because their own party was losing votes while the PC was gaining. Supressing the Communists also removed justifications for right-wing military plots against the government. Moreover, many Radicals had grown closer to the propertied elites since the inception of popular-front politics. State intervention in the economy created more common interests than conflicts between leading Radicals and the traditional privileged groups. The main policy Radicals had shared with Marxists, economic growth, had also brought them into harmony with the Right. However, not all upper- and middle-class sectors hailed González Videla's persecution of the Communists. Some preferred stricter respect for party and union rights, believing accommodation wiser than exclusion. For example, the Grand Master of the Masons denounced the president's attacks on the PC.[50]

González Videla's betrayal of the Communists was also a campaign against organized labor. Outlawing the PC scaled down working-class demands on scarce resources in a period of economic uncertainty, as occurred most acutely during the deep recession of 1947. It

49. Sotomayor, pp. 59-61; Partido Comunista, *Ricardo,* p. 164; Durán, pp. 428-29; Alexander, *Latin,* p. 100.

50. Olavarría Bravo, *Chile,* II, pp. 44-52; Durán, pp. 426-28, 478-97; Partido Comunista, *Ricardo,* pp. 152-57; Pinto, "Desarrollo," pp. 25-26; Petras, pp. 131-32; Clissold, *Chilean,* p. 63.

gave the government greater freedom from labor interference to pursue a policy of industrialization linked to foreign interests. Furthermore, it lessened the pressures on galloping inflation by making workers the most vulnerable victims. Non-Communist, often Socialist, unions and workers also felt the weight of repression. As a result, workers' wages were even harder pressed to keep pace with the rocketing cost of living.[51]

As expected by proponents of the policy, ejection of the Communists bettered economic relations with the United States. Not only right-wing Radicals but also some leftist leaders from that party, the Falange, and the Socialists foresaw economic advantages in following North American wishes. Partly in response to the demobilization of the PC, U.S. technological assistance, loans, and investments in Chile rose. Union pressures and demands for greater state involvement in the copper companies diminished, while production climbed upward. Taxes which the multinational corporations were willing to pay the financially beleaguered government also increased. In 1950 González Videla visited the United States and made new arrangements for state participation in the copper companies and more credits for industrialization. In 1952 he also signed a military assistance pact with Washington that brought Chile's armed forces more modern equipment and training.[52]

In response to their expulsion from the cabinet in 1947, the Communists launched protests and strikes, notably in the coal mines. The government hit back with military repression of the strikers. A few Socialists even helped break the coal strike in hopes of capturing unions from the PC. González Videla also escalated the conflict by severing relations with the Soviet Union, arresting Communist leaders, and persuading Congress to pass the "Law for the Defense of Democracy" in 1948. This bill banned the PC and expunged its voters from the electoral rolls. A handful of Socialists violated party discipline to vote for that law, just as a few Conservatives and Radicals broke ranks to vote against it. In general, however, it passed with the backing of the Conservatives, Liberals, Radicals, and minor rightist parties and over the opposition of the Communists, Socialists, and Falange. It kept the PC illegal for a decade. Populist mobilization, coalitions, and programs had been dwindling in significance through-

51. Angell, p. 59; Jobet, "El Partido," p. 45.

52. Moran, pp. 57-88, 174-79. On United States–Chilean relations throughout this period, see Claude G. Bowers, *Chile through Embassy Windows* (New York, 1958), esp. pp. 166-75, 309-29. Johnson, *Political Change*, p. 88; Partido Comunista, *Ricardo*, pp. 157-66; Aranda and Martínez, p. 111; Durán, pp. 428-29, 478-97, 549-89.

out the forties, and now popular-front politics was clearly on its way out.[53]

Being banned from participating did not radicalize the Communists. When they did counter with strikes, the military squashed the resistance. This deepened the old enmity of the armed forces toward the PC and its worker followers.[54] Some more-leftist Communists, especially youth, advocated armed struggle. Official party policy, however, prescribed retreat into clandestine activities in order to preserve their cadres, draw other parties over to their side, and thus regain their legal status. The PC's explanation for rejecting confrontation in favor of gradual rebuilding was that the masses were unprepared mentally, politically, or militarily for insurrection. According to the party, a majority of the workers were resigned and passive in the face of González Videla's assault on the Communists and the labor movement. The PC's retiring strategy belied the president's claims that the Communists had to be slapped down because they were planning, in league with the Soviet Union, a violent uprising against the state.[55]

The Communists' continued acceptance of the rules of the Chilean political game, despite their suspension, was evident in the 1949 congressional elections. Those members who thought the party should respond to exclusion by abstaining in revolutionary isolation lost to those who felt the party should help its cause as much as possible by exerting whatever marginal influence it could on the elections. It was the leaders representing the worker wing of the PC who prevailed over intellectual dissidents in this decision to work through any cracks in the system.[56]

Moreover, the party continued to call for a coalition of Marxist and middle- to upper-class reform parties. This was still intended to initiate a bourgeois, industrial, democratic revolution in Chile as the first step toward socialism in a semi-feudal, dependent country. For the future, the PC argued that such a heterogeneous front could finally succeed if the proletariat and its vanguard parties took more of a leadership role.[57]

Socialist Division over González Videla and the Cold War, 1946-49

During Ampuero's reconstruction, the Socialists hunted for an independent path between the Radicals and the Communists, between

53. Partido Comunista, *Ricardo*, pp. 159-61; Guiñez, p. 175; Petras, p. 129.
54. Bravo Ríos, pp. 185-202.
55. Halperin, pp. 55-57; Partido Comunista, *Ricardo*, pp. 166-68.
56. Upon the death of Ricardo Fonseca, long-time working-class leader Galo González Díaz became secretary-general in 1949. Partido Comunista, *Ricardo*, pp. 174-78.
57. Partido Comunista, *Ricardo*, pp. 15-19.

the United States and the Soviet Union. Some party leaders, particularly those most concerned about losses among the workers, wanted the PS to define itself in more radical Marxist terms. Others, particularly those most concerned about losses among the middle strata, leaned more toward democratic socialism or populism to revive the PS as a mass party. The PS officially stepped away from past populist brethren, notably APRA, as insufficiently socialist, but it continued to grope for alternative models, such as the British Labour Party, Peronism, and Tito's independent communism in Yugoslavia.[58]

Once again, aggravated by the Cold War, the Socialists agonized over their posture toward a Radical government and toward communism. The PS officially opposed González Videla's vendetta against the PC and labor.[59] However, Bernardo Ibáñez and a small group of followers challenged the regular leadership. The rebels wanted to join the government and its anticommunist crusade. They wanted cabinet posts to be able to enjoy the perquisites of office, to balance the influence of the Right, and to pull labor unions away from the PC. In addition, they disobeyed party orders because of resentment against Ampuero's discipline. Although the dissidents were a little more conservative than the regular party leadership, the cleavage was not primarily ideological. The Ibáñez faction was only slightly more committed to anticommunism and to economic growth over social change. Neither side adamantly opposed coalitions with the Radicals or the middle class. Indeed, the insurgent wing was stronger with labor than was the Ampuero group and rallied its workers to attack the established leadership. As in the past, another highly personalistic conflict was infused with ideological charges and countercharges, which, however, failed to place either faction in a starkly purist position or to preclude either combatant from later shifts in tactics. This latest friction climaxed in one of the worst ruptures in Socialist history.[60]

Before the end of 1948 Ibáñez quit the regular party. He took three of its six congressional deputies, but neither of its two senators. By joining the administration, the rebels won legal recognition of their splinter group as the official Socialist Party of Chile. Consequently the regular Socialists adopted the name Popular Socialist Party (PSP).

58. Partido Socialista, *La palabra del Partido;* Raúl Ampuero Díaz, *En defensa del partido y del socialismo* ([Santiago?], 1948); Astolfo Tapia Moore, *¡El socialismo triunfará!* (Santiago, 1948); Álvarez Villablanca, *Objetivos;* Chelén, *Trayectoria,* p. 119.

59. Eugenio González Rojas, *El Partido Socialista Popular y la política del actual gobierno* (Santiago, 1949), pp. 3-4; Partido Socialista Popular, *El Partido Socialista Popular lucha contra las facultades extraordinarias* (Santiago, 1949); Partido Socialista Unificado, *Declaración de principios, estatutos y reglamentos, tesis política, tesis sindical e himno del partido* (Santiago, 1947); Grove, *Declaraciones;* Partido Socialista, *Por una democracia de trabajadores* (Santiago, 1948).

60. Ampuero, *En defensa;* Ibáñez, *El movimiento;* Waiss, *El drama,* pp. 82-87.

Ibáñez ran off not only with the party name but also with a majority of its unions and left the PSP with significant organized labor strength only among copper workers. Nevertheless, Ampuero's Socialists, which included Allende, retained most of the original party's leaders, members, and voters.[61]

After the schism, Ampuero's PSP continued to reject invitations to enter the cabinet and support government efforts to quell worker and employee complaints against the rising cost of living. The PSP faltered, however, in attempts to concoct a viable alternative to popular-front politics with the Radicals and Communists. The Popular Socialists experimented with alliances with dissident Radicals and Democratics; they also tried to develop closer relations with the Social Christians, recent offshoots from the Conservatives, and the Falange, earlier offshoots. Despite lingering Catholic apprehensions over Masonry, PSP leaders argued that the evaporation of clerical issues had brought some Catholic reformers closer to the Left than Liberals. At the end of the 1940s, these prescient Socialists feared the rise of a competing Christian Democrat reform movement for the middle classes and sectors of the lower strata. Consequently, most PSP leaders foresaw refurbished nationalist, populist appeals to a wide social spectrum as the best immediate hope for party resurgence.[62]

A minority of PSP leaders, however, emphasized a turn toward more orthodox Marxism—a species of "nationalist communism" —aimed at recovering worker more than middle-class support. Through such radicalization, some Popular Socialists hoped to overcome great worker "apathy and indifference toward the political parties." Frustrated PSP organizers complained that years of multi-party opportunism had left laborers even more cynical than the politicians. For example, Ampuero lamented "the tendency to forget our reason for existence, our revolutionary mission." Some Socialist labor leaders had acquired a reputation among workers of being coopted and corrupted. Leftist critics characterized Bernardo Ibáñez as a friend of the ruling groups who was constantly junketing abroad. His wing of the CTCH (with U.S. help) and both Socialist parties made some union gains after the outlawing of the PC, but many apparent Socialist successes represented only temporary shelter for Communist labor groups. Despite the Socialists' inability to reignite the 1930s' enthusiasm of the working classes, the PSP remained a predominately worker-based party. The laborers had few alternatives left, and the

61. Partido Socialista, *Proyecto de programa del Partido Socialista chileno* (Santiago, 1947); Chelén, *Trayectoria*, pp. 116-19; Angell, pp. 99-101.
62. González Rojas, *El Partido*, pp. 2-5; Barría, *El movimiento;* Mayorga, "Primeros," p. 19; Partido Socialista, *Tareas para un buen militante* (Santiago, 1948).

party's losses had apparently been even greater among the middle sectors.[63]

The Socialists also tried to revive by intensifying appeals to under-privileged groups in the resentful regions. Their special target was the far southern Channels area provinces of Aysén and Magallanes. Allende was a senator from that region, which became one of the last bastions of the shrinking party.[64]

Further Socialist Congressional Decline in the 1949 Elections

The 1949 congressional elections revealed general political disin-tegration. New, ephemeral, and Lilliputian parties proliferated. In addition to the Socialists, all major organizations had splinter groups running separately from the parent body. Women voted for congres-sional representatives for the first time. Counting all the Conservative and Liberal factions, the Right, with 42.1%, dropped slightly from 1945 (43.7%). The Radicals, momentarily sliced into three electoral fragments, rose collectively from 20.0% in 1945 to 27.7% in 1949. They attracted a few stray ballots from the proscribed Communists and many from the Socialists. The regular Socialists in the PSP stum-bled from 7.2% of the vote in 1945 to 4.8% in 1949. They barely outdistanced the rebel PS (3.4%) and the disappearing PSA (1.1%). Even combining the Socialist segments, then, gave the movement only 9.3% of the national ballots, well below its already depressed 12.8% figure of 1945.[65]

At the regional level, the Socialists were weak everywhere except Magallanes, as Table 26 shows. There, Ampuero's party collected a majority of the votes. Throughout the 1940s, the most consistently high percentage regions for the regular party were the Channels and, despite notable losses, the Urban Center.

At the *comuna* level, all three Socialist parties displayed a similar pattern in 1949. By this measure, they were not sharply distinguished from one another at their social bases. Moreover, the shifting, mitotic mother party did not undergo any drastic transformation of its elec-

---

63. Ampuero, *En defensa;* Partido Socialista, *La palabra del Partido;* Chelén, *Trayec-toria,* pp. 125-31; Angell, pp. 104-5; Hochwald, p. 79.

64. Salvador Allende, *Las provincias enjuician el porvenir de Chile* (Santiago, 1947); Salvador Allende, *Aysén, presente y futuro* (Santiago, 1948).

65. In 1949, only 79% of the registered voters cast ballots, though this was a higher turnout than in the congressional elections of 1937, 1941, or 1945. González Videla's new governing coalition with the Right retained control of Congress. The Socialists at least attracted a higher percentage of the votes than in the 1945 presidential race or the 1947 municipal contests. Chile, Dirección del Registro Electoral, "Elección ordinaria de Congreso Nacional" (Santiago, 1949); Cruz-Coke, pp. 12, 76-85.

TABLE 26: VOTES FOR SOCIALISTS BY REGION, 1941, 1945, 1949

Region	1941		1945		1949	
	PS	PS & PST	PS	PS & PSA	PSP	PSP, PS, & PSA
Great North	15.7%	18.6%	6.5%	14.9%	4.5%	11.5%
Small North	18.0	20.7	4.2	7.5	8.1	13.2
Urban Center	18.1	20.1	7.8	15.3	4.9	9.9
North Center	18.1	19.8	0.7	5.8	4.5	6.9
South Center	12.5	12.4	4.5	5.3	1.1	1.4
Frontier	14.2	20.1	4.8	8.2	3.5	5.9
Lakes	29.9	30.6	3.5	13.7	2.7	3.7
Channels	42.8	42.9	23.5	28.4	27.3	27.3
National total	17.9%	20.7%	7.2%	12.8%	4.8%	9.3%

toral foundation. Instead, the general pattern in this decade of dis-integration showed the regular Socialists shriveling to a hard core in their communities of traditional strength; they grew even weaker in districts with a record of low votes for the party. The results from these selected *comunas* indicated that the Socialists survived mainly as a vehicle for the urban workers. They lost the most support in the peasant and middle- to upper-class occupational areas considered in Table 27.[66] In 1949 the Socialists, especially the regular party (PSP), withdrew even more than in 1945 to their original pattern of notably higher percentages of deputy votes in the selected urban *comunas* than in rural *comunas*. Confirming provincial and regional trends, both the PSP and the combined Socialist parties scored much better in these miner and urban worker zones than in the middle- to upper–strata urban areas or in the peasant districts considered in Table 27. The big gain from 1945 to 1949 came in miner communities, perhaps because of the Communists' submersion. In the mining districts, all three Socialist parties collected low average percentages in the main coal *comunas*, the regular PSP did best in the copper zones (12.5% of the votes), and Grove's PSA led in the nitrate areas (14.0%). As in 1945, the supposedly more conservative rebel faction (the PS in 1949) ran better overall than the regular party in the mining *comunas* consid-ered. By far the strongest areas for the Socialists, as always, were the selected industrial-worker communities. As in the 1930s, the Socialists also ended the 1940s with the rural and peasant zones returning relatively low percentages to them. In further comparison with the

66. See Appendix A. As one example of Socialist durability in areas of traditional strength, in the regular Socialists' best *comunas* in the 1941 election (all those where they received at least 40% of the votes), they won an average vote of 13.2% in 1949, compared to 4.9% nationally and compared to a 1949 average of 0.7% in all those *comunas* where they received under 5% of the votes in 1941.

TABLE 27: VOTES FOR SOCIALISTS BY TYPE OF *COMUNA*, 1941, 1945, 1949

	1941			1945			1949			
	PS	PST	PS & PST	PS	PSA	PS & PSA	PSP	PS	PSA	PSP, PS, & PSA
Urban										
comunas	17.5%	5.7%	23.2% (−11.5%)	9.0%	6.4%	15.4% (−33.6%)	9.1%	4.9%	2.9%	16.9% (+9.7%)
Rural										
comunas	22.7	0.9	23.6 (+402.1)	6.9	5.9	12.8 (−45.8)	3.2	3.9	1.1	8.2 (−35.9)
Middle- to upper-class										
comunas	14.4	1.5	15.9 (−50.0)	3.9	6.3	10.2 (−35.8)	3.6	1.5	0.3	. 5.4 (−47.1)
Industrial-worker										
comunas	26.1	7.0	33.1 (−15.3)	17.1	7.1	24.2 (−26.9)	10.6	8.0	5.1	23.7 (−2.1)
Miner										
comunas	13.9	3.0	16.9 (+38.5)	6.3	5.5	11.8 (−30.2)	5.2	6.6	3.9	15.7 (+33.1)
Peasant										
comunas	24.4	0.8	25.2 (+472.7)	4.7	3.4	8.1 (−67.9)	3.4	1.7	0.8	5.9 (−27.2)
National total	17.9%	2.8%	20.7% (+16.9%)	7.2%	5.6%	12.8% (−38.2%)	4.8%	3.4%	1.1%	9.3% (−26.6%)

NOTE: The numbers in parentheses show the changes in average percentages from the previous congressional election for the combined Socialist parties. The figures for 1941 refer to changes from those percentages won by Grove in the 1932 presidential election.

party's early years, in 1949 these miner districts gave the Socialists far higher relative and absolute percentages than before, while these middle- to upper-class communities gave them far lower. The desire of some Socialists to build further on their urban and working-class base and the desire of others to reawaken middle-class ardor for the party were both understandable. The erosion of rural, peasant, and middle- to upper-class support noted in the tables, while not denoting any precise national percentages for the Socialists, suggested that voters in those selected areas may have backed the party earlier because of opportunism or loyalty to electoral *caciques*. Those *comunas* were not permanently converted to the Socialists or, apparently, to their professed ideology. Through the ordeals and vicissitudes of the 1940s, as populism waned, all types of communities studied withdrew some support from the Socialists. The allegiance of the selected urban worker *comunas*, however, proved most durable. Interpreting the limited information in these tables cautiously, in conjunction with other materials, indicates that the Socialists retained significant backing in working-class areas even at the party's low ebb.

Consequences of Radical Rule for Socialism and Populism

By 1952 fourteen years of Radical rule in coalition governments had failed to yield the promised harvest of economic growth and social reform.[67] Despite the expansion of a potential urban constituency with plentiful grounds for discontent, the strength of the Marxist movement dwindled in the 1940s. The Left was unable to effectively mobilize the dissatisfied masses and regional groups until the 1950s when it shed the stale popular-front approach and returned to being the opposition.[68]

By the end of the 1940s the uneven, disappointing results of the popular-front formula culminated in epidemic political disenchantment. Out of that malaise, the electorate turned to strong personalities, not to radical Marxists, for new solutions. Once again, as in the Great Depression, populist appeals became more attractive to voters when multiparty politics was discredited. Confronted with the personalistic resurgence of Carlos Ibáñez in 1952, the Marxist parties would once again return to the dilemma of populism versus socialism.[69]

From the 1930s through the 1940s, both the rise and fall of the Communists and Socialists took place through participation in socially mixed political coalitions. Most Socialist critics blamed their party's decay in the 1940s on its obedience to Chilean political culture and traditions instead of to Marxist principles. In retrospect, Socialist diagnoses argued that electoral victories secured through charismatic leadership and populist coalitions were counterproductive. Such victories allegedly distracted the party from revolutionary social struggles. In this view, the PS degenerated into little more than just another political machine and employment agency. According to these Socialist critics, mainly from the left wing of the party, alliances with centrist governments increasingly devoted to capitalist economic and industrial growth alienated the workers. To the extent that elections measured working-class reactions, however, it was not really clear that laborers turned away from the Socialists because of the party's dedica-

67. Chile, Universidad, Instituto de Economía, *Desarrollo,* esp. p. 4; Partido Radical, *14;* Jorge Ahumada C., *En vez de la miseria* (5th ed., Santiago, 1965), pp. 49-50, 87-183; Durán, pp. 600-605; Petras, pp. 132-35; Pinto, *Chile, un caso,* pp. 138-39; Cademártori, pp. 244-57; Varela, "Distribución del ingreso nacional en Chile."
68. Chile, Universidad, Instituto de Economía, *La migración,* pp. 1-9.
69. Guiñez, pp. 178-79.

tion to moderate, multiclass coalitions and to personalism over Marxism. Indeed, the Socialists' electoral decline occurred after they had discarded the Popular Front coalition and their charismatic leader. Moreover, there is some evidence that urban workers remained at least as loyal to the party as did other social sectors. Coalition-derived concessions and programmatic shortcomings alone could not explain worker alienation and party decline.[70]

The complex issue of participation in traditional politics and in the bureaucratic state affected the Socialists' worsening position in three distinct ways. First, the restrictions and compromises intrinsic to coalition electoral politics accounted in large part for the Socialists' inability to meet their substantive goals for the workers. Second, the debate over the efficacy of participation, which was mainly focused on cabinet positions, was a major cause of splits among Socialist leaders, although causes other than ideological differences were at least as important in these leadership brawls. Third, the failure to meet worker needs was less significant than party divisions as an explanation for the Socialists' loss of mass support.

Almost inevitably, the conventional electoral and bureaucratic methods which won the Socialists' popular backing and high offices failed to achieve their higher programmatic aspirations. In a late-industrializing country with a multiparty democracy, the Socialists and their coalitions were socially as well as ideologically diverse. Chile's worker movement had a more militant tradition and greater independent muscle than labor in most Latin American countries. Nevertheless, it remained frail and highly dependent on alliances with centrist forces. In the 1930s and 1940s, the Chilean working classes were mobilized enough to be important partners with the middle sectors in intraparty and interparty coalitions, but they were not mobilized enough to claim a role commensurate with their numbers or consistent with the ideologies of the Marxists. The major stumbling block was Socialist and Communist ineffectiveness at galvanizing the peasants into action with urban labor.

The inhibitions built into broad reform coalitions were not the only impediments to implementing a socialist program. Particularistic factors, such as leadership, also sidetracked the Socialists. The thrusts and parries of the rightist opposition were often devastating. Moreover, international economic and political influences, such as trade, war, and ideologies, also derailed radical reforms.

Socialist leaders divided the party not only because of ideological dissatisfaction with the fruits of coalition politics for the under-

70. Chelén, *Trayectoria;* Jobet, *El Partido Socialista de Chile;* Waiss, *El drama.*

privileged. Of at least equal importance were other reasons, including crucial personal conflicts over power and position. Furthermore, in spite of appearances, the intraparty dispute over the possibility of moderate means accomplishing declared radical ends was rarely, if ever, a debate about participation in versus abstention from traditional politics. Rather, the debate concerned types of participation. The party burst apart over the issue of collaborating with the Communists as much as over the issue of collaborating with the Radicals. Undoubtedly the theoretical, social, or strategic substance of most of the Socialist feuds from 1932 to 1952 was difficult for voters to discern. The inadequacy of highly ideological explanations for party divisions was revealed by the changing positions of various leaders and factions on the participation issue over the years; with rare exceptions, yesterday's purists became tomorrow's pragmatists, as in all political organizations. During the rancor and fragmentation from the 1930s into the 1950s, few ideological continuities underlay the permutations of most prominent Socialists. For example, Ampuero's apparently more leftist PSP joined the mildly reformist government of former antagonist Carlos Ibáñez in the early 1950s. Meanwhile the Socialists who had departed with Bernardo Ibáñez rejected that personalistic, multiclass, integrative populist approach and instead joined their former enemies, the Communists, in a "workers' front." Another case in point was the failure of Godoy's PST in its independent attempt to challenge reformist coalition politics. The reversion of the PST to the popular-front approach also raised doubts about the practical capacity or ideological will of Socialist dissidents to reject standard political competition, compromises, and temptations.[71]

Tensions between personalities, between the national and local branches of the Socialist Party, between its ideological and clientelistic commitments, between mobilization and institutionalization, and between leaders and followers repeatedly splintered the organization. Opposition to Grove's domination was held in check during the party's construction in the 1930s, but success unleashed ambitions and animosities by the 1940s. Grove, Schnake, Godoy, Ampuero, Allende, and Ibáñez, without being eminent ideologists, played enormous personalistic roles in the party's destiny. Resentment of the power exerted by the privileged group lodged at the top of the party and well connected to the national government ruptured Socialist unity. In an economy of relative scarcity and limited opportunities, politics was a

71. The shifting personalities on various sides of issues and divisions within the Socialist Party can be followed, without discovering many ideological continuities, in Jobet, *El Partido Socialista de Chile;* Halperin, pp. 135-44, 229.

critical avenue for social mobility. This was especially true for the middle class or those with middle-class aspirations. Elevation to public offices by directing the party or its offspring tended to improve the socioeconomic status of individual Socialist leaders, not unlike the Radicals.[72]

The motivations of leaders in dividing the party and the motivations of voters in deserting it cannot be equated automatically. The failure of popular-front politics to gratify working-class desires undoubtedly alienated some Socialist followers as well as leaders. The best evidence is, however, that other factors were more important in the erosion of mass support. To varying degrees, both middle- and lower-class Socialists gravitated to other reformist camps, often the Radicals, instead of turning against the system of coalition politics. For laborers, reform movements from the 1920s to the 1970s fell short of their promises. Nevertheless, the workers continued to participate, at least electorally, in established political processes. In many cases, they continued to back the same reform parties, mainly the Marxists. The workers, like their political spokesmen, did not resolve the dilemma between means and ends; nor were they generally attracted to more radical alternatives.

At the beginning of the 1940s, the Socialist Party reached an electoral pinnacle while engaging in conventional political arrangements which were not keeping programmatic faith with working-class supporters. The renegade PST, denouncing collaboration for not addressing the problems of the poor, was rejected at the polls, partly by working-class voters. In the 1940s the Communists were at least as eager as the Socialists to take part in most aspects of multiparty politics, and the PC was often less publicly critical of the results. Nevertheless, until their proscription, the Communists gained more with labor than did the Socialists. For example, during the 1947 municipal elections while the Socialists were disdaining participation in opportunistic political associations the Communists were sharing fully in the Radical government, and the PC far outran the PS at the polls. At least in the short run, collaboration seemed to offer more electoral advantages than did autonomous opposition. Both mobilization and institutionalization always had their benefits as well as drawbacks. Ultimately, participation in ideologically questionable electoral or administrative coalitions did not provide a satisfactory explanation for the difference in worker support for the Communists and

72. Petras, p. 161; Chelén, *Trayectoria,* pp. 184-92; Michels; Waiss, *El drama,* pp. 3-7, 16-43; Gil, pp. 260-63, 284-90; Simón Olavarría Alarcón, *La gran culpa del Partido Radical* (Santiago, 1951); Merle Kling, "Toward a Theory of Power and Political Instability in Latin America," in Petras and Zeitlin, eds., *Latin America,* pp. 76-93.

Socialists. Instead, party unity best explained it. The Socialist Party's electoral collapse was traceable to its loss of unity and of Grove more than to mass repudiation of the institutionalization of the PS.[73]

It might be argued, as some leftist critics implied, that the Marxist parties and the workers should have rejected accommodations with the prevailing political system as a result of the disappointments of the 1940s, but there is almost no evidence that they did. Furthermore, even dissident Marxists did not make it fully clear how the system should or could have been successfully opposed. Whether because of tradition, commitment, the absence of viable alternatives, or the lack of a politically radical consciousness, the overwhelming majority of working-class voters and Marxist leaders remained wedded to Chile's political institutions and culture. The failures during the Radical era did not force a resolution of the conflicts between electoral success and ideological purity, between political-social accommodation and revolutionary rhetoric, or between populist and socialist tendencies. On the contrary, the dilemma, not surprisingly, persisted. The Socialists, after all, had the greatest success at winning middle- and lower-class support in the period when they indulged in populistic modes of participation in traditional politics.

Chile's relatively high levels of political and socioeconomic development, by Latin American standards, both inhibited and assisted socialism in some ways. It not only rendered social upheaval less likely but also facilitated the institutionalization of the Marxist movement. That institutionalization drew the wrath of some Socialists. At the same time, it gave the party certain opportunities within boundaries erected by the traditional elites. Despite great setbacks, the Socialists achieved continuity and durability. Even when the rebels seceded with the founding leader or the party trademark, the parent body ultimately prevailed, with the potential to rebuild.[74]

The first era of the Socialist Party, 1932-52, ended as ultimately bitter as it had been initially exhilarating. Without fully divesting themselves of past tendencies, the Socialists from 1946 on headed in the direction of becoming more of a Marxist vanguard party and less of a populist mass movement. This metamorphosis led them from popular-front politics in the 1940s toward worker-front politics in the 1950s. Their transformation coincided with an eventual slowdown in import-substituting industrialization and increasing rigidities in the

73. Waiss, *El drama*, pp. 143-46, 166-84; Halperin, pp. 59-61, 117-62, 229; Sunkel, esp. pp. 130-34.
74. Hennessy, pp. 28-61; Love, pp. 3-24; Paul W. Drake, "The Chilean Socialist Party and Coalition Politics, 1932-1946," *Hispanic American Historical Review*, LIII, no. 4 (Nov., 1973), pp. 619-43.

economy. At the same time, urbanization and industrialization, combined with a gradual awakening of the peasants, made more strictly working-class politics viable for the Marxists. From the early 1950s, as times ripened for more emphasis on class conflict over coalitions and on redistribution over growth, Chilean socialism, through patient efforts, revived.

The period from 1932 to 1952 formed a coherent story of the rise of a populist socialist movement in an industrializing country, its acculturation into the existing power structure, and its subsequent unraveling. Just as the years from World War I to the Great Depression contained the roots of this political experience, the era from 1952 to 1973 brought forth the later consequences. In this era the Socialists, in alliance with the Communists, rose and fell again. Despite new tactics, the Marxists once more climbed to power through the Chilean multiparty system and, therefore, they never satisfactorily resolved the seemingly inescapable dilemmas of the past. Popular-front politics conditioned the patterns of the future. In various ways, the PS and the PC tried to emulate or to transcend their heritage, but neither moderate coalitions in the 1930s and 1940s nor more radical combinations in the 1950s to 1970s enabled the Chilean Socialists to consummate their dreams of "revolution."

Epilogue

The Tragedy of Socialism and Populism, 1952-73

In their second two decades, the Socialists and the Communists came back to life through the four presidential campaigns of Salvador Allende and were destroyed with their attempt to govern directly after his victory in 1970. From the 1950s to the 1970s, the electorate moved leftward, as evidenced by increasing votes both for Marxist candidates and for progressively more radical platforms espoused by even centrist groups. This time, the Left tried to use democratic means to bring about far more revolutionary changes than during the popular-front era. The PS shifted from identification with APRA and populism to identification with Fidel Castro's Cuba and socialist revolution. The Marxists came to place far greater stress on ideological and social confrontation than on compromise. In practice, this radicalization meant that the PS and PC relied on coalitions dominated by Marxists and their worker followers instead of centrist reformers and the middle classes. In response, the elites and the declining Right began to abandon flexibility. By the 1970s the system based on the unequal accommodation of increasingly hostile forces within the established hierarchy became more and more brittle. The Marxists and their adversaries seemingly threatened to extinguish each other as legitimate contenders. Unable to resolve or transcend their long-standing contradictions, the Socialists' electoral trajectory ended in 1973 as it had begun in 1932, through a military coup. When the system came crashing down, the armed forces expelled the Marxists and thus buried socialism and populism in Chile.

The following brief treatment of Chilean socialism's second era makes no pretense of complete coverage, in-depth analysis, or exhaustive original research. Although based on a wide range of secondary materials, substantial primary sources, and field observations, the interpretations offered in this capsule summary may in some cases be modified and in others even overturned by future researchers with the benefit of richer hindsight. In particular, the condensation of the Popular Unity episode—still boiling in controversy over facts as well as explanations—must be seen as a modest and preliminary attempt to place recent events in the context of the history already much more thoroughly developed in preceding chapters. In many ways, the Allende experience of the 1970s and its aftermath was unique. In other respects, it echoed issues faced by socialist movements abroad, it reflected similar pressures for social democratization or for authoritarian containment found elsewhere in Latin America and. throughout much of the Third World, and it carried on certain recognizable patterns from the Chilean past. The Allende years and the entire 1952-73 period have already attracted and will deserve many more books in their own right. Far less ambitious and unavoidably somewhat speculative, this epilogue merely suggests ways in which some currents from 1932 to 1952 flowed into the succeeding two decades.

Emergence of Allende, the Workers' Front, and the FRAP, 1952-58

In the 1952 presidential campaign, the splintered Socialists were torn between populism and Marxism as means of replenishing their electoral assets. Ampuero's PSP joined the ground swell behind the old war-horse Carlos Ibáñez. It hoped to reach the middle and lower classes, who were already rallying to Ibáñez's paternalistic banner. Attempting to avoid the kind of alienation from the masses suffered by the Argentine Socialists because of their opposition to the populist Perón, the PSP gave Ibáñez his only firm party support. In addition, some Socialists were taken with peronism. They and others envisioned swinging Ibáñez's vague, mystical, nationalist movement more toward the left. Once again, populist mobilization was seen as a bridge to future efforts toward real socialism. The purely personalistic campaign of the "General of Victory" succeeded because of the deterioration of the parties and the economy. Drawing votes away from both leftist and rightist candidates, Ibáñez finished first with 46.8% of the ballots and was declared president-elect by the Congress.[1]

When Ampuero's regular Socialists enlisted in the Ibáñez cam-

1. Eighty-seven percent of the registered voters cast ballots in 1952, but that turnout still only represented 16% of the national population. The two major losing candidates were Arturo Matte Larraín, backed by the Liberals and Conservatives, who finished second with 27.8% of the votes, and Pedro Enrique Alfonso Barrios, nominated by the Radicals, who attracted 19.9%. Daugherty, pp. 15, 33; Carlos Ibáñez del Campo, *Lo que haremos por Chile* (Santiago, 1952); Chelén, *Trayectoria*, pp. 125-31; Olavarría Bravo, *Chile*, II, pp. 76-97; Alfonso Stephens Freire, *El irracionalismo político en Chile* (Santiago, 1957); Halperin, pp. 128-31.

paign, Allende and a handful of colleagues bolted the PSP. They joined the PS, which had been launched by Bernardo Ibáñez in the 1940s. Incongruously, the Allende dissidents, who had good connections with the proscribed Communists, made common cause with the once virulently anticommunist PS. They nominated Allende, with Communist support, as a token challenge to the opportunism of the PSP. It was, in part, a blow against populism. Although most Socialist and Communist votes went to Carlos Ibáñez, Allende's "People's Front" staked out an independent future strategy for the Marxists. For the first time, the Communists united with their most acerbic enemies in the Socialist camp to run an avowedly Marxist candidate for president. The People's Front aimed primarily at the worker vote and opposed coalitions with traditional reform movements. In contrast to the 1940s, the Allende campaign laid more emphasis on collectivist social changes than on industrialization to reduce the privileges of foreign and domestic elites and to improve the lot of the masses. Allende's symbolic alternative fetched only 5.5% of the ballots, a few more from men than women, who were allowed to vote for president for the first time.[2]

President Ibáñez failed to cure the ills, such as dependence on foreign capital, inflation, rural stagnation, and working-class poverty, which had sent him and previous reformers to office. According to one estimate for the years from 1953 to 1959, slower economic growth helped bring the workers' share of national income down from 30.0% to 25.5% and that of the middle strata from 26.4% to 25.2%, while the share of property-owners, financiers, and top executives rose from 43.6% to 49.3%. The consequent erosion of Ibáñez's popularity with the masses mainly benefited the emerging Christian Democrats and the resurgent Marxists. They offered competing concepts of reform to the middle and lower classes. Two former spinoffs from the Conservatives, the Falange and the Social Christians, fused to found the Christian Democrat Party (PDC) in 1957. With their youthful, ideological appeal and the charisma of Eduardo Frei, they rapidly displaced the Radicals as the dominant centrist party in Chile, gaining especially among the middle classes and among newly mobilizing sectors such as women, peasants, and urban squatters.[3]

The Marxists took wing, as they had in the mid-1930s, with the

2. Sandra Sue Powell, "Social Structure and Electoral Choice in Chile, 1952-1964" (Ph.D. dissertation, Northwestern University, Evanston, Ill., 1966), pp. 86-105; Glaucio Soares and Robert L. Hamblin, "Socioeconomic Variables and Voting for the Radical Left: Chile, 1952," *American Political Science Review*, LXI, no. 4 (Dec., 1967), pp. 1053-65; Hochwald, pp. 68-69; Halperin, pp. 57-58; Gil, p. 77.

3. Petras, pp. 31, 197-255; Halperin, pp. 192-201; Angell, pp. 174-82.

unification of the national trade union movement in 1953. Reacting chiefly to the inequities caused by inflation, the Central Federation of Chilean Workers (Central Única de Trabajadores de Chile, or CUTCH) replaced the moribund CTCH. The CUTCH was a loose, multiparty grouping of both white- and blue-collar unions. Within it, the Socialists and Communists quickly established supremacy, based on their strength among older unions in mining, construction, and manufacturing. Despite a decade underground, the PC later became the leading single party in the federation.[4]

While Ibáñez's first-year popularity lasted, the independent People's Front launched by the Allende group in 1952 evoked little resonance among the electorate; an isolated socialist alternative seemed to be having no more success than in prior decades under Recabarren or the PST. In the 1953 congressional elections, Ampuero's Socialist faction in the Ibáñez administration gained along with all the government groups. The PSP rose from 4.8% of the votes in 1949 to 8.3% in 1953. Allende's PS, which was outside the governing coalition, claimed only 1.5% of the ballots. Meanwhile, the Conservatives and Liberals slumped to roughly 10% each, and the Radicals to 14%. In contrast to past collaborations, however, this time the Socialists divorced themselves from the Ibáñez government as soon as it rotated away from its campaign promises and toward the right. The PSP entered the opposition before the end of 1953.[5]

By 1955 the Socialists adopted the thesis of a "Workers' Front." This new strategy eschewed compacts with the upper class or the Right, large sections of the middle classes (especially the professional and more prosperous sectors), and, above all, the centrist reform parties, particularly the Radicals. The PSP sought electoral, congressional, and administrative alliances only with working-class parties, mainly the Communists. Although still directed toward some segments of the middle strata, the new policy corresponded to the widening gap between the middle and lower classes. It recognized that the Socialists' constituency had been shorn of some of its middle-class elements and mainly reduced to a residue among organized laborers. Moreover, economic and social modernization was expanding the mobilizable working sectors receptive to Marxist overtures. The Workers' Front also entailed a more radical commitment to a socialist program of nationalization and redistribution.[6]

4. Petras, pp. 168-73; Angell, pp. 84-85, 155.
5. Urzúa Valenzuela, *Los partidos,* p. 94; Waiss, *Nacionalismo,* pp. 143-44; Halperin, pp. 132-33.
6. Although the Socialists now officially expected the proletariat to lead leftist movements, they still defined "manual and intellectual workers" broadly enough to

In 1956, the two Socialist parties formed the Popular Action Front (FRAP), an enduring electoral alliance with the Communists, who were increasingly amenable to cooperation in accord with de-Stalinization. The Socialists' Workers' Front approach prevailed in this alliance. Major centrist reformers were excluded from the FRAP, despite Communist desires for a broader coalition. The Chilean Socialists were turning more radical, while Latin American populists, such as APRA, and Communists were becoming less so.[7]

With the Communists still outside the law in the 1957 elections, the Socialists split nearly 11% of the votes. The PSP took 6.3% and the PS 4.4%. With the waning of *ibañismo,* the traditional parties rebounded to 18% for the Conservatives, 15% for the Liberals, and 22% for the Radicals. The Christian Democrats' percentage of deputy votes jumped from roughly 3% in 1953 to over 9% in 1957.[8] Shortly afterward in 1957 the two Socialist parties reunited, no longer divided by disagreements over coalition tactics and divested of some of the antagonistic personalities from the past (such as Bernardo Ibáñez), in spite of continuing tensions between Allende and the more anti-communist Ampuero. The FRAP was further strengthened by 1958 because President Ibáñez had kept his promise to restore the Communists to legal participation.[9]

FRAP's Quest for the Presidency, 1958-64

In the 1958 presidential contest, the FRAP came within a hair's breadth of victory. The Conservatives and Liberals nominated the paternalistic, austere businessman Jorge Alessandri Rodríguez, son of the deceased Lion of Tarapacá. In the center, the Radicals offered Luis Bossay Leyva and the Christian Democrats, Eduardo Frei. The FRAP, with some small parties and some *ibañistas* in tow, ran Allende. He advocated comprehensive state intervention to reshape Chile's economy and society, a more radical program than any major candidate had ever offered.[10]

Three main electoral forces defeated the FRAP: (1) Bossay's 15.2%

embrace lower layers of the middle strata, especially many white-collar employees. Chelén, *Trayectoria,* pp. 142-43; Jobet, *El Partido Socialista de Chile,* II, pp. 39-40; Barría, *El movimiento;* Hochwald, pp. 160-232.

7. Gil, pp. 204-5; Petras, pp. 182-86.

8. Of those registered, only 68% voted in 1957. Chile, Dirección del Registro Electoral, "Variación porcentual de los partidos políticos, 1957-1971" (n.p., n.d.).

9. At the reunification of the Socialist parties, old leaders such as Schnake and Hidalgo were readmitted. Jobet, *El socialismo chileno,* pp. 86-101; Chelén, *Trayectoria,* pp. 135-48.

10. Olavarría Bravo, *Chile,* II, pp. 390-97; Chelén, *Trayectoria,* pp. 154-55.

of the votes; (2) a defrocked populistic priest, with a following among the poor, whose 3.3% of the ballots exceeded the 2.6% separating Allende from Alessandri; and (3) women voters, who gave Allende only 22.3% of their ballots while men were contributing 32.4%. The Marxists barely missed capturing the executive branch on their own terms, winning 28.6% of the national electorate to 31.2% for Alessandri and 20.5% for Frei.[11] Regionally, Allende ran best in the Great North and the Channels and also scored well in the Small North and the Frontier. His lowest percentages accrued in the South Center and Lakes, with the Urban Center also a relatively disappointing zone. The FRAP's highest percentage in the provinces came from Magallanes. At the *comuna* level, miner and urban worker areas were strongly favorable to Allende. Like Ibáñez in 1952, he gathered impressive pluralities in the highly working-class communities within Santiago. Allende lost the more middle- to upper-class *comunas* there by equally wide margins. Rural peasant zones continued to be the Right's stronghold, although Ibáñez had made inroads. Nevertheless, one of the most significant changes in 1958 was the growth of the vote in peasant communities for Allende, who had promised to parcel out the great estates.[12]

For the first time since the end of World War I the historic rightist parties directly reoccupied the presidency. They returned with a mildly reformist, rather independent, personalistic representative. The Right's brief tenure, however, failed to solve the socioeconomic problems which fueled the Left or to reverse the decline of the Conservative and Liberal electorate.[13]

In the 1961 congressional elections, the Conservatives sank to 11%, the Liberals rose to 16%, and the Radicals, also serving in the Alessandri administration, held at 21%. The advancing Christian Democrats accounted for 15% of the deputy votes. For the FRAP, the Socialists and Communists each tallied roughly 11%. In their first legal congressional foray since 1945, the Communists showed they had weathered a decade of prohibition with their electoral strength intact.[14]

Since the 1925 constitution prevented Alessandri from succeeding himself directly, the Right feared an Allende victory in the 1964 presidential competition. Reluctantly but shrewdly, the Conservatives and Liberals chose the defensive route of tossing their support behind Christian Democrat Frei. Besides the Right and his own party, Frei

11. Of those registered, 83.5% voted in 1958. Daugherty, pp. 34-35.
12. Powell, pp. 121-68; Olavarría Bravo, *Chile*, II, p. 399; Affonso et al., I, p. 199.
13. Chelén, *Trayectoria*, pp. 156-57; Petras, pp. 11, 104-13.
14. In 1961, 74.5% of those registered voted. Chile, Dirección del Registro Electoral, *Variación;* Gil, pp. 81-83, 233-43.

drew substantial but unofficial backing from the Church and the United States. He campaigned on the still popular theme of anticommunism. Frei also promised Chileans a "revolution in liberty," the social reforms awaited since World War I but without Marxism or Allende's more far-reaching proposals. In a populistic, charismatic appeal, Frei wooed all sectors of society with visions of tandem economic prosperity and social justice. Not unlike Arturo Alessandri in 1920 and Aguirre Cerda in 1938, Frei was explicitly promising evolution to preclude revolution.[15]

For the first time in Chilean history, the Marxist parties and the conservative and centrist forces were involved in a polar confrontation. Partly inspired by Castro's Cuba, the FRAP set out detailed, rather radical proposals for nationalization of mines and industries, redistribution, agrarian reform, and independence from the United States. In the face of rumors that the military would intervene if Allende won, the FRAP and the CUTCH, consistent with leftist tradition, promised resistance and general strikes if their opponents unleashed violence.[16]

Frei's program and personality won by a landslide that permeated all regional and social groups. Thanks to the support of the rightist parties, he defeated Allende 56% to 39%; the latter's total included 31.9% of the national votes from women and 44.8% from men. Of the registered voters, 87%, 32% of the national population, cast ballots. At the regional level, Frei ran best in the Urban Center (accounting for roughly 44% of the national population and 53% of the national votes cast), Allende's weakest zone. The FRAP only accumulated a higher regional percentage than Frei in the Great North. At the *comuna* level, Frei received strong support from all types. He did especially well in urban middle- to upper-class districts and in rural zones. Although both major candidates naturally attracted mixed followings, Allende still tended to score his best percentages in communities exceptionally noteworthy for miners, urban workers, and slum dwellers. The FRAP generally exceeded its 1958 showing throughout all *comuna* categories, but its rise was most dramatic in rural peasant areas. Several studies indicate that Allende improved much less in miner and urban working-class districts than he did nationally. This did not

15. As a token gesture, the rightist Radical Julio Antonio Durán Neumann sustained a third candidacy throughout the 1964 contest. Federico G. Gil and Charles J. Parrish, *The Chilean Presidential Election of September 4, 1964* (Washington, D.C., 1965), pp. 24-40; Gil, pp. 239-43; Olavarría Bravo, *Chile*, III, esp. pp. 257-320, IV, pp. 147-277; *New York Times*, Sept. 8-20, 1974.

16. Chelén, *Trayectoria*, pp. 158-63; Olavarría Bravo, *Chile*, III, pp. 314-19, IV, pp. 237-82; Gil., pp. 298-307.

suggest massive radicalization of the proletariat. Even with the Workers' Front strategy, the Marxists continued to rely on significant assistance from middle-class (especially white-collar employees) and regional groups.[17]

The Socialist Dilemma under Frei, 1964-70

With a third loss but rising percentages behind Allende's banner, the Socialists debated their perennial dilemma between electoral means and revolutionary ends more strenuously than ever. The example of Cuba exerted pressure for more rapid and radical action, as did the competing reformist successes of the Christian Democrats. According to left-wing Socialists, their defeats in presidential races indicated the need to establish a clearer radical Marxist position based almost exclusively on the workers and peasants. They argued for radicalization so that the FRAP could unify the working classes, whose loyalties were still scattered among many parties. Learning different lessons, more moderate Socialists, closer to the Communists and old popular-front approaches, concluded that excessively strict application of the Workers' Front thesis had denied them the presidency. Therefore, they favored stretching the coalition to encompass more centrist groups, at least in a subordinate role.[18]

The left wing of the PS won the theoretical debate at the 1967 party congress. There the Socialists declared their adherence to revolutionary Marxism-Leninism, outflanking the gradualist Communists. They reaffirmed the Workers' Front, meant to include students, intellectuals, the poorer sectors of the middle classes, and peasants, with the proletariat as the leader of the coalition. They rejected any cooperation with the national bourgeoisie or centrist reformers, specifically the Radicals and Christian Democrats. Moreover, the PS subscribed to the possibility of nonelectoral means: "Revolutionary violence is inevitable and legitimate. . . . Pacific or legal means of struggle alone do not lead to power. The Socialist Party considers them as limited instruments of action, incorporated in the political process which carries us to the armed struggle."[19] This turn to the

17. The isolated Durán took 5% of the ballots. The only provinces in which Allende topped Frei were Tarapacá, Antofagasta, Atacama, Concepción, Arauco, and Magallanes. Chile, Dirección del Registro Electoral, "Elección presidencial" (Santiago, 1964); Gil and Parrish; Powell, pp. 134-207; Zemelman, pp. 50-60.

18. Jobet and Chelén; interviews with Garay and Chelén, Santiago, 1970; Partido Socialista, *¡Frei no es Chile!* (Santiago, 1966); Partido Socialista, *El socialismo ante el mundo de hoy* (Santiago, 1964); Luis Corvalán, *Un Partido Comunista fuerte es garantía para el pueblo* (Santiago, 1967).

19. Jobet, *El Partido Socialista de Chile*, II, p. 130; also pp. 128-49; interviews with Jobet, Garay, and Almeyda, Santiago, 1970.

left in party theory did not resolve the Socialists' long-standing contradictions. Instead, it mainly widened the gap between their revolutionary doctrines and democratic reformist actions. The party
pragmatists, such as Allende, kept the PS on the path of electoral
coalitions. Even after the 1967 declarations against popular-front
politics, the Socialists followed the Communists into another alliance
for the 1970 presidential race, including the Radicals as junior
partners.[20]

In the wake of the 1964 defeat, continuing Socialist devotion to the
electoral route was one cause of two offshoots to the left of the PS.
Largely inspired by guerrilla theorists and activists, a small band of
younger, mainly middle- to upper-class Socialists departed to consolidate the Movement of the Revolutionary Left (MIR) in 1964-65. The
MIR, a tiny vanguard party, abstained from national elections and
prepared for the violent confrontation with the bourgeoisie which it
deemed inevitable.[21] In late 1967, partly out of personal disagreements over leadership and partly out of opposition to any pact with
the Radicals which violated PS doctrines, Ampuero and a handful of
followers also seceded and founded the miniscule Popular Socialist
Union (USP). Assuming that Allende would lose a fourth time in 1970,
both the MIR and the USP stayed out of the leftist coalition. Claiming
to speak for the truly revolutionary workers, they criticized the PS for
reverting to populism, accepting Communist strategies, and tolerat-
ing the Radicals. Like past electoral challengers to the mother party,
the USP failed to muster a credible alternative.[22]

Despite doctrinal radicalization, the Socialists' social composition
changed very little in the fifties and sixties. Available evidence showed
that middle- and upper-middle-class intellectuals and professionals
continued to lead the PS. This was true even though the Socialists, of
all the major parties from World War I through the 1960s, displayed
the greatest turnover in leadership personnel. Meanwhile, the Communists experienced the least circulation of leaders. From 1932 to
1965, two-thirds of the Socialists elected to Congress improved their
social standing. They did so by attaining those seats and by securing
better subsequent employment. Through the PS, lower-middle-class
and lower-class party leaders clambered into the middle strata, and
those from the middle class enhanced their status. Moreover, many of

20. Hochwald, pp. 72-73, 117-21; Halperin, pp. 39-40, 135-42; Eduardo Labarca
Goddard, *Chile al rojo* (Santiago, 1971), p. 190.

21. Jobet, *El Partido Socialista de Chile*, II, pp. 100-123.

22. Interviews with Garay, Santiago, 1970; Mario Garay, *La cuestión de la unidad*
(Santiago, 1968); Union Socialista Popular, *La clase obrera y la elección, 1970* (n.p., 1970);
Ampuero, *La izquierda*, pp. 9-11, 105-28; Halperin, pp. 170-76.

them lost their ideological zeal in the process. Especially during the period of popular-front–style coalitions, a majority of Socialist congressmen either deserted the party or became more conservative after their terms expired. From the 1930s to 1953, only 21% continued to back the PS after leaving office; 36% switched to more conservative groups and 3% to other leftist vehicles; the remaining 40% vanished from politics.[23]

In the fifties and sixties, Socialist congressional and party leadership continued to overlap. One student was able to track down 39 of the 93 persons on the central committee from 1940 to 1965 and found 13 lawyers, 11 teachers, 7 professionals, 6 government employees, and 2 trade union leaders. Although the middle- to upper-class bias of standard biographical sources always made it difficult to discover working-class leaders, the traceable middle-class intellectuals and professionals were unquestionably powerful and gave the PS respectability and expertise. They provided links with public and private institutions, such as CORFO and the University of Chile, and their influence over the party even exceeded their high numerical proportion at the top, although a few more working-class leaders surfaced by the start of the 1970s. Still far more middle class than the Communists, Socialist congressional and party leaders also exhibited less university-level education and more working-class origins than the heads of the Radicals, Liberals, or Conservatives. In contrast to the other major parties from the 1930s through the 1960s, Socialist and Communist leaders were much more likely to come from provinces other than Santiago. The PS continued to offer geographic as well as social mobility to its leaders.[24]

At the level of members and voters, later studies indicated that the Socialists still straddled the middle and lower classes. By the 1960s, the party rank-and-file included teachers, students, technicians, professionals, retired military officers, and many lower-middle-class employees. More a working-class party at the level of followers, the PS attracted new urban and rural laborers. Nevertheless, its strength in the proletariat remained inferior to that of the Communists. One

---

23. Petras, pp. 161-63; interview with Almeyda, Santiago, 1970; Reimer.

24. Many Socialist leaders, especially those in Congress, continued to come from the provincial middle class. For example, one study found that three-fourths of the traceable Socialist congressional representatives from 1932 to 1966 were born outside Santiago. For the 1957, 1961, and 1965 congressional contests, the following percentages of senators elected from each major party were born in Santiago: 75% of the Conservatives, 55% of the Liberals, 50% of the Radicals, 31% of the Christian Democrats, 22% of the Socialists, and 14% of the Communists. Hochwald, pp. 58-61; Urzúa Valenzuela, *Los partidos,* esp. p. 194; Gil, pp. 281-94; Chelén, *Trayectoria,* pp. 189-90; Agor, pp. 34-35; interview with Barría, Santiago, 1973.

Socialist concentration was still in the copper mines, where workers were better off than most of their counterparts. While the PS held best in more traditional unions, such as railroad workers and printers, the PC scored gains in more modern industrial sectors such as textiles and construction, a phenomenon which differed from the pattern of the early 1930s. The Communists also maintained a large following in the mines, especially in nitrates and coal, as well as among recently mobilized peasant and rural-to-urban migrant groups. In addition, the Socialists counted some supporters among port workers and squatter slum dwellers, and they preserved a near monopoly on the electorate in Magallanes, based on "semiindustrial workers" mainly in cattle and sheep enterprises. Indeed, the PS was compensating for its losses in Santiago with gains in the outlying regions, particularly among the provincial middle classes and agricultural laborers. The Socialists became more of a rural and less of an urban party than in the decade of their birth.[25]

The political opposition to the Marxists eroded electorally in the late 1960s. After a high tide in the honeymoon congressional elections of 1965, the Christian Democrats suffered the typical ebbing of a party in power. Despite opposition from both the Right and the Marxists, the Frei administration instituted unparalleled reforms, most notably in the countryside, but the accumulated problems of decades persisted. For example, inflation, spotty economic growth, structural inequalities, a burgeoning foreign debt, inadequate housing, and working-class discontent remained. At the same time, the Radicals continued to decline. Only behind the lure of a reprise by Jorge Alessandri did the traditional Right show even faint signs of revival. However, calculated flexibility remained one keynote of conservative strategy: the elites identified themselves with selected reforms and techno-cratic, capitalist economic modernization. In the 1960s many rightist leaders were willing to bargain even on limited land reform. Frei, however, went farther than they thought necessary to undercut the Marxists. Most of the Right still recoiled from extensive redistributive measures or state monopolies over finance and banking. The

25. Halperin, pp. 39-40; Casanueva and Fernández, p. 223; Partido Socialista, *Cartilla campesina* (Santiago, 1966); Aniceto Rodríguez A., *1966: año de la organización y las luchas campesinas* (Santiago, 1966); Faletto and Ruiz, esp. p. 226; Zemelman, pp. 50-60; Tomás Moulian, *Estudio sobre Chile* (Santiago, 1965); James Petras and Maurice Zeitlin, *El radicalismo político de la clase trabajadora chilena* (Buenos Aires, 1969); Alejandro Portes, "Leftist Radicalism in Chile (A Test of Three Hypotheses)," *Comparative Politics*, II (Jan., 1970), pp. 251-74; James Prothro and Patricio E. Chaparro, "Public Opinion and the Movement of Chilean Government to the Left, 1952-72," *Journal of Politics*, XXXVI (Feb., 1974), pp. 2-43.

conservative elites backed the PDC reformers only so long as that support appeared mandatory to block the threat of socialism.[26]

By the fifties and sixties, the upper class and the Right had altered their strategies and composition little since the 1930s. The agricultural and industrial magnates remained tied to each other and to government at many junctures. For example, it was estimated in the 1960s that nearly half the large businessmen in Chile either owned extensive farms or were related to *latifundistas*. Urban financial institutions served as a primary nexus for all these interconnections. The congressional leadership of the Right was still highly aristocratic and homogeneous. Substantial evidence suggested that the Conservatives and Liberals were dominated by agricultural elites. Many party spokesmen also sported professional titles, especially law degrees. Numerous Conservative and Liberal congressmen, as well as some Radicals, served as directors on the boards of major banks and corporations. In many cases, upper-class leaders became prominent in state enterprises and agencies previously created as reform measures. Compared to the Conservatives; the Liberals were only slightly more urban and commercially oriented. The major background differences were still religious and educational ties. Finally, after over thirty years of close collaboration, the Conservatives and Liberals officially joined forces in 1966 to form the National Party (PN).[27]

By the end of the 1960s, the electoral scene did not reveal any glacial shifts in voter loyalties. Instead, the division of voters into Right, Center, or Left camps persisted, as Table 28 shows.[28] Marxist gains were small but steady. The Communists were outstripping the Socialists at the polls as well as in the unions, but Marxist advances were much less striking in congressional than in presidential races, where Allende had soared from 6% to 29% to 39%. This indicated that voter identification of his name and his personal appeal, while scarcely charismatic, were not to be discounted. In congressional

26. Petras, pp. 108-13, 158-255, 338-55; Robert R. Kaufman, *The Chilean Political Right and Agrarian Reform: Resistance and Moderation* (Washington, D.C., 1967), pp. i, 41-46.

27. Urzúa Valenzuela, *Los partidos,* pp. 125-46; Petras, pp. 38-55, 100-104; Gil, pp. 294-95; Lagos Escobar, pp. 7-16, 95-172; Johnson, "Industrialization,"; Menges, pp. 343-65; Agor, pp. 34-35; Casanueva and Fernández, p. 206. For a description of many of the forces in play in the 1960s, see Ben G. Burnett, *Political Groups in Chile* (Austin, Tex., 1970).

28. The USP drew only 2% of the votes in 1969. Chile, Dirección del Registro Electoral, "Variación"; Chile, Dirección del Registro Electoral, "Résultado elección ordinaria de diputados" (Santiago, 1969); Chile, Dirección del Registro Electoral, "Resultado elección ordinaria de senadores" (Santiago, 1969); Garcés, *1970;* Faletto and Ruiz.

TABLE 28: NATIONAL CONGRESSIONAL VOTES FOR PARTIES, 1961, 1965, 1969

	1961	1965	1969
Conservatives & Liberals	30.4%	12.5%	20.0%
Radicals	21.4	13.3	13.0
Christian Democrats	15.4	42.3	29.8
Communists	11.4	12.4	15.9
Socialists	10.7	10.3	12.2

percentages, by 1969, the Socialists were back up to their 1937 and 1945 levels, and the Communists were higher than ever before.

The Popular Unity and the Chilean Road to Socialism, 1970

For the 1970 presidential election, the Right tried to recoup power alone through the popular but aged figure of Alessandri. The campaign relied on personalism and, once again, anticommunism. A formal platform was never issued. Still, even Alessandri promised, along with liberal capitalism, a heftier dose of reform than he had given the country in the late 1950s.[29]

In the center, Christian Democrat Radomiro Tomic Romero aspired to succeed Frei. Tomic was from the left wing of the PDC and his platform promises were barely distinguishable from Allende's. Although a PDC-FRAP alliance was discussed with the Communists, the Socialists apparently vetoed it.[30]

A coalition reminiscent of 1938 emerged on the left, though with the Communists and Socialists leading and the shrunken Radical Party in tow. On the one hand, the inclusion of the Radicals was a tribute to the Communists' belief that Chile, given its economic underdevelopment and small proletariat, still needed a broad multiclass front to move it through a reformist, industrial, state capitalist transformation before a leap toward socialism was conceivable. On the other hand, the subordination of the Radicals and the exclusion of the PDC was a tribute to the Socialists' belief that Chile, given its existing

29. For general coverage of the 1970 election and its aftermath as discussed in the following pages, see Richard E. Feinberg, *The Triumph of Allende* (New York, 1972); David Morris, *We Must Make Haste–Slowly* (New York, 1973); Newton Carlos et al., *Chile com Allende: ¿para onde vai?* (Rio de Janeiro, 1970); Carlos Núñez, *Chile: ¿la última opción electoral?* (Santiago, 1970); Luis Vitale, *¿Y después del 4, qué?* (Santiago, 1970); Labarca Goddard. All the sections on the victory and administration of Allende also rely on personal observations and interviews in November, 1969–October, 1970, and June–August, 1973, as well as a wide reading of newspapers and magazines. For particular coverage of the Right's 1970 campaign, see *El Mercurio*, Nov., 1969–Sept., 1970; *El Diario Ilustrado*, Nov., 1969–Sept., 1970; *La Segunda*, Nov., 1969–Sept. 1970; *New York Times*, Sept. 8, 1974; Chile Joven, *La palmada en la frente* (Santiago, 1970).

30. *La Nación*, Nov., 1969–Sept., 1970; *La Tarde*, Nov., 1969–Sept., 1970; *El Clarín*, Nov., 1969–Sept., 1970; Faletto and Ruiz, pp. 217-25.

entanglement with international capitalism and its lack of a dynamic entrepreneurial bourgeoisie, needed immediate strides toward state socialism for the working class. Three minor parties, notably one of left-wing rebels from the Christian Democrats, rounded out the coalition. It was christened the Popular Unity (UP).[31]

The UP promised a government in transition toward socialism. It sought rapid transfer of the means and fruits of production from foreign and indigenous elites to the middle and especially lower classes.[32] After agreeing on a program, the coalition nominated Allende, a professional politician of four decades' experience, who was famous for his agility and durability. As a Socialist, Allende had opposed Godoy in 1940, Grove in 1943, Bernardo Ibáñez in 1948, and Ampuero in 1952 and 1967. Throughout these years, though seen as a party firebrand at the end of the 1930s, he was usually associated with the moderate mainstream of PS thought and practice. By 1970, Allende was identified with the social-democrat style of the right wing of the party. Nevertheless, he had moved or stayed further left over the years than contemporaries and friends like Rómulo Betancourt of AD and Haya de la Torre of APRA. He developed close personal, if not ideological, bonds with Castro's Cuba. In his fourth and final try for the presidency, Allende conducted a restrained campaign. He did so because that was his style—the opposite of Grove's earlier style—and because more stridency might have frightened the Right and the Center into reviving their compact of 1964.[33]

Compared to the Popular Front, the Popular Unity boasted a far more socialistic program and was far more dedicated to it. At the same time, the UP faced similar problems of coalition formation and maintenance. As in the 1930s, the Marxists were plagued by the issue of making the alliance broad enough to win without diluting its program and class character. The UP bore seeds of problems similar to those of the Popular Front: incompatible ideological and social interests. Moreover, the PS and PC still quarreled with each other almost as much as with more moderate coalition allies or opponents. In hopes of not repeating the programmatic disappointments of thirty years earlier, the two Marxist groups relied on the domination of the UP by themselves and their worker followers. In contrast to the polarized contest of 1938, the Socialists and Communists were able to reach for

31. A fraction of the Radicals also broke away to back Alessandri. *El Clarín*, Nov., 1969–Sept., 1970; *Última Hora*, Nov., 1969–Sept., 1970; *El Siglo*, Nov., 1969–Sept., 1970; *Puro Chile*, 1970; Luis Corvalán, *El poder popular* (Santiago, 1969).
32. La Unidad Popular, *Programa básico de gobierno de la Unidad Popular* (Santiago, 1970); Garcés, *1970*, pp. 72-128.
33. Debray, pp. 62-121.

the presidency in 1970 with far less middle-sector support because it was a three-way race.[34]

Election night brought the electrifying news that Allende had finally eked out a victory. After nearly forty years, the Socialists won the presidency directly and democratically. Over one-third of the national population—83.5% of the registered voters—cast ballots. In a reversal of the photo finish in 1958, Allende came in first with 36% of the votes (42% from men and 31% from women), a slight drop from his 39% national total in 1964. Alessandri finished second with 35% and Tomic third with 28%.[35]

Regionally, just as in 1964, Allende performed best in the Great North and worst in the agrarian Lakes zone south of Concepción. He rolled up his highest provincial percentages in the three northern mining provinces of Tarapacá, Antofagasta, and Atacama, urban Concepción and its coal-mining and farming neighbor Arauco, and, inevitably, Magallanes. Elsewhere, the UP maintained or approached its national percentage in both heavily rural and urban areas.

In conjunction with regional and provincial data, some evidence from selected *comunas* suggests that Allende's percentage slippage from 1964 to 1970 took place largely in rural peasant zones, where Alessandri's paternalistic appeal often attracted large shares of the ballots. Also, Allende's male vote dropped slightly more than his female. Although more in-depth studies are needed, it appears that Allende's support in traditionally favorable miner and urban worker–slum dweller *comunas* held steady and still led all other categories by a wide margin. For example, within the capital city he carried the more identifiably working-class communities, while Alessandri pocketed the central downtown and the highly middle- to upper-class districts. All types of provinces and *comunas* gave strong votes to all three candidates. This indicated the mixed nature of most of the voting units and the multiclass backing for all the contenders. Thus while Allende could by no means claim to speak for all the lower classes, especially those tilling the earth, he could claim to be mainly the president-elect of the workers, especially those in the mines and the cities, and even of some portions of the middle groups. In 1970 there was no dramatic shift in electoral patterns, and the Marxists won with the same basic constituency they had been cultivating since the 1930s. More than reflecting profound sociopolitical changes, Allende's electoral triumph initiated them.[36]

34. Garcés, *1970*, pp. 67-71; Debray, pp. 70-118.
35. Chile, Dirección del Registro Electoral, "Elección ordinaria de Presidente de la República" (Santiago, 1970).
36. For example, at least in the rural zones of Putaendo, La Cruz, Isla de Maipo,

Defeating their opponents at the polls was only the first step toward national office for the UP. Once again, the Right warned the nation of the horrors of communism and threatened to annul the verdict of the ballots. Plots to negate the UP's victory through congressional, unorthodox, or violent means prompted mass demonstrations and promises of counterviolence from the Left. With even greater intensity than in 1938, the Marxists urged calm and advised their less intransigent adversaries to ratify their victory. Simultaneously the Popular Unity conjured up the cataclysm of social upheaval and civil war in defense of their right to the presidency. Behind the apocalyptic warnings and bluffs from both sides, the military deliberated as a latent arbiter.

The Right, with U.S. support, tried to stop Allende both through manipulations to certify the runner-up, Alessandri, and through military maneuvers. As in 1938, the falling stock market reflected uncertainty. Extreme right-wing terrorists, reportedly in collusion with the U.S. Central Intelligence Agency, worked to create a climate of violence and anarchy. They assassinated the constitutionalist commander-in-chief of the armed forces, Army General René Schneider, in the first killing of a major Chilean governmental leader in over 130 years. Once again, Chile pulled back from the brink when a majority of the Christian Democrats and the military signaled a preference for honoring the tradition of peacefully transferring power to the top vote-recipient. In return for ratification, the PDC extracted guarantees from the UP that its government would respect democratic proprieties. Torn between those hopeful for the incoming administration's reforms and those fearful of its ideological objectives, the PDC shied away from disrupting the relative social tranquility underpinned by four decades of constitutional regularity. Apparently, a pivotal argument in the hotly contested Christian Democrat

---

Pichidegua, Palmilla, Teno, Longaví, Coihueco, Hualqui, Los Alamos, Santa Barbara, Lumaco, Frutillar, and Achao, where Allende's percentage had risen without exception from 1958 to 1964, his percentage dropped (in 10 of the 14 *comunas*) from 1964 to 1970. Conversely, in the selected miner–worker–urban slum dweller areas of Arica, Tocopilla, Loa, Andacollo, Calera, San Miguel, Quinta Normal, Puente Alto, San Antonio, San Bernardo, Barrancas, La Granja, and La Cisterna, where Allende's percentage (which was generally higher in these zones to begin with) had risen in 11 out of 13 from 1958 to 1964, his percentage dropped in only 4 from 1964 to 1970. Zemelman, pp. 50-60; Gil and Parrish; Petras and Alexander, pp. 72-81. In 1970, Alessandri finished first among the three presidential candidates in 8 of the 14 rural communities; in the 13 worker–miner–urban slum dweller areas, Allende finished first in all of them in 1970, though of course he did not do as well in all communities of that type, and the few mentioned here fell far short of any full national sample. Published after this book was virtually finished, a valuable collection of additional studies of the political and social forces which shaped Allende's Chile can be found in Arturo Valenzuela and J. Samuel Valenzuela, eds.. *Chile: Politics and Society* (New Brunswick, N.J., 1976).

decision to accept Allende was that denying him might justify more violent means of gaining power. Preliminary evidence suggests that the armed forces stayed in their barracks, to the disappointment of some civilians, because of their traditions, internal divisions, good relations with some leaders of the UP, and reluctance to incur the potentially horrendous costs of intrusion. The time-honored practice of admitting reformers but not their more radical programs was now put to the ultimate test, however, and proved a poor gamble with Allende.[37]

Chilean Socialism in the Presidency, 1970-73

Far more than in the past, the Marxists in office faced the predicament of fulfilling their promises of social reform and mobilization while conforming to constitutional norms and protecting their position in the executive branch from constant conservative assaults. They needed to retain power within constitutional bounds while stretching those bounds as far as possible. Despite the Socialists' radicalization in the 1960s and the fears of their opponents, the Popular Unity was very unlikely to switch to more violent means. The Marxists adhered to constitutional institutions partly because of their long socialization into Chilean party politics. Moreover, many of them clung to ingrained democratic beliefs. After all, they had achieved great party successes through that system. Their moderate approach was also a response to such institutional constraints as the military's and Congress's toleration of the PS and PC only within defined limits. Adopting more radical methods was not only undesirable to many Marxists, it also appeared extremely difficult and perhaps suicidal. In many respects, what was most surprising was not the timidity of the government but rather the bold reforms it achieved through the given system. Within those limits, the more gradual, compromising approach was most championed, inside the UP, by the Communists. They emphasized institutionalized changes routed through the government, party, and union hierarchies. The PC proposed achieving those reforms in cooperation with progressive members of the middle and upper classes, mainly the Christian Democrats. The more radical approach was advocated most consistently by left-wing Socialists. They preferred speedier reforms propelled by new mass mobilizations based on class conflict.[38]

37. Feinberg; Labarca Goddard; Bicheno; Robert Moss, *Chile's Marxist Experiment* (Newton Abbot, England, 1973); *New York Times*, Sept. 8-20, 1974.
38. Arturo Valenzuela, "Political Constraints and the Prospects for Socialism in Chile," in Douglas A. Chalmers, ed., *Changing Latin America* (n.p., 1972), pp. 65-82.

Ambivalent toward the alternatives of institutionalization and mobilization, the Marxists, especially the Socialists, swore that the Popular Unity would be more radical than the Popular Front. The PS explicitly denounced populism and emphasized ideology and class struggle over nationalism and personalism. As a symbol of the party's greater commitment to social conflict than to national integration, Allende, once inaugurated, pointedly said, "I am not the president of all Chileans." Further underlining the upsurge of the workers envisioned by his government, Allende declared: "The process in Chile is neither paternalistic nor charismatic. . . . I am not a messiah, nor am I a *caudillo*. We know that popular power is built from the base upwards."[39]

The Socialists also publicized their rising militance by electing Carlos Altamirano Orrego secretary-general of the party in 1971. A lawyer and intellectual, Altamirano was a lean, fiery representative of the Socialist wing to the left of Allende. Under Altamirano's leadership, the PS adopted the slogan "Advance without Compromise." The party vowed to overcome vestiges of populism in itself and the UP: ". . . the Socialist Party recognizes that . . . the Popular Unity reflects a multiclass composition . . . where worker, petty-bourgeois, and bourgeois tendencies come together. These class contradictions . . . will be surpassed by the revolutionary dynamic of the working masses led by their class parties."[40]

President Allende himself, while rejecting personalistic populism or dictatorial Marxism, never made a firm choice between more cautious Communist and more daring Socialist approaches. In his first year, Allende instituted some short-term populistic measures such as the distribution of liters of milk to undernourished children and the rapid transfer of consumer power to the lower classes. These policies were not totally unlike the old Popular Front. Far more significant, Allende also carried out vast structural changes which shoved Chile toward socialism, for instance the nationalization of foreign and domestic oligopolies and the eradication of private latifundia. These actions were a sharp departure from popular-front politics.

During the first year of the Popular Unity government, the experiment, contrary to all predictions, seemed to be working. With unanimous congressional approval, Chile nationalized the U.S. copper companies. While national production and employment went up, inflation tapered off. More land passed out of the hands of the rural

39. Debray, pp. 94-123. On the PS, also see Alejandro Chelén Rojas, *El Partido Socialista de Chile* (Santiago, 1972).

40. Jobet, *El Partido Socialista de Chile,* II, pp. 172-77.

elites than during Frei's entire pioneering six years. The administration took over numerous factories and banks under legal auspices. It began to redress regional inequities and symbolized this by temporarily running the government from Valparaíso. By repressing prices and hiking wage readjustments, the UP increased the wage-earners' share of national income from approximately 53% in 1970 to 59% in 1971. Ninety-five percent of the population benefited from this consumers' revolution at the expense of the wealthiest 5%.[41]

In the "honeymoon-period" municipal elections of 1971, the UP's share of the votes soared to 50%. The long-run dream of building a socialist state and society through democratic procedures appeared to be attainable. In comparison to 1969, votes for the Right (18%), the Christian Democrats (26%), and the Radicals (8%) dropped a bit. The Communists inched forward to 17%, and the Socialists spurted to 22%, making them electorally the second largest party in Chile. As during the Popular Front, PS membership snowballed, while party leaders worried about the quality and commitment of their recruits.[42]

However, these first-year successes were pregnant with severe problems for 1972-73. As demand outran production, imports rose, debts soared, and inflation skyrocketed, thus eroding the workers' initial gains. At the same time, traditional sources of investment and of foreign credit, aid, and replacement parts were cut off. Allende's multiplying economic woes resulted partly from natural dislocations during a process of radical and abrupt change. Falling world copper prices compounded the agonies of an economy in transition. In addition, the government's errors, poor planning, spoils system, and inadequate control over certain major sectors of production and distribution kept the economy in a tailspin. Equally important as a cause of mounting stagnation, shortages, and prices was harassment—including withdrawal of capital, sabotage, hoarding, speculation, and black marketing—by the UP's domestic and foreign enemies. The

41. Debray, pp. 190-91; Thomas G. Sanders, "The Process of Partisanship in Chile," *American Universities Field Staff Reports*, XX, no. 1 (Oct., 1973); Thomas G. Sanders, "Urban Pressure, Natural Resource Constraints, and Income Redistribution in Chile," *American Universities Field Staff Reports*, XX, no. 2 (Dec., 1973); Gonzalo Martner, ed., *El pensamiento económico del gobierno de Allende* (Santiago, 1971); Unidad Proletaria, *El primer año del gobierno popular* (n.p., 1972); North American Congress on Latin America, *New Chile* (n.p., 1972); Eric J. Hobsbawm, "Chile: Year One," *New York Review of Books*, XVII, no. 4 (Sept. 23, 1971), pp. 23-32; Solon Barraclough et al., *Chile: reforma agraria y gobierno popular* (Buenos Aires, 1973); Dale L. Johnson, ed., *The Chilean Road to Socialism* (Garden City, N.Y., 1973); J. Ann Zammit, ed., *The Chilean Road to Socialism* (Austin, Tex., 1973); Salvador Allende, *Su pensamiento político* (Santiago, 1972).
42. Chile, Dirección del Registro Electoral, "Resultado elección ordinaria de regidores" (Santiago, 1971); Jobet, *El Partido Socialista de Chile*, II, pp. 169-82.

spark for all this tinder was opposition strikes which were partly underwritten by the United States and led by property owners, professionals, truckers, merchants, and some privileged sectors of organized labor. An increasingly polarized social battle raged over a finite amount of goods and power, with little room left for compromise. Unable to correct the economy or stifle the increasingly subversive opposition, Allende went on the defensive in his second two years in office. He tried to fend off or outwit a united and revitalized Right-Center coalition. Given the multifaceted forces against the Popular Unity, it was perhaps more surprising that it achieved so many successes in the first year than that it encountered so many failures in the next two. The vaunted and maligned Chilean road to socialism, theoretically running through the democratic system with the acquiescence of the capitalists, proved efficacious for a short time, but then it ran into a quagmire because of the inherent conceptual shortcomings of the model, the mistakes of its practitioners, and the opposition's determination to wreck it.[43]

Frightened but tenacious conservative elites weighed three main possibilities for contending with the UP. First, to some it appeared that accommodation and cooptation were bankrupt. The remaining upper-class leaders knew that the growth of the interventionist state since the 1930s meant that capture of that apparatus by the Left was far more ominous than in 1932 or 1938. Moreover, the Popular Unity was devoted not just to industrialization and economic growth but specifically to redistribution and economic takeover. It could cut deeply into upper-class sanctuaries during a six-year term, and Al-

43. North American Congress on Latin America, *NACLA's Latin America and Empire Report*, VII, no. 1 (Jan., 1973); Paul E. Sigmund, "The 'Invisible Blockade' and the Overthrow of Allende," *Foreign Affairs*, Jan., 1974, pp. 322-40; Richard R. Fagen, "The United States and Chile: Roots and Branches," *Foreign Affairs*, Jan., 1975, pp. 297-313; Paul N. Rosenstein-Rodan, "Why Allende Failed," *Challenge*, XVII (May-June, 1974), pp. 7-13; *New York Times*, Sept. 8-20, 1974; United States, House of Representatives, Committee on Foreign Affairs, Subcommittee on Inter-American Affairs, *United States and Chile during the Allende Years, 1970-1973* (Washington, D.C., 1975); Escuela de Negocios de Valparaíso, Fundación Adolfo Ibáñez, *La economía de Chile durante el período de gobierno de la Unidad Popular* (n.p., 1974); Alberto Baltra Cortés, *Gestión económica del gobierno de la Unidad Popular* (Santiago, 1973); Unidad Proletaria, *El segundo año del gobierno popular* (n.p., 1972); Paul M. Sweezy and Harry Magdoff, eds., *Revolution and Counter-Revolution in Chile* (New York, 1974); Amidst the flood of new books on the Allende years arriving too late for full consideration in this chapter, the following seem especially noteworthy: James Petras and Morris Morley, *The United States and Chile: Imperialism and the Overthrow of the Allende Government* (New York, 1975); Francisco Orrego Vicuña, ed., *Chile: The Balanced View* (Santiago, 1975); Stefan de Vylder, *Allende's Chile: The Political Economy of the Rise and Fall of the Unidad Popular* (New York, 1976); Ian Roxborough, Philip O'Brien, and Jackie Roddick, *Chile: The State and Revolution* (New York, 1977).

lende moved with far greater celerity than most had expected. Consequently, many prosperous Chileans abandoned the country, although often with hopes of returning.[44]

A second option for the upper class and the Right was not surrender or retreat but an open fight against the UP. From the day the ballots were counted, conspiracies brewed. Some conservative groups began arming. A small neofascist organization dubbed "Fatherland and Liberty" set its sights on the overthrow of the Popular Unity. Most leaders on the Right, however, were unable or unwilling to organize a coup in the first two years. They had to cultivate the chiefs of the armed forces, who were usually from the middle classes and isolated from the intimate social circles of the elites. Another restraint was that many affluent Chileans were chary of the long-range consequences of scrapping legal stability. Worse, they might not be able to win an overt clash, whether through military or paramilitary means. Even those who desired an insurrection bided their time until more of the middle classes and the Center could be convinced that a violent solution was preferable to allowing Allende to stay in office. Therefore, as so often in the past, many conservative groups, particularly in the early stages, tended toward a third set of strategies, one between capitulation and counterrevolution.[45]

The third approach by the privileged sectors was to rely primarily on more conventional tactics to help them survive the Popular Unity's mandate and to set up the possible conditions for a coup as insurance. The Right tried to ally the anti-Marxist middle strata and bureaucracy against the UP, and conservatives constantly ambushed and demoralized the administration. Many rightists also sought assistance from the United States, Brazil, and Argentina. Through delaying tactics, shackling Allende in Congress, and fanning economic and international troubles, they hoped to keep change within bearable limits until the next presidential election. Before Allende's persistence made intolerable changes appear irreversible, his foes pursued these multiple strategies, but by the third year most of the administration's opponents had long stopped merely sniping. Instead, they launched a frontal assault on the government's legitimacy and existence. Most important in the crisis, the old elites and the Right accumulated increasing support from the centrist groups.[46]

44. Drake, "The Political," pp. 336-37; *El Mercurio*, 1970–Sept., 1973; Hobsbawm, esp. p. 30; Hernán Millas and Emilio Filippi, *Chile '70-'73: crónica de una experiencia* (Santiago, 1974); Luis Maira, *Chile: dos años de Unidad Popular* (Santiago, 1973).

45. Chamudes, esp. pp. 32-34; North American Congress on Latin America, *NACLA's Latin America and Empire Report*, VII, no. 1 (Jan., 1973).

46. Garcés, esp. pp. 15-19; Mauricio Solaún and Fernando Cepeda, "Alternative

When Allende first took office, nongovernmental representatives of the traditional elites were more prone than the political Right to try to dispel drastic reforms by seeking accommodation. For example, the Church, no longer strongly identified with the upper class, tried to play a mediating role, as it had with Aguirre Cerda in 1938-41 and with Alessandri in the 1920s. The SNA provided another prime example of a malleable posture toward the Popular Unity, one similar to its posture toward the Popular Front. The aristocratic president of the landowners' association gave early, selective cooperation to Allende. Through conciliation with the UP, he tried to subdue its rural reforms as well as landholder hostility. He assisted in the division of great estates and the expansion of relations with Cuba. The SNA, however, found neither the governing coalition nor the landowners at all reconcilable as they had been in the days of Aguirre Cerda. The UP expropriated and redistributed latifundia with startling speed, and in response, the SNA members ejected their peace-making president. The SNA joined other functionalist, *"gremial"* groups, the SOFOFA, the Confederation of Production and Commerce, and a welter of professional associations, in a concerted campaign to break the government. The SNA's former president himself abandoned flexibility in favor of membership in Fatherland and Liberty.[47]

The party opponents of Allende used their legislative majority to defeat nearly all measures introduced by the Popular Unity. Charges against and impeachment of cabinet ministers had recreated the instability and immobility of the Parliamentary Republic by the third year. On the eve of the coup d'etat in 1973, these attacks culminated in accusations against all of Allende's ministers. More to make the executive appear illegitimate than to safeguard democratic norms, legislators accused the administration of violations of the constitution. They also hurled charges of corruption and mismanagement. On its part, the Left retorted that the Congress was violating constitutional ethics and urged Allende to circumvent, replace, or close it, perhaps through a plebiscite. The institutional crisis mounted.[48]

In a thickening atmosphere of mutual paranoia and guile, both sides tried to discredit their opponents as handmaidens of foreign enemies. Conservative groups claimed that the UP was selling Chile out to international Marxism, especially the Cuban variety. In turn,

Strategies in Allende's Chile: On the Politics of Brinkmanship," *Land Tenure Center Special Report* (Madison, Wisc., 1973).

47. *La tragedia chilena: testimonios* (Buenos Aires, 1973), pp. 95-96; Patricio García F., ed., *Los gremios patronales* (Santiago, [1973?]); Barraclough.

48. Sanders, "The Process"; Paul E. Sigmund, "Seeing Allende through the Myths," *Worldview* (Apr., 1974), pp. 16-21; Eduardo Valle, *Allende, cronología* (Mexico, 1974).

the Socialists and Communists painted the Right as puppets of North American imperialism. Increasingly, both camps were trying to undermine each other before the court of military as well as civilian opinion.[49]

The battle between the Right and the Left converged on the centrist parties and social groups. The UP, somewhat like the Popular Front before it, argued that many in the middle classes were also disadvantaged by dependent capitalism and underdevelopment. The Left tried to win over the middle sectors, especially the less-prosperous segments, to build an electoral majority and to deny the opposition the social base for a military dictatorship, but attempts to cater to middle-class reformers caused alarm among left-wing Socialists. They remembered the concessions of the Popular Front and opposed accords with the Christian Democrats. Many PS leaders argued that the government should siphon off the middle- and lower-class followers of the PDC through sweeping reforms for those social groups, not through negotiations with the party chieftains. However, appeals to class interests failed to produce a majority for the UP. Consequently, Allende and the Communists continued to seek a *détente* with the PDC, or at least its left wing. By 1973, many of the middle classes and their political spokesmen were as resolutely set against compromise as were the more militant Socialists. The middle groups were reluctant to accept a subordinate role in a coalition and in an emerging society that challenged their security and values. The Popular Unity's venture in greater class exclusiveness may have kept the government more dedicated than past administrations to the momentum of fundamental reforms for the masses. It did not, however, keep the UP in office.[50]

The Popular Unity's Responses to the Siege by the Opposition

Allende circumvented the congressional blockade, especially in 1971, by intensifying the application of laws already on the books, for example in the area of agrarian reform. Like Aguirre Cerda decades before him, the president dusted off obscure legislation from the 1932

49. *Sepa*, (1973); Chile, Secretaria General de Gobierno, *Libro blanco del cambio de gobierno en Chile* (2nd ed., Santiago, 1973); Salvador Allende, *La conspiración contra Chile* (Buenos Aires, 1973).

50. On the Christian Democrats and other centrist (increasingly rightist) politics, see *La Prensa*, 1972-73; *La Tercera de la Hora*, 1970-73; *Las Últimas Noticias*, 1970-73; *Ercilla* (1970-73); *Qué Pasa* (1972-73); Radomiro Tomic, *Intervención de . . . en reunión del Partido Demócrata Cristiana el 7 de noviembre de 1973* (Mexico, 1974); Carlos Altamirano, *Decisión revolucionaria* (Santiago, 1973); Partido Socialista, *Boletín*, no. 1 (Mexico, Oct., 1974); *La tragedia*, esp. pp. 99-128; Sigmund, "Seeing," pp. 16-21; Laurence Birns, ed., *The End of Chilean Democracy* (New York, 1974), pp. 9-18.

Socialist Republic. This tactic allowed the UP to nationalize major sectors of the economy and to clamp down on consumer prices. Unlike Aguirre Cerda, Allende also tolerated direct action by workers and peasants to achieve their objectives—for instance, control of factories and lands—prior to deliberation and adjudication by the legal institutions, which increasingly joined the opposition parties in denouncing such changes. The Popular Unity's other main response to its legislative handicap was to work toward victory in the 1973 mid-term elections.[51]

While coping with the ever more unified Right and Center parties, the Allende coalition also prepared to defend itself in the event of paramilitary or military clashes. Although militias were probably less active than under Alessandri in the 1930s or the Popular Front, some of the UP supporters, as well as some of their opponents, armed and trained themselves. The hope lingered that both military and nonmilitary armed loyalists, combined with an uprising of the working class, could, as a last resort, protect the government. Nevertheless, the Popular Unity concentrated far more energy on the venerable tactics of multiparty politics than on any conversion to armed force. Allende himself relied far less on private cadres than on the faithfulness of top professional officers, who indeed squelched coup attempts until they hatched their own.

In addition to the threat of counterforce, the Popular Unity employed positive appeals to the military. The Ministry of Defense stayed in the hands of middle-class politicians and officers, often Masons and never Communists. Allende's own charm, diplomacy, and social affiliations wooed many officers for a time. Furthermore, the UP boasted of raising salaries and perquisites over those granted by the Frei administration. The jump in expenditures on the armed services in Allende's opening year, however, was followed by a decline in the next two. Worsening economic conditions eroded Allende's ability to satisfy multiple groups.[52]

The Marxists' attempt to court the regular military was two-pronged. First, they coaxed generals and admirals with benefits and personal favors. Second, they appealed to enlisted men with better treatment and exhortations to class loyalty. This dual approach was

51. Hobsbawm, pp. 23-32. For further information on the UP's strategies and leftist critiques of same, see *La Nación*, 1971–Sept., 1973; *El Clarín*, 1970–Sept., 1973; *Puro Chile*, 1971–Sept., 1973; *El Siglo*, 1970–Sept., 1973; *Última Hora*, 1970–Sept., 1973; *Nueva Estrategia* (1970); *Punto Final* (1969–Sept., 1973); *El Rebelde*, 1973; *La Aurora de Chile*, 1973; *De Frente*, 1973; *Tarea Urgente*, 1973; *Chile Hoy* (1972-73).

52. Carlos, pp. 255-56; *La tragedia*, p. 128; United States, Department of State, *World Military Expenditures and Arms Trade, 1963-1973* (Washington, D.C., 1975), pp. 26, 84.

another instance of contradictory Marxist efforts to work through the administrative hierarchy at the top while simultaneously trying to disrupt that hierarchy by fomenting independent action among the masses at the bottom. Leftist propaganda aimed at soldiers and sailors outside the chain of command fueled officers' fears of rebellion within their ranks, as did, for that matter, rightist propaganda. Appeals to the rank-and-file to disobey the conspiracies of conservative officers probably cost the Marxists more armed support than it gained, if there was ever much to be won. Although the Left's inducements were ultimately in vain, they did retain military adherence to the UP government for a surprisingly long time.

The best Popular Unity hope for winning over segments of the military probably lay with the Socialists, who had long nurtured relatively good relations with the armed services. As a highly nationalistic movement, they were more acceptable to the military than were the Communists. Even Altamirano, whose radicalism was anathema to many officers, tried to draw on that past friendliness now that the UP and its foes were in open competition for military sympathies. Altamirano pointed to the PS's support for improved incomes and conditions for the armed services, who were restless under the press of inflation. He also recalled Grove's connections with the men in uniform. The Right punctured such Socialist claims by noting that Grove's ghost had not been resurrected in decades and that he had left the PS when it began edging away from populist nationalism toward more doctrinaire Marxism. The Right also spotlighted the Socialists' identification with Latin American revolutionaries, who had long viewed the military as a central enemy. As it turned out, earlier bonds between the Socialists and sections of the armed forces had withered by the 1970s.[53]

Once again, the Marxist parties failed to coordinate institutionalization and mobilization. In the Popular Front, the Marxists gained access to the political upper echelons, but at the cost of putting a lid on worker organizations and programs. In the Popular Unity, they mobilized, or allowed the mobilization of, the workers behind massive social changes, but at the cost of being disbarred from government. The predicament of the "Chilean road to socialism" was to convert the party participation attained through popular-front politics into an instrument for structural reforms and real worker participation —ultimately command—in the Popular Unity. Under Allende, the working classes won unprecedented participation in the economy,

53. *El Clarín*, June 24, 1973; *La Tribuna*, June 27, 1973.

society, and politics, but not enough to enable them to make the major
national decisions or to perpetuate their new share of power.

During the UP's tenure, fresh forms of working-class activism and
organization proliferated, making it look as though traditional deference or resignation was finally disappearing. While frightening
the elites, this ferment also often disturbed the government and the
established parties and unions, especially the Communists. Populism
had proved to be a force which could be deflected or absorbed by
the traditional system, but it appeared that socialism might break the
bounds of political order. Many in the upper and middle classes, and
even privileged or non-Marxist sectors of the lower strata, feared an
end to zero-sum politics with them as the final losers. The long-
standing Chilean combination of ideological and clientelistic politics
encouraged stasis and had its drawbacks for all members. Nevertheless, it at least assured everyone of a portion, however unequal, of the
nation's scarce resources. By contrast, the mobilizations which seemed
to be undermining and overloading timeworn political patterns in the
early 1970s jeopardized the wealthy few, moderate reformers, and
even many organizations in the established Left.

Novel forms of worker militance reflected both competition within
the Left and autonomous efforts to break through the entrenched
party and bureaucratic network. Virtually an arm of the UP government, the CUTCH also preferred to mobilize the masses through
hierarchical organizations captained by official leaders. Such organizations multiplied under Allende, in the countryside, factories,
schools, and neighborhoods. For example, new bureaucratic appendages sprang up to distribute scarce commodities in working-class
communities, to oversee factories taken away from private owners,
and to organize local health care. Less manageable by state, party, and
union officials were seizures of the means of production and local
organizational efforts outside the UP machinery. Both in the countryside and in the cities, these more independent actions—sometimes of
dubious legality or even illegal—were often inspired by the MIR and
even left-wing members of the governing coalition. More significant,
they were frequently propelled by members of the working classes
themselves, which surpassed traditional Chilean notions of populist or
popular-front politics. Such independent expressions of class conflict
were seen by many as the symbol and substance of the deepest threat
to the old order. Most noteworthy were industrial "cordons" or belts.
They were created largely outside standard political structures as
loose but aggressive factory-zone federations of workers to meet local

problems of shortages, mobilization, and defense.[54] Although probably less spontaneous and weaker than the partisan press suggested, the
cordones represented a profound departure by segments of the urban
masses and thus imperiled clientelistic politics, as one of their leaders explained: "We do not want the cordons to be paternalized by
any government organism. We want them to be independent so
that they can make their own decisions, issued from the workers
themselves...."[55]

These sentiments were echoed by Socialist Secretary-General Altamirano. Without making crystal clear the more radical path to be
taken, he tirelessly prodded the UP from the left:[56]

> [We must deliver] power to the masses of peasants and workers....
> Only this mobilization, contrary to all bourgeois paternalism, will make
> the transformation [to socialism] viable.... Do not forget that the great
> enemy of revolution is reformism, and that reformism, cloaked in its
> paternalistic populism and in its merely redistributive economic dema-
> gogy, is a false, although possible, solution, not totally foreign to certain
> tendencies in the Left.... The parties of the Left have lived all their
> political lives accepting, without protests, the electoral, parliamentary,
> and bourgeois game.... the Chilean revolution will only be possible to
> the extent that the vanguards of the working class know how to revo-
> lutionize themselves....[57]

According to a French observer in the 1970s, the Chilean Socialists not
only swerved to the ideological left of their European counterparts but
also recruited more mixed support with a larger proletarian component. A rough estimate was that the PS's followers were about 50%
workers, 30% middle class and intellectuals, and 20% lower-middle
class.[58] By contrast, the Chilean Communists' secretary-general
claimed in 1973 that 76% of his party were workers, 14% peasants,

54. *Tarea Urgente*, 1973; *Chile Hoy*, esp. año II, nos. 60, 61 (Aug., 1973); Partido
Socialista, *Boletín*, no. 1 (Mexico, Oct., 1974), p. 2; Betty and James F. Petras, "Ballots
into Bullets: Epitaph for a Peaceful Revolution," *Ramparts*, XII, no. 4 (Nov., 1973),
pp. 21-28, 59-62; Landsberger and McDaniel.

55. *La tragedia*, p. 119.

56. Available evidence indicates that some arming of the PS took place, but it was
poorly planned and executed, intended far more to defend the government in case of a
coup than to launch a violent revolution; in a few cases, the armaments were reportedly
used to jockey for intraparty power rather than to prepare to confront the opposition.
Partido Socialista, *Boletín*, no. 1 (Mexico, Oct., 1974), esp. p. 4; Jobet, *El Partido Socialista
de Chile*, II, pp. 177-78, 182-89; Altamirano; Hugo Blanco et al., *La tragedia chilena*
(Buenos Aires, 1973).

57. Casanueva and Fernández, pp. 240-41.

58. Catherine Lamour, *Le pari chilien* (Paris, 1972), pp. 180-201; Jobet, *El Partido
Socialista de Chile*, II, pp. 174-82; Partido Socialista, *Estatutos...* (Santiago, 1972). Also
see Alain Labrousse, *L'experience chilienne* (Paris, 1972).

and 10% artisans, small merchants, and intellectuals.[59] The most significant feature of the Popular Unity may not have been how moderate and legalistic it was compared to more radical models such as Cuba, but how far-reaching the Allende government's reforms were within the context of democratic socialism. Within Latin American history, the changes advanced under the UP exceeded those under any other formally democratic government and almost all authoritarian ones. For that reason, Chilean socialism's survival would have been more astonishing than its demise.

Final Breakdown of the Chilean Political System, 1973

For both the government and the opposition, the 1973 congressional elections marked an apogee of conflict and testing. The conservative forces claimed that the UP could not be trusted to conduct fair elections, despite its preservation of full democratic freedoms. To insure tranquility, Allende maintained military personnel in his cabinet, where they had been serving to promote order since previous opposition strikes nearly brought Chile to a standstill in 1972. The Popular Unity's adversaries pressured the administration to reduce leftist mobilization and agitation. In the depths of darkening economic conditions, it was reasonable to expect the UP to suffer at least the typical mid-term losses from their prior presidential total, and the Right-Center coalition envisioned compiling a two-thirds majority, enough to depose Allende through impeachment by the Congress.

Instead, the UP shocked its opponents by increasing its 36% in 1970 to 44% in 1973. Over one-third of the national population voted, and the group now included illiterates and citizens between 18 and 21 years of age. Like Aguirre Cerda and unlike other presidents since 1941, Allende raised his mid-term congressional voter support 8% over his coalition's presidential tally. The UP gained everywhere, but slightly more among women than men. Still, however, the coalition's highest percentages came from male (48%) rather than female (39%) voters. At the provincial level, the Popular Unity outdistanced the PN-PDC alliance only in the four northernmost provinces and in Concepción. Returns from the provinces and selected *comunas* suggested that the UP still relied most on miner and urban worker–slum dweller areas but was making striking gains in peasant districts. Nevertheless, the government's percentage improved in some identi-

59. *La tragedia,* pp. 12-13.

fiably middle- to upper-class as well as working-class urban communities. Whatever the precise ecological or social composition of the UP's backing, it revealed a nation sorely divided. Polarization left all minor parties, including now the fractured Radicals, with trifling shares. For example, the Popular Socialist Union tapped less than 1% of the electorate. The Right, Christian Democrats, and Communists hovered around the same percentages they'd had in 1969. The Socialists improved from 12% to over 18%, their highest congressional peak since 1941.[60]

Because both sides claimed victory, the balloting of 1973 failed to resolve the political stalemate. Since the legal means to hobble a minority government bent on audacious reforms were nearly exhausted, the opposition accelerated its campaign to stamp the administration as illegitimate: for example, they charged electoral fraud. Brinkmanship on both sides again threatened to demolish the fading consensus over democratic procedures. Most important, the military, encouraged by many rightist leaders, began solidifying plans for a coup against Allende.[61]

From June through August of 1973, the battle between the government and the opposition escalated on three fronts. First, the fight between the executive and other political institutions increased its tempo. The president and the Congress were at loggerheads over state transferral of businesses and properties out of the private domain and over related procedural issues. The high courts and the bureaucracy, most vocally the Supreme Court and the national comptroller, joined the legislature in a chorus of criticism. Both sides swapped charges of illegality and immorality. Extreme right-wing elements suggested, as did some on the far Left, that the only remaining alternative was dictatorship by either the military or the Marxists. Some leaders of the PN and the PDC called for Allende's resignation.

60. See footnote #36 above for comments on the 1970 election and sources of *comuna* analyses. As a very limited indication of voter patterns in at least a few selected areas, it is worth noting that in the miner–worker–urban slum dweller districts of Arica, Tocopilla, Andacollo, Calera, Quinta Normal, San Miguel, Puente Alto, San Bernardo, San Antonio, Barrancas, La Granja, Cisterna, and Lota, the UP rose an average of roughly 6% from 1970 to 1973. At the same time, it rose an average of about 12% in the rural areas of Putaendo, La Cruz, Isla de Maipo, Pichidegua, Palmilla, Teno, Longaví, Coihueco, Lumaco, Santa Barbara, Los Alamos, Hualqui, and Achao. In the Santiago middle- to upper-class communities of Providencia, Nuñoa, and Las Condes, Allende's coalition increased 5% from 1970 to 1973, although it still scored well below its averages in the previously mentioned working-class and rural zones. Chile, Dirección del Registro Electoral, "Resultado elección ordinaria de diputados" (Santiago, 1973); Chile, Dirección del Registro Electoral, "Resultado elección ordinaria de senadores" (Santiago, 1973).

61. Birns, esp. pp. 60-65; *La tragedia,* esp. pp. 23-28; Chile, Secretaria.

A few openly vowed to "knock on the doors of the barracks" if he continued in office.[62]

The second front was an expansion of the quasi-corporatist, functionalist movement of property-owner, employer, and professional organizations which helped align the middle strata with the economic elites. Mobilization of these interest groups countered the leftist mobilization of the working classes. The mainly upper- and middle-class occupational *gremios* used their combined power to protest government economic policies and to undermine Allende by strangling the weak economy. In the last months of his government, a chain of strikes by truck owners, chauffeurs, professionals, and other functional organizations built to a crescendo. Middle-class women also demonstrated for Allende's abdication or removal. The College of Lawyers and other professional associations declared the president unfit to govern. In the first week of September, the Grand Master of the Chilean Masons, although Allende and three of his cabinet members belonged to the lodge, publicly announced his organization's opposition to Marxism and class conflict.[63]

The third front, established by the most extreme members of the opposition, consisted of conspiracies with sympathetic military officers and of sabotage and terrorism, at times replied to in kind by factions within or akin to the UP. A premature "pronouncement" by a Santiago tank corps at the end of June was foiled by the commanders of the regular armed forces. Neither the primary leaders of the National Party nor the Christian Democrats roundly condemned the aborted coup in public. In its aftermath, the UP still vacillated between the Socialists' insistence on accelerated worker conquests and the Communists' prescription for cautious consolidation to give respite from the opposition's bombardment. On the one hand, Allende reluctantly allowed most workers to keep the additional factories they had seized in defense against the coup attempt. On the other, he called for moderation and devotion to production by his supporters. At the urging of the Church and sectors of the military, he also began an eleventh-hour "dialogue among the deaf" with the Christian Democrats. Unceasing psychological warfare precluded compromise and created an atmosphere of violence. The impression grew that Chile, as the Communists had warned, was careening toward civil war.[64]

62. *La tragedia,* esp. pp. 24-179; *Punto Final* (July-Aug., 1973); *El Mercurio,* July-Sept., 1973; *La Segunda,* July-Aug., 1973; *La Tribuna,* July-Aug., 1973.

63. García, *Los gremios;* Petras and Petras, pp. 21-28, 59-62; *El Mercurio,* Aug.-Sept., 1973; *La Prensa,* Aug.-Sept., 1973.

64. Birns, pp. 9-18; Patricio García F., ed., *El tancazo de ese 29 de junio . . .* (Santiago, 1973).

Even under enormous pressures for de-escalation, expropriations and other direct actions by ostensibly independent worker cadres continued. This activism projected the image of mass participation achieving a momentum of its own and escaping institutional channels. Rampant mobilization battered the accommodative political arrangements of the past without going far enough to prepare the working classes for revolution or counterrevolution. However, the failure of the UP resulted at least as much from the destabilizing efforts of its domestic and foreign antagonists as from the errors or excesses of its supporters. Both sides were breaking the rules of the game. The economy and the government lacked the resources to assuage all competing demands. Accordingly, the opposition stiffened in defense of its share of national goods, services, and power, while the UP debated its next move.

In the impasse of the final months, the Communists proposed a slowdown in mobilization to master the crisis. They wanted to shore up the administration, existing reforms, and the economy. They stressed production over redistribution. The PC hoped to lessen the entrenchment of two diametrically opposed Chiles through negotiations with the Christian Democrats. By contrast, the more-leftist Socialists, mainly supported outside the coalition by the MIR, advocated increased mobilization and reforms. They contended that compromises would display weakness to their adversaries and betrayal to their supporters. Without recommending immediate armed struggle, many Socialists indicated that Allende's backers should be ready to fight rather than abandon their program as the perceived price of staying in office. At the end, disunity within the UP was so great that the PS appeared on the verge of leaving the administration or dividing. Allende wavered fatally between these defensive and offensive approaches but basically held to the more cautious Communist formula. He also retained the military in his cabinet, but that ploy served to neither diminish the crisis nor insure officer loyalty. The government never fully chose the traditional Chilean solution of bargaining with the moderate Center—which would have delayed socialism—or the new Chilean solution of swift social change through revolutionary use of bourgeois institutions—which, given the opposition's determination and strength, was straining the fragile democracy to the breaking point. In any case, by the end, formal democracy, though still intact, was not the most burning issue. Rather, so it seemed, the social order was at stake. Indeed, it is doubtful that any representative democracy anywhere could have withstood the forces rending Chile. Unwilling or unable to either abandon its quest toward socialism or jettison traditional political tools, Allende's coalition fell prey to opponents theoretically and physically capable of smashing the multiparty system. The existing evidence is that the president had prepared to broadcast, on the very day the military suddenly foreclosed any chances for a peaceful democratic solution, a call for an extraordinary plebiscite to resolve the standoff. When brinkmanship climaxed in bloodshed, it was the Right, not the Left, that scrapped any pretense of fundamental democratic processes. The Marxist dilemma between institutionalization and mobilization ended when the military terminated the Left's participation in both the halls of government and the streets.[65]

The End of Socialism and Populism, September, 1973

On September 11, 1973, President Allende died defending his government against one of the most brutal coups in Latin American history. In light of the disintegration of the economy (with inflation racing at over 1% per day), the extreme polarization of the society and the polity, the near paralysis of governing institutions, and the pressures from the UP's domestic and North American foes, the *golpe de estado* was not as surprising as was its ferocity. Perhaps the main reasons for the military's Draconian use of force were its fears of mounting lower-class militance and of the decline of its own institutional solidity and integrity. Lightning repression was a response to the actual and legendary mobilization powers of the Marxists and the workers, the existence or dread of armed resistance, and Allende's personal refusal to surrender. Apparently it was assumed that far greater firepower would be needed than, for example, in Brazil in 1964 to depoliticize Chile in 1973. In a society and institution unaccustomed to military rule, the Chilean armed forces instantly established their authority and unity through extraordinary measures. It may also have been partly because of its inexperience at intervening in and managing political pluralism that the Chilean military struck like an armed force at war, instead of merely a typical Latin American instrument to change chief executives. For that reason, in addition to its perception of the adversary's powers, the junta dealt with its opponents as enemies to be obliterated rather than as dissidents to be simply ousted and controlled. To an extent, the UP's tactic of warning against civil war to discourage physical confrontation backfired. Com-

65. Sigmund, "Seeing," p. 18; *La tragedia;* interviews with Socialist and Christian Democrat survivors of the coup, currently not for attribution; Mauricio Solaún and Michael A. Quinn, *Sinners and Heretics: The Politics of Military Intervention in Latin America* (Urbana, Ill., 1973).

bined with the Right's caricature of the "Marxist hordes," the civil war scenario provided one rationalization for seizing power savagely to an uneasy military determined to extirpate socialism and communism. It was, in part, a preemptive strike against a phantom red army.[66]

Causing the death of perhaps three thousand initially and an estimated five to ten thousand in the ensuing months, the military takeover produced a slaughter, not a civil war. The failure of the expected protracted battle to materialize was primarily due to the blitzkrieg and subsequent reign of terror by the armed forces, but also to the Popular Unity's lack of preparedness. Moreover, the military did not divide as the UP had hoped. Nevertheless, a few officers, as indicated by subsequent trials, apparently stood by the president even at the end. Except in rare cases, the military did not encounter any "popular army," parallel to the legal armed forces and ready for combat, which the opposition had alleged was being assembled under Allende as a challenge to the regular troops. Even if Popular Unity preparations had been more extensive, it would have proved very difficult to translate a basically electoral movement into an effective armed force. According to nearly all accounts, the resistance to the coup that did occur was uncoordinated, isolated, and futile, and it never approached the magnitude of a Spanish-style civil war predicted in the event of a final clash. Witnessing the demise of the Popular Unity, Peruvian guerrilla leader Hugo Blanco bitterly observed that it was true that most of the arms in Chile were in the hands of peasants and workers, but those peasants and workers were enrolled in the regular armed services; they obeyed the orders of their officers rather than appeals to class solidarity.[67]

Following the initial bloody struggles and the vast loss of life by Allende's scattered supporters, the military's decimation of the UP's established party and governmental leadership left the Marxist movement largely incapacitated. Further research into relations between the leftist parties and the workers may reveal to what extent populism, clientelism, and popular-front politics, along with class conflict, had served as motor forces of the UP. In many ways, Chilean

66. *New York Times,* Sept. 12-15, 1973; Birns, pp. 18-32; Chile, Secretaria; Fidel Castro and Beatriz Allende, *Homenaje a Salvador Allende* (Buenos Aires, 1973); Gabriel García Márquez, "The Death of Salvador Allende," *Harper's,* no. 1486 (Mar., 1974), pp. 46-53; Frederick M. Nunn, "New Thoughts on Military Intervention in Latin American Politics: The Chilean Case, 1973," *Journal of Latin American Studies,* VII (Nov., 1975), pp. 271-304. Although published too late to take into full account in this study, also worth consulting is Frederick M. Nunn, *The Military in Chilean History: Essays on Civil-Military Relations, 1810-1973* (Albuquerque, N.M., 1976).

67. Blanco, pp. 29-54; Tomic, pp. 5-9; Birns, pp. 18-70; *La Opinión* (Buenos Aires) Nov., 1973–1974, for example see Mar. 29, 1974.

socialism, despite major innovations, undoubtedly remained riveted to the multiparty practices of the past.[68]

Once in power, the junta and its president, Army General Augusto Pinochet Ugarte, dismantled all the mechanisms of democracy and mass mobilization. As in 1924-25, though far more decisively now, the military had come in to change the system. The armed forces blamed especially the Left but also all the political developments of the last forty years for what they saw as excessive "politicization" of society and themselves. Chile's new rulers outlawed the UP parties, "recessed" all others, closed Congress, suppressed unions, silenced the leftist press, crushed *cordones,* purged the bureaucracy and education, packed concentration camps with suspected Allende sympathizers, and placed all facets of national life under military supervision. Nevertheless, the partisan Supreme Court, which had accused the UP government of illegalities, recognized the dictatorship as a legitimate regime. The *gremialista* groups, such as the SNA, the SOFOFA, and the Confederation of Production and Commerce, supported the junta, though they could not control all its decisions. They backed its efforts to supplant mass mobilization with corporatist demobilization. The oft-repeated themes of the disaffected Right—functionalism, decentralization, aristocratic nationalism, morality, efficiency, opposition to party politics, authoritarianism, anticommunism, and neoorthodox capitalism —became the junta's creed. The carnage of September, 1973, did not deliver power to the Christian Democrats or middle-class civilians but rather to aloof military dictators, relying mainly on their own advice or that of conservative elites. The junta turned back many of the supposedly irreversible reforms of the Allende years. For example, they restored most factories and some land to their former owners. U.S. aid increased, and the copper companies received compensation. Foreign investment was encouraged by Pinochet, but the response was disappointing in the unfavorable international economic climate of the 1970s. Income distribution became more regressive, and unemployment soared. Although production rose, copper prices tumbled and inflation continued at world-record levels. In the first years of the junta's efforts at permanent "national reconstruction," Chile's future looked bleak.[69]

68. Blanco; Manuel Mejido, *Esto pasó en Chile* (Mexico, 1974); J. Posada, *Chile: conclusiones del golpe military y la resistencia del proletariado* (Buenos Aires, 1974); Les Evans, ed., *Disaster in Chile: Allende's Strategy and Why It Failed* (New York, 1974).

69. *La Opinión* (Buenos Aires), Feb.-Mar., 1974; Bicheno; Chile, La Junta de Gobierno, *Declaración de principios del gobierno de Chile* (Santiago, 1974); Fuerzas Armadas y Carabineros, *Septiembre de 1973: los cien combates de una batalla* (Santiago, 1974); Augusto Pinochet Ugarte, *Un año de construcción* (Santiago, 1974); *Algunos fundamentos de la intervención militar en Chile, septiembre, 1973* (2nd ed., Santiago, 1974); Chile,

Immediately after the coup, it still appeared that Chile, given the lengthy and intensive politicization of the working classes, might be ripe for social revolution. Neither tradition, geography, nor prevailing conditions, however, were conducive to a prompt counteroffensive from the Left. The Marxists were probably even less likely to mount a mass army under the junta's repression than they had been when they controlled the presidency. The coup wreaked havoc on the always undisciplined and vulnerable Socialist Party. A majority of its regional organizations were destroyed. The coup also injured and drove underground the more tightly organized and therefore less damaged Communists, as well as the MIR and other Allende sympathizers. The military exterminated, jailed, tortured, or exiled thousands of leftist leaders and followers. Although the peaceful road to socialism had been blocked by tanks, it was not surprising that there were only isolated, infrequent reports of armed resistance during the first years of the military's state of siege against the Left and labor.[70]

Following their defeat, the Chilean Marxists made the formation of a broad, antijunta front, rather than guerrilla warfare, their first priority. Even the more leftist MIR reluctantly joined the front. At least publicly, the Popular Unity members, especially the Communists, talked about the need to increase the political liberty, consciousness, and organization of the masses before more revolutionary methods could be adopted. Once more, the Marxist parties encountered problems of scope and maintenance with their coalition. All agreed that sectors of the Christian Democrats, also sometimes persecuted by the junta, had to be attached to the front, but the left wing of the coalition, notably many Socialists and the MIR, worried that too eclectic an alliance would subordinate Marxist goals to political expediency. The Communists were inclined to postpone thorny ideological and strategic debates in the interest of the more urgent need to isolate and undermine the dictatorship, but in the opening years of the underground and exiled resistance movement the Marxists had grave problems winning over many Christian Democrats, smoothing over their own personal and doctrinal differences, and challenging the junta.[71]

Secretaria; *Latin America*, (1973-75); Non-Intervention in Chile, *Chile Newsletter*, (1973-74).

70. Blanco, pp. 29-33; *La Opinión* (Buenos Aires), Jan. 8, Feb. 19, and Feb. 22, 1974.

71. *Chile en la Resistencia* (Mexico, 1974-75); *Chile Informativo Internacional* (Buenos Aires, 1974); Non-Intervention in Chile, *Chile Newsletter* (1973-74). Birns, pp. 93-106; Partido Socialista, *Boletín*, no. 1 (Mexico, 1974); Partido Socialista, *Conclusiones del torneo partidario del Partido Socialista chileno realizado en la Habana, Cuba* (Cuba, 1974).

Conclusions on the Failure of Chilean Socialism

The Chilean disaster of 1973 was a tragedy of classic proportions. Within the context of the forces arrayed against them, the UP and Allende were protagonists and victims of their own dilemma and distress. Their anguish issued from the historical record of Chilean socialism, which, from the 1930s into the 1970s, revealed significant continuities. Democratic socialism as well as populism proved unsuccessful.

For the Marxists, the contradiction of using the evolutionary institutions of a formal democracy in a highly dependent capitalist system to pursue a theoretically revolutionary ideology aimed at the ultimate replacement of that system was never resolved. It could be argued that the Socialists and Communists might have been more successful in both 1938 and 1970 if they had been more radical in their means or more moderate in their ends. In light of the history of Chilean politics, the realistic options, and the context of the Allende government, however, it was probably impossible for the UP either to switch to more violent means or to abandon socialism as its goal. The radical means that might have led on to socialism, for instance armed revolution or accelerated factory seizures, were not very live options, especially by September, 1973. Conversely, the more moderate means that might have kept the Popular Unity in office until 1976 would not, even after the heady first year, have led to full-blown socialism. Over four decades, the Marxists, particularly the Socialists, had come too far, electorally and ideologically, to sacrifice their *raison d'être*. In all probability, means and ends were simply and ultimately irreconcilable. In large part, the significance of the socialist venture lay in the challenge to work through their historic dilemma between means and ends. It was the challenge to be "revolutionary" in an intrinsically Chilean way. For whatever length of time, that remained a challenge for the future, even though the coup's banishment of Chilean socialism also broke the peculiarly hopeful but frustrating political system in which that movement thrived.

A fundamental tragedy in Chile was that the very processes of modernization which socialism and populism had earlier responded to and helped promote later obstructed their political success. Prior to World War I, in a less articulated, literate, and urban society, many in the lower and even middle classes were politically ignored at relatively low cost to government authority. By the twenties and thirties, the price of continued exclusion—for example strikes, protests, and radical ideologies—appeared greater than the dangers of gradual incorporation of the most militant urban groups. Therefore, populism, even infused with Marxism, arose in Latin America as a widespread and coherent response to the initial acceleration of industrialization, social differentiation, and pressures from the middle and working classes. Populists reflected and fueled those pressures by promising simultaneous welfare measures and protected industrial growth.[72]

From the 1930s into the 1940s in Chile, populism's accommodationist, integrationist strategy was tenable. It did not require direct assaults on domestic capitalists, latifundia, or the vital foreign sector. For a time, populist import-substituting industrialization was able, in varying degrees, to pacify manufacturers with protection and credit, agriculturalists with expanding urban markets and restrictions on peasant organization, the middle classes and the military with state growth and nationalism, and the more skilled urban workers with consumer, welfare, and union benefits superior to those accorded other lower-class groups. These compromises postponed any showdown over scarce resources as long as the relatively easy stage of replacing consumer goods from abroad lasted. Politically, institutionalization stayed well ahead of mobilization. By failing to confront established elites or dependency on the unreliable, foreign-dominated export sector, however, popular-front politics left obstacles to later development intact.

Once in office, populist movements downplayed social welfare in favor of industrialization because that pleased part of their constituency without alarming powerful vested interests. From the 1920s through the 1940s, Chilean reformers failed to deliver on most campaign promises to the underprivileged, largely because of the rules of the political game. Those "rules" permitted reformist coalitions to take office but not to overthrow established elites or carry out significant redistributive measures for the workers. Populist mixtures of social classes and program planks allowed politicians great latitude in shifting from leftist campaign behavior to conservative administrative behavior. This gap between rhetoric on the hustings and action in office grew as those dominating electoral resources and those dominating other levers of power became separate groups. To reach office in the period after World War I, it became increasingly necessary to appeal to the workers. However, to function effectively and survive once in office, it remained necessary to satisfy the controllers of the major means of production, distribution, communication, and coercion.

72. This entire conclusion draws heavily on the analyses of Guillermo A. O'Donnell, *Modernization and Bureaucratic-Authoritarianism: Studies in South American Politics* (Berkeley, Calif., 1973), esp. pp. 55-78.

From World War II into the 1950s, the possibilities of such populist approaches dimmed. Import-substituting industrialization began running into bottlenecks. This led to relative stagnation, spiraling inflation, and continued reliance on fluctuations in the international mineral and credit markets. At the same time, the proliferation of urban dwellers and politically relevant actors, which had given birth to populism, continued and soon outstripped the economy's capacity for absorption. Added to the demands raised and frustrated by reformers earlier were expectations from peasants and rural-urban migrants. Mobilization began outdistancing institutionalization. In a zero-sum game played out in an economy of scarcity, populism lost its capacity to reconcile diverging class interests. Instead, it came to be seen as an impediment to noninflationary economic growth. As a result, populist coalitions among industrializers, the middle classes, and urbanized workers unraveled. Politicians started considering ways to reduce the load on the overburdened government. By the end of the 1940s, this approach began surfacing in González Videla's exclusion of peasants and Communists as well as in the Marxists' rising determination to dislodge the upper classes. Although a populist campaign style was revived at times, as under Carlos Ibáñez in 1952, its popularity subsided, while broad coalitions and integrative programs became less sustainable.

From the 1950s to the 1960s, unsatisfactory economic growth, chronic inflation, mushrooming pressures from the socially mobilized lower classes, and competitive bidding on the left continued. In response, President Frei finally began implementing many of the social reforms promised since World War I. His attempts at integrative development through unprecedented redress of the balance between rich and poor only mildly encroached on domestic and foreign elites. Nevertheless, in a fragile and unexpansive economy those overdue reforms were enough to erode upper-class tolerance while further raising lower-class expectations.

Allende then inherited the discontent of decades as well as the domestic and international constraints faced by previous reformers. Partly because of the growth in social mobilization since World War II, the Marxists had radicalized. They appealed more exclusively to the working classes, rejected alliances behind centrist reformers, and provided their followers with a more structured, programmatic movement dedicated to development through conflict with the upper class and foreign capital. However, the Socialists and Communists, like all politicians, did not carry their new tactics to the point of totally abandoning the practices learned through years of political socialization. Not surprisingly, established patterns, as well as innovations, guided their behavior. Whether mainly out of predilection or necessity, Allende pursued his radical redistributive policies within most of the confines set by the existing system, and the very political system which allowed his minority coalition to reach office and institute reforms placed limits on progress toward its vision of socialism. Yet, far more than the Christian Democrats before it, the UP broke the implicit "rules of the game" by pushing through sweeping reforms to contend with the social pluralism which years of modernization and populist policies had nurtured. Despite cultural continuities, paternalism seemed to be losing its grip, and sectors of the lower classes became more assertive than ever in the past. As in much of Latin America and the Third World, multiplying claims on socioeconomic benefits and political participation, rising population pressures, growing resource scarcities, galloping inflation, galling dependence on an unstable foreign sector, and uncontrollable international economic difficulties rendered the maintenance of political pluralism and formal democracy extremely precarious. In a far more developed economy, more needs and demands might have been met simultaneously. Instead, in an ideologically charged atmosphere Chile underwent rapid social and political polarization, which potentially threatened reformers as well as reactionaries. Important groups on both the Left and the Right came to favor the expulsion or drastic curtailment of their opponents in the political arena. However, neither populism nor democratic socialism ever won over all the urban and rural workers or prepared them to oust the native and foreign elites. Instead, the potential of the socialist movement for elevating the poor at the expense of most of the upper and middle classes convinced besieged elites that suppression was preferable to accommodation. For the upper class and for large segments of the middle strata, the perceived price of including the masses—for example wages, inflation, and property transfers, not to mention the ultimate possibility of radical social displacement—now appeared greater than the risks of overt conflict. If an ostensibly prerevolutionary situation made it appear that the standoff was going to end, the relatively privileged groups did not intend to be the losers.

While moving a significant distance beyond earlier populist styles, coalitions, and policies, the Marxists made great strides through democratic socialism. At the same time, they maintained and approached, but never fully defined or acted upon, their more revolutionary socialist aspirations. Resolving the dilemma between means and ends more easily, the domestic and foreign elites opted decisively for economic growth for themselves over social gains for those beneath. With apparently widespread middle-class backing, they created the conditions for and supported a military takeover which ejected the lower classes from active participation. Indeed, the armed forces initially seemed determined to shove almost everyone off the crowded political stage. Despite the sophisticated, high levels of politicization and organization achieved over great obstacles by Chilean leftists and workers, the Right and the military were willing and able to eliminate them, even at extraordinarily severe social-political costs. By 1973, the level of social and political mobilization reached by the masses since the 1930s was sufficient to invite extreme oppression but insufficient to prevent it, at least for the moment. Over the course of more than four decades, Chile's difficult journey from attempts at democratic, populist inclusion of the workers to efforts at authoritarian, corporatist exclusion took a more radical turn toward socialism along the way than anywhere else in South America. Whether a conservative coercive system can long endure in an under-developed nation as intensely politicized as Chile—and what alternatives may succeed the junta—will reveal still more about the final historical fruits of populism and socialism.

Appendix A

Methodological Note on the Construction of the *Comuna* Tables

The purpose of the *comuna* tables is merely to trace trends among the Socialists in the selected districts from the benchmark election of 1932 into the 1940s. The results will be used only in conjunction with manifold other sources to draw limited conclusions about social-political trends. The national censuses did not satisfactorily define their categories or criteria, and marginal cases (e.g., 50-60% "urban") would probably be unreliable examples of voting patterns in particular coherent settings. In Tables 7 and 8, only those *comunas* with consistent characteristics in the era and with reliable voting data from the 1920s to the 1930s were used to compare broad electoral tendencies over time. The object of the *comuna* data is to probe more deeply voting patterns discerned at the regional and provincial levels, where data are very gross and give little clue to internal variation. For example, if it were discovered that Grove in 1932 ran very poorly in the most highly urbanized communities of Chile and within the central urban provinces actually scored best in the most rural districts, then the patterns suggested by the provincial and regional returns would be cast in doubt; of course the opposite *comuna* findings would tend to reinforce the trends perceived in larger, more mixed voting units.

Although useful in these ways and for showing that the particular selected *comunas* had certain voting characteristics, none of the *comuna* tables establish firm national trends through all degrees of urban and rural areas. Not a scientific sample or set of correlations, all these tables merely represent a partial measure of voting patterns just in these most clearly identifiable ecological units. Given the mixed nature of most of the *comunas* and the deficiencies of much of the census and electoral data over the time period studied, these limited community results were only developed to supplement, buttress, or contradict other information on social-political tendencies extracted from national, regional, and provincial electoral returns, from party leadership and membership data, and from qualitative contemporary observations. As in Tables 10 and 15 on party leaders, the primary goal was to discover possible broad trends rather than precise, subtle characteristics, with the heaviest emphasis always on the Socialists. Although other *comunas* analyzed in other ways would generate different percentages, there is substantial evidence from these tables and abundant corroborative materials that the fundamental conclusions reached in the text—such as the urban orientation of the newborn Socialists—will stand. Moreover, those conclusions are quite cautious, as all interpretations of the data presented here should be. For example, it is conceivable that communities with extreme social characteristics, such as 100% urban, might vote quite differently from those farther down the scale, say 70% urban.

To measure only the impact of extremely urban or rural settings on community voting habits, only those thirteen communities with reliable data consistently comparable in the period and ranked as 75-100% "urban" by the 1930 census, a degree of urbanization far above the national figure of 49% in 1930, were used in Tables 7 and 8 to calculate and compare average voting percentages for those particular areas. The thirteen *comunas* which met those criteria included Tocopilla (89% urban) (in the Great North province of Antofagasta), Valparaíso (97%), Viña del Mar (94%), Quilpué (78%), Quillota (75%) (all four in the Urban Center provinces of Aconcagua-Valparaíso), Providencia (84%), San Miguel (82%), Nuñoa (78%) (all three in the Urban Center province of Santiago), Chillán (76%) (in the South Center province of Ñuble), Concepción (99%), Talcahuano (87%), Lota (90%) (all three in the Frontier province of Concepción), and Valdivia (79%) (in the Lakes province of Valdivia). For contrast, all the comparable nearly totally rural (90-100%) *comunas* with usable electoral returns across time were selected out in the same manner. The following twenty-nine communities were all ranked 100% "rural" except where otherwise noted in parentheses: El Tránsito, Freirina (both in the Small North province of Atacama), La Higuera, Paihuano, Los Vilos (in the Small North province of Coquimbo), Petorca, Catemu, Panquehue (in the Urban Center provinces of Aconcagua-Valparaíso), Tiltil, Colina, Lampa, Isla de Maipo (in Santiago), Olívar, Pichilemu (in the North Center province of Colchagua), Teno (91%), Vichuquén (in the North Center province of Curicó),

Pencahue (in the North Center province of Talca), Yerbas Buenas (in the South Center province of Maule), San Fabián, San Nicolás, Pinto (in the South Center province of Ñuble), Florida (in the Frontier province of Concepción), Santa Fe, Quilleco, Quilaco (in the Frontier province of Bío-Bío), San José de la Mariquina (93%), San Pablo (in the Lakes provinces of Valdivia-Osorno), Maullín (93%), and Achao (in the Lakes provinces of Llanquihue-Chiloé). Chile, Dirección General de Estadística, *Resultados del X censo de la población* (3 vols., Santiago, 1931), I, pp. 40-47, 51-55; Robert McCaa, comp., *Chile. XI censo de población (1940)* (Santiago, n.d.), esp. pp. 76-319; Oscar Álvarez Andrews, *Historia del desarrollo industrial de Chile* (Santiago, 1936), p. 234.

For Table 9 and all the subsequent ones using *comuna* types selected mainly by occupational profiles, if the limited community data showed very low votes for Socialist candidates in the most solidly working-class *comunas* in Chile, that would not say anything conclusive about the national voting patterns among workers, but it would certainly raise doubts about PS claims of vast worker support. Conversely, a very high Socialist vote in those same areas would show that at least in those selected *comunas* the claim of strong support in working-class districts had validity, as already more indirectly indicated by regional and provincial data, not to mention qualitative observations, leadership backgrounds, membership information, trade union affiliations, and other evidence.

For the era, it is impossible to isolate relatively pure *comunas* by class composition. The dearth of sharp, consistent measures of occupation and class for *comunas* that span all the elections from the 1920s through the 1940s, the impurities in the census categories and data, and even the widespread use of bribes in the elections discouraged the use of highly sophisticated manipulations and correlations. Although the 1940 census contained *comuna* data susceptible to more elaborate analysis, adequate materials did not exist to do the same for the other periods in the study. Therefore, only those *comunas* comparable over time with the most graphic possible social characteristics and differences (e.g., 100% urban vs. 100% rural) have been used here to at least derive some partial refutations or corroborations of larger political trends. Realizing inherent ecological fallacies and difficulties, these categories of selected types of *comunas* will be used to calculate average electoral percentages to provide explicitly limited insights into voting behavior in those particular communities. The emphasis will be on widely divergent voting trends rather than marginal differences.

Comparable selective *comuna* data, instead of wider national samples subjected to quantification techniques of correlation and regression analysis, have been used to study Chilean voting patterns in similar ways by other scholars. See Ricardo Cruz-Coke, *Geografía electoral de Chile* (Santiago, 1952), pp. 78-82; Hugo Zemelman Merino, "Problemas ideológicos de la izquierda," *Arauco,* no. 58 (Nov., 1964), pp. 50-60; Federico G. Gil and Charles J. Parrish, *The Chilean Presidential Election of September 4, 1964* (Washington, D.C., 1965), pp. 47-48; James Petras and Robert J. Alexander, "Two Views of Allende's Victory," *New Politics,* VIII, no. 4 (Fall, 1970), pp. 72-81.

To get at least some indication over time of the social appeals of political alternatives, the tables here use *comuna* types which have been selected by combining 1930 and 1940 census materials and by combing contemporary observations on the character of various communities. Throughout the period, newspaper comments on the character of *comunas,* especially in Santiago and the mining zones, helped confirm the selections. For example see *Bandera Roja,* Dec. 4 and Dec. 16, 1931; *El Mercurio,* Nov. 2, 1932; *Claridad,* Apr. 4-5, 1938; *La Nación,* Apr. 16, 1938. Some characterizations of these communities were also found in reports from the U.S. Embassy; see U.S., Dept. of State Archives, Santiago, Oct. 7, 1931, 825.00/702. Then these unavoidably rough social definitions of *comunas* and their voting proclivities were further checked against a wide variety of narrative and secondary accounts, provincial data, and other ecological voting studies for the 1940s, '50s, and '60s. For example, especially on mining communities, see Humberto Fuenzalida et al., *Chile* (Buenos Aires, 1946), particularly pp. 30-68, 180-81, 299-311.

The category of *comunas* most likely to reveal electoral preferences in selected middle- to upper-class areas is disappointingly small because of the difficulty of safely isolating such districts. Of course Grove's receiving higher than average voting percentages in these few *comunas* in 1932 does not establish how the middle to upper classes voted nationwide or even what proportion of them in those selected districts cast Socialist ballots; all it shows is Grove's ability to attract significant electoral support in these unusually non–working-class zones, thus lending credence to the widespread observation that the Socialist banner was rallying social sectors above the proletariat. This method, with all its limitations, is far preferable to more impressionistic attempts to discuss the social composition of political movements. In all Chile, only three *comunas,* all in the Urban Center, could be confidently selected for the first category based on: (1) according to the exceptionally useful though imprecise 1940 occupational census, a percentage of manual workers (a relatively reliable census classification) in the *comuna's* active male population well below the national figure of 63%, and conversely a relatively high percentage of white-collar employees (compared to the national 13%) and of a very mixed group of employers and self-employed (compared to the national 24%); (2) over 75% urban in 1930 and 1940; (3) crude indications from the 1930 census that these were indeed likely centers of the middle to upper classes, especially provincial data referred to in the text showing Santiago and Aconcagua-Valparaíso to be the homes of the urban elites and community data showing that these three *comunas* had the highest percentage in the nation of private automobiles to total population in 1930 (when the national number of private automobiles was equivalent to 0.4% of the total population); and (4) contemporary commentators agreeing that these *comunas* represented the epitome of higher-class residential zones throughout the era. These three *comunas* were:

	1930 Urban	1930 Autos	1940 Urban	1940 Workers
Urban Center				
Aconcagua				
Viña del Mar	93%	1.8%	96%	58%
Santiago				
Providencia	84	2.6	100	39
Nuñoa	78	1.9	92	49

The category of industrial-worker *comunas* is equally small, partly because industry at the time was very concentrated geographically. For 1932 this group includes the only three communities which had: (1) census figures showing them over 70% urban in both 1930 and 1940; (2) a proportion of private automobiles to population in 1930 well beneath that of the three middle- to upper-class *comunas;* (3) a 1940 percentage of workers out of the *comuna's* total active male population at least equal to the national worker share of 63%; (4) at least 30% of those workers in each community occupied in manufacturing (compared to 17% nationally in 1940); (5) the combined percentage in construction (3% nationally) and manufacturing equal to 40% or more (compared to 20% nationally) of the *comuna's* worker population; and (6) confirmation from contemporary observers, often politicians, that these were working-class areas. These three comunas used in Table 9 were:

	1930 Urban	1930 Autos	1940 Urban	1940 Worker	1940 Mfg.	1940 Constr.
Urban Center						
Santiago						
San Miguel	82%	0.7%	97%	63%	47%	20%
Quinta Normal	100	0.2	100	67	44	18
Renca	71	0.2	81	71	30	18

More easily selected and more numerous than these two urban categories for Table 9 were fourteen mining *comunas* clearly designated by 1940 census materials and by earlier and later descriptive accounts with: (1) over 70% of their active population considered workers and (2) over 65% (compared to 5% nationally) occupied in extractive industries. They represented all the provinces recognized in the 1930 census and elsewhere as major mining zones, all the most famous mines, and the main types of mining in Chile:

	1940 Worker	1940 Extractive
Great North		
Tarapacá		
General Lagos	72%	65%
Huara	75	85
Pozo Almonte	80	82
Antofagasta		
Toco	87	84
Calama	76	71
Sierra Gorda	84	89
Small North		
Atacama		
Chañaral	81	73
Freirina	86	79
Coquimbo		
La Higuera	78	75
Andacollo	83	82
North Center		
O'Higgins		
Machalí	82	74
Frontier		
Concepción		
Coronel	81	68
Lota	87	80

	1940 Worker	1940 Extractive
Arauco		
Curanilahue	83	68

In 1932 Grove and Lafertte scored fairly evenly in the main nitrate *comuna* (Pozo Almonte) for which electoral results were available; in the three main copper areas of Calama (home of the famous Chuquicamata mine), Chañaral (the Potrerillos mine), and Machalí (El Teniente), Grove's average vote was 10.4% to 0.4% for Lafertte; in the three famous coal communities of Coronel, Lota, and Curanilahue, Grove took 15.0% and Lafertte 9.5%.

Nineteen *comunas,* which only partially overlapped with the general "rural" category used earlier in Tables 7 and 8, were placed in the relatively solid column of peasant zones for Table 9 as a result of: (1) at least 60% rural in both the 1930 and 1940 censuses; (2) at least 70% of their 1940 active population listed as workers; and (3) at least 80% working in agriculture (compared to 35% nationally), again substantiated as much as possible by earlier information for the twenties and thirties, by the absence of any contradictory indications at any level, and, to a much lesser extent, by other primary and secondary accounts:

	1930 Rural	1940 Rural	1940 Worker	1940 Agriculture
Urban Center				
Aconcagua				
Panquehue	100%	100%	89%	90%
Calle Larga	71	86	77	92
Santiago				
Quilicura	100	79	79	87
Colina	100	88	87	86
Curacaví	84	77	80	85
Isla de Maipo	100	60	73	84
Melipilla	67	69	79	86
North Center				
O'Higgins				
Requínoa	85	86	84	85
Colchagua				
Chimbarongo	77	72	78	93
Nancagua	71	84	75	89
Curicó				
Teno	75	87	79	94

	1930 Rural	1940 Rural	1940 Worker	1940 Agriculture
Talca				
San Clemente	87	88	82	94
Pencahue	100	95	71	90
South Center				
Linares				
Yerbas Buenas	100	93	70	96
Ñuble				
San Fabián	100	92	73	96
San Nicolás	100	96	71	94
Coihueco	89	90	71	94
Frontier				
Bío-Bío				
Quilaco	100	92	78	96
Lakes				
Valdivia				
San Pablo	100	88	75	90

Not surprisingly, most of the *comunas* fitting the "peasant" criteria turned up in the three central regions of traditional latifundia.

For 1932, usable voting returns were found and used for all three of the middle- to upper-class *comunas,* all three of those for industrial laborers, ten of the fourteen mining areas (General Lagos, Toco, Sierra Gorda, and Andacollo, mainly nitrate zones, had to be omitted), and all but one (Quilicura) of the peasant communities. The major sources used to select and analyze these *comunas* included Chile, Dirección General de Estadística, *Resultados del X censo,* I, esp. pp. 40-47, 51-55; Chile, Dirección General de Estadística, *Sinopsis geográfico-estadística de la República de Chile* (Santiago, 1933); Chile, *Geografía descriptiva de la vista panorámica en la exposición histórico-cultural del progreso de Chile* (Santiago, 1934); Álvarez Andrews, *Historia;* McCaa, esp. pp. 76-319; Karl H. Brunner, *Santiago de Chile* (Santiago, 1932), pp. 9-17, 85-119; newspapers, esp. *El Mercurio,* for example Oct. 21, 1932; Armand Mattelart,*Manual de análisis demográfico* (Santiago, 1964); Mattei Dogan and Stein Rokkan, eds., *Quantitative Ecological Analysis in the Social Sciences* (Cambridge, Mass., 1969).

All the subsequent tables on *comunas* in this book were constructed in the same way, for the same reasons, from the same basic sources, with the same criteria, and with the same virtues and drawbacks. Beginning with Table 13, the fundamental source for the *comuna* types used to analyze all the elections from 1938 through the 1940s

was McCaa, again supplemented by other earlier and later information on community characteristics. All the electoral data were taken
from official returns. All twenty-two of the communities ranked as
75-100% urban by the 1940 census were used for the "urban" *comunas*
from 1938 through the 1940s (Table 13 onward). The following list of
those *comunas* notes their urban percentage in parentheses; an asterisk
signifies that a *comuna* was also used in Tables 7 and 8 for 1932:
Iquique (97%) (in the Great North province of Tarapacá), Tocopilla*
(89%), Antofagasta (96%) (both in the Great North province of Antofagasta), Copiapó (78%) (in the Small North province of Atacama),
Coquimbo (82%) (in the Small North province of Coquimbo), Los
Andes (78%), Valparaíso* (97%), Viña del Mar* (96%) (in the Urban
Center provinces of Aconcagua-Valparaíso), Conchalí (92%), Providencia* (100%), Nuñoa* (92%), San Miguel* (97%), Quinta Normal
(omitted from the 1932 urban table because the 1920 electoral data
did not permit a comparison) (100%), Renca (81%), Cisterna (89%)
(in the Urban Center province of Santiago), Rancagua (81%) (in the
North Center province of O'Higgins), Talca (89%) (in the North
Center province of Talca), Chillán* (75%) (in the South Center province of Ñuble), Talcahuano* (89%), Concepción* (97%), Lota* (90%)
(in the Frontier province of Concepción), and Puerto Natales (86%)
(in the Channels province of Magallanes). Using the same percentage
criteria as in 1932 also produced a somewhat different list of rural
comunas due to changing patterns of urbanization. The twenty-five
communities used from the 1938 election through the 1940s (Table 13
onward) because of their ranking in the 1940 census as 90-100%
"rural" were General Lagos (100%), Pozo Almonte (96%) (in the Great
North province of Tarapacá), Sierra Gorda (96%) (in the Great North
province of Antofagasta), La Higuera* (94%) (in the Small North
province of Coquimbo), Panquehue* (100%), Catemu* (95%) (in the
Urban Center provinces of Aconcagua-Valparaíso), Florida (100%),
Pirque (100%) (in the Urban Center province of Santiago), Machalí
(91%) (in the North Center province of O'Higgins), Vichuquén*
(90%) (in the North Center province of Curicó), Pencahue* (95%) (in
the North Center province of Talca), Yerbas Buenas* (93%) (in the
South Center province of Linares), San Fabián* (92%), San Nicolás*
(96%), Coihueco (90%) (in the South Center province of Ñuble),
Florida* (97%) (in the Frontier province of Concepción), Quilleco*
(92%), Quilaco* (92%) (in the Frontier province of Bío-Bío), Lanco
(90%), Los Lagos (91%), Puerto Octay (90%) (in the Lakes province
of Valdivia), Fresia (95%), Maullín* (91%) (in the Lakes province of
Llanquihue), Quellón (95%), and Achao* (96%) (in the Lakes province of Chiloé).

As mentioned in the text, the three middle- to upper-class *comunas* remained the same selections from 1932 through the 1940s. In Table 14, three more industrial worker *comunas* were added to those used in Chapter 4 (Table 9) for all the electoral analyses from 1938 through the 1940s. These three were added because their census ranking shifted from a majority of their population being rural in 1930 to a majority being urban in 1940 and because the percentages of their active male populations in the working class and in industrial activities were so high. These three additional industrial-worker communities were Puente Alto, Tomé, and Corral.

	1930 Urban	1940 Urban	1940 Worker	1940 Mfg.	1940 Constr.
Urban Center					
Santiago					
Puente Alto	33%	58%	79%	43%	5%
Frontier					
Concepción					
Tomé	34	57	70	44	10
Lakes					
Valdivia					
Corral	45	52	80	57	2

The fourteen mining communities used from 1938 through the 1940s were the same ones tested in 1932 (Table 9). The twenty peasant *comunas* used in Table 14 were also the same as in 1932, with the addition of Puerto Octay in the Lakes province of Valdivia, a community which the 1940 censuses found to have a population 90% rural, 76% worker, and 87% agricultural.

All the *comunas* in Tables 18, 19, and 20 were the same as those for the 1938 election (Tables 13 and 14) except where electoral returns were unavailable in 1941. Only eighteen instead of twenty-two "urban" communities were included in the 1941 tables because Iquique, Antofagasta, Rancagua, and Talca lacked complete electoral data. Only twenty-three instead of twenty-five "rural" communities were used because of insufficient returns from Florida and Pirque in Santiago province. The middle- to upper-class, industrial-worker, miner, and peasant areas were totally identical to those used in 1938. Within the mining *comunas,* the Communists ran best in the three main nitrate districts of Pozo Almonte, Toco (home of the María Elena mine), and Sierra Gorda (home of the Pedro de Valdivia mine), where they averaged 62.3% of the votes in 1941, and in the three main coal-mining communities of Coronel, Lota, and Curanilahue, where they averaged 63.9%. In the three main copper communities of

Calama, Chañaral, and Machalí, the PC averaged 15.3% of the ballots. By contrast, both Socialist parties scored best in the copper *comunas*, the PS with 17.3% and the PST with 6.6%, for a combined average of 23.9%. In the nitrate zones covered in the tables, the PS averaged 12.6% and the PST 1.7% (14.3% together), and in the coal communities the PS averaged 7.5% and the PST 4.0% (together 11.5%) in 1941.

All the communities used in 1945 (Table 24) were the same as those for the 1938 and 1941 elections, except that only twenty-three rural *comunas* were included because electoral data were unavailable for Pozo Almonte and Quellón and only thirteen mining districts were included, again because of a lack of data on Pozo Almonte. The regular Socialists ran poorly in 1945 in all mining areas, plummeting most sharply in the copper zones. In the two main nitrate districts with voting returns available (Toco and Sierra Gorda), the regular PS averaged only 1.8% while Grove's PSA took 11.5%, for a total of 13.3%. Running second best among these mining *comunas* in the three primary copper areas, the PS claimed 1.7% to 10.2% for the PSA, a total of 11.9%. And in the three major coal communities, the PS averaged 3.5%, the PSA 0.8%, and the two Socialist parties together 4.3%.

Finally, all the communities used in 1949 (Table 27) were the same as those in 1941, except that only thirteen mining zones were included because Huara lacked official electoral returns. In the three main copper communities in the tables, the regular PSP (12.5% of the votes there) well outdistanced the rival PS (5.7%) and Grove's PSA (1.5%). By contrast, Ampuero's PSP and Ibáñez's PS had identical averages of 5.3% of the deputy votes each in 1949 in the three major nitrate areas, while the PSA won 14.0%, perhaps because of Communist support. All three Socialist parties scored poorly in the three main coal *comunas*, the PSP claiming 5.3%, the PS 2.0%, and the PSA 0.7%. The figures in parentheses in the tables show average percentage changes. The 1949 *comuna* tables should be interpreted with even greater caution than the previous ones because changes after the 1940 censuses might have altered the composition of a few of the *comunas* used, especially those in the rural and peasant groups. However, other studies for the late 1940s and subsequent decades indicate no change in the fundamental character of most of the communities used, especially those in the urban and mining areas. In particular see Cruz-Coke, pp. 78-82; Fuenzalida, pp. 30-68, 180-81, 299-311; Zemelman, pp. 50-60; Petras and Alexander, pp. 72-81.

Appendix B

Methodological Note on the Construction of the Tables of Background Information on Political Leaders

As a supplement to the judgments of observers in the era, party programs, provincial and community electoral data, membership information, lists of leaders' occupations in various time periods, and sketches of individual public figures, Tables 10 and 15 help flesh out the social content of party politics. The main purpose of the tables is to evaluate the composition of the Socialists' leadership in comparison with that of the other Chilean parties. Given the newborn Socialists' weakness in Congress, it was necessary to augment the sample for Table 10 with as many recognized noncongressional party leaders as possible to extract a meaningful picture of top personnel. Therefore, to achieve broad coverage of each party's national leadership without dipping down to middle-level cadres or local notables, each original sample was drawn up by adding to the 1932 congressional representatives other national personnel with a clear functional or public role as leaders. These noncongressional leaders included national party officers, members of party directorates and major committees, and a smaller group cited in the press or party literature as key leaders without specific posts at the moment, for instance, prominent party intellectuals and spokesmen.

Except in the case of the newcomer Socialists, the overwhelming majority of these noncongressional leaders included in the original and final samples for Table 10 had held numerous ministerial and congressional seats and some were unsuccessful candidates in 1932. Not including leaders aside from those elected in 1932 would have barred from the samples such towering figures as Marmaduke Grove of the Socialists, Pedro Aguirre Cerda of the Radicals, and Arturo Alessandri of the Liberals. Consequently, the greater precision in group definition that would have been obtained by only investigating the 1932 senators and deputies was sacrificed in favor of a wider, richer, yet still reliable sample. This approach furnished a fuller in-depth picture of party leadership, but for those who might prefer a narrower sample of just congressional representatives, a breakdown separating the two components of each party's sample is given below. The resulting combined clusters of congressional and noncongressional leadership characteristics for each major party in 1931-33 are broadly representative of the social tendencies of each party's top personnel as compared to those in the forefront of the other parties in the tables.

The strength of the tables lies in the general patterns revealed more than in the precise percentages. Not necessarily reflecting "scientific samples," the selections presented here are inevitably imperfect because of the insurmountable difficulties of tracking down party leaders and data on them. Adding or deleting some party leaders about whose importance scholars might disagree would doubtless produce slightly different percentages in particular categories for each party, but there is very strong evidence that such changes in the composition of the samples would not significantly alter the fundamental profile of any of the parties or the basic comparisons drawn among them.

The reliability of the large outlines of each party's leadership profile is established by the breakdowns below of the makeup of each sample. These breakdowns show that the inclusion of recognized internal, noncongressional party leaders along with those elected to Congress in 1932 tilted the samples in certain ways but in no case distorted the major conclusions and contrasts reached in the text. For example, just including the Radicals' 1932 congressional representatives in Table 10 without other intraparty dignitaries would have reduced the Radical Party's percentage of leaders belonging to the aristocratic Union Club, but that smaller percentage would still have been notably higher than the percentage of Democrat or Socialist congressmen in the Union Club and notably lower than that of Conservative or Liberal congressmen; in other words, the relative positions of the parties would have remained virtually the same. While disaggregating the data lumped in the tables points to the reliability of the samples used, so does the inclusion below of all the fragmentary information uncovered on those leaders from the original samples who were not tabulated in the final tables because of insufficient data. Furthermore, the findings in Tables 10 and 15 are compatible in most respects with those derived by other scholars comparing the leadership of these parties based on other samples in other years. For example, see Joan

Reimer, *Circulación de las elites en Chile* (Santiago, [1971?]) and Germán Urzúa Valenzuela, *Los partidos políticos chilenos* (Santiago, 1968).

For the original sample used to construct Table 10, lists of 1932 congressional candidates and winners were compiled primarily from Chile, Tribunal Calificador, "Elecciones extraordinarias generales" (Santiago, 1933). Then names of noncongressional leaders were culled from a vast multitude of sources, mainly party publications, party histories, newspapers, and interviews. For instance, Luis Palma Zúñiga, *Historia del Partido Radical* (Santiago, 1967) and Julio César Jobet, *El Partido Socialista de Chile* (2 vols., Santiago, 1971) were especially useful for finding the names of internal leaders in those two parties; abundant similar sources are footnoted throughout this study. A particularly helpful general treasure of names was Ricardo Donoso, *Alessandri, agitador y demoledor* (2 vols., Mexico and Buenos Aires, 1952, 1954); also rewarding were reports from the U.S. Embassy, for example as found in U.S., Dept. of State Archives, Santiago, Mar. 21, 1932, 825.00/722. Not surprisingly, the widespread digging for internal party leaders turned up lists of noncongressional notables of varying sizes for the parties. Because of the vagaries of the availability of reliable names of leaders and other factors such as differing party organizational and leadership structures, even the numbers of leaders in the original samples for the parties other than the Socialists were not directly, precisely proportionate to the congressional-electoral strength of each party. For example, the Conservatives elected 44 senators and deputies together in 1932 and the Liberals only 34, but the Conservatives' original leadership sample of congressional and noncongressional figures contained 64 names and the Liberals' 98; this was mainly because of the somewhat capricious availability of names but also because the Conservatives had a smaller, more concentrated, tightly knit leadership, fewer cabinet members in the early 1930s, and fewer publicly recognized noncongressional spokesmen, intellectuals, and writers. For instance, in the 1932 congressional contests the Conservatives elected 10 of their 14 candidates to the senate with 56,149 votes; they also elected 34 of their 70 candidates to the house with 55,259 votes. By contrast, the more dispersed Liberals campaigning under three main factional labels (Liberal, United Liberal, and Doctrinaire Liberal) elected 7 of their 24 nominees to the Senate with 58,378 votes; they also elected 27 of their 102 deputy candidates to the House with 58,859 votes. Possessing more party organizations, officers, candidates, and votes than the Conservatives, the Liberals won fewer congressional seats. At the same time, they took the presidency.

For all parties, congressional, electoral, and broader political strengths were not necessarily equivalent commodities. As a result, it was impossible to determine exactly how large each party sample should have been with the inclusion of noncongressional leaders, especially when the primary purpose was to compare them with the Socialists, whose leadership was predominantly noncongressional. Moreover, as will be demonstrated in the breakdowns below, the varying sizes of the original and final samples for the different parties did not undermine the broad comparisons drawn among the upper echelons. In both the original and the final samples, leaders who belonged to a closely akin faction or splinter group—particularly common among the Liberals and Democrats—were tabulated under the parent party.

After accumulating an original sample of clear-cut leaders which totaled 64 Conservatives, 98 Liberals, 105 Radicals, 40 Democrats, and 97 Socialists, the size of the final sample included in Table 10 was determined by the availability of sound biographical information, verified from more than one source as often as possible. In all the tables, only those leaders were included whose birthdate and geographic origins could be discovered as a minimal base of information. Then all the other data, however incomplete, available on those leaders were inserted in the subsequent tables on occupations, political positions, education, and organizations. In most cases, those leaders for whom there was information on birthdates and provincial roots also had the most data available in other categories. The biographical sources on political leaders were inherently biased toward middle- to upper-class figures, particularly of the established, less leftist parties. Nevertheless, qualitative materials from the period, interviews, and other studies do not indicate that the discovery of the few lower-middle- and working-class leaders of the parties hidden by the elitism of the sources would strikingly alter the general portrait and comparisons offered in the tables. Furthermore, the partial material unearthed on those ultimately left out of the tables will be noted below; these separate calculations for omitted leaders did not reveal sharp deviations from the patterns shown in the tables. In all the tables except those on provinces and ages, a leader may be counted more than once if, for example, he was heavily occupied in law practice as well as running a *fundo* or had attended both the Catholic and a foreign university. These duplications, although very few, have been kept because the purpose of the tables is to reflect the propensity of competing political groups to, for example, own great estates or belong to labor organizations. For this reason, as well as the absence of data at some points, the figures, which are rounded to the nearest whole percentage point, do not necessarily equal 100%.

In Tables 10a-10e, the numbers refer to the percentages of 54 Conservatives, 85 Liberals, 93 Radicals, 28 Democrats, 54 Socialists, and 141 congressional winners in 1932 in the final sample who were found to have each particular trait. Another word of caution about interpreting the tables is that aggregate figures can be deceptive, since they do not isolate factions, opinion leaders, or decision makers within the parties. The leaders and the data on them in the tables were gleaned from a wide variety of sources, among which the following were the most productive: Empresa Periodística "Chile," eds., *Diccionario biográfico de Chile* (1st-9th eds., Santiago, 1936-55); Luis Valencia Avaria, *Anales de la república* (2 vols., Santiago, 1951); *Chilean Who's Who* (Santiago, 1937); Jordi Fuentes and Lia Cortes, *Diccionario político de Chile* (Santiago, 1967); Virgilio Figueroa, *Diccionario histórico y biográfico de Chile* (5 vols., Santiago, 1925); Osvaldo López, *Diccionario biográfico obrero de Chile* (Santiago, 1912); Carlos Pinto Durán, *Diccionario personal de Chile* (Santiago, 1921); M. Alberto Parada G., *Los presidenciables* (Santiago, 1937); La Sociedad de Fomento Fabril, *Rol de industriales de Chile* (Santiago, 1932); Pedro Luis González, *50 años de labor de la Sociedad de Fomento Fabril* (Santiago, 1933); Pedro Luis González and Miguel Soto Núñez, eds., *Albúm gráfico e histórico de la Sociedad de Fomento Fabril y de la industria nacional* (Santiago, 1926); La Sociedad Nacional de Agricultura, *Memoria* (Santiago, 1932); Club de la Unión, El Directorio, *Septuagésima sexta memoria* (Santiago, 1932); Club de la Unión, El Directorio, *Septuagésima séptima memoria* (Santiago, 1933); Guillermo Edwards Matte, *El Club de la Unión en sus ochenta años (1864-1944)* (Santiago, 1944); Club de la Unión, *Nómina de socios . . .* (Santiago, 1935, 1940, 1946). For the names of all those political leaders included in the final sample for Table 10, see Paul W. Drake, "Socialism and Populism in Chile: The Origins of the Leftward Movement of the Chilean Electorate, 1931-1933" (Ph.D. dissertation, Stanford University, Stanford, Calif., 1971).

The original Conservative sample, for Table 10, of 64 leaders included 31 of the 34 deputies elected in 1932 (three of those reported elected could not be identified beyond a reasonable doubt as to name and party affiliation) and all 10 of the senators elected in 1932; in addition to the 41 congressional representatives there were 23 Conservatives who were party officers or widely recognized spokesmen, usually having served previously in high government posts. From these original 64 external and internal leaders, the birthdates and provincial origins were hunted down for 54, who were therefore included in the final sample for the tables, which summarized all the data available on their primary occupations, past political positions, educations, and organizational memberships. The 10 original leaders discarded from the final sample included 5 of the 1932 deputies and 1 of the senators along with 1 cabinet minister (in 1931), 1 leading former senator, and 2 with previous experience merely as internal party leaders. Spotty biographical information on those 10 Conservatives uncovered 2 from Santiago, 2 professionals (a doctor and a lawyer), 1 who had attended both the University of Chile and the Catholic University, 2 in the Union Club (neither were members of the 1932 Congress), 2 in the SNA (again neither of them 1932 congressmen), and 1 in the Viña del Mar Club. This sketchy information on the small number of Conservative leaders rejected from the final sample revealed no patterns contrary to those recorded in the tables.

Of the 54 Conservative leaders included in the final sample, there were 26 deputies and 9 senators elected in 1932 for a congressional total of 35 (65% of the final sample). Of the final 19 Conservatives outside the current Congress, 12 were from Santiago (a slightly higher proportion than the 55% of the entire final sample of 54), 3 were from Aconcagua, and the other 4 were scattered in the provinces south of the capital city; 6 of the noncongressional 19 vs. 10 of the congressional 35 were engaged in large-scale agriculture, or about the same percentage; 7 of the 19 were heavily involved in business and commerce, only a marginally higher percentage than that for the group of 54 as a whole; 1 of the 19 was in industry vs. 3 of the congressional 35; 15 (79%) of the 19 were professionals vs. 75% of the entire sample of 54; 0 of the 19 vs. 1 of the congressional 35 were employees; 3 of the 19 had no current or previous service in high-level government posts, while the remaining 16 noncongressional leaders together boasted 7 former or current cabinet posts, 7 previous Senate seats, and 14 prior House seats; 10 of the 19 had gone to the University of Chile, slightly higher than among the entire group of 54; 7 had gone to the Catholic University, slightly lower; only 1 of the 19 vs. 7 of the congressional 35 had attended a foreign educational institution, one of the widest numerical gaps between the two segments of the Conservative sample; 2 of the 19 vs. 4 of the 35 clearly stopped their formal education beneath the university level; 14 (74%) of the noncongressional 19 vs. 19 (54%) of the congressional 35 (vs. 61% of the total 54) belonged to the Union Club; 7 (37%) of the 19 vs. 15 (43%) of the 35 belonged to the SNA, so while the Union Club figures made the noncongressional segment look somewhat more aristocratic, the SNA figures had the opposite effect; 3 of the 19 vs. 2 of the 35 belonged to the SOFOFA; 2

of the 19 vs. 1 of the 35, the Viña del Mar Club; 2 of the 19 vs. 2 of the 35, the Auto Club; 11% of the 19 vs. 9% of the total 54, regional clubs; 32% of the 19 vs. 40% of the 54 belonged to professional organizations; finally, the noncongressional 19 had an average age in 1932 of 48 vs. 44 for the entire sample of 54, presumably because the 19 were more representative of the party's old guard. Despite some minor differences between the noncongressional and congressional Conservative leaders in 1932, the combination of these two categories produced a representative sample overall and did not warp either the general findings for that party or its relative social position vis-à-vis the other parties in Table 10.

The original sample of 98 Liberal leaders for Table 10 included all of the 27 deputies and 7 senators elected in 1932; in addition to the 34 congressional representatives there were 64 noncongressional Liberals, making the latter group weightier in this sample than among the Conservatives. From these original 98 leaders, sufficient biographical data were found to place 85 in the final sample. The 13 original Liberal leaders dropped from the final sample included 5 of the 1932 deputies and 1 of the senators, 4 who had entered President Alessandri's cabinet in the early 1930s (one of whom had been a deputy and a senator previously), and 3 who were simply party leaders. Partial information on these 13 showed 1 from Santiago and 1 from Valdivia, 1 in agriculture, 1 in business, 4 in the professions, 1 bureaucrat, 1 employee, 2 who had attended the University of Chile, 1 educated in the military, 1 whose education had terminated below the university level, 4 in the Union Club (none of them in the 1932 Congress), 2 in the SNA, 1 in the SOFOFA, and 1 member of a regional organization.

Of the 85 Liberals included in the final sample, there were 22 deputies and 6 senators elected in 1932 for a congressional total of 28 (33% of the final sample, much smaller than among the Conservatives). Of the 57 final Liberals outside the 1932 Congress, 44 (77%) were from Santiago vs. 6 (21%) of the congressional 28 (vs. 59% of the total 85), this wide discrepancy indicating that congressmen were more likely to come from the outlying provinces and that, as many observers often remarked, party leadership was nonetheless concentrated around the capital city; 7 more of the noncongressional 57 came from the two provinces (Aconcagua and Colchagua) north and south of Santiago; 20 *fundos* were held by the noncongressional 57 vs. 10 by the congressional 28, for a minimal difference of 35% vs. 36%; 11 (19%) of the 57 were in business and commerce vs. 5 (18%) of the congressional 28; 3 of the 57 vs. 3 of the 28 were in industry; 48 (84%)

of the 57 vs. 14 (50%) of the 28 were professionals; 1 of the 57 vs. 0 of the 28 were bureaucrats; 1 of the 57 vs. 0 of the 28 were employees; 5 of the noncongressional 57 had no current or previous top government experience, while the remaining 52 noncongressional Liberal leaders had held or were holding cumulatively 57 cabinet positions, 14 past Senate seats, and 32 deputyships (a group total of 102 major government posts); 41 (72%) of the noncongressional 57 had gone to the University of Chile vs. 13 (46%) of the congressional 28; 2 of the 57 vs. 0 of the 28 had gone to the Catholic University; 5 of the 57 vs. 4 of the 28 had had foreign education; 1 of the 57 vs. 1 of the 28 had attended military schools; 5 of the 57 vs. 4 of the 28 had stopped their schooling beneath the university level; 45 (79%) of the 57 vs. 21 (75%) of the 28 belonged to the Union Club, no noteworthy difference between the two segments; 18 (32%) of the 57 vs. 11 (39%) of the 28 were enrolled in the SNA; 9 of the 57 vs. only 2 of the 28 were in the SOFOFA, a sharp proportional difference but one hard to generalize about based on such small numbers; there were no striking differences between the two segments in the Viña, Auto, September, or regional clubs, in each of which some members of both the noncongressional and congressional groups could be found; 26 of the 57 vs. only 4 of the 28 belonged to professional associations, again a sharp but not obviously salient difference, apparently reflecting the higher percentage of professionals among the noncongressional Liberals; finally, the noncongressional 57 had a 1932 average age of 53 vs. 49 for the entire sample of 85, a four-year gap equivalent to that among the Conservatives. Despite some significant differences between the two Liberal segments (especially in terms of provincial ties, higher education, professionals, and age), their major separate and joint characteristics were reflected accurately in the tables as compared to the other parties' leadership. For example, even using just 1932 congressional representatives would have shown 21% of the Liberals as opposed to 10% of the Radicals from Santiago; the result would have been different percentages than in the existing tables but a similar comparative pattern of roughly twice as many Liberal as Radical leaders from Santiago.

The original sample of 105 Radical leaders for Table 10 included all of the 34 deputies and 13 senators elected in 1932; in addition to these 47 congressmen there were 58 noncongressional leaders. Adequate information on province and age was found to include 93 of these original Radicals in the final sample. The 12 left out of the final sample included 4 1932 deputies and 3 senators, 1 1932 member of Alessandri's cabinet who had also been a former senator and deputy, 2 other pre-1932 deputies, and 2 who were merely internal party leaders. The very thin data on these 12 Radicals revealed 1 businessman, 4 professionals, 1 government bureaucrat–employee, 1 whose education had halted before reaching any university, and 2 members of the Union Club (1 in the 1932 Congress and 1 not).

Of the 93 Radicals in the final sample, there were 30 deputies and 10 senators for a 1932 congressional total of 40 (43% of the final sample). Of the 53 final Radicals outside the 1932 Congress (including such figures as Guillermo Labarca Hubertson, vice-president of the party in 1931-32), 17 (32%) were from Santiago vs. 4 (10%) of the 1932 congressional 40, a notable difference, but this still left the 53 noncongressional Radical leaders strung out among the other provinces far more than the noncongressional leaders of the rightist parties; 14 *fundos* were owned by the noncongressional 53 vs. 7 by the congressional 40, for a slight difference of 26% vs. 18%; 7 (13%) of the noncongressional 53 vs. 6 (15%) of the congressional 40 were in business and commerce; 3 of the 53 vs. 3 of the 40 were in industry; 47 (87%) of the 53 vs. 25 (63%) of the 40 were in the professions, another noteworthy difference; 3 of the 53 vs. 3 of the 40 were bureaucrats; 3 of the 53 vs. 3 of the 40, employees; 12 of the 53 had no current or previous high government experience, while the remaining 41 Radical noncongressional leaders together claimed 38 cabinet positions, 11 past Senate seats, and 30 House seats; 42 (79%) of the 53 vs. 18 (45%) of the 40 had attended the University of Chile, establishing a higher pattern of education among the noncongressional Radical leaders; 6 of the 53 vs. 1 of the 40 had been educated abroad; 2 of the 53 vs. 3 of the 40 had gone to military schools; 2 of the 53 vs. 10 of the 40 had not reached the university level; 28 (53%) of the 53 vs. 12 (30%) of the 40 belonged to the Union Club, again suggesting that the noncongressional Radicals were a somewhat higher status group than those in the 1932 congress; 8 (15%) of the 53 vs. 4 (10%) of the 40 were in the SNA; 5 of the 53 vs. only 1 of the 40 were in the SOFOFA; 1 of the 53 vs. 1 of the 40 in the Viña del Mar Club; 4 of the 53 vs. 0 of the 40 in the Auto Club; 7 of the 53 vs. 0 of the 40 in the September Club; 4 of the 53 vs. 7 of the 40 in regional clubs; 23 (43%) of the 53 vs. 19 (48%) of the 40 in professional organizations; and 0 of the 53 vs. 2 of the 40 in employee-worker associations; finally, the noncongressional 53 had a 1932 average age of 47 vs. 45 for the entire sample of 93, once more showing that the noncongressional segment represented older party leaders. Thus, compared to the 1932 congressional Radicals in the sample, these 53 other Radical leaders appeared to be somewhat higher class, especially in terms of location in Santiago, education, and organizational affiliations. But either of the segments alone or the entire sample combined still seemed representative of the mixed Radical Party and still placed it in an intermediate social position between the Right and the Left. Even looking at just the 1932 Radical congressional representatives, while providing a narrower sample, would not change any of the basic contrasts among the parties in the text.

The original sample of 40 Democrat leaders for Table 10 suggests that both their names and characteristics were harder to find because of their lower social standing. Of those 40, there were 19 of the 20 deputies elected in 1932 and all 7 of the senators; in addition to these 26 congressmen there were 14 noncongressional leaders. Sufficient information on province and age was uncovered to include 28 of these Democrats in the tables. The 12 left out of the final sample included 9 1932 deputies and 1 senator, about whom absolutely no information could be found, except that one was an employee; the other Democrat was an internal party leader, a member of Alessandri's early 1930s' cabinet, and a journalist. Of the 28 Democrats in the final sample, there were 10 1932 deputies and 6 senators for a congressional total of 16 (57% of the final sample).

Of the 12 final Democrats outside the 1932 Congress, 3 were from Santiago vs. 6 of the congressional 16, so, in contrast to the three previous parties considered, the congressional group revealed a higher tendency to come from the province of the capital city; 2 of the noncongressional 12 vs. 5 of the congressional 16 were in business and commerce, again, even dealing with very small numbers, indicating slightly higher status among the Democrats' 1932 senators and deputies; 5 of the noncongressional 12 vs. 6 of the other 16 were in the professions; 0 of the 12 vs. 3 of the congressional 16 were bureaucrats; 3 of the 12 vs. 3 of the 16 were employees; 3 of the 12 vs. 3 of the 16 were workers; 3 of the 12 were simply party leaders with no previous high government posts, while the remaining 9 noncongressional leaders had together held 10 cabinet seats, 2 Senate seats, and 6 House seats; 2 of the noncongressional 12 vs. 4 of the congressional 16 had attended the University of Chile; 0 of the 12 vs. 3 of the 16 had gone to foreign schools; 4 of the 12 vs. 7 of the 16 had attained only lower educational levels; 1 of the 12 vs. 1 of the 16 belonged to the SOFOFA; 2 of the 12 vs. 1 of the 16 to professional organizations; and 9 unions were belonged to by the 12 vs. 13 by the 16, or nearly the same percentage of both segments; finally, as in the other parties, the noncongressional group had a higher average age in 1932, 51 years for the 12 vs. 47 for the entire sample of 28. Given such small numbers in both Democrat segments, it is risky to make any generalizations; both segments appeared fairly similar and, if any trend was discernible, the congressional half seemed to be slightly higher in social status, a reverse of the tendency among the other parties' leaders already examined.

The original Socialist sample of 97 leaders in 1931-33 included many of the prominent figures in the Socialist Republic and in the new parties behind Grove's 1932 campaign, but only when they also helped found the PS in 1933, from whose chief founders and early leaders most of the names in the sample for Table 10 were drawn. In those 97 were included the 4 of the 5 1932 deputies whose party affiliation at the time could be firmly established and both of the 2 senators, for a congressional total of 6, to whom were added 91 noncongressional socialist leaders. At this early point in the party's career, many could be found claiming leadership roles. Sufficient information was found on province and age for only 54 of the 97. The 43 Socialists exempted from the final sample included 1 1932 deputy on whom no information was discovered; the data on the other 42 left out was too sketchy to perceive any patterns, though there were 1 each from Antofagasta, Aconcagua, and Santiago, 2 professionals, 1 employee, 3 workers or artisans (maybe suggesting that Socialists lacking public biographical information tended to hail more frequently from the working class), 1 former deputy for another party, and 1 member of a trade union.

Of the 54 Socialists in the final sample, there were 3 deputies and 2 senators, for a congressional total of 5 (9% of the final sample). Since 91% of the final were noncongressional leaders, there is no point in examining their traits separately from those of the sample as a whole. Suffice it to say that of those 5 in the 1932 Congress, 3 were from Santiago, 4 were professionals, 1 a worker, they had held 2 previous cabinet positions and 1 deputy seat, 3 had attended the University of Chile, 1 belonged to a professional organization, and 2 were affiliated with trade unions. Even relying on such a high proportion of noncongressional leaders, the Socialist sample in its entirety had a notably younger average age in 1932 than the other parties in the tables because the infant PS could not have had a substantial old guard.

As compared to the five party samples in Table 10, the 1932 congressional winners sample is less significant and therefore given little weight in the text. To achieve a general portrait of the Congress elected during the realignments of 1932, the original and final samples were mainly derived from the five previous party samples. For the 1932 winners, the original sample included 31 of the 34 Conservative deputies elected and all 10 of the senators, all of the Liberals' 27 deputies and 7 senators, all of the Radicals' 34 deputies and 13 senators, 19 of the Democrats' 20 deputies and all 7 of their senators, 4 of the Socialists' 5 deputies and both of their senators. In addition, minor party winners were included, with all 8 of the Radical Socialists' deputies and their 5 senators (the party rapidly disintegrated in the 1930s, its fragments mainly falling into the orbit of either the Radicals or Socialists), the Social Republicans' 4 deputies and 1 senator (the party quickly dissolved, mainly to the benefit of the Radicals), the Agrarians' 4 deputies (a tiny rightist regionalist party), 1 deputy for the Communists, 1 deputy for the Democratic Socialists, and 4 other deputies of undefined party orientations, for a total original sample of 182 congressmen (137 of the 142 deputies, plus 45 senators). Sufficient data on age and province were found to include 141 congressmen in the final sample: 26 Conservative deputies and 9 senators, 22 Liberal deputies and 6 senators, 30 Radical deputies and 10 senators, 10 Democrat-Democratic deputies and 6 senators, 3 Socialist deputies and 2 senators, 7 Radical Socialist deputies and 1 senator, 4 Social Republican deputies and 1 senator, 3 Agrarian deputies, and 1 Communist deputy, for a final sample total of 106 deputies and 35 senators. The fragmentary information available on those congressmen not included in the final sample from the five major parties has already been noted.

For the other congressmen dropped from the final sample (4 Radical Socialist senators and 1 deputy, 1 Agrarian deputy, 1 Democratic Socialist deputy, and 4 non-party deputies), virtually no information was found. The resulting final sample of 1932 congressional winners roughly reflected the parties' relative congressional strengths. The relatively younger average age of these congressmen compared to all the other party samples except the Socialists confirms the pattern found previously within each party sample.

Table 15 was put together in the same way as Table 10, with the same basic objectives, procedures, strengths, limitations, types of data, and sources. In both cases, the two most useful references were Empresa Periodística "Chile," eds., *Diccionario* and Valencia Avaria, along with a panoply of other biographical collections, organizational listings, party pamphlets and histories, newspapers, and secondary works, already footnoted for Table 10 or elsewhere. As additional examples of party publications particularly useful for collecting the names of internal leaders for Table 15, see Partido Socialista, *IX congreso* ([Santiago?], 1943) and Partido Radical, *Posición política y estatuto del Partido Radical* (Santiago, 1941). Especially helpful for 1941 congressional representatives were Donoso, *Alessandri*, II, pp. 386-90 and U.S., Dept. of State Archives, Santiago, Feb. 19, 1941, 825.00/ 1306. The 1941 congressional winners from all parties were not calculated as a separate group for Table 15 because that election was not as much of a turning point as the one in 1932. Also, the Democrat parties are not repeated here because they shrank to insignificance. With extensive, reliable information available on fewer than 20 Communist leaders, it was impossible to derive meaningful percentages on their social backgrounds for inclusion in the tables, though their major traits are noted in the text.

Although still broadly representative of leadership composition and of relative national political weight, most of the original samples and all the final samples for 1940-42 are smaller than in 1931-33, mainly because of the vagaries of name and data availability but also because of the rise of small new parties which are not included in Table 15, such as the Falange and the PST. With figures in parentheses showing changes from the 1931-33 table, the original samples for each party in Table 15 contained the following numbers of leaders: 50 (−14) Conservatives, 80 (−18) Liberals, 112 (+7) Radicals, and 89 (−8) Socialists. The final 1940-42 samples contained 41 (−13) Conservatives, 57 (−28) Liberals, 83 (−10) Radicals, and 48 (−6) Socialists, to which all the percentages in Tables 15a-15e refer. Throughout, as before, percentages do not necessarily add up to 100%. Some provinces are combined in Table 15a to make them as equivalent as possible to the units used in the 1931-33 table, where Aysén and Magallanes were excluded. Once more, the breakdowns by parties, which follow, will indicate the composition and reliability of the leadership groups tested.

For the Conservatives, the original 1940-42 sample of 50 leaders included all 29 of their deputies and all 11 of their senators serving in 1941; in addition to these 40 congressional representatives there were 10 clear-cut internal party leaders. Adequate information was found on birth and province to place 41 in the final sample. The 9 Conservatives left out of the final sample in Table 15 included 6 1941 deputies and 3 internal leaders with no previous high government experience. Very scanty information on those 9 revealed 1 from Santiago, 1 businessman, 1 professional, and 1 who had attended the University of Chile. Of the 41 Conservative leaders in the final sample, there were 23 deputies and 11 senators serving in 1941 for a congressional total of 34 (83% of the sample vs. 65% in 1932); 18 of the final 41 had previously turned up in the 1931-33 tables. Of the 7 final Conservatives outside the 1941 Congress, 4 were from Santiago and 1 from Aconcagua vs. 18 of the congressional 34 from Santiago and 5 from

Aconcagua, a similar pattern in both segments; 1 great estate was found among the noncongressional 7 vs. 13 among the congressional 34, making the latter group look more aristocratic; 2 (29%) of the noncongressional 7 vs. 5 (15%) of the congressional 34 were in business and commerce; 1 of the 7 vs. 2 of the 34, in industry; 5 (71%) of the 7 vs. 24 (71%) of the 34, in the professions; 0 of the 7 vs. 1 of the 34, bureaucrats; 0 of the 7 vs. 2 of the 34, employees; 5 of the noncongressional 7 had no previous experience in top government positions, while 1 had been a deputy and the other had been a deputy five times and a senator twice; 0 of the 7 vs. 15 of the 34 had gone to the University of Chile, a sharp difference; 5 of the 7 vs. 21 of the 34, to the Catholic University, a higher percentage among the noncongressional leaders; 1 of the 7 vs. 3 of the 34 had been educated abroad; 1 of the 7 vs. 6 of the 34 had never reached the university level; 2 (29%) of the 7 vs. 12 (35%) of the 34 belonged to the Union Club; 0 of the 7 vs. 11 of the 34 were in the SNA, again suggesting more landholding and aristocratic ties among the congressional leaders; 0 of the 7 vs. very few of the 34 were in the remaining elite organizations; 1 of the 7 vs. 6 of the 34 in regional organizations; and 2 (29%) of the 7 vs. 9 (26%) of the 34 in professional organizations; finally, the noncongressional 7 had an average 1941 age of 42 vs. 43 for the sample as a whole.

In general, these small numbers in the two 1940-42 Conservative segments and the differences between them do not lend themselves to strong contrasts. The breakdown does not show the same noncongressional vs. congressional patterns as in 1931-33 nor does it suggest that this mixed 1940-42 sample is in any significant way unrepresentative or unsuited to establishing a viable portrait of Conservative leaders at the time to contrast in broad outlines with those of other parties.

For the Liberals, the original 1940-42 sample of 80 leaders included 20 of their 22 deputies (2 of them simply could not be firmly identified as to name and party affiliation) and all 8 of their senators serving in 1941; added to these 28 congressmen were 52 noncongressional leaders. Sufficient data were found to enroll 57 in Table 15. The 23 Liberals excluded from the final sample included 6 1941 deputies, 9 internal leaders with no prior major government posts, and 8 who had held a total of 11 cabinet ministries, 4 Senate seats, and 10 deputy seats; the partial information uncovered on these 23 showed 1 from Valdivia, 1 *latifundista*, 2 businessmen, 3 professionals, 1 University of Chile, 1 foreign school, 1 military school, 1 lower education, 2 Union Club, 1 September Club, 1 regional organization, and 1 professional association, nothing to hint at any strikingly different pattern from those in the tables. Of the 57 Liberals in the final sample, there were 14 deputies and 8 senators for a 1941 congressional total of 22 (39% of the final sample vs. 33% in 1932); 27 of these final 57 appeared before in the 1931-33 tables. Of the 35 noncongressional Liberals in the final 1940-42 sample, 21 (60%) vs. 10 (45%) of the congressional 22 were from Santiago, so the noncongressional segment tipped the Liberal group more toward the province of the capital city; 11 (31%) of the noncongressional 35 boasted *fundos* vs. 9 (41%) of the congressional 22; 4 of the 35 vs. 5 of the 22 were in business and commerce, showing a higher proportion of the congressional group active in that field as well as in big agriculture; 2 of the 35 vs. 4 of the 22, in industry; 27 (77%) of the 35 vs. 19 (86%) of the 22, in the professions, which made the congressional segment appear to have slightly higher social status based on all the occupational measures; 1 of the 35 vs. 0 of the 22 was a bureaucrat; 12 of the noncongressional 35 were merely party officers or otherwise recognized spokesmen with no previous high government positions, while the remaining 23 outside the 1941 Congress had together filled 2 presidencies, 30 cabinet posts, 13 Senate seats, and 38 deputy seats; 20 (57%) of the noncongressional 35 vs. 16 (73%) of the congressional 22 had gone to the University of Chile; 4 of the 35 vs. 2 of the 22, to the Catholic University; 4 of the 35 vs. 4 of the 22, to foreign schools; 0 of the 35 vs. 1 of the 22, to military institutes; 5 (14%) of the 35 vs. 4 (18%) of the 22 had clearly stopped their formal education beneath the university level; 22 (63%) of the 35 vs. 15 (68%) of the 22 were in the Union Club; 11 (31%) of the 35 vs. 5 (23%) of the 22, in the SNA, a bit surprising since the congressional 22 held more *fundos* than did the noncongressional 35; 2 of the 35 vs. 0 of the 22, in the SOFOFA; 1 of the 35 vs. 2 of the 22, in the Viña del Mar Club; 3 of the 35 vs. 1 of the 22, in the Auto Club; 6 of the 35 vs. 3 of the 22, in the September Club; 7 of the 35 vs. 8 of the 22, in regional associations, a logical but not dramatic lead in that category among congressmen; and 12 of the 35 vs. only 3 of the 22 were in professional organizations, indicating that the noncongressional group held more memberships overall; finally, the noncongressional 35 had an average age of 53 vs. 50 for the sample as a whole, again pointing to the noncongressional segment as more representative of the old guard.

As among the Conservatives, the two Liberal segments appeared fairly similar to each other or displayed differences which cut different ways in different categories, for example with certain occupations making the congressional group look more upper class and certain organizations having the same impact on the noncongressional group. As throughout, the combination of the two segments gave a deeper picture of the Liberals while distorting neither their fundamental profile in the tables nor their basic contrasts with the leaders of other parties.

The original sample of 112 Radical leaders for Table 15 included 41 of their 43 deputies and all 13 of their senators for a 1941 congressional total of 54, to whom were added 58 noncongressional leaders. The 29 Radicals left out of the final sample of 83 included 14 of the 1941 deputies, 10 noncongressional leaders who had held no prior top government offices, and 5 more who among them had served in 7 cabinet posts and 4 House seats; the miniscule data discovered on these 29 Radicals revealed 4 professionals, 1 with foreign education, 1 member of a regional organization, and 1 member of a professional association. Of the 83 Radicals in the final sample, there were 27 deputies and 13 senators who had been elected to serve in the 1941-45 Congress; this congressional total of 40 represented 48% of the final sample vs. 43% in 1931-33; 36 of these final 83 were also in the previous Radical tables for Chapter 4. Of the 43 noncongressional Radicals in the final 1940-42 sample, 11 (26%) were from Santiago and 5 from Aconcagua vs. 3 (8%) and 5 respectively of the congressional 40, so the noncongressional segment slanted the Radical leadership slightly more toward Santiago but still far less than the Conservatives or Liberals, thus causing no basic change in the comparative patterns; the rest of the noncongressional Radicals were scattered throughout the other provinces, far more dispersed than the noncongressional Conservatives or Liberals and far closer to the Socialist pattern in terms of regional diversity; 12 (28%) *fundos* belonged to the noncongressional 43 vs. 18 (45%) to the congressional 40, making the latter group appear somewhat more upper class, the reverse of the 1931-33 intraparty distribution; 6 of the 43 vs. only 2 of the 40 were in business and commerce; 1 of the 43 vs. 2 of the 40, in industry; 30 (70%) of the 43 vs. 30 (75%) of the 40, in the professions; 4 of the 43 vs. 5 of the 40 were bureaucrats; 6 of the 43 vs. 4 of the 40 were employees; 22 of the noncongressional 43 were simply internal party leaders with no previous major government offices, while the remaining 21 together claimed 1 presidency, 26 cabinet posts, 14 Senate seats, and 35 House seats; 22 (51%) of the noncongressional 43 vs. 27 (68%) of the congressional 40 had attended the University of Chile; 3 of the 43 vs. 1 of the 40 had gone to foreign schools; 1 of the 43 vs. 2 of the 40, military schools; 12 (28%) of the 43 vs. 10 (25%) of the 40 had ceased education beneath the university level, so there were no great differences between the two segments at any point on the education scale; 10 (23%) of the 43 vs. 8 (20%) of the 40 belonged to the Union Club; 5 of the 43 vs. 6 of the 40, to the SNA; 2 of the 43 vs. 1 of the 40, to the SOFOFA; 4 of the 43 vs. 1 of the 40, to the Auto Club; 5 of the 43 vs. 0 of the 40, to the September Club; 13 of the 43 vs. 12 of the 40, to regional clubs; 14 of the 43 vs. 16 of the 40, to professional associations; and 0 of the 43 vs. 1 of the 40, to a trade union; finally, the average age of the noncongressional 43 was 47, a shade above the average of 46 for the entire sample.

The original 89 Socialist leaders included all 15 of their deputies and all 5 of their senators elected to serve in the 1941 Congress, along with 69 noncongressional leaders. The 41 Socialists excluded from the final sample in Table 15 because of insufficient data on birth and province included 7 of the deputies elected in 1941, 32 internal leaders with no past national government positions, and 2 more who had together held 3 deputy seats; the available information on these 41 leaders showed 1 from Atacama, 2 from Santiago, 3 professionals, 1 employee, 3 workers, 3 with less than university-level education, 1 in a professional organization, and 1 in a trade union. Of the 48 Socialists in the final sample, there were 8 deputies and 5 senators for a 1941 congressional total of 13 (27% of the final sample vs. 9% in 1931-33; thus the Socialists' sample echoed that of the other three parties by being far more proportionately congressional in 1941 than in 1932, but it remained in both instances far more noncongressional than the other parties' samples); 19 of these final 48 had previously appeared in the Socialists' 1932 tables. Of the 35 noncongressional Socialists in the final 1940-42 sample, 6 (17%) came from Santiago and 5 from Aconcagua-Valparaíso vs. 3 (23%) and 0 respectively of the congressional 13, with the rest of the noncongressional leaders spread throughout the other provinces in no particular pattern; 2 of the noncongressional 35 vs. 1 of the congressional 13 possessed large landholdings; 1 of the 35 vs. 2 of the 13 were in business and commerce; 26 (74%) of the 35 vs. 9 (69%) of the 13 were professionals; 4 of the 35 vs. 1 of the 13 were bureaucrats; 8 (23%) of the 35 vs. 2 (15%) of the 13 were employees; 1 of the 35 vs. 5 of the 13 was a worker, indicating that inclusion of the noncongressional 35 made the PS sample look a bit more professional and middle class; 23 of the noncongressional 35 were party leaders who had never served in national government slots, while the 12 others had filled a total of 10 cabinet positions, 1 Senate seat, and 9 deputy seats; 14 (40%) of the 35 had gone to the University of Chile vs. 4 (31%) of the 13, again suggesting slightly higher social status among the noncongressional group; 1 of the 35 vs. 1 of the 13 had attended the Catholic University; 7 of the 35 vs. 0 of the 13 had gone abroad for education; 1 of the 35 vs. 1 of the 13 had gone to military institutes; 12 (34%) of the 35 vs. 7

(54%) of the 13 had not reached any university; 5 of the 35 vs. 1 of the 13 joined regional organizations; 14 of the 35 vs. 4 of the 13, professional associations; and 4 of the 35 vs. 9 of the 13, employee-worker organizations, again consistently indicating slightly lower social status and greater worker orientation within the congressional segment; finally, the noncongressional 35 had an average age in 1941 of 38, a bit younger than the sample as a whole, perhaps reflecting the rise of a new generation within the PS, which still could not possess an old guard as aged as in the other three parties.

Bibliography

Interviews

The following scholars and public figures particularly contributed to the information and ideas used in this study. Since many formal and informal conversations and correspondence took place with these Chileans in Santiago from December, 1969, through September, 1970, and from June, 1973, through August, 1973, no precise dates are given.

Almeyda, Clodomiro
Barría, Jorge
Charlín Ojeda, Carlos
Chelén Rojas, Alejandro
Garay, Mario
Grove, Hiram and Blanca Elena
Jara, Aníbal
Jobet, Julio César
Keller, Carlos
Mandujano Navarro, Manuel
Tapia Moore, Astolfo
Tapia Videla, Jorge Ivan
Urzúa F., Raúl
Urzúa Valenzuela, Germán

Unpublished and Manuscript Sources

Chile. Dirección del Registro Electoral. "Elección extraordinaria de Presidente de la República." Santiago, [1925?].

———. "Elección extraordinaria de Presidente de la República." Santiago, [1931?].

———. "Elección extraordinaria de Presidente de la República." Santiago, 1932.

———. "Elección extraordinaria de Presidente de la República." Santiago, 1942.

———. "Elección extraordinaria de Presidente de la República." Santiago, 1946.

————. "Elección ordinaria de Congreso Nacional." Santiago, 1949.
————. "Elección ordinaria de municipalidades." Santiago, 1948
————. "Elección ordinaria de Presidente de la República." Santiago, 1970.
————. "Elección ordinaria general de senadores y diputados al Congreso Nacional." Santiago, 1945.
————. "Elección presidencial." Santiago, 1964.
————. "Poder electoral de la República." Santiago, 1932.
————. "Resultado elección ordinaria de diputados." Santiago, 1969.
————. "Resultado elección ordinaria de diputados." Santiago, 1973.
————. "Resultado elección ordinaria de regidores." Santiago, 1971.
————. "Resultado elección ordinaria de senadores." Santiago, 1969.
————. "Resultado elección ordinaria de senadores." Santiago, 1973.
————. "Resultado general de las elecciones de Congreso Nacional . . . y de municipalidades . . . ." Valparaíso, 1942.
————. "Variación porcentual de los partidos políticos, 1957-1971." n.p., n.d.
Chile. Tribunal Calificador. "Elecciones extraordinarias generales." Santiago, 1933.
Drake, Paul W. "Socialism and Populism in Chile: The Origins of the Leftward Movement of the Chilean Electorate, 1931-1933." Ph.D. dissertation, Stanford University, Stanford, Calif., 1971.
Hochwald, Miriam Ruth. "Imagery in Politics: A Study of the Ideology of the Chilean Socialist Party." Ph.D. dissertation, University of California at Los Angeles, 1971.
Landsberger, Henry A., and McDaniel, Tim. "Mobilization as a Double-Edged Sword: The Allende Government's Uneasy Relationship with Labor, 1970-1973." Paper presented at the Latin American Studies Association Fifth National Meeting, San Francisco, 1974.
Partido Socialista. "Rejistro de fundadores." Santiago, 1933.
Powell, Sandra Sue. "Social Structure and Electoral Choice in Chile, 1952-1964." Ph.D. dissertation, Northwestern University, Evanston, Ill., 1966.
Raven, Ronald E. "El 4 de junio: Birth of a Legend." M.A. thesis, Wayne State University, Detroit, 1973.
Tapia Videla, Jorge Ivan. "Bureaucratic Power in a Developing Country: The Case of the Chilean Social Security Administration." Ph.D. dissertation, University of Texas, Austin, 1969.
Tarr, Terrence Stephen. "Military Intervention and Civilian Reaction in Chile, 1924-1936." Ph.D. dissertation, University of Florida, Gainesville, 1960.
Thomas, Jack Ray. "Marmaduke Grove: A Political Biography." Ph.D. dissertation, Ohio State University, Columbus, 1962.
United States. Department of State Archives. Record Group 59. "Chile, 1930-1944." National Archives. Washington, D.C.

Printed Government Sources

Alessandri Palma, Arturo. *Mensaje leído por S.E. del Presidente de la República.* Santiago, 1921, 1933.

Chile. *Constitución política.* Santiago, 1925.

———. *El Diario Oficial.* Santiago, 1919-73.

———. *Geografía descriptiva de la vista panorámica en la exposición histórico-cultural del progreso de Chile.* Santiago, 1934.

———. *Recopilación de decretos-leyes.* XIII. Santiago, 1925.

———. *Recopilación de leyes.* VII. Santiago, 1914.

Chile. Cámara de Diputados. *Boletín de Sesiones.* Santiago, 1932-73.

Chile. Cámara de Senadores. *Boletín de Sesiones.* Santiago, 1932-73.

Chile. Congreso Pleno. *Boletín y actas de las sesiones celebradas por el Congreso Nacional en 1920 con motivo de la elección de Presidente de la República.* Santiago, 1921.

Chile. Dirección General de Estadística. |*Estadística anual de administración, justicia y educación.* Santiago, [1932?]. |

———. *Estadística anual de administración y justicia.* Santiago, 1934.

———. *Estadística anual de comercio interior y comunicaciones.* [Santiago?], 1934.

———. *Estadística anual de finanzas, bancos, y cajas sociales.* [Santiago?], 1929-36.

———. *Población total por provincias. Chile. 1885-1960.* Santiago, 1964.

———. *Política, administración, justicia y educación.* Santiago, 1938-39.

———. *Política y administración.* Santiago, 1922, 1929, 1935.

———. *Resultados del X censo de la población.* 3 vols. Santiago, 1931.

———. *Sinopsis geográfico-estadística de la República de Chile.* Santiago, 1933.

———. *Veinte años de legislación social.* Santiago, 1945.

Chile. La Junta de Goberno. *Declaración de principios del gobierno de Chile.* Santiago, 1974.

Chile. Ministerio de Hacienda. *Cuentas fiscales de Chile, 1925-1957.* Santiago, 1959.

Chile. Oficina Central de Estadística. *Censo electoral 1921.* Santiago, 1922.

———. *Política y administración.* Santiago, 1918, 1922, 1927.

Chile. Secretaria General de Gobierno. *Libro blanco del cambio de gobierno en Chile.* 2nd ed. Santiago, 1973.

Corporación de Fomento de la Producción. *Cinco años de labor, 1939-1943.* Santiago, 1944.

———. *Cuentas nacionales de Chile: 1940-1954.* Santiago, 1957.

———. *Geografía económica de Chile.* 4 vols. Santiago, 1950, 1962.

———. *Renta nacional, 1940-1945.* 2 vols. Santiago, 1946.

Great Britain. Department of Overseas Trade. *Economic Conditions in Chile.* London, 1932, 1935.

———. *Report on Economic and Commercial Conditions in Chile.* London, 1936, 1937.

———. *Report on the Industrial and Economic Situation in Chile.* London, 1922, 1925.

Ibáñez del Campo, Carlos. *Mensaje con que el Presidente de la República da cuenta al Congreso Nacional. . . .* Santiago, 1931.

Montero, Juan E. *Mensaje del Presidente de la República al Congreso Nacional.* Santiago, 1932.

United States. Department of State. *Foreign Relations of the United States. Diplomatic Papers. 1932.* 5 vols. Washington, D.C., 1948.

————. *World Military Expenditures and Arms Trade, 1963-1973.* Washington, D.C., 1975.

United States. House of Representatives. Committee on Foreign Affairs. Subcommittee on Inter-American Affairs. *United States and Chile during the Allende Years, 1970-1973.* Washington, D.C., 1975.

Printed Social Organization Sources

Club de la Unión. *Nómina de socios . . . .* Santiago, 1935, 1940, 1946.

Club de la Unión. El Directorio. *Septuagésima séptima memoria.* Santiago, 1933.

————. *Septuagésima sexta memoria.* Santiago, 1932.

La Confederación de Trabajadores de Chile. *La Confederación de Trabajadores de Chile y el proletariado de América latina.* Santiago, 1939.

————. *Manifiesto de la Confederación de Trabajadores de Chile a las clases laboriosas del país.* Santiago, 1940.

————. *Memoria . . . .* Santiago, 1946.

————. *¿Por qué salimos a la calle el 21 de mayo de este año?* Santiago, 1940.

————. *Treinta meses de acción en favor del proletariado de Chile.* Santiago, 1939.

Gran Logia de Chile. *Cuarta conferencia dada por el serenísimo gran maestro . . . .* Santiago, [1935?].

————. *Tercera conferencia dada por el serenísimo gran maestro . . . .* Santiago, [1935?].

La Sociedad de Fomento Fabril. *Boletín . . . .* Santiago, 1932.

————. *Industria.* Santiago, 1938-42.

————. *Plan de fomento de la producción.* Santiago, 1932.

————. *Rol de industriales de Chile.* Santiago, 1932.

————. *La Sociedad de Fomento Fabril de Chile.* Santiago, 1935.

La Sociedad Nacional de Agricultura. *Boletín . . . .* Santiago, 1932.

————. *El Campesino.* 1938-42.

————. *Memoria . . . .* Santiago, 1932.

La Sociedad Nacional de Minería. *Boletín Minero . . . .* Santiago, 1939-42.

Newspapers

Acción. Nacimiento, Chile, 1933.

Acción. Santiago, 1925.

Acción Socialista. Santiago, 1934.

La Aurora de Chile. Santiago, 1973.

Bandera Roja. Santiago, 1931-33.

La Batalla. Temuco, Chile, 1940.

El Chileno. Chuquicamata, Chile, 1931-32.

Claridad. Santiago, 1937-38.

El Clarín. Santiago, 1969-73.

Consigna. Santiago, 1934-37.

La Crítica. Santiago, 1939-42.

Crónica. Santiago, 1931-32.

De Frente. Santiago, 1973.

El Debate. Santiago, 1932.
El Diario Ilustrado. Santiago, 1920-70.
Frente Popular. Santiago, 1936-40.
Frente Único. Santiago, 1934-35.
La Hora. Santiago, 1936-37.
El Imparcial. Santiago, 1932.
Izquierda. Santiago, 1934-36.
Jornada. Santiago, 1934-35.
El Mercurio. Santiago, 1919-74.
La Nación. Santiago, 1924-73.
New York Times. New York, 1920-75.
La Opinión. Buenos Aires, 1973-74.
La Opinión. Santiago, Iquique, and Tocopilla, Chile, 1932-33.
El País. Santiago, 1932.
La Prensa. Santiago, 1972-73.
El Proletario. Arica, Chile, 1934-35.
Puro Chile. Santiago, 1970-73.
El Rebelde. Santiago, 1973.
La Segunda. Santiago, 1969-73.
El Siglo. Santiago, 1940-41, 1969-73.
South Pacific Mail. Valparaíso, 1920, 1931-32.
La Tarde. Santiago, 1969-70.
Tarea Urgente. Santiago, 1973.
La Tercera de la Hora. Santiago, 1969-73.
La Tribuna. Santiago, 1973.
La Última Hora. Santiago, 1969-73.
La Unión. Valparaíso, 1931.

Periodicals

Acción. Santiago, 1932.
Acción. Santiago, 1933.
Arauco. Santiago, 1960-67.
Atenea. Concepción, Chile, 1924–.
Barricada. Santiago, 1943.
Bases. Valparaíso, 1937.
Célula. Santiago, 1932-33.
Chile. Universidad. *Anales* . . . . Santiago, 1931–.
Chile en la Resistencia. Mexico, 1974-75.
Chile Hoy. Santiago, 1972-73.
Chile Informativo Internacional. Buenos Aires, 1974.
Chile Pan-American. New York, 1932-33.
Cuadernos de la Realidad Nacional. Santiago, 1969-73
Ercilla. Santiago, 1933-75.
Espartaco. Santiago, 1939-47.
Hoy. Santiago, 1931-43.

Latin America. London, 1971-75.
Memorial del Ejército de Chile. Santiago, 1932.
Mensaje. Santiago, 1969-71.
Non-Intervention in Chile. *Chile Newsletter.* Berkeley, Calif., 1973-74.
North American Congress on Latin America. *NACLA's Latin America and Empire Report.* New York, 1971-75.
Núcleo. Valparaíso, 1934.
Nueva Estrategia. Santiago, 1970.
Nuevos Rumbos. Santiago, 1954–.
Panorama Económico. Santiago, 1959-73.
Partido Socialista. *Boletín.* Mexico, 1974.
———. *Boletín del comité central* . . . . Santiago, 1963.
———. *Boletín interno* . . . . Santiago, 1943.
———. *Boletín Socialista.* Magallanes, Chile, 1936.
Política y Espíritu. Santiago, 1945-64.
Portada. Santiago, 1970-73.
Principios. Santiago, 1933-34.
Punto Final. Santiago, 1968-73.
Qué Pasa. Santiago, 1972-73.
Revista de la Universidad Técnica del Estado. Santiago, 1971-73.
Rumbo. Santiago, 1939.
Ruta. Antofagasta, Chile, 1935.
Sepa. Santiago, 1973.
El Socialista. Concepción, Chile, 1932-34.
El Socialista. Magallanes, Chile, 1938.
El Socialista. Puerto Natales, Chile, 1935.
El Socialista. Valparaíso, 1935.
Topaze. Santiago, 1931-70.
Zig-Zag. Santiago, 1931-52.

Articles

Affonso, Almino. "Trayectoria del movimiento campesino chileno," *Cuadernos de la Realidad Nacional,* no. 1 (Sept., 1969), pp. 15-31.
Allende, Salvador. "Trayectoria del Partido Socialista," Partido Socialista, *Boletín interno* . . . , (Oct., 1943), pp. 3-7.
Aranda, Sergio, and Martínez, Alberto. "Estructura económica: algunas características fundamentales," in Aníbal Pinto et al., *Chile, hoy,* pp. 55-172.
Barría, Jorge. "Chile. La cuestión política y social. 1920-1926," Chile, Universidad, *Anales* . . . , no. 116 (4th trimester, 1959), pp. 56-73.
Berman B., Natalio. "Eugenio Matte Hurtado," in Comité Regional del Partido Socialista de Santiago, eds., *Homenaje* . . . , pp. 11-14.
Bicheno, H. E. "Anti-Parliamentary Themes in Chilean History: 1920-70," *Government and Opposition,* VII, no. 3 (Summer, 1972), pp. 351-88.
Borón, Atilio. "Movilización política y crisis política en Chile," *Aportes,* no. 20 (Apr., 1971), pp. 41-69.

Casali Castillo, Lucy. "Los partidos populares como expresión del norte de Chile," *Occidente,* año XIV, no. 121 (Nov.-Dec., 1959), pp. 23-29.

Castillo, Leonardo; Sáez, Arturo; and Rogers, Patricio. "Notas para un estudio de la historia del movimiento obrero en Chile," *Cuadernos de la Realidad Nacional,* no. 4 (June, 1970), pp. 3-30.

Chapman, Charles Edward. "The Chilean Elections," *The Nation,* CXI, no. 2885 (Oct. 20, 1920), pp. 445-46.

Cifuentes Solar, Oscar. "Declaración," *Núcleo,* no. 6 (Nov. 1, 1934), pp. 3-20.

Cumplido, Francisco. "Constitución política de 1925: hoy, crisis de las instituciones políticas chilenas," *Cuadernos de la Realidad Nacional,* no. 5 (Sept., 1970), pp. 25-40.

Dávila, Carlos G. "The Montevideo Conference. Antecedents and Accomplishments," *International Conciliation,* no. 300 (May, 1934), pp. 121-58.

Di Tella, Torcuato. "Populism and Reform in Latin America," in Claudio Veliz, ed., *Obstacles to Change in Latin America,* pp. 47-74.

Doyle, Henry Grattan. "Chilean Dictatorship Overthrown," *Current History,* XXXIV (Sept., 1931), pp. 918-22.

———. "The Chilean Elections," *Current History,* XXXVII (Dec., 1932), pp. 344-45.

———. "The Chilean Scramble for Power," *Current History,* XXXVI (Aug., 1932), pp. 591-95.

———. "Chile in a New Revolution," *Current History,* XXXVI (July, 1932), pp. 477-80.

———. "Fascism in South America," *Current History,* XXXVIII (Aug., 1933), p. 599.

Drake, Paul W. "The Chilean Socialist Party and Coalition Politics, 1932-1946," *Hispanic American Historical Review,* LIII, no. 4 (Nov., 1973), pp. 619-43.

———. "The Political Responses of the Chilean Upper Class to the Great Depression and the Threat of Socialism, 1931-1933," in Frederic Cople Jaher, ed., *The Rich, the Well Born, and the Powerful: Elites and Upper Classes in History.* Urbana, Ill., 1973. Pp. 304-37.

Edelman, Murray. "Symbols and Political Quiescence," *American Political Science Review,* LIV, no. 3 (Sept., 1960), pp. 695-704.

Fagen, Richard R. "The United States and Chile: Roots and Branches," *Foreign Affairs* (Jan., 1975), pp. 297-313.

Faletto, Enzo, and Ruiz, Eduardo. "Conflicto político y estructura social," in Aníbal Pinto et al., *Chile, hoy,* pp. 213-54.

Feliú Cruz, Guillermo. "La evolución política, económica y social de Chile," Chile, Universidad, *Anales . . . ,* no. 119 (3rd trimester, 1960), pp. 45-85.

Galarza, Ernest. "The Economic Crisis in Latin America," *Foreign Policy Bulletin,* XI, no. 22 (Apr. 1, 1932), pp. 1-2.

———. "Latin America in Turmoil," *Foreign Policy Bulletin,* XI, no. 48 (Sept. 30, 1932), pp. 1-2.

———. "Socialists Seize Government in Chile," *Foreign Policy Bulletin,* XI, no. 33 (June 17, 1932), pp. 1-2.

García Márquez, Gabriel. "The Death of Salvador Allende," *Harper's*, no. 1486 (Mar., 1974), pp. 46-53.

Gray, Richard B., and Kirwin, Frederick R. "Presidential Succession in Chile: 1817-1966," *Journal of Inter-American Studies*, XI, no. 1 (Jan., 1969), pp. 144-59.

Grove Vallejo, Marmaduke. "Discurso . . . ," *Núcleo*, no. 1 (June 1, 1934), pp. 1-20.

———. "La elección presidencial de 1932," *Claridad*, Apr. 24, 1938, p. 2.

Guerra, Gregorio. "Revolución y crisis de la racionalización," *Cuadernos de la Economía Mundial*, no. 6 (1932), pp. 1-32.

Haring, C. H. "Chilean Politics, 1920-1928," *Hispanic American Historical Review*, XI, no. 1 (Feb., 1931), pp. 1-26.

———. "The Chilean Revolution of 1931," *Hispanic American Historical Review*, XIII, no. 2 (May, 1933), pp. 197-203.

———. "Chile Moves Left," *Foreign Affairs*, XVII, no. 3 (Apr., 1939), pp. 618-24.

Heise González, Julio. "La constitución de 1925 y las nuevas tendencias político-sociales," Chile, Universidad, *Anales . . .* , no. 80 (4th trimester, 1950), pp. 95-234.

Hennessy, Alistair. "Latin America," in Ghita Ionescu and Ernest Gellner, eds., *Populism: Its Meanings and National Characteristics*, pp. 28-61.

Hobsbawm, Eric J. "Chile: Year One," *New York Review of Books*, XVII, no. 4 (Sept. 23, 1971), pp. 23-32.

"Los jefes del socialismo: Carlos Alberto Martínez," *Bases*, no. 2 (Nov., 1937), pp. 5-10.

"Los jefes del socialismo: Schnake," *Bases*, no. 1 (Oct., 1937), pp. 9-16.

Jobet, Julio César. "Alejandro Escobar Carvallo y el movimiento obrero chileno," *Arauco*, no. 84 (Jan., 1967), pp. 53-60.

———. "La juventud de 1930 y el socialismo," *Arauco*, no. 9 (July, 1960), pp. 29-32.

———. "Movimiento social obrero," in Chile, Universidad, *Desarrollo . . .* , I, pp. 51-106.

———. "Notas sobre la historiografía chilena," in Luis Durand et al., *Historiografía chilena*. [Santiago?], 1949. Pp. 345-77.

———. "Origenes y primeros congresos del Partido Socialista," *Arauco*, no. 12 (Oct., 1960), pp. 5-19.

———. "El Partido Socialista y el Frente Popular en Chile," *Arauco*, no. 85 (Feb., 1967), pp. 13-47.

———. "La penetración imperialista y el movimiento obrero en Chile," *Espartaco*, nos. 2-3 (July 30, 1947), pp. 29-37.

———. "La personalidad de Oscar Schnake y los primeros años del Partido Socialista," *Arauco*, no. 73 (Feb., 1966), pp. 2-20.

———. "La personalidad socialista de Eugenio González Rojas," *Arauco*, no. 42 (July, 1963), pp. 8-11.

———. "Revolución socialista del 4 de junio de 1932," *Arauco*, no. 8 (June, 1960), pp. 49-50.

————. "Semblanza de Eugenio Matte Hurtado," *Arauco*, no. 15 (Jan.-Feb., 1961), pp. 41-43.

————. "Trayectoria del Partido Socialista de Chile," *Arauco*, no. 63 (Apr., 1965), pp. 5-15.

————. "Tres semblanzas de socialistas chilenas," *Arauco*, no. 69 (Oct., 1965), pp. 22-42.

Johnson, Dale L. "Industrialization, Social Mobility, and Class Formation in Chile," *Studies in Comparative International Development*, III (1967-68).

Kenworthy, Eldon. "Coalitions in the Political Development of Latin America," in Sven Groennings, E. W. Kelley, and Michael Leiserson, eds., *The Study of Coalition Behavior*. New York, 1970. Pp. 103-40.

Kling, Merle. "Toward a Theory of Power and Political Instability in Latin America," in James Petras and Maurice Zietlin, eds., *Latin America*, pp. 76-93.

Labarca H., Amanda. "Apuntes para estudiar la clase media en Chile," *Atenea*, XCIX, nos. 305-306 (Nov.-Dec., 1950), pp. 239-57.

Levine B., Flavián. "Indices de producción física," *Economía*, año V, nos. 10-11 (July, 1944), pp. 69-98.

————. "La renta nacional," in Francisco Méndez, ed., *Chile: tierra y destino*, pp. 643-61.

Levine B., Flavián, and Crocco Ferrari, Juan. "La población chilena," *Economía*, año V, nos. 10-11 (July, 1944), pp. 31-68.

————. "La población chilena como fuerza de trabajo," *Economía*, año VI, no. 14 (1st trimester, 1945), pp. 15-85.

Love, Joseph L. "Political Participation in Brazil," *Luso-Brazilian Review*, VII, no. 2 (Dec., 1970), pp. 3-24.

McKenzie, Robert T., and Silver, Allan. "The Delicate Experiment," in Seymour Martin Lipset and Stein Rokkan, eds., *Party Systems and Voter Alignments*, pp. 115-25.

"Manuel Hidalgo, primer embajador socialista," *Rumbo*, no. 2 (July, 1939), pp. 13-16.

"¡La masonería traiciona a Chile!" *Trabajo*, Jan. 6, 1954, p. 4.

Mayorga, Wilfredo. "Las asambleas del hambre," *Ercilla*, no. 1567 (June 2, 1965), pp. 4-5, 10.

————. "Los caciques electorales," *Ercilla*, no. 1706 (Feb. 28, 1968), p. 15.

————. "Caímos por no armar el pueblo," *Ercilla*, no. 1603 (Feb. 23, 1966), pp. 14-15.

————. "El camino a la Moneda," *Ercilla*, no. 1588 (Oct. 27, 1965), pp. 14-15.

————. "Chile bloqueado por los chilenos," *Ercilla*, no. 1702 (Jan. 31, 1968), p. 15.

————. "Crisis con sangre," *Ercilla*, no. 1682 (Aug. 30, 1967), p. 15.

————. "Cuando el ejército 'dio pase' a don Pedro," *Ercilla*, no. 1687 (Oct. 4, 1967), p. 15.

————. "Cuando el PS gritaba viva el ejército," *Ercilla*, no. 1613 (May 4, 1966), pp. 14-15.

————. "Cuando Montero 'se somete,'" *Ercilla*, no. 1598 (Jan. 19, 1966), pp. 18-19.

————. "Cuatro cartas de triunfo para don Pedro," *Ercilla*, no. 1622 (July 6, 1966), pp. 23-25.

————. "La derecha deseaba la dictadura," *Ercilla*, no. 1693 (Nov. 29, 1967), p. 15.

————. "La difícil generación del 20," *Ercilla*, no. 1720 (June 5-11, 1968), pp. 43-44.

————. "Don Arturo y los cuarteles," *Ercilla*, no. 1745 (Nov. 27-Dec. 3, 1968), p. 41.

————. "Entre la pluma y el sable," *Ercilla*, no. 1726 (July 17-23, 1968), pp. 43-44.

————. "El fantasma de Vignola en Santiago," *Ercilla*, no. 1606 (Mar. 16, 1966), pp. 18-19.

————. "Fuego contra la milicia," *Ercilla*, no. 1610 (Apr. 13, 1966), pp. 18-19.

————. "La fugaz violencia del nacismo," *Ercilla*, no. 1611 (Apr. 20, 1966), pp. 18-19.

————. "La generación sacrificada," *Ercilla*, no. 1681 (Aug. 23, 1967), p. 13.

————. "El golpe de estado de 1939," *Ercilla*, no. 1701 (Jan. 24, 1968), p. 15.

————. "Las intrigas electorales de 1938," *Ercilla*, no. 1619 (June 15, 1966), pp. 18-19.

————. "El jesuita rebelde," *Ercilla*, no. 1713 (Apr. 17, 1968), p. 15.

————. "Jorge González von Marées," *Ercilla*, no. 1740 (Oct. 23-29, 1968), pp. 41-42.

————. "La Milicia Republicana," *Ercilla*, no. 1609 (Apr. 6, 1966), pp. 18-19.

————. "París contra Ibáñez," *Ercilla*, no. 1579 (Aug. 25, 1965), pp. 4-6.

————. "Por qué falló el avión rojo," *Ercilla*, no. 1580 (Sept. 1, 1965), pp. 4-5.

————. "Primeros pasos falangistas en la Moneda," *Ercilla*, no. 1624 (July 20, 1966), pp. 17-19.

————. "Rafael Luis Gumucio," *Ercilla*, no. 1730 (Aug. 14-20, 1968), pp. 41-42.

————. "Rafael Luis Gumucio, el amigo," *Ercilla*, no. 1731 (Aug. 21-27, 1968), pp. 41-42.

————. "Se equivocó el estado y ganó la iglesia," *Ercilla*, no. 1597 (Jan. 12, 1966), pp. 18-19.

————. "Todos bailamos el año veinte," *Ercilla*, no. 1561 (Apr. 21, 1965), pp. 4-5.

————. "Todos fuimos anarquistas," *Ercilla*, no. 1676 (July 19, 1967), p. 15.

————. "Los últimos caciques," *Ercilla*, no. 1709 (Mar. 20, 1968), p. 15.

————. "Y don Pedro se subió a la troika," *Ercilla*, no. 1618 (June 8, 1966), pp. 16-17.

Menges, Constantine. "Public Policy and Organized Business in Chile," *Journal of International Affairs*, XX (1966), pp. 343-65.

Montero Moreno, René. "Los principios comunistas . . . ," *Memorial del Ejército de Chile*, (Jan., 1932), pp. 45-53.

Newton, Ronald. "On 'Functional Groups,' 'Fragmentation,' and 'Pluralism' in Spanish American Political Society," *Hispanic American Historical Review,* L, no. 1 (Feb., 1970), pp. 1-29.

"Nitrogen," *Fortune,* VI, no. 2 (Aug., 1932), pp. 43-70, 90-91.

Nun, José. "The Middle-Class Military Coup," in Claudio Veliz, ed., *The Politics of Conformity in Latin America,* pp. 66-118.

Nunn, Frederick M. "Military Rule in Chile: The Revolutions of September 5, 1924, and January 23, 1925," *Hispanic American Historical Review,* XLVII, no. 1 (Feb., 1967), pp. 1-21.

————. "New Thoughts on Military Intervention in Latin American Politics: The Chilean Case, 1973," *Journal of Latin American Studies,* VII (Nov., 1975), pp. 271-304.

Petras, Betty and James F. "Ballots into Bullets: Epitaph for a Peaceful Revolution," *Ramparts,* XII, no. 4 (Nov., 1973), pp. 21-28, 59-62.

Petras, James, and Alexander, Robert J. "Two Views of Allende's Victory," *New Politics,* VIII, no. 4 (Fall, 1970), pp. 72-81.

Pinto, Aníbal. "Desarrollo económico y relaciones sociales," in Aníbal Pinto et al., *Chile, hoy,* pp. 5-52.

Portes, Alejandro. "Leftist Radicalism in Chile (A Test of Three Hypotheses)," *Comparative Politics,* II (Jan., 1970), pp. 251-74.

Prothro, James, and Chaparro, Patricio E. "Public Opinion and the Movement of Chilean Government to the Left, 1952-72," *Journal of Politics,* XXXVI (Feb., 1974), pp. 2-43.

Ratinoff, Luis. "The New Urban Groups: The Middle Classes," in Seymour Martin Lipset and Aldo Solari, eds., *Elites in Latin America,* pp. 61-93.

Rosenstein-Rodan, Paul N. "Why Allende Failed," *Challenge,* XVII (May-June, 1974), pp. 7-13.

Sánchez, Luis Alberto. "Marmaduke Grove," *Zig-Zag,* año XLVII, no. 2424 (Sept. 8, 1951), p. 39.

Sanders, Thomas G. "The Process of Partisanship in Chile," *American University Field Staff Reports,* XX, no. 1 (Oct., 1973).

————. "Urban Pressure, Natural Resource Constraints, and Income Redistribution in Chile," *American Universities Field Staff Reports,* XX, no. 2 (Dec., 1973).

Sartori, Giovanni. "European Political Parties," in Joseph LaPalombara and Myron Weiner, eds., *Political Parties and Political Development,* pp. 137-76.

————. "From the Sociology of Politics to Political Sociology," in Seymour Martin Lipset, ed., *Politics and the Social Sciences,* pp. 65-100.

Schnake, Oscar. "No somos un partido más," in Comité Regional del Partido Socialista de Santiago, eds., *Homenaje . . . ,* pp. 5-6.

Scott, Robert E. "Political Elites and Political Modernization: The Crisis of Transition," in Seymour Martin Lipset and Aldo Solari, *Elites in Latin America,* pp. 117-45.

————. "Political Parties and Policy-Making in Latin America," in Joseph LaPalombara and Myron Weiner, eds., *Political Parties and Political Development,* pp. 331-67.

Sigmund, Paul E. "Allende in Retrospect," *Problems of Communism* (May-June, 1974), pp. 45-62.

———. "The 'Invisible Blockade' and the Overthrow of Allende," *Foreign Affairs* (Jan., 1974), pp. 322-40.

———. "Seeing Allende through the Myths," *Worldview* (Apr., 1974), pp. 16-21.

Soares, Glaucio, and Hamblin, Robert L. "Socio-economic Variables and Voting for the Radical Left: Chile, 1952," *American Political Science Review*, LXI, no. 4 (Dec., 1967), pp. 1053-65.

Solaún, Mauricio, and Cepeda, Fernando. "Alternative Strategies in Allende's Chile: On the Politics of Brinkmanship," *Land Tenure Center Special Report*, University of Wisconsin-Madison, 1973.

"South America III: Chile," *Fortune*, XVII, no. 5 (May, 1938), pp. 74-83, 148-72.

Sunkel, Osvaldo. "Change and Frustration in Chile," in Claudio Veliz, ed., *Obstacles to Change in Latin America*, pp. 116-44.

Teitelboim, Volodia. "Algunas experiencias chilenas sobre el problema de la burguesía nacional," *Principios*, no. 59 (July, 1959), pp. 20-30.

Thomas, Jack Ray. "The Evolution of a Chilean Socialist: Marmaduke Grove," *Hispanic American Historical Review*, XLVII, no. 1 (Feb., 1967), pp. 22-37.

———. "Marmaduke Grove and the Chilean National Election of 1932," *The Historian*, XXIX, no. 1 (Nov., 1966), pp. 22-33.

———. "The Socialist Republic of Chile," *Journal of Inter-American Studies*, VI, no. 2 (Apr., 1964), pp. 203-20.

Thomson, Charles A. "Chile Struggles for National Recovery," *Foreign Policy Reports*, IX, no. 25 (Feb. 14, 1934), pp. 282-92.

Valenzuela, Arturo. "Political Constraints and the Prospects for Socialism in Chile," in Douglas A. Chalmers, ed., *Changing Latin America*. N.p., 1972. Pp. 65-82.

———. "The Scope of the Chilean Party System," *Comparative Politics*, IV, no. 2 (Jan., 1972), pp. 179-99.

Varela Carmona, Héctor. "Distribución del ingreso nacional," *Panorama Económico*, año XIII, no. 207 (Oct., 1959), p. 405.

———. "Distribución del ingreso nacional en Chile a través de las diversas clases sociales," *Panorama Económico*, año XII, no. 199 (Feb., 1959), pp. 61-70.

Vera, González. "Meditación electoral," *Célula*, no. 5 (Oct. 26, 1932), pp. 1-2.

Viera-Gallo, José Antonio, and Villela, Hugo. "Consideraciones preliminares para el estudio del estado en Chile," *Cuadernos de la Realidad Nacional*, no. 5 (Sept., 1970), pp. 3-24.

Weffort, Francisco. "El populismo en la política brasileña," in Celso Furtado et al., *Brasil: hoy*. Mexico, 1968. Pp. 54-84.

Winkler, Max. "Session on Investments and National Policy of the United States in Latin America," *American Economic Review: Supplement*, XXII, no. 1 (Mar., 1932), pp. 144-51.

Zeitlin, Maurice. "The Social Determinants of Political Democracy in Chile," in James Petras and Maurice Zeitlin, eds., *Latin America*, pp. 220-34.
Zemelman Merino, Hugo. "Problemas ideológicos de la izquierda," *Arauco*, no. 58 (Nov., 1964), pp. 50-60.

Books and Pamphlets

Abovich, Miguel. *Reflexiones inherentes al momento actual.* Valparaíso, 1932.
Acción Nacionalista de Chile. *Ideología.* Santiago, 1932.
Acción Republicana. *Programa y estatutos.* Santiago, 1937.
Adhel, Malek. *La campaña electoral en la provincia de Santiago.* Santiago, 1932.
Affonso, Almino. *Esbozo histórico del movimiento campesino.* Santiago, 1973.
Affonso, Almino, et al., *Movimiento campesino chileno.* 2 vols. Santiago, 1970.
Agor, Weston H. *The Chilean Senate.* Austin, Tex., and London, 1971.
La Agrupación Económica-Social de la Clase Media. *Programa.* Valparaíso, [1931?].
Aguilar, Luis E., ed. *Marxism in Latin America.* New York, 1968.
Aguirre Cerda, Pedro. *El problema industrial.* Santiago, 1933.
Ahumada C., Jorge. *En vez de la miseria.* 5th ed. Santiago, 1965.
Alarcón Pino, Raúl. *La clase media en Chile.* Santiago, 1947.
Aldunate Phillips, Arturo. *Un pueblo en busca de su destino.* Santiago, 1947.
Aldunate Phillips, Raúl. *Ruído de sables.* Santiago, [1971?].
———. *Sentido moderno de liberalismo.* Santiago, 1943.
Alegría, Fernando. *Como un arbol rojo.* Santiago, 1968.
———. *Mañana los guerreros* .... Santiago, 1964.
Alessandri Palma, Arturo. *El alma de Alessandri.* Santiago, 1925.
———. *Discurso de incorporación.* Santiago, 1935.
———. *El Presidente Alessandri.* Santiago, 1926.
———. *Rectificaciones al tomo IX.* Santiago, 1941.
———. *Recuerdos de gobierno.* 3 vols. Santiago, 1952.
———. *Revolución de 1891.* Santiago, 1950.
Alexander, Robert J. *Aprismo.* Kent, Ohio, 1973.
———. *Communism in Latin America.* New Brunswick, N.J., 1957.
———. *Labor Parties of Latin America,* New York, 1942.
———. *Labor Relations in Argentina, Brazil, and Chile.* New York, 1962.
———. *Latin American Political Parties.* New York, 1973.
———. *Prophets of the Revolution.* New York, 1962.
———. *Trotskyism in Latin America.* Stanford, Calif., 1973.
———. *The Venezuelan Democratic Revolution.* New Brunswick, N.J., 1964.
Alford, Robert R. *Party and Society.* Chicago, 1963.
Algunos fundamentos de la intervención militar en Chile, septiembre, 1973. 2nd. ed. Santiago, 1974.
Allende, Salvador. *Aysén, presente y futuro.* Santiago, 1948.
———. *La conspiración contra Chile.* Buenos Aires, 1973.
———. *La contradicción de Chile.* Santiago, 1943.

———. *Las provincias enjuician el porvenir de Chile.* Santiago, 1947.

———. *La realidad médico-social chilena.* N.p., 1939.

———. *Su pensamiento político.* Santiago, 1972.

Altamirano, Carlos. *Decisión revolucionaria.* Santiago, 1973.

Alterman P., León. *El movimiento demográfico en Chile.* Santiago, 1946.

Álvarez Andrews, Oscar. *Bases para una constitución funcional.* Santiago, 1932.

———. *Chile monografía sociológica.* Mexico, 1965.

———. *Historia del desarrollo industrial de Chile.* Santiago, 1936.

Álvarez Villablanca, Agustín. *Objetivos del socialismo en Chile.* Santiago, 1946.

———. *El tercer frente.* Santiago, 1945.

Alzamora Ríos, Ramón. *Manifiesto del ex-diputado.* Antofagasta, Chile, 1932.

Amadeo Aracena, Luis. *Ensayos económicos, políticos y sociales.* Santiago, 1941.

Ampuero Díaz, Raúl. *Los ascensos militares ante el senado.* Santiago, 1966.

———. *En defensa del partido y del socialismo.* [Santiago?], 1948.

———. *La izquierda en punto muerto.* Santiago, 1969.

———. *La juventud en la frente del pueblo.* Santiago, 1939.

Amunátegui Jordán, Gabriel. *El liberalismo y su misión social.* Santiago, 1933.

Amunátegui Solar, Domingo. *El progreso intelectual y político de Chile.* Santiago, 1936.

———. *La segunda presidencia de Arturo Alessandri.* Santiago, 1961.

Anderson, Charles W. *Politics and Economic Change in Latin America.* Princeton, 1967.

Angell, Alan. *Politics and the Labour Movement in Chile.* London, 1972.

Antonioletti, Mario. *Cooperativismo.* Santiago, 1954.

———. *La moneda, el crédito y los bancos.* Santiago, 1934.

Arancibia Laso, Héctor. *La doctrina radical.* Santiago, 1937.

Araneda Bravo, Fidel. *El Arzobispo Errázuriz y la evolución política y social de Chile.* Santiago, 1956.

Aránguiz Latorre, Miguel. *El 4 de junio.* Santiago, 1933.

Arce G., Leopoldo. *La crisis chilena.* Santiago, 1932.

Arias Escobedo, Osvaldo. *La prensa obrera en Chile.* Santiago, 1970.

Arriagada, Genaro. *La oligarquía patronal chilena.* Santiago, 1970.

Arrieta Cañas, Luis. *El liberalismo y la cuestión social.* Santiago, 1932.

———. *El marxismo y la cuestión social.* Santiago, 1932.

La Asamblea Nacional de Acción Cívica. *Primera memoria semestral.* Santiago, 1932.

La Asamblea Radical de Iquique. *Don Arturo Alessandri.* Iquique, Chile, 1920.

Baily, Samuel L. *Labor, Nationalism, and Politics in Argentina.* New Brunswick, N.J., 1967.

Baltra Cortés, Alberto. *Gestión económica del gobierno de la Unidad Popular.* Santiago, 1973.

Bañados, Guillermo M. *¡Avancemos!* . . . . 2nd. ed. N.p., 1924.

———. *Las ideas se combaten con ideas* . . . . Santiago, 1933.

Barbosa, Enrique O. *Los liberales democráticos y la candidatura de don Enrique Zañartu Prieto.* Santiago, 1932.

Barraclough, Solon, et al. *Chile: reforma agraria y gobierno popular.* Buenos Aires, 1973.

Barría, Jorge. *Breve historia del sindicalismo chileno.* Santiago, 1961.

———. *El movimiento obrero en Chile.* Santiago, 1971.

Barría Soto, Francisco Conrado. *El Partido Radical.* Santiago, 1957.

Barros Ortiz, Tobías. *Recuerdos oportunos.* Santiago, 1938.

Barrueto, Héctor D. *Mi cuenta.* N.p., 1944.

Bauer, Arnold J. *Chilean Rural Society from the Spanish Conquest to 1930.* New York, 1975.

Beals, Carleton. *Lands of the Dawning Morrow.* Indianapolis and New York, 1948.

———. *Rio Grande to Cape Horn.* Boston, 1943.

Bedoya, Manuel. *Grove, su vida, su ejemplo, su obra.* N.p., [1944?].

Bello Codesido, Emilio. *Recuerdos políticos.* Santiago, 1954.

Beltrame Curubetto, Humberto. *Aspiraciones populares.* Iquique, Chile, [1938?].

Bennet, Juan Pablo. *La revolución del 5 de septiembre de 1924.* Santiago, [1926?].

Bentjerodt B., Jorge. *El desafío chileno.* Santiago, 1970.

Berman B., Natalio. *Berman al servicio del pueblo.* Santiago, 1945.

———. *Digo lo que pienso; hago lo que digo.* N.p., n.d.

———. *El Diputado Berman defiende a los obreros del carbón.* Santiago, 1941.

Bermúdez Miral, Oscar. *El drama político de Chile.* Santiago, 1947.

Birns, Laurence, ed. *The End of Chilean Democracy.* New York, 1974.

Blanco, Hugo, et al. *La tragedia chilena.* Buenos Aires, 1973.

Blanco-Amor, Eduardo. *Chile a la vista.* 3rd ed. Santiago, 1957.

Blanksten, George I. *Perón's Argentina.* Chicago, 1953.

Blondel, J. *Voters, Parties, and Leaders.* Middlesex, England, 1965.

Bobillier, Guillermo. *Diálogos de FEBO.* N.p., 1946.

Boizard, Ricardo. *Cuatro retratos en profundidad.* Santiago, 1950.

———. *La democracia cristiana en Chile.* Santiago, 1963.

———. *Doctrinas sociales.* Santiago, 1933.

———. *Hacia el ideal político de una juventud.* Santiago, 1931.

———. *Historia de una derrota.* Santiago, 1941.

———. *Voces de la política, del púlpito y la calle.* Santiago, 1939.

Bonilla, Frank, and Glazer, Myron. *Student Politics in Chile.* New York and London, 1970.

Bowers, Claude G. *Chile through Embassy Windows.* New York, 1958.

Bravo, Alfredo Guillermo. *El 4 de junio: el festín de los audaces.* 2nd ed. Santiago, 1932.

Bravo, Enrique. *Actuación del senador por Aconcagua.* Santiago, 1935.

Bravo G., Alejandro. *Cincuenta años de vida masónica en Chile.* Santiago, 1951.

Bravo Lavín, Mario. *Chile frente al socialismo y al comunismo.* Santiago, 1934.

Bravo Ríos, Leonidas. *Lo que supo un auditor de guerra.* Santiago, 1955.

Brigada Parlamentaria Socialista. *Boletín informativo.* N.p., 1942.

Browne, C. G., and Cohn, Thomas S., eds. *The Study of Leadership.* Danville, Ill., 1958.

Brunner, Karl H. *Santiago de Chile*. Santiago, 1932.

Bureau Sudamericano de la Internacional Comunista. *Las grandes luchas revolucionarias del proletariado chileno*. Santiago, 1932.

Burgos Varas, Enrique. *A los radicales de mi patria*. Santiago, 1938.

Burnett, Ben G. *Political Groups in Chile*. Austin, Tex., 1970.

Butland, Gilbert J. *Chile*. London, 1953.

Cabero, Alberto. *Chile y los chilenos*. Santiago, 1926.

———. *Recuerdos de don Pedro Aguirre Cerda*. Santiago, 1948.

Cabezas Cabezas, Clodomiro. *Nuestro socialismo*. Santiago, 1932.

Cademártori, José. *La economía chilena*. Santiago, 1968.

Campaña presidencial de 1920. Candidatura del señor don Luis Barros Borgoño. Santiago, 1920.

Campbell, Angus, et al. *The American Voter*. New York and London, 1960.

Campos Harriet, Fernando. *Historia constitucional de Chile*. Santiago, 1956.

Carlos, Newton, et al. *Chile com Allende: ¿para onde vai?* Rio de Janeiro, 1970.

Caro, José María. *La iglesia está con el pueblo*. Valparaíso, 1940.

———. *El misterio de la masonería*. Santiago, 1926.

Casanueva Valencia, Fernando, and Fernández Canque, Manuel. *El Partido Socialista y la lucha de clases en Chile*. Santiago, 1973.

Castro, Baltazar. *¿Me permite una interrupción?* Santiago, 1962.

Castro, Fidel, and Allende, Beatriz. *Homenaje a Salvador Allende*. Buenos Aires, 1973.

Castro D., Juan E. *Conciencia socialista*. Antofagasta, Chile, 1939.

Catilina. Santiago, 1920.

Celis Maturana, Armando. *El Diputado Armando Celis Maturana rinde cuenta de su mantado . . . .* Santiago, 1936.

Cerda, José M. *Relación histórica de la revolución de la armada de Chile*. Concepción, Chile, 1934.

Chamudes, Marcos. *Chile, una advertencia americana*. [Santiago?], [1972?].

Charlín O., Carlos. *Del avión rojo a la república socialista*. Santiago, 1972.

Chelén Rojas, Alejandro. *Aspectos históricos de la revolución mexicana*. Chañaral, Chile, 1938.

———. *Flujo y reflujo del socialismo chileno*. Santiago, 1961.

———. *El Partido de la victoria*. Chañaral, Chile, 1939.

———. *El Partido Socialista de Chile*. Santiago, 1972.

———. *Trayectoria del socialismo*. Buenos Aires, 1967.

———. *Tres hombres. Carlos Marx, Recabarren y Grove*. Chañaral, Chile, 1940.

Chile. Universidad. *Desarrollo de Chile en la primera mitad del siglo XX*. 2 vols. Santiago, 1953.

Chile. Universidad. Instituto de Economía. *Desarrollo económico de Chile, 1940-1956*. Santiago, 1956.

———. *La migración interna en Chile en el período 1940-1952*. Santiago, 1959.

Chile-American Association. *Chile in 1930*. New York, 1930.

Chilean Who's Who. Santiago, 1937.

Chile Joven. *La palmada en la frente*. Santiago, 1970.

Cifuentes, Antonio. *Evolución de la economía chilena desde la crisis hasta nuestros días.* Santiago, 1935.

Cifuentes, José María. *La propiedad.* Santiago, 1932.

Clagett, Helen L. *A Guide to the Law and Legal Literature of Chile, 1917-1946.* Washington, D.C., 1947.

Clever, F. B. *¡Atras!* Valparaíso, 1932.

Clissold, Stephen. *Chilean Scrap-Book.* London, 1952.

———, ed. *Soviet Relations with Latin America, 1918-1968.* London, 1970.

La Comisión de Agit. Prop. del C. C. del Partido Comunista. Sección Chilena de I. C. *Plan de estudios de un curso de capacitación.* Santiago, 1933.

El Comité Central del Partido Comunista. *¡Contra la dictadura fascista de Ibáñez!* N.p., 1931.

El Comité de Estudiantes Universitarios. *Al tirano y sus secuaces.* N.p., 1931.

———. *Camaradas universitarios.* N.p., 1931.

El Comité de los Estudiantes Universitarios. *Camaradas universitarios.* N.p., 1931.

Comité Ejecutivo de la Internacional Comunista. *Tesis y resoluciones.* Buenos Aires, 1931.

Comité Regional del Partido Socialista de Santiago, eds. *Homenaje al 6th aniversario del Partido Socialista.* Santiago, 1939.

El complot abortado. Santiago, 1934.

El comunismo. Santiago, [1934?].

Concha, Aquiles. *A mis amigos y correligionarios de la provincia de Atacama.* [Santiago?], [1937?].

———. *A mis electores.* N.p., [1932?].

Congreso extraordinario del Partido Socialista. Santiago, 1944.

Congreso Nacional del Partido Comunista. *En defensa de la revolución.* Santiago, 1933.

Contreras Labarca, Carlos. *Alessandri, portavoz de las fuerzas reaccionarias y profascistas.* Santiago, 1945.

———. *¡Este es Schnake!* Santiago, 1941.

———. *Por la paz, por nuevas victorias del Frente Popular.* Santiago, 1939.

———. *El programa del Frente Popular debe ser realizado.* Santiago, [1940?].

———. *La traición de los jefes socialistas al descubierto.* N.p., 1941.

———. *El trotzkismo.* Santiago, 1937.

———. *Unidad para defender la victoria.* Santiago, 1938.

———. *Unión nacional y partido único.* Santiago, 1943.

Convención provincial radical de Chiloé. Ancud, Chile, 1940.

Corbalán González, Salomón. *Partido Socialista.* Santiago, 1957.

Correa, Ulises. *Discurso pronunciado . . . .* Santiago, 1941.

Correa Prieto, Luis. *El Presidente Ibáñez.* Santiago, 1962.

Corvalán, Luis. *Un Partido Comunista fuerte es garantía para el pueblo.* Santiago, 1967.

———. *El poder popular.* Santiago, 1969.

Cox Balmaceda, Ricardo. *Discurso.* Santiago, 1932.

Cruz-Coke, Ricardo. *Geografía electoral de Chile.* Santiago, 1952.
Cruz Salas, Luis. *Historia social de Chile: 1931-1945. Los partidos populares: 1931-1941.* Santiago, 1969.
Cuadra Poisson, Jorge de la. *Magia financiera.* Santiago, 1938.
―――. *Prolegomenos a la sociología y bosquejo de la evolución de Chile desde 1920.* Santiago, 1957.
―――. *La revolución que viene.* Santiago, 1931.
―――. *La verdad de las incidencias milicianas.* Santiago, 1935.
Daugherty, Charles H., ed. *Chile: Election Factbook.* Washington, D.C., 1963.
Dávila, Carlos G. *Chile no está arruinado.* N.p., 1932.
―――. *Latin-American Trade Development with the United States.* New York, 1928.
―――. *North American Imperialism.* New York, 1930.
―――. *We of the Americas.* Chicago. 1949.
Dávila de cuerpo entero. Santiago, 1932.
de Alas, Claudio. *Arturo Alessandri.* Santiago, 1915.
Debray, Regis. *The Chilean Revolution.* New York, 1971.
La defensa del obrero. Santiago, 1932.
Dell'Orto Prieto, Julio. *Un chileno al servicio de Chile.* Santiago, 1937.
de Petris Giesen, Héctor. *Historia del Partido Democrático.* Santiago, 1942.
Dimitroff, George. *¡Frente popular en todo el mundo!* Santiago, 1936.
Doctrina rossiana. Santiago, 1938.
Dogan, Mattei, and Rokkan, Stein, eds. *Quantitative Ecological Analysis in the Social Sciences.* Cambridge, Mass., 1969.
Domínguez, Eliodoro. *¿Que quiere el socialismo?* Santiago, 1937.
―――. *Un movimiento ideológico en Chile.* Santiago, 1935.
Donoso, Armando. *Conversaciones con don Arturo Alessandri.* Santiago, 1934.
―――, ed. *Recuerdos de cincuenta años.* Santiago, 1947.
Donoso, Luis. *La masonería.* Santiago, [1934?].
Donoso, Ricardo. *Alessandri, agitador y demoledor.* 2 vols. Mexico and Buenos Aires, 1952, 1954.
―――. *Desarrollo político y social de Chile desde la constitución de 1833.* Santiago, 1942.
―――. *La sátira política en Chile.* Santiago, 1950.
Duhalde Vásquez, Alfredo. *Gobiernos de izquierda.* Santiago, 1951.
Durán Bernales, Florencio. *El Partido Radical.* Santiago, 1958.
Durand, Georgina. *Mis entrevistas.* 2 vols. Santiago, 1943.
Durand, Luis. *Don Arturo.* Santiago, 1952.
―――. *Gente de mi tiempo.* Santiago, 1953.
Echaíz, René León. *Evolución histórica de los partidos políticos chilenos.* Santiago, 1939.
―――. *Liberalismo y conservantismo.* Curicó, Chile, 1936.
Echeverría de Larraín, Inés. *Alessandri.* Santiago, 1932.
Editorial "El Amigo del Pueblo." *El socialismo y el comunismo ante el sentido común.* 4 vols. Santiago, 1939.
Edwards, Agustín. *Las corporaciones y la doctrina liberal.* Santiago, 1934.

————. *Recuerdos de mi persecución.* Santiago, 1932.

Edwards Bello, Joaquín. *Criollos en París.* 3rd ed. Santiago, 1933.

————. *Crónicas del centenario.* Santiago, 1968.

————. *Nacionalismo continental.* Santiago, 1968.

————. *El roto.* 4th ed. Santiago, 1927.

Edwards Matte, Guillermo. *El Club de la Unión en sus ochenta años (1864-1944).* Santiago, 1944.

Edwards Vives, Alberto. *La fronda aristocrática.* 6th ed. Santiago, 1966.

Edwards Vives, Alberto, and Frei Montalva, Eduardo. *Historia de los partidos políticos chilenos.* Santiago, 1949.

Ellsworth, P. T. *Chile, an Economy in Transition.* New York, 1945.

Empresa Periodística "Chile," eds. *Diccionario biográfico de Chile.* 1st-9th eds. Santiago, 1936-55.

Errázuriz, Ladislao. *Los deberes del Partido Liberal en la hora actual.* Santiago, 1934.

Escobar Carvallo, Alejandro. *Un precursor socialista.* Santiago, 1932.

Escobar Zenteno, Aristodemo. *Compendio de la legislación social y desarrollo del movimiento obrero en Chile.* Santiago, 1940.

Escuela de Negocios de Valparaíso. Fundación Adolfo Ibáñez. *La economía de Chile durante el período de gobierno de la Unidad Popular.* N.p., 1974.

Espinosa, Januario. *Figuras de la política chilena.* Santiago, 1945.

Espinoza, Manuel. *Humanismo socialista.* Santiago, 1962.

Espoz, Diego. *Ante el abismo . . . .* Valparaíso, 1936.

Evans, Les, ed. *Disaster in Chile.* New York, 1974.

Eyzaguirre, Jaime. *Fisonomía histórica de Chile.* Mexico, 1948.

Faletto, Enzo; Ruiz, Eduardo; and Zemelman, Hugo. *Genesis histórica del proceso político chileno.* Santiago, 1971.

Feinberg, Richard E. *The Triumph of Allende.* New York, 1972.

Feliú Cruz, Guillermo. *Alessandri, personaje de la historia.* Santiago, 1950.

Fergusson, Erna. *Chile.* New York, 1943.

Fernández C., Juan F. *Pedro Aguirre Cerda y el Frente Popular chileno.* Santiago, 1938.

Fernández Larraín, Sergio. *Informe sobre el comunismo.* Sántiago, 1954.

————. *El Partido Conservador en la vida nacional.* Santiago, 1940.

————. *33 meses de gobierno de Frente Popular.* Santiago, 1941.

Fetter, Frank Whitson. *Monetary Inflation in Chile.* Princeton, 1931.

Figueroa, Virgilio. *Diccionário histórico y biográfico de Chile.* 5 vols. Santiago, 1925.

La Fracción Comunista del Grupo Avance. *¿Quién dividió el grupo avance?* Santiago, 1932.

Frank, André Gunder. *Capitalism and Underdevelopment in Latin America.* New York, 1966.

Frank, Waldo. *South American Journey.* New York, 1943.

Frei Montalva, Eduardo. *Chile desconocido.* Santiago, 1937.

Frente Funcional Socialista. *Manifiesto del Frente Funcional Socialista.* Santiago, 1934.

Frías Ojeda, René. *Ubicación histórica del cuatro de junio.* Santiago, 1939.
Fuentes, Jordi, and Cortes, Lia. *Diccionario político de Chile.* Santiago, 1967.
Fuenzalida, Humberto, et al. *Chile.* Buenos Aires, 1946.
Fuerzas Armadas y Carabineros. *Septiembre de 1973: los cien combates de una batalla.* Santiago, 1974.
Las fuerzas productoras ante la elección presidencial. Santiago, 1938.
Furtado, Celso, et al. *Brazil: hoy.* 2nd ed. Mexico, 1970.
Gaete Leighton, Julio. *Tarapacá y Antofagasta ante las consecuencias del pasado.* Iquique, Chile, 1931.
Gajardo Contreras, Samuel. *Alessandri y su destino.* Santiago, 1951.
Galdames, Luis. *A History of Chile.* Chapel Hill, N.C., 1941.
Garafulic Y., Andrés. *Carnalavaca.* Santiago, 1932.
Garay, Mario. *La cuestión de la unidad.* Santiago, 1968.
Garcés, Joan E. *Desarrollo político y desarrollo económico. Los casos de Chile y Colombia.* Santiago, 1972.
―――. *1970. La pugna política por la presidencia en Chile.* Santiago, 1971.
García F., Patricio, ed. *Los gremios patronales.* Santiago, [1973?].
―――. *El tancazo de ese 29 de junio . . . .* Santiago, 1973.
Garrido Merino, Edgardo. *Espíritu y acción del liberalismo.* Santiago, 1934.
Gil, Federico G. *The Political System of Chile.* Boston, 1966.
Gil, Federico G., and Parrish, Charles J. *The Chilean Presidential Election of September 4, 1964.* Washington, D.C., 1965.
Godoy Urrutia, César. *¿A dónde va el socialismo?* 2nd ed. Santiago, 1939.
―――. *Hombres y pueblos.* Santiago, 1966.
―――. *Manifiesto al magisterio de Chile.* Santiago, 1931.
―――. *¿Qué es el inconformismo?* 2nd ed. Santiago, 1940.
―――. *Los sucesos del 5 de septiembre.* Santiago, 1939.
Godoy Urzúa, Hernán. *Estructura social de Chile.* Santiago, 1971.
González, Pedro Luis. *50 años de labor de la Sociedad de Fomento Fabril.* Santiago, 1933.
González, Pedro Luis, and Soto Núñez, Miguel, eds. *Albúm gráfico e histórico de la Sociedad de Fomento Fabril y de la industria nacional.* Santiago, 1926.
González Díaz, Galo. *El congreso de la victoria.* Santiago, 1938.
―――. *La lucha por la formación del Partido Comunista de Chile.* Santiago, 1958.
González Echenique, Guillermo. *Reflexiones de la hora presente.* Santiago, 1934.
González Rojas, Eugenio. *Hombres.* Santiago, 1935.
―――. *El Partido Socialista Popular y la política del actual gobierno.* Santiago, 1949.
González Rojas, Eugenio, and Ampuero Díaz, Raúl. *La controversia permanente: socialismo y liberalismo. El socialismo único fundamento de la democracia. Carácter de la revolución chilena.* Santiago, 1957.
González Videla, Gabriel. *El Partido Radical y la evolución social de Chile.* Santiago, 1938.
González von Marées, Jorge. *La concepción nacista del estado.* Santiago, 1934.
―――. *La hora de la decisión.* Santiago, 1937.
―――. *El mal de Chile.* Santiago, 1940.

———. *La mentira democrática.* Santiago, 1936.

———. *El Movimiento Nacional-Socialista de Chile.* Santiago, 1932.

Grayson, George W., Jr. *El Partido Demócrata Cristiano Chileno.* Buenos Aires, 1968.

Grote, Federico. *¿Quiere ser socialista?* Santiago, 1933.

Grove Vallejo, Jorge. *Descorriendo el velo.* Valparaíso, 1933.

Grove Vallejo, Marmaduke. *Declaraciones del Senador Marmaduke Grove al "conflicto del carbón."* Santiago, 1947.

———. *Grove explica el peligro de una falsa unificación socialista.* Santiago, 1946.

———. *Manifiesto socialista.* Santiago, 1934.

———. *Reforma agraria.* Santiago, 1939.

———. *La relegación de Grove.* Valparaíso, 1933.

———. *Toda la verdad.* Paris, 1929.

Grupo Universitario Renovación. *Renovación. Declaración de principios.* Santiago, 1932.

Guilisasti Tagle, Sergio. *Partidos políticos chilenos.* 2nd ed. Santiago, 1964.

Guiñez Carrasco, Julio Enrique. *Interpretación de la evolución social y política de Chile desde 1932 a 1952.* Concepción, Chile, 1963.

Gumucio V., Rafael Luis. *El deber político.* Santiago, 1933.

———. *Me defiendo.* Santiago, 1939.

———. *No más.* Santiago, 1932.

Gunther, John. *Inside Latin America.* New York and London, 1941.

Guzmán Cortés, Leonardo. *Un episodio olvidado de la historia nacional.* Santiago, 1966.

Halperin, Ernst. *Nationalism and Communism in Chile.* Cambridge, Mass., 1965.

Hanson, Earl Parker. *Chile. Land of Progress.* New York, 1941.

Harrington, Michael. *Socialism.* New York, 1970.

Heredia M., Luis. *Como se construirá el socialismo.* Valparaíso, 1936.

Herring, Hubert. *Chile en la presidencia de don Pedro Aguirre Cerda.* Buenos Aires, 1971.

———. *Good Neighbors.* New Haven, 1941.

Hidalgo, Manuel, and Zapata, Emilio. *2 discursos en el parlamento.* Santiago, 1933.

Hirschman, Albert O. *Journeys toward Progress.* Garden City, N.Y., 1965.

Historia íntima de la revolución. Santiago, n.d.

Hofstadter, Richard. *The Age of Reform.* New York, 1955.

Hormachea Reyes, Armando. *El Frente Popular de 1938.* Santiago, 1968.

Horowitz, Irving Louis, ed. *Masses in Latin America.* New York, 1970.

Hott Kindermann, Erico. *Las sociedades agrícolas nacionales y su influencia en la agricultura de Chile.* Santiago, 1944.

Hubner, Manuel Eduardo, et al. *Forjando la unión nacional.* Santiago, 1944.

Huidobro, Vicente. *Obras completas . . . .* 2 vols. Santiago, 1964.

Huntington, Samuel P. *Political Order in Changing Societies.* New Haven, 1968.

Ianni, Octavio. *Crisis in Brazil.* New York and London, 1970.

———. *La formación del estado populista en América latina.* Mexico, 1975.

Ibáñez, Bernardo. *Discurso pronunciado por el Secretario General de la Confederación de Trabajadores de Chile.* Santiago, 1946.

———. *El movimiento sindical internacional y la fundación de la C.I.T.* Santiago, 1949.

———. *El socialismo y el porvenir de los pueblos.* Santiago, 1946.

Ibáñez B., Adolfo. *Santiago y las provincias.* Valparaíso, 1936.

Ibáñez del Campo, Carlos. *Lo que haremos por Chile.* Santiago, 1952.

———. *Programa presidencial.* Santiago, 1938.

Iglesias Mascaregno, Augusto. *Alessandri, una etapa de la democracia en América.* Santiago, 1960.

Illanes Benítez, Francisco. *La economía chilena y el comercio exterior.* Santiago, 1944.

El imperialismo extranjero en Chile. Santiago, 1937.

Infante Barros, Marta. *Testigos del treinta y ocho.* Santiago, 1972.

Ionescu, Ghita, and Gellner, Ernest. *Populism: Its Meanings and National Characteristics.* London, 1969.

Jiles Pizarro, Jorge. *Partido Comunista de Chile.* Santiago, 1957.

Jobet, Julio César. *Ensayo crítico del desarrollo económico-social de Chile.* Santiago, 1955.

———. *El Partido Socialista de Chile.* 2 vols. Santiago, 1971.

———. *El Partido Socialista frente a la penetración imperialista en Chile.* N.p., 1939.

———. *Los precursores del pensamiento social de Chile.* 2 vols. Santiago, 1955.

———. *Recabarren.* Santiago, 1955.

———. *Significado del Partido Socialista en la realidad nacional.* Santiago, 1940.

———. *El socialismo chileno a través de sus congresos.* Santiago, 1965.

———. *El socialismo en Chile.* Santiago, 1956.

———. *Socialismo y comunismo.* Santiago, 1952.

Jobet, Julio César, and Chelén Rojas, Alejandro. *Pensamiento teórico y político del Partido Socialista de Chile.* Santiago, 1972.

Johnson, Dale L., ed. *The Chilean Road to Socialism.* Garden City, N.Y., 1973.

Johnson, John J. *Political Change in Latin America.* Stanford, Calif., 1958.

Joxe, Alain. *Las fuerzas armadas en el sistema político de Chile.* Santiago, 1970.

La junta de gobierno al país. Santiago, 1932.

Kaempffer Villagran, Guillermo. *Así sucedió, 1850-1925.* Santiago, 1962.

Kantor, Harry. *The Ideology and Program of the Peruvian Aprista Movement.* Berkeley, Calif. 1953.

Kaufman, Robert R. *The Chilean Political Right and Agrarian Reform: Resistance and Moderation.* Washington, D.C., 1967.

———. *The Politics of Land Reform in Chile, 1950-1970.* Cambridge, Mass., 1972.

Keller R., Carlos. *Como salir de la crisis.* Santiago, 1932.

———. *La eterna crisis chilena.* Santiago, 1931.

———. *Nuestro problema monetario.* Santiago, 1932.

———. *Un país al garete.* Santiago, 1932.

Kinsbruner, Jay. *Chile: A Historical Interpretation.* New York, 1973.

Klaren, Peter F. *Modernization, Dislocation, and Aprismo*. Austin, Tex., 1973.

Klein Reidel, Federico. *Las nacionalizaciones y la democracia cristiana*. Santiago, 1964.

Krimerman, Leonard I., and Perry, Lewis, eds. *Patterns of Anarchy*. Garden City, N.Y. 1966.

Krüger, Viktor. *¡Leer o perecer!* Valdivia, Chile, 1932.

Labarca, Santiago. *Figuras de agitadores*. N.p., 1923.

Labarca Fuentes, Osvaldo. *Los enanos de la libertad*. 2nd ed. Santiago, 1932.

Labarca Goddard, Eduardo. *Chile al rojo*. Santiago, 1971.

Labrousse, Alain. *L'experience chilienne*. Paris, 1972.

Lafertte, Elías. *Como triunfaremos en las elecciones de 1941*. Santiago, 1940.

———. *Vida de un comunista*. Santiago, 1961.

Lafertte, Elías, and Contreras Labarca, Carlos. *Los comunistas, el Frente Popular y la independencia nacional*. Santiago, 1937.

———. *El Frente Popular vive y vencerá*. Santiago, 1941.

Lagos Escobar, Ricardo. *La concentración del poder económico*. Santiago, 1961.

Lagos Valenzuela, Tulio. *Bosquejo histórico del movimiento obrero en Chile*. Santiago, 1941.

Lamour, Catherine. *Le pari chilien*. Paris, 1972.

LaPalombara, Joseph, and Weiner, Myron, eds. *Political Parties and Political Development*. Princeton, 1966.

Larraín, Jaime. *Orientación de nuestra política agraria*. Santiago, 1932.

Larraín Bravo, Ricardo. *Biografías sucintas de algunos próceres de Chile*. Santiago, 1939.

Lasswell, Harold D. *Psychopathology and Politics*. Chicago, 1930.

Lasswell, Harold D., and Kaplan, Abraham. *Power and Society*. New Haven, 1950.

Latcham, Ricardo A. *Chuquicamata, estado yankee*. Santiago, 1926.

Lavín, Carlos. *Chile visto por los extranjeros*. Santiago, 1949.

Lechner, Norbert. *La democracia en Chile*. Buenos Aires, 1970.

El liberalismo. Santiago, 1939.

Liga de Asalariados Pro-Patria. *¿Revolución o paz? Año 1932*. N.p., 1932.

Lipset, Seymour Martin, ed. *Politics and the Social Sciences*. New York, 1969.

Lipset, Seymour Martin, and Hofstadter, Richard. *Sociology and History: Methods*. New York, 1968.

Lipset, Seymour Martin, and Rokkan, Stein, eds. *Party Systems and Voter Alignments*. New York, 1967.

Lipset, Seymour Martin, and Solari, Aldo, eds. *Elites in Latin America*. New York, 1967.

Lira Urquieta, Pedro. *El futuro del país y el Partido Conservador*. Santiago, 1934.

Lo que dijo Grove. Santiago, 1934.

López, Osvaldo. *Diccionario biográfico obrero de Chile*. Santiago, 1912.

Loveman, Brian. *Struggle in the Countryside: Politics and Rural Labor in Chile, 1919-1973*. Bloomington, Ind., 1976.

Loyola Acuña, Ernesto. *El hombre que frustró una revolución*. Talca, Chile, 1942.

———. *La verdad en marcha*. Talca, Chile, 1938.

Luco, Germán. *Desde Alessandri hasta Alessandri.* Concepción, 1932.

Luksic Savoia, Zarko. *La conducta del votante y sus razones sociales.* Santiago, 1961.

McBride, George M. *Chile: Land and Society.* New York, 1936.

McCaa, Robert, comp. *Chile. XI censo de población (1940).* Santiago, n.d.

Macchiavello Varas, Santiago. *Política económica nacional.* 2 vols. Santiago, 1931.

Maira, Luis. *Chile: dos años de Unidad Popular.* Santiago, 1973.

Mallol Pemjean, Mario. *La verdad sobre los dirigentes regionales de Iquique del año 1941 del Partido Socialista chileno.* Iquique, Chile, 1942.

Mamalakis, Markos. *The Growth and Structure of the Chilean Economy.* New Haven and London, 1976.

Mamalakis, Markos, and Reynolds, Clark Winton. *Essays on the Chilean Economy.* New York, 1965.

Mandujano Tobar, Luis. *Luis Mandujano Tobar, candidato a senador por Cautín y Bío-Bío.* Santiago, n.d.

Manifiesto de la asamblea demócrata departamental de San Fernando . . . . San Fernando, Chile, 1932.

Manifiesto de las mujeres aguirristas de Coquimbo . . . . Coquimbo, Chile, 1938.

Mann, Wilhelm. *Chile luchando por nuevas formas de vida.* 2 vols. Santiago, 1935.

Manns, Patricio. *La revolución de la escuadra.* Santiago, 1972.

Marín Balmaceda, Raúl. *La administración que termina.* Santiago, 1939.

———. *La caída de un régimen, julio de 1931.* Santiago, 1933.

———. *El 4 de junio de 1932.* Santiago, 1933.

Marín Balmaceda, Raúl, and Vega, Manuel. *La futura presidencia de la república.* Santiago, 1938.

Martin, Gene Ellis. *La división de la tierra en Chile central.* Santiago, 1960.

Martner, Daniel. *Economía política.* 2nd ed. Santiago, 1934.

Martner, Gonzalo, ed. *El pensamiento económico del gobierno de Allende.* Santiago, 1971.

Mattelart, Armand. *Manual de análisis demográfico.* Santiago, 1964.

Mattelart, Armand; Castillo, Carmen; and Castillo, Leonardo. *La ideología de la dominación en una sociedad dependiente.* Buenos Aires, 1970.

Mattelart, Armand, and Garretón, Manuel A. *Integración nacional y marginalidad.* 2nd ed. Santiago, 1969.

Matthei, Adolfo. *La agricultura en Chile y la política agraria chilena.* Santiago, 1939.

Maturana Barahona, Venturana. *Mi ruta.* Buenos Aires, 1936.

Maza, José. *Discurso.* Santiago, 1932.

———. *Liberalismo constructivo.* Santiago, 1942.

Mejido, Manuel. *Esto pasó en Chile.* Mexico. 1974.

Melfi, Domingo. *Dictadura y mansedumbre.* Santiago, 1931.

———. *Sin brújula.* Santiago, 1932.

Mena L., Aníbal. *Fuerte antinacionalismo del gobierno. Delictuoso constitución de la COSACH.* Santiago, 1933.

Méndez, Francisco, ed. *Chile: tierra y destino.* Santiago, [1947?].

Mendoza, Humberto. *Socialismo, camino de la libertad.* Santiago, 1945.

———. *¿Y ahora?* Santiago, 1942.

Michels, Robert. *Political Parties.* New York, 1962.

Milbrath, Lester W. *Political Participation.* Chicago, 1965.

La Milicia Republicana. *Albúm conmemorativo de su presentación pública.* Santiago, 1933.

Millas, Hernán, and Filippi, Emilio. *Chile '70-'73: crónica de una experiencia.* Santiago, 1974.

Millas R., Columbano. *Los secretos que divulga un secretario privado de los Ministros de Guerra* . . . . Santiago, 1923.

Molina, Enrique. *La revolución, los estudiantes y la democracia.* Santiago, 1931.

Monreal, Enrique, *Historia completa y documentada del período revolucionario, 1924-1925.* N.p., 1927.

Montecinos Rozas, Edmundo. *Apuntaciones para el estudio de la evolución de los partidos políticos chilenos y de su proyección jurídica.* Santiago, 1942.

Montero Moreno, René. *Confesiones políticas.* 2nd ed. Santiago, 1959.

———. *La verdad sobre Ibáñez.* Buenos Aires, 1953.

Morales C., Ramón. *Democracia chilena triunfante.* Santiago, 1939.

Moran, Theodore H. *Multinational Corporations and the Politics of Dependence: Copper in Chile.* Princeton, 1974.

Moreno, Francisco José. *Legitimacy and Stability in Latin America.* New York, 1969.

Morris, David. *We Must Make Haste–Slowly.* New York, 1973.

Morris, George. *CIA and American Labor.* New York, 1967.

Morris, James O. *Elites, Intellectuals, and Consensus.* Ithaca, N.Y., 1966.

Morris, James O., and Oyaneder C., Roberto. *Afiliación y finanzas sindicales en Chile, 1932-1959.* Santiago, 1962.

Moss, Robert. *Chile's Marxist Experiment.* Newton Abbot, England, 1973.

Moulian, Tomás. *Estudio sobre Chile.* Santiago, 1965.

El Movimiento Nacional-Socialista de Chile. Santiago, 1932, 1933.

Mujica, Gustavo. *Rebelión en la armada.* Santiago, 1959.

Müller Rivera, Carlos. *El jefe de la brigada parlamentaria contesta, en defensa del Partido Socialista, los ataques derechistas.* Santiago, 1940.

Mundt, Tito. *Yo lo conocí.* Santiago, 1965.

Muñoz, Diego. *La avalancha.* Santiago, 1932.

Muñoz Gomá, Oscar. *Crecimiento industrial de Chile, 1941-1965.* [Santiago?], [1968?].

Nazaré, Jacobo. *Destrucción.* Valparaíso, n.d.

North, Liisa. *Civil-Military Relations in Argentina, Chile, and Peru.* Berkeley, Calif., 1966.

North American Congress on Latin America. *New Chile.* N.p., 1972.

Nueva Acción Pública. *Declaración de principios y estatuto orgánico.* Santiago, 1932.

Núñez, Carlos. *Chile: ¿la última opción electoral?* Santiago, 1970.

Nunn, Frederick M. *Chilean Politics, 1920-1931.* Albuquerque, N.M., 1970.
———. *The Military in Chilean History: Essays on Civil-Military Relations, 1810-1973.* Albuquerque, N.M., 1976.
Ochoa Mena, H. *La revolución de junio.* Santiago, 1931.
O'Donnell, Guillermo A. *Modernization and Bureaucratic-Authoritarianism: Studies in South American Politics.* Berkeley, Calif., 1973.
Olavarría Alarcón, Simón. *La gran culpa del Partido Radical.* Santiago, 1951.
Olavarría Bravo, Arturo. *Casos y cosas de la política.* Santiago, 1950.
———. *Chile entre dos Alessandri.* 4 vols. Santiago, 1962, 1965.
———. *La cuestión social en Chile.* Santiago, 1923.
———. *Debe y haber.* Santiago, 1936.´
———. *Durante la tiranía.* Santiago, 1931.
Olivares, René. *Alessandri, precursor y revolucionario.* Valparaíso, 1942.
———. *Ibáñez.* Valparaíso, 1937.
Orden Socialista. *Principios fundamentales.* Santiago, 1931.
La Organización Política, Económica y Social de la Clase Media. *Programa mínimo provisional.* Valparaíso, 1934.
Orrego Barros, Carlos. *La organización gremial y el poder político.* Santiago, 1932.
Orrego Vicuña, Eugenio. *El escritor y la sociedad.* Santiago, 1937.
———. *Perspectiva del desenvolvimiento socialista en América y en el mundo.* Santiago, 1932.
Orrego Vicuña, Francisco, ed. *Chile: The Balanced View.* Santiago, 1975.
Ortega y Gasset, José. *The Revolt of the Masses.* New York, 1932.
Ovalle Castillo, Francisco Javier. *Hacia la política chilena.* Santiago, 1922.
Palacios M., Bartolomé. *El Partido Conservador y la democracia cristiana.* Santiago, 1933.
Palma Zúñiga, Luis. *Historia del Partido Radical.* Santiago, 1967.
———. *Pedro Aguirre Cerda.* Santiago, 1963.
Pan, techo, abrigo. Dos años de gobierno popular. Valparaíso, 1941.
Parada G., M. Alberto. *Los presidenciables.* Santiago, 1937.
Partido Agrario. *Acción corporativa.* Chillán, Chile, 1941.
———. *Declaración de principios y programa.* Temuco, Chile, 1934.
Partido Comunista. *Cartilla electoral.* Santiago, 1941.
———. *Hacia la formación de un verdadero partido de clase.* Santiago, 1933.
———. *XI congreso . . . .* Santiago, 1940.
———. *Problemas de organización.* Santiago, 1939.
———. *Ricardo Fonseca.* Santiago, [1952?].
———. *El tercer frente ha sido alquilado por el imperialismo norteamericano . . . .* Santiago, 1946.
Partido Conservador. *Falange Nacional.* Santiago, 1938.
———. *Programa y estatutos.* Santiago, 1933.
Partido Liberal. *La crisis.* Santiago, 1932.
———. *Programa y estatuto.* Santiago, 1933.
———. *Proyecto de estatuto orgánico del Partido Liberal.* Santiago, 1931.
———. *Quinta convención.* Santiago, 1932.
———. *7.a convención.* Santiago, 1939.

Partido Obrero Revolucionario. *¿A dónde va la C.T.CH.?* Santiago, 1944.

Partido Radical. *14 años de progreso, 1938-1952.* Santiago, 1952.

——. *Convención extraordinaria del Partido Radical.* Santiago, 1937.

——. *En defensa de los principios.* N.p., 1946.

——. *El Partido Radical ante el "acuerdo de caballeros" Ross-Calder.* Santiago, 1936.

——. *El Partido Radical en el gobierno, en su organización y en el Frente Popular.* Santiago, 1940.

——. *Posición política y estatuto del Partido Radical.* Santiago, 1941.

——. *Programa, estatutos, reglamento.* Santiago, 1933.

——. *¡Radicales en la acción!* Vallenar, Chile, 1932.

Partido Radical Doctrinario. *Manifiesto del Partido Radical Doctrinario a los radicales del país.* Santiago, 1938.

Partido Radical Socialista. *Programa y estatuto orgánico.* Santiago, 1932.

Los Partidos Liberal y Conservador. *¿Por qué nos abstenemos?* Santiago, 1940.

Partido Socialista. *A los camaradas de Bío-Bío.* Los Angeles, Chile, 1934.

——. *Cartilla campesina.* Santiago, 1966.

——. *Cartilla sindical campesina.* Santiago, 1941.

——. *Chile y América en la órbita espiritual del socialismo.* Santiago, 1941.

——. *Concepción económica del Partido Socialista.* Santiago, 1941.

——. *Conclusiones del torneo partidario del Partido Socialista chileno realizado en La Habana.* Cuba, 1974.

——. *Contestamos a los enemigos del pueblo chileno.* Santiago, 1939.

——. *IV congreso extraordinario del Partido Socialista.* Santiago, 1943.

——. *4 de junio.* Santiago, 1933.

——. *Estatutos.* Santiago, 1936.

——. *Estatutos.* Santiago, 1940.

——. *Estatutos . . . .* Santiago, 1972.

——. *¡Frei no es Chile!* Santiago, 1966.

——. *Grove a la presidencia.* Santiago, 1937.

——. *Grove, el militar y el ciudadano.* Santiago, 1937.

——. *Informe sobre posición política del Partido Socialista.* Santiago, 1943.

——. *El libro negro del Partido Comunista.* Santiago, 1941.

——. *La línea política del Partido Socialista.* Santiago, 1941.

——. *Manifiesto.* Santiago, 1940.

——. *IX congreso.* [Santiago?], 1943.

——. *La palabra del Partido Socialista en la lucha sindical.* Santiago, 1947.

——. *La palabra de Oscar Schnake V. en la convención radical de La Serena.* Santiago, 1939.

——. *Para deshacer la ola de calumniosas informaciones . . . .* Santiago, 1940.

——. *Partido Socialista Marxista.* Concepción, Chile, 1931.

——. *El Partido Socialista y su 6.° congreso ordinario.* Santiago, 1940.

——. *Política sindical del Partido Socialista.* Santiago, 1939.

——. *Por una democracia de trabajadores.* Santiago, 1948.

——. *Primer congreso de los partidos democráticos de latinoamérica.* Santiago, 1940.

————. *Primer congreso regional del Partido Socialista en la provincia de Tarapacá.* Santiago, 1939.

————. *Programa.* Santiago, 1936.

————. *Proyecto de programa del Partido Socialista chileno.* Santiago, 1947.

————. *Significado de la república socialista del 4 de junio.* Santiago, 1939.

————. *Sobre la moral revolucionaria.* Santiago, 1939.

————. *El socialismo ante el mundo de hoy.* Santiago, 1964.

————. *Tareas para un buen militante.* Santiago, 1948.

————. *Tesis política.* Santiago, 1939.

————. *33 años por el socialismo.* Santiago, 1966.

————. *Una etapa de clarificación socialista.* Santiago, 1944.

Partido Socialista Auténtico. *Primer congreso extraordinario.* Santiago, 1946.

————. *Sobre la unidad socialista.* Santiago, 1946.

Partido Socialista Auténtico y Partido Comunista de Chile. *Pacto de acción política.* Santiago, 1946.

Partido Socialista de Trabajadores. *El camino del pueblo.* Santiago, 1942.

————. *Construyendo el partido único.* Santiago, 1944.

Partido Socialista Popular. *El Partido Socialista Popular lucha contra las facultades extraordinarias.* Santiago, 1949.

Partido Socialista Unificado. *Declaración de principios, estatutos y reglamentos, tesis política, tesis sindical e himno del partido.* Santiago, 1947.

Partido Social Republicano. *Programa del Partido Social Republicano.* Santiago, 1932.

————. *Programa y estatutos.* Valparaíso, 1933.

El Personal de la Empresa de "El Mercurio" en Asamblea. *Considerando . . . .* n.p., 1932.

Petras, James. *Politics and Social Forces in Chilean Development.* Berkeley, Calif. 1969.

Petras, James, and Morley, Morris. *The United States and Chile: Imperialism and the Overthrow of the Allende Government.* New York, 1975.

Petras, James, and Zeitlin, Maurice. *El radicalismo político de la clase trabajadora chilena.* Buenos Aires, 1969.

————, eds. *Latin America: Reform or Revolution?* New York, 1968.

Pike, Fredrick B. *Chile and the United States, 1880-1962.* South Bend, Ind., 1963.

Pike, Fredrick B., and Stritch, Thomas, eds. *The New Corporatism.* Notre Dame, Ind., 1974.

Pinochet, Tancredo. *Aguirre Cerda.* Santiago, 1938.

Pinochet Ugarte, Augusto. *Un año de construcción.* Santiago, 1974.

Pinto Durán, Carlos. *Diccionario personal de Chile.* Santiago, 1921.

————. *Plan de gobierno de la república.* Santiago, 1932.

————. *La revolución chilena.* Santiago, 1925.

Pinto Lagarrigue, Fernando. *La masonería: su influencia en Chile.* 3rd ed. Santiago, 1966.

Pinto Salvatierra, Francisco. *Clase media y socialismo.* Valparaíso, 1941.

Pinto Santa Cruz, Aníbal, ed. *Antecedentes sobre el desarrollo de la economía chilena, 1925-1952.* Santiago, 1954.

————. *Chile, un caso de desarrollo frustrado.* Santiago, 1962.

————. *Hacia nuestra independencia económica.* Santiago, 1953.

Pinto Santa Cruz, Aníbal, et al. *Chile, hoy.* Mexico City, 1970

Poblete, Nicanor. *Descentralización económica de las provincias.* Santiago, 1937.

Podlech Davison, Jorge. *Panorama político del momento.* Santiago, 1936.

La política de la Alianza Liberal juzgada por sus propios hombres. Santiago, 1920.

Ponce Cumplido, Jaime J. *La desconcentración administrativa.* Santiago, 1965.

¿Por qué cayó Grove? Santiago, 1932.

Posada, J. *Chile: conclusiones del golpe militar y la resistencia del proletariado.* Buenos Aires, 1974.

Prat, Arturo. *Causas políticas de la crisis.* Santiago, 1935.

Prat, Jorge. *El fracaso de un triunfo.* Santiago, 1943.

Primera Convención de las Provincias de Chile. *Un paso hacia la decentralización administrativa del país.* [Valparaíso?], [1946?].

Programa de trabajo de los candidatos a regidores del Partido Regionalista de Magallanes. Magallanes, Chile, [1938?].

¿Qué es el Partido Agrario? Talca, Chile, 1935.

Quezada Acharán, Armando. *El socialismo.* Valparaíso, 1932.

Quijada Cerda, Osvaldo. *La pascua trágica de Copiapó y Vallenar.* Santiago, 1932.

Ramírez Necochea, Hernán. *Origen y formación del Partido Comunista de Chile.* Santiago, 1965.

Ravines, Eudocio. *La gran estafa.* 2nd ed. Santiago, 1954.

Reglamentos del Frente Popular. Santiago, 1937.

Reimer, Joan. *Circulación de las elites en Chile.* Santiago, [1971?].

Una revolución en la paz, 1932-1937. Santiago and Valparaíso, 1937.

Ríos, Juan Antonio. *Durante el gobierno del General Ibáñez.* Santiago, 1931.

————. *¡Expulsado!* Concepción, Chile, 1932.

Rippy, J. Fred. *British Investments in Latin America, 1822-1949.* Minneapolis, 1959.

Rivas Vicuña, Francisco. *Nacionalismo social.* Santiago, 1932.

Riveros Cruz, Mariano. *La industria salitrera frente al proyecto de ley sobre Corporación de Ventas de Salitre y Yodo.* Santiago, 1933.

Robeca, A. *Perfiles de presidenciables.* Santiago, 1925.

Rodríguez A., Aniceto. *1966: año de la organización y las luchas campesinas.* Santiago, 1966.

Rodríguez Corces, José. *Ética socialista.* Santiago, 1939.

Rodríguez de la Sotta, Héctor. *Crisis política, económica y moral.* Santiago, 1932.

Rodríguez Lazo, Raúl. *Aspectos sobre centralismo y descentralización en Chile.* Santiago, 1935.

Rodríguez Mendoza, Emilio. *Como si fuera ahora . . . .* Santiago, 1929.

————. *El golpe de estado de 1924.* Santiago, 1938.

Rojas Mery, Eulojio. *Recuerdos de un joven "octogenario."* Santiago, 1958.

Rojo Indo, Carlos. *Boceto histórico político de Chile de los últimos veinte años.* Santiago, 1939.

Romualdi, Serafino. *Presidents and Peons.* New York, 1967.

Ross Santa María, Gustavo. *Palabras de un estadista.* Santiago, 1938.

Roxborough, Ian; O'Brien, Philip; and Roddick, Jackie. *Chile: The State and Revolution.* New York, 1977.

Ruiz Urbina, Antonio; Zorbas D., Alejandro; and Donoso Varela, Luis. *Estratificación y movilidad sociales en Chile.* Rio de Janeiro, 1961.

Sáez Morales, Carlos. *Recuerdos de un soldado.* 3 vols. Santiago, 1934.

————. *Y así vamos . . . .* Santiago, 1938.

Sanfuentes Carrión, Marcial. *El Partido Conservador.* Santiago, 1957.

Santos Salas, José. *Alessandri y el pueblo.* Santiago, 1950.

————. *Carta del Dr. José Santos Salas al Diputado César Godoy Urrutia.* Santiago, 1940.

Sarmiento, Pedro Elías. *Descorriendo el velo de los hermanos Grove en la Isla de Pascua.* Valparaíso, 1938.

Schnake Vergara, Oscar. *América y la guerra.* Santiago, 1941.

————. *Chile y la guerra.* Santiago, 1941.

————. *El Partido Socialista y el problema de las tierras de Magallanes.* Santiago, 1937.

————. *Política socialista.* Santiago, 1938.

Schneider, Carlos Oliver. *Hacia la cultura colectiva.* Concepción, Chile, 1932.

Sesión inaugural de la convención de la producción y del comercio. Santiago, 1934.

Siegfried, André. *Impressions of South America.* New York, 1933.

Silva, Jorge Gustavo. *Nuestra evolución político-social (1900-1930).* Santiago, 1931.

Silva Castro, Raúl. *Prensa y periodismo en Chile (1812-1956).* Santiago, 1958.

Silvert, Kalman H. *Chile.* New York, 1965.

Simón, Marcelo. *Allende detrás de la muerte.* Buenos Aires, 1973.

Simón, Raúl. *Determinación de la entrada nacional de Chile.* Santiago, 1935.

Simón, Raúl, et al. *El concepto de industria nacional y la protección del estado.* Santiago, 1939.

Siquieros, Juan. *El grovismo.* N.p., [1933?].

Skidmore, Thomas. *Politics in Brazil.* New York, 1967.

Solaún, Mauricio, and Quinn, Michael A. *Sinners and Heretics: The Politics of Military Intervention in Latin America.* Urbana, Ill., 1973.

Solberg, Carl. *Immigration and Nationalism, Argentina and Chile, 1890-1914.* Austin, Tex., 1970.

Sotomayor A., Sergio. *Carta abierta de un ex militante al Partido Comunista.* Santiago, 1953.

Spengler, Oswald. *Man and Technics.* New York, 1932.

Spoerer C., Jerman. *Simbiosis del capital y el trabajo.* Santiago, 1938.

Stephens Freire, Alfonso. *El irracionalismo político en Chile.* Santiago, 1957.

Stevenson, John Reese. *The Chilean Popular Front.* Philadelphia, 1942.

Subercaseaux, Benjamín. *Contribución a la realidad.* Santiago, 1939.

Subercaseaux, Guillermo. *Historia de las doctrinas económicas en América y en especial en Chile.* Santiago, 1924.

————. *La política social nacionalista moderna.* Santiago, 1932.

Subercaseaux, Ramón. *Memorias de ochenta años.* 2 vols. 2nd ed. Santiago, 1936.

Sweezy, Paul M., and Magdoff, Harry, eds. *Revolution and Counter-Revolution in Chile.* New York, 1974.

Talesnik Rabinovich, Gregorio. *Intervenciones del estado y control del precios por el mismo.* Santiago, 1941.

Tannenbaum, Frank. *Whither Latin America?* New York, 1934.

Tapia Moore, Astolfo. *¡El socialismo triunfará!* Santiago, 1948.

Téllez, Indalecio. *Recuerdos militares.* Santiago, 1949.

Tomic, Radomiro. *Intervención de . . . en reunión del Partido Demócrata Cristiana el 7 de noviembre de 1973.* Mexico, 1974.

Torreblanca, Edecio. *Ante la próxima elección presidencial.* Santiago, 1938.

Torres, Isauro, and Opitz, Pedro. *Defensa de los gobiernos de izquierda.* Santiago, 1942.

Townsend y Onel. *La inquisición chilena, 1925-31.* Valparaíso, 1932.

La tragedia chilena: testimonios. Buenos Aires, 1973.

Los 30 puntos. N.p., 1932.

Troncoso, Moisés Poblete, and Burnett, Ben G. *The Rise of the Latin American Labor Movement.* New York, 1960.

Turri, Enrique. *Frente Popular.* N.p., n.d.

Ugarte y E. E., R. V. *La lucha de clases.* Santiago, 1932.

La Unidad Popular. *Programa básico de gobierno de la Unidad Popular.* Santiago, 1970.

Unidad Proletaria. *El primer año del gobierno popular.* N.p., 1972.

————. *El segundo año del gobierno popular.* N.p., 1972.

Unión Republicana. Santiago, 1932.

Unión Republicana. Valparaíso, 1932.

Unión Republicana. *Declaraciones de sus juntas generales de directorios.* Santiago, [1936?].

Unión Social de Chile. *Procedimientos comunistas para obtener adaptos a su causa.* Santiago, 1933.

Unión Social del Personal en Retiro de las Fuerzas Armadas de Chile. *Declaración de principios.* Santiago, 1932.

Unión Socialista Popular. *La clase obrera y la elección, 1970.* N.p., 1970.

Urzúa Valenzuela, Germán. *El Partido Radical.* Santiago, 1961.

————. *Los partidos políticos chilenos.* Santiago, 1968.

Valdés, Renato. *Seis cartas al Presidente Alessandri.* Santiago, 1935.

————. *Tres cartas.* Santiago, 1932.

Valdés Larraín, Luis. *El sufragio.* Santiago, 1940.

Valdés M., Salvador. *Cinco años de gobierno de izquierda, 1939 a 1943,* I. Puente Alto, Chile, 1944.

Valencia Avaria, Luis. *Anales de la república.* 2 vols. Santiago, 1951.

Valencia Courbis, Luis. *Sobre las rutas del porvenir.* Santiago, 1932.

Valenzuela, Arturo, and Valenzuela, J. Samuel, eds. *Chile: Politics and Society.* New Brunswick, N.J., 1976.

Valle, Eduardo. *Allende, cronología*. Mexico, 1974.

Van Niekerk, A. E. *Populism and Political Development in Latin America*. Rotterdam, 1974.

Varas, José Miguel. *Chacón*. Santiago, 1968.

Veliz, Claudio, ed. *Obstacles to Change in Latin America*. London, 1965.

———. *The Politics of Conformity in Latin America*. London, 1967.

Vera, González, et al. *"Célula." Hechos y sorpresas de la política criolla*. Santiago, 1932.

Vera Riquelme, Enrique. *Evolución del radicalismo chileno*. Santiago, 1943.

Vergara, Marta. *Memorias de una mujer irreverente*. Santiago, 1961.

Vergara Herrera, Roberto. *Descentralización administrativa*. Santiago, 1932.

Vergara Montero, Ramón. *Perspectiva trágica*. Santiago, 1939.

———. *Por rutas extraviadas*. Santiago, 1933.

Vergara V., Sergio. *Decadencia o recuperación*. Santiago, 1945.

Vergara Vicuña, Aquiles. *Candidatura a diputado por Santiago*. Santiago, 1932.

———. *Mi defensa ante el congreso*. Santiago, 1932.

Vial Solar, Javier. *El diluvio*. Santiago, 1934.

Vico, Vicente, et al. *Hidalgo-Alessandri-Montero*. Chillán, Chile, 1931.

Vicuña Fuentes, Carlos. *La caída del coronel*. N.p., 1951.

———. *En las prisiones políticas de Chile*. Santiago, 1946.

———. *La tiranía en Chile*. 2 vols. Santiago, 1938.

Villagra, Víctor M. *Discurso del presidente del Partido Liberal de Bulnes*. Chillán, Chile, 1938.

Vitale, Luis. *Esencia y apariencia de la democracia cristiana*. Santiago, 1964.

———. *Historia del movimiento obrero*. Santiago, 1962.

———. *¿Y después del 4, que?* Santiago, 1970.

Viviani Contreras, Guillermo. *Sociología chilena*. Santiago, 1926.

Von Schroeders, Almirante. *El delegado del gobierno y el motín de la escuadra*. Santiago, 1933.

Vylder, Stefan de. *Allende's Chile: The Political Economy of the Rise and Fall of the Unidad Popular*. New York, 1976.

Waiss, Oscar. *El drama socialista*. N.p., 1948.

———. *Nacionalismo y socialismo en América latina*. Santiago, 1954.

———. *Presencia del socialismo en Chile*. Santiago, 1952.

———. *Socialismo sin gerentes*. 3rd ed. Santiago, 1961.

Walker Valdés, Alejandro. *La verdad sobre el motín militar*. Santiago, 1919.

Wilson Hernández, Santiago. *Nuestra crisis económica y la desocupación obrera*. Santiago, 1933.

Würth Rojas, Ernesto. *Ibáñez. Caudillo enigmático*. Santiago, 1958.

Zaleg, Mig. *Recuerdos provincianos, apolíticos, del año 1920*. Rancagua, Chile, 1931.

Zammit, J. Ann, ed. *The Chilean Road to Socialism*. Austin, Tex., 1973.

Zañartu Prieto, Enrique. *Hambre, miseria e ignorancia*. Santiago, 1938.

———. *El proyecto Ross*. Santiago, 1933.

Zegers Baeza, Antonio. *Sobre nuestra crisis política y moral*. Santiago, 1934.

Zúñiga. Luis. *El Partido Socialista en la política chilena*. Santiago, 1938.

Index

Achao, 317n, 330n
Aconcagua, 21, 99, 263
Advance Group, 63, 138, 162
Afuerinos, 28
Agrarian reform: agricultural elites, 24, 88, 116, 191; naval revolt, 64; Socialist Republic, 75–79 *passim*; middle class, 89–90, 192; Communist Party, 96, 283, 288; Radical Party, 115; Nazis, 124; Socialist Party, 144–49 *passim*, 170, 195, 210–12 *passim*, 239, 256; Popular Front, 179, 180, 202, 219, 221; Allende, 307, 308, 319–25 *passim*, 335; Frei, 312. *See also* Agriculture; Peasants
Agricultural elites: populism, 11, 25, 115, 116, 338; upper class, 22–24, 41–43 *passim*, 86n, 88, 109–25 *passim*, 189–92 *passim*, 220, 221, 250, 313; agrarian reform, 24, 88, 116, 191; election of 1920, 54; during Great Depression, 62; Montero, 66; Socialist Republic, 78–79; election of 1932, 91, 97, 102, 103; Masons, 128; Radical Party, 131, 132, 175, 186, 187, 210, 235, 249; Democrats, 135; Socialist Party, 170, 183, 248; Popular Front, 181, 187, 202, 217, 221–24 *passim*, 249; peasants, 193–95 *passim*; regionalism, 32–36 *passim*, 196, 197; Ríos, 269, 270; González Videla, 283n; Popular Unity, 313, 319–23 *passim*; mentioned, 338. *See also* SNA
Agriculture: as percentage of economy, 16, 17, 24, 25, 28, 192, 269, 285; upper class, 23–25 *passim*, 86n, 88, 109–17 *passim*, 125, 190, 221, 246, 248, 313; middle class, 26, 127, 192; regionalism, 32–36 *passim*, 196; election of 1920, 52; during Great Depression, 62; Dávila, 82; Communist Party, 136, 251; Socialist Party, 142, 147, 149n, 152, 156, 169, 172n, 177, 256; Popular Front, 216–22 *passim*, 245; election of

Agriculture *(continued)*
1941, 259–62; election of 1946, 282; election of 1970, 316. *See also* Agrarian reform; Agricultural elites; Peasants
Aguirre Cerda, Pedro: Popular Front, 179, 186, 187, 201, 265, 267, 275; agricultural elites, 181, 187, 202–49 *passim*, 254, 283n, 323; election of 1938, 185, 186, 192, 193, 198–213, 259; Radical Party, 186, 208, 211, 268; as president, 1938–41, 210n, 215–45 *passim*, 254, 257, 265, 270, 274, 285, 308, 323–25 *passim*, 329
Air Force. *See* Military
Los Alamos, 317n, 330n
Alessandri Palma, Arturo: populism, 12, 45–53 *passim*, 69, 84, 90, 134, 159, 308; election of 1915, 45; upper class, 45–47 *passim*, 121, 165, 167, 190, 191, 232; Radical Party, 45–49, 131, 171, 175; middle class, 45–49 *passim*, 89, 93, 126–30 *passim*, 157, 166, 167; working class, 45–54 *passim*, 89, 92, 93, 134, 158, 166, 167, 194; election of 1920, 47–54 *passim*, 208; military, 48, 55, 56, 83, 161, 194, 209; as president, 1920–24, 54–59 *passim*, 137n, 323; constitution of 1925, 56, 197; Carlos Ibáñez, 63; election of 1931, 66–69; socialism, 69–72 *passim*, 92, 165; Marmaduke Grove, 73, 75, 159; election of 1932, 84, 90–108 *passim*; as president, 1932–38, 98, 142, 165–67, 173, 189, 203, 215, 228, 277, 325; Masons, 129, 179; Democrats, 131, 135; Socialist Party, 139–41 *passim*, 161–63; foreign capital and trade, 166, 167, 200; election of 1938, 206–10 *passim*; election of 1942, 268; election of 1946, 281
Alessandri Rodríguez, Fernando, 281, 282
Alessandri Rodríguez, Jorge, 306, 307, 312, 315n, 316, 317

090140